I0885269

Multi-Criteria Decision Making Models and Techniques:

Neutrosophic Approaches

Mohamed Abdel-Basset
Zagazig University, Egypt

Abduallah Gamal
Zagazig University, Egypt

Florentin Smarandache
University of New Mexico, USA

A volume in the Advances in Systems Analysis, Software Engineering, and High Performance Computing (ASASEHPC) Book Series

IGI Global
PUBLISHER of TIMELY KNOWLEDGE

Published in the United States of America by
IGI Global
Engineering Science Reference (an imprint of IGI Global)
701 E. Chocolate Avenue
Hershey PA, USA 17033
Tel: 717-533-8845
Fax: 717-533-8661
E-mail: cust@igi-global.com
Web site: http://www.igi-global.com

Library of Congress Cataloging-in-Publication Data

Names: Abdel-Basset, Mohamed, 1985- editor. | Gamal, Abduallah, editor. | Smarandache, Florentin, editor.
Title: Multi-criteria decision making models and techniques : neutrosophic approaches / edited by Mohamed Abdel-Basset, Abduallah Gamal, Florentin Smarandache.
Description: Hershey, PA : Engineering Science Reference, [2025] | Includes bibliographical references and index. | Summary: "The objectives of the book are to introduce new strategies in the process of decision making, such as alpha-discounting method for MCDM, soft set theories and neutrosophic and plithogenic sets, logics, probability and statistics helpful in taking a decision"-- Provided by publisher.
Identifiers: LCCN 2024007204 (print) | LCCN 2024007205 (ebook) | ISBN 9798369320853 (hardcover) | ISBN 9798369320860 (ebook)
Subjects: LCSH: Decision making--Statistical methods.
Classification: LCC HD30.215 .M85 2024 (print) | LCC HD30.215 (ebook) | DDC 519.5/42--dc23/eng/20240422
LC record available at https://lccn.loc.gov/2024007204
LC ebook record available at https://lccn.loc.gov/2024007205

British Cataloguing in Publication Data
A Cataloguing in Publication record for this book is available from the British Library.

All work contributed to this book is new, previously-unpublished material.
The views expressed in this book are those of the authors, but not necessarily of the publisher.

For electronic access to this publication, please contact: eresources@igi-global.com.

Table of Contents

Detailed Table of Contents

TOPSIS (technique for order preference by similarity to ideal solution) is a mathematical approach employed in the context of multi-criteria decision-making. Its primary purpose is to establish a ranking among various alternatives by taking into consideration multiple attributes or criteria. This method utilizes distance metrics to gauge the nearness of each alternative to both the ideal and anti-ideal solutions. Ultimately, its goal is to facilitate the identification of the most optimal alternative. In this era of uncertainty, many parents grapple with myriad uncertainties when it comes to selecting the right educational institution for their children. This chapter provides an initial glimpse into the neutrosophic pythagorean plithogenic hypersoft set (N_pphs) along with its fundamental definition. Additionally, an algorithm has been devised for the TOPSIS methodology, accompanied by a practical numerical illustration. This is intended to assist parents in making an informed decision when choosing the most suitable school for their children with their set of criteria.

The use of plithogenic cognitive maps is instrumental in tackling intricate decision-making structures. These models, utilizing plithogenic representations, enable the examination of interconnected influences among decision-making factors. This chapter introduces a novel type of plithogenic cognitive maps employing plithogenic Fermatean sets representations. The suggested decision-making model is employed to analyze the effects of digitalized educational system on the learning community. A comparative assessment of the effectiveness and competence of this model against plithogenic cognitive maps with alternative representations is conducted. The outcomes exhibit greater promise for the proposed model. Consequently, this chapter advocates for the adoption of this decision-making approach to address problems involving complex interrelated factors.

Digital authentication and key encapsulation mechanisms (KEM) are two basic primitives for the security level of all robotic and IoT systems. Dilithium and Kyber are two post-quantum algorithms to establish secure communication. The use of uniform random sampling in these algorithms is very important. The finalists Dilithium and Kyber use SHAKE and AES to generate the random sequence at multiple stages of the algorithm. Here, the authors characterize one of the sampling techniques available in Dilithium with the help of the neutrosophic Boolean function. The idea of the neutrosophic Boolean function came from the theory of neutrosophy, and it is useful to study any ternary distributions. The authors present the non-existence of neutrobalanced bent functions specifically with respect to the sampling named SampleInBall in Dilithium.

In neutrosophic soft relation, if only the parameters or alternatives are processed, the relations may not give the desired clear result. In this chapter, in order to overcome this problem, a cartesian product is defined on neutrosophic soft sets with a different approach. With this approach, both alternatives and parameters are processed. Then, the concept of neutrosophic soft relation is denoted by using the definition of Cartesian product. The important features of the presented structures are examined, and various examples are given. In addition, the basic method that can be used in decision-making problems is presented by using the concept of neutrosophic soft relation.

The interval-valued complex neutrosophic set (IVCNS), an expansion of the interval-valued neutrosophic set (IVNS), provides a more precisecharacterisation of uncertainty than traditional fuzzy sets. Fuzzy control can use it in a variety of ways. In this research study, the authors also introduce the adjacency matrix IVCNGS notion as well as the idea of an isomorphic adjacency matrix. They also introduce interval-valued complex neutrosophic graph structures (IVCNGS). They use an example to investigate a number of IVCNGS adjacency matrix properties. In addition, they introduce the ideas of edge regular and totally edge regular adjacency matrix IVCNGS. The conditions under which edge regular adjacency matrix IVCNGS and totally edge regular adjacency matrix IVCNGS are equal are described. Finally, in order to make the proposed IVCNGS principles more understandable, they give specific instances of how virtual social networks impact cross-cultural communication and evaluate the effectiveness and performance of the organisation.

Decision-making analysis is one of the best ways to choose the perfect alternative for any specified purpose. Fuzzy theory overcomes the vague and uncertain conditions. Neutrosophic set was an extension of fuzzy set theory. Application of neutrosophic hyper soft set is a major tool in solving the multi-criteria decision-making problem. In this chapter, a numerical example has been framed to select the best school in the certain locality using the proposed algorithm. The parameters have been given in the form of neutrosophic hyper soft set. Comparison was done with the existing method.

Neutrosophic sets are a type of mathematical object that can be used to model indeterminacy and inconsistent information. They are defined using three degrees of membership: truthfulness, indeterminacy, and falsity. Single-valued Fermatean neutrosophic sets (SVFNSs) and interval-valued Fermatean neutrosophic sets (IVFNSs) are two specific cases of neutrosophic sets that have been shown to be useful in a variety of applications. In this chapter, a new Python toolbox is proposed under the neutrosophic environment, which consists in some Python code for single-valued Fermatean neutrosophic matrices and interval-valued Fermatean neutrosophic matrices. Some definitions of interval-valued Fermatean neutrosophy are vague sets such as union, complement, and intersection, which are presented. Furthermore, the related examples are included.

In this research work, a new neutrosophic probability model named a neutrosophic Topp-Leone exponentiated generalized exponential distribution is proposed to model the normalized difference vegetation index (NDVI) of Pakistan in the year 2022. The MODIS was used in this research, which gave spatial and spectral information on NDVI in the Earth. NDVI maps were produced from the acquired data, and NDVI sensors computed the normalized difference vegetation index. Mathematical characteristics of the proposed model of NDVI are derived, including central tendency measures, dispersion estimators, inferential statistics, moment generating function, order statistics, reliability measures, quantile-based statistical measures, and renyi entropy and graphical representations of the density function are also presented. The maximum likelihood technique is used to estimate the parameters for the proposed probability model.

The ramifications of making decisions are more noteworthy due to the abundance and intricacy of data in everyday challenges. Hence, it is imperative to make sound and effective decision by developing innovative mathematical approaches to resolve these tasks. In this chapter, a problem is identified in the current scenario and a novel technique is proposed to make efficacious decision through the utilization of compactness in neutrosophic generalized topology. For that, initially, μN-compact space is introduced, and its characteristics are analyzed. Subsequently, μN-feebly compact space is presented along with its properties and examined its relationships with some existing notions.

Education is a crucial aspect in determining the progress of a nation. However, selecting a good school is a challenge. Therefore, the chapter offers a solution by applying the theories of single-valued neutrosophic numbers (S-VNNs) and the additive ratio assessment (ARAS) method for a school evaluation. This performance evaluation is viewed as a process involving a committee of school performance judgments and a list of senior high schools. The committee gives professional assessments of the school's performance by using S-VNNs. To conquer this, the chapter first presents the basic theory of S-VNNs with some of their mathematical operations and their two Einstein aggregation operators. The chapter then proposes an improved ARAS method based on S-VNNs to handle a multi-criteria group decision-making problem. Next, the chapter demonstrates an illustrative example using the improved ARAS method to select the favorite school. Finally, comparison analysis with other decision-making methods is presented to prove the feasibility and capability of the proposed ARAS method.

Preface

As editors of this edited reference book on *Multi-Criteria Decision Making Models and Techniques: Neutrosophic Approaches*, we are pleased to present a comprehensive exploration of innovative strategies in decision-making processes. This book brings together the expertise of scholars and researchers from Zagazig University, Egypt, and the University of New Mexico, USA, to delve into advanced concepts that revolutionize how decisions are made across diverse fields of knowledge.

The world of decision-making is constantly evolving, demanding sophisticated methodologies to handle complex scenarios. In this context, our book introduces cutting-edge approaches such as alpha-discounting MCDM, soft set theories, and neutrosophic and plithogenic sets. These methodologies extend beyond traditional frameworks, offering a nuanced understanding of decision parameters and criteria.

The objectives of this book are manifold. Firstly, it aims to elucidate the alpha-discounting method for MCDM, providing readers with insights into its applications and advantages over conventional techniques. Additionally, it delves into soft set theories, highlighting their relevance and efficacy in decision-making contexts. Furthermore, it explores neutrosophic and plithogenic sets, offering readers a deep dive into these innovative concepts and their practical implications.

Our target audience encompasses a wide range of professionals and scholars, including students, professors, engineers, technicians, and researchers. Whether you're in academia, industry, or government, the insights and methodologies presented in this book are designed to enhance your decision-making capabilities and drive impactful outcomes.

To supplement the theoretical discussions, we have included links to resources that delve deeper into specific topics covered in this book. These resources provide additional context, examples, and applications, enriching the reader's understanding and facilitating further exploration.

We believe that this book will serve as a valuable resource for anyone seeking to navigate the complexities of decision-making in today's dynamic and interconnected world.

CHAPTER OVERVIEW

Chapter 1: TOPSIS Methodology in Multi-Criteria Decision Making

TOPSIS (Technique for Order Preference by Similarity to Ideal Solution) is a mathematical approach crucial in multi-criteria decision-making scenarios. This chapter delves into its application, which involves establishing a ranking among alternatives based on multiple criteria. It employs distance metrics to evaluate how close each alternative is to both the ideal and anti-ideal solutions, aiding in identifying the most optimal choice. Using a practical example, this chapter showcases the TOPSIS algorithm's efficacy, particularly in assisting parents in selecting the most suitable educational institution for their children.

Chapter 2: Plithogenic Cognitive Maps for Complex Decision Structures

Plithogenic cognitive maps offer a sophisticated toolset for addressing complex decision-making structures. This chapter introduces a new variant of plithogenic cognitive maps utilizing plithogenic Fermatean sets representations. By analyzing the impacts of digitalized educational systems, it compares this model's effectiveness against alternative representations. The results highlight the promise of this approach, advocating for its adoption in solving problems with intricate interdependencies.

Chapter 3: Neutrosophic Approach to Digital Authentication and Key Encapsulation Mechanisms

This chapter explores the application of neutrosophic concepts in digital authentication and key encapsulation mechanisms (KEM) for secure communication. Focusing on algorithms like Dilithium and Kyber, it investigates the use of neutrosophic Boolean functions to enhance sampling techniques and addresses specific challenges within Dilithium's framework.

Chapter 4: Neutrosophic Soft Relations for Enhanced Decision Making

The chapter delves into neutrosophic soft relations, emphasizing the importance of considering both alternatives and parameters for clearer results. It introduces a novel approach using Cartesian products on neutrosophic soft sets, defining and exploring neutrosophic soft relations to aid decision-making processes.

Chapter 5: Interval-Valued Complex Neutrosophic Sets for Precise Uncertainty Characterization

This chapter introduces Interval-Valued Complex Neutrosophic Sets (IVCNS) as a refined model for uncertainty characterization. It delves into IVCNS properties, adjacency matrices, and their application in understanding complex systems such as virtual social networks.

Chapter 6: Neutrosophic Hyper Soft Set for Multi-Criteria Decision Making

Neutrosophic Hyper Soft Set emerges as a powerful tool for addressing multi-criteria decision-making challenges. This chapter presents a numerical example utilizing Neutrosophic Hyper Soft Sets to select the best school in a locality, showcasing its effectiveness through comparison with existing methods.

Chapter 7: Python Toolbox for Single-Valued and Interval-Valued Fermatean Neutrosophic Matrices

This chapter introduces a Python toolbox under the neutrosophic environment for single-valued and interval-valued Fermatean neutrosophic matrices. It provides definitions, operations, and examples to facilitate understanding and practical application.

Chapter 8: Neutrosophic Probability Modeling for Earth Observation Data

Focused on Earth observation data modeling, this chapter proposes a new neutrosophic probability model for Normalized Difference Vegetation Index (NDVI). It explores mathematical characteristics, inferential statistics, reliability measures, and graphical representations, showcasing its utility in analyzing environmental data.

Chapter 9: Compactness in Neutrosophic Generalized Topology for Effective Decision Making

This chapter introduces a novel technique utilizing compactness in Neutrosophic Generalized Topology for efficacious decision-making. It defines μN-compact and μN-feebly compact spaces, analyzing their properties and relationships, offering a valuable approach to resolving complex decision tasks.

Chapter 10: Single-Valued Neutrosophic Numbers for School Evaluation and Decision Making

Using single-valued neutrosophic numbers (S-VNNs) and the Additive Ratio Assessment (ARAS) method, this chapter proposes a comprehensive framework for school evaluation and decision-making. It presents mathematical operations, aggregation operators, and a comparative analysis with other methods to demonstrate its effectiveness.

Chapter 11: Configurational Analysis in Neutrosophic Decision Making

This chapter explores a configurational approach in decision-making, integrating neutrosophic logic, statistics, and probability analysis. It discusses the interplay between configurational analysis and neutrosophy, offering insights into resolving complex and uncertain problems.

CONCLUSION

In concluding this preface and chapter overview for our edited reference book on *Multi-Criteria Decision Making Models and Techniques: Neutrosophic Approaches*, we are excited about the depth and breadth of insights offered within these pages. Our collaboration with esteemed scholars from Zagazig University, Egypt, and the University of New Mexico, USA, has resulted in a collection of chapters that push the boundaries of decision-making methodologies.

The chapters in this book traverse a wide spectrum of innovative approaches, from TOPSIS methodology to plithogenic cognitive maps, and from digital authentication using neutrosophic concepts to interval-valued complex neutrosophic sets for uncertainty characterization. Each chapter is crafted to not only inform but also inspire further exploration and application of these advanced techniques.

We believe that this book will be a valuable asset to professionals and academics across various domains, providing them with the tools and frameworks needed to navigate complex decision landscapes with confidence and precision. The inclusion of practical examples, algorithms, and theoretical discussions ensures a well-rounded understanding of the topics at hand.

As editors, we extend our gratitude to the contributors for their dedication and expertise in shaping this comprehensive resource. We are confident that readers will find immense value in the theories, methodologies, and insights presented here, paving the way for more informed and impactful decision-making processes in the future.

Mohamed Abdel-Basset
Zagazig University, Egypt

Abduallah Gamal
Zagazig University, Egypt

Florentin Smarandache
University of New Mexico, USA

Chapter 1
Enhancing Decision-Making for Parents:
A Neutrosophic Pythagorean Plithogenic Hypersoft Set Approach to School Selection With TOPSIS Method

R. Narmada Devi
https://orcid.org/0000-0001-6472-3003
Vel Tech Rangarajan Dr. Sagunthala R&D Institute of Science and Technology, India

Parthiban Yamini
https://orcid.org/0009-0001-8802-129X
Vel Tech Rangarajan Dr. Sagunthala R&D Institute of Science and Technology, India

ABSTRACT

TOPSIS (technique for order preference by similarity to ideal solution) is a mathematical approach employed in the context of multi-criteria decision-making. Its primary purpose is to establish a ranking among various alternatives by taking into consideration multiple attributes or criteria. This method utilizes distance metrics to gauge the nearness of each alternative to both the ideal and anti-ideal solutions. Ultimately, its goal is to facilitate the identification of the most optimal alternative. In this era of uncertainty, many parents grapple with myriad uncertainties when it comes to selecting the right educational institution for their children. This chapter provides an initial glimpse into the neutrosophic pythagorean plithogenic hypersoft set (N_pphs) along with its fundamental definition. Additionally, an algorithm has

DOI: 10.4018/979-8-3693-2085-3.ch001

been devised for the TOPSIS methodology, accompanied by a practical numerical illustration. This is intended to assist parents in making an informed decision when choosing the most suitable school for their children with their set of criteria.

1. INTRODUCTION

In today's dynamic world, parents are confronted with the daunting task of selecting the most suitable educational institution for their children. This decision, laden with uncertainties and complexities, is often fraught with anxiety and indecision. The multitude of factors to consider, ranging from academic reputation and teaching methodologies to extracurricular offerings and location, only serve to exacerbate the challenge. It is within this context of uncertainty that our study seeks to provide a solution.

Existing approaches to decision-making, while valuable, often struggle to adequately address the multifaceted nature of the decision-making process involved in selecting educational institutions. Traditional methods may overlook crucial factors or fail to account for the inherent uncertainties and ambiguities in the decision-making environment. This gap in the literature underscores the need for a more comprehensive and nuanced approach.

The methodologies of fuzzy sets, neutrosophic sets, and soft sets offer a promising avenue for addressing the complexities of decision-making under uncertainty. By allowing for the representation of vague, imprecise, or conflicting information, these methodologies provide a more nuanced understanding of the decision space. Moreover, their flexibility and adaptability make them well-suited for integrating multiple criteria and preferences, essential in the context of educational decision-making.

Prior studies have addressed the challenges inherent in decision-making under uncertainty, particularly in the context of selecting educational institutions for children. These studies have underscored the multifaceted nature of the decision-making process and the need for comprehensive frameworks to guide parents in their choices (Zadeh, 1965; Zadeh, 1978; Atanassov, 2012).

Zadeh's seminal work on fuzzy sets laid the groundwork for handling imprecise and uncertain information in decision-making (Zadeh, 1965). Subsequent research by Atanassov (2012) extended this framework to intuitionistic fuzzy sets, which incorporate degrees of hesitation or non-membership. These methodologies have been applied in various domains to address decision-making challenges influenced by fuzziness and ambiguity (Bellman & Zadeh, 1970).

The introduction of neutrosophic sets by Smarandache (2017) offered a further extension of fuzzy logic, allowing for the representation of indeterminacy, contradiction, and incomplete information. This approach has found applications in diverse fields, including decision-making under uncertainty (Smarandache, 2017; Devi & Muthumari, 2021). Moreover, the concept of neutrosophic soft sets introduced by Broumi (2013) has provided a flexible framework for handling uncertain and imprecise data.

Building upon these foundational works, researchers have explored novel constructs such as plithogenic sets and logic introduced by Smarandache (2017, 2018). These developments have spurred significant scholarly interest, with researchers investigating their practical applications in decision-making contexts (Martin & Smarandache, 2020; Martin, Smarandache, & Broumi, 2021; Sankar, Sujatha, & Nagarajan, 2020).

Despite these advancements, existing approaches to decision-making in the context of selecting educational institutions may overlook certain factors or fail to adequately address the complexities inherent in the decision space. A comprehensive survey of prior literature reveals potential areas for improvement, such as the integration of multiple criteria and preferences, the consideration of uncertainty and ambiguity, and the need for practical decision-making frameworks tailored to real-world scenarios (Smarandache & Pramanik, 2016).

By synthesizing and analyzing prior studies, we aim to identify gaps in existing knowledge and inform the development of our proposed decision-making framework. Through a comprehensive literature review, we can draw upon the strengths of previous approaches while addressing their limitations, ultimately contributing to the advancement of decision-making methodologies in uncertain environments.

This study is significant not only for its potential to enhance the decision-making process for parents but also for its broader implications in other domains characterized by uncertainty. By offering a systematic framework for navigating uncertainty, our research aims to empower decision-makers across various sectors to make more informed and effective choices.

In the subsequent sections of this paper, we will delve into the intricacies of our proposed decision-making framework, drawing upon the principles of fuzzy sets, neutrosophic sets, and soft sets. We will demonstrate the practical application of this framework through a real-world scenario: the selection of educational institutions for children. Through empirical analysis and numerical examples, we will illustrate the efficacy of our approach and its potential to revolutionize decision-making in uncertain environments.

2. PRELIMINARIES

This section describes the definition of neutrosophic set$(\mathscr{N}_{\mathfrak{s}})$, neutrosophic Pythagorean set $(\mathscr{N}_{\mathfrak{ps}})$ and Plithogenic set$(\mathscr{P}_{\mathfrak{s}})$.

Definition 2.1.

Let $\mathscr{H}$ be an non empty set over an universal set $\mathscr{G}$ and $\mathscr{J}$ is said to be an $\mathscr{N}_{\mathfrak{s}}$. Then

$$\mathscr{J} = \{\langle h, \aleph(h), \partial(h), \Upsilon(h)\rangle : h \in \mathscr{H}\}$$

where $\aleph, \eth, \Upsilon : \mathscr{H} \to [0,1]$ and $0 \le \aleph(h) + \eth(h) + \Upsilon(h) \le 3$. Here $\aleph(h), \partial(h)$ and $\Upsilon(h)$ are degree of true membership, degree of indeterminacy and degree of falsity.

Definition 2.2.

Let $\mathscr{H}$ be an non empty set and $\mathscr{J}$ is said to be an $\mathscr{N}_{\mathfrak{ps}}$. Then

$$\mathscr{J} = \{\langle h, \aleph(h), \precsim(h), \Upsilon(h)\rangle : h \in \mathscr{H}\}$$

where $,\eth, \Upsilon : \mathscr{H} \to [0,1]$ and $0 \le \aleph(h) + \eth(h) + \Upsilon(h) \le 2$. Here $0 \le \aleph(h)^2 + \eth(h)^2 \le 1$ and $\le \Upsilon(h)^2 \le 1$.

Definition 2.3.

A set *X* earns the classification of being a plithogenic set when all its constituents are characterized by specific attributes, and each attribute can accommodate a variable number of attribute values ($\rtimes$)[24]. Each attribute value is linked to a corresponding degree of association concerning the element *x* in relation to set *X*, considering specific criteria. Furthermore, to enhance the precision of aggregation procedures for plithogenic sets, a contradiction degree function is introduced, which assesses the relationship between each attribute value and the predominant attribute value within an attribute. These degrees of association and contradiction can exhibit fuzzy, intuitionistic fuzzy, or neutrosophic characteristics.

Definition 2.4.

A Plithogenic set $(\mathscr{P}_{\mathfrak{s}})$ serves as a comprehensive extension of various set types, including crisp sets, fuzzy sets $(\mathscr{F}_{\mathfrak{s}})$, intuitionistic fuzzy sets $(\mathscr{I}_{\mathfrak{f}\mathfrak{s}})$, and neutrosophic sets $(\mathscr{N}_{\mathfrak{s}})$. These distinct categories are distinguished by their specific attribute values: a single value (belonging) for crisp sets and fuzzy sets, two values (belonging and non-belonging) for intuitionistic fuzzy sets, and three values (belonging, non-belonging, and indeterminacy) for neutrosophic sets. In a broader sense, a $\mathscr{P}_{\mathfrak{s}}$ is characterized by its members being determined through a collection of elements with four or more attribute values.

3. NEUTROSOPHIC PYTHAGOREAN PLITHOGENIC HYPERSOFT SET

This section clearly explains new concepts of neutrosophic pythagorean plithogenic set$(\mathscr{N}_{\mathfrak{pp}\mathfrak{s}})$, neutrosophic pythagorean plithogenic hypersoft set$(\mathscr{N}_{\mathfrak{pp}\mathfrak{h}\mathfrak{s}})$ and its operations.

Definition 3.5.

A neutrosophic pythagorean plithogenic set$(\mathscr{N}_{\mathfrak{pp}\mathfrak{s}})$ is be defined as a collection where its constituents are characterized by attributes encompassing a variety of attribute values. Moreover, these attributes and their associated values have the capacity to encompass degrees of uncertainty and ambiguity in accordance with the principles of neutrosophic pythagorean. This innovative framework proves to be highly beneficial in addressing intricate, uncertain, and indistinct information across a range of practical applications, including decision-making and the representation of knowledge.

Let $\mathfrak{P}$ a non-empty set of elements over $\mathscr{G}$,i.e., $\mathfrak{P} \subset \mathscr{G}\mathscr{N}_{\mathfrak{pp}\mathfrak{h}\mathfrak{s}}$

Definition 3.6.

$A\,\mathscr{N}_{\mathfrak{pp}\mathfrak{s}}$ is termed a $\mathscr{N}_{\mathfrak{pp}\mathfrak{h}\mathfrak{s}}$ when $\mathfrak{I}(\rtimes) \in \mathscr{P}([0,1])$, where $\mathscr{P}([0,1])$ signifies the power set of $\mathscr{N}_{\mathfrak{pp}\mathfrak{h}\mathfrak{s}}$.

Definition 3.7. (Attribute Value Spectrum)

Consider a set of uni-dimensional attributes denoted as $\mathscr{Z}$, where $\mathscr{Z}$ comprises attributes such as $\mathfrak{Z}_1, \mathfrak{Z}_2, \ldots, \mathfrak{Z}_\mathfrak{g}$, with $\mathfrak{g} \geq 1$. Among these attributes, let $\mathfrak{Z}$ be a specific attribute. The spectrum of all possible values or states for $\mathfrak{Z}$ is represented by the non-empty set $\mathfrak{W}$. The set $\mathfrak{W}$ can take on one of the following forms:

a) For a finite discrete set, $\mathfrak{W}$ is defined as $\mathfrak{W} = \{\mathfrak{w}_1, \mathfrak{w}_2, \ldots, \mathfrak{w}_l\}$, where l is a positive integer less than infinity.
b) For an infinitely countable set, $\mathfrak{W}$ is given as $\mathfrak{W} = \{\mathfrak{w}_1, \mathfrak{w}_2, \ldots, \mathfrak{w}_\infty\}$.
c) For an infinitely uncountable (continuum) set, $\mathfrak{W}$ is expressed as $\mathfrak{W} =]\mathfrak{c}, \mathfrak{d}[$, where $\mathfrak{c}$ is less than $\mathfrak{d}$, and]... [can represent an open, semi-open, or closed interval taken from the set of real numbers or another general set.

Definition 3.8. (Attribute Value Range)

Let ξ be a non-empty subset of $\mathfrak{W}$, where ξ is the range of all attribute values needed by the experts for their application. Each element $\mathfrak{x} \in \mathfrak{P}$ is characterized by all attribute values in $\xi = \{\mathfrak{v}_1, \mathfrak{v}_2, \ldots, \mathfrak{v}_\mathfrak{n}\}$, for $\mathfrak{n} \geq 1$.

Definition 3.9. (Dominant Attribute Value $(\rtimes_{\mathfrak{b}i})$)

Within the set of attribute values, denoted as ξ, it is customary to identify a predominant attribute value, a determination typically made by experts as they apply their expertise. The term "predominant attribute value" signifies the attribute value of utmost significance to the experts and aligning with their specific interests.

Nevertheless, there arise situations where in the consideration of such a predominant attribute value is not a given or may not even have relevance. Alternatively, multiple predominant (significant) attribute values may come into play. In such instances, an alternative approach becomes necessary.

Definition 3.10. (Appurtenance Attribute Value $(\rtimes)$ Degree Function $(\mathfrak{I}(\rtimes))$)

For each attribute value $\mathfrak{v} \in \xi$, there exists a corresponding degree of affiliation denoted as $d(\mathfrak{x}, \mathfrak{v})$ for the element $\mathfrak{x}$ concerning the set $\mathfrak{P}$, all within the context of specified criteria.

The degree of affiliation can be expressed as a neutrosophic pythagorean degree of affiliation with respect to the plithogenic set.

Consequently, the attribute value's degree of affiliation function can be defined as follows: For all $\mathfrak{x} \in \mathfrak{P}$, the function $d\colon \mathfrak{P} \times \xi \to \mathscr{P}([0,1])$ So, $d(\mathfrak{x}, \mathfrak{v})$ represents a subset of [0,1].

In essence, this function quantifies the extent to which an element $\mathfrak{x}$ is associated with various attribute values in ξ, taking into consideration a neutrosophic pythagorean measures of affiliation within the plithogenic set.

Definition 3.11. (Attribute Value Contradiction (Dissimilarity) Degree Function)

Let the cardinality $|\xi| = 3$. The attribute value for neutrosophic puthagorean plithogenic dissimilarity degree function, denoted as $\mathfrak{a}: \xi \times \xi \to [0,1]$, which quantifies the level of contradiction or dissimilarity between any two attribute values, $\mathfrak{v}_1$ and $\mathfrak{v}_2$. This function, represented as $\mathfrak{a}(\mathfrak{v}_1, \mathfrak{v}_2)$, adheres to the following principles:

1. $\mathfrak{a}(\mathfrak{v}_1, \mathfrak{v}_1) = 0$: The contradiction degree between identical attribute values is set to zero.
2. $\mathfrak{a}(\mathfrak{v}_1, \mathfrak{v}_2) = \mathfrak{a}(\mathfrak{v}_2, \mathfrak{v}_1)$

In essence, this newly introduced function quantifies the extent of dissimilarity or contradiction between attribute values $\mathfrak{v}_1$ and $\mathfrak{v}_2$ within the set ξ, where $|\xi| = 3$.

Primarily, we calculate the degree of dissimilarity between one-dimensional attribute values. In the case of multi-dimensional attribute values, we break them down into their respective one-dimensional attribute values for the purpose of computation. In essence, our focus is primarily on quantifying the level of contradiction or dissimilarity among attribute values that are one-dimensional. When dealing with multi-dimensional attributes, can disassemble them into their individual one-dimensional components before conducting the dissimilarity assessments.

Definition 3.12.

The attribute is denoted as $\mathfrak{z}$ and set of all attributes is defined as "appurtenance."

The set of possible attribute values is represented by ξ, which includes the values $\{\aleph, \eth, \Upsilon\}$, and the cardinality of ξ is $|\xi| = 3$.

The predominant attribute value for $\mathfrak{z}$ is $\aleph$. The attribute value appurtenance degree function is defined as follows:

For all $\mathfrak{x} \in \mathfrak{P}$, the function $d: \mathfrak{P} \times \xi \to [0,1]$ where $-0 \leq d(\mathfrak{x}, \aleph)^2 + d(\mathfrak{x}, \Upsilon)^2 \leq 1$ and $-0 \leq d(\mathfrak{x}, \eth)^2 \leq 1$. Note that the sum of these appurtenance degrees for any $\mathfrak{x}$ must satisfy the condition $0 \leq d(\mathfrak{x}, \aleph)^2 + d(\mathfrak{x}, \eth)^2 + d(\mathfrak{x}, \Upsilon)^2 \leq 2$.

Definition 3.13.

The function that assesses the degree of dissimilarity or contradiction between attribute values is denoted as $\mathfrak{a}$ and is formally defined as:

$$\mathfrak{a}:\xi \times \xi \rightarrow [0,1]$$

The specific values assigned to this function $\mathfrak{a}$ are as follows:

$$\mathfrak{a}(\aleph,\aleph) = \mathfrak{a}(\eth,\eth) = \mathfrak{a}(\Upsilon,\Upsilon) = 0$$

$$\mathfrak{a}(\aleph,\Upsilon) = 1$$

$$\mathfrak{a}(\aleph,\eth) = \mathfrak{a}(\Upsilon,\eth) = 0.5$$

In essence, the function $\mathfrak{a}$ quantifies the level of dissimilarity or contradiction between various attribute values. The assigned values indicate the degree of dissimilarity, where values of 0 represent no contradiction, 0.5 denote moderate contradiction, and a value of 1 signifies complete contradiction.

Definition 3.14.

Let $\mathcal{J}$ and $\mathcal{K}$ are two Neutrosophic Pythagorean set under plithogenic condition is defined as

$$\mathcal{J} = \{h_1, \aleph(h_1), \eth(h_1), \Upsilon(h_1) : h_1 \in \mathcal{H}\}$$

$$\mathcal{K} = \{h_2, \aleph(h_2), \eth(h_2), \Upsilon(h_2) : h_2 \in \mathcal{H}\}$$

Then the union, intersection, compliment operations is defined in terms of t_{norm} (Δ) and t_{conorm} (∇) as follows:

<u>**UNION**</u>

$$\mathcal{J} \mathcal{V} \mathcal{K} = \left\{h_1, \aleph(h_1) \nabla \aleph(h_2), \tfrac{1}{2}[\eth(h_1)\Delta\eth(h_2) + \eth(h_1) \nabla \eth(h_2)], \Upsilon(h_1)\Delta\Upsilon(h_2) : h_1, h_2 \in \mathcal{H}\right\}$$

INTERSECTION

$$\mathcal{J}\delta\mathcal{K} = \left\{h_1, \aleph(h_1)\Delta\aleph(h_2), \tfrac{1}{2}[\eth(h_1)\Delta\eth(h_2) + \eth(h_1) \ \nabla \ \eth(h_2)], \Upsilon(h_1) \ \nabla \ \Upsilon(h_2): h_1, h_2 \in \mathcal{H}\right\}$$

COMPLIMENT

$\mathcal{J}^{C} = \left\{h_1, \Upsilon(h_1), \eth(h_1), \aleph(h_1): h_1 \in \mathcal{H}\right\}$ where, $\aleph(\mathbf{h}_1)\Delta\aleph(\mathbf{h}_2) = (\aleph(\mathbf{h}_1))(\aleph(\mathbf{h}_2))$ and $\aleph(\mathbf{h}_1) \ \nabla \ \aleph(\mathbf{h}_2) =$

$$\aleph(\mathbf{h}_1) + \aleph(\mathbf{h}_2) - (\aleph(\mathbf{h}_1))(\aleph(\mathbf{h}_2))$$

Example 3.1: Let $\mathcal{Y} = \{\mathfrak{y}_1, \mathfrak{y}_2, \mathfrak{y}_3\}$ be a set of three house and $\xi = \{\text{Price}(\mathfrak{z}_1), \text{Model}(\mathfrak{z}_2), \text{Colour}(\mathfrak{z}_3)\}$
where,

$$\mathfrak{z}_1 = \{\text{low}(\mathfrak{z}_{11}), \text{Moderate}(\mathfrak{z}_{12}), \text{Costly}(\mathfrak{z}_{13})\},$$

$$\mathfrak{z}_2 = \{\text{Old}(\mathfrak{z}_{21}), \text{Latest}(\mathfrak{z}_{22})\}$$

$$\mathfrak{z}_3 = \{\text{Red}(\mathfrak{z}_{31}), \text{Blue}(\mathfrak{z}_{32}), \text{Pink}(\mathfrak{z}_{33}), \text{Black}(\mathfrak{z}_{34})\}$$

$$\mathcal{B}_1(\mathfrak{z}_{11}, \mathfrak{z}_{22}, \mathfrak{z}_{34}) = \{(\mathfrak{z}_{11}, \mathfrak{z}_{22}, \mathfrak{z}_{34}), \mathfrak{y}_1(0.5,0.6,0.2),(0.7,0.8,0.2),(0.6,0.9,0.1),$$

$$\mathfrak{y}_3((0.6,0.6,0.3),(0.5,0.9,0.4),(0.9,0.9,0.1))$$

$$\mathcal{B}_2(\mathfrak{z}_{11}, \mathfrak{z}_{22}, \mathfrak{z}_{34}) = \{(\mathfrak{z}_{11}, \mathfrak{z}_{22}, \mathfrak{z}_{34}), \mathfrak{y}_1(0.5,0.6,0.2),(0.5,0.7,0.4),(0.3,0.6,0.4),$$

$$\mathfrak{y}_3\langle(0.4,0.6,0.1),(0.5,0.9,0.4),(0.3,0.9,0.5)\rangle\}$$

$$\mathcal{B}_3(\mathfrak{z}_{11}, \mathfrak{z}_{22}, \mathfrak{z}_{34}) = \{(\mathfrak{z}_{11}, \mathfrak{z}_{22}, \mathfrak{z}_{34}), \mathfrak{y}_1(0.4,0.5,0.3),(0.5,0.7,0.4),(0.5,0.7,0.3),$$

$\mathfrak{y}_3\langle(0.6,0.9,0.2),(0.5,0.9,0.4),(0.3,0.9,0.6)\rangle\}$

Table 1. Examples for contradiction, union, intersection, compliment

Contradiction	$[(\mathfrak{z}_1,\mathfrak{z}_2) = 0,(\mathfrak{z}_1,\mathfrak{z}_1) = 1],\left[(\mathfrak{z}_{11},\mathfrak{z}_{12}) = \frac{1}{3},(\mathfrak{z}_{12},\mathfrak{z}_{13}) = \frac{2}{3}\right]$
Union	$\mathscr{B}_1\mathscr{V}\mathscr{B}_2(\mathfrak{z}_{11},\mathfrak{z}_{22},\mathfrak{z}_{34}) = \{(\mathfrak{z}_{11},\mathfrak{z}_{22},\mathfrak{z}_{34}),\mathfrak{y}_1\langle(0.8,0.6,0.4),(0.85,0.75,0.04),(0.72,0.75,0.04)\rangle$ $\mathfrak{y}_3\langle(0.76,0.6,0.03),(0.75,0.9,0.16),(0.93,0.9,0.05)\rangle\}$
Intersection	$\mathscr{B}_1\delta\mathscr{B}_2(\mathfrak{z}_{11},\mathfrak{z}_{22},\mathfrak{z}_{34}) = \{(\mathfrak{z}_{11},\mathfrak{z}_{22},\mathfrak{z}_{34}),\mathfrak{y}_1\langle(0.25,0.6,0.36),(0.35,0.75,0.36),(0.18,0.75,0.46)\rangle$ $\mathfrak{y}_3\langle(0.24,0.6,0.037),(0.25,0.9,0.64),(0.27,0.9,0.55)\rangle\}$
Compliment	$\mathscr{B}_3(\mathfrak{z}_{11},\mathfrak{z}_{22},\mathfrak{z}_{34})^C = \{(\mathfrak{z}_{11},\mathfrak{z}_{22},\mathfrak{z}_{34}),\mathfrak{y}_1\langle(0.3,0.5,0.4),(0.4,0.7,0.5),(0.3,0.7,0.5)\rangle,$ $\mathfrak{y}_3\langle(0.2,0.9,0.6),(0.4,0.9,0.5),(0.6,0.9,0.3)\rangle\}$

4. FLOWCHART

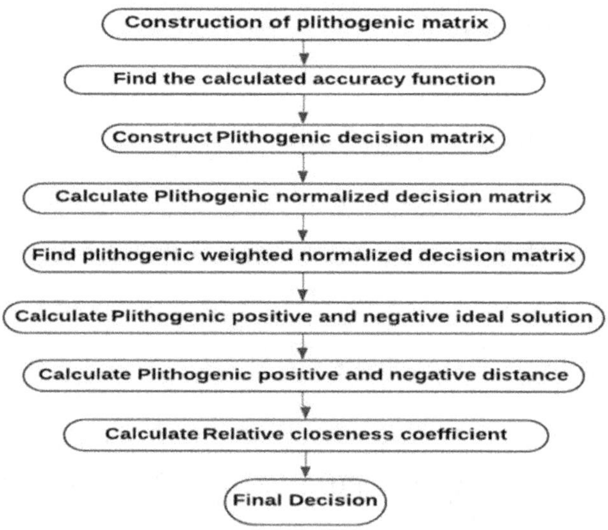

5. ALGORITHM FOR $\mathscr{N}_{\mathfrak{pph}\mathfrak{z}}$ TOPSIS METHOD

Using a real-world example like evaluating job candidates helps to illustrate the application of the framework in a tangible and relevant context. It allows readers to see how the theoretical concepts and steps of the framework translate into practical decision-making processes that they may encounter in their own professional or personal lives.

Furthermore, the example of evaluating job candidates showcases the versatility and broad applicability of the framework beyond theoretical discussions. It demonstrates how the framework can be used to address specific decision-making challenges, such as selecting the best candidate from a pool of applicants based on multiple criteria like qualifications, experience, and communication skills.

While it's true that the authors could have explained the basic steps of the framework without resorting to the problem of evaluating candidates, using a concrete example adds depth and richness to the explanation. It provides context and relevance to the theoretical concepts, making them more engaging and easier to grasp for readers.

Overall, the choice to address the problem of evaluating potential candidates for a job serves to enhance the clarity, relevance, and practicality of the explanation of the framework, ultimately aiding readers in understanding and applying it effectively.

TOPSIS (Technique for Order Preference by Similarity to Ideal Solution) was likely chosen for its well-established theoretical foundation, simplicity, and widespread use in decision-making literature. Despite the emergence of newer approaches, TOPSIS remains a popular and extensively studied method for multi-criteria decision-making.

One reason for choosing TOPSIS could be its ease of understanding and implementation. TOPSIS offers a straightforward methodology that is accessible to a wide range of users, including practitioners and researchers who may not have specialized knowledge in advanced decision-making techniques. Its simplicity makes it an attractive choice for illustrating the steps of the framework and demonstrating how the $\mathcal{N}_{\mathfrak{pphs}}$ methodology can be applied in practice.

Additionally, TOPSIS has been extensively validated and applied in various real-world decision-making contexts across different domains. Its effectiveness in handling multi-criteria decision-making problems has been demonstrated in numerous studies, further reinforcing its suitability for the task at hand.

While newer approaches may offer certain advantages or advancements over TOPSIS, such as enhanced computational efficiency or the ability to handle more complex decision-making scenarios, TOPSIS remains a valuable tool in the decision-makers toolkit. Its continued relevance and widespread use make it a pragmatic choice for illustrating the steps of the $\mathcal{N}_{\mathfrak{pphs}}$ framework and showcasing its practical application in evaluating alternatives and selecting the best option. The steps for the $\mathcal{N}_{\mathfrak{pphs}}$-based TOPSIS method as follows:

Step 1:

Construct a matrix ($\mathscr{L}$) of order $\mathfrak{e} \times \mathfrak{m}$, whose entries are the neutrosophic degree of appurtenance of each attribute value, with respect to each alternative under consideration.

Step 2:

Utilize the newly developed accuracy function $\mathscr{A}_{\mathfrak{i}}$ on each element of the matrix obtained in Step 1. This is done with the aim of converting each element into a single, well-defined value, as follows:

$$\mathscr{A}_{\mathfrak{i}} = \frac{\aleph_{\rtimes i} + \eth_{\rtimes i} + \Upsilon_{\rtimes i}}{3} + \frac{\aleph_{\rtimes_{(b)i}} + \eth_{\rtimes_{(b)i}} + \Upsilon_{\rtimes_{(b)i}}}{3}\left[\mathfrak{a}\left(\rtimes i, \rtimes_{(b)i}\right)\right]$$

where $\rtimes i, \rtimes_{(b)i}$ and $\mathfrak{a}\left(\rtimes i, \rtimes_{(b)i}\right)$ are appurtenance attribute values, dominant attibutes values, and degree of contradiction between appurtenance attribute values and dominant attribute values.

Step 3:

Perform the transposition operation on the plithogenic accuracy matrix to derive the plithogenic decision matrix $\left(\mathscr{D}_{\mathfrak{p}} = \left[\mathfrak{f}_{\mathfrak{t}j}\right]_{\mathfrak{t}\times\mathfrak{u}}\right)$. This matrix encapsulates the relationships between alternatives and criteria.

Step 4:

Construction of a plithogenic normalized decision matrix $\left(\mathfrak{G}_{\mathfrak{p}}\right)$ to illustrate the relative performance of alternatives. The elements of this matrix are determined in the following manner:

$$\mathfrak{G}_{\mathfrak{p}} = \frac{\mathfrak{f}_{\mathfrak{j}}}{\sqrt{\sum_{\mathfrak{t}=1}^{\mathfrak{q}} \mathfrak{f}_{\mathfrak{tj}}^{2}}} \quad \mathfrak{j} = 1,2,3,\ldots,\mathfrak{u}$$

Step 5:

Construct a plithogenic weighted normalized decision matrix $\mathscr{Q}_{\mathfrak{p}} = \left[\mathfrak{q}_{\mathfrak{tj}}\right]_{\mathfrak{t}\times\mathfrak{u}} = \mathscr{W}_{\mathfrak{r}} \mathfrak{G}_{\mathfrak{p}}$, in which $\mathscr{W}_{\mathfrak{r}} = \left\{\mathscr{W}_1, \mathscr{W}_2, \mathscr{W}_3, \ldots, \mathscr{W}_{\mathfrak{h}}\right\}$ and represents a row vector denoting the allocated weights attributed to the criteria, $\mathscr{W}_{\mathfrak{o}}(\mathfrak{o} = 1,2,3,\ldots,\mathfrak{h})$ and $\sum_{\mathfrak{o}=1}$

$\mathcal{W}_{o} = 1$. Additionally, the decision maker assigns varying weights to each selection criterion, reflecting their respective importance in the decision-making process.

Step 6:

Calculate the plithogenic positive ideal solution $\mathcal{Q}_p^+$ and the plithogenic negative ideal solution $\mathcal{Q}_p^-$ utilizing the subsequent formula:

For benificial criteria:

$$\mathcal{Q}_p^+ = \left\{\max_{\iota=1}^{t} q_{\iota j}\right\}; j = 1,2,3,\ldots,u \ \mathcal{Q}_p^- = \left\{\min_{\iota=1}^{t} q_{\iota j}\right\}; j = 1,2,3,\ldots,u$$

For cost criteria:

$$\mathcal{Q}_p^+ = \left\{\min_{\iota=1}^{t} q_{\iota j}\right\}; j = 1,2,3,\ldots,u, \mathcal{Q}_p^- = \left\{\max_{\iota=1}^{t} q_{\iota j}\right\}; j = 1,2,3,\ldots,u$$

Step 7:

Determine the plithogenic positive distance $\mathcal{R}^+$ and the plithogenic negative distance $\mathcal{R}^-$ for each alternative in relation to $\mathcal{Q}_p^+$ and $\mathcal{Q}_p^-$ respectively, utilizing the subsequent mathematical formulas:

$$\mathcal{R}_\iota^+ = \sqrt{\sum_{j=1}^{u} \left(q_{\iota j} - q_\iota^+\right)^2}; \iota = 1,2,3,\ldots,t$$

$$\mathcal{R}_\iota^- = \sqrt{\sum_{j=1}^{u} \left(q_{\iota j} - q_\iota^-\right)^2}; \iota = 1,2,3,\ldots,t$$

Step 8:

Determine the relative closeness coefficient $\mathcal{C}_\iota$ for each alternative utilizing the subsequent mathematical expression:

$$\mathcal{C}_\iota = \frac{\mathcal{R}_\iota^-}{\mathcal{R}_\iota^+ + \mathcal{R}_\iota^-}; \iota = 1,2,3,\ldots,t$$

Step 9:

The alternative possessing the greatest closeness coefficient is considered the most appropriate option.

6. NUMERICAL APPLICATION

Assessment of Alternatives: The assessment of alternatives/schools according to the given criteria was conducted by constructing a plithogenic decision matrix based on the relationship between attributes and criteria. Each school was evaluated based on its performance across the selection attributes, such as fees, distance, popularity, and educational qualities. The plithogenic decision matrix quantifies the relative performance of each school in relation to these criteria.

Scale and Linguistic Terms: The scale used for evaluation was represented by plithogenic values, which consist of three components denoting the truth, indeterminacy, and falsity. The linguistic terms associated with the plithogenic values, such as "Low," "Moderate," "High," "Very-near," "Almost-near," etc., provide a qualitative understanding of the performance of each school across the criteria.

Comparison with Other Approaches: While the numerical application demonstrates the effectiveness of the proposed framework in selecting the best school based on the parent's criteria, incorporating a discussion section comparing the results with other decision-making approaches would provide additional insights. This comparison could highlight the strengths and limitations of the $\mathcal{N}_{\mathfrak{pph s}}$ TOPSIS method relative to alternative methods, further validating its efficacy in real-world scenarios. Additionally, discussing the advantages and disadvantages of different decision-making approaches can help readers better understand the unique features and applicability of the proposed framework.

Selection-attributes = { Fees, Distance, Popularity, Educational qualities }. Each attribute has sub-attributes as follows:

Fees= {Low(t_1), Moderate(t_2), High(t_3)]

Distance= {Very Near(d_1), Almost Near(d_2), Near(d_3), Almost Long(d_4), Long(d_5), Very Long(d_6)]

Popularity= {Non Popular(p_1), More Popular(p_2)], and

$$\text{Educational - qualities} = \{\text{Poor}(e_1), \text{Moderate}(e_2), \text{High}(e_3)\}$$

Contradiction: $a(t_1, t_2) = \frac{1}{3}, a(t_1, t_3) = \frac{2}{3}.$

$$a(d_1, d_2) = \frac{1}{3}, a(d_1, d_3) = \frac{2}{3}, a(p_1, p_2) = \frac{1}{2}, a(e_1, e_2) = \frac{1}{3}, a(e_1, e_3) = \frac{2}{3}$$

Let the schools are denoted as $\{\mathscr{E}_1, \mathscr{E}_2, \mathscr{E}_3, \mathscr{E}_4\}$

Table 2. Relation between attributes and criteria

Variables	$\mathscr{E}_1$	$\mathscr{E}_2$	$\mathscr{E}_3$	$\mathscr{E}_4$
t_1	(0.4,0.2,0.2)	(0.5,0.1,0.4)	(0.1,0.6,0.8)	(0.2,0.3,0.7)
t_2	(0.8,0.9,0.2))	(0.7,0.4,0.3)	(0.2,0.5,0.6)	(0.7,0.8,0.4)
t_3	(0.5,0.5,0.2)	(0.1,0.2,0.5)	(0.2,0.3,0.7)	(0.5,0.7,0.4)
d_1	(0.9,0.3,0.1)	(0.9,0.3,0.0)	(0.9,0.5,0.1)	(0.8,0.4,0.1)
d_2	(0.8,0.4,0.1)	(0.6,0.1,0.3)	(0.5,0.2,0.4)	(0.7,0.5,0.3)
d_3	(0.9,0.5,0.1)	(0.8,0.2,0.2)	(0.6,0.4,0.4)	(0.2,0.4,0.6)
p_1	(0.3,0.4,06)	(0.3,0.2,0.4)	(0.2,0.7,0.3)	(0.7,0.4,0.1)
p_2	(1.0,0.3,0.0)	(0.7,0.5,0.3)	(0.4,0.5,0.4)	(0.6,0.3,0.3)
e_1	(0.2,0.3,0.5)	(0.4,0.5,0.6)	(0.7,0.9,0.3)	(0.2,0.7,0.6)
e_2	(0.2,0.2,0.7)	(0.3,0.3,0.6)	(0.3,0.7,0.2)	(0.2,0.7,0.7)
e_3	(0.5,0.6,0.5)	(0.9,0.8,0.1)	(0.9,0.8,0.0)	(0.7,0.7,0.2)

(i) **Construction of plithogenic matrix**

$$\mathscr{L}(t_2, d_2, p_2, e_3) = \begin{bmatrix} (0.8,0.9,0.2) & (0.7,0.4,0.3) & (0.2,0.5,0.6) & (0.7,0.8,0.4) \\ (0.8,0.4,0.1) & (0.6,0.1,0.3) & (0.5,0.2,0.4) & (0.7,0.5,0.3) \\ (1.0,0.3,0.0) & (0.7,0.5,0.3) & (0.4,0.5,0.4) & (0.6,0.3,0.3) \\ (0.5,0.6,0.5) & (0.9,0.8,0.1) & (0.9,0.8,0.0) & (0.7,0.7,0.2) \end{bmatrix}$$

(ii) **The accuracy function is calculated as below:**

$$\begin{bmatrix} 0.7221 & 0.5777 & 0.5999 & 0.7666 \\ 0.5777 & 0.4666 & 0.5332 & 0.6444 \\ 0.6499 & 0.6500 & 0.6333 & 0.6000 \\ 0.7555 & 0.9333 & 0.9888 & 0.8666 \end{bmatrix}$$

(iii) **Plithogenic decision matrix:**

$$\begin{bmatrix} 0.7221 & 0.5777 & 0.6499 & 0.7555 \\ 0.5777 & 0.4666 & 0.6500 & 0.9333 \\ 0.5999 & 0.5332 & 0.6333 & 0.9888 \\ 0.7666 & 0.6444 & 0.6000 & 0.8666 \end{bmatrix}$$

Table 3. Relation between attributes and criteria required for the parents

	t_2	d_2	p_2	e_3
$\mathscr{E}_1$	0.7221	0.5777	0.6499	0.7555
$\mathscr{E}_2$	0.5777	0.4666	0.6500	0.9333
$\mathscr{E}_3$	0.5999	0.5332	0.6333	0.9888
$\mathscr{E}_4$	0.7666	0.6444	0.6000	0.8666

(iv) **Plithogenic normalized decision matrix**

$$\mathfrak{G}_{\mathfrak{p}} = \begin{bmatrix} 0.5378 & 0.5165 & 0.5128 & 0.4242 \\ 0.4302 & 0.4171 & 0.5129 & 0.5241 \\ 0.4468 & 0.4767 & 0.4997 & 0.5553 \\ 0.5709 & 0.5761 & 0.4734 & 0.4866 \end{bmatrix}$$

(v) **Plithogenic weighted normalized decision matrix**

$$\mathscr{W}_{\mathbf{r}} = [0.23, 0.22, 0.15, 0.4]$$

$$\mathscr{Q}_{\mathfrak{p}} = \begin{bmatrix} 0.1236 & 0.1136 & 0.0769 & 0.1697 \\ 0.0989 & 0.0917 & 0.0770 & 0.2096 \\ 0.1027 & 0.1048 & 0.0749 & 0.2221 \\ 0.1313 & 0.1267 & 0.0710 & 0.1946 \end{bmatrix}$$

(vi) **Plithogenic positive and negative ideal solution**

$$\mathcal{Q}_{p^+} = [0.1313 \quad 0.1267 \quad 0.0770 \quad 0.2221]$$

$$\mathcal{Q}_{p^-} = [0.0989 \quad 0.0917 \quad 0.0710 \quad 0.1697]$$

(vii) **Plithogenic positive and negative distance**

$$\mathcal{R}_\iota^+ = \begin{bmatrix} 0.0545 \\ 0.0493 \\ 0.0360 \\ 0.0281 \end{bmatrix}$$

$$\mathcal{R}_\iota^- = \begin{bmatrix} 0.0335 \\ 0.0403 \\ 0.0542 \\ 0.0538 \end{bmatrix}$$

(viii) **relative closeness coefficient**

$$\mathcal{C}_\iota = \begin{bmatrix} 0.3806 \\ 0.4497 \\ 0.6008 \\ 0.6568 \end{bmatrix}$$

(ix) **Final decision**

Table 4. Relative closeness coefficient $\mathcal{C}_1$ for each alternative.

	$\mathcal{R}_\iota^+$	$\mathcal{R}_\iota^-$	$\mathcal{C}_\iota$	**Ranking**	**Decision**
$\mathcal{E}_1$	0.0545	0.0335	0.3806	4	$\mathcal{E}_4 > \mathcal{E}_3 > \mathcal{E}_2 > \mathcal{E}_1$
$\mathcal{E}_2$	0.0493	0.0403	0.4497	3	
$\mathcal{E}_3$	0.0360	0.0542	0.6008	2	
$\mathcal{E}_4$	0.0281	0.0538	0.6568	**1**	

Thus, the result shows that school $\mathscr{E}_4$ is the best school for the children with their parent's attributes.

7. RESULTS AND DISCUSSION

The final decision, as depicted in Table 4, presents a comprehensive evaluation of the alternative schools based on the parent-defined attributes, namely Fees, Distance, Popularity, and Educational Qualities. The relative closeness coefficients ($\mathscr{C}_{\mathfrak{l}}$) calculated for each school offer valuable insights into their suitability for children, guiding parents in making informed decisions regarding school selection.

Upon analyzing the results, it is evident that school $\mathscr{E}_4$ emerges as the most favorable option, with a notably high relative closeness coefficient of 0.6568. This indicates that $\mathscr{E}_4$ the closest alignment with the parent's criteria, demonstrating superior performance across the evaluated attributes. Notably, its plithogenic positive distance ($\mathscr{R}_{\mathfrak{l}}^{+}$) is the lowest among the alternatives, reflecting its proficiency in meeting the specified requirements.

Following closely behind is school $\mathscr{E}_3$, which achieves a relative closeness coefficient of 0.6008. While not surpassing $\mathscr{E}_4$, $\mathscr{E}_3$ demonstrates commendable performance across the criteria, positioning it as a strong contender for consideration.

In contrast, schools $\mathscr{E}_2$ and $\mathscr{E}_1$ rank lower in the evaluation, with relative closeness coefficients of 0.4497 and 0.3806, respectively. While both schools exhibit positive attributes, they fall short of $\mathscr{E}_4$and $\mathscr{E}_3$in terms of overall suitability based on the parent's preferences.

These findings underscore the importance of a systematic evaluation framework in assisting parents in making informed decisions regarding school selection for their children. By considering a comprehensive set of attributes and employing the $\mathscr{N}_{\mathfrak{pphs}}$TOPSIS method, parents can prioritize schools that best align with their specific requirements, ultimately enhancing the educational experience and outcomes for their children.

The numerical application of the $\mathscr{N}_{\mathfrak{pphs}}$ TOPSIS method in selecting the best school for children based on parent-defined criteria offers valuable insights into the decision-making process. By comparing the results obtained with traditional decision-making methods, such as traditional TOPSIS or Analytic Hierarchy Process (AHP), we can evaluate the effectiveness of the $\mathscr{N}_{\mathfrak{pphs}}$ TOPSIS approach in handling complex decision scenarios.

Moreover, conducting sensitivity analysis reveals the robustness of the method to variations in input data and criteria weights. This analysis provides insights into the stability of rankings and decisions, enhancing confidence in the reliability of the $\mathscr{N}_{\mathfrak{pphs}}$ TOPSIS method.

Interpreting the results sheds light on the significance of each criterion and sub-criterion in influencing the final decision. Attributes like educational qualities or popularity may carry more weight in the decision-making process for parents, reflecting their priorities and preferences.

However, it is crucial to acknowledge any limitations or assumptions made in the application of the $\mathcal{N}_{\mathfrak{pphs}}$ TOPSIS method. Future research could focus on refining the accuracy function or incorporating additional attributes to further improve decision outcomes.

Practically, the findings have implications for both parents and educational institutions. Parents can make more informed decisions about their children's education, while schools can use the insights to enhance their offerings and attract more students.

Comparing the $\mathcal{N}_{\mathfrak{pphs}}$ TOPSIS method with other decision-making approaches highlights its advantages and disadvantages. While traditional methods may have their merits, the $\mathcal{N}_{\mathfrak{pphs}}$ TOPSIS method offers a robust framework for handling subjective and contradictory criteria in decision-making contexts.

In conclusion, the numerical application demonstrates the effectiveness and relevance of the $\mathcal{N}_{\mathfrak{pphs}}$ TOPSIS method in real-world decision-making scenarios. By addressing these points in the discussion section, we provide a comprehensive analysis that enhances our understanding of the method's strengths and limitations.

8. CONCLUSION

Ultimately, the aim is to empower parents to make informed choices regarding their children's education, allowing them to navigate the complexities of school selection with confidence and precision. The integration of mathematical rigor and practical illustration serves as a bridge between theory and real-life decision-making, addressing the uncertainties that parents commonly encounter in this important aspect of their children's lives. TOPSIS stands as a robust mathematical tool for addressing the complexities of multi-criteria decision-making, offering a structured approach to rank alternatives based on diverse attributes. This approach considers uncertainties inherent in real-world scenarios, aiding in the identification of optimal solutions. The summary succinctly points out that, given the unique attributes and preferences of the parents, $\mathscr{E}_4$ stands out as the optimal educational institution for their children. This conclusion arises from a meticulous evaluation of various factors, ultimately leading to the selection of this particular school as the best fit for their children. In a similar vein $\mathcal{N}_{\mathfrak{pphs}}$ TOPSIS method is extends across a variety of domains, encompassing fields like medicine, industry, and construction etc.

FUNDING

This research received no external funding

ACKNOWLEDGMENT

We extend our gratitude to Mr. G. Nirmal and Mrs. N. Suganya for their valuable assistance in gathering data to demonstrate a numerical application in support of our contribution.

REFERENCES

Ahmad, M. R., Saeed, M., Afzal, U., & Yang, M. S. (2020). A novel MCDM method based on plithogenic hypersoft sets under fuzzy neutrosophic environment. *Symmetry*, 12(11), 1855. DOI:10.3390/sym12111855

Ali, M. I., Feng, F., Liu, X., Min, W. K., & Shabir, M. (2009). On some new operations in soft set theory. *Computers & Mathematics with Applications (Oxford, England)*, 57(9), 1547–1553. DOI:10.1016/j.camwa.2008.11.009

Atanassov, K. T. (2012). *On intuitionistic fuzzy sets theory* (Vol. 283). Springer. DOI:10.1007/978-3-642-29127-2

Bellman, R. E., & Zadeh, L. A. (1970). Decision-making in a fuzzy environment. *Management Science*, 17(4), B-141–B-164. DOI:10.1287/mnsc.17.4.B141

Broumi, S. (2013). *Generalized neutrosophic soft set*. Infinite Study. https://doi.org//arXiv.1305.2724DOI:10.48550

Christianto, V., Boyd, R. N., & Smarandache, F. (2020). *Three possible applications of neutrosophic logic in fundamental and applied sciences.* Infinite Study. https://doi.org/DOI:10.5281/zenodo.3692037

Devi, R., & Muthumari, G. (2021). View On Neutrosophic Over Topologized Domination Graphs. *Neutrosophic Sets and Systems, 47*(1), 33. https://dio.org/10.5281/zenodo.5775174

Devi, R. N., & Muthumari, G. (2022, November). Dominating energy in neutrosophic over topologized graphs. In AIP Conference Proceedings: Vol. 2516. *No. 1* (p. 210010). AIP Publishing LLC. DOI:10.1063/5.0108812

Maji, P. K., Biswas, R., & Roy, A. R. (2003). Soft set theory. *Computers & Mathematics with Applications (Oxford, England)*, 45(4-5), 555–562. DOI:10.1016/S0898-1221(03)00016-6

Martin, N., & Smarandache, F. (2020). *Introduction to combined plithogenic hypersoft sets.* Infinite Study. https://digitalrepository.unm.edu/nss_journal/vol35/iss1/28

Martin, N., Smarandache, F., & Broumi, S. (2021). Covid-19 decision-making model using extended plithogenic hypersoft sets with dual dominant attributes. *International Journal of Neutrosophic Science, 13*(2), 75-86. https://dio.org/10.5281/zenodo.4553562

Molodtsov, D. (1999). Soft set theory first results. *Computers & Mathematics with Applications (Oxford, England)*, 37(4-5), 19–31. DOI:10.1016/S0898-1221(99)00056-5

Sankar, C., Sujatha, R., & Nagarajan, D. (2020). *Topsis by using plithogenic set in COVID-19 decision making*. Infinite Study. htts://DOI:10.5281/zenodo.4011772

Smarandache, F. (2017). *Plithogeny, plithogenic set, logic, probability, and statistics*. Infinite Study. https://doi.org//arXiv.1808.03948DOI:10.48550

Smarandache, F. (2018). *Plithogenic set, an extension of crisp, fuzzy, intuitionistic fuzzy, and neutrosophic sets-revisited*. Infinite Study. https://doi.org/DOI:10.5281/zenodo.1408740

Smarandache, F., & Pramanik, S. 2016. *New trends in neutrosophic theory and applications (Vol. 1)*. Infinite Study. https://doi.org//arXiv.1611.08555DOI:10.48550

Zadeh, L. A. (1965). Fuzzy sets. *Information and Control*, 8(3), 338–353. DOI:10.1016/S0019-9958(65)90241-X

Zadeh, L. A. (1978). Fuzzy sets as a basis for a theory of possibility. *Fuzzy Sets and Systems*, 1(1), 3–28. DOI:10.1016/0165-0114(78)90029-5

Chapter 2
Plithogenic Fermatean-Based Plithogenic Cognitive Map Decision-Making Model

Nivetha Martin
Arul Anandar College (Autonomous), Karumathur, India

N. Angel
https://orcid.org/0000-0003-1182-3371
Department of Mathematics, Madurai Kamaraj University, India

P. Pandiammal
G.T.N. Arts College (Autonomous), India

Ramila Gandhi
PSNA College of Engineering and Technology, India

Florentin Smarandache
https://orcid.org/0000-0002-5560-5926
University of New Mexico, USA

ABSTRACT

The use of plithogenic cognitive maps is instrumental in tackling intricate decision-making structures. These models, utilizing plithogenic representations, enable the examination of interconnected influences among decision-making factors. This chapter introduces a novel type of plithogenic cognitive maps employing plithogenic Fermatean sets representations. The suggested decision-making model is employed to analyze the effects of digitalized educational system on the learning community.

DOI: 10.4018/979-8-3693-2085-3.ch002

A comparative assessment of the effectiveness and competence of this model against plithogenic cognitive maps with alternative representations is conducted. The outcomes exhibit greater promise for the proposed model. Consequently, this chapter advocates for the adoption of this decision-making approach to address problems involving complex interrelated factors.

1. INTRODUCTION

The well-constructed theory of Plithogeny has intense applications in the broad and comprehensive field of decision making. The efficacy of the decision-making models is measured by the extent of optimal resultants obtained on using suitable methods. Cognitive Maps are one such excellent decision-making tools primarily applied in investigating the causal relationship existing between the factors of the considered decision-making problem. These cognitive maps are basically graphical structures with nodes and edges representing the factors and causal effects respectively. The positive, negative and null associational impacts between the factors are represented by the edge weights belonging to the set {1,0,-1}. The extension of this cognitive maps into fuzzy, intuitionistic and neutrosophic differ by the representations of the edge weights. Nivetha and Smarandache (Martin, Smarandache, 2020) discussed Plithogenic cognitive maps and applied in developing a decision making model. Plithogeny based cognitive maps are widely employed in exploring the causal effect relationship in the context of problems pertinent to disease diagnosis and education. However, Plithogenic cognitive maps has dealt with Plithogenic fuzzy representations. In a Plithogenic cognitive map decision model, the initial constructions of factors and associational impacts are based on the intuition of the experts. The data representations must possess the competency of reflecting the expert's opinion and the Fermatean sets are the best choice of it. Senapati and Yager (Senapati, Yager, 2020) introduced Fermatean sets which are the extended version of Pythagorean sets. These Fermatean sets facilitate experts to express their consent and dissent more effectively and this has made the researchers to develop and extend the theory of Fermatean sets.

Antony and Jansi (Sweety, Jansi, 2021) developed the theory of Fermatean Neutrosophic sets and also discussed the algebraic operations and applications in decision making. However, the Fermatean sets are not discussed under Plithogenic environment. This chapter introduces the concept of Plithogenic Fermatean sets. As Plithogenic cognitive maps are primarily based on expert's opinion, the Plithogenic Fermatean representations will be so beneficial in constructing the initial data sets. The integration of Plithogenic Fermatean representations with Plithogenic cognitive maps will set new benchmarks in building decision making models based on Plithogenic Cognitive Maps.

The remaining content of the chapter is structured as follows, section 2 presents the state of art of work of Plithogenic Cognitive maps and applications of Fermatean sets. Section 3 sketches out the conceptualization of Plithogenic Fermatean sets. Section 4 presents the methodology of the proposed decision-making method. Section 5 applies the proposed method to a decision-making problem on finding the effects of digitalized educational system on the learners. Section 6 discusses the results with different cases. Section 7 discourses the applications of the proposed model in other domains and the last section concludes the work with future scope.

2. STATE OF ART OF WORK

This section presents the literature review of the research works concerned with the developments of Plithogenic cognitive maps, applications of Fermatean sets and Fermatean neutrosophic sets. The research gaps and the significant contributions also forms a part of this section.

The conceptualization of Plithogenic Cognitive maps is the resultant of the advancement in the field of Fuzzy Cognitive Maps FCM. Kosko introduced Fuzzy Cognitive Maps by integrating fuzzy concepts with the domain of Cognitive Maps. The FCMs are further extended into intuitionistic FCM and later on to Neutrosophic Cognitive Maps. The extensions are basically dependent over the nature of the edge weights. Different kinds of Fuzzy Cognitive Maps are constructed with various representations such as soft sets and hypersoft sets. FCMs are also integrated with both fuzzy and neutrosophic sociogram approach of decision making. Nivetha and Smarandache (Martin, Priya, Smarandache, 2021) discussed FCM approach in a plithogenic environment and developed a decision-making model to investigate the interrelational impacts between the factors of the study. Based on this work Sujatha et al (Sujatha, Poomagal, Kuppuswami, Broumi, 2020) framed a COVID 19 disease diagnosis model. Priya, et al (Priya, Martin, 2021) took a unique approach by applying Plithogenic cognitive analysis to explore the development of spiritual intelligence in the context of smart age youth. This work showcased the broader philosophical and ethical implications of Plithogenic cognitive maps. Nivetha et al (Priya, Martin, Kishore, 2022) expanded upon the Plithogenic cognitive maps by introducing a sub-cognitive maps approach that considered mediating factors in a COVID-19 diagnostic model. This research extended the application of Plithogenic cognitive maps in healthcare decision-making. Priya et al (Martin, Priya, Smarandache, 2021) introduced Induced Plithogenic Cognitive Maps to investigate the issues in online learning systems, which highlights the adaptability of Plithogenic cognitive maps to address problems in the education sector. Gomathy et al. (Gomathy, Rajkumar, Nagarajan, Said, 2023) introduced Plithogenic Combined Disjoint Block Fuzzy Cognitive Maps, which represents a further development of the Plithogenic cognitive map framework. Angel et al.(Angel, Pandiammal, Gandhi, Martin, Smarandache, 2023) extended the use of Plithogenic cognitive maps by incorporating linguistic contradiction degree representations in decision-making related to academic stress factors. The contributions in the field of Plithogenic cognitive maps are highly progressive and proliferate the applications in diverse sectors. The Plithogenic Cognitive maps have not dealt with Fermatean sets as of now in literature.

Fermatean sets are basically intuitionistic sets with a specific condition and it is an extension of the Pythagorean sets. The Fermatean sets are discussed in both Fuzzy and neutrosophic forms. Senapati and Yager (Senapati, Yager, 2020) have laid the foundation for the development of Fuzzy Fermatean sets. The flexibility, compatibility and varied kind of representations of these sets have made the researchers to apply in developing the multi criteria decision making models. Akram et al (Akram, Bibi, Deveci, 2023) have applied 2-tuple linguistic Fermatean sets in extended CODAS method and outranking approach of multi attribute decision making. Qahtan et al. (Qahtan, Alsattar, Zaidan, Deveci, Pamucar, Delen, Pedrycz, 2023) evaluated Agriculture-Food 4.0 supply chain approaches using Fermatean probabilistic hesitant-fuzzy sets. Zaman et al (Zaman, Ghani, Khan, Abdullah, Khan, 2023) and Akram et al (Akram, Amjad, Alcantud, Santos-Garcia, 2023) have discussed more on the applications of complex Fermatean sets. Kiptum et al. (Kiptum, Bouraima, Badi, Zonon, Ndiema, Qiu, 2023) conducted an assessment of challenges to urban sustainable development utilizing an interval-valued Fermatean fuzzy approach. In addition to Fuzzy Fermatean sets, researchers also apply Fermatean neutrosophic sets in developing decision making models. Broumi et al (Broumi, 2023) introduced complex Fermatean neutrosophic graphs, showcasing their application in decision-making contexts. Raut et al [17] focused on the calculation of the shortest path on Fermatean neutrosophic networks. Broumi (Broumi, Prabha, Uluçay, 2023) explored Fermatean neutrosophic matrices and their basic operations, contributing foundational knowledge to the field. Saeed et al (Saeed, Nisa, Saeed, Alballa, Khalifa, 2023) focused on detecting patterns of infection-induced fertility using Fermatean neutrosophic sets and similarity analysis. Kirişci et al (Kirişci, 2022) introduced a pioneering Multi-Attribute Group-Decision Making (MAGDM) method employing the Technique for Order of Preference by Similarity to Ideal Solution (TOPSIS). This approach integrated Fermatean Fuzzy Hypersoft Sets and correlation coefficients, offering a novel perspective on decision-making processes, especially in complex environments requiring precise evaluations and comparisons. Building upon the foundation laid by Kirişci, (Kirişci) a further refinement emerged with a Novel TOPSIS Method based on Fermatean Fuzzy Hypersoft Sets and Correlation Coefficients. Joice et al (Joice, Pricilla, Broumi, 2023) explored generalized pre-closed sets within Fermatean neutrosophic hypersoft topological spaces. This research delved into the intricate aspects of topology, revealing the nuanced relationships within Fermatean neutrosophic spaces. Broumi et al (Broumi, Mohanaselvi, Witczak, Talea, Bakali, Smarandache, 2023) addressed a specific challenge in network optimization by formulating the interval-valued Fermatean neutrosophic shortest path problem. These studies not only expanded the theoretical foundations of the field but also demonstrated the applicability of fuzzy Fermatean and Fermatean neutrosophic sets in solving complex decision-making problems.

2.1 Research Gaps and Novel Contributions

The aforementioned literature clearly exhibits the applications of Fermatean sets and the theory of Plithogeny in several domains of decision-making. However, this review of literature finds few research gaps which are as follows

- The concept of Plithogenic Fermatean sets is not discussed
- Decision making models based on Plithogenic cognitive maps with the representations of Fermatean sets are not explored

This has made the authors to make the following significant contributions in this chapter

- Conceptualization of Plithogenic Fermatean sets and Plithogenic Fermatean Neutrosophic sets
- Development of Plithogenic cognitive models integrated with Plithogenic Fermatean representations.
- Extended method of Plithogenic cognitive approach in finding the optimal solution.

3. CONCEPTUALIZATION OF PLITHOGENIC FERMATEAN SET

3.1 Fermatean Sets (Senapati, Yager, 2020; Sweety, Jansi, 2021)

A Fermatean is basically a special kind of intuitionistic set of the form $A=\{\langle x, u_A(x), v_A(x) : x \in X\rangle\}$ where X is the universal sets, the functions $u_A : X \rightarrow [0,1]$ and

v_A:X→ [0,1] denote respectively the degree of membership and degree of non-membership of each element x ∈ X to the set P, and 0≤ $(u_A(x))^3 + (v_A(x))^3$ ≤ 1 for each x ∈ X.

3.2 Plithogenic Set (Smarandache, 2018)

A Plithogenic set is a 5-tuple of the form (P,a,V,d,c), where P is the set, a is the attribute, V is the set of attribute values, d is the degree of appurtenance of the elements of P with the dominant attribute value, c is the contradiction degree between the attribute values.

3.3 Plithogenic Fermatean Sets

From the above two conceptualizations of Fermatean sets and Plithogenic sets, A Plithogenic Fermatean set is a kind of Plithogenic set with Fermatean degree of appurtenance.

i.e$d: P\times V\rightarrow[0,1]\times[0,1]$, where $d(x,a_1) =$ (

u(x),v(x)), x∈ P, a_1 ∈ V, u:P→ [0,1] and

v:P→ [0,1], $(u(x))^3 + (v(x))^3 \leq 1$ and also $c: V\times V\rightarrow[0,1]$

3.4 Plithogenic Fermatean Neutrosophic Set

A Plithogenic Fermatean set is said to be Plithogenic Fermatean neutrosophic if the degree of appurtenance is Fermatean neutrosophic in nature.

i.e$d: P\times V\rightarrow[0,1]\times[0,1]\times[0,1]$, where $d(x,a_1) =$ (

u(x),v(x),w(x)), x∈ P, a_1 ∈ V, u:P→ [0,1] and v:P→ [0,1], w: P→ [0,1], $0\leq (u(x))^3 + (v(x))^3 \leq 1$ and $0\leq (w(x))^3 \leq 1$.

Then $0\leq (u(x))^3 + (v(x))^3 + (w(x))^3 \leq 2$ for all x in P and also $c: V\times V\rightarrow[0,1]$

The conventional Plithogenic operators presented for Intuitionistic and neutrosophic representations by Smarandache (Smarandache, 2018) shall be used for Plithogenic Fermatean and Plithogenic Fermatean neutrosophic representations respectively.

4. METHODOLOGY OF PLITHOGENIC FERMATEAN BASED PLITHOGENIC COGNITIVE MAP

This section presents the steps involved in the proposed method.

Step 1: The decision making problem is well defined and the factors say $F_1, \ldots F_n$ associated with the problem are well stated with expert's assistance.

Step 2: The aspects to which the factors are subjected are also initially determined and they are labelled as the attributes say $a_1, a_2, \ldots, a_m$ with the attribute set of values say $\{a_{11}, a_{12}, \ldots a_{1k}\}$, $\{a_{21}, a_{22}, \ldots a_{2h}\}, \ldots \{a_{m1}, a_{m2}, \ldots a_{mp}\}$

Step 3: The Plithogenic connection matrices say $PLa_1, PLa_2, ..PLa_m$ are constructed with the degrees of appurtenance pertaining to each of the factors with respect to the dominant attribute values of each of the attributes. The degree of appurtenance may be of either Fermatean representations or Fermatean neutrosophic representations.

Step 4: Let us assume an instantaneous vector of the form X = ((1,0), (0,1), (0,1), (0,1), (0,1), (0,1), (0,1), (0,1), (0,1), (0,1)) and it is passed to each of the Plithogenic connections matrices PLa_1, $PLa_2, ..PLa_m$ to determine the interrelational impacts between the factors of the problem with respect to the dominant attribute value of each of the attributes.

Step 5: On passing the vector into the matrix, a new vector X1 is obtained using $(1\text{-}c(aD,a_{ij})).\ [d_X(x,(a,b))\ V_F\ dPLa(y,(g,e))] + c(aD,a_{ij}).\ [d_X(x,(a,b))\wedge_F dPLa(y,(g,e))]$

Here the c(aD,aij) is the contradiction degree of the attribute value with respect to the dominant attribute value. $d_X(x,(a,b))$ is the Fermatean degree of appurtenance of the elements of the vector X with respect to the dominant attribute value. dPLA(y, (g,e)) refers to the degree of appurtenance of the connection matrix PLA with respect to the dominant attribute value, V_F denotes the t-conorm $aV_F\, g = a+g-ag$ and $a\wedge_F g$ denotes the t norm $\wedge_F = ag$

$$(a, b) \vee_{FS} (g, e) = (a\vee_F g, b\wedge_F e),$$

$$(a, b) \wedge_{FS} (g,e) = (a\wedge_F g, b\vee_F e)$$

Step 6: The updated vector X1 is again passed onto the matrix and the procedure is repeated until two vectors obtained are alike.

Step 7: The similar procedure is repeated with other Plithogenic matrices to find the interrelational impacts between the factors with respect to the dominant attribute values of other attributes.

5. DECISION MAKING ON FINDING THE EFFECTS OF DIGITALIZED EDUCATIONAL SYSTEM ON THE LEARNERS

This section presents the application of Plithogenic Fermatean based Plithogenic Cognitive maps in finding the effects of digitalized educational system on the learners. This section also throws light on the changes caused by the digital system of education.

5.1 Overview of Digitalized Educational System

The conventional educational system turns digitalized when the traditional process of teaching and learning embraces technology. The digitalized system of education represents a transformative shift in the way knowledge is disseminated and acquired, leveraging technology to enhance learning experiences. In this modern educational landscape, traditional classrooms are complemented or even replaced by online platforms, interactive learning tools, and digital resources. Students can access a wealth of information at their fingertips, enabling personalized learning experiences tailored to individual needs and preferences. Digital platforms facilitate real-time collaboration, allowing students to engage in discussions, group projects, and virtual classrooms regardless of geographical boundaries. Moreover, educators can employ innovative teaching methods, incorporating multimedia elements, simulations, and gamified content to make learning more engaging and effective. The digitalized system of education not only fosters global connectivity but also equips learners with essential digital skills, preparing them for the challenges of the 21st century. The outspread of COVID has created the channels of digitalizing the system of education and now this has commenced to govern the educational system.

5.2 State of Art of Digitalized Educational System

The recent researches on digitalization of educational system have outlined the pros and cons of such a technology embraced education. Tække (Smarandache, 2018) introduces the concept of the "three waves" theory in digitalization of education. This theoretical framework provides a foundation for understanding the evolutionary stages of digitalization, offering valuable insights into the progression of educational technology adoption. Sadjadi (Sadjadi, 2023) delves into the challenges and opportunities faced by education systems during the COVID-19 pandemic. The study critically analyzes the impact of digitalization, highlighting its role in addressing the unprecedented challenges posed by the global health crisis. Mukhitdinova (Mukhitdinova, 2023) emphasizes the significance of implementing digitalization in educational systems and explores its direct impact on the development of teaching processes. The study sheds light on the transformative potential of digital technologies in enhancing pedagogical approaches. Alenezi et al (Alenzezi, Wardat, Akour, 2023) specifically focus on higher education, discussing the need to integrate digital education by addressing the challenges and opportunities associated with digitalization in higher education institutions, emphasizing sustainability and technological integration. Timotheou et al (Timotheou, Miliou, Dimitradis, Sobrino, Giannoutsou, Cachia, Ioannou, 2023) conducted a comprehensive literature review on the impacts of digital technologies on education. Davronovich and Mansurjonovich (Davronovich, Mansurjonovich, 2023) delineate the important advantages of organizing the educational process within a digital technology environment. Their work highlights the positive aspects of digitalization, focusing on the benefits reaped by educational institutions and learners alike. Rivas (Rivas, 2023) introduces the concept of "platformization of education" and offers a framework to map the new directions of hybrid education systems. The study explores emerging trends in educational platforms and hybrid learning environments, providing a forward-looking perspective on the future of digital education. Butin et al (Butin, Tselykovskiy, Kuzankov, Pogodina, 2023) examine the transformation of the education system in the context of digitalization. Chidinmma and Matthew (Chidinmma, Matthew, 2023) critically evaluate the pros and cons of revitalizing education through digitalization. Their study provides a balanced perspective, considering both the benefits and challenges associated with the widespread adoption of digital technologies in educational contexts.

5.3 Positive and Negative Impacts of Digitalized Educational System

Based on the aforementioned studies (Tække, 2023; Sadjadi, 2023; Mukhitdinova 2023; Alenezi, Wardat, Akour, 2023; Timotheou, Miliou, Dimitriadia, Sobrino, Giannoutsou, Cachia, Ioannou, 2023; Davronovich, Mansurjonovich, 2023) the positive and negative impacts of digitalized educational system are sketched as follows. The digitalized educational system has ushered in a new era of learning, offering several positive impacts. It has enhanced accessibility, making education available to diverse learners residing worldwide, breaking down geographical barriers. Personalized learning experiences cater to individual needs, ensuring a more effective understanding of concepts. Interactive and engaging digital tools promote active participation and collaboration among students, fostering crucial skills for the future workforce. Additionally, the wealth of online resources enriches the learning process, providing a vast array of materials for students and educators alike.

However, this digital transformation also comes with negative impacts. Excessive screen time can lead to health issues, such as eye strain and digital fatigue. The digital divide exacerbates inequalities, as not all students have equal access to technology and a reliable internet connection. Distractions from social media and online entertainment can hinder focused learning. Moreover, concerns about data privacy and online security raise ethical questions, demanding careful consideration in the digital educational landscape. Balancing the positive and negative impacts requires thoughtful integration of technology, ensuring that the benefits of digitalized education are maximized while mitigating its drawbacks.

5.4 Factors Representing the Effects of Digitalized Educational System on the Learners

From the aforementioned literature of the contributions made in the domain of digitalized system of learning, it is very evident that this new system is both advantageous and disadvantageous. However, the contributions have not devised or framed any mathematical model to make investigations of the interrelational impacts between the positive and negative consequences of this digitalized educational system. This has induced the authors to take up this decision instance to apply the proposed model as Plithogenic Fermatean sets based Plithogenic Cognitive maps has room for accommodating the opinion of the experts with less constraints. To determine the optimal solutions to the problem considered, a decision -making model is framed with the assistance of three experts specialized in the areas of education to identify ten significant factors. These factors reflect the effects of digitalized educational system. The details of the experts are presented in the Table 1.

Table 1. Profile of the experts

S. No	Areas of Expertise	Years of Experience
Expert 1	ICT Teaching Pedagogy	23
Expert 2	Multimedia Learning	20
Expert 3	Computer-based instruction	18

The three experts together determined the following factors PL1,PL2,..Pl10 stating the effects of digitalized system on the learners. The brief description of the factors are as follows:

PL1 Learning takes place at the pace of learners: Personalized learning is essential in today's educational landscape. Individuals have different learning speeds and styles, and education should adapt to accommodate these variances. By allowing learners to progress at their own pace, they can grasp concepts thoroughly before moving forward, ensuring a more comprehensive understanding of the material.

PL2 Learners shall collaborate more effectively: Collaboration is a crucial skill in the modern world. Educational environments that encourage effective collaboration among learners provide opportunities for students to exchange ideas, solve problems collectively, and develop social skills. Collaborative learning enhances communication abilities and prepares individuals for teamwork, fostering a sense of community and mutual understanding.

PL3 Learners get isolated from societal settings: While personalized learning is beneficial, isolation from societal settings can be detrimental. It's important for learners to engage with the real world, interact with diverse communities, and develop social skills. A balanced approach that integrates classroom learning with real-world experiences ensures that students are not only academically proficient but also socially adept and culturally aware.

PL4 Learners get addicted to digital gadgets: The widespread use of digital devices in education has its advantages, but excessive reliance can lead to addiction and adverse effects on mental and physical health. It is crucial to strike a balance, encouraging the responsible use of technology while promoting offline activities, physical exercise, and face-to-face interactions. Educators and parents play a vital role in guiding learners toward a healthy relationship with digital gadgets.

PL5 Learning completely depends on technology: While technology has transformed education, it should not be the sole focus. Traditional teaching methods, hands-on experiences, and human interaction are equally important. A well-rounded education incorporates a variety of approaches, ensuring that learners receive a comprehensive and holistic learning experience.

PL6 Disparities between resource sharing: Disparities in resource allocation can hinder the educational progress of certain communities. Addressing these inequalities is crucial to ensuring that all learners have access to high-quality education, regardless of their socioeconomic background. Efforts to bridge the resource gap can level the playing field and provide equal opportunities for every student.

PL7 Learners get exposure to enhanced learning resources: Access to diverse and enhanced learning resources enriches the educational experience. Modern technology enables learners to explore a wide range of materials, including interactive simulations, virtual tours, and online courses. Exposure to these resources broadens knowledge horizons, encouraging curiosity and a lifelong love for learning.

PL8 Personalized learning gets enriched: Personalized learning tailors educational experiences to individual learners, catering to their unique strengths, weaknesses, and interests. Enriching personalized learning involves understanding each student's needs, providing tailored support, and offering challenging tasks to foster continuous growth. By addressing individual learning styles, personalized education ensures that students reach their full potential.

PL9 Learning gets escalated with subject expert's assistance and support: Subject expert guidance enhances the learning journey significantly. Educators, mentors, and specialists provide valuable insights, answer questions, and offer support, helping learners navigate complex topics. Collaboration with subject experts not only deepens understanding but also inspires students, motivating them to explore subjects in greater depth and pursue their passions.

PL10 Acceleration of learner's engagement with learning: Engaging learners is essential for effective education. Interactive and stimulating learning experiences capture attention, sustain interest, and encourage active participation. By accelerating learner engagement, educators can create a positive and motivating environment, fostering a love for learning that extends beyond the classroom. Engaged learners are more likely to retain information, develop critical thinking skills, and apply knowledge in real-world situations, leading to a more profound and meaningful educational experience

The interrelational impacts between the aforementioned factors shall be discussed under the aspects of *cognitive, social and affective* effect over the learners. The three different effects namely cognitive, social and affective are assumed to be the attributes and the nature of the effects are considered to be positive (PO), negative (NE) and null (Nu) which are the attribute values of each of the attribute. In this case the dominant attribute value is positive and the contradiction degrees with respect to other attribute values are

c(PO,PO) = 0, c(PO, NE) = 1/3, c(PO,NU) = 2/3

The Plithogenic Fermatean connection matrix stating the interrelationship between the factors with respect to the cognitive aspect of the learners is presented as follows in Table 2.

Table 2. Connection matrix of the associational impacts of the factors with respect to cognitive aspect of the learners

	PL1	PL2	PL3	PL4	PL5	PL6	PL7	PL8	PL9	PL10
PL1	(0, 1)	(0.6, 0.2)	(0.2, 0.8)	(0.2, 0.8)	(0.1, 0.8)	(0.1, 0.8)	(0.9, 0.1)	(0.8, 0.2)	(0.9, 0.1)	(0.9, 0.1)
PL2	(0.8, 0.2)	(0, 1)	(0.2, 0.7)	(0.2, 0.7)	(0.1, 0.7)	(0.1, 0.8)	(0.8, 0.2)	(0.9, 0.1)	(0.8, 0.2)	(0.9, 0.1)
PL3	(0.1, 0.8)	(0.1, 0.8)	(0, 1)	(0.1, 0.8)	(0.1, 0.9)	(0.1, 0.9)	(0.1, 0.8)	(0.1, 0.9)	(0.1, 0.8)	(0.1, 0.9)

continued on following page

Table 2. Continued

	PL1	PL2	PL3	PL4	PL5	PL6	PL7	PL8	PL9	PL10
PL4	(0.1, 0.8)	(0.1, 0.9)	(0.1, 0.7)	(0, 1)	(0.1, 0.9)	(0.1, 0.9)	(0.1, 0.8)	(0.1, 0.9)	(0.1, 0.8)	(0.1, 0.9)
PL5	(0.1, 0.8)	(0.1, 0.9)	(0.1, 0.7)	(0.1, 0.9)	(0, 1)	(0.1, 0.9)	(0.1, 0.9)	(0.1, 0.9)	(0.1, 0.9)	(0.1, 0.9)
PL6	(0.1, 0.9)	(0.1, 0.9)	(0.1, 0.9)	(0.1, 0.9)	(0.1, 0.9)	(0, 1)	(0.1, 0.9)	(0.1, 0.9)	(0.1, 0.9)	(0.1, 0.9)
PL7	(0.9, 0.1)	(0.9, 0.1)	(0.1, 0.9)	(0.1, 0.9)	(0.1, 0.9)	(0.1, 0.9)	(0, 1)	(0.9, 0.1)	(0.9, 0.1)	(0.9, 0.1)
PL8	(0.9, 0.1)	(0.9, 0.1)	(0.1, 0.9)	(0.1, 0.9)	(0.1, 0.9)	(0.1, 0.9)	(0.9, 0.1)	(0, 1)	(0.9, 0.1)	(0.9, 0.1)
PL9	(0.9, 0.1)	(0.9, 0.1)	(0.1, 0.9)	(0.1, 0.9)	(0.1, 0.9)	(0.1, 0.9)	(0.9, 0.1)	(0.9, 0.1)	(0, 1)	(0.9, 0.1)
PL10	(0.9, 0.1)	(0.9, 0.1)	(0.1, 0.9)	(0.1, 0.9)	(0.1, 0.9)	(0.1, 0.9)	(0.9, 0.1)	(0.9, 0.1)	(0.9, 0.1)	(0, 1)

The Plithogenic Fermatean connection matrix stating the interrelationship between the factors with respect to the social aspect of the learners is presented in Table 3.

Table 3. Connection matrix of the associational impacts of the factors with respect to social aspect of the learners

	PL1	PL2	PL3	PL4	PL5	PL6	PL7	PL8	PL9	PL10
PL1	(0, 1)	(0.7, 0.1)	(0.3, 0.6)	(0.2, 0.6)	(0.1, 0.7)	(0.1, 0.7)	(0.1, 0.7)	(0.4, 0.6)	(0.6, 0.2)	(0.3, 0.6)
PL2	(0.2, 0.8)	(0, 1)	(0.2, 0.7)	(0.2, 0.7)	(0.2, 0.7)	(0.2, 0.7)	(0.4, 0.6)	(0.4, 0.6)	(0.9, 0.1)	(0.2, 0.7)
PL3	(0.4, 0.6)	(0.1, 0.8)	(0, 1)	(0.1, 0.8)	(0.1, 0.8)	(0.1, 0.9)	(0.1, 0.8)	(0.1, 0.9)	(0.1, 0.8)	(0.1, 0.8)
PL4	(0.1, 0.8)	(0.1, 0.8)	(0.1, 0.8)	(0, 1)	(0.1, 0.8)	(0.1, 0.8)	(0.1, 0.9)	(0.1, 0.9)	(0.1, 0.9)	(0.1, 0.9)
PL5	(0.1, 0.9)	(0.1, 0.7)	(0.1, 0.8)	(0.1, 0.9)	(0, 1)	(0.1, 0.8)	(0.1, 0.7)	(0.1, 0.8)	(0.1, 0.9)	(0.1, 0.9)
PL6	(0.2, 0.6)	(0.1, 0.8)	(0.2, 0.6)	(0.2, 0.6)	(0.2, 0.6)	(0, 1)	(0.1, 0.8)	(0.1, 0.9)	(0.1, 0.8)	(0.1, 0.8)
PL7	(0.1, 0.9)	(0.1, 0.7)	(0.1, 0.8)	(0.1, 0.7)	(0.1, 0.9)	(0.1, 0.7)	(0, 1)	(0.1, 0.8)	(0.1, 0.7)	(0.1, 0.8)
PL8	(0.1, 0.9)	(0.1, 0.7)	(0.1, 0.8)	(0.1, 0.7)	(0.1, 0.9)	(0.1, 0.7)	(0.1, 0.8)	(0, 1)	(0.2, 0.7)	(0.2, 0.8)
PL9	(0.2, 0.7)	(0.1, 0.9)	(0.1, 0.8)	(0.2, 0.7)	(0.2, 0.8)	(0.1, 0.7)	(0.2, 0.8)	(0.2, 0.7)	(0, 1)	(0.1, 0.8)
PL10	(0.1, 0.9)	(0.1, 0.7)	(0.1, 0.8)	(0.1, 0.7)	(0.1, 0.9)	(0.1, 0.8)	(0.2, 0.7)	(0.2, 0.9)	(0.2, 0.9)	(0, 1)

The Plithogenic Fermatean connection matrix stating the interrelationship between the factors with respect to the technological aspect of the learners is represented in Table 4.

Table 4. Connection matrix of the associational impacts of the factors with respect to technical aspect of the learners

	PL1	PL2	PL3	PL4	PL5	PL6	PL7	PL8	PL9	PL10
PL1	(0, 1)	(0.7, 0.2)	(0.1, 0.8)	(0.1, 0.5)	(0.2, 0.6)	(0.1, 0.7)	(0.6, 0.2)	(0.5, 0.2)	(0.6, 0.2)	(0.6, 0.2)
PL2	(0.1, 0.7)	(0, 1)	(0.2, 0.6)	(0.1, 0.8)	(0.1, 0.8)	(0.1, 0.7)	(0.1, 0.7)	(0.1, 0.9)	(0.1, 0.8)	(0.1, 0.9)
PL3	(0.1, 0.8)	(0.1, 0.7)	(0, 1)	(0.1, 0.8)	(0.1, 0.7)	(0.1, 0.9)	(0.1, 0.8)	(0.1, 0.7)	(0.1, 0.8)	(0.1, 0.7)
PL4	(0.1, 0.9)	(0.1, 0.8)	(0.1, 0.7)	(0, 1)	(0.1, 0.9)	(0.1, 0.8)	(0.1, 0.7)	(0.1, 0.8)	(0.1, 0.8)	(0.1, 0.9)
PL5	(0.1, 0.8)	(0.1, 0.7)	(0.1, 0.8)	(0.1, 0.9)	(0, 1)	(0.1, 0.9)	(0.1, 0.7)	(0.1, 0.8)	(0.1, 0.9)	(0.2, 0.7)
PL6	(0.1, 0.8)	(0.1, 0.7)	(0.1, 0.8)	(0.1, 0.8)	(0.1, 0.9)	(0, 1)	(0.2, 0.7)	(0.2, 0.8)	(0.1, 0.9)	(0, 1)
PL7	(0.1, 0.9)	(0.2, 0.8)	(0.2, 0.7)	(0, 1)	(0.1, 0.9)	(0.2, 0.8)	(0, 1)	(0.1, 0.8)	(0.1, 0.8)	(0.1, 0.9)
PL8	(0.2, 0.6)	(0.1, 0.8)	(0.1, 0.9)	(0.2, 0.8)	(0.1, 0.8)	(0.1, 0.9)	(0.1, 0.8)	(0, 1)	(0.1, 0.8)	(0.1, 0.9)
PL9	(0.1, 0.8)	(0.1, 0.7)	(0.1, 0.8)	(0.1, 0.8)	(0.1, 0.9)	(0.1, 0.9)	(0.2, 0.8)	(0.1, 0.8)	(0, 1)	(0.2, 0.7)
PL10	(0.1, 0.9)	(0.2, 0.8)	(0.1, 0.8)	(0.1, 0.7)	(0.1, 0.8)	(0.1, 0.8)	(0.1, 0.9)	(0.1, 0.8)	(0.1, 0.9)	(0, 1)

Let us pass this vector into the Plithogenic Fermatean connection matrix PFC_C

Let us assume $X = ((1,0), (0,1), (0,1), (0,1), (0,1), (0,1), (0,1), (0,1), (0,1), (0,1))$

In the vector X, the first element represents the ON position of the factor PL1 and the remaining elements represent the OFF position of other factors PL2,..PL10. The value (1,0) indicates the ON state of PL1 with respect to the attribute value of the positive cognitive effects of the learners. The remaining elements of the vector are with respect to the attribute value of the null cognitive effects of the learners. Let us pass this vector into the Plithogenic Fermatean connection matrix PFC_C

$X^* \; PFC_C = \{a,b,c,d,e,f,g,h,i,j\}$

Where each a is of the form Fermatean set

a=max{ (1,0) ^(0,1),(0,1) ^(0.8,0.2), (0,1) ^(0.1,0.8), (0,1) ^(0.1,0.8), (0,1) ^(0.1,0.8), (0,1) ^(0.1,0.9), (0,1) ^(0.9,0.1),(0,1) ^(0.9,0.1),(0,1) ^(0.9,0.1),(0,1) ^(0.9,0.1)}

a=max{(0, 1), (0.533, 0.133), (0.067, .867), (0.067, 0.867), (0.067, 0.867), (0.067, 0.933), (0.6, 0.4), (0.6, 0.4), (0.6, 0.4), (0.6, 0.4) }

a=(0.6, 0.133)

b=max{ (1, 0) ^(0.6, 0.2), (0, 1) ^(0, 1), (0, 1) ^(0.1, 0.8), (0, 1) ^(0.1, 0.9, (0, 1) ^(0.1, 0.9), (0, 1) ^(0.1, 0.9), (0, 1) ^(0.9, 0.1), (0, 1) ^(0.9, 0.1), (0, 1) ^(0.9, 0.1), (0, 1) ^(0.9, 0.1)}

b=max{(.6, .2), (0, 1), (.067, .867), (0.067, 0.933), (0.067, 0.933), (0.067, 0.933), (0.6, 0.4), (0.6, 0.4), (0.6, 0.4), (0.6, 0.4)}

b=(.6, .2)

c=max{(1, 0) ^(0.2, 0.8), (0, 1) ^(0.2, 0.7), (0, 1) ^(0, 1), (0, 1) ^(0.1, 0.7), (0, 1) ^(0.1, 0.7), (0, 1) ^(0.1, 0.9), (0, 1) ^(0.1, 0.9), (0, 1) ^(0.1, 0.9), (0, 1) ^(0.1, 0.9) (0, 1) ^(0.1, 0.9)}

c=max{(.2, .8), (.133, .8), (0, 1), (0.067, 0.8), (0.067, .8), (0.067, .933),), (0.067, .933),), (0.067, .933),), (0.067, .933),), (0.067, .933), }

c={.2, .8)

d=max{(1, 0) ^(0.2, 0.8), (0, 1) ^(0.2, 0.7), (0, 1) ^(0.1, 0.8), (0, 1) ^(0, 1), (0, 1) ^(0.1, 0.9), (0, 1) ^(0.1, 0.9), (0, 1) ^(0.1, 0.9), (0, 1) ^(0.1, 0.9), (0, 1) ^(0.1, 0.9), (0, 1) ^(0.1, 0.9)}

d=max{(.2, .8), (.13, .8), (.067, .867), (0, 1), (.067, .933), (.067, .933), (.067, .933), (.067, .933), (.067, .933), (.067, .933)}

d=(.2, .8)

e=max{(1, 0) ^(0.1, 0.8), (0, 1) ^(0.1, 0.7), (0, 1) ^(0.1, 0.9), (0, 1) ^(0.1, 0.9), (0, 1) ^(0, 1), (0, 1) ^(0.1, 0.9), (0, 1) ^(0.1, 0.9), (0, 1) ^(0.1, 0.9), (0, 1) ^(0.1, 0.9), (0, 1) ^(0.1, 0.9)}

e=max{(.1, .8), (.067, .8), (.067, .933), (.067, .933), (0, 1), (.067, .933), (.067, .933), (.067, .933), (.067, .933), (.067, .933)} e=(.1, .8)

f=max{(1, 0) ^(0.1, 0.8), (0, 1) ^(0.1, 0.8), (0, 1) ^(0.1, 0.9), (0, 1) ^(0.1, 0.9), (0, 1) ^(0.1, 0.9), (0, 1) ^(0, 1), (0, 1) ^(0.1, 0.9), (0, 1) ^(0.1, 0.9), (0, 1) ^(0.1, 0.9), (0, 1) ^(0.1, 0.9)}

f=max{(.1, .8), (.067, .867), (.067, .933), (.067, .933), (.067, .933), (0, 1), (.067, .867), (.067, .867), (.067, .867), (.067, .867)}

f=(.1, .8)

g=max{(1, 0) ^(0.9, 0.1), (0, 1) ^(0.8, 0.2), (0, 1) ^(0.1, 0.8), (0, 1) ^(0.1, 0.8), (0, 1) ^(0.1, 0.9), (0, 1) ^(0.1, 0.9), (0, 1) ^(0, 1), (0, 1) ^(0.9, 0.1), (0, 1) ^(0.9, 0.1), (0, 1) ^(0.9, 0.1)}

g=max{(.9, .1), (.533, .467), (.067, .867), (.067, .867), (.067, .933), (.067, .933), (0, 1), (0.16, 0.4), (0.16, 0.4), (0.16, 0.4)}

g=(.9, .1)

h=max{(1, 0) ^(0.8, 0.2), (0, 1) ^(0.9, 0.1), (0, 1) ^(0.1, 0.9), (0, 1) ^(0.1, 0.9), (0, 1) ^(0.1, 0.9), (0, 1) ^(0.1, 0.9), (0, 1) ^(0.9, 0.1), (0, 1) ^(0, 1), (0, 1) ^(0.9, 0.1), (0, 1) ^(0.9, 0.1)}

h=max{(.8, .2), (.6, .4), (.067, .933), (0.067, .933), (.067, .933), (.067, .933), (.6, .4), (0, 1), (.6, .4), (.6, .4)}

h=(.8, .2)

i=max{(1, 0) ^(0.9, 0.1), (0, 1) ^(0.8, 0.2), (0, 1) ^(0.1, 0.8), (0, 1) ^(0.1, 0.8), (0, 1) ^(0.1, 0.9), (0, 1) ^(0.1, 0.9), (0, 1) ^(0.9, 0.1), (0, 1) ^(0.9, 0.1), (0, 1) ^(0, 1), (0, 1) ^(0.9, 0.1)}

i=max{(.9, .1), (.533, .467), (.067, .867), (.067, .867), (.067, .933), (.067, .933), (.6, .4), (.6, .4), (0, 1), (.6, .4)

i=(.9, .1)

j=max{(1, 0) ^(0.9, 0.1), (0, 1) ^(0.9, 0.1), (0, 1) ^(0.1, 0.9), (0, 1) ^(0.1, 0.9), (0, 1) ^(0.1, 0.9), (0, 1) ^(0.1, 0.9), (0, 1) ^(0.9, 0.1), (0, 1) ^(0.9, 0.1), (0, 1) ^(0.9, 0.1), (0, 1) ^(0, 1)} j=max{(.9, .1), (.6, .4), (.067, .933), (.067, .933), (.067, .933), (.067, .933), (.067, .933), (.6, .4), (.6, .4), (.6, .4), (0, 1)}

j=(.9, .1)

X^{1}={(.6, .133), (.6, .2), (.2, .8), (.2, .8), (.1, .8), (.1, .8), (.9, .1), (.8, .2), (.9, .1), (.9, .1)}

→{(1, 0), (.6, .2), (.2, .8), (.2, .8), (.1, .8), (.1, .8), (.9, .1), (.8, .2), (.9, .1), (.9, .1)}

$X^{1=}${(1, 0), (.6, .2), (.2, .8), (.2, .8), (.1, .8), (.1, .8), (.9, .1), (.8, .2), (.9, .1), (.9, .1)}

II-Iteration

X^{11}={(.93, .07), (.93, .07), (.637, .346), (.637, .343), (.637, .346), (.637, .363), (.93, .07), (.93, .07), (.93, .07), (.93, .07)}

→{(1, 0), (.93, .07), (.637, .346), (.637, .343), (.637, .346), (.637, .363), (.93, .07), (.93, .07), (.93, .07), (.93, .07)}

X^{11}={(1, 0), (.93, .07), (.637, .346), (.637, .343), (.637, .346), (.637, .363), (.93, .07), (.93, .07), (.93, .07), (.93, .07)}

III-Iteration

X^{111}={(.941, .059), (.941, .059), (.691, .273), (.691, .273), (.656, .273), (.656, .308), (.905, .094), (.941, .059), (.905, .904), (.941, .059)}

→{(1, 0), (.941, .059), (.691, .273), (.691, .273), (.656, .273), (.656, .308), (.905, .094), (.941, .059), (.905, .904), (.941, .059)}

X^{111}={(1, 0), (.941, .059), (.691, .273), (.691, .273), (.656, .273), (.656, .308), (.905, .094), (.941, .059), (.905, .904), (.941, .059)}

IV-Iteration

X^{IV}={(.941, .059), (.945, .055), (.698, .266), (.698, .266), (.662, .266), (.662, .302), (.945, .055), (.945, .055), (.945, .055), (.945, .055)}

→{(.941, .059), (.945, .055), (.698, .266), (.698, .266), (.662, .266), (.662, .302), (.945, .055), (.945, .055), (.945, .055), (.945, .055)}

X^{IV}={(1, 0), (.945, .055), (.698, .266), (.698, .266), (.662, .266), (.662, .302), (.945, .055), (.945, .055), (.945, .055), (.945, .055)}

IV-Iteration

X^{IV}={(.941, .059), (.945, .055), (.698, .266), (.698, .266), (.662, .266), (.662, .302), (.945, .055), (.945, .055), (.945, .055), (.945, .055)}

→{(.941, .059), (.945, .055), (.698, .266), (.698, .266), (.662, .266), (.662, .302), (.945, .055), (.945, .055), (.945, .055), (.945, .055)}

X^{IV}={(1, 0), (.945, .055), (.698, .266), (.698, .266), (.662, .266), (.662, .302), (.945, .055), (.945, .055), (.945, .055), (.945, .055)}

On converting to the crisp form the final vector obtained using the score function is

(1, 0.844, 0.321, 0.321, 0.271, 0.263, 0.844, 0.844, 0.844, 0.844)

The vector states that the factor PL1 in ON position has 84% of impact on PL2, 32% of impact on PL3 and PL4 and similarly the percentage of associational impacts over other factors shall be inferred from the above vector.

6. DISCUSSIONS

By repeating the similar procedure, the impacts of other factors shall be determined with respect to both social and technological effects of the learners. The cumulative effects of the factors shall also be obtained by finding the aggregate matrix of cognitive, social and technological effects. The impacts of the factors over one another are presented in the following tables 5,6,7 and 8 as linguistic variable for making quick inferences. [Very High (VH) – Range of values [0.9,1], High (H) – [0.7,0.9), Moderate (M) – [0.5,0.7), Low (L) – [0.3,0.5), Very Low (VL) – [0, 0.3)]

Table 5. Linguistic associational impacts of the factors with respect to cognitive aspects of the learners

	PL1	PL2	PL3	PL4	PL5	PL6	PL7	PL8	PL9	PL10
PL1	VH	H	L	L	VL	VL	H	H	H	H
PL2	H	VH	VL	L	VH	H	H	H	H	H
PL3	L	VL	VH	L	L	L	L	L	L	L
PL4	L	L	L	VH	L	M	L	L	L	L
PL5	VH	VH	L	L	VH	VL	VH	VH	VH	VH
PL6	VL	H	L	M	VL	VH	L	L	H	H
PL7	H	H	L	L	VH	L	VH	VH	VH	VH
PL8	H	H	L	L	VH	L	VH	VH	VH	VH
PL9	H	H	L	L	VH	H	VH	VH	VH	VH
PL10	H	H	L	L	VH	H	VH	VH	VH	VH

Table 6. Linguistic associational impacts of the factors with respect to social aspects of the learners

	PL1	PL2	PL3	PL4	PL5	PL6	PL7	PL8	PL9	PL10
PL1	VH	VH	L	L	H	VL	H	H	H	H
PL2	VH	VH	VL	L	H	VH	H	H	H	H
PL3	L	VL	VH	L	L	L	L	L	L	L
PL4	L	L	L	VH	L	M	L	L	L	L
PL5	H	H	L	L	VH	VL	VH	VH	VH	VH
PL6	VL	VH	L	M	VL	VH	L	L	VH	VH
PL7	H	H	L	L	VH	L	VH	VH	VH	VH
PL8	H	H	L	L	VH	L	VH	VL	VH	VH
PL9	H	H	L	L	VH	H	VH	VH	VH	VH
PL10	H	H	L	L	VH	VH	VH	VH	VH	VH

Table 7. Linguistic associational impacts of the factors with respect to technological aspects of the learners

	PL1	PL2	PL3	PL4	PL5	PL6	PL7	PL8	PL9	PL10
PL1	VH	L	VH	H	H	VL	L	L	L	L
PL2	L	VH	VL	H	H	L	L	L	L	L
PL3	VH	VL	VH	H	H	VH	VH	VH	VH	VH

continued on following page

Table 7. Continued

	PL1	PL2	PL3	PL4	PL5	PL6	PL7	PL8	PL9	PL10
PL4	H	H	H	VH	H	M	H	H	H	H
PL5	H	H	H	H	VH	VL	VH	VH	VH	VH
PL6	VL	L	VH	M	VL	VH	VL	L	L	L
PL7	L	L	VH	H	L	L	VH	L	L	L
PL8	L	L	VH	H	L	L	L	VH	L	L
PL9	L	L	VH	H	L	L	L	L	VH	L
PL10	L	L	VH	H	L	L	L	L	L	VH

Table 8. Linguistic associational impacts of the factors with respect to aggregate aspects of the learners

	PL1	PL2	PL3	PL4	PL5	PL6	PL7	PL8	PL9	PL10
PL1	VH	H	L	L	VH	VL	H	H	H	H
PL2	H	VH	VL	L	VH	H	H	H	H	H
PL3	L	VL	VH	L	L	L	L	L	L	L
PL4	L	L	L	VH	L	M	L	L	L	L
PL5	VH	VH	L	L	VH	VL	VH	VH	VH	VH
PL6	VL	H	L	M	VL	VH	L	L	H	H
PL7	H	H	L	L	VH	L	VH	VH	VH	VH
PL8	H	H	L	L	VH	L	VH	VH	VH	VH
PL9	H	H	L	L	VH	H	VH	VH	VH	VH
PL10	H	H	L	L	VH	H	VH	VH	VH	VH

Figure 1 represents the Associational Impacts of the Factors with respect to Cognitive Aspects of the Learners graphically.

Figure 1. Graphical representation of associational impacts of the factors with respect to cognitive aspects of the learners

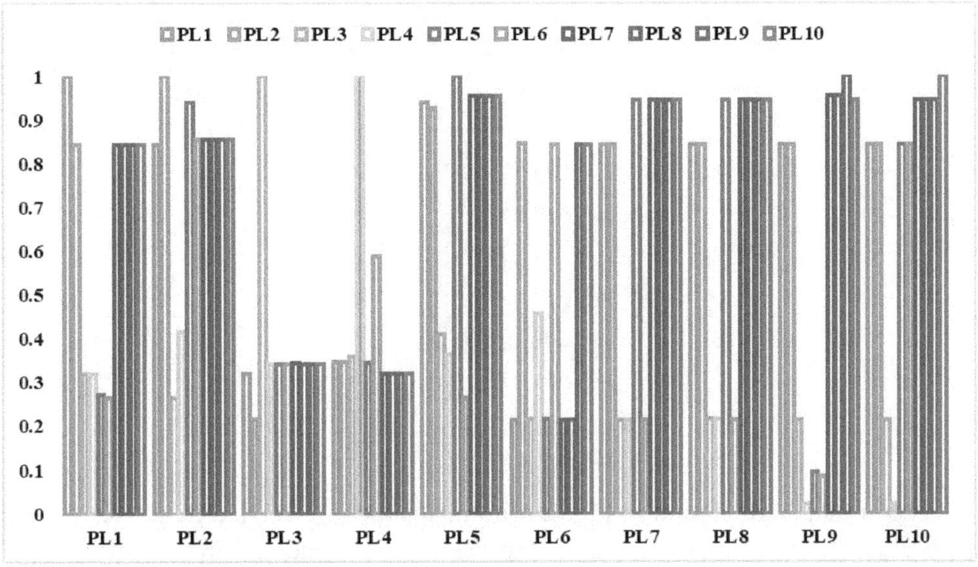

The visual representation illustrates the interconnected relationships among key factors influencing learners' cognitive experiences. The graph captures the varying degrees of influence and the intensity of associations between different factors. This graphical representation serves as a visual aid to comprehend the complex web of factors contributing to cognitive impacts, offering a concise overview of the intricate dynamics at play in the digital learning environment.

Figure 2 represents the Associational Impacts of the Factors with respect to Social Aspects of the Learners graphically.

Figure 2. Graphical representation of associational impacts of the factors with respect to social aspects of the learners

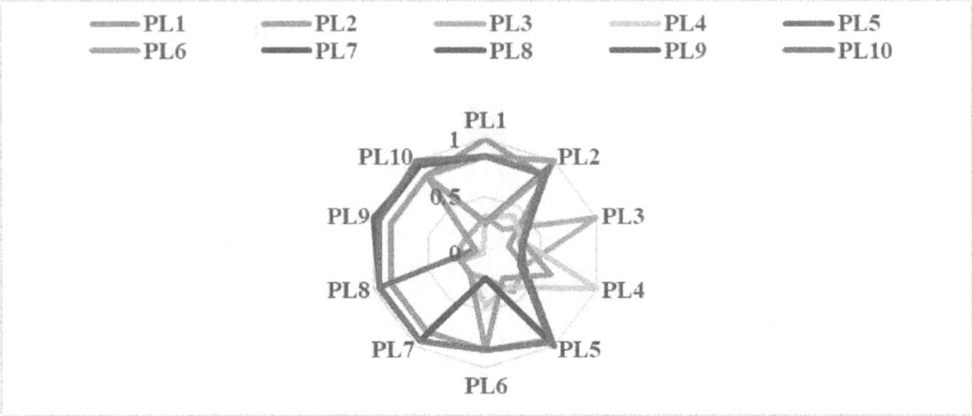

The graphical depiction in Fig. 2 illuminates the interrelated dynamics among pivotal factors that shape the social experiences of learners. Through varying degrees of influence and the robust connections between factors, the graph visually communicates the intricate relationships impacting the social aspects within the digital learning environment. This visual representation acts as a helpful tool for grasping the complex network of factors contributing to social impacts, providing a succinct overview and enhancing understanding of the nuanced dynamics present in the realm of digital learning.

Fig.3 represents the Associational Impacts of the Factors with respect to Technical Aspects of the Learners graphically.

Figure 3. Graphical representation of associational impacts of the factors with respect to technical aspects of the learners

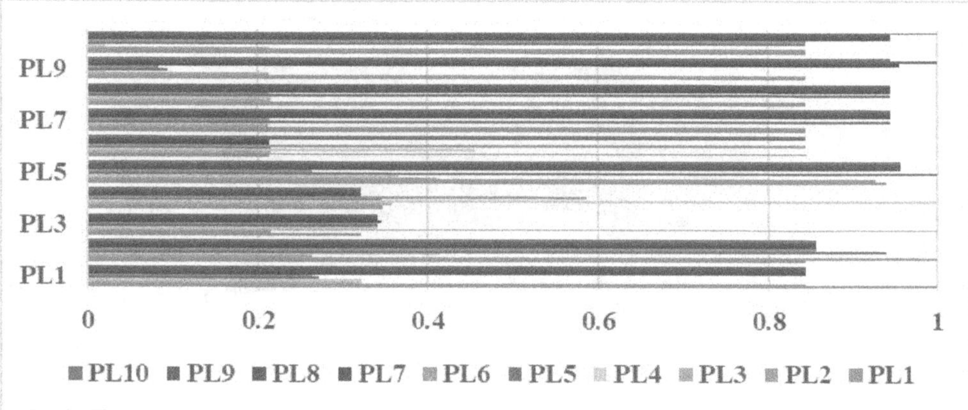

The graph visually conveys the Associational Impacts of Factors related to the Technical Aspects of Learners, offering insights into the interconnected relationships among key factors influencing learners' technical experiences. It effectively communicates varying degrees of influence and the strength of associations between different technical factors. Serving as a concise and informative tool, the visual representation provides a clear overview of the complex elements contributing to technical impacts on learners. It enhances understanding of the intricate dynamics within the technical dimension of the digital learning environment.

Fig.4 represents the Aggregate Impacts of the Factors with respect to Cognitive, Social and Technical Aspects of the Learners graphically.

Figure 4. Graphical representation of the aggregate impacts of the factors with respect to cognitive, social, and technical aspects of the learners

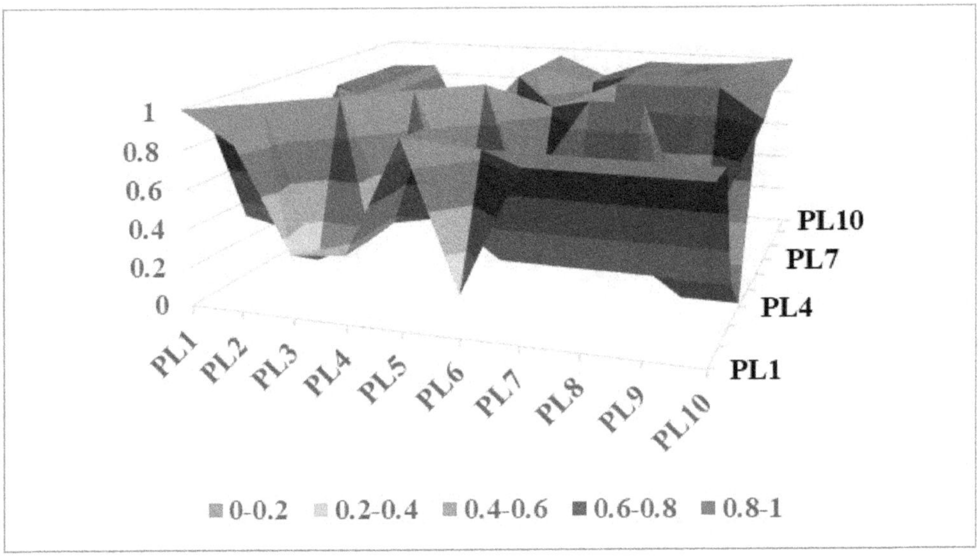

Fig. 4 visually portrays the Aggregate Impacts of Factors on Cognitive, Social, and Technical Aspects of Learners. This graph succinctly captures the interconnected relationships among key factors that collectively influence learners across cognitive, social, and technical dimensions. By presenting a comprehensive overview, the visual representation illustrates the varying degrees of influence and associations between different elements. Serving as an informative tool, the graph enhances understanding of the complex interplay of factors contributing to the holistic impacts on learners within the learning environment.

6.1 Inferences

From the above results the following inferences are obtained with respect to the application of the proposed approach to the decision-making problem.

- The interrelationship between the factors considered for study are determined.
- The linguistic quantification of the relational impacts helps the decision makers to identify the most influential factor.
- The interrelational impacts between the factors with respect to the cognitive, social and technological effects are determined.
- The specific relational impacts and generic impacts are also identified

It is very evident that on applying this proposed decision model, a decision-maker will certainly arrive at optimal results in making investigations on relational impacts.

7. OTHER DOMAINS OF APPLICATIONS

The Plithogenic Fermatean-based Plithogenic Cognitive Map Decision Making Model holds significant promise across various industries due to its capacity to navigate intricate decision-making structures. These sets shall be applied in the decision-making scenarios of supply chain management, logistics, supplier selection and many others. In healthcare, the model could be applied to optimize patient care by assessing the impact of digitalized medical records on treatment outcomes and resource allocation. In finance, the model may prove invaluable for analyzing complex market trends and guiding investment strategies amidst the evolving landscape of digital finance. Within manufacturing, the decision-making model could enhance efficiency by evaluating the interplay of technological advancements and workforce dynamics. Additionally, in the energy sector, it could aid in optimizing sustainable practices and navigating the transition to renewable energy sources. The versatility of the Plithogenic Fermatean-based model positions it as a valuable tool for industries seeking to navigate multifaceted decision landscapes and adapt to evolving paradigms.

8. CONCLUSION

The Plithogenic Fermatean-based Plithogenic Cognitive Map Decision Making Model emerges as a promising and versatile approach to address complex decision-making challenges across various industries. Its ability to dissect interconnected influences among factors provides a robust framework for analyzing and optimizing systems in healthcare, finance, manufacturing, and energy. The comparative assessment conducted in this chapter underscores the efficacy and competence of the proposed model, indicating its superiority over alternative representations in navigating intricate decision landscapes. The findings advocate for the widespread adoption of this innovative decision-making approach, offering industries a powerful tool to tackle dynamic and interconnected problems in the ever-evolving technological and organizational landscape. The Plithogenic Fermatean-based model stands as a beacon for enhanced decision-making in the face of complex interdependencies, paving the way for more informed and strategic industry practices.

REFERENCES

Akram, M., Amjad, U., Alcantud, J. C. R., & Santos-García, G. (2023). Complex fermatean fuzzy N-soft sets: A new hybrid model with applications. *Journal of Ambient Intelligence and Humanized Computing*, 14(7), 8765–8798. DOI:10.1007/s12652-021-03629-4 PMID:35136452

Akram, M., Bibi, R., & Deveci, M. (2023). An outranking approach with 2-tuple linguistic Fermatean fuzzy sets for multi-attribute group decision-making. *Engineering Applications of Artificial Intelligence*, 121, 105992. DOI:10.1016/j.engappai.2023.105992

Alenezi, M., Wardat, S., & Akour, M. (2023). The Need of Integrating Digital Education in Higher Education: Challenges and Opportunities. *Sustainability (Basel)*, 15(6), 4782. DOI:10.3390/su15064782

Angel, N., Pandiammal, P., Gandhi, N. R., Martin, N., & Smarandache, F. (2023). PCM with Linguistic Contradiction Degree Representations in Decision making on Academic Stress causing Factors. *International Journal of Neutrosophic Science*, 21(3), 126–26. DOI:10.54216/IJNS.210312

Antony Crispin Sweety, C., & Jansi, R., R. (2021). Fermatean Neutrosophic Sets. *International Journal of Advanced Research in Computer and Communication Engineering*, 10(6), 24–27.

Broumi, S. (2023). Fermatean Neutrosophic Matrices and Their Basic Operations. *Neutrosophic Sets and Systems*, 58(1), 35.

Broumi, S., Mohanaselvi, S., Witczak, T., Talea, M., Bakali, A., & Smarandache, F. (2023). Complex fermatean neutrosophic graph and application to decision making. *Decision Making: Applications in Management and Engineering*, 6(1), 474–501. DOI:10.31181/dmame24022023b

Broumi, S., Prabha, S., & Uluçay, V. (2023). Interval-Valued Fermatean Neutrosophic Shortest Path Problem via Score Function. *Neutrosophic Systems with Applications*, 11, 1–10. DOI:10.61356/j.nswa.2023.83

Butin, A. V., Tselykovskiy, A. A., Kuzenkov, S. E., & Pogodina, E. K. (2023, June). Transformation of the Education System in the Context of Digitalization. In *2023 3rd International Conference on Technology Enhanced Learning in Higher Education (TELE)* (pp. 294-296). IEEE. DOI:10.1109/TELE58910.2023.10184366

Chidinmma, A. E., & Matthew, O. O. (2023). Revitalizing Education through Digitalization: Its Pros and Cons. *Journal of Advances in Education and Philosophy*, 7(2), 52–55. DOI:10.36348/jaep.2023.v07i02.004

Davronovich, A. D., & Mansurjonovich, J. M. (2023). Important Advantages Of Organizing The Educational Process In A Digital Technology Environment. *Galaxy International Interdisciplinary Research Journal*, 11(2), 149–154.

Gomathy, S., Rajkumar, A., Nagarajan, D., & Said, B. (2023). Plıthogenıc Combıned Dısjoınt Block Fuzzy Cognıtıve Maps (Pcdbfcm). *International Journal of Neutrosophic Science*, 20(1).

Joice, P. R., Pricilla, M. T., & Broumi, S. (2023). Generalized Pre-closed Sets in Fermatean Neutrosophic Hypersoft Topological Spaces. *International Journal of Neutrosophic Science*, 20(3), 82–2. DOI:10.54216/IJNS.200308

Kiptum, C. K., Bouraima, M. B., Badi, I., Zonon, B. I. P., Ndiema, K. M., & Qiu, Y. (2023). Assessment of the Challenges to Urban Sustainable Development Using an Interval-Valued Fermatean Fuzzy Approach. *Systemic Analytics*, 1(1), 11–26. DOI:10.31181/sa1120233

Kirişci, M. (2022). Novel Multi-Attribute Group-Decision Making Method with TOPSIS: A Fermatean Fuzzy Hypersoft Sets and Correlation Coefficients Approach. In *Applied Mathematics, Modeling and Computer Simulation* (pp. 952-960). IOS Press. DOI:10.3233/ATDE221119

Martin, N., Priya, R., & Smarandache, F. (2021). *New Plithogenic sub cognitive maps approach with mediating effects of factors in COVID-19 diagnostic model.* Infinite Study.

Martin, N., & Smarandache, F. (2020). *Plithogenic cognitive maps in decision making*. Infinite Study.

Mukhitdinova, N. A. (2023). The Importance of Implementing Digitalization into Educational System and its Impact on the Development of Teaching Process. Best Journal of Innovation in Science. *Research for Development*, 2(7), 27–32.

Priya, R., & Martin, N. (2021). *Induced Plithogenic Cognitive Maps with Combined Connection Matrix to investigate the glitches of online learning system*. Infinite Study.

Priya, R., Martin, N., & Kishore, T. E. (2022, May). Plithogenic cognitive analysis on instigating spiritual intelligence in smart age youth for humanity redemption. In *AIP Conference Proceedings* (Vol. 2393, No. 1). AIP Publishing. DOI:10.1063/5.0074105

Qahtan, S., Alsattar, H. A., Zaidan, A. A., Deveci, M., Pamucar, D., Delen, D., & Pedrycz, W. (2023). Evaluation of agriculture-food 4.0 supply chain approaches using Fermatean probabilistic hesitant-fuzzy sets based decision making model. *Applied Soft Computing*, 138, 110170. DOI:10.1016/j.asoc.2023.110170

Raut, P. K., Behera, S. P., Broumi, S., & Mishra, D. (2023). Calculation of shortest path on Fermatean Neutrosophic Networks. *Neutrosophic Sets and Systems*, 57(1), 22.

Rivas, A. (2023). The platformization of education: A framework to map the new directions of hybrid education systems 1. In *The New Digital Education Policy Landscape* (pp. 191–209). Routledge. DOI:10.4324/9781003373018-13

Sadjadi, E. N. (2023). Challenges and Opportunities for Education Systems with the Current Movement toward Digitalization at the Time of COVID-19. *Mathematics*, 11(2), 259. DOI:10.3390/math11020259

Saeed, M., Nisa, M. U., Saeed, M. H., Alballa, T., & Khalifa, H. A. E. W. (2023). Detecting Patterns of Infection-Induced Fertility Using Fermatean Neutrosophic Set with Similarity Analysis. *IEEE Access : Practical Innovations, Open Solutions*, 11, 112320–112333. DOI:10.1109/ACCESS.2023.3323024

Senapati, T., & Yager, R. R. (2020). Fermatean fuzzy sets. *Journal of Ambient Intelligence and Humanized Computing*, 11(2), 663–674. DOI:10.1007/s12652-019-01377-0

Smarandache, F. (2018). *Plithogenic set, an extension of crisp, fuzzy, intuitionistic fuzzy, and neutrosophic sets-revisited.* Infinite Study.

Sujatha, R., Poomagal, S., Kuppuswami, G., & Broumi, S. (2020). *An Analysis on Novel Corona Virus by a Plithogenic Approach to Fuzzy Cognitive Map*. Infinite Study.

Tække, J. (2023, July). Digitalization of education-the theory of the three waves. In *7 International ISEKI-Food Conference* (p. 1). Academic Press.

Timotheou, S., Miliou, O., Dimitriadis, Y., Sobrino, S. V., Giannoutsou, N., Cachia, R., Monés, A. M., & Ioannou, A. (2023). Impacts of digital technologies on education and factors influencing schools' digital capacity and transformation: A literature review. *Education and Information Technologies*, 28(6), 6695–6726. DOI:10.1007/s10639-022-11431-8 PMID:36465416

Zaman, M., Ghani, F., Khan, A., Abdullah, S., & Khan, F. (2023). Complex Fermatean fuzzy extended TOPSIS method and its applications in decision making. *Heliyon*, 9(9), e19170. DOI:10.1016/j.heliyon.2023.e19170 PMID:37809522

Chapter 3
Neutrosophic Analysis of Rejection Sampling in Post Quantum Cryptography (PQC)

Shashi Kant Pandey
https://orcid.org/0000-0002-0818-6984
Society for Electronic Transaction and Security, Chennai, India

ABSTRACT

Digital authentication and key encapsulation mechanisms (KEM) are two basic primitives for the security level of all robotic and IoT systems. Dilithium and Kyber are two post-quantum algorithms to establish secure communication. The use of uniform random sampling in these algorithms is very important. The finalists Dilithium and Kyber use SHAKE and AES to generate the random sequence at multiple stages of the algorithm. Here, the authors characterize one of the sampling techniques available in Dilithium with the help of the neutrosophic Boolean function. The idea of the neutrosophic Boolean function came from the theory of neutrosophy, and it is useful to study any ternary distributions. The authors present the non-existence of neutrobalanced bent functions specifically with respect to the sampling named SampleInBall in Dilithium.

1. INTRODUCTION

Any equation or a function having class symbols $x, y, \ldots$ is termed a "logical equation" or a "logical function" by Georg Boole (1815-1864). Every logical function f(x) can be written as $f(x) = ax + b(1 - x)$, under the convention for the law of

DOI: 10.4018/979-8-3693-2085-3.ch003

symbols by George Boole (Boole,1957). If a and b are equal then this function is a balanced function. The extension of the idea of Boole's representation of a Boolean function for two variables x and y is

$$f(x,y)=f(1,1)xy+f(1,0)x(1-y)+f(0,1)(1-x)y+f(0,0)(1-x)(1-y)$$

With the abuse of notation, a Boolean function in cryptography is termed as a function f from an n dimensional vector space F_2^n to the base field F_2 of order 2. Later on, the development of cryptography produces many such mathematical properties of Boolean functions (Kolmogorov et al,1992; Carlet,2020; Dillon,1974; Kavut,2008; Cusick et al,2009). To a certain extent, the enumeration of cryptographic properties of a Boolean function starts with an important transformation of a Boolean function named Walsh transformation(*WT*). This transformation depends on the first-order correlation of a bit stream of a Boolean function. Another important cryptographic requirement of a Boolean function is its nonlinearity *(NL)* and it is based on the maximum value of the Walsh transformation. Those Boolean functions having maximum nonlinearity are called bent Boolean functions. Other than the correlation nature of the input-output of a Boolean function, there is a well-known feature of algebraic resistance and it is named Algebraic immunity (AI) (Courtois,2003;Carlet et al,2006). The generalization of the Boolean function and its other cryptographic features is an interesting area of work. These functions are named as Generalized Boolean function (GBF) in the literature (Tăndăreanu,1981;Budaghyan et al,2018;-Carlet et al, 2006;Stanica et al, 2011). The generalization of the bent Boolean function proposed by O.S. Rothus in (Rothaus,1976). A generalization of Boolean function based on neutrosophy and logic is presented in (Smarandache, 2003;Vadiraja et al, 2022) and termed as a neutrosphic Boolean function.

The idea of neutrosophy came from the classification of a set (Smarandache et al, 2020; Smarandache et al, 2019; Smarandache et al, 2003; Smarandache et al, 2020). An imagination of three disjoint classifications refers that any set S can be classified as P_1, P_2 and P_3 such that the given condition for a set is satisfied by elements in P_1, not satisfied by elements in P_2 and undefined or not decidable for elements in P_3. In this way, any set with any condition uniformly obeys the idea of neutrality or neutrosophy. This partition leads us to define a neutrosphic function ψ from any set S to any arbitrary set K, where ψ is defined on the partition P_1, not defined on P_2 and indeterminate on P_3. The same analogy is useful for studying every rejection sampling where some condition is fixed for the selection of the sample. In particular, any arbitrary evaluation of a function $f(x)$ can be used to reject or accept in the sampling procedure. One simple example for the partition of the sample can be seen as three sets $P_0 = \{x:0 = f(x)mod2\}, P_1 = \{x:0 \neq f(x)mod2\}$ and $P_3 =$

$\{x{:}rejection\}$. These three sets can be seen as ternary distribution and the principal of neutrosphic statistics are useful in study of their properties (Afzal et al, 2023).

The threat from quantum computing and its power of computing to cryptographic community is growing day by day after the scalability of q-bits. NIST has organized the open call for the upgradation of all vulnerable classical algorithms for digital authentication and key encapsulation in the year 2018. After fourth round of evaluation, they listed two algorithms Dilithium and KYBER for authentication and key encapsulation mechanism respectively (Avanzi et al, 2021; Ducas et al, 2021). Here we focus on the sampling function SampleInBall of Dilithium for sampling of one of the main random vectors c during the signing process in the algorithm (Ducas et al, 2021). Both of the listed algorithms ae based on lattice-based cryptography and refer the algebraic problem named as learning with errors (LWE). In section (2), we introduce the LWE problem and its background for lattice-based problems. The sampling in Dilithium with the analogy of neutrosphic Boolean function is presented in subsection (2.1). Further in section (3) we present the analysis of the extendable output function (XOF) and SampleInBall function of Dilithium with the characterization of the neutrosphic bent Boolean function. Our contributions in this chapters are as follows:

- A comprehensive survey on Neutropohic Boolean function is presented
- The analogy of neutroosphic Boolean function with rejection sampling in post quantum algorithm is explained for all version of Dilithium
- The generalizations of neutrosphic bent Boolean function is presented
- Proof of non-existence of neutrosphic bent Boolean functions is presented
- The experimental results for the analysis of SampleInBall in Dilithium is presented using and open-source implementation of Dilithium

2. LEARNING WITH ERROR PROBLEM

The reduction of hard maths problems in the classical domain is an ongoing and open-ended problem. Learning with error is one of those hard maths problems about which more discussion is after the NIST PQC competition. However, it is one of the types of uniformity in the finalists of the PQC competition. Oded Regev was the person who coined this in (Regev, 2009). The problem of LWE is framed as to find a vector $s \in Z_2^n$ for some integer $n \geq 1$ and a real number ϵ such that the following set of linear equations with errors,

$$< a_1, s > =_\varepsilon b_1 (\text{mod} 2)$$
$$< a_2, s > =_\varepsilon b_2 (\text{mod} 2)$$

where each a_i are sampled from the uniform distribution on Z_2^n and the inner product $< a_i, s >$ is defined as $\sum_{j=1}^{n} s_j a_i^j$ on modulo 2. Here, the meaning of an equation with errors is that each equation is correct independently with probability $1 - \epsilon$. The case of zero error can be easily solvable by Gaussian elimination therefore the insertion of hardness in this problem comes from the sampling of errors. The sampling of a is independently and uniformly on $Z_2^n$and b is independent with probability $1 - \epsilon$. Sampling independently and deterministically is interesting in cryptography. Various designs of deterministic random number generators (DRBG) serve this for cryptographic purpose. The design of DRBG is based on hash functions like SHA-1, SHA-2, XOF etc. Outcomes of a hash function plays a key role in the uniform distribution for the sampling of vector $a \in Z_2^n$. In the next section, we elaborate on the sampling techniques in post-quantum algorithms.

2.1 Sampling of Errors in Post-Quantum Solutions

The future of Quantum computing is a great threat to the available cryptographic infrastructure. Taking this threat into mind NIST has started an open competition for the possible solutions for public key cryptographic (PKC) algorithms and signature schemes. Most of the finalists in the available procedures are based on the LWE problem proposed by Regev in (Regev, 2009). This problem refers to the idea of introducing some error with some randomized sampling. In every design of PQC which is based on the LWE problem, there is a provision for the randomization of the public key or secret key. This process is based on the various classical rejection sampling techniques (Decru et al, 2019; Zheng et al, 2021;Agrawal et al, 2022). The trade-off between the parameters of rejection sampling and security is interesting for every design. KYBER and Dilithium are the two finalists in the list of NIST final rounds of public key encryption decryption algorithm and digital signature algorithm (Avanzi et al, 2021; Ducas et al, 2021). Both of the algorithms are based on hard problem learning with errors.

2.2 Rejection Sampling in Dilithium

Dilithium is a finalist algorithm in the NIST competition for post-quantum cryptography. It is an algorithm for digital signature and is based on the hard lattice problem named learning with errors. The core idea of this problem is to solve a linear system of equations having intentionally inserted errors in their coefficients.

Dilithium Algorithm

KeyGen:

$1.A \leftarrow R_q^{k\times l}, (s_1, s_2) \leftarrow S_\eta^l \times S_\eta^k$

$2.t = As_1 + s_2$

$3.\mathrm{Re}turn(pk = A, t), (sk = A, t, s_1, s_2)$

Sign(sk,M):

$4.Initialize(z = \perp)$

$5.while(z = \perp)$

$6.y \leftarrow S_{\gamma_1}^l, \omega_1 = HighBits(Ay, 2\gamma_2)$

$7.\widehat{c} \in \{0,1\}^{256} = H(M\|2\gamma_2), c \in B_\tau = SampleInBall(\widehat{c})$

$8.z = y + cs_1$

$9.if(\|z\|_\infty \leq \gamma_1 - \beta) or(\|LowBits(Ay - cs_2, 2\gamma_2)\|_\infty \geq \gamma_2 - \beta) then(z = \perp)$

$10.return(\rho = z, c)$

Verification(pk,M,ρ):

$11.w_1^{'} = HighBits(Az - ct, 2\gamma_2)$

$12.if[\|Z\|_\infty \prec \gamma_2 - \beta] and[\widehat{c} = H(M\|\omega_1^{'})]$

A short explanation of the algorithm of Dilithium is presented in the above block. Here A represents a matrix of size $k \times l$, where each of the elements a_{ij} is a polynomial taken from the ring $R_q, Z_q[x]/\langle x^n - 1\rangle$, where $n = 256$ and $q = 8380417$ for every version of Dilthium algorithm. The key generation part of the algorithm uses sampling of the public key and secret key from the output of the hash function. However, the optimization in terms of the size of the keys in all versions of Dilithium is an open problem for the researchers. In (Kaushik et al, 2023) and (Bos et al, 2022) authors have proposed faster algorithms for authentication in memory constraints IOT and robotics devices. The matrix A is sampled from the output of the extendable output function (XOF) and it is part of the public as well as secret key. (s_1, s_2) are part of the secret key and they are sampled from the XOF function denoted as S_η^l and S_η^k. Secret keys s_1 and s_2 are elements of the same ring R_q. Other parameters for security leveling are presented in Table 1.

Table 1. Security Parameters

NIST Security level	**q**	**d**	τ	γ_1	γ_2	**(k, l)**	η	β	ω
1	8380417	13	39	2^{17}	(q-1)/88	(4,4)	2	78	80
2	8380417	13	49	2^{19}	(q-1)/32	(6,5)	4	196	55
3	8380417	13	60	2^{19}	(q-1)/32	(8,7)	2	120	75

The function *ExpandS* computes each of the $l + k$polynomials in s_1 and s_2 independently. For the i-th polynomial, $0 \le i \le l + k$, it absorbs the 64 bytes of ρ concatenated with 2 bytes representing i in little-endian byte order into SHAKE-256. Then the output bytes are used to create a sequence of uniformly random positive numbers in the range $\{0, ..., 2\eta\}$ by performing rejection sampling. Concretely, the lower and upper four bits of each output byte are interpreted as two integers in $\{0, ..., 15\}$. Then, in the case of $\eta = 2$, an integer is accepted when it is less than 15 and then reduced modulo 5. In the case of $\eta = 4$, an integer is accepted when it is less than $2\eta + 1 = 9$. Finally, the polynomial coefficients are obtained by subtracting the positive numbers from η.

Dilithium-5

This is the final version of Dilithium and security parameter η is 2, therefore the sampling function for this version is S_2. The function *ExpandS*, used for generating the secret vectors in key generation, maps a seed ρ' to $(s_1, s_2) \in S_2^8 \times S_2^7$.

Similar to the explanation in Dilithium-2, the mapping without little-endian byte order input can be treated as a generalized Boolean function $f{:}Z_2^4 \mapsto Z_5$. The mapping with little-endian order can be treated as a generalized Boolean function $f{:}Z_2^{16} \mapsto Z_5$.

Dilithium-2

This is the first version of Dilithium and here the security parameter η is selected as 2, therefore the sampling function for this version is S_2. The function *ExpandS*, used for generating the secret vectors in key generation, maps a seed ρ' to $(s_1, s_2) \in S_\eta^l \times S_\eta^k$. The value of k and l is 4, therefore the sampling of vectors s_1 and $s_2$independently with the help of XOF uniform distribution. In total there is l+k polynomial needs to be sampled from the output of XOF therefore for this version, eight polynomials have to be sampled from index $0 \leq i \leq 7$. Since ρ' is fixed 64 bytes for all input of XOF function, therefore, we assume this to be known and constant, therefore to generate each polynomial or 256 integer sequence we feed only 2 bytes representing i in little-endian byte order into SHAKE-256. For the sake of convenience in the case of version-2, where $0 \leq i \leq 7$, the input vector of SHAKE-256 can be taken as three bits, and if we take little-endian order then they are of sixteen bits. The mapping without little-endian byte order input can be treated as a Boolean function $f{:}Z_2^3 \mapsto Z_5$. The mapping with little-endian order can be treated as a generalized Boolean function $f{:}Z_2^{16} \mapsto Z_5$.

Dilithium-3

This is the second version of Dilithium and here η is selected as 4, therefore the sampling function for this version is S_4. The function *ExpandS*, used for generating the secret vectors in key generation, maps a seed ρ' to $(s_1, s_2) \in S_4^6 \times S_4^5$.

Similar to the explanation in Dilithium-2, the mapping without little-endian byte order input can be treated as a Boolean function $f{:}Z_2^4 \mapsto Z_9$. The mapping with little-endian order can be treated as a Boolean function $f{:}Z_2^{16} \mapsto Z_9$.

Now we present a discussion on the sampling technique of s_1 and s_2 for three versions of Dilithium named security levels 2,3 and 5. Here we frame some generalized Boolean functions w.r.t these sampling techniques.

Now we explore the balancedness property of a generalized Boolean function coined from the rejection sampling *SampleInBall* in all three cases of the Dilithium-2,3 and 5. However, unbalanced generalized Boolean functions are only bent functions and they achieve the highest nonlinearity. It refers to the idea of nonlinearity analysis of all these Boolean functions for cryptanalysis of this algorithm. Noise in KYBER is sampled from centered binomial distributions and specifically compress and decompress function can be relooked with the idea of neutrosphic Boolean functions.

3. XOF FUNCTION AND NEUTROSPHIC BOOLEAN FUNCTION

XOF or extendable output functions are hash functions where we can change the length of the output based on our choice. There are many places in PQC algorithms Kyber and Dilithium where XOF is used for random sampling. The technique of sampling mentioned in section 2.2 is based on the uniformity of output of XOF functions. therefore, the efficiency of PQC algorithms depends on the efficient implementation of these XOF functions.

The performance of rejection sampling for the selection of vectors s_1 and s_2 depends on the SHAKE256. In every version of the Dilithium, the rejection sampling SampleInBall can be treated as a neutrosphic Boolean function. Here in the Dilithium algorithm steps 9 is for the sampling of a vector c. In the final proposed algorithm from "[20]", this c is sampled from another vector c^. The function named SampleInBall ($c^\wedge$) gives the output c. After signing the message $\hat{c}$ becomes the part of the signature and c will be safe as a secret. The proposed algorithm fixed security parameters for the sampling of c. The condition is directly related to frequency distribution in a vector of length 256 having entry $\{1,-1,0\}$. More specifically the security parameter τ is the total count of 1 and -1 in c. The value of τ in all three versions of Dilithium is presented in Table-2. We made an analogy of Boolean function to *SampleInBall*($c^\wedge$) function based on the distribution of 1, -1, and 0 in the outcome of that function which is c. Since the outcomes of the SampleInBall function are of 256 lengths, therefore, we can treat them as a truth table of a Boolean function, in the next definition we present the idea to analyze the *SampleInBall* function as a Boolean function, However, the inputs are not of the size of eight bits but the length of output c is 256, therefore, we have taken it as an eight-bit Boolean function.

> **Definition 3.1**(*SampleInBall* Boolean function): A *SampleInBall* is a generalized Boolean function *f* from Z_2^8 to Z_3.

Now the Walsh transformation of Boolean function f from Z_2^8 to Z_3 can be defined as,

Definition 3.2(Walsh Transformation): The Walsh Transformation of *SampleInBall* is defined as

$$WT_f(a) = \sum_{x \in Z_2^8} (-1)^{<x,a>} \omega^{f(x)} \quad (1)$$

where ω is 3rd root of unity which is $(-1 + \sqrt{3}\, i)/2$.

A generalized Boolean $f{:}Z_2^n \mapsto Z_3$ function is called balanced if the cardinality of every set $\{x{:}f(x) = i\}$ is $3^n - 1$ for every $0 \leq i \leq 2$. The flat Walsh spectrum i.e., $|WT_f(a)| = 2^n$ for all $a \in Z_2^n$ is the condition for f to be bent function. This can be generalized for a Boolean function f from Z_q^n *to* Z_3 for any prime q.

In the case of a generalized Boolean function f from Z_q^n to Z_q, where q is a prime number, the generalized Walsh transformation is defined as

$$WT_f(a) = \sum_{x \in Z_q^n} (\varsigma)^{<x,a>+f(x)}, \quad (2)$$

where $\zeta is\, q^{th}$ root of unity. Following is an example of a generalized Boolean function $f{:}Z_3^2 \mapsto Z_3$ with its Walsh spectrum

Table 2.

x	**(0,0)**	**(1,0)**	**(1,1)**	**(-1,1)**	**(0, -1)**	**(-1,0)**	**(-1, -1)**	**(1,0)**	**(0,1)**
$f(x)$	1	-1	-1	-1	-1	0	0	0	0
$WT_f(x)$	2.99̇	3	3	3	3	3	3	3	3

A Boolean function f: $Z_3^2 \mapsto Z_3$

A generalized Boolean $f{:}Z_q^n \mapsto Z_q$ function is called balanced if the cardinality of every sets $\{x{:}f(x) = i\}$ is q^{n-1} for every $0 \leq i \leq q-1$. Now in the next section, we present the results for the existence of bent functions with various other generalized properties of neutrobalancedness.

3.1 Classicalbalanced Bent Function

Definition 3.3(Classicalbalanced function): A function $f{:}Z_q^n \mapsto Z_3$ is said to be a Classicalbalanced function if it takes an equal number of 1's, 0's, and -1's.

Theorem3.4: A Classicalbalanced function $f{:}Z_q^n \mapsto Z_q$ never be a bent function.

Proof: From the definition (3.3) we know that a function $f{:}Z_q^n \mapsto Z_q$ is Classicalbalanced if and only if

$\sum_{x\in Z_2^n, f(x)=k} 1 = q^{n-1}$ (3)for all $0 \leq k < q$. Using (3) it is proved in (Pandey et al, 2017), that the Classicalbalanced function never be bent function. Now in the next section, we explore other generalizations of balancedness and bent functions. In the case of a neutrosphic Boolean function $f{:}Z_2^n \mapsto Z_3$, it is obvious to say that no classical balanced function exists.

3.2 Neutrobalanced Bent Function

Definition 3.5 A function is said to be a Neutrobalanced function if the number of 1's, 0's, and -1's are not the same but exactly two of them are equal.

Theorem 3.6 The Neutrobalanced bent function $f{:}Z_2^n \mapsto Z_3$does not exist for odd n.

Proof: Let a, b and c be the cardinality of

$\{x \in Z_2^n{:} f(x) = 1 = \alpha\}$, $\{x \in Z_2^n{:} f(x) = -1 = \beta\}$

and $\{x \in Z_2^n{:} f(x) = 0 = \gamma\}$

respectively. We can observe that

$$a + b + c = |Z_2^n| = 2^n \tag{4}$$

Here f is Neutrobalanced therefore any of two from a, b and c are always equal therefor taking symbolic equality of a and c, we can write that

$$a + b = 2^n. \tag{5}$$

From (1) the Walsh transformation of a Neutrobalanced function at $t \in Z_3^n$can be written as

$$WT_f(t) = \sum_{x\in Z_3^n} \omega^{f(x)}(-1)^{t.x}.$$

Walsh transformation at$t = 0$

$$WT_f(0) = \sum_{x\in Z_3^n} \omega^{f(x)}$$

It can be written as,

$$WT_f(0) = \sum_{x \in Z_3^n} \omega^{f(x)} = a\,\omega^{\alpha} + b\,\omega^{\beta} + c\,\omega^{\gamma} \tag{6}$$

where ω is the 3rd root of unity. Now since f is Neutrobalanced and bent after taking the symbolic equality of a and c

$$WT_f(0) = a(\omega^{\alpha} + \omega^{\beta}) + b\,\omega^{\gamma} \tag{7}$$

and

$$|WT_f(0)|^2 = 3^n. \tag{8}$$

Now using (7) and (8), we can characterize the necessary condition for the Neutrobalanced bent function in the Diophantine equations. For all values of (α, β, γ), (7) and (8) implies that

$$|a(1 + \omega) + b\,\omega^2| = 3^{n/2}$$

implies $|b - a|^2 = 3^n$ (9)

Now from (5) and (9)

$$a = \frac{3^n - \sqrt{3^n}}{3}$$

and

$$b = \frac{3^n + 2\sqrt{3^n}}{3}. \tag{10}$$

a and b are irrational numbers for odd values of n. Hence the theorem is proved.

It is interesting to see the construction of symmetric and rotational symmetric Neutrobalanced bent Boolean functions for even values of n. In (Pandey et al, 2017), for n=2, the list of eight symmetric and rotational symmetric bent Boolean functions is presented. From the available list of bent functions, we can say that f_5, f_6, f_7 and f_8

presented in (Pandey et al, 2017) are neutrobalanced symmetric and rotational bent Boolean functions. Their Algebraic Normal Form is presented as

Neutrobalanced symmetric and rotational symmetric bent Boolean function $f{:}Z_3^2 \mapsto Z_3$

$f(x_1,x_2) = 1 - x_1x_2,$
$f(x_1,x_2) = 1 + x_1 + x_2 + x_1x_2,$
$f(x_1,x_2) = x_1 + x_2 - x_1x_2 - 1,$
$f(x_1,x_2) = x_1x_2 - 1.$

3.3 Antibalanced Bent Function

Definition 3.7: A function is said to be an Antibalanced function if the number of 1's, 0's, and -1's are all distinct from each other.

Theorem 3.8: There does not exist any Antibalanced bent function $f{:}Z_2^n \mapsto Z_3$.

Walsh transformation of the Antibalanced function $f{:}Z_2^n \mapsto Z_3$ at t=0

$$WT_f(0) = \sum_{x \in Z_3^n} \omega^{f(x)} = a\omega^{\alpha} + b\omega^{\beta} + c\omega^{\gamma} \tag{11}$$

where ω is the 3rd root of unity. Now for all possible values of (α,β,γ), (11) implies that

$$WT_f(0) = \frac{2a + b + c + i\sqrt{3(b - c)}}{2} \tag{12}$$

Therefore, the Walsh transformation of bent Antibalanced function satisfy

$$4\left|WT_f(0)\right| = (2a + b + c)^2 + 3(b - c)^2$$

or

$$(a + 3^n)^2 + 3(b - c)^2 = 4(3^n). \tag{13}$$

Using (4) and (13) we can get a quadratic equation in b,

$$b^2 - (3^n + c)b + 3^{2n} + c^2 - (3^n)c - 3^n = 0$$

After solving this quadratic equation for b, we get

$$b = \frac{(3^n + c) \pm i\sqrt{(3^{2n+1} + 3c^2 + 2c(3^n) + 4(3^n))}}{2}. \quad (14)$$

Here b is a positive integer, therefore,

$$(3^{2n+1} + 3c^2 + 2c(3^n) + 4(3^n)) = 0. \quad (15)$$

Now solving (15), for the integer values of c, we found that the real roots do not exist. Hence no Anitibalanced bent function $f{:}Z_2^n \mapsto Z_3$ exist.

4. CONCLUSION: SAMPLEINNBALL FUNCTION AND NEUTROBALANCED BENT FUNCTION

τ is an important security parameter in Dilithium and its value reflects the distribution of 1, -1 and 0. It is interesting to use the observation in this article to characterize the SampleInBall function in Dilithium based on the security parameter τ. In all three versions of Dilithium, the value of $\tau$is 39, 49, and 60. Therefore it is straightforward that in the security level, 2 and 3, the SampleInBall function never be a Neutrobalanced bent function and achieves the highest nonlinearity. Consequently, SampleInBall for τ=39, 49 is an Antibalanced Boolean function, and from theorem 3.8, no Antibalanced Bent function exists, therefore SampleInBall has not achieved the highest nonlinearity.

In the case of Dilithium of security level, 5 the value of τ is 60, therefore the sampling may or may not be highly nonlinear based on the frequency distribution of 1 and -1 in c. In case of τ=60, SampleInBall is Neutrobalanced if \# 1 = 30 = \# -1. Now from theorem 3.6, if SampleInBall is bent then it is sampled through an even number of bits only to achieve bentness. SampleInBall for $\tau = 60$ is Antibalanced if \#1 $\neq$ \# $-$ 1 and from theorem (3.8), SampleInBall is not a bent function.

We have done experiments through the available implementation of Dilithium in (github_link, 2022) and found that out of 122 test vectors, $\hat{c}$ in Dilithium-5 only 22 are neutrobalanced therefore they are not with the highest nonlinearity. It would be interesting to study another rejection sampling with respect to the idea of corresponding generalized Boolean function and neutrosphy. The finalist of fourth round of PQC algorithm are Dilithium and KYBER. Both of them are based on the LWE problem and in the algorithms the sampling of errors and other binary vectors are available. It would be interesting to analyse those sampling in KYBER through the idea of neutrosphic Boolean function.

REFERENCES

Afzal. (2023). New Statistical Methodology for Capacitor Data Analysis via LCR Meter. *Neutrosphic System With Applications, 8*, 26-34. Doi.org/10.61356/j.nsw .2023.19

Agrawal, A., Stehlé, S., & Yadav, A. (2022). Round-optimal lattice-based threshold signatures, revisited. *49th EATCS International Conference on Automata, Languages, and Programming*.

Avanzi. (2021). CRYSTALS-Kyber (version 3.02) – Submission to round 3 of the NIST post-quantum project. Specification document (update from August 2021).

Boole, G. (1957). *An investigation of the laws of thought, on which are founded the mathematical theories of logic and probabilities*. Dover Publications, Inc.

Bos. (2022). Dilithium for memory constrained devices. *Lecture Notes in Comput. Sci., 13503*.

Budaghyan. (2018). Arithmetic of finite fields. *7th International Workshop, WAIFI 2018*.

Carlet, C. (2006). Vectorial Boolean functions for cryptography. In *Boolean Methods and Models*. Cambridge Univ. Press. Available http://www-roc.inria.fr/secret/ Claude.Carlet/pubs.html

Carlet, C. (2020). *Boolean functions for cryptography and coding theory*. Cambridge University Press.

Carlet, C., Dalai, D. K., Gupta, K. C., & Maitra, S. (2006). Algebraic immunity for cryptographically significant Boolean functions: analysis and construction. *IEEE Trans. Inform. Theory, 52*(7), 3105–3121.

Courtois & Meier. (2003). Algebraic attacks on stream ciphers with linear feedback. Advances in cryptology—EUROCRYPT 2003, 345–359.

Cusick & Stănică. (2009). *Cryptographic Boolean functions and applications*. Elsevier/Academic Press.

Decru, T. Panny, L., & Vercauteren, F. (2019). Faster SeaSign signatures through improved rejection sampling. *Post-quantum cryptography*, 271–285.

Dillon, J. F. (1974). *Elementary Hadamard difference-sets* [PhD Thesis]. University of Maryland.

Ducas. (2021). CRYSTALS-Dilithium – Algorithm Specifications and Supporting Documentation (Version 3.1). Specification document (update from February 2021).

Kaushik. (2023). Post Quantum Public and Private Key Cryptography Optimized for IoT Security. *Wireless Pers Commun, 129*, 893–909. https://doi.org/DOI:10.1007/s11277-022-10162-w

Kavut. (2008). *Boolean functions with excellent cryptographic properties in autocorrelation and walsh spectra* [PhD thesis]. Middle East Technical University.

Kolmogorov & Yushkevich. (1992). *Mathematics of the 19th century, Mathematical logic Algebra Number Theory Probability theory*. Springer Basel AG.

Pandey. (2017). Count and cryptographic properties of generalized symmetric Boolean functions. *Ital. J. Pure Appl. Math., 37*, 173–182.

Regev. (2009). Oded On lattices, learning with errors, random linear codes, and cryptography. *J. ACM, 56*(6).

Rothaus, O. S. (1976). On "bent" functions. *J. Combinatorial Theory Ser., A20*(3), 300–305.

Smarandache, F. (2003). *A unifying field in logics: neutrosphic logic, neutrosophy, neutrosphic set, neutrosphic probability.* Academic Press.

Smarandache, F. (2013). *A unifying field in logics: neutrosphic logic, neutrosophy, neutrosphic set, neutrosphic probability*. American Research Press.

Smarandache, F. (2019). Introduction to NeutroAlgebraic Structures and AntiAlgebraic Structures. In *Advances of Standard and Nonstandard Neutrosphic Theories*. Academic Press.

Smarandache, F. (2020a). Introduction to NeutroAlgebraic Structures and AntiAlgebraic Structures (revisited). *Neutrosphic Sets and Systems*, 31, 1–16.

Smarandache, F. (2020b). NeutroAlgebra is a Generalization of Partial Algebra. *International Journal of Neutrosphic Science*, 2(1), 8–17.

Stanica & Martinsen. (2011). Octal Bent Generalized Boolean Functions. arXiv:1102.4812v2

Tăndăreanu, N. (1981). On generalized Boolean functions. *I. Discrete Math., 34*(3), 293–299.

Vadiraja. (2022). Classical Balanced, Anti Balanced and Neutro Balanced functions. *Neutrosphic Sets and Systems, 48*, 386-398. Retrieved from https://fs.unm.edu/NSS2/index.php/111/article/view/2111

Zheng, Z., Wang, A., & Qin, L. (2021). Rejection sampling revisit: how to choose parameters in lattice-based signature. *Math. Probl. Eng.*

Chapter 4
Some New Results on Neutrosophic Soft Relations and Its Applications

Aysun Benek
https://orcid.org/0000-0001-8131-6178
Kafkas University, Turkey

Taha Yasin Öztürk
https://orcid.org/0000-0003-2402-6507
Kafkas University, Turkey

Adem Yolcu
https://orcid.org/0000-0002-4317-652X
Kafkas University, Turkey

ABSTRACT

In neutrosophic soft relation, if only the parameters or alternatives are processed, the relations may not give the desired clear result. In this chapter, in order to overcome this problem, a cartesian product is defined on neutrosophic soft sets with a different approach. With this approach, both alternatives and parameters are processed. Then, the concept of neutrosophic soft relation is denoted by using the definition of Cartesian product. The important features of the presented structures are examined, and various examples are given. In addition, the basic method that can be used in decision-making problems is presented by using the concept of neutrosophic soft relation.

DOI: 10.4018/979-8-3693-2085-3.ch004

1. INTRODUCTION

In 1965, Zadeh (Zadeh, 1965), introduced the idea of fuzzy set theory, which is used to address uncertainty in many real-world applications. Zadeh specified that there is a considerable amount of ambiguity in most real-life situations and physical problems that the classical set theory and its normal mathematical theories centered on such set theory did not give us the necessary knowledge and inferences. Later, the fuzzy set is generalized as the concept of the intuitionistic fuzzy set by Atanassov (Atanassov, 1986).

Molodtsov described soft set theory (Molodtsov, 1999) in 1999 as a new mathematical instrument for dealing with uncertainty, and how soft set theory is free of the parameterization inadequacy syndrome of fuzzy set theory and probability theory. In soft set theory, the challenge of determining the membership function, among other related issues, does not arise. As a result, the theory is highly straightforward and simple to use in practice. In line with this, Maji et al., presented a viewpoint on fuzzy soft sets and intuitionistic fuzzy soft sets (Maji et al., 2001a, 2001b). Soft sets and other set structures used in hybrid architectures are still being investigated extensively (Mehmood et al., 2022; Feng et al., 2010; Yolcu & Ozturk, 2021,2022; Yolcu et al., 2021a; Ozturk, 2016, 2018; Ozturk & Bayramov, 2017)

In 1999, Smarandache was established the concept of neutrospohic set (Smarandache, 1999). A membership function, an indeterminacy function, and a non membership function characterize a neutrosophic set. The functions are connected separately, with membership, indeterminacy, and non-membership functional values belonging to [0,1]. Later, Maji (Maji, 2013). proposed a combined notion called Neutrosophic soft set (NSS), which was later extended and generalized by (Bui et al., 2022; Tran et al., 2022; Yolcu et al., 2021b, 2023a, 2023b; Broumi, 2013; Broumi & Smarandache, 2013; Hussain & Shabir, 2015; Maji, 2015; Ozturk et al., 2021a, 2021b; Gunduz et al., 2019) and others. Presently, work on this NSS theory is progressing rapidly in different branches of Mathematics.

The use of fuzzy relations (Zadeh, 1965) arose from the realization that real-world items might be connected to each other to some extent. In the sense that they provide the degree to which two items are connected to each other, fuzzy relations can describe ambiguity. They cannot, however, model uncertainty. As a result, Bustince and Burillo (Bustince & Burillo, 1996) defined intuitionistic fuzzy relations, and Dinda and Samanta (Dinda & Samanta, 2012) defined intuitionistic fuzzy soft relations. This allows for the inclusion of uncertainty to some extent, but it does not manage indeterminacy of membership degree. As a result, Deli and Broumi (Deli & Broumi, 2015) launched neutrosophic soft connections. Many academics have recently explored fuzzy relations (Di Nola et al. 1988; Dutta & Chakraborty, 2015), fuzzy soft relations (Borah et al., 2012) and neutrosophic soft relations (Al-Quran & Hassan, 2018; Dalkılıç, 2021).

Previous studies on the neutrosophic soft relation have some disadvantages and structural deficiencies. In the studies (Deli & Broumi, 2015; Dalkılıç, 2021), it is seen that only the parameters are multiplied in the Cartesian product definitions given in the concept of relations on neutrosophic soft sets. There is no Cartesian multiplication on the alternatives. In this chapter, the concept of neutrosophic soft Cartesian product will be redefined in a way that both parameters and alternatives are multiplied. Additionally, the concept of neutrosophic flexible relation will be constructed using this Cartesian product concept. Along with this concept, the concepts of inverse correlation and composition will also be redefined. Moreover, on the concept of neutrosophic soft relation, the properties of reflection, transition and symmetry will be examined and the definition of equivalence relation will be made based on these properties. Additionally, some important theorems on the neutrosophic soft relation will be given and various examples will be presented. Finally, an application will be made on decision-making methods using these newly defined concepts.

2. PRELIMINARIES

Definition 2.1 (Deli & Broumi, 2015) Let X be an initial universe set and E be a set of parameters. Let $P(X)$ denote the set of all neutrosophic sets of X. Then, a neutrosophic soft set (F,E) over X is a set defined by a set valued function F representing a mapping F: $E \rightarrow P(X)$ where F is called approximate function of the neutrosophic soft set (F,E). In other words, the neutrosophic soft set is a parameterized family of some elements of the set $P(X)$ and therefore it can be written as a set of ordered pairs,

$$(F,E) = \left\{ \left(e, \left\langle x, T_{F(e)}(x), I_{F(e)}(x), F_{F(e)}(x) \right\rangle \right) : e \in E \right\}$$

where, $T_{F(e)}(x), I_{F(e)}(x), F_{F(e)}(x) \in [0,1]$, respectively called the truth - membership, indeterminacy - membership, falsity - membership function of $F(e)$.

Since supremum of each T, I, F is so the inequality $0 \leq T_{F(e)}(x) + I_{F(e)}(x) + F_{F(e)}(x) \leq 3$ is obvious.

Definition 2.2 (Ozturk et al., 2019) 1. A neutrosophic soft set (F,E) over the universe set X is said to be null neutrosophic soft set if $T_{F(e)}(x) = 0$, $I_{F(e)}(x) = 0$, $F_{F(e)}(x) = 1$; $\forall e \in E$, $\forall x \in X$. It is denoted by $0_{(X,E)}$.

2. A neutrosophic soft set (F,E) over the universe set C is said to be absolute neutrosophic soft set if $T_{F(e)}(x) = 1$, $I_{F(e)}(x) = 1$, $F_{F(e)}(x) = 0$; $\forall e \in E$, $\forall x \in X$. It is denoted by $1_{(X,E)}$.

Clearly, $0^c_{(X,E)} = 1_{(X,E)}$ and $1^c_{(X,E)} = 0^c_{(X,E)}$.

Definition 2.3 (Maji, 2013) Let (F,E) and (G,E) be two neutrosophic soft sets over the universe set X. (F,E) is said to be neutrosophic soft subset of (G,E) if $T_{F(e)}(x) \leq T_{G(e)}(x)$, $I_{F(e)}(x) \leq I_{G(e)}(x)$, $F_{F(e)}(x) \geq F_{G(e)}(x)$, $\forall e \in E$, $\forall x \in X$.

It is denoted by $(F,E) \subseteq (G,E)$. (F,E) is said to be neutrosophic soft equal to (G,E) if (F,E) is neutrosophic soft subset of (G,E) and (G,E) is neutrosophic soft subset of (F,E). It is denoted by $(F,E) = (G,E)$.

Definition 2.4 (Ozturk et al., 2019) Let (F_1,E) and (F_2,E) be two neutrosophic soft sets over the universe set X. Then their union is denoted by $(F_1,E) \cup (F_2,E) = (F_3,E)$ and is defined by:

$$(F_3,E) = \left\{\left(e, < x, T_{F_3(e)}(x), I_{F_3(e)}(x), F_{F_3(e)}(x) > : x \in X\right) : e \in E\right\}$$

where

$$T_{F_3(e)}(x) = \max\left\{T_{F_1(e)}(x), T_{F_2(e)}(x)\right\}$$

$$I_{F_3(e)}(x) = \max\left\{I_{F_1(e)}(x), I_{F_2(e)}(x)\right\}$$

$$F_{F_3(e)}(x) = \min\left\{F_{F_1(e)}(x), F_{F_2(e)}(x)\right\}.$$

Definition 2.5 (Ozturk et al., 2019) Let (F_1,E) and (F_2,E) be two neutrosophic soft sets over the universe set X. Then their intersection is denoted by $(F_1,E) \cap (F_2,E) = (F_3,E)$ and is defined by:

$$(F_3,E) = \left\{\left(e, \left\langle x, T_{F_3(e)}(x), I_{F_3(e)}(x), F_{F_3(e)}(x)\right\rangle : x \in X\right) : e \in E\right\}.$$

where

$$T_{F_3(e)}(x) = \min\left\{T_{F_1(e)}(x), T_{F_2(e)}(x)\right\}$$

$$I_{F_3(e)}(x) = \min\{I_{F_1(e)}(x), I_{F_2(e)}(x)\}$$

$$F_{F_3(e)}(x) = \max\{F_{F_1(e)}(x), F_{F_2(e)}(x)\}.$$

Definition 2.6 (Gunduz et al., 2019) Let *NSS(X,E)* be the family of all neutrosophic soft sets over the universe set *X*. Then neutrosophic soft set $x^e_{(\alpha,\beta,\gamma)}$ is called a neutrosophic soft point, for every *x*∈*X*, $0 < \alpha,\beta,\gamma \leq 1$, *e*∈*E*, and is defined as follows:

$$x^e_{(\alpha,\beta,\gamma)}(e')(y) = \begin{cases} (\alpha,\beta,\gamma) & if\ e' = e\ and\ y = x \\ (0,0,1) & if\ e' \neq e\ or\ y \neq x \end{cases}$$

Definition 2.7 (Gunduz et al., 2019) Let *(F,E)* be a neutrosophic soft set over the universe set *X*. We say that $x^e_{(\alpha,\beta,\gamma)} \in (F,E)$ read as belonging to the neutrosophic soft set *(F,E)* whenever $\alpha \leq T_{F(e)}(x), \beta \leq I_{F(e)}(x)$ and $\gamma \geq F_{F(e)}(x)$.

3. NEUTROSOPHIC SOFT RELATION

Definition 3.1 Let *X* be a universe and *E* be a parameter sets. *(F,A)* and *(G,B)* be two neutrosophic soft set over the common universe *X* and $A,B \subseteq E$. Then their cartesian product is *(F,A)*× *(G,B)*= *(H,X)* where *C*=*A*×*B*, *H*: *A*×*B*→ *NS*(*X*×*X*). Then *(H,C)* is defined as follows;

$$(H,C) = \left\{ \begin{array}{l} (e_k,e_l), \langle (x_i,x_j), T_{H(e_k,e_l)}(x_i,x_j), I_{H(e_k,e_l)}(x_i,x_j), F_{H(e_k,e_l)}(x_i,x_j) \rangle : x_i \in (F,A), \\ x_j \in (G,B), e_k \in A, e_l \in B \end{array} \right\}$$

$$T_{H(e_k,e_l)}(x_i,x_j) = \min\{T_{F(e_k)}(x_i), T_{G(e_l)}(x_j)\}$$

$$I_{H(e_k,e_l)}(x_i,x_j) = \min\{I_{F(e_k)}(x_i), I_{G(e_l)}(x_j)\}$$

$$F_{H(e_k,e_l)}(x_i,x_j) = \max\{F_{F(e_k)}(x_i), F_{G(e_l)}(x_j)\}$$

Example 3.1 Let $X = \{x_1, x_2, x_3\}$ be a universe and $E = \{e_1, e_2, e_3, e_4\}$ and $A = \{e_1, e_2, e_3\}$, $B = \{e_1, e_3\}$. We define (*F,A*) and (*G,B*) as follows:

$$(F,A) = \left\{\begin{array}{l} \left(e_1, \langle x_1, 0.3, 0.7, 0.6\rangle, \langle x_2, 0.4, 0.3, 0.8\rangle, \langle x_3, 0.2, 0.5, 0.4\rangle\right) \\ \left(e_2, \langle x_1, 0.4, 0.6, 0.8\rangle, \langle x_2, 0.3, 0.7, 0.2\rangle, \langle x_3, 0.3, 0.3, 0.7\rangle\right) \\ \left(e_3, \langle x_1, 0.6, 0.5, 0.4\rangle, \langle x_2, 0.4, 0.2, 0.3\rangle, \langle x_3, 0.7, 0.9, 0.5\rangle\right) \end{array}\right\}$$

$$(G,B) = \left\{\begin{array}{c} \left(e_1, \langle x_1, 0.6, 0.6, 0.8\rangle, \langle x_2, 0.1, 0.2, 0.4\rangle, \langle x_3, 0.7, 0.9, 0.5\rangle\right) \\ \left(e_3, \langle x_2, 0.5, 0.5, 0.4\rangle, \langle x_3, 0.3, 0.2, 0.3\rangle\right) \end{array}\right\}$$

Then (*F,A*)×(*G,B*)=(*H,C*) calculated as follows:

$$(H,C) = \left\{\begin{array}{l}
\left((e_1,e_1), \left(\begin{array}{l} <(x_1,x_1),0.3,0.6,0.8>, <(x_1,x_2),0.1,0.2,0.6>, <(x_1,x_3),0.3,0.7,0.6>, \\ <(x_2,x_1),0.4,0.3,0.8>, <(x_2,x_2),0.1,0.2,0.8>, <(x_2,x_3),0.4,0.3,0.8>, \\ <(x_3,x_1),0.2,0.5,0.8>, <(x_3,x_2),0.1,0.2,0.4>, <(x_3,x_3),0.2,0.5,0.5>, \end{array}\right)\right) \\
\left((e_1,e_3), \left(\begin{array}{l} <(x_1,x_2),0.3,0.5,0.6>, <(x_1,x_3),0.3,0.2,0.6>, \\ <(x_2,x_2),0.4,0.3,0.8>, <(x_2,x_3),0.3,0.2,0.8>, \\ <(x_3,x_2),0.2,0.5,0.4>, <(x_3,x_3),0.2,0.2,0.4> \end{array}\right)\right) \\
\left((e_2,e_1), \left(\begin{array}{l} <(x_1,x_1),0.4,0.6,0.8>, <(x_1,x_2),0.1,0.2,0.8>, <(x_1,x_3),0.4,0.6,0.8>, \\ <(x_2,x_1),0.3,0.6,0.8>, <(x_2,x_2),0.1,0.2,0.4>, <(x_2,x_3),0.3,0.7,0.5>, \\ <(x_3,x_1),0.3,0.3,0.8>, <(x_3,x_2),0.1,0.2,0.7>, <(x_3,x_3),0.3,0.3,0.7>, \end{array}\right)\right) \\
\left((e_2,e_3), \left(\begin{array}{l} <(x_1,x_2),0.4,0.5,0.8>, <(x_1,x_3),0.3,0.2,0.8>, \\ <(x_2,x_2),0.3,0.5,0.4>, <(x_2,x_3),0.3,0.2,0.3>, \\ <(x_3,x_2),0.3,0.3,0.7>, <(x_3,x_3),0.3,0.2,0.7>, \end{array}\right)\right) \\
\left((e_3,e_1), \left(\begin{array}{l} <(x_1,x_1),0.6,0.5,0.8>, <(x_1,x_2),0.1,0.2,0.4>, <(x_1,x_3),0.6,0.5,0.5>, \\ <(x_2,x_1),0.4,0.2,0.8>, <(x_2,x_2),0.1,0.2,0.4>, <(x_2,x_3),0.4,0.2,0.5>, \\ <(x_3,x_1),0.6,0.6,0.8>, <(x_3,x_2),0.1,0.2,0.5>, <(x_3,x_3),0.7,0.9,0.5>, \end{array}\right)\right) \\
\left((e_3,e_3), \left(\begin{array}{l} <(x_1,x_2),0.5,0.5,0.4>, <(x_1,x_3),0.3,0.2,0.4>, \\ <(x_2,x_2),0.4,0.2,0.4>, <(x_2,x_3),0.3,0.2,0.3>, \\ <(x_3,x_2),0.5,0.5,0.5>, <(x_3,x_3),0.3,0.2,0.5>, \end{array}\right)\right)
\end{array}\right\}$$

Remark 3.1 Definition 3.1 is also provided in case of taking different universal sets and different parameter set. Assuming that in Example 3.1, there are two different universal set *X* and *Y*, and two different parameters *E* and E', we get $F{:}E \times E' \rightarrow X \times Y$.

As a result, it is clear that Definition 3.1 is provided. When other neutrosophic soft cartesian product definitions (Deli & Broumi, 2015; Dalkılıç, 2021) are examined, ıt is clear that the neutrosophic soft cartesian product is not a product on both parameters and alternatives.

Definition 3.2 (*F,A*) and (*G,B*) be two neutrosophic soft set over the common universe *X*. If (*H,C*) is a neutrosophic soft subset of (*F,A*)×(*G,B*), where $C \subseteq A \times B$ and (*H,C*) $\subseteq$ (*F,A*) × (*G,B*), then (*H,C*) is called a neutrosophic soft relation on *X*.

Example 3.2 We consider the Example 3.1. Then *R* is neutrosophic soft relation and defined as follows:

$$R = \left\{ \begin{array}{l} \left((e_1,e_3), \left\{ \begin{array}{l} \langle (x_1,x_2), 0.3, 0.5, 0.6 \rangle, \langle (x_1,x_3), 0.3, 0.2, 0.6 \rangle, \\ \langle (x_2,x_2), 0.4, 0.3, 0.8 \rangle, \langle (x_2,x_3), 0.3, 0.2, 0.8 \rangle, \\ \langle (x_3,x_2), 0.2, 0.5, 0.4 \rangle, \langle (x_3,x_3), 0.2, 0.2, 0.4 \rangle \end{array} \right\} \right) \\ \left((e_2,e_1), \left\{ \begin{array}{l} \langle (x_1,x_1), 0.4, 0.6, 0.8 \rangle, \langle (x_1,x_2), 0.1, 0.2, 0.8 \rangle, \langle (x_1,x_3), 0.4, 0.6, 0.8 \rangle, \\ \langle (x_2,x_1), 0.3, 0.6, 0.8 \rangle, \langle (x_2,x_2), 0.1, 0.2, 0.4 \rangle, \langle (x_2,x_3), 0.3, 0.7, 0.5 \rangle, \\ \langle (x_3,x_1), 0.3, 0.3, 0.8 \rangle, \langle (x_3,x_2), 0.1, 0.2, 0.7 \rangle, \langle (x_3,x_3), 0.3, 0.3, 0.7 \rangle, \end{array} \right\} \right) \\ \left((e_2,e_3), \left\{ \begin{array}{l} \langle (x_1,x_2), 0.4, 0.5, 0.8 \rangle, \langle (x_1,x_3), 0.3, 0.2, 0.8 \rangle, \\ \langle (x_2,x_2), 0.3, 0.5, 0.4 \rangle, \langle (x_2,x_3), 0.3, 0.2, 0.3 \rangle, \\ \langle (x_3,x_2), 0.3, 0.3, 0.7 \rangle, \langle (x_3,x_3), 0.3, 0.2, 0.7 \rangle, \end{array} \right\} \right) \\ \left((e_3,e_3), \left\{ \begin{array}{l} \langle (x_1,x_2), 0.5, 0.5, 0.4 \rangle, \langle (x_1,x_3), 0.3, 0.2, 0.4 \rangle, \\ \langle (x_2,x_2), 0.4, 0.2, 0.4 \rangle, \langle (x_2,x_3), 0.3, 0.2, 0.3 \rangle, \\ \langle (x_3,x_2), 0.5, 0.5, 0.5 \rangle, \langle (x_3,x_3), 0.3, 0.2, 0.5 \rangle, \end{array} \right\} \right) \end{array} \right\}$$

Definition 3.3 Let (F,A) and (G,B) be two neutrosophic soft sets over the universe X and let R be neutrosophic soft relation from (F,A) to (G,B). Then R^{-1} is a inverse neutrosophic soft relation from (G,B) to (F,A) and defined as follows:

$$R^{-1} = \left\{ (e_l, e_k), \left\langle (x_j, x_i), T_{R^{-1}(e_l,e_k)}(x_j, x_i), I_{R^{-1}(e_l,e_k)}(x_j, x_i), F_{R^{-1}(e_l,e_k)}(x_j, x_i) \right\rangle : e_k \in A, e_l \in B \right\}$$

$$T_{R^{-1}(e_l,e_k)}(x_j, x_i) = \min\left\{ T_{G(e_l)}(x_j), T_{F(e_k)}(x_i) \right\}$$

$$I_{R^{-1}(e_l,e_k)}(x_j, x_i) = \min\left\{ I_{G(e_l)}(x_j), I_{F(e_k)}(x_i) \right\}$$

$$F_{R^{-1}(e_l,e_k)}(x_j, x_i) = \max\left\{ F_{G(e_l)}(x_j), F_{F(e_k)}(x_i) \right\}$$

Example 3.3 We consider the Example 3.2. Then we get R^{-1} as follows:

$$R^{-1} =$$

$$\left\{ \begin{array}{l} \left((e_3,e_1), \left\{ \begin{array}{l} \langle (x_2,x_1), 0.3, 0.5, 0.6 \rangle, \langle (x_2,x_2), 0.4, 0.3, 0.8 \rangle, \langle (x_2,x_3), 0.2, 0.5, 0.4 \rangle, \\ \langle (x_3,x_1), 0.3, 0.2, 0.6 \rangle, \langle (x_3,x_2), 0.3, 0.2, 0.8 \rangle, \langle (x_3,x_3), 0.2, 0.2, 0.4 \rangle \end{array} \right\} \right) \\ \left((e_1,e_2), \left\{ \begin{array}{l} \langle (x_1,x_1), 0.4, 0.6, 0.8 \rangle, \langle (x_1,x_2), 0.3, 0.6, 0.8 \rangle, \langle (x_1,x_3), 0.3, 0.3, 0.8 \rangle, \\ \langle (x_2,x_1), 0.1, 0.2, 0.8 \rangle, \langle (x_2,x_2), 0.1, 0.2, 0.4 \rangle, \langle (x_2,x_3), 0.1, 0.2, 0.7 \rangle, \\ \langle (x_3,x_1), 0.4, 0.6, 0.8 \rangle, \langle (x_3,x_2), 0.3, 0.7, 0.5 \rangle, \langle (x_3,x_3), 0.3, 0.3, 0.7 \rangle, \end{array} \right\} \right) \\ \left((e_3,e_2), \left\{ \begin{array}{l} \langle (x_2,x_1), 0.4, 0.5, 0.8 \rangle, \langle (x_2,x_2), 0.3, 0.5, 0.4 \rangle, \langle (x_2,x_3), 0.3, 0.3, 0.7 \rangle, \\ \langle (x_3,x_1), 0.3, 0.2, 0.8 \rangle, \langle (x_3,x_2), 0.3, 0.2, 0.3 \rangle, \langle (x_3,x_3), 0.3, 0.2, 0.7 \rangle \end{array} \right\} \right) \\ \left((e_3,e_3), \left\{ \begin{array}{l} \langle (x_2,x_1), 0.5, 0.5, 0.4 \rangle, \langle (x_2,x_2), 0.4, 0.2, 0.4 \rangle, \langle (x_2,x_3), 0.5, 0.5, 0.5 \rangle, \\ \langle (x_3,x_1), 0.3, 0.2, 0.4 \rangle, \langle (x_3,x_2), 0.3, 0.2, 0.3 \rangle, \langle (x_3,x_3), 0.3, 0.2, 0.5 \rangle \end{array} \right\} \right) \end{array} \right\}$$

Proposition 3.1 Let (F,A) and (G,B) be two neutrosophic soft sets over the common universe X and R be neutrosophic soft relation from (F,A) to (G,B). Then R^{-1} is a neutrosophic soft relation from (G,B) to (F,A).

Proof. For $x_i \in (F,A)$, $x_j \in (G,B)$, $e_k \in A$, $e_l \in B$, we have

$$T_{R^{-1}(e_l,e_k)}(x_j,x_i) = \min\{T_{G(e_l)}(x_j), T_{F(e_k)}(x_i)\}$$

$$= \min\{T_{F(e_k)}(x_i), T_{G(e_l)}(x_j)\}$$

$$= T_{R(e_k,e_l)}(x_i,x_j)$$

$$I_{R^{-1}(e_l,e_k)}(x_j,x_i) = \min\{I_{G(e_l)}(x_j), I_{F(e_k)}(x_i)\}$$

$$= \min\{I_{F(e_k)}(x_i), I_{G(e_l)}(x_j)\}$$

$$= I_{R(e_k,e_l)}(x_i,x_j)$$

$$F_{R^{-1}(e_l,e_k)}(x_j,x_i) = \max\{F_{G(e_l)}(x_j), F_{F(e_k)}(x_i)\}$$

$$= \max\{F_{F(e_k)}(x_i), F_{G(e_l)}(x_j)\}$$

$$= F_{R(e_k,e_l)}(x_i,x_j)$$

Then, R^{-1} is a neutrosophic soft relation from (G,B) to (F,A).

Proposition 3.2 Let (F,A) and (G,B) be two neutrosophic soft sets over the common universe X and R_1, R_2 be neutrosophic soft relation from (F,A) to (G,B). Then

1. $(R_1^{-1})^{-1} = R_1$
2. $R_1 \subseteq R_2 \Rightarrow R_1^{-1} \subseteq R_2^{-1}$

Proof. 1. Let $x_i \in (F,A)$ and $x_j \in (G,B)$, $e_k \in A$, $e_l \in B$. From the Proposition 3.1,

$$T_{R_1(e_k,e_l)}(x_i,x_j) = T_{R_1^{-1}(e_l,e_k)}(x_j,x_i)$$

$$I_{R_1(e_k,e_l)}(x_i,x_j) = I_{R_1^{-1}(e_l,e_k)}(x_j,x_i)$$

$$F_{R_1(e_k,e_l)}(x_i,x_j) = F_{R_1^{-1}(e_l,e_k)}(x_j,x_i)$$

Then we have,

$$T_{R_1(e_k,e_l)}(x_i,x_j) = T_{R_1^{-1}(e_l,e_k)}(x_j,x_i) = T_{(R_1^{-1})^{-1}(e_k,e_l)}(x_i,x_j)$$

$$I_{R_1(e_k,e_l)}(x_i,x_j) = I_{R_1^{-1}(e_l,e_k)}(x_j,x_i) = I_{(R_1^{-1})^{-1}(e_k,e_l)}(x_i,x_j)$$

$$F_{R_1(e_k,e_l)}(x_i,x_j) = F_{R_1^{-1}(e_l,e_k)}(x_j,x_i) = F_{(R_1^{-1})^{-1}(e_k,e_l)}(x_i,x_j)$$

It follows that $(R_1^{-1})^{-1} = R_1$.
If $R_1 \subseteq R_2$, then

$$T_{R_1(e_k,e_l)}(x_i,x_j) = T_{R_2(e_k,e_l)}(x_i,x_j)$$

$$I_{R_1(e_k,e_l)}(x_i,x_j) = I_{R_2(e_k,e_l)}(x_i,x_j)$$

$$F_{R_1(e_k,e_l)}(x_i,x_j) = F_{R_2(e_k,e_l)}(x_i,x_j)$$

Thus

$$T_{R_1(e_k,e_l)}(x_i,x_j) = T_{R_1^{-1}(e_l,e_k)}(x_j,x_i) \leq T_{R_2(e_k,e_l)}(x_i,x_j) = T_{R_2^{-1}(e_l,e_k)}(x_j,x_i)$$

$$I_{R_1(e_k,e_l)}(x_i,x_j) = I_{R_1^{-1}(e_l,e_k)}(x_j,x_i) \leq I_{R_2(e_k,e_l)}(x_i,x_j) = I_{R_2^{-1}(e_l,e_k)}(x_j,x_i)$$

$$F_{R_1(e_k,e_l)}(x_i,x_j) = F_{R_1^{-1}(e_l,e_k)}(x_j,x_i) \geq F_{R_2(e_k,e_l)}(x_i,x_j) = F_{R_2^{-1}(e_l,e_k)}(x_j,x_i)$$

so,

$$T_{R_1^{-1}(e_l,e_k)}(x_j,x_i) \leq T_{R_2^{-1}(e_l,e_k)}(x_j,x_i)$$

$$I_{R_1^{-1}(e_l,e_k)}(x_j,x_i) \leq I_{R_2^{-1}(e_l,e_k)}(x_j,x_i)$$

$$F_{R_1^{-1}(e_l,e_k)}(x_j,x_i) \geq F_{R_2^{-1}(e_l,e_k)}(x_j,x_i)$$

Hence, we have $R_1^{-1} \subseteq R_2^{-1}$. This completes of the conditions.

Definition 3.4 Let X be a universe and E be a parameter sets. (F,A), (G,B) and (H,C) be neutrosophic soft sets over the common universe X and $A,B \subseteq E$. R and S be two neutrosophic soft relations from (F,A) to (G,B) and (G,B) to (H,C), respectively. Then their neutrosophic soft composition is denoted by $R \circ S$ and defined by

$$R \circ S = \left\{ \begin{array}{l} (e_k, e_m), \left\langle (x_i,x_j), T_{R\circ S(e_k,e_m)}(x_i,x_j), I_{R\circ S(e_k,e_m)}(x_i,x_j), F_{R\circ S(e_k,e_m)}(x_i,x_j) \right\rangle \\ : x_i \in (F,A),\ x_j \in (H,C) : e_k \in A, e_m \in C \end{array} \right\}$$

where;

$$T_{R\circ S(e_k,e_m)}(x_i,x_j) = \max\left\{\min\left\{T_{R(e_k,e_l)}(x_i,x_j), T_{S(e_l,e_m)}(x_i,x_j)\right\}\right\}$$

$$I_{R\circ S(e_k,e_m)}(x_i,x_j) = \max\left\{\min\left\{I_{R(e_k,e_l)}(x_i,x_j), I_{S(e_l,e_m)}(x_i,x_j)\right\}\right\}$$

$$F_{R\circ S(e_k,e_m)}(x_i,x_j) = \min\left\{\max\left\{F_{R(e_k,e_l)}(x_i,x_j), F_{S(e_l,e_m)}(x_i,x_j)\right\}\right\}$$

$\forall e_k \in A$, $\forall e_l \in B$ and $\forall e_m \in C$.

Remark 3.2 When examining the composition of two relations, the following situations should be considered.

1. If a parameter pair such as (e_k,e_l) in the composition consist of a single match, the common alternative pairs in the relations forming the (e_k,e_l) parameter are taken into account. Other alternative pairs take the value of membership 0.
2. If a parameter pair such as (e_k,e_l) in the composition consist of more than one match, all the alternative pairs in the relations forming the (e_k,e_l) pairs in the relations forming the (e_k,e_l) parameter are taken into account.

The following example illustrates this more clearly.

Example 3.4 We consider the Example 3.1. Let (F,D) be given as follows;

$$(F,D) = \left\{ \begin{array}{c} (e_1, (\langle x_1, 0.4, 0.2, 0.6\rangle, \langle x_2, 0.2, 0.5, 0.7\rangle, \langle x_3, 0.3, 0.4, 0.9\rangle,)) \\ e_2, (\langle x_1, 0.7, 0.2, 0.5\rangle, \langle x_2, 0.5, 0.4, 0.6\rangle, \langle x_3, 0.6, 0.2, 0.3\rangle,) \end{array} \right\}$$

Let $R \subseteq (F,A) \times (G,B)$, $S \subseteq (G,B) \times (F,D)$ relations be defined as below.

$$R = \left\{ \begin{array}{l} \left((e_1,e_3), \left\{ \begin{array}{l} \langle (x_1,x_2), 0.3, 0.5, 0.6\rangle, \langle (x_1,x_3), 0.3, 0.2, 0.6\rangle, \\ \langle (x_2,x_2), 0.4, 0.3, 0.8\rangle, \langle (x_2,x_3), 0.3, 0.2, 0.8\rangle, \\ \langle (x_3,x_2), 0.2, 0.5, 0.4\rangle, \langle (x_3,x_3), 0.2, 0.2, 0.4\rangle \end{array} \right\} \right) \\ \left((e_2,e_1), \left\{ \begin{array}{l} \langle (x_1,x_1), 0.4, 0.6, 0.8\rangle, \langle (x_1,x_2), 0.1, 0.2, 0.8\rangle, \langle (x_1,x_3), 0.4, 0.6, 0.8\rangle, \\ \langle (x_2,x_1), 0.3, 0.6, 0.8\rangle, \langle (x_2,x_2), 0.1, 0.2, 0.4\rangle, \langle (x_2,x_3), 0.3, 0.7, 0.5\rangle, \\ \langle (x_3,x_1), 0.3, 0.3, 0.8\rangle, \langle (x_3,x_2), 0.1, 0.2, 0.7\rangle, \langle (x_3,x_3), 0.3, 0.3, 0.7\rangle, \end{array} \right\} \right) \\ \left((e_2,e_3), \left\{ \begin{array}{l} \langle (x_1,x_2), 0.4, 0.5, 0.8\rangle, \langle (x_1,x_3), 0.3, 0.2, 0.8\rangle, \\ \langle (x_2,x_2), 0.3, 0.5, 0.4\rangle, \langle (x_2,x_3), 0.3, 0.2, 0.3\rangle, \\ \langle (x_3,x_2), 0.3, 0.3, 0.7\rangle, \langle (x_3,x_3), 0.3, 0.2, 0.7\rangle, \end{array} \right\} \right) \\ \left((e_3,e_3), \left\{ \begin{array}{l} \langle (x_1,x_2), 0.5, 0.5, 0.4\rangle, \langle (x_1,x_3), 0.3, 0.2, 0.4\rangle, \\ \langle (x_2,x_2), 0.4, 0.2, 0.4\rangle, \langle (x_2,x_3), 0.3, 0.2, 0.3\rangle, \\ \langle (x_3,x_2), 0.5, 0.5, 0.5\rangle, \langle (x_3,x_3), 0.3, 0.2, 0.5\rangle, \end{array} \right\} \right) \end{array} \right\}$$

$$S = \left\{ \begin{array}{l} \left((e_1,e_1), \left\{ \begin{array}{l} \langle (x_1,x_1), 0.4, 0.2, 0.8\rangle, \langle (x_1,x_2), 0.2, 0.5, 0.8\rangle, \langle (x_1,x_3), 0.3, 0.4, 0.9\rangle, \\ \langle (x_2,x_1), 0.1, 0.2, 0.6\rangle, \langle (x_2,x_2), 0.1, 0.2, 0.7\rangle, \langle (x_2,x_3), 0.1, 0.2, 0.9\rangle, \\ \langle (x_3,x_1), 0.4, 0.2, 0.6\rangle, \langle (x_3,x_2), 0.2, 0.5, 0.7\rangle, \langle (x_3,x_3), 0.3, 0.4, 0.9\rangle, \end{array} \right\} \right) \\ \left((e_1,e_2), \left\{ \begin{array}{l} \langle (x_1,x_1), 0.6, 0.2, 0.8\rangle, \langle (x_1,x_2), 0.5, 0.4, 0.8\rangle, \langle (x_1,x_3), 0.6, 0.2, 0.8\rangle, \\ \langle (x_2,x_1), 0.1, 0.2, 0.5\rangle, \langle (x_2,x_2), 0.1, 0.2, 0.6\rangle, \langle (x_2,x_3), 0.1, 0.2, 0.4\rangle, \\ \langle (x_3,x_1), 0.7, 0.2, 0.5\rangle, \langle (x_3,x_2), 0.5, 0.4, 0.6\rangle, \langle (x_3,x_3), 0.6, 0.2, 0.5\rangle, \end{array} \right\} \right) \\ \left((e_3,e_2), \begin{array}{l} \langle (x_2,x_1), 0.5, 0.2, 0.5\rangle, \langle (x_2,x_2), 0.5, 0.4, 0.6\rangle, \langle (x_2,x_3), 0.5, 0.2, 0.4\rangle, \\ \langle (x_3,x_1), 0.3, 0.2, 0.5\rangle, \langle (x_3,x_2), 0.3, 0.2, 0.6\rangle, \langle (x_3,x_3), 0.3, 0.2, 0.3\rangle, \end{array} \right) \end{array} \right\}$$

The parameters of $R \circ S$ system is provided as;

$$\{(e_1,e_3) \circ (e_3,e_2)\} = (e_1,e_2)$$

$$\{(e_2,e_1) \circ (e_1,e_1)\} = (e_2,e_1)$$

$$\{(e_2,e_1)\circ(e_1,e_2)\} = \{(e_2,e_3)\circ(e_3,e_2)\} = (e_2,e_2)$$

$$\{(e_3,e_3)\circ(e_3,e_2)\} = (e_3,e_2)$$

Here according to Remark 3.2 (1. condition), we examine $R \circ S$ to (e_1,e_2). Parameter pair (e_1,e_2) in the composition consist of a single match $\{(e_1,e_3)\circ(e_3,e_2)\}$. For the (e_1,e_2) parameter, we should investigate the (e_1,e_3) parameter in R relation and (e_3,e_2) parameter in S relation.

Common alternative pairs for the (e_1,e_3) parameter in R relation and (e_3,e_2) parameter in S relation are (x_2,x_2), (x_2,x_3), (x_3,x_2) and (x_3,x_3).

The membership values of other alternatives according to (e_1,e_2) parameter becomes 0 by the definition of composition. Some calculations are provided as follow,

$$T_{R\circ S(e_1,e_2)}(x_2,x_2) = \max\left\{\min\left\{T_{R(e_1,e_3)}(x_2,x_2),T_{S(e_3,e_2)}(x_2,x_2)\right\}\right\}$$

$$= \max\{\min\{0.4,0.5\}\} = 0.4$$

$$I_{R\circ S(e_1,e_2)}(x_2,x_2) = \max\left\{\min\left\{I_{R(e_1,e_3)}(x_2,x_2),I_{S(e_3,e_2)}(x_2,x_2)\right\}\right\}$$

$$= \max\{\min\{0.3,0.4\}\} = 0.3$$

$$F_{R\circ S(e_1,e_2)}(x_2,x_2) = \min\left\{\max\left\{F_{R(e_1,e_3)}(x_2,x_2),F_{S(e_3,e_2)}(x_2,x_2)\right\}\right\}$$

$$= \min\{\max\{0.8,0.6\}\} = 0.8$$

$$T_{R\circ S(e_1,e_2)}(x_2,x_3) = \max\left\{\min\left\{T_{R(e_1,e_3)}(x_2,x_3),T_{S(e_3,e_2)}(x_2,x_3)\right\}\right\}$$

$$= \max\{\min\{0.3,0.5\}\} = 0.3$$

$$I_{R\circ S(e_1,e_2)}(x_2,x_3) = \max\left\{\min\left\{I_{R(e_1,e_3)}(x_2,x_3),I_{S(e_3,e_2)}(x_2,x_3)\right\}\right\}$$

$$= \max\{\min\{0.2, 0.2\}\} = 0.2$$

$$F_{R \circ S(e_1,e_2)}(x_2, x_3) = \min\left\{\max\left\{F_{R(e_1,e_3)}(x_2, x_3), F_{S(e_3,e_2)}(x_2, x_3)\right\}\right\}$$

$$= \min\{\max\{0.8, 0.4\}\} = 0.8$$

$$T_{R \circ S(e_1,e_2)}(x_3, x_2) = \max\left\{\min\left\{T_{R(e_1,e_3)}(x_3, x_2), T_{S(e_3,e_2)}(x_3, x_2)\right\}\right\}$$

$$= \max\{\min\{0.2, 0.3\}\} = 0.2$$

$$I_{R \circ S(e_1,e_2)}(x_3, x_2) = \max\left\{\min\left\{I_{R(e_1,e_3)}(x_3, x_2), I_{S(e_3,e_2)}(x_3, x_2)\right\}\right\}$$

$$= \max\{\min\{0.5, 0.2\}\} = 0.2$$

$$F_{R \circ S(e_1,e_2)}(x_3, x_2) = \min\left\{\max\left\{F_{R(e_1,e_3)}(x_3, x_2), F_{S(e_3,e_2)}(x_3, x_2)\right\}\right\}$$

$$= \min\{\max\{0.4, 0.6\}\} = 0.6$$

$$T_{R \circ S(e_1,e_2)}(x_3, x_3) = \max\left\{\min\left\{T_{R(e_1,e_3)}(x_3, x_3), T_{S(e_3,e_2)}(x_3, x_3)\right\}\right\}$$

$$= \max\{\min\{0.2, 0.3\}\} = 0.2$$

$$I_{R \circ S(e_1,e_2)}(x_3, x_3) = \max\left\{\min\left\{I_{R(e_1,e_3)}(x_3, x_3), I_{S(e_3,e_2)}(x_3, x_3)\right\}\right\}$$

$$= \max\{\min\{0.2, 0.2\}\} = 0.2$$

$$F_{R \circ S(e_1,e_2)}(x_3,x_3) = \min\left\{\max\left\{F_{R(e_1,e_3)}(x_3,x_3), F_{S(e_3,e_2)}(x_3,x_3)\right\}\right\}$$

$$= \min\{\max\{0.4, 0.3\}\} = 0.4$$

Now, we examine $R \circ S$ according to (e_2,e_2). Parameter pair (e_2,e_2) in the composition consist of more than one match. We see that it consist of product $\{(e_2,e_1) \circ (e_1,e_2)\}$ and $\{(e_2,e_3) \circ (e_3,e_2)\}$. For parameters consisting of such multi-parameter product, any alternatives cannot be ignored.

Some calculations for the (e_2,e_2) parameter are as follow;

$$T_{R \circ S(e_2,e_2)}(x_1,x_1) = \max\left\{\begin{matrix} \min\left\{T_{R(e_2,e_1)}(x_1,x_1), T_{S(e_1,e_2)}(x_1,x_1)\right\} \\ \min\left\{T_{R(e_2,e_3)}(x_1,x_1), T_{S(e_3,e_2)}(x_1,x_1)\right\} \end{matrix}\right\}$$

$$= \max\{\min\{0.4, 0.6\}, \min\{0, 0\}\}$$

$$= \max\{0.4, 0\} = 0.4$$

$$I_{R \circ S(e_2,e_2)}(x_1,x_1) = \max\left\{\begin{matrix} \min\left\{T_{R(e_2,e_1)}(x_1,x_1), T_{S(e_1,e_2)}(x_1,x_1)\right\} \\ \min\left\{T_{R(e_2,e_3)}(x_1,x_1), T_{S(e_3,e_2)}(x_1,x_1)\right\} \end{matrix}\right\}$$

$$= \max\{\min\{0.6, 0.2\}, \min\{0, 0\}\}$$

$$= \max\{0.2, 0\} = 0.2$$

$$F_{R \circ S(e_2,e_2)}(x_1,x_1) = \min\left\{\begin{matrix} \max\left\{T_{R(e_2,e_1)}(x_1,x_1), T_{S(e_1,e_2)}(x_1,x_1)\right\} \\ \max\left\{T_{R(e_2,e_3)}(x_1,x_1), T_{S(e_3,e_2)}(x_1,x_1)\right\} \end{matrix}\right\}$$

$$= \min\{\max\{0.8, 0.8\}, \max\{1, 1\}\}$$

$$= \min\{0.8, 1\} = 0.8$$

$$T_{R\circ S(e_2,e_2)}(x_2,x_2) = \max\left\{ \begin{array}{l} \min\left\{T_{R(e_2,e_1)}(x_2,x_2), T_{S(e_1,e_2)}(x_2,x_2)\right\} \\ \min\left\{T_{R(e_2,e_3)}(x_2,x_2), T_{S(e_3,e_2)}(x_2,x_2)\right\} \end{array} \right\}$$

$$= \max\{\min\{0.1, 0.1\}, \min\{0.3, 0.5\}\}$$

$$= \max\{0.1, 0.3\} = 0.3$$

$$I_{R\circ S(e_2,e_2)}(x_2,x_2) = \max\left\{ \begin{array}{l} \min\left\{T_{R(e_2,e_1)}(x_2,x_2), T_{S(e_1,e_2)}(x_2,x_2)\right\} \\ \min\left\{T_{R(e_2,e_3)}(x_2,x_2), T_{S(e_3,e_2)}(x_2,x_2)\right\} \end{array} \right\}$$

$$= \max\{\min\{0.2, 0.2\}, \min\{0.5, 0.4\}\}$$

$$= \max\{0.2, 0.4\} = 0.2$$

$$F_{R\circ S(e_2,e_2)}(x_2,x_2) = \min\left\{ \begin{array}{l} \max\left\{T_{R(e_2,e_1)}(x_2,x_2), T_{S(e_1,e_2)}(x_2,x_2)\right\} \\ \max\left\{T_{R(e_2,e_3)}(x_2,x_2), T_{S(e_3,e_2)}(x_2,x_2)\right\} \end{array} \right\}$$

$$= \min\{\max\{0.4, 0.6\}, \max\{0.4, 0.6\}\}$$

$$= \min\{0.6, 0.6\} = 0.6$$

Other calculations can easily be done similarly. The composition $R \circ S$ is shown in Table 1 below;

Table 1. The Composition RoS

$R \circ S$	(e_1, e_2)	(e_2, e_1)	(e_2, e_2)	(e_3, e_2)
(x_1, x_1)	$(0,0,1)$	$(0.4,0.2,0.8)$	$(0.4,0.2,0.8)$	$(0,0,1)$
(x_1, x_2)	$(0,0,1)$	$(0.1,0.2,0.8)$	$(0.1,0.2,0.8)$	$(0,0,1)$
(x_1, x_3)	$(0,0,1)$	$(0.3,0.4,0.9)$	$(0.4,0.2,0.8)$	$(0,0,1)$
(x_2, x_1)	$(0,0,1)$	$(0.1,0.2,0.8)$	$(0.1,0.2,0.8)$	$(0,0,1)$
(x_2, x_2)	$(0.4,0.3,0.8)$	$(0.1,0.2,0.7)$	$(0.3,0.4,0.6)$	$(0.4,0.2,0.6)$
(x_2, x_3)	$(0.3,0.2,0.8)$	$(0.1,0.2,0.9)$	$(0.3,0.2,0.4)$	$(0.3,0.2,0.4)$
(x_3, x_1)	$(0,0,1)$	$(0.3,0.2,0.8)$	$(0.3,0.2,0.8)$	$(0,0,1)$
(x_3, x_2)	$(0.2,0.2,0.6)$	$(0.1,0.2,0.7)$	$(0.3,0.2,0.7)$	$(0.3,0.2,0.6)$
(x_3, x_3)	$(0.2,0.2,0.4)$	$(0.3,0.3,0.9)$	$(0.3,0.2,0.7)$	$(0.3,0.2,0.5)$

Proposition 3.3 Let X be a universe and E be a parameter sets. (F,A), (G,B) and (H,C) be neutrosophic soft sets over the common universe X and $A,B \subseteq E$. R and S be two neutrosophic soft relations from (F,A) to (G,B) and (G,B) to (H,C), respectively. Then $R \circ S$ is neutrosophic soft relation from (F,A) to (H,C).

Proof. By Definition 3.4, for all $e_1 \in A$, $e_2 \in B$ and $e_3 \in C$.

$$T_{R\circ S(e_1,e_3)}(x_i, x_j) = \max\left\{\min\left\{T_{R(e_1,e_2)}(x_i, x_j), T_{S(e_2,e_3)}(x_i, x_j)\right\}\right\}$$

$$= \max\left\{\min\left\{T_{F(e_1)}(x_i), T_{G(e_2)}(x_j)\right\}, \min\left\{T_{G(e_2)}(x_i), T_{H(e_3)}(x_j)\right\}\right\}$$

$$= \max\left\{\min\left\{T_{F(e_1)}(x_i), T_{G(e_2)}(x_j), T_{H(e_3)}(x_j)\right\}\right\}$$

$$\leq \max\left\{\min\left\{T_{F(e_1)}(x_i), 1, T_{H(e_3)}(x_j)\right\}\right\}$$

$$\leq \max\left\{\min\left\{T_{F(e_1)}(x_i), T_{H(e_3)}(x_j)\right\}\right\}$$

$$\leq \min\left\{T_{F(e_1)}(x_i), T_{H(e_3)}(x_j)\right\}$$

$$I_{R\circ S(e_1,e_3)}(x_i, x_j) = \max\left\{\min\left\{I_{R(e_1,e_2)}(x_i, x_j), I_{S(e_2,e_3)}(x_i, x_j)\right\}\right\}$$

$$= \max\left\{\min\left\{I_{F(e_1)}(x_i), I_{G(e_2)}(x_j)\right\}, \min\left\{I_{G(e_2)}(x_i), I_{H(e_3)}(x_j)\right\}\right\}$$

$$= \max\left\{\min\left\{I_{F(e_1)}(x_i), I_{G(e_2)}(x_j), I_{H(e_3)}(x_j)\right\}\right\}$$

$$\leq \max\left\{\min\left\{I_{F(e_1)}(x_i), 1, I_{H(e_3)}(x_j)\right\}\right\}$$

$$\leq \max\left\{\min\left\{I_{F(e_1)}(x_i), I_{H(e_3)}(x_j)\right\}\right\}$$

$$\leq \min\left\{I_{F(e_1)}(x_i), I_{H(e_3)}(x_j)\right\}$$

$$F_{R \circ S(e_1,e_3)}(x_i, x_j) = \min\left\{\max\left\{F_{R(e_1,e_2)}(x_i, x_j), F_{S(e_2,e_3)}(x_i, x_j)\right\}\right\}$$

$$= \min\left\{\max\left\{F_{F(e_1)}(x_i), F_{G(e_2)}(x_j)\right\}, \max\left\{F_{G(e_2)}(x_i), F_{H(e_3)}(x_j)\right\}\right\}$$

$$= \min\left\{\max\left\{F_{F(e_1)}(x_i), F_{G(e_2)}(x_j), F_{H(e_3)}(x_j)\right\}\right\}$$

$$\leq \min\left\{\max\left\{F_{F(e_1)}(x_i), 1, F_{H(e_3)}(x_j)\right\}\right\}$$

$$\leq \min\left\{\max\left\{F_{F(e_1)}(x_i), F_{H(e_3)}(x_j)\right\}\right\}$$

$$\leq \max\left\{F_{F(e_1)}(x_i), F_{H(e_3)}(x_j)\right\}$$

Hence, $R \circ S \subseteq (F,A) \times (H,C)$.

Proposition 3.4 The neutrosophic soft composition is associate. If R, S and T are three neutrosophic soft relations from (F,A) to (G,B), (G,B) to (H,C) and (H,C) to (F,D), respectively. Then $(R \circ S) \circ T = R \circ (S \circ T)$.

Proof. For all $e_1 \in A$, $e_2 \in B$, $e_3 \in C$ and $e_4 \in D$.

$$T_{(R\circ S)\circ T(e_1,e_4)}(x_i,x_j) \;=\; \max\left\{\min\left\{T_{R\circ S(e_1,e_3)}(x_i,x_j),T_{T(e_3,e_4)}(x_i,x_j)\right\}\right\}$$

$$= \max\left\{\min\left\{T_{R(e_1,e_2)}(x_i,x_j),T_{S(e_2,e_3)}(x_i,x_j),T_{T(e_3,e_4)}(x_i,x_j)\right\}\right\}$$

$$= \max\left\{\min\left\{T_{R(e_1,e_2)}(x_i,x_j),T_{S\circ T(e_2,e_4)}(x_i,x_j)\right\}\right\}$$

$$= T_{R\circ(S\circ T)(e_1,e_4)}(x_i,x_j)$$

$$I_{(R\circ S)\circ T(e_1,e_4)}(x_i,x_j) \;=\; \max\left\{\min\left\{I_{R\circ S(e_1,e_3)}(x_i,x_j),I_{T(e_3,e_4)}(x_i,x_j)\right\}\right\}$$

$$= \max\left\{\min\left\{I_{R(e_1,e_2)}(x_i,x_j),I_{S(e_2,e_3)}(x_i,x_j),I_{T(e_3,e_4)}(x_i,x_j)\right\}\right\}$$

$$= \max\left\{\min\left\{I_{R(e_1,e_2)}(x_i,x_j),I_{S\circ T(e_2,e_4)}(x_i,x_j)\right\}\right\}$$

$$= I_{R\circ(S\circ T)(e_1,e_4)}(x_i,x_j)$$

$$F_{(R\circ S)\circ T(e_1,e_4)}(x_i,x_j) \;=\; \min\left\{\max\left\{F_{R\circ S(e_1,e_3)}(x_i,x_j),F_{T(e_3,e_4)}(x_i,x_j)\right\}\right\}$$

$$= \min\left\{\max\left\{F_{R(e_1,e_2)}(x_i,x_j),F_{S(e_2,e_3)}(x_i,x_j),F_{T(e_3,e_4)}(x_i,x_j)\right\}\right\}$$

$$= \min\left\{\max\left\{F_{R(e_1,e_2)}(x_i,x_j),F_{S\circ T(e_2,e_4)}(x_i,x_j)\right\}\right\}$$

$$= F_{R\circ(S\circ T)(e_1,e_4)}(x_i,x_j)$$

Hence $(R \circ S) \circ T = R \circ (S \circ T)$.

Proposition 3.5 Let $R \subseteq (F,A) \times (G,B)$ and $S,T \subseteq (G,B) \times (H,C)$ be three neutrosophic soft relations defined over X. Then, $R \circ (S \cup T) = (R \circ S) \cup (R \circ T)$.

Proof. Let $S \cup T \neq \varnothing$. For all $e_1 \in A$, $e_2 \in B$ and $e_3 \in C$, we have,

$$T_{R\circ(S\cup T)(e_1,e_3)}(x_i,x_j) = \max\left\{\min\left\{T_{R(e_1,e_2)}(x_i,x_j), T_{(S\cup T)(e_2,e_3)}(x_i,x_j)\right\}\right\}$$

$$= \max\left\{\min\left\{\max\left\{T_{R(e_1,e_2)}(x_i,x_j), T_{S(e_2,e_3)}(x_i,x_j), T_{T(e_2,e_3)}(x_i,x_j)\right\}\right\}\right\}$$

$$= \max\left\{\min\left\{\max\left\{\begin{matrix}\min\left\{T_{F(e_1)}(x_i), T_{G(e_2)}(x_j)\right\}\\ \min\left\{T_{G(e_2)}(x_i), T_{H(e_3)}(x_j)\right\}\\ \min\left\{T_{G(e_2)}(x_i), T_{H(e_3)}(x_j)\right\}\end{matrix}\right\}\right\}\right\}$$

$$= \max\left\{\min\left\{\begin{matrix}\min\left\{T_{F(e_1)}(x_i), T_{G(e_2)}(x_j)\right\}\\ \min\left\{T_{G(e_2)}(x_i), T_{H(e_3)}(x_j)\right\}\end{matrix}\right\}\right\}$$

$$= \max\left\{\min\left\{T_{F(e_1)}(x_i), T_{G(e_2)}(x_j), T_{H(e_3)}(x_j)\right\}\right\}$$

$$I_{R\circ(S\cup T)(e_1,e_3)}(x_i,x_j) = \max\left\{\min\left\{I_{R(e_1,e_2)}(x_i,x_j), I_{(S\cup T)(e_2,e_3)}(x_i,x_j)\right\}\right\}$$

$$= \max\left\{\min\left\{\max\left\{I_{R(e_1,e_2)}(x_i,x_j), I_{S(e_2,e_3)}(x_i,x_j), I_{T(e_2,e_3)}(x_i,x_j)\right\}\right\}\right\}$$

$$= \max\left\{\min\left\{\max\left\{\begin{matrix}\min\left\{I_{F(e_1)}(x_i), I_{G(e_2)}(x_j)\right\}\\ \min\left\{I_{G(e_2)}(x_i), I_{H(e_3)}(x_j)\right\}\\ \min\left\{I_{G(e_2)}(x_i), I_{H(e_3)}(x_j)\right\}\end{matrix}\right\}\right\}\right\}$$

$$= \max\left\{\min\left\{\begin{matrix}\min\left\{I_{F(e_1)}(x_i), I_{G(e_2)}(x_j)\right\}\\ \min\left\{I_{G(e_2)}(x_i), I_{H(e_3)}(x_j)\right\}\end{matrix}\right\}\right\}$$

$$= \max\left\{\min\left\{I_{F(e_1)}(x_i), I_{G(e_2)}(x_j), I_{H(e_3)}(x_j)\right\}\right\}$$

$$F_{R\circ(S\cup T)(e_1,e_3)}(x_i, x_j) = \min\left\{\max\left\{F_{R(e_1,e_2)}(x_i, x_j), F_{(S\cup T)(e_2,e_3)}(x_i, x_j)\right\}\right\}$$

$$= \min\left\{\max\left\{\min\left\{F_{R(e_1,e_2)}(x_i, x_j), F_{S(e_2,e_3)}(x_i, x_j), F_{T(e_2,e_3)}(x_i, x_j)\right\}\right\}\right\}$$

$$= \min\left\{\max\left\{\min\left\{\begin{array}{l}\max\left\{F_{F(e_1)}(x_i), F_{G(e_2)}(x_j)\right\}\\ \max\left\{F_{G(e_2)}(x_i), F_{H(e_3)}(x_j)\right\}\\ \max\left\{F_{G(e_2)}(x_i), F_{H(e_3)}(x_j)\right\}\end{array}\right\}\right\}\right\}$$

$$= \min\left\{\max\left\{\begin{array}{l}\max\left\{F_{F(e_1)}(x_i), F_{G(e_2)}(x_j)\right\}\\ \max\left\{F_{G(e_2)}(x_i), F_{H(e_3)}(x_j)\right\}\end{array}\right\}\right\}$$

$$= \min\left\{\max\left\{F_{F(e_1)}(x_i), F_{G(e_2)}(x_j), F_{H(e_3)}(x_j)\right\}\right\}$$

Then,

$$T_{R\circ(S\cup T)(e_1,e_3)}(x_i, x_j) = \max\left\{\min\left\{T_{F(e_1)}(x_i), T_{G(e_2)}(x_j), T_{H(e_3)}(x_j)\right\}\right\}$$

$$I_{R\circ(S\cup T)(e_1,e_3)}(x_i, x_j) = \max\left\{\min\left\{I_{F(e_1)}(x_i), I_{G(e_2)}(x_j), I_{H(e_3)}(x_j)\right\}\right\}$$

$$F_{R\circ(S\cup T)(e_1,e_3)}(x_i, x_j) = \min\left\{\max\left\{F_{F(e_1)}(x_i), F_{G(e_2)}(x_j), F_{H(e_3)}(x_j)\right\}\right\}$$

on the other hand, let $(R \circ S) \cap (R \circ T) \neq \varnothing$. Then,

$$T_{(R\circ S)\cup(R\circ T)(e_1,e_3)}(x_i, x_j) = \max\left\{T_{(R\circ S)(e_1,e_3)}(x_i, x_j), T_{(R\circ T)(e_1,e_3)}(x_i, x_j)\right\}$$

$$= \max\left\{ \begin{array}{l} \max\left\{\min\left\{T_{R(e_1,e_2)}(x_i,x_j), T_{S(e_2,e_3)}(x_i,x_j)\right\}\right\}, \\ \max\left\{\min\left\{T_{R(e_1,e_2)}(x_i,x_j), T_{T(e_2,e_3)}(x_i,x_j)\right\}\right\} \end{array} \right\}$$

$$= \max\left\{ \begin{array}{l} \max\left\{ \min\left\{ \begin{array}{l} \min\left\{T_{F(e_1)}(x_i), T_{G(e_2)}(x_j)\right\} \\ \min\left\{T_{G(e_2)}(x_i), T_{H(e_3)}(x_j)\right\} \end{array} \right\} \right\}, \\ \max\left\{ \min\left\{ \begin{array}{l} \min\left\{T_{F(e_1)}(x_i), T_{G(e_2)}(x_j)\right\} \\ \min\left\{T_{G(e_2)}(x_i), T_{H(e_3)}(x_j)\right\} \end{array} \right\} \right\} \end{array} \right\}$$

$$= \max\left\{ \min\left\{ \begin{array}{l} \min\left\{T_{F(e_1)}(x_i), T_{G(e_2)}(x_j)\right\} \\ \min\left\{T_{G(e_2)}(x_i), T_{H(e_3)}(x_j)\right\} \end{array} \right\} \right\}$$

$$= \max\left\{\min\left\{T_{F(e_1)}(x_i), T_{G(e_2)}(x_j), T_{H(e_3)}(x_j)\right\}\right\}$$

Membership functions I and F can also be found in the same way.

Then, we have $R \circ (S \cup T) = (R \circ S) \cup (R \circ T)$.

Definition 3.5 Let X be a universe and E be a parameter sets. The neutrosophic soft relation $\Delta \in NSR(X \times X)_{E\times E}$ is called identity relation if;

$$T_{\Delta(e_k,e_l)}(x_i,x_j) = \begin{cases} 1, & if\ i = j = k = l \\ 0, & if\ i \neq j \neq k \neq l \end{cases}$$

$$I_{\Delta(e_k,e_l)}(x_i,x_j) = \begin{cases} 1, & if\ i = j = k = l \\ 0, & if\ i \neq j \neq k \neq l \end{cases}$$

$$F_{\Delta(e_k,e_l)}(x_i,x_j) = \begin{cases} 0, & if\ i = j = k = l \\ 1, & if\ i \neq j \neq k \neq l \end{cases}, \forall (x_i,x_j) \in X \times X$$

Where $(x_i,x_j) \in (X,E) \times (X,E)$.

4. NEUTROSOPHIC SOFT EQUIVALENCE RELATION

Definition 4.1 Let X be a universe and E be a parameter sets. The neutrosophic soft relation R on $(F,A) \in NSS(X,E)$ is called to be neutrosophic soft reflexive if $\left(x^{e_i}_{i(\alpha,\beta,\gamma)}, x^{e_i}_{i(\alpha,\beta,\gamma)}\right)$, $\forall x^{e_i}_{i(\alpha,\beta,\gamma)} \in (F,A)$.

Definition 4.2 Let X be a universe and E be a parameter sets. The neutrosophic soft relation R on $(F,A) \in NSS(X,E)$ is called to be neutrosophic soft symmetric if

$$\left(x^{e_1}_{1(\alpha,\beta,\gamma)}, x^{e_2}_{2(\alpha,\beta,\gamma)}\right) \Rightarrow \left(x^{e_2}_{2(\alpha,\beta,\gamma)}, x^{e_1}_{1(\alpha,\beta,\gamma)}\right),$$

$$\forall x^{e_1}_{1(\alpha,\beta,\gamma)}, x^{e_2}_{2(\alpha,\beta,\gamma)} \in (F,A).$$

Definition 4.3 Let X be a universe and E be a parameter sets. The neutrosophic soft relation R on $(F,A) \in NSS(X,E)$ is called to be neutrosophic soft transitive if

$$\left(x^{e_1}_{1(\alpha,\beta,\gamma)}, x^{e_2}_{2(\alpha,\beta,\gamma)}\right)$$

and

$$\left(x^{e_2}_{2(\alpha,\beta,\gamma)}, x^{e_3}_{3(\alpha,\beta,\gamma)}\right) \Rightarrow \left(x^{e_1}_{1(\alpha,\beta,\gamma)}, x^{e_3}_{3(\alpha,\beta,\gamma)}\right),$$

$$x^{e_1}_{1(\alpha,\beta,\gamma)}, x^{e_2}_{2(\alpha,\beta,\gamma)}, x^{e_3}_{3(\alpha,\beta,\gamma)} \in (F,A)$$

Definition 4.4 A neutrosophic soft relation R is called to be neutrosophic soft equivalence relation if it is neutrosophic soft symmetric, neutrosophic soft transitive and neutrosophic soft reflexive.

Example 4.1 Let $X = \{x_1, x_2, x_3\}$ and $E = \{e_1, e_2\}$. Assume that a neutrosophic soft set on X as;

$$(F,E) = \left\{ \begin{array}{l} (e_1, \langle x_1, 0.2, 0.8, 0.7\rangle, \langle x_2, 0.5, 0.7, 0.8\rangle, \langle x_3, 0.4, 0.3, 0.7\rangle) \\ (e_2, \langle x_1, 0.5, 0.3, 0.8\rangle, \langle x_2, 0.4, 0.7, 0.9\rangle, \langle x_3, 0.7, 0.6, 0.5\rangle) \end{array} \right\}$$

Then we get a neutrosophic soft relation R on (F,E) as follows;

$$R = \left\{ \begin{array}{l} \left\{ (e_1,e_1), \left\{ \begin{array}{l} \langle (x_1,x_1), 0.2, 0.8, 0.7 \rangle, \langle (x_1,x_2), 0.2, 0.7, 0.8 \rangle, \langle (x_1,x_3), 0.2, 0.3, 0.7 \rangle, \\ \langle (x_2,x_1), 0.2, 0.7, 0.8 \rangle, \langle (x_2,x_2), 0.5, 0.7, 0.8 \rangle, \langle (x_2,x_3), 0.4, 0.3, 0.8 \rangle, \\ \langle (x_3,x_1), 0.2, 0.3, 0.7 \rangle, \langle (x_3,x_2), 0.4, 0.3, 0.8 \rangle, \langle (x_3,x_3), 0.4, 0.3, 0.7 \rangle, \end{array} \right\} \right\} \\ \left\{ (e_1,e_2), \left\{ \begin{array}{l} \langle (x_1,x_1), 0.2, 0.3, 0.8 \rangle, \langle (x_1,x_2), 0.2, 0.7, 0.9 \rangle, \langle (x_1,x_3), 0.2, 0.6, 0.7 \rangle, \\ \langle (x_2,x_1), 0.5, 0.3, 0.8 \rangle, \langle (x_2,x_2), 0.4, 0.7, 0.9 \rangle, \langle (x_2,x_3), 0.5, 0.6, 0.8 \rangle, \\ \langle (x_3,x_1), 0.4, 0.3, 0.8 \rangle, \langle (x_3,x_2), 0.4, 0.3, 0.9 \rangle, \langle (x_3,x_3), 0.4, 0.3, 0.7 \rangle, \end{array} \right\} \right\} \\ \left\{ (e_2,e_1), \left\{ \begin{array}{l} \langle (x_1,x_1), 0.2, 0.3, 0.8 \rangle, \langle (x_1,x_2), 0.5, 0.3, 0.8 \rangle, \langle (x_1,x_3), 0.4, 0.3, 0.8 \rangle, \\ \langle (x_2,x_1), 0.2, 0.7, 0.9 \rangle, \langle (x_2,x_2), 0.4, 0.7, 0.9 \rangle, \langle (x_2,x_3), 0.4, 0.3, 0.9 \rangle, \\ \langle (x_3,x_1), 0.2, 0.6, 0.7 \rangle, \langle (x_3,x_2), 0.5, 0.6, 0.8 \rangle, \langle (x_3,x_3), 0.4, 0.3, 0.7 \rangle, \end{array} \right\} \right\} \\ \left\{ (e_2,e_2), \left\{ \begin{array}{l} \langle (x_1,x_1), 0.5, 0.3, 0.8 \rangle, \langle (x_1,x_2), 0.4, 0.3, 0.9 \rangle, \langle (x_1,x_3), 0.5, 0.3, 0.8 \rangle, \\ \langle (x_2,x_1), 0.4, 0.3, 0.9 \rangle, \langle (x_2,x_2), 0.4, 0.7, 0.9 \rangle, \langle (x_2,x_3), 0.4, 0.6, 0.9 \rangle, \\ \langle (x_3,x_1), 0.5, 0.3, 0.8 \rangle, \langle (x_3,x_2), 0.4, 0.6, 0.9 \rangle, \langle (x_3,x_3), 0.7, 0.6, 0.5 \rangle, \end{array} \right\} \right\} \end{array} \right\}$$

R on (F,E) is a neutrosophic soft equivalence relation because it is neutrosophic soft symmetric, neutrosophic soft transitive and neutrosophic soft reflexive.

Definition 4.5 Let R be an equivalence relation on a neutrosophic soft set $(F,A) \in NSS(X,E)$ and $e_i \in A$. Then neutrosophic soft equivalence class of $x^{e_i}_{i(\alpha,\beta,\gamma)} \in (F,A)$ denoted by $[x^{e_i}_{i(\alpha,\beta,\gamma)}]$, is defined as;

$$[x^{e_i}_{i(\alpha,\beta,\gamma)}] = \left\{ x^{e_i'}_{i(\alpha',\beta',\gamma')} : \left(x^{e_i}_{i(\alpha,\beta,\gamma)}, x^{e_i'}_{i(\alpha',\beta',\gamma')} \right) \in R \right\}$$

The set of $\left\{ [x^{e_i}_{i(\alpha,\beta,\gamma)}] : x^{e_i}_{i(\alpha,\beta,\gamma)} \in (F,A) \right\}$ is called the quotient neutrosophic soft set of (F,A) and denoted by $(F,A)/R$.

Lemma 4.1 Let R be an equivalence relation on a neutrosophic soft set $(F,A) \in NS$-$S(X,E)$ and $e_1, e_2 \in A$. For any

$$x^{e_1}_{1(\alpha,\beta,\gamma)}, x^{e_2}_{2(\alpha,\beta,\gamma)} \in (F,A),$$

$$\left(x^{e_1}_{1(\alpha,\beta,\gamma)}, x^{e_2}_{2(\alpha,\beta,\gamma)} \right)$$

iff

$$[x^{e_1}_{1(\alpha,\beta,\gamma)}] = [x^{e_2}_{2(\alpha,\beta,\gamma)}].$$

Proof. Suppose $[x^{e_1}_{1(\alpha,\beta,\gamma)}] = [x^{e_2}_{2(\alpha,\beta,\gamma)}]$. Since R is neutrosophic soft reflexive

$$\left(x^{e_2}_{2(\alpha,\beta,\gamma)}, x^{e_2}_{2(\alpha,\beta,\gamma)} \right).$$

Hence, $x^{e_2}_{2(\alpha,\beta,\gamma)} \in [x^{e_2}_{2(\alpha,\beta,\gamma)}] = [x^{e_1}_{1(\alpha,\beta,\gamma)}]$ which gives $\left(x^{e_1}_{1(\alpha,\beta,\gamma)}, x^{e_2}_{2(\alpha,\beta,\gamma)} \right)$.

Conversely, suppose $\left(x^{e_1}_{1(\alpha,\beta,\gamma)}, x^{e_2}_{2(\alpha,\beta,\gamma)}\right)$. Let $x^{e_1}_{1(\alpha,\beta,\gamma)} \in \left[x^{e_1}_{1(\alpha,\beta,\gamma)}\right]$.

Then $x^{e_1}_{1(\alpha,\beta,\gamma)} \in x^{e_1}_{1(\alpha,\beta,\gamma)}$. Using the transitive property of R this gives $x^{e_1}_{1(\alpha,\beta,\gamma)} \in \left[x^{e_2}_{2(\alpha,\beta,\gamma)}\right]$.

Hence $\left[x^{e_1}_{1(\alpha,\beta,\gamma)}\right] \subseteq \left[x^{e_2}_{2(\alpha,\beta,\gamma)}\right]$. Using the similar argument $\left[x^{e_2}_{2(\alpha,\beta,\gamma)}\right] \subseteq \left[x^{e_1}_{1(\alpha,\beta,\gamma)}\right]$.

Hence $\left[x^{e_1}_{1(\alpha,\beta,\gamma)}\right] = \left[x^{e_2}_{2(\alpha,\beta,\gamma)}\right]$.

Definition 4.6 A collection $P = \{(F_i,A_i):i \in I\}$ of nonempty neutrosophic soft subset of neutrosophic soft set $(F,A) \in NSS(X,E)$ is called a neutrosophic soft partition of (F,A) if,

1. $\bigcup_{i \in I}(F_i,A_i) = (F,A)$
2. $(F_i,A_i) \cap (F_j,A_j) = \emptyset$ if $i \neq j$

The members of partition are called a block of (F,A).

Theorem 4.1 Corresponding to every equivalence relation defined on a neutrosophic soft set (F,A). The exists a partition on (F,A) and this partition precisely consist of the equivalence clases of R.

Proof. Let $\left[x^{e}_{(\alpha,\beta,\gamma)}\right]$ be a equivalence class w.r.t a relation R on (F,A). Let A_ρ denote all those elements in A corresponding to $\left[x^{e}_{(\alpha,\beta,\gamma)}\right]$. $A_\rho = \left\{e_2 \in A: \left(\left(x^{e_2}_{2(\alpha,\beta,\gamma)}, x^{e_1}_{1(\alpha,\beta,\gamma)}\right)\right)\right\}$ .Thus we can denote $\left[x^{e}_{(\alpha,\beta,\gamma)}\right]$ as (F,A_ρ). So we have to show that the collection $\left\{(F,A_\rho):e_1 \in A\right\}$ of such distinct sets forms a partition P of (F,A). In order to prove this we should prove,

i. $\bigcup_{i \in I}(F_i,A_i) = (F,A)$
ii. $(F_i,A_i) \cap (F_j,A_j) = \emptyset$ whenever $i \neq j$

Since R neutrosophic soft reflexive $\left(x^{e}_{(\alpha,\beta,\gamma)}, x^{e}_{(\alpha,\beta,\gamma)}\right)$, $\forall e \in A$ so that part (*ii*) can prove easily. Now part (*iii*). Let $e \in A_i \cap A_j$ then $x^{e_i}_{i(\alpha,\beta,\gamma)} \in (F_i,A_i)$ and $x^{e_j}_{j(\alpha,\beta,\gamma)} \in (F_j,A_j)$ then $\left(x^{e_i}_{i(\alpha,\beta,\gamma)}, x^{e_j}_{j(\alpha,\beta,\gamma)}\right)$ and $\left(x^{e_j}_{j(\alpha,\beta,\gamma)}, x^{e_i}_{i(\alpha,\beta,\gamma)}\right)$. Using neutrosophic soft transitive property of R we have $\left((F_i,A_i),(F_j,A_j)\right)$.

Now using the Lemma 4.1, we have $\left[x^{e_1}_{1(\alpha,\beta,\gamma)}\right] = \left[x^{e_2}_{2(\alpha,\beta,\gamma)}\right]$. This gives $x^{e_1}_{1(\alpha,\beta,\gamma)} = x^{e_2}_{2(\alpha,\beta,\gamma)}$.

5. DECISION-MAKING METHOD

In this section, we present an application of neutrosophic soft relation in a decision-making problem. Some of it is quoted from in (Deli & Broumi, 2015; Dalkılıç, 2021).

Now, we can construct a decision making method on neutrosophic soft relation by the following algorithm;

1. Input the neutrosophic soft (F,A) and (G,B).
2. Obtain the neutrosophic soft matrix R (relational table) corresponding to cartesian product of (F,A) and (G,B) respectively.
3. Compute the comparison table using the following formula $T+I-F$
4. Select the highest numerical grades from comparison table for each column.
5. Find the score table which having the following form *Table 2*:

Table 2. Form of the Score Table

	(e_1,e_1)	...	...	...	(e_n,e_m)
Object	(x_i,x_j)	...	...	...	...
Highest Numerical Grade	...	...	...	...	...

Where e_n denotes the parameters of (F,A) and e_m denotes the parameters of (G,B).

6. Compute the score of each objects by taking the sum of these numerical grades.
7. The decision is any one of the elements in M where $M = \max_{(x_i,x_j)\in R}\left\{S_{(x_i,x_j)}\right\}$.

Now, we use this algorithm to find the best choice in decision making system.

Example 5.1 Let $X = \{x_1,x_2,x_3\}$={Erzurum, Ardahan, Iğdır} be a set of three city. Let's assume that two friends want to choose one of these highways for city Kars according to the preference parameters $A = \{e_1,e_2,e_3\}$={expensive, moderate, inexpensive} and $B = \{e'_1,e'_3\}$={asphalt road, gravel road}, respectively. We then choose a path based on parameter sets using the neutrosophic soft relation decision making method.

The first friend evaluates the cities according to the turnpike parameters, and the second friend evaluates the cities according to the road features parameters.

1. We input the neutrosophic soft (F,A) and (G,B) as;

$$(F,A) = \begin{Bmatrix} (e_1,\langle x_1,0.3,0.7,0.6\rangle,\langle x_2,0.5,0.4,0.6\rangle,\langle x_3,0.2,0.5,0.4\rangle) \\ (e_2,\langle x_1,0.4,0.8,0.5\rangle,\langle x_2,0.3,0.7,0.2\rangle,\langle x_3,0.3,0.3,0.7\rangle) \\ (e_3,\langle x_1,0.6,0.5,0.4\rangle,\langle x_2,0.4,0.2,0.3\rangle,\langle x_3,0.7,0.9,0.5\rangle) \end{Bmatrix}$$

and

$$(G,B) = \begin{Bmatrix} (e'_1,\langle x_1,0.6,0.6,0.8\rangle,\langle x_2,0.3,0.7,0.4\rangle,\langle x_3,0.7,0.9,0.5\rangle) \\ (e'_3,\langle x_2,0.6,0.5,0.4\rangle,\langle x_3,0.6,0.5,0.3\rangle) \end{Bmatrix}$$

2. In *Table 3*. we obtain the neutrosophic soft matrix R corresponding to cartesian product of (F,A) and (G,B), respectively.

Table 3. Neutrosophic soft matrix R (Relational Table)

R	(e_1,e'_3)	(e_2,e'_1)	(e_2,e'_3)	(e_3,e'_3)
(x_1,x_1)	$(0,0,1)$	$(0.4,0.6,0.8)$	$(0,0,1)$	$(0,0,1)$
(x_1,x_2)	$(0.3,0.5,0.6)$	$(0.3,0.7,0.5)$	$(0.4,0.5,0.5)$	$(0.6,0.5,0.4)$
(x_1,x_3)	$(0.3,0.5,0.6)$	$(0.4,0.8,0.5)$	$(0.4,0.5,0.5)$	$(0.6,0.5,0.4)$
(x_2,x_1)	$(0,0,1)$	$(0.3,0.6,0.8)$	$(0,0,1)$	$(0,0,1)$
(x_2,x_2)	$(0.5,0.4,0.6)$	$(0.3,0.7,0.4)$	$(0.3,0.5,0.4)$	$(0.4,0.2,0.4)$
(x_2,x_3)	$(0.5,0.4,0.6)$	$(0.3,0.7,0.5)$	$(0.3,0.5,0.3)$	$(0.4,0.2,0.3)$
(x_3,x_1)	$(0,0,1)$	$(0.3,0.3,0.8)$	$(0,0,1)$	$(0,0,1)$
(x_3,x_2)	$(0.2,0.5,0.4)$	$(0.3,0.3,0.7)$	$(0.3,0.3,0.7)$	$(0.6,0.5,0.5)$
(x_3,x_3)	$(0.2,0.5,0.4)$	$(0.3,0.3,0.7)$	$(0.3,0.3,0.7)$	$(0.6,0.5,0.5)$

3. By using the *Table 3*., we compute the comparison as *Table 4*;

Table 4. Comparison Table

R	(e_1,e'_3)	(e_2,e'_1)	(e_2,e'_3)	(e_3,e'_3)
(x_1,x_1)	-1	0.2	-1	-1
(x_1,x_2)	0.2	0.5	0.4	**0.7**
(x_1,x_3)	0.2	**0.7**	0.4	**0.7**
(x_2,x_1)	-1	0.1	-1	-1
(x_2,x_2)	**0.3**	0.6	0.4	0.2
(x_2,x_3)	**0.3**	0.5	**0.5**	0.3
(x_3,x_1)	-1	-0.2	-1	-1
(x_3,x_2)	**0.3**	-0.1	-0.1	0.6
(x_3,x_3)	**0.3**	-0.1	-0.1	0.6

4. The highest numerical grades for each column in *Table 4*. is written in bold.
5. We find the score table which having the following form *Table 5*;

Table 5. Score Table

R	(e_1,e'_3)	(e_2,e'_1)	(e_2,e'_3)	(e_3,e'_3)
(x_i,x_j)	(x_2,x_2), (x_2,x_3), (x_3,x_2), (x_3,x_3)	(x_1,x_3)	(x_2,x_3)	(x_1,x_2), (x_1,x_3)
Highest Numerical Grade	0.3	0.7	0.5	0.7

6. We compute the score of each objects by taking the sum of these numerical grades as;

$$S_{(x_1,x_2)} = 0.7$$

$$S_{(x_1,x_3)} = 0.7 + 0.7 = 1.4$$

$$S_{(x_2,x_2)} = 0.3$$

$$S_{(x_2,x_3)} = 0.3 + 0.5 = 0.8$$

$$S_{(x_3,x_2)} = 0.3$$

$$S_{(x_3,x_3)} = 0.3$$

Hence $M = \max_{(x_i,x_j)\in R}\left\{S_{(x_i,x_j)}\right\} = S_{(x_1,x_3)}$. Thus, the decision is to choose the associated object (x_1, x_3), as the appropriate solution for selecting the most suitable city.

CONCLUSION

In this chapter, we redefined the concept of relation on neutrosophic soft sets. Also, we give some properties of the neutrosophic soft relation concept that we redefined. Finally a decision making method on neutrosophic soft relation is presented. In addition, the neutrosophic soft relation concept that we have redefined can be applied on the neutrosophic soft function defined in study (Ozturk et al., 2021a). It can be applied to problems of many fields that contain uncertainty such as computer science, decision making and so on.

REFERENCES

Al-Quran, A., & Hassan, N. (2018). The complex neutrosophic soft expert relation and its multiple attribute decision-making method. *Entropy (Basel, Switzerland)*, 20(2), 101. DOI:10.3390/e20020101 PMID:33265192

Atanassov, K. T. (1986). Intutionistic fuzzy sets. *Fuzzy Sets and Systems*, 20(1), 87–96. DOI:10.1016/S0165-0114(86)80034-3

Borah, M. J., Neog, T. J., & Sut, D. K. (2012). Relations on fuzzy soft sets. *J. Math. Comput. Sci.*, 2(3), 515–534.

Broumi, S. (2013). Generalized neutrosophic soft set. *International Journal of Computer Science Engineering and Information Techonology*, 3(2), 17–30.

Broumi, S., & Smarandache, F. (2013). Intuitionistic neutrosophic soft set. *Infinite Study*, 130-140.

Bui, Q. T., Ngo, M. P., Snasel, V., Pedrycz, W., & Vo, B. (2022). The sequence of neutrosophic soft sets and a decision-making problem in medical diagnosis. *International Journal of Fuzzy Systems*, 24(4), 2036–2053. DOI:10.1007/s40815-022-01257-4

Bustince, H., & Burillo, P. (1996). Structures on intuitionistic fuzzy relations. *Fuzzy Sets and Systems*, 78(3), 293–303. DOI:10.1016/0165-0114(96)84610-0

Dalkılıç, O. (2021). Relations on neutrosophic soft set and their application in decision making. *Journal of Applied Mathematics & Computing*, 67(1-2), 257–273. DOI:10.1007/s12190-020-01495-5

Deli, I., & Broumi, S. (2015). Neutrosophic soft relations and some properties. *Annals of Fuzzy Mathematics and Informatics, 9*(1), 169-182.

Di Nola, A., Pedrycz, W., & Sessa, S. (1988). Fuzzy relation equations with equality and difference composition operators. *Fuzzy Sets and Systems*, 25(2), 205–215. DOI:10.1016/0165-0114(88)90188-1

Dinda, B., & Samanta, T. K. (2012). Relations on intuitionistic fuzzy soft sets. *arXiv preprint arXiv:1202.4649.*

Dutta, S., & Chakraborty, M. K. (2015). Fuzzy relation and fuzzy function over fuzzy sets: A retrospective. *Soft Computing*, 19(1), 99–112. DOI:10.1007/s00500-014-1356-z

Feng, F., Li, C., Davvaz, B., & Ali, M. I. (2010). Soft sets combined with fuzzy sets and rough sets: A tentative approach. *Soft Computing*, 14(9), 899–911. DOI:10.1007/s00500-009-0465-6

Gunduz, Ç., Ozturk, T. Y., & Bayramov, S. (2019). Separation axioms on neutrosophic soft topological spaces. *Turkish Journal of Mathematics*, 43(1), 498–510. DOI:10.3906/mat-1805-110

Hussain, A., & Shabir, M. (2015). Algebraic structures of neutrosophic soft sets. *Neutrosophic Sets and Systems*, 7, 53–61.

Maji, P. K. (2013). Neutrosophic soft set. *Ann. Fuzzy Math. Inform.*, 5(1), 157–168.

Maji, P. K. (2015). An application of weighted neutrosophic soft sets in a decision-making problem. In *Facets of Uncertainties and Applications: ICFUA, Kolkata, India, December 2013* (pp. 215-223). Springer India. DOI:10.1007/978-81-322-2301-6_16

Maji, P. K., Biswas, R., & Roy, A. R. (2001b). Intuitionistic fuzzy soft sets. *Journal of Fuzzy Mathematics, 9*(3), 677-692.

Maji, P. K., Biswas, R. K., & Roy, A. (2001a). *Fuzzy soft sets*. Academic Press.

Mehmood, A., Abdullah, S., & Park, C. (2022). A New Approach to Vague Soft Bi-Topological Spaces. *CMES-Computer Modeling in Engineering & Sciences, 131*(1).

Molodtsov, D. (1999). Soft set theory—First results. *Computers & Mathematics with Applications (Oxford, England)*, 37(4-5), 19–31. DOI:10.1016/S0898-1221(99)00056-5

Ozturk, T. Y. (2016). On defining soft spaces by weak soft neighborhood systems. *New Trends in Mathematical Sciences*, 4(2), 113–124. DOI:10.20852/ntmsci.2016217822

Ozturk, T. Y. (2018). Soft Mappings on soft generalized topological spaces. *Creat. Math. Inform, 27*(2).

Ozturk, T. Y., Aras, C. G., & Bayramov, S. (2019). *A new approach to operations on neutrosophic soft sets and to neutrosophic soft topological spaces*. Infinite Study.

Ozturk, T. Y., & Bayramov, S. (2017). Topology on soft continuous function spaces. *Mathematical & Computational Applications*, 22(2), 32. DOI:10.3390/mca22020032

Ozturk, T. Y., Benek, A., & Ozkan, A. (2021b). Neutrosophic soft compact spaces. *Afrika Matematika*, 32(1-2), 301–316. DOI:10.1007/s13370-020-00827-9

Ozturk, T. Y., Karataş, E., & Yolcu, A. (2021a). On neutrosophic soft continuous mappings. *Turkish Journal of Mathematics*, 45(1), 81–95. DOI:10.3906/mat-1912-113

Smarandache, F. (1999). A unifying field in Logics: Neutrosophic Logic. In *Philosophy* (pp. 1–141). American Research Press.

Tran, T. B., Ngo, M. P., Bui, Q. T., Snasel, V., & Vo, B. (2022). A new approach for operations on neutrosophic soft sets based on the novel norms for constructing topological structures. *AIMS Mathematics*, 7(6), 9603–9626. DOI:10.3934/math.2022534

Yolcu, A., Benek, A., & Ozturk, T. Y. (2023a). A new approach to neutrosophic soft rough sets. *Knowledge and Information Systems*, 65(5), 2043–2060. DOI:10.1007/s10115-022-01824-z

Yolcu, A., & Büşra, A. K. A. (2023b). On Neutrosophic Soft Multisets and Neutrosophic Soft Multi Topological Spaces. *Erzincan University Journal of Science and Technology*, 16(1), 89–109. DOI:10.18185/erzifbed.1114721

Yolcu, A., Karatas, E., & Ozturk, T. Y. (2021b). A new approach to neutrosophic soft mappings and application in decision making. *Neutrosophic Operational Research: Methods and Applications*, 291-313.

Yolcu, A., & Ozturk, T. Y. (2021). Fuzzy hypersoft sets and its application to decision-making. *Theory and application of hypersoft set, 50.*

Yolcu, A., & Ozturk, T. Y. (2022). Separation axioms and connectedness on fuzzy parameterized fuzzy soft topological spaces. In *Handbook of research on advances and applications of fuzzy sets and logic* (pp. 412–427). IGI Global. DOI:10.4018/978-1-7998-7979-4.ch019

Yolcu, A., Smarandache, F., & Ozturk, T. Y. (2021a). Intuitionistic fuzzy hypersoft sets. *Communications Faculty of Sciences University of Ankara Series A1 Mathematics and Statistics, 70*(1), 443-455..

Zadeh, L. A. (1965). Fuzzy sets. *Information and Control*, 8(3), 338–353. DOI:10.1016/S0019-9958(65)90241-X

Chapter 5

A Novel on Virtual Social Network Analysis Utilising Interval-Valued Complex Neutrosophic Graph Structures

Suber Bathusha
Sadakathullah Appa College, Manonmaniam Sundaranar University, India

Sowndharya Jayakumar
Cauvery College of Women, India

S. Angelin Kavitha Raj
Sadakathullah Appa College, India

ABSTRACT

The interval-valued complex neutrosophic set (IVCNS), an expansion of the interval-valued neutrosophic set (IVNS), provides a more precisecharacterisation of uncertainty than traditional fuzzy sets. Fuzzy control can use it in a variety of ways. In this research study, the authors also introduce the adjacency matrix IVCNGS notion as well as the idea of an isomorphic adjacency matrix. They also introduce interval-valued complex neutrosophic graph structures (IVCNGS). They use an example to investigate a number of IVCNGS adjacency matrix properties. In addition, they introduce the ideas of edge regular and totally edge regular adjacency matrix IVCNGS. The conditions under which edge regular adjacency matrix IVCNGS and totally edge regular adjacency matrix IVCNGS are equal are described. Finally, in order to make the proposed IVCNGS principles more understandable, they give specific

DOI: 10.4018/979-8-3693-2085-3.ch005

instances of how virtual social networks impact cross-cultural communication and evaluate the effectiveness and performance of the organisation.

1. INTRODUCTION

In 1965, L.A. Zadeh (1965) developed fuzzy sets to solve the problems associated with handling uncertainty in fuzzy sets. Since then, other scholars have investigated more real-world issues involving ambiguous and uncertain conditions in an effort to solve them using fuzzy sets and fuzzy logic. A fuzzy set development that the author initiated in Turksen (1986) in 1986 is interval-valued fuzzy sets. It also takes into account the values of number intervals to account for uncertainty as a result of using numbers as the membership function. Normally, it is denoted by the symbol $[\mu_{AL}^{-}(x), \mu_{AL}^{+}(x)]$. To express the degree of membership of the fuzzy set A use the formula $0 \leq \mu_{AL}^{-}(x) + \mu_{AL}^{+}(x) \leq 1$. The list of components that make up fuzzy sets was expanded by T. Atanassov in Atanassove and Gargov (1989) by include a non-membership function, which is represented as intuitionistic fuzzy sets. He also included interval valued intuitionistic fuzzy sets in the definition of intuitionistic fuzzy sets (Atanassove & Gargov, 1989). Interval-valued intuitionistic fuzzy sets, as opposed to classical fuzzy sets, are preferable for representing uncertainty. The phase of the process that requires the greatest processing is defuzzification, a method used in fuzzy control in various ways. For the purpose of interpreting the degree of true and false membership functions, it is defined as a pair of intervals $[\mu^{-}, \mu^{+}], 0 \leq \mu^{-} + \mu^{+} \leq 1$ and $[\lambda^{-}, \lambda^{+}], 0 \leq \lambda^{-} + \lambda^{+} \leq 1$ with $0 \leq \mu^{-} + \lambda^{+} \leq 1$. These theories have the common flaw of not being able to model two-dimensional occurrences, despite being applicable to a wide number of scientific subjects. The fuzzy set (FS) theory is a useful tool for coping with uncertainties that occur in many different spheres of life. However, this theory cannot always reproduce the precise and irregular information of a two-dimensional or periodic nature seen in the real world. To solve this issue, Ramot (Rani & Garg, 2017) proposed the idea of a complex fuzzy set (CFS) in 2012. This idea's membership grade, which has the notation $re^{i\theta}$, where r denotes the amplitude term and θ the phase term, is a helpful generalisation of FS. There is a restriction that values may only come from the unit circle of the complex plane. The phase term of CFS is significant since it is better able to control recurrent problematic phenomena or cyclical problems. Because the phase term is present in CFS, it is guaranteed that there may be situations where the second dimension is necessary. CFS stands out from every other type of currently available information due to this phrase. A CF representation of solar activity is an example of this use that best illustrates the unique idea. time series forecasting and signal processing applications. In 2012, Alkouri and Salleh (2012) first introduced the notions of complex intuitionistic fuzzy sets (CIFSs), which they translated to complex intuitionistic fuzzy sets using the degree of complex valued non-membership functions. In recent years, Harish Garg and Dimple Rani (2019) proposed the concepts of Complex Interval-Valued Intuitionistic Fuzzy Sets (CIVIFSs) and associated Aggregation Operator. For the purpose of interpreting the complex degree of true and false membership functions, it is defined as a pair of intervals

$$[\mu^- \; e^{i\alpha^-}, \; \mu^+ \; e^{i\alpha^+}], 0 \leq \mu^- + \mu^+ \leq 1, \; 0 \leq \alpha^- + \alpha^+ \leq 2\pi,$$

and

$$[\lambda^- e^{i\beta^-}, \; \lambda^+ e^{i\beta^+}], 0 \leq \lambda^- + \lambda^+ \leq 1, 0 \leq \beta^- + \beta^+ \leq 2\pi,$$

With

$$0 \leq \mu^+ + \lambda^+ \leq 1$$

And

$$0 \leq \alpha^+ + \beta^+ \leq 1.$$

The aforementioned limitations, which only permit the retention of partial data, do not prevent the handling of confusing information.

The neutrosophic set, introduced by author Smarandache, has been thoroughly studied regarding neutrosophic set (Satham Hussain, 2021; Shamim Kaiser, 2018; Shannon & Atanassov, 1994; Smarandache, 1998; Smarandache, 2010) and is used in various domains to handle the uncertain and inconsistent information. In the neutrosophic set, the indeterminacy value is quantified directly, and truth membership, indeterminacy membership, and false membership are defined completely independently if the sum of these values is between 0 and 3. Broumi, S., et al. (2023a) introduced the idea of a complex fermatean neutrosophic graph and its application to decision-making. It is recommended to look up more information at the research papers. Some useful information about these kinds of structures can be found in the following studies(Broumi et al., n.d.; 2023b; 2023c). A helpful method for representing object relationship structures is the study on generalized graph representations of complex neutrosophic information presented by Akram, M., et al. (2021).

We have developed Interval-Valued Complex Neutrosophic Set (IVCNS), a novel generalisation of CIVIFS. To deal with the unexpected nature, it has greater variety. The list of components that make up IVCIFS was expanded by the addition of the indeterminate-membership function, which is represented by IVCNS. Using the amplitude term of IVCN notions, It is utilised in various ways by fuzzy control. The aforementioned restrictions only allow keeping partial data, but processing uncertain information is still required.

The concept of Graph Structure was first introduced by Sampath Kumar (2006). It is a tool used to study various structures, including ratified graphs and graphs. T. Dinesh and T. V. Ramakrishnan introduced the idea of a fuzzy graph structure in 2011 (Dinesh & Ramakrishnan, 2011). Muhammad Akram recently introduced the concepts of Operations on Intuitionistic FGSs and Single-Valued NGSs (Akram & Akmal, 2016; Akram & Sitara, 2017). Bathusha, S. N. S., et al. (2024a; 2024b) introduced the concept of Edge Regular Complex Neutrosophic Graph Structure and its Application, along with the energy of interval-valued Complex NGS.

Novelties

Although fuzzy graphs with edge properties have been the subject of numerous publications in the field of research, there is still much to be done in terms of devolving the adjacency matrix IVCNGS with edge regular properties. This work's specific goal is to introduce the adjacency matrix IVCNGS as it relates to the Edge Regular concept. Further, the computation of δ_J-degree of vertex and δ_J-degree of edges in the adjacency matrix IVCNGS was examined. Moreover, we present the notion of an isomorphic, identical, δ_J-edge regular adjacency matrix of IVCNGS with properties.

Motivation

Pair wise relations of objects are considered seriously in many graph theory problems. Certain properties of the objects can be connected in a way that results in irreflexive, symmetric, and mutually disjoint relations. This kind of information loss can be avoided by graphically representing as a GS. The need to manage complex decision-making scenarios when presented with imprecise information drives the study of IVCNS as it relates to the GS and their applications. This helps the demonstration of the edge of the graph construct's uniqueness using real-world issues. IVCNGSs provide a more flexible tool for controlling uncertainty, even though existing fuzzy models offer some flexibility. The values for true, false, and indeterminate membership in the interval-valued complex are considered into account in the interval-valued complex Neutrosophic set (IVCNS). This study is primarily focused on the characteristics and constraints of the edge regular adjacency matrix of IVCNGS with properties.

This model can be rewritten in an abstract version for usage in IVCNGS. The work's primary contribution is the following:

- The Interval-Valued Complex Neutrosophic Set (IVCNS), an extension of the Interval-Valued Neutrosophic Set (IVCNS), offers a more accurate description of uncertainty than conventional fuzzy sets. It can be applied in various ways through fuzzy control.
- We also introduce the IVCNGS adjacency matrix concept and the idea of an isomorphic adjacency matrix in this research work. Interval-valued complex neutrosophic graph structures (IVCNGS) are also introduced. We look into some IVCNGS adjacency matrix properties using an example.
- In addition, we introduce the ideas of edge regular and totally edge regular adjacency matrix IVCNGS. The conditions under which edge regular adjacency matrix IVCNGS and totally edge regular adjacency matrix IVCNGS are equal are described.
- Finally, we define the advantages of the IVCNGS and how social contexts might use it to investigate the impacts of growing social media platform usage. Additionally, we create an algorithm that clarifies the application's fundamental functions.

We encouraged readers to read this paper so that scholars might further explore this hypothesis using analysis of the isomorphic adjacency matrix, the edge regular adjacency matrix, and the total edge regular adjacency matrix IVCNGS.

2. PRELIMINARIES

The description of some basic definitions and properties in this area will aid in the development of the research work.

Definition 1 (Bathusha et al., 2024a) Let's say that conversation is the universe *Y*. Interval-Valued Complex Neutrosophic Set (IVCNS) *A* defined on *Y* is the object of the form.

$$A = \Big\{ (a, \left[\mu^-_{A_1}(a)\,e^{i\alpha^-_{A_1}(a)}, \mu^+_{A_1}(a)\,e^{i\alpha^+_{A_1}(a)}\right],$$
$$\left[\mu^-_{A_2}(a)\,e^{i\alpha^-_{A_2}(a)}, \mu^+_{A_2}(a)\,e^{i\alpha^+_{A_2}(a)}\right], \left[\mu^-_{A_3}(a)\,e^{i\alpha^-_{A_3}(a)}, \mu^+_{A_3}(a)\,e^{i\alpha^+_{A_3}(a)}\right] / \, a \in Y \Big\}$$

where

$i = \sqrt{-1}, \mu^-_{A_1}(a), \mu^+_{A_1}(a), \mu^-_{A_2}(a), \mu^+_{A_2}(a), \mu^-_{A_3}(a), \mu^+_{A_3}(a) \in [0,1],$

$\alpha^-_{A_1}(a), \alpha^+_{A_1}(a), \alpha^-_{A_2}(a), \alpha^+_{A_2}(a),$

$\alpha^-_{A_3}(a), \alpha^+_{A_3}(a) \in [0, 2\pi], 0 \leq ((\mu^+_{A_1}(a)) + ((\mu^+_{A_2}(a)(\mu^+_{A_3}(a))) \leq 3.$

Definition 2 (Siddique et al., 2021) Let

$$A = \Big\{ (a, \left[\mu^-_{A_1}(a) e^{i\alpha^-_{A_1}(a)}, \mu^+_{A_1}(a) e^{i\alpha^+_{A_1}(a)}\right], \left[\mu^-_{A_2}(a) e^{i\alpha^-_{A_2}(a)}, \mu^+_{A_2}(a) e^{i\alpha^+_{A_2}(a)}\right],$$

$$\left[\mu^-_{A_3}(a) e^{i\alpha^-_{A_3}(a)}, \mu^+_{A_3}(a) e^{i\alpha^+_{A_3}(a)}\right])/ a \in Y\Big\}$$

$$\text{and } B = \Big\{ (a, \left[\mu^-_{B_1}(a) e^{i\alpha^-_{B_1}(a)}, \mu^+_{B_1}(a) e^{i\alpha^+_{B_1}(a)}\right]$$

$$\left[\mu^-_{B_2}(a) e^{i\alpha^-_{B_2}(a)}, \mu^+_{B_2}(a) e^{i\alpha^+_{B_2}(a)}\right], \left[\mu^-_{B_3}(a) e^{i\alpha^-_{B_3}(a)}, \mu^+_{B_3}(a) e^{i\alpha^+_{B_3}(a)}\right]]/ a \in Y\Big\}$$

be the two IVCNSs in *Y*, then

$A \subseteq B$ if and only if

$\mu^-_{A_1}(a) \leq \mu^-_{B_1}(a), \mu^+_{A_1}(a) \leq \mu^+_{B_1}(a), \mu^-_{A_2}(a) \leq \mu^-_{B_2}(a), \mu^+_{A_2}(a) \leq \mu^+_{B_2}(a)$

$\mu^-_{A_3}(a) \leq \mu^-_{B_3}(a), \mu^+_{A_3}(a) \leq \mu^+_{B_3}(a)$ for amplitude terms and $\alpha^-_{A_1}(a) \leq \alpha^-_{B_1}(a),$

$\alpha^+_{A_1}(a) \leq \alpha^+_{B_1}(a), \alpha^-_{A_2}(a) \leq \alpha^-_{B_2}(a), \alpha^+_{A_2}(a) \leq \alpha^+_{B_2}(a),$

$\alpha^-_{A_3}(a) \leq \alpha^-_{B_3}(a), \alpha^+_{A_3}(a) \leq \alpha^+_{B_3}(a)$

for phase terms, for all $a \in Y$;

$A{=}B$ if and only if $\mu^-_{A_1}(a) = \mu^-_{B_1}(a), \mu^+_{A_1}(a) = \mu^+_{B_1}(a),$

$\mu^-_{A_2}(a) = \mu^-_{B_2}(a), \mu^+_{A_2}(a) = \mu^+_{B_2}(a)$

$\mu^-_{A_3}(a) = \mu^-_{B_3}(a), \mu^+_{A_3}(a) = \mu^+_{B_3}(a)$ for amplitude terms and $\alpha^-_{A_1}(a) = \alpha^-_{B_1}(a),$

$\alpha^+_{A_1}(a) = \alpha^+_{B_1}(a), \alpha^-_{A_2}(a) = \alpha^-_{B_2}(a), \alpha^+_{A_2}(a) = \alpha^+_{B_2}(a),$

$\alpha^-_{A_3}(a) = \alpha^-_{B_3}(a), \alpha^+_{A_3}(a) = \alpha^+_{B_3}(a).$

for phase terms, for all $a \in Y$;

For simplicity, the

$$\left(\left[\mu^-_{A_1}(a)\, e^{i\alpha^-_{A_1}(a)}, \mu^+_{A_1}(a)\, e^{i\alpha^+_{A_1}(a)}\right],\right.$$

$$\left.\left[\mu^-_{A_2}(a)\, e^{i\alpha^-_{A_2}(a)}, \mu^+_{A_2}(a)\, e^{i\alpha^+_{A_2}(a)}\right], \left[\mu^-_{A_3}(a)\, e^{i\alpha^-_{A_3}(a)}, \mu^+_{A_3}(a)\, e^{i\alpha^+_{A_3}(a)}\right]\right),$$

is called the IVCNS, where $\mu^+_{A_1}, \mu^+_{A_2}, \mu^+_{A_3} \in [0.1]$ such that $\mu^+_{A_1} + \mu^+_{A_2} + \mu^+_{A_3} \leq 3$.

Definition 3 (Broumi et al., 2023b) A Interval-valued complex Neutrosophic relation in Y is described as a IVCNS X in $Y{\times}Y$ and is characterised by

$$X = \left\{ (ab, \left[\mu^-_{X_1}(ab)\, e^{i\alpha^-_{X_1}(ab)}, \mu^+_{X_1}(ab)\, e^{i\alpha^+_{X_1}(ab)}\right], \left[\mu^-_{X_2}(ab)\, e^{i\alpha^-_{X_2}(ab)}, \mu^+_{X_2}(ab)\, e^{i\alpha^+_{X_2}(ab)}\right]\right.$$

$$\left.\left[\mu^-_{X_3}(ab)\, e^{i\alpha^-_{X_3}(ab)}, \mu^+_{X_3}(ab)\, e^{i\alpha^+_{X_3}(ab)}\right] / ab \in Y \times Y\right\}$$

where the Inter-valued complex Neutrosophic truth-membership, complex indeterminate-membership and complex false-membership functions of X are mapping to [0,1], such that

$\mu^+_{X_1}(ab) + \mu^+_{X_2}(ab) + \mu^+_{X_3}(ab) \leq 3$ for all $ab \in Y{\times}Y$.

Definition 4 (Bathusha et al., 2024a) On a non-empty set *X*, a Interval-valued complex Neutrosophic graph is a pair *G=(A,B)*, where *A* and *B* are complex Neutrosophic sets on *X* and a Interval-valued complex Neutrosophic relation on *X*, respectively, such that:

i. $\mu^-_{B_1}(ab)\, e^{i\alpha^-_{B_1}(ab)} \le min\{\mu^-_{A_1}(a), \mu^-_{A_1}(b)\}\, e^{i min\{\alpha^-_{A_1}(a),\ \alpha^-_{A_1}(b)\}}$,
ii. $\mu^+_{B_1}(ab)\, e^{i\alpha^+_{B_1}(ab)} \le min\{\mu^+_{A_1}(a), \mu^+_{A_1}(b)\}\, e^{i min\{\alpha^+_{A_1}(a),\ \alpha^+_{A_1}(b)\}}$,
iii. $\mu^-_{B_2}(ab)\, e^{i\alpha^-_{B_2}(ab)} \le max\{\mu^-_{A_2}(a), \mu^-_{A_2}(b)\}\, e^{i max\{\alpha^-_{A_2}(a),\ \alpha^-_{A_2}(b)\}}$,
iv. $\mu^+_{B_2}(ab)\, e^{i\alpha^+_{B_2}(ab)} \le max\{\mu^+_{A_2}(a), \mu^+_{A_2}(b)\}\, e^{i max\{\alpha^+_{A_2}(a),\ \alpha^+_{A_2}(b)\}}$,
v. $\mu^-_{B_3}(ab)\, e^{i\alpha^-_{B_3}(ab)} \le max\{\mu^-_{A_3}(a), \mu^-_{A_3}(b)\}\, e^{i max\{\alpha^-_{A_3}(a),\ \alpha^-_{A_3}(b)\}}$,
vi. $\mu^+_{B_3}(ab)\, e^{i\alpha^+_{B_3}(ab)} \le max\{\mu^+_{A_3}(a), \mu^+_{A_3}(b)\}\, e^{i max\{\alpha^+_{A_3}(a),\ \alpha^+_{A_3}(b)\}}$

$\mu^+_{X_1}(ab) + \mu^+_{X_2}(ab) + \mu^+_{X_3}(ab) \le 3$ for all $ab \in Y \times Y$.

3. EDGE REGULAR ADJACENCY MATRIX OF IVCNGS

In this part, the concept of routine IVCNGS is introduced. To further explain some of the fundamental IVCNGS features, examples are also provided.

Definition 5 Let $\zeta = \{\eta, \delta_1, \delta_2, ..., \delta_k\}$ is referred to as an IVCNGS of graph structure (GS)

$$\zeta^* = \{Q, R_1, R_2, ..., R_k\}$$

if

$$\eta = (\eta_1, \eta_2, \eta_3) = ([\eta_1^- e^{i\alpha_1^-}, \eta_1^+ e^{i\alpha_1^+}], [\eta_2^- e^{i\alpha_2^-}, \eta_2^+ e^{i\alpha_2^+}], [\eta_3^- e^{i\alpha_3^-}, \eta_3^+ e^{i\alpha_3^+}])$$

is an IVCNS on *Q* and

$$\delta_J = (\delta_{1J}, \delta_{2J}, \delta_{3J})$$
$$= \left([\delta_{1J}^- e^{i\beta_{1J}^-},\ \delta_{1J}^+ e^{i\beta_{1J}^+}], [\delta_{2J}^- e^{i\beta_{2J}^-},\ \delta_{2J}^+ e^{i\beta_{2J}^+}], [\delta_{3J}^- e^{i\beta_{3J}^-},\ \delta_{3J}^+ e^{i\beta_{3J}^+}]\right)$$

are IVCNSs on *Q* and R_J such that

i. $\delta^-_{1J}(a,b)\, e^{i\beta^-_{1J}(ab)} \le min\{\eta^-_1(a), \eta^-_1(b)\}\, e^{i min\{\alpha^-_1(a),\ \alpha^-_1(b)\}}$,
ii. $\delta^+_{1J}(a,b)\, e^{i\beta^+_{1J}(ab)} \le min\{\eta^+_1(a), \eta^+_1(b)\}\, e^{i min\{\alpha^+_1(a),\ \alpha^+_1(b)\}}$
iii. $\delta^-_{2J}(a,b)\, e^{i\beta^-_{2J}(ab)} \le max\{\eta^-_2(a), \eta^-_2(b)\}\, e^{i max\{\alpha^-_2(a),\ \alpha^-_2(b)\}}$,
iv. $\delta^+_{2J}(a,b)\, e^{i\beta^+_{2J}(ab)} \le max\{\eta^+_2(a), \eta^+_2(b)\}\, e^{i max\{\alpha^+_2(a),\ \alpha^+_2(b)\}}$,

v. $\delta_{3J}^{-}(a,b)\,e^{i\beta_{3J}^{-}(ab)} \leq max\{\eta_3^{-}(a),\eta_3^{-}(b)\}\,e^{i\max\{\alpha_3^{-}(a),\ \alpha_3^{-}(b)\}}$,
vi. $\delta_{3J}^{+}(a,b)\,e^{i\beta_{3J}^{+}(ab)} \leq max\{\eta_3^{+}(a),\eta_3^{+}(b)\}\,e^{i\max\{\alpha_3^{+}(a),\ \alpha_3^{+}(b)\}}$

$$\delta_{1J}^{+}(a,b) + \delta_{2J}^{+}(a,b) + \delta_{3J}^{+}(a,b) \leq 3,\ \forall\,(a,b) \in R_J \text{ and } J = 1,2,\ldots,k.$$

Note: $\delta_{1J}^{-},\delta_{1J}^{+},\ \delta_{2J}^{-},\ \delta_{2J}^{+}$ and $\delta_{3J}^{-},\ \delta_{3J}^{+}$ are function from R_J to [0,1] such that

$$\delta_{1J}^{-}(a,b) \leq \delta_{1J}^{+}(a,b),\ \delta_{2J}^{-}(a,b) \leq \delta_{2J}^{+}(a,b),\ \delta_{3J}^{-}(a,b) \leq \delta_{3J}^{+}(a,b)$$

and

$$\beta_{1J}^{-}(a,b) \leq \beta_{1J}^{+}(a,b),\ \beta_{2J}^{-}(a,b) \leq \beta_{2J}^{+}(a,b),\ \beta_{3J}^{-}(a,b) \leq \beta_{3J}^{+}(a,b)$$

for all $(a,b)\in R_J$ and J=1,2,…,k.

Definition 6 The adjacency matrix $A\zeta = \{A\eta, A\delta_1,\ A\delta_2,\ldots,A\delta_k\}$ of a IVCNGS

$$\zeta = \{\ \eta,\ \delta_1,\ \ \delta_2,\ldots,\delta_k\}$$

where $A\delta_J$, (J=1,2,…,k) is a square matrix as $[u_{jk}]$ in which

$$u_{jk} = ([\delta_{1J}^{-}(u_j,u_k)\,e^{i\beta_{1J}^{-}(u_j,u_k)},\delta_{1J}^{+}(u_j,u_k)\,e^{i\beta_{1J}^{+}(u_j,u_k)}],$$

$$[\delta_{2J}^{-}(u_j,u_k)\,e^{i\beta_{2J}^{-}(u_j,u_k)},\delta_{2J}^{+}(u_j,u_k)\,e^{i\beta_{2J}^{+}(u_j,u_k)}],$$

$$([\delta_{3J}^{-}(u_j,u_k)\,e^{i\beta_{3J}^{-}(u_j,u_k)},\delta_{3J}^{+}(u_j,u_k)\,e^{i\beta_{3J}^{+}(u_j,u_k)}]),$$

where $\delta_{1J}^{-}(u_ju_k)$, $\delta_{1J}^{+}(u_ju_k)$ is represent the strength of interval-valued truth membership amplitude term between u_j and u_k and $\delta_{2J}^{-}(u_ju_k)$, $\delta_{2J}^{+}(u_ju_k)$ is represent the strength of interval-valued indeterminate membership amplitude term between u_j and u_k and $\delta_{3J}^{-}(u_ju_k)$, $\delta_{3J}^{+}(u_ju_k)$ is represent the strength of interval-valued false membership amplitude term between u_j and u_k and $\beta_{1J}^{-}(u_ju_k)$, $\beta_{1J}^{+}(u_ju_k)$ is represent the strength of interval-valued truth membership phase term u_j and u_k and $\beta_{2J}^{-}(u_ju_k)$, β_{2J}^{+} (u_ju_k) is represent the strength of interval-valued indeterminate membership phase term between u_j and u_k and $\beta_{3J}^{-}(u_ju_k)$, $\beta_{3J}^{+}(u_ju_k)$ is represent the strength of interval-valued false membership phase term between u_j and u_k.

Definition 8 The adjacency matrix $A\zeta = \{A\eta, A\delta_1,\ A\delta_2,\ldots,A\delta_k\}$ of a IVCNGS

$\zeta = \{\eta, \delta_1, \delta_2, \ldots, \delta_k\}$.

Then the δ_J- degree of vertex u in $A(\zeta)$ is defined as

$$Ad_{\delta_J}(u)\, e^{iAd_{\beta_J}(u)} = ([Ad_{\delta_{1J}^-}(u)\, e^{iAd_{\beta_{1J}^-}(u)}, Ad_{\delta_{1J}^+}(u)\, e^{iAd_{\beta_{1J}^+}(u)}],$$

$$[Ad_{\delta_{2J}^-}(u)\, e^{iAd_{\beta_{2J}^-}(u)}, Ad_{\delta_{2J}^+}(u)\, e^{iAd_{\beta_{2J}^+}(u)}]$$

$$[Ad_{\delta_{3J}^-}(u)\, e^{iAd_{\beta_{3J}^-}(u)}, Ad_{\delta_{3J}^+}(u)\, e^{iAd_{\beta_{3J}^+}(u)}],$$

where

$$Ad_{\delta_{1J}^-}(u)\, e^{iAd_{\beta_{1J}^-}(u)} = \sum \delta_{1J}^-(u_{jz})_{z=1}^{k}\ e^{\sum \beta_{1J}^-(u_{jz})_{z=1}^{k}},$$

$$Ad_{\delta_{1J}^+}(u)\, e^{iAd_{\beta_{1J}^+}(u)} = \sum \delta_{1J}^+(u_{jz})_{z=1}^{k}\ e^{\sum \beta_{1J}^+(u_{jz})_{z=1}^{k}},$$

$$Ad_{\delta_{2J}^-}(u)\, e^{iAd_{\beta_{2J}^-}(u)} = \sum \delta_{2J}^-(u_{jz})_{z=1}^{k}\ e^{\sum \beta_{2J}^-(u_{jz})_{z=1}^{k}},$$

$$Ad_{\delta_{2J}^+}(u)\, e^{iAd_{\beta_{2J}^+}(u)} = \sum \delta_{2J}^+(u_{jz})_{z=1}^{k}\ e^{\sum \beta_{2J}^+(u_{jz})_{z=1}^{k}},$$

$$Ad_{\delta_{3J}^-}(u)\, e^{iAd_{\beta_{3J}^-}(u)} = \sum \delta_{3J}^-(u_{jz})_{z=1}^{k}\ e^{\sum \beta_{3J}^-(u_{jz})_{z=1}^{k}},$$

$$Ad_{\delta_{3J}^+}(u)\, e^{iAd_{\beta_{3J}^+}(u)} = \sum \delta_{3J}^+(u_{jz})_{z=1}^{k}\ e^{\sum \beta_{3J}^+(u_{jz})_{z=1}^{k}}$$

Example 1 An IVCNGS $\zeta = \{\eta, \delta_1, \delta_2\}$ of a GS $\zeta^* = \{Q, R_1, R_2\}$ given Figure-1 is a IVCNGS

$\zeta = \{\eta, \delta_1, \delta_2\}$

such that

$$\eta = \left\{ u_1\left(\left[.4e^{i.3\pi}, .7e\text{^}(i.4\pi)\right], \left[.3e^{i.1\pi}, .6e^{i.3\pi}\right], \left[.2e^{i.1\pi}, .4e^{i.3\pi}\right]\right),\right.$$

$$u_2\left(\left[.4e^{i.2\pi}, .6e^{i.4\pi}\right], \left[.3e^{i.5\pi}, .5e^{i.5\pi}\right], \left[.4e^{i.3\pi}, .6e\text{^}(i.4\pi)\right]\right),$$

$$u_3([.5e^{i.3\pi}, .6e^{i.4\pi}], [.5e^{i.\pi}, .7e^{i.2\pi}],$$

$$\left.[.3e^{i.4\pi}, .4e^{i.5\pi}]), u_4([.3e^{i.6\pi}, .6e^{i.7\pi}], [.4e^{i.4\pi}, .5e^{i.5\pi}], [.2e^{i.3\pi}, .5e^{i.5\pi}])\right\}$$

Figure 1. $\zeta = \{\eta, \delta_1, \delta_2\}$

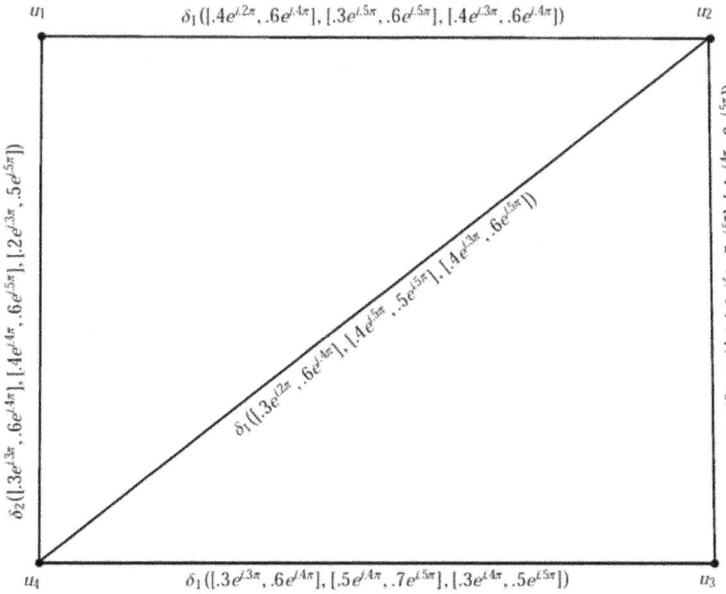

The adjacency matrix of amplitude term of a IVCNGS given in Figure 1 is:

$$A\delta_1 = \begin{bmatrix} \begin{pmatrix} 0 & 0 \\ 0 & 0 \\ 0 & 0 \end{pmatrix} & \begin{pmatrix} .4 & .6 \\ .3 & .6 \\ .4 & .6 \end{pmatrix} & \begin{pmatrix} 0 & 0 \\ 0 & 0 \\ 0 & 0 \end{pmatrix} & \begin{pmatrix} 0 & 0 \\ 0 & 0 \\ 0 & 0 \end{pmatrix} \\ \begin{pmatrix} .4 & .6 \\ .3 & .6 \\ .4 & .6 \end{pmatrix} & \begin{pmatrix} 0 & 0 \\ 0 & 0 \\ 0 & 0 \end{pmatrix} & \begin{pmatrix} 0 & 0 \\ 0 & 0 \\ 0 & 0 \end{pmatrix} & \begin{pmatrix} .3 & .6 \\ .4 & .5 \\ .4 & .6 \end{pmatrix} \\ \begin{pmatrix} 0 & 0 \\ 0 & 0 \\ 0 & 0 \end{pmatrix} & \begin{pmatrix} 0 & 0 \\ 0 & 0 \\ 0 & 0 \end{pmatrix} & \begin{pmatrix} 0 & 0 \\ 0 & 0 \\ 0 & 0 \end{pmatrix} & \begin{pmatrix} .3 & .6 \\ .5 & .7 \\ .3 & .5 \end{pmatrix} \\ \begin{pmatrix} 0 & 0 \\ 0 & 0 \\ 0 & 0 \end{pmatrix} & \begin{pmatrix} .3 & .6 \\ .4 & .5 \\ .4 & .6 \end{pmatrix} & \begin{pmatrix} .3 & .6 \\ .5 & .7 \\ .3 & .5 \end{pmatrix} & \begin{pmatrix} 0 & 0 \\ 0 & 0 \\ 0 & 0 \end{pmatrix} \end{bmatrix}$$

The adjacency matrix of phase term of a IVCNGS given in Figure 1 is:

$$A\beta_1 = \begin{bmatrix} \begin{pmatrix} 0 & 0 \\ 0 & 0 \\ 0 & 0 \end{pmatrix} & \begin{pmatrix} .2 & .4 \\ .5 & .5 \\ .3 & .4 \end{pmatrix} & \begin{pmatrix} 0 & 0 \\ 0 & 0 \\ 0 & 0 \end{pmatrix} & \begin{pmatrix} 0 & 0 \\ 0 & 0 \\ 0 & 0 \end{pmatrix} \\ \begin{pmatrix} .2 & .4 \\ .5 & .5 \\ .3 & .4 \end{pmatrix} & \begin{pmatrix} 0 & 0 \\ 0 & 0 \\ 0 & 0 \end{pmatrix} & \begin{pmatrix} 0 & 0 \\ 0 & 0 \\ 0 & 0 \end{pmatrix} & \begin{pmatrix} .2 & .4 \\ .5 & .5 \\ .3 & .6 \end{pmatrix} \\ \begin{pmatrix} 0 & 0 \\ 0 & 0 \\ 0 & 0 \end{pmatrix} & \begin{pmatrix} 0 & 0 \\ 0 & 0 \\ 0 & 0 \end{pmatrix} & \begin{pmatrix} 0 & 0 \\ 0 & 0 \\ 0 & 0 \end{pmatrix} & \begin{pmatrix} .3 & .4 \\ .4 & .5 \\ .4 & .5 \end{pmatrix} \\ \begin{pmatrix} 0 & 0 \\ 0 & 0 \\ 0 & 0 \end{pmatrix} & \begin{pmatrix} .2 & .4 \\ .5 & .5 \\ .3 & .6 \end{pmatrix} & \begin{pmatrix} .3 & .4 \\ .4 & .5 \\ .4 & .5 \end{pmatrix} & \begin{pmatrix} 0 & 0 \\ 0 & 0 \\ 0 & 0 \end{pmatrix} \end{bmatrix}$$

The δ_1- degree of vertex u_i in $A(\zeta)$ is (i=1,2,3,4).

$$A d_{\delta_1}(u_1) e^{iAd_{\beta_1}(u_1)} = \begin{pmatrix} \left[\mathrm{Ad}_{\delta_{11}^-}(u_1) e^{iAd_{\beta_{11}^-}(u_1)}, \mathrm{Ad}_{\delta_{11}^+}(u_1) e^{iAd_{\beta_{11}^+}(u_1)}\right] \\ \left[\mathrm{Ad}_{\delta_{21}^-}(u_1) e^{iAd_{\beta_{21}^-}(u_1)}, \mathrm{Ad}_{\delta_{21}^+}(u_1) e^{iAd_{\beta_{21}^+}(u_1)}\right] \end{pmatrix}$$

$$[\mathrm{Ad}_{\delta_{31}^-}(u_1) e^{iAd_{\beta_{31}^-}(u_1)}, \mathrm{Ad}_{\delta_{31}^+}(u_1) e^{iAd_{\beta_{31}^+}(u_1)}]$$

$$= ([.4 e^{i.2\pi}, .6 e^{i.4\pi}],[.3 e^{i.5\pi}, .6 e^{i.5\pi}],[.4 e^{i.3\pi}, .6 e^{i.4\pi}])$$

$$A d_{\delta_1}(u_2) e^{iAd_{\beta_1}(u_2)} =$$

$$([.7 e^{i.4\pi}, 1.2 e^{i.8\pi}],[.7 e^{i1.0\pi}, 1.1 e^{i1.0\pi}],[.8 e^{i.6\pi}, 1.2 e^{i1.0\pi}])$$

$$Ad_{\delta_1}(u_3)\, e^{iAd_{\beta_1}(u_3)} =$$

$$([.3\, e^{i.3\pi},\ .6\, e^{i.4\pi}],[.5\, e^{i.4\pi}, .7\, e^{i.5\pi}],[.3\, e^{i.4\pi}, .5\, e^{i.5\pi}])$$

$$Ad_{\delta_1}(u_4)\, e^{iAd_{\beta_1}(u_4)} =$$

$$([.6\, e^{i.5\pi}, 1.2\, e^{i.8\pi}],[.9\, e^{i.9\pi}, 1.2\, e^{i1.0\pi}],[.7\, e^{i.7\pi}, 1.1\, e^{i1.1\pi}])$$

Similarly, we calculate

The adjacency matrix of amplitude term of a IVCPFGS given in Figure 1 is

$$A\delta_2 = \begin{bmatrix} \begin{pmatrix} 0 & 0 \\ 0 & 0 \\ 0 & 0 \end{pmatrix} & \begin{pmatrix} 0 & 0 \\ 0 & 0 \\ 0 & 0 \end{pmatrix} & \begin{pmatrix} 0 & 0 \\ 0 & 0 \\ 0 & 0 \end{pmatrix} & \begin{pmatrix} .3 & .6 \\ .4 & .6 \\ .2 & .5 \end{pmatrix} \\ \begin{pmatrix} 0 & 0 \\ 0 & 0 \\ 0 & 0 \end{pmatrix} & \begin{pmatrix} 0 & 0 \\ 0 & 0 \\ 0 & 0 \end{pmatrix} & \begin{pmatrix} .4 & .6 \\ .5 & .7 \\ .4 & .6 \end{pmatrix} & \begin{pmatrix} 0 & 0 \\ 0 & 0 \\ 0 & 0 \end{pmatrix} \\ \begin{pmatrix} 0 & 0 \\ 0 & 0 \\ 0 & 0 \end{pmatrix} & \begin{pmatrix} .4 & .6 \\ .5 & .7 \\ .4 & .6 \end{pmatrix} & \begin{pmatrix} 0 & 0 \\ 0 & 0 \\ 0 & 0 \end{pmatrix} & \begin{pmatrix} 0 & 0 \\ 0 & 0 \\ 0 & 0 \end{pmatrix} \\ \begin{pmatrix} .3 & .6 \\ .4 & .6 \\ .2 & .5 \end{pmatrix} & \begin{pmatrix} 0 & 0 \\ 0 & 0 \\ 0 & 0 \end{pmatrix} & \begin{pmatrix} 0 & 0 \\ 0 & 0 \\ 0 & 0 \end{pmatrix} & \begin{pmatrix} 0 & 0 \\ 0 & 0 \\ 0 & 0 \end{pmatrix} \end{bmatrix}$$

The adjacency matrix of phase term of a IVCNGS given in Figure 1 is

$$A\delta_2 = \begin{bmatrix} \begin{pmatrix}0&0\\0&0\\0&0\end{pmatrix} & \begin{pmatrix}0&0\\0&0\\0&0\end{pmatrix} & \begin{pmatrix}0&0\\0&0\\0&0\end{pmatrix} & \begin{pmatrix}.3&.4\\.4&.5\\.3&.5\end{pmatrix} \\ \begin{pmatrix}0&0\\0&0\\0&0\end{pmatrix} & \begin{pmatrix}0&0\\0&0\\0&0\end{pmatrix} & \begin{pmatrix}.2&.4\\.5&.5\\.4&.5\end{pmatrix} & \begin{pmatrix}0&0\\0&0\\0&0\end{pmatrix} \\ \begin{pmatrix}0&0\\0&0\\0&0\end{pmatrix} & \begin{pmatrix}.2&.4\\.5&.5\\.4&.5\end{pmatrix} & \begin{pmatrix}0&0\\0&0\\0&0\end{pmatrix} & \begin{pmatrix}0&0\\0&0\\0&0\end{pmatrix} \\ \begin{pmatrix}.3&.4\\.4&.5\\.3&.5\end{pmatrix} & \begin{pmatrix}0&0\\0&0\\0&0\end{pmatrix} & \begin{pmatrix}0&0\\0&0\\0&0\end{pmatrix} & \begin{pmatrix}0&0\\0&0\\0&0\end{pmatrix} \end{bmatrix}$$

The δ_2- degree of vertex u_i in $A(\zeta)$ is (i=1,2,3,4).

$$Ad_{\delta_2}(u_1)\, e^{iAd_{\beta_2}(u_1)}$$

$$= \begin{pmatrix} \left[\mathrm{Ad}_{\delta_{12}^-}(\mathrm{u}_1)\,\mathrm{e}^{iAd_{\beta_{12}^-}(u_1)}, \mathrm{Ad}_{\delta_{12}^+}(u_1)\,\mathrm{e}^{iAd_{\beta_{12}^+}(u_1)}\right] \\ \left[\mathrm{Ad}_{\delta_{22}^-}(u_1)\,\mathrm{e}^{iAd_{\beta_{22}^-}(u_1)}, \mathrm{Ad}_{\delta_{22}^+}(u_1)\,\mathrm{e}^{iAd_{\beta_{22}^+}(u_1)}\right] \end{pmatrix}$$

$$[\mathrm{Ad}_{\delta_{32}^-}(u_1)\,\mathrm{e}^{iAd_{\beta_{32}^-}(u_1)}, \mathrm{Ad}_{\delta_{32}^+}(u_1)\,\mathrm{e}^{iAd_{\beta_{32}^+}(u_1)}]$$
$$= ([.3\,e^{i.3\pi}, .6\,e^{i.4\pi}][.4\,e^{i.4\pi}, .6\,e^{i.5\pi}], [.2\,e^{i.3\pi}, .5\,e^{i.5\pi}])'$$

$$Ad_{\delta_2}(u_2)\, e^{iAd_{\beta_2}(u_2)} =$$

$$([.4\,e^{i.2\pi}, .6\,e^{i.4\pi}],[.5\,e^{i.5\pi}, .7\,e^{i.5\pi}],[.4\,e^{i.4\pi}, .6\,e^{i.5\pi}]),$$

$Ad_{\delta_2}(u_3)\, e^{iAd_{\beta_2}(u_3)}=$

$([.4e^{i.2\pi}, .6e^{i.4\pi}],[.5e^{i.5\pi}, .7e^{i.5\pi}],[.4e^{i.4\pi}, .6e^{i.5\pi}]),$

$Ad_{\delta_2}(u_4)\, e^{iAd_{\beta_2}(u_4)}=$

$([.3e^{i.3\pi}, .6e^{i.4\pi}],[.4e^{i.4\pi}, .6e^{i.5\pi}],[.2e^{i.3\pi}, .5e^{i.5\pi}])$

Definition 8 Let $\zeta = \{\eta, \delta_1, \delta_2, ..., \delta_k\}$ be a IVCNGS of GS $\zeta^* = \{Q, R_1, R_2, ..., R_k\}$ is isomorphic to IVCNGS $\zeta_2 = \{\widetilde{\eta}, \widetilde{\delta_1}, \widetilde{\delta_2}, ..., \widetilde{\delta_k}\}$ of GS $\zeta_2^* = \{\widetilde{Q}, \widetilde{R_1}, \widetilde{R_2}, ..., \widetilde{R_k}\}$ if we have (f,Ψ) where $f:\eta \rightarrow \widetilde{\eta}$ is bijection and Ψ is a permutation on set $\{1,2,\ldots,k\}$ and following relation are satisfied

$\eta_1^S(u_i) = \widetilde{\eta_1^S}\,(f(u_i)), \eta_2^S(u_i) = \widetilde{\eta_2^S}\,(f(u_i))$ and $\eta_3^S(u_i) = \widetilde{\eta_3^S}\,(f(u_i))$

is amplitude term of IVCNGS and

$\beta_1^S(u_i) = \widetilde{\beta_1^S}\,(f(u_i)), \beta_2^S(u_i) = \widetilde{\beta_2^S}\,(f(u_i))$ and $\beta_3^S(u_i) = \widetilde{\beta_3^S}\,(f(u_i))$

is amplitude term of IVCNGS for all $u_i \in Q_1$ and

$\delta_{1J}^S(u_i u_j) = \widetilde{\delta_{1J}^S}(f(u_i)f(u_j)),\ \delta_{2J}^S(u_i u_j) = \widetilde{\delta_{2J}^S}(f(u_i)f(u_j))$

and

$\delta_{3J}^S(u_i u_j) = \widetilde{\delta_{3J}^S}(f(u_i)f(u_j))$

is amplitude term of IVCNGS and

$\beta_{1J}^S(u_i u_j) = \widetilde{\beta_{1J}^S}(f(u_i)f(u_j)),\ \beta_{2J}^S(u_i u_j) = \widetilde{\beta_{2J}^S}(f(u_i)f(u_j))$

and

$\beta_{3J}^S(u_i u_j) = \widetilde{\beta_{3J}^S}(f(u_i)f(u_j))$

is phase term of IVCNGS for all S= -,+ and $u_i \in Q_1$.

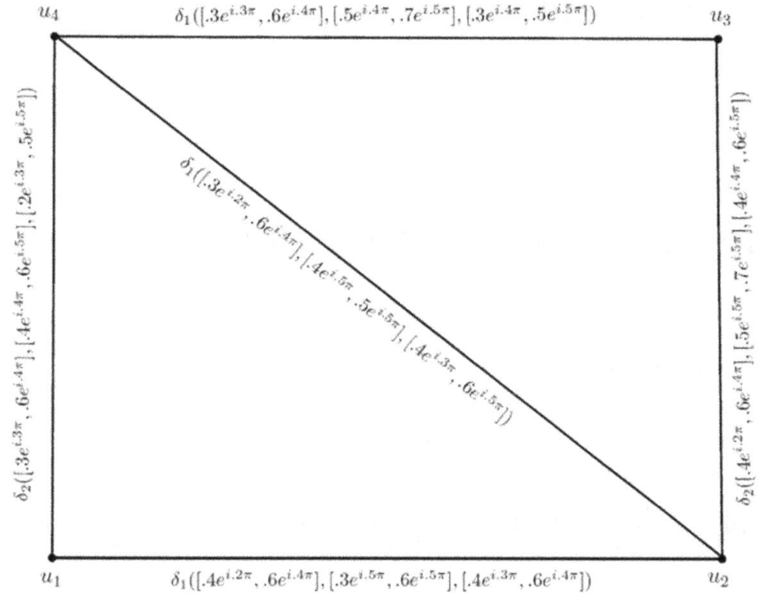

Remark 1 If two adjacency matrix of IVCNGS are $A\zeta = \{A\delta_1, A\delta_2, ..., A\delta_k\}$ and $A\zeta_2 = \{A\widetilde{\delta_1}, A\widetilde{\delta_2}, ..., A\widetilde{\delta_k}\}$ they are isomorphic if

$$\sum_{i=1}^{n} \mathrm{Ad}_{\delta^S_{1J}}(u_i) = \sum_{i=1}^{n} \mathrm{Ad}_{\widetilde{\delta^S_{1J}}}(f(u_i)), \sum_{i=1}^{n} \mathrm{Ad}_{\delta^S_{2J}}(u_i) = \sum_{i=1}^{n} \mathrm{Ad}_{\widetilde{\delta^S_{2J}}}(f(u_i)),$$

$$\sum_{i=1}^{n} \mathrm{Ad}_{\delta^S_{3J}}(u_i) = \sum_{i=1}^{n} \mathrm{Ad}_{\widetilde{\delta^S_{3J}}}(f(u_i)), \sum_{i=1}^{n} \mathrm{Ad}_{\beta^S_{1J}}(u_i) = \sum_{i=1}^{n} \mathrm{Ad}_{\widetilde{\beta^S_{1J}}}(f(u_i)),$$

$$\sum_{i=1}^{n} \mathrm{Ad}_{\beta^S_{2J}}(u_i) = \sum_{i=1}^{n} \mathrm{Ad}_{\widetilde{\beta^S_{2J}}}(f(u_i)), \sum_{i=1}^{n} \mathrm{Ad}_{\delta^S_{3J}}(u_i) = \sum_{i=1}^{n} \mathrm{Ad}_{\widetilde{\delta^S_{3J}}}(f(u_i)),$$

$\forall S$= -,+ and J=1,2,…,k.

Example 2 The adjacency matrix $A\zeta = \{A\delta_1, A\delta_2\}$ of a IVCNGS $\zeta = \{\eta, \delta_1, \delta_2\}$ is isomorphic to the adjacency matrix $A\zeta_2 = \{A\widetilde{\delta_1}, A\widetilde{\delta_2}\}$ of a IVCNGS $\zeta_2 = \{\widetilde{\eta}, \widetilde{\delta_1}, \widetilde{\delta_2}\}$ as shown in Figure-1 under (f,Ψ) where $f{:}\delta \rightarrow \widetilde{\delta}$ is a bijection and Ψ is a permutation on set {1,2} defined as Ψ(1)=2, Ψ(2)=1 and following relations are satisfied, by above Definition-[8], Remark-1. Such that

$$\tilde{\eta} = \{ u_4([.3e^{i.6\pi}, .6e^{i.7\pi}], [.4e^{i.4\pi}, .5e^{i.5\pi}], [.2e^{i.3\pi}, .5e^{i.5\pi}]),$$

$$u_3([.5e\text{^}(i.3\pi), .6e^{i.4\pi}], [.5e^{i.\pi}, .7e^{i.2\pi}], [.3e^{i.4\pi}, .4e^{i.5\pi}]),$$

$$u_2([.4e^{i.2\pi}, .6e^{i.4\pi}], [.3e^{i.5\pi}, .5e^{i.5\pi}], [.4e^{i.3\pi}, .6e^{i.4\pi}]), u_1([.4e^{i.3\pi}, .7e^{i.4\pi}],$$

$$[.3e^{i.1\pi}, .6e^{i.3\pi}], [.2e^{i.1\pi}, .4e^{i.3\pi}]) \}.$$

as show in Figure-1, we can easy to verify

$$\sum_{i=1}^{4} \mathrm{Ad}_{\delta_{1J}^{S}}(\mathrm{u_i}) = \sum_{i=1}^{4} \mathrm{Ad}_{\widetilde{\delta_{1J}^{S}}}(\mathrm{f(u_i)}), \sum_{i=1}^{4} \mathrm{Ad}_{\delta_{2J}^{S}}(\mathrm{u_i}) = \sum_{i=1}^{4} \mathrm{Ad}_{\widetilde{\delta_{2J}^{S}}}(\mathrm{f(u_i)}),$$

$$\sum_{i=1}^{4} \mathrm{Ad}_{\delta_{3J}^{S}}(\mathrm{u_i}) = \sum_{i=1}^{4} \mathrm{Ad}_{\widetilde{\delta_{3J}^{S}}}(\mathrm{f(u_i)}), \sum_{i=1}^{4} \mathrm{Ad}_{\beta_{1J}^{S}}(\mathrm{u_i}) = \sum_{i=1}^{4} \mathrm{Ad}_{\widetilde{\beta_{1J}^{S}}}(\mathrm{f(u_i)}),$$

$$\sum_{i=1}^{4} \mathrm{Ad}_{\beta_{2J}^{S}}(\mathrm{u_i}) = \sum_{i=1}^{4} \mathrm{Ad}_{\widetilde{\beta_{2J}^{S}}}(\mathrm{f(u_i)}), \sum_{i=1}^{4} \mathrm{Ad}_{\delta_{3J}^{S}}(\mathrm{u_i}) = \sum_{i=1}^{4} \mathrm{Ad}_{\widetilde{\delta_{3J}^{S}}}(\mathrm{f(u_i)}),$$

$\forall S$= -,+ and J=1,2.

Hence, $A\zeta$ is isomorphic to the adjacency matrix $A\tilde{\zeta}$.

Definition 9 Let $A\zeta = \{A\delta_1, A\delta_2, ..., A\delta_k\}$ be an adjacency matrix of a IVCNGS $\zeta = \{\eta, \delta_1, \delta_2, ..., \delta_k\}$ If $Ad_{\delta_J}(u\_i) = ([a_1, b_1], [a_2, b_2], [a_3, b_3])$ is amplitude term of each δ_J- degree of vertex u_i in $A(\zeta)$ and $Ad_{\beta_J}(u\_i) = ([c_1, d_1], [c_2, d_2], [c_3, d_3])$ is phase term of each β_J- degree of vertex u_i in $A(\zeta)$. Then $A(\zeta)$ is said to be δ_J - regular adjacency matrix of amplitude term IVCNGS and β_J- regular adjacency matrix of phase term IVCNGS for all J=1,2,…,k.

Theorem 10 The adjacency matrix $A\zeta = \{A\delta_1, A\delta_2, ..., A\delta_k\}$ of a IVCNGS $\zeta = \{\eta, \delta_1, \delta_2, ..., \delta_k\}$

Then

$$\sum_{i=1}^{n} A d_{\delta_J}(u_i)\, e^{i\sum_{i=1}^{n} Ad_{\beta_J}(u_i)} = ([2\sum_{(u_i,v)\in R_J} \delta_{1J}^{-}(u_i,v)\, e^{i\sum_{(u_i,v)\in R_J}\beta_{1J}^{-}(u_i,v)},$$

$$2\sum_{(u_i,v)\in R_J} \delta_{1J}^{+}(u_i,v)\, e^{i\sum_{(u_i,v)\in R_J}\beta_{1J}^{+}(u_i,v)}],[2\sum_{(u_i,v)\in R_J} \delta_{2J}^{-}(u_i,v)\, e^{i\sum_{(u_i,v)\in R_J}\beta_{2J}^{-}(u_i,v)},$$

$$[2\sum_{(u_i,v)\in R_J} \delta_{2J}^{+}(u_i,v)\, e^{i\sum_{(u_i,v)\in R_J}\beta_{2J}^{+}(u_i,v)}],[2\sum_{(u_i,v)\in R_J} \delta_{3J}^{-}(u_i,v)\, e^{i\sum_{(u_i,v)\in R_J}\beta_{3J}^{-}(u_i,v)}$$

$$\left[2\sum_{(u_i,v)\in R_J} \delta_{3J}^{+}(u_i,v)\, e^{i\sum_{(u_i,v)\in R_J}\beta_{3J}^{+}(u_i,v)}\right]) \text{ for all J=1, 2,...,k.}$$

Definition 11 Let $A\zeta = \{A\delta_1, A\delta_2, ..., A\delta_k\}$ be an adjacency matrix of a IVCNGS $\zeta = \{\eta, \delta_1, \delta_2, ..., \delta_k\}$. Then the degree of an δ_J-edge, $e_{ij}\in R_J$ is defined as $A d_{\delta_J}(e_{ij})\, e^{iA\beta_J(e_{ij})}=$

$$([A d_{\delta_{1J}^{-}}(e_{ij})\, e^{iA\beta_{1J}^{-}(e_{ij})},\ A d_{\delta_{1J}^{+}}(e_{ij})\, e^{iA\beta_{1J}^{+}(e_{ij})}],$$

$$[A d_{\delta_{2J}^{-}}(e_{ij})\, e^{iA\beta_{2J}^{-}(e_{ij})},\ A d_{\delta_{2J}^{+}}(e_{ij})\, e^{iA\beta_{2J}^{+}(e_{ij})}],$$

$$[A d_{\delta_{3J}^{-}}(e_{ij})\, e^{iA\beta_{3J}^{-}(e_{ij})},\ A d_{\delta_{3J}^{+}}(e_{ij})\, e^{iA\beta_{3J}^{+}(e_{ij})}]),$$

$$A d_{\delta_{1J}^{s}}(e_{ij})\, e^{iA\beta_{1J}^{s}(e_{ij})} = A d_{\delta_{1J}^{s}}(u_i)$$

$$+ A d_{\delta_{1J}^{s}}(u_j) - 2A\,\delta_{1J}^{S}(e_{ij})\, \mathrm{e}^{\mathrm{i}\, Ad_{\beta_{1J}^{s}}(u_i) + Ad_{\beta_{1J}^{s}}(u_j) - 2A\beta_{1J}^{s}(e_{ij})}$$

(or)

$$A d_{\delta_{1J}^{s}}(e_{ij})\, e^{iA\beta_{1J}^{s}(e_{ij})} = \sum_{u_i,u_k\in R_J, k\neq j} A\,\delta_{1J}^{S}(e_{ik})$$

$$+\sum_{u_k u_j\in R_J, k\neq i} A\,\delta_{1J}^{S}(e_{kj})\, e^{i\sum_{u_i,u_k\in R_J,k\neq j} A\beta_{1J}^{S}(e_{ik}) + \sum_{u_k u_j\in R_J,k\neq i} A\beta_{1J}^{S}(e_{kj})},$$

$$A\,d_{\delta^S_{2J}}(e_{ij})\,e^{iA\beta^S_{2J}(e_{ij})} = A\,d_{\delta^S_{2J}}(u_i)$$

$$+ A\,d_{\delta^S_{2J}}(u_j) - 2A\,\delta^S_{2J}(e_{ij})\,\mathrm{e}^{i\,Ad_{\beta^S_{2J}}(u_i)+Ad_{\beta^S_{2J}}(u_j)-2A\beta^S_{2J}(e_{ij})}$$

(or)

$$A\,d_{\delta^S_{2J}}(e_{ij})\,e^{iA\beta^S_{2J}(e_{ij})} = \sum_{u_i,u_k\in R_J,k\neq j} A\,\delta^S_{2J}(e_{ik})$$

$$+\sum_{u_k u_j\in R_J,k\neq i} A\,\delta^S_{2J}(e_{kj})\,e^{i\sum_{u_i,u_k\in R_J,k\neq j}A\beta^S_{2J}(e_{ik})+\sum_{u_k u_j\in R_J,k\neq i}A\beta^S_{2J}(e_{kj})},$$

$$A\,d_{\delta^S_{3J}}(e_{ij})\,e^{iA\beta^S_{3J}(e_{ij})} = A\,d_{\delta^S_{3J}}(u_i)$$

$$+ A\,d_{\delta^S_{3J}}(u_j) - 2A\,\delta^S_{3J}(e_{ij})\,\mathrm{e}^{i\,Ad_{\beta^S_{3J}}(u_i)+Ad_{\beta^S_{3J}}(u_j)-2A\beta^S_{3J}(e_{ij})}$$

(or)

$$A\,d_{\delta^S_{3J}}(e_{ij})\,e^{iA\beta^S_{3J}(e_{ij})} = \sum_{u_i,u_k\in R_{1J},k\neq j} A\,\delta^S_{3J}(e_{ik})$$

$$+\sum_{u_k u_j\in R_J,k\neq i} A\,\delta^S_{3J}(e_{kj})\,e^{i\sum_{u_i,u_k\in R_{1J},k\neq j}A\beta^S_{3J}(e_{ik})+\sum_{u_k u_j\in R_J,k\neq i}A\beta^S_{3J}(e_{kj})},$$

$\forall S$= -,+ and J=1,2,…,k.

Notation: An δ_J -edge of an IVCNGS is denoted by $e_{ij}\in R_J$ or $(u_i, u_j)\in R_J$.

Definition 12 Let $A\zeta = \{A\delta_1, A\delta_2, ..., A\delta_k\}$ be an adjacency matrix of a IVCNGS $\zeta = \{\eta, \delta_1, \delta_2, ..., \delta_k\}$. Then the total degree of an δ_J-edge, $e_{ij}\in R_J$ is defined as

$$tA\,d_{\delta_J}(e_{ij})\,e^{itA\beta_J(e_{ij})} =$$

$$([tA\,d_{\delta^-_{1J}}(e_{ij})\,e^{itA\beta^-_{1J}(e_{ij})}, t\,A\,d_{\delta^+_{1J}}(e_{ij})\,e^{itA\beta^+_{1J}(e_{ij})}],$$

$$[tA\,d_{\delta_{2J}^-}(e_{ij})\,e^{itA\beta_{2J}^-(e_{ij})},\ tA\,d_{\delta_{2J}^+}(e_{ij})\,e^{itA\beta_{2J}^+(e_{ij})}],$$

$$[tA\,d_{\delta_{3J}^-}(e_{ij})\,e^{itA\beta_{3J}^-(e_{ij})},\ tA\,d_{\delta_{3J}^+}(e_{ij})\,e^{itA\beta_{3J}^+(e_{ij})}]),$$

$$tA\,d_{\delta_{1J}^S}(e_{ij})\,e^{iA\beta_{1J}^S(e_{ij})} = \sum_{u_i u_k \in R_J, k\neq j} A\,\delta_{1J}^S(e_{ik}) + \sum_{u_k u_j \in R_J, k\neq i} A\,\delta_{1J}^S(e_{kj})$$

$$+A\,\delta_{1J}^S(e_{ij})\,e^{i\sum_{u_i u_k \in R_J, k\neq j} A\beta_{1J}^S(e_{ik})+\sum_{u_k u_j \in R_J, k\neq i} A\beta_{1J}^S(e_{kj})+A\beta_{1J}^S(e_{ij})},$$

$$tA\,d_{\delta_{2J}^S}(e_{ij})\,e^{itA\beta_{2J}^S(e_{ij})} = \sum_{u_i u_k \in R_J, k\neq j} A\,\delta_{2J}^S(e_{ik})$$

$$+\sum_{u_k u_j \in R_J, k\neq i} A\,\delta_{2J}^S(e_{kj}) + \delta_{2J}^S(e_{ij})\,e^{i\sum_{u_i u_k \in R_J, k\neq j} A\beta_{2J}^S(e_{ik})+\sum_{u_k u_j \in R_J, k\neq i} A\beta_{2J}^S(e_{kj})+A\beta_{2J}^S(e_{ij})},$$

$$tA\,d_{\delta_{3J}^S}(e_{ij})\,e^{iA\beta_{3J}^S(e_{ij})} = \sum_{u_i u_k \in R_J, k\neq j} A\,\delta_{3J}^S(e_{ik})$$

$$+\sum_{u_k u_j \in R_J, k\neq i} A\,\delta_{3J}^S(e_{kj}) + \delta_{3J}^S(e_{ij})\,e^{i\sum_{u_i u_k \in R_J, k\neq j} A\beta_{3J}^S(e_{ik})+\sum_{u_k u_j \in R_J, k\neq i} A\beta_{3J}^S(e_{kj})+A\beta_{3J}^S(e_{ij})},$$

$\forall S=$ -,+ and $J=1,2,\ldots,k$.

Definition 13 Let $A\zeta = \{A\delta_1, A\delta_2, \ldots, A\delta_k\}$ be an adjacency matrix of a IVCNGS $\zeta = \{\eta, \delta_1, \delta_2, \ldots, \delta_k\}$. If

$$A\,d_{\delta_J}(e_{ij}) = ([p_1, q_1],[p_2, q_2],[p_3, q_3])$$

for all $e_{ij} \in R_J$ each edge has amplitude term δ_J-degree of vertex u_i in $A(\zeta)$ and

$$A\,d_{\beta_J}(e_{ij}) = ([r_1, s_1],[r_2, s_2],[r_3, s_3])$$

for all $e_{ij} \in R_J$ each edge has phase term δ_J-degree of vertex u_i in $A(\zeta)$. Then $A(\zeta)$ is said to be δ_J -edge regular adjacency matrix of IVCNGS for all $J=1,2,\ldots,k$.

Example 3 Next, we show the example of the above definition-1. Let us Consider $A\zeta = \{A\delta_1, A\delta_2\}$ be an adjacency matrix of a IVCPFGS $\zeta = \{\eta, \delta_1, \delta_2\}$ as shown in Figure - 3 is δ_J -edge regular adjacency matrix of IVCPFGS such that

$$\eta = \{\ u_1 = u_2 = u_3 = u_4 = ([.4e^{i.3\pi}, .7e^{i.4\pi}], [.3e^{i.1\pi}, .6e^{i.3\pi}], [.2e^{i.1\pi}, .4e^{i.3\pi}])$$

Figure 3. $\zeta = \{\eta, \delta_1, \delta_2\}$

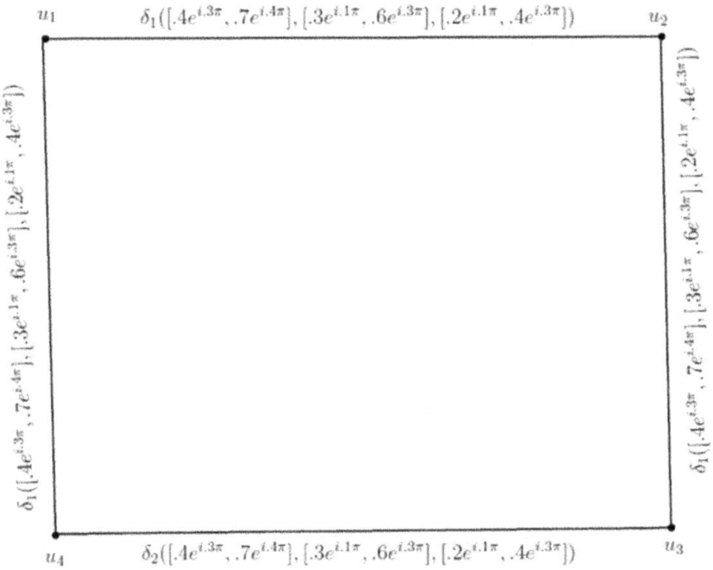

The adjacency matrix of amplitude term of a IVCNGS given in Figure 3 is

$$Ad_{\delta_J}(e_{12})e^{iA\beta_J(e_{12})} = ([Ad_{\delta_{1J}^-}(e_{12})e^{iA\beta_{1J}^-(e_{12})}, Ad_{\delta_{1J}^+}(e_{12})e^{iA\beta_{1J}^+(e_{12})}],$$

$$[Ad_{\delta_{2J}^-}(e_{12})e^{iA\beta_{2J}^-(e_{12})}, Ad_{\delta_{2J}^+}(e_{12})e^{iA\beta_{2J}^+(e_{12})}],$$

$$[Ad_{\delta_{3J}^-}(e_{12})e^{iA\beta_{3J}^-(e_{12})}, Ad_{\delta_{3J}^+}(e_{12})e^{iA\beta_{3J}^+(e_{12})}]),$$

$$Ad_{\delta_{1J}^S}(e_{12})e^{iA\beta_{1J}^S(e_{12})} = Ad_{\delta_{1J}^S}(u_1) + Ad_{\delta_{1J}^S}(u_2)$$

$$- 2Ad_{\delta_{1J}^{s}}(e_{12})\,e^{i\,Ad_{\beta_{1J}^{s}}(u_1)+Ad_{\beta_{1J}^{s}}(u_2)-2Ad_{\beta_{1J}^{s}}(e_{12})}=.4e^{i.3\pi}$$

Similarly, we can calculate

$$Ad_{\delta_{1J}^{s}}(e_{12})\,e^{iA\beta_{1J}^{s}(e_{12})}$$
$$= Ad_{\delta_{1J}^{s}}(e_{23})\,e^{iA\beta_{1J}^{s}(e_{23})} = Ad_{\delta_{1J}^{s}}(e_{34})\,e^{iA\beta_{1J}^{s}(e_{34})} = Ad_{\delta_{1J}^{s}}(e_{14})\,e^{iA\beta_{1J}^{s}(e_{14})}$$

$$= ([.4e^{i.3\pi},.7e^{i.4\pi}],[.3e^{i.1\pi},.6e^{i.3\pi}],[.2e^{i.1\pi},.4e^{i.3\pi}])$$

In the above Example-3 is δ_J-edge regular adjacency matrix of IVCNGS for all J=1,2

Definition 14 Let $A\zeta = \{A\delta_1, A\delta_2, ..., A\delta_k\}$ be an adjacency matrix of a IVCNGS $\zeta = \{\eta, \delta_1, \delta_2, ..., \delta_k\}$. If $tAd_{\delta_J}(e_{ij})$= $([x_1,y_1],[x_2,y_2],[x_3,y_3])$ for all $e_{ij}\in R_J$ each edge has amplitude term δ_J-degree of vertex u_i in $A(\zeta)$ and $tAd_{\beta_J}(e_{ij})$= $([z_1,l_1],[z_2,l_2],[z_3,l_3])$ for all $e_{ij}\in R_J$ each edge has phase term δ_J-degree of vertex u_i in $A(\zeta)$. Then $A(\zeta)$ is said to be totally δ_J -edge regular adjacency matrix of IVCNGS for all J=1,2,…,k.

Example 4. Let us Consider $A\zeta = \{A\delta_1, A\delta_2\}$ be an adjacency matrix of a IVCPFGS $\zeta = \{\eta, \delta_1, \delta_2\}$

as shown in Figure-3 in Example-3 is totally δ_J -edge regular adjacency matrix of IVCNGS for all J=1,2. The amplitude term of total degree of an δ_J -edge is

$$tAd_{\delta_{1J}^{s}}(e_{12})\,e^{itA\beta_{1J}^{s}(e_{12})}$$
$$= tAd_{\delta_{1J}^{s}}(e_{23})\,e^{itA\beta_{1J}^{s}(e_{23})} = tAd_{\delta_{1J}^{s}}(e_{34})\,e^{itA\beta_{1J}^{s}(e_{34})} = tAd_{\delta_{1J}^{s}}(e_{14})\,e^{itA\beta_{1J}^{s}(e_{14})}$$

$$= ([.8e^{i.6\pi},1.4e^{i.8\pi}],[.6e^{i.2\pi},1.2e^{i.6\pi}],[.4e^{i.2\pi},.8e^{i.6\pi}])$$

Hence, $A(\zeta)$ is totally δ_J -edge regular adjacency matrix of IVCNGS.

Theorem 15 Let $A\zeta = \{A\delta_1, A\delta_2, ..., A\delta_k\}$ be an adjacency matrix of a IVCNGS $\zeta = \{\eta, \delta_1, \delta_2, ..., \delta_k\}$ and ζ is cycle. Then

$$\sum_{i=1}^{n} Ad_{\delta_J}(u_i)\,e^{i\sum_{i=1}^{n} Ad_{\beta_J}(u_i)} = \sum_{i=1}^{n} Ad_{\delta_J}(e_{ij})\,e^{i\sum_{i=1}^{n} Ad_{\beta_J}(e_{ij})}$$

for all J=1,2,…,k and j=i+1.

Proof Given That $A\zeta = \{A\delta_1, A\delta_2, ..., A\delta_k\}$ be an adjacency matrix of a IVCNGS $\zeta = \{\eta, \delta_1, \delta_2, ..., \delta_k\}$ and ζ is cycle $u_1,u_2,\ldots,u_n$. Then

$$\sum_{i=1}^{n} Ad_{\delta_J}(u_i)\, e^{i\sum_{i=1}^{n} Ad_{\beta_J}(u_i)}$$

$$= ([\sum_{i=1}^{n} Ad_{\delta_{1J}^-}(e_{ij})\, e^{i\sum_{i=1}^{n} A\beta_{1J}^-(e_{ij})}, \sum_{i=1}^{n} Ad_{\delta_{1J}^+}(e_{ij})\, e^{i\sum_{i=1}^{n} A\beta_{1J}^+(e_{ij})}],$$

$$([\sum_{i=1}^{n} Ad_{\delta_{2J}^-}(e_{ij})\, e^{i\sum_{i=1}^{n} A\beta_{2J}^-(e_{ij})}, \sum_{i=1}^{n} Ad_{\delta_{2J}^+}(e_{ij})\, e^{i\sum_{i=1}^{n} A\beta_{2J}^+(e_{ij})}],$$

$$([\sum_{i=1}^{n} Ad_{\delta_{3J}^-}(e_{ij})\, e^{i\sum_{i=1}^{n} A\beta_{3J}^-(e_{ij})}, \sum_{i=1}^{n} Ad_{\delta_{3J}^+}(e_{ij})\, e^{i\sum_{i=1}^{n} A\beta_{3J}^+(e_{ij})}]),$$

Consider,

$$\sum_{i=1}^{n} Ad_{\delta_{1J}^S}(e_{ij})\, e^{i\sum_{i=1}^{n} A\beta_{1J}^S(e_{ij})} =$$

$$Ad_{\delta_{1J}^S}(e_{12}) + Ad_{\delta_{1J}^S}(e_{23}) + \cdots + Ad_{\delta_{1J}^S}(e_{n1})\ e^{i\,(A\beta_{1J}^S(e_{12}) + A\beta_{1J}^S(e_{23}) + \cdots + A\beta_{1J}^S(e_{n1}))}$$

$$= Ad_{\delta_{1J}^S}(u_1) + Ad_{\delta_{1J}^S}(u_2) - 2Ad_{\delta_{1J}^S}(e_{12})$$
$$+ \cdots + Ad_{\delta_{1J}^S}(u_n) + Ad_{\delta_{1J}^S}(u_1) - 2Ad_{\delta_{1J}^S}(e_{n1})$$

$$e^{i\left(Ad_{\beta_{1J}^s}(u_1) + Ad_{\beta_{1J}^s}(u_2) - 2Ad_{\beta_{1J}^s}(e_{12}) + \cdots + Ad_{\beta_{1J}^s}(u_n) + Ad_{\beta_{1J}^s}(u_1) - 2Ad_{\beta_{1J}^s}(e_{1n1})\right)}$$

$$= 2\sum_{u_i \in Q} Ad_{\delta_{1J}^S}(u_i) - 2\sum_{i=1}^{n} Ad_{\delta_{1J}^S}(e_{ii+1})\, e^{i2\sum_{u_i \in Q} Ad_{\beta_{1J}^s}(u_i) - 2\sum_{i=1}^{n} Ad_{\beta_{1J}^s}(e_{ii+1})}$$

$$= \sum_{u_i \in Q} Ad_{\delta_{1J}^S}(u_i) + 2\sum_{i=1}^{n} Ad_{\delta_{1J}^S}(e_{ii+1}) - 2\sum_{i=1}^{n} Ad_{\delta_{1J}^S}(e_{ii+1})$$

$$e^{i\sum_{u_i \in Q} Ad_{\beta_{1J}^s}(u_i) + 2\sum_{i=1}^{n} Ad_{\beta_{1J}^s}(e_{ii+1}) - 2\sum_{i=1}^{n} Ad_{\beta_{1J}^s}(e_{ii+1})}$$

$$= \sum_{u_i \in Q} Ad_{\delta_{1J}^S}(u_i)\ e^{i\sum_{u_i \in Q} Ad_{\beta_{1J}^s}(u_i)}.$$

Similarly, we derive the equation

$$\sum_{i=1}^{n} Ad_{\delta_{2J}^{s}}(e_{ij})\, e^{i\sum_{i=1}^{n} A\beta_{2J}^{S}(e_{ij})} = \sum_{u_i\in Q} Ad_{\delta_{2J}^{S}}(u_i)\; e^{i\sum_{u_i\in Q} Ad_{\beta_{2J}^{s}}(u_i)}$$

$$\sum_{i=1}^{n} Ad_{\delta_{3J}^{s}}(e_{ij})\, e^{i\sum_{i=1}^{n} A\beta_{3J}^{S}(e_{ij})} = \sum_{u_i\in Q} Ad_{\delta_{3J}^{S}}(u_i)\; e^{i\sum_{u_i\in Q} Ad_{\beta_{3J}^{s}}(u_i)}$$

Hence, $\sum_{i=1}^{n} Ad_{\delta_J^{s}}(e_{ij})\, e^{i\sum_{i=1}^{n} A\beta_J^{S}(e_{ij})} = \sum_{u_i\in Q} Ad_{\delta_J^{s}}(u_i)\; e^{i\sum_{u_i\in Q} Ad_{\beta_J^{s}}(u_i)}$ for all J=1,2,…,k and j=I+1, S = −,+.

Theorem 16 Let $A\zeta = \{A\delta_1, A\delta_2,\ldots,A\delta_k\}$ be an adjacency matrix of a IVCNGS $\zeta = \{\eta, \delta_1, \delta_2,\ldots,\delta_k\}$ Then

$$\sum_{i=1}^{n} Ad_{\delta_J}(e_{ij})\, e^{i\sum_{i=1}^{n} Ad_{\beta_J}(e_{ij})} = (\sum_{e_{ij}\in R_J} Ad_{R_J}^{*}(e_{ij}) Ad_{\delta_{1J}}^{S}(e_{ij})\, e^{i\sum_{e_{ij}\in R_J} Ad_{R_J}^{*}(e_{ij}) Ad_{\beta_{1J}}^{S}(e_{ij})},$$

$$\sum_{e_{ij}\in R_J} Ad_{R_J}^{*}(e_{ij}) Ad_{\delta_{2J}}^{S}(e_{ij})\, e^{i\sum_{e_{ij}\in R_J} Ad_{R_J}^{*}(e_{ij}) Ad_{\beta_{2J}}^{S}(e_{ij})},$$

$$\sum_{e_{ij}\in R_J} Ad_{R_J}^{*}(e_{ij}) Ad_{\delta_{3J}}^{S}(e_{ij})\, e^{i\sum_{e_{ij}\in R_J} Ad_{R_J}^{*}(e_{ij}) Ad_{\beta_{3J}}^{S}(e_{ij})})$$

for all J=1,2,…,k and j=i+1, S= -,+.

Proof $A\zeta = \{A\delta_1, A\delta_2,\ldots,A\delta_k\}$ be an adjacency matrix of a IVCNGS

$\zeta = \{\eta, \delta_1, \delta_2,\ldots,\delta_k\}$

We know that as

$$Ad_{\delta_J}(e_{ij})\, e^{iA\beta_J(e_{ij})} = ([Ad_{\delta_{1J}^{-}}(e_{ij})\, e^{iA\beta_{1J}^{-}(e_{ij})}, Ad_{\delta_{1J}^{+}}(e_{ij})\, e^{iA\beta_{1J}^{+}(e_{ij})}],$$

$$[Ad_{\delta_{2J}^{-}}(e_{ij})\, e^{iA\beta_{2J}^{-}(e_{ij})}, Ad_{\delta_{2J}^{+}}(e_{ij})\, e^{iA\beta_{2J}^{+}(e_{ij})}],$$

$$[Ad_{\delta_{3J}^{-}}(e_{ij})\, e^{iA\beta_{3J}^{-}(e_{ij})}, Ad_{\delta_{3J}^{+}}(e_{ij})\, e^{iA\beta_{3J}^{+}(e_{ij})}]),$$

where $Ad_{\delta_J}(e_{ij})\, e^{iA\beta_J(e_{ij})}$ is sum of the adjacency matrix of a IVCNGS δ_J-edge in $A(\zeta)$.

Therefore, in $\sum_{e_{ij}\in R_J} Ad_{\delta_J}(e_{ij})\, e^{i\sum_{e_{ij}\in R_J} A\beta_J(e_{ij})}$, every δ_J -edge in $A(\zeta)$is adjacent to that δ_J -edge times.

Thus, in $\sum_{e_{ij}\in R_J} Ad_{\delta_J}(e_{ij})\, e^{i\sum_{e_{ij}\in R_J} A\beta_J(e_{ij})}$ each $Ad_{\delta_J}(e_{ij})\, e^{iA\beta_J(e_{ij})}$ appears $Ad^*_{R_J}(e_{ij})\, e^{iAd^*_{R_J}(e_{ij})}$

Hence, $\sum_{e_{ij}\in R_J} Ad_{\delta^S_{1J}}(e_{ij})\, e^{i\sum_{e_{ij}\in R_J} A\beta^S_{1J}(e_{ij})}$

$$= \sum_{e_{ij}\in R_J} Ad^*_{R_J}(e_{ij}) Ad^S_{\delta_{1J}}(e_{ij})\, e^{i\sum_{e_{ij}\in R_J} Ad^*_{R_J}(e_{ij}) Ad^S_{\beta_{1J}}(e_{ij})},$$

$$\sum_{e_{ij}\in R_J} Ad_{\delta^S_{2J}}(e_{ij})\, e^{i\sum_{e_{ij}\in R_J} A\beta^S_{2J}(e_{ij})}$$

$$= \sum_{e_{ij}\in R_J} Ad^*_{R_J}(e_{ij}) Ad^S_{\delta_{2J}}(e_{ij})\, e^{i\sum_{e_{ij}\in R_J} Ad^*_{R_J}(e_{ij}) Ad^S_{\beta_{2J}}(e_{ij})}$$

$$\sum_{e_{ij}\in R_J} Ad_{\delta^S_{3J}}(e_{ij})\, e^{i\sum_{e_{ij}\in R_J} A\beta^S_{3J}(e_{ij})}$$

$$= \sum_{e_{ij}\in R_J} Ad^*_{R_J}(e_{ij}) Ad^S_{\delta_{3J}}(e_{ij})\, e^{i\sum_{e_{ij}\in R_J} Ad^*_{R_J}(e_{ij}) Ad^S_{\beta_{3J}}(e_{ij})},$$

$\forall J=1,2,\ldots,k$ and $S= =,+$

Theorem 17 Let $A\zeta = \{A\delta_1, A\delta_2, \ldots, A\delta_k\}$ be an adjacency matrix of a IVCNGS $\zeta = \{\eta, \delta_1, \delta_2, \ldots, \delta_k\}$ Then

$$\sum_{i=1}^{n} Ad_{\delta_J}(e_{ij})\, e^{i\sum_{i=1}^{n} Ad_{\beta_J}(e_{ij})} =(k-1\sum_{u_i\in Q} Ad_{\delta^S_{1J}}(u_i)\, e^{ik-1\sum_{u_i\in Q} Ad_{\beta^S_{1J}}(u_i)},$$

$$k-1\sum_{u_i\in Q} Ad_{\delta^S_{2J}}(u_i)\, e^{ik-1\sum_{u_i\in Q} Ad_{\beta^S_{2J}}(u_i)}, k-1\sum_{u_i\in Q} Ad_{\delta^S_{3J}}(u_i)\, e^{ik-1\sum_{u_i\in Q} Ad_{\beta^S_{3J}}(u_i)}),$$

$\forall J=1,2,\ldots,k$ and $j=i+1$, $S= -,+$.

Proof By Theorem-16

$$\sum_{i=1}^{n} Ad_{\delta_J}(e_{ij})\, e^{i\sum_{i=1}^{n} Ad_{\beta_J}(e_{ij})} = (\sum_{e_{ij}\in R_J} Ad^*_{R_J}(e_{ij}) Ad^S_{\delta_{1J}}(e_{ij})\, e^{i\sum_{e_{ij}\in R_J} Ad^*_{R_J}(e_{ij}) Ad^S_{\beta_{1J}}(e_{ij})},$$

$$\sum_{e_{ij}\in R_J} Ad^*_{R_J}(e_{ij}) Ad^S_{\delta_{2J}}(e_{ij})\, e^{i\sum_{e_{ij}\in R_J} Ad^*_{R_J}(e_{ij}) Ad^S_{\beta_{2J}}(e_{ij})},$$

$$\sum_{e_{ij}\in R_J} Ad^*_{R_J}(e_{ij}) Ad^S_{\delta_{3J}}(e_{ij})\, e^{i\sum_{e_{ij}\in R_J} Ad^*_{R_J}(e_{ij}) Ad^S_{\beta_{3J}}(e_{ij})})$$

$$\sum_{e_{ij}\in R_J} Ad^*_{R_J}(e_{ij}) Ad^S_{\delta_{1J}}(e_{ij})\, e^{i\sum_{e_{ij}\in R_J} Ad^*_{R_J}(e_{ij}) Ad^S_{\beta_{1J}}(e_{ij})} =$$

$$\sum_{e_{ij}\in R_J} Ad^*_{R_J}(u_i) + \sum_{e_{ij}\in R_J} Ad^*_{R_J}(u_j) - 2\, Ad^S_{\delta_{1J}}(e_{ij})\, e^{i\sum_{e_{ij}\in R_J} Ad^*_{R_J}(u_i) + \sum_{e_{ij}\in R_J} Ad^*_{R_J}(u_j) - 2\, Ad^S_{\beta_{1J}}(e_{ij})},$$

$$\sum_{e_{ij}\in R_J} Ad^*_{R_J}(e_{ij}) Ad^S_{\delta_{2J}}(e_{ij})\, e^{i\sum_{e_{ij}\in R_J} Ad^*_{R_J}(e_{ij}) Ad^S_{\beta_{2J}}(e_{ij})} =$$

$$\sum_{e_{ij}\in R_J} Ad^*_{R_J}(u_i) + \sum_{e_{ij}\in R_J} Ad^*_{R_J}(u_j) - 2\, Ad^S_{\delta_{2J}}(e_{ij})\, e^{i\sum_{e_{ij}\in R_J} Ad^*_{R_J}(u_i) + \sum_{e_{ij}\in R_J} Ad^*_{R_J}(u_j) - 2\, Ad^S_{\beta_{2J}}(e_{ij})},$$

$$\sum_{e_{ij}\in R_J} Ad^*_{R_J}(e_{ij}) Ad^S_{\delta_{3J}}(e_{ij})\, e^{i\sum_{e_{ij}\in R_J} Ad^*_{R_J}(e_{ij}) Ad^S_{\beta_{3J}}(e_{ij})} =$$

$$\sum_{e_{ij}\in R_J} Ad^*_{R_J}(u_i) + \sum_{e_{ij}\in R_J} Ad^*_{R_J}(u_j) - 2\, Ad^S_{\delta_{3J}}(e_{ij})\, e^{i\sum_{e_{ij}\in R_J} Ad^*_{R_J}(u_i) + \sum_{e_{ij}\in R_J} Ad^*_{R_J}(u_j) - 2\, Ad^S_{\beta_{3J}}(e_{ij})}.$$

Since, $\tilde{\zeta}$ is a ζ regular adjacency matrix of IVCNGS, $Ad^S_{\delta_{1J}}(u_i) = k$ for all $u_i \in Q$.

$$\sum_{e_{ij}\in R_J} Ad^*_{R_J}(e_{ij}) Ad^S_{\delta_{1J}}(e_{ij})\, e^{i\sum_{e_{ij}\in R_J} Ad^*_{R_J}(e_{ij}) Ad^S_{\beta_{1J}}(e_{ij})} = (k + k - 2) \sum_{e_{ij}\in R_J} Ad^S_{\delta_{1J}}(e_{ij})$$

$$e^{i(k+k-2)\sum_{e_{ij}\in R_J} Ad^S_{\beta_{1J}}(e_{ij})} = 2(k-1) \sum_{e_{ij}\in R_J} Ad^S_{\delta_{1J}}(e_{ij})\, e^{i2(k-1)\sum_{e_{ij}\in R_J} Ad^S_{\beta_{1J}}(e_{ij})}$$

$$= k - 1 \sum_{u_i \in Q} A\, d_{\delta_{1J}^{S}}(u_i)\, e^{ik-1\sum_{u_i\in Q} Ad_{\beta_{1J}^{S}}(u_i)}$$

Likewise, we can demonstrate that

$$\sum_{e_{ij}\in R_J} A\, d_{R_J}^{*}(e_{ij}) A\, d_{\delta_{2J}}^{S}(e_{ij})\, e^{i\sum_{e_{ij}\in R_J} Ad_{R_J}^{*}(e_{ij}) Ad_{\beta_{2J}}^{S}(e_{ij})} = k - 1 \sum_{u_i \in Q} A\, d_{\delta_{2J}^{S}}(u_i)\, e^{ik-1\sum_{u_i\in Q} Ad_{\beta_{2J}^{S}}(u_i)},$$

$$\sum_{e_{ij}\in R_J} A\, d_{R_J}^{*}(e_{ij}) A\, d_{\delta_{3J}}^{S}(e_{ij})\, e^{i\sum_{e_{ij}\in R_J} Ad_{R_J}^{*}(e_{ij}) Ad_{\beta_{3J}}^{S}(e_{ij})} = k - 1 \sum_{u_i \in Q} A\, d_{\delta_{3J}^{S}}(u_i)\, e^{ik-1\sum_{u_i\in Q} Ad_{\beta_{3J}^{S}}(u_i)}),$$

$\forall J$=1,2,…,k and j=i+1, S= -,+.

Theorem 18 Let $A\zeta = \{A\delta_1, A\delta_2, \ldots, A\delta_k\}$ be an adjacency matrix of a IVCNGS $\zeta = \{\eta, \delta_1, \delta_2, \ldots, \delta_k\}$ on a δ_J regular crisp graph $\tilde{\delta}$ of GS ζ^*. Then

$$\sum_{i=1}^{n} tA\, d_{\delta_J}(e_{ij})\, e^{i\sum_{i=1}^{n} tAd_{\beta_J}(e_{ij})} =$$

$$(\sum_{e_{ij}\in R_J} A\, d_{R_J}^{*}(e_{ij}) A\, d_{\delta_{1J}}^{S}(e_{ij}) + \sum_{e_{ij}\in R_J} A\, d_{\delta_{1J}}^{S}(e_{ij})\, e^{i\sum_{e_{ij}\in R_J} Ad_{R_J}^{*}(e_{ij}) Ad_{\beta_{1J}}^{S}(e_{ij}) + \sum_{e_{ij}\in R_J} Ad_{\beta_{1J}}^{S}(e_{ij})},$$

$$\sum_{e_{ij}\in R_J} A\, d_{R_J}^{*}(e_{ij}) A\, d_{\delta_{2J}}^{S}(e_{ij}) + \sum_{e_{ij}\in R_J} A\, d_{\delta_{2J}}^{S}(e_{ij})\, e^{i\sum_{e_{ij}\in R_J} Ad_{R_J}^{*}(e_{ij}) Ad_{\beta_{2J}}^{S}(e_{ij}) + \sum_{e_{ij}\in R_J} Ad_{\beta_{2J}}^{S}(e_{ij})},$$

$$\left(\sum_{e_{ij}\in R_J} A\, d_{R_J}^{*}(e_{ij}) A\, d_{\delta_{3J}}^{S}(e_{ij}) + \sum_{e_{ij}\in R_J} A\, d_{\delta_{3J}}^{S}(e_{ij})\, e^{i\sum_{e_{ij}\in R_J} Ad_{R_J}^{*}(e_{ij}) Ad_{\beta_{3J}}^{S}(e_{ij}) + \sum_{e_{ij}\in R_J} Ad_{\beta_{3J}}^{S}(e_{ij})}\right)$$

$\forall J$=1,2,…,k and j=i+1, S= -,+.

Proof By Definition-14 of total degree of δ_J -edge of $A(\zeta)$.

$$\sum_{i=1}^{n} tA\, d_{\delta_J}(e_{ij})\, e^{i\sum_{i=1}^{n} tAd_{\beta_J}(e_{ij})}$$

$$= (\sum_{i=1}^{n} tA\, d_{\delta_{1J}^{S}}(e_{ij})\, e^{i\sum_{i=1}^{n} tA\beta_{1J}^{S}(e_{ij})},\ \sum_{i=1}^{n} tA\, d_{\delta_{2J}^{S}}(e_{ij})\, e^{i\sum_{i=1}^{n} tA\beta_{1J}^{S}(e_{ij})},$$

$$\sum_{i=1}^{n} tA\,d_{\delta_{3J}^{S}}(e_{ij})\,e^{i\sum_{i=1}^{n} tA\beta_{1J}^{S}(e_{ij})}),$$

$$\sum_{i=1}^{n} tA\,d_{\delta_{1J}^{S}}(e_{ij})\,e^{i\sum_{i=1}^{n} tA\beta_{1J}^{S}(e_{ij})} = \sum_{i=1}^{n} A\,d_{\delta_{1J}^{S}}(e_{ij}) + A\,\delta_{1J}^{S}(e_{ij})\,e^{i\sum_{i=1}^{n} A\beta_{1J}^{S}(e_{ij})+A\beta_{1J}^{S}(e_{ij})},$$

$$\sum_{i=1}^{n} tA\,d_{\delta_{2J}^{S}}(e_{ij})\,e^{i\sum_{i=1}^{n} tA\beta_{2J}^{S}(e_{ij})} = \sum_{i=1}^{n} A\,d_{\delta_{2J}^{S}}(e_{ij}) + A\,\delta_{2J}^{S}(e_{ij})\,e^{i\sum_{i=1}^{n} A\beta_{2J}^{S}(e_{ij})+A\beta_{2J}^{S}(e_{ij})},$$

$$\sum_{i=1}^{n} tA\,d_{\delta_{3J}^{S}}(e_{ij})\,e^{i\sum_{i=1}^{n} tA\beta_{3J}^{S}(e_{ij})} = \sum_{i=1}^{n} A\,d_{\delta_{3J}^{S}}(e_{ij}) + A\,\delta_{3J}^{S}(e_{ij})\,e^{i\sum_{i=1}^{n} A\beta_{3J}^{S}(e_{ij})+A\beta_{3J}^{S}(e_{ij})},$$

$\forall J=1,2,\ldots,k$ and $j=i+1$, $S=-,+$.

By Theorem-16 we get

$$\sum_{i=1}^{n} A\,d_{\delta_J}(e_{ij})\,e^{i\sum_{i=1}^{n} Ad_{\beta_J}(e_{ij})} = (\sum_{e_{ij}\in R_J} A\,d_{R_J}^{*}(e_{ij})A\,d_{\delta_{1J}}^{S}(e_{ij})\,e^{i\sum_{e_{ij}\in R_J} Ad_{R_J}^{*}(e_{ij})Ad_{\beta_{1J}}^{S}(e_{ij})},$$

$$\sum_{e_{ij}\in R_J} A\,d_{R_J}^{*}(e_{ij})A\,d_{\delta_{2J}}^{S}(e_{ij})\,e^{i\sum_{e_{ij}\in R_J} Ad_{R_J}^{*}(e_{ij})Ad_{\beta_{2J}}^{S}(e_{ij})},$$

$$\sum_{e_{ij}\in R_J} A\,d_{R_J}^{*}(e_{ij})A\,d_{\delta_{3J}}^{S}(e_{ij})\,e^{i\sum_{e_{ij}\in R_J} Ad_{R_J}^{*}(e_{ij})Ad_{\beta_{3J}}^{S}(e_{ij})}),$$

$\forall J=1,2,\ldots,k$ and $j=i+1$, $S=-,+$.

Theorem 19 Let $A\zeta = \{A\delta_1, A\delta_2, \ldots, A\delta_k\}$ be an adjacency matrix of a IVCNGS $\zeta = \{\eta, \delta_1, \delta_2, \ldots, \delta_k\}$. Then δ_J-edge is a constant function if and only if the following are equivalent:

1. $A(\zeta)$ is an δ_J-edge regular IVCNGS.
2. $A(\zeta)$ is a totally δ_J-edge regular IVCNGS.

Proof Assume that δ_J-edge is a constant function. Then

$$A\,d_{\delta_J}(e_{ij})\,e^{iAd_{\beta_J}(e_{ij})} = (c_1, c_2, c_3, c_4, c_5, c_6)$$

where

$c_1, c_2, c_3, c_4, c_5, c_6$ are constant (1)

Assume that $A(\zeta)$ is δ_J -edge regular IVCNGS. Then

$$A d_{\delta_J}(e_{ij}) e^{iAd_{\beta_J}(e_{ij})} = (p_1, q_1, p_2, q_2, p_3, q_3)$$

for all $e_{ij} \in E_j$. (2)

Consider,

$$\sum_{i=1}^{n} tA d_{\delta_J}(e_{ij}) e^{i\sum_{i=1}^{n} tAd_{\beta_J}(e_{ij})}$$

$$= (\sum_{i=1}^{n} tA d_{\delta_{1J}^S}(e_{ij}) e^{i\sum_{i=1}^{n} tA\beta_{1J}^S(e_{ij})}, \sum_{i=1}^{n} tA d_{\delta_{2J}^S}(e_{ij}) e^{i\sum_{i=1}^{n} tA\beta_{1J}^S(e_{ij})},$$

$$\sum_{i=1}^{n} tA d_{\delta_{3J}^S}(e_{ij}) e^{i\sum_{i=1}^{n} tA\beta_{1J}^S(e_{ij})})$$
$$= (p_1 + c_1,\ q_1 + c_2,\ p_2 + c_3,\ q_2 + c_4,\ p_3 + c_5,\ q_3 + c_6)$$

for all $e_{ij} \in R_J$ by equation (1) and (2)
Which implies $A(\zeta)$ is a totally δ_J -edge regular IVCNGS.
Let $A(\zeta)$ be totally δ_J -edge regular IVCNGS. Then

$$tA d_{\delta_J}(e_{ij}) e^{itA\beta_J(e_{ij})} = (x_1, y_1, x_2, y_2, x_3, y_3) \text{ for all } e_{ij} \in R_J.$$

$$tA d_{\delta_J}(e_{ij}) e^{itAd_{\beta_J}(e_{ij})} = (A d_{\delta_{1J}^S}(e_{ij}) + A\, \delta_{1J}^S(e_{ij})\, e^{iAd_{\beta_{1J}^S}(e_{ij}) + A\beta_{1J}^S(e_{ij})},$$

$$A d_{\delta_{2J}^S}(e_{ij}) + A\, \delta_{2J}^S(e_{ij})\, e^{iAd_{\beta_{2J}^S}(e_{ij}) + A\beta_{2J}^S(e_{ij})},$$

$$A d_{\delta_{3J}^S}(e_{ij}) + A\, \delta_{3J}^S(e_{ij})\, e^{iAd_{\beta_{3J}^S}(e_{ij}) + A\beta_{3J}^S(e_{ij})})$$

Now,

$$Ad_{\delta_J}(e_{ij})\,e^{iAd_{\beta_J}(e_{ij})} = (Ad_{\delta^s_{1J}}(e_{ij})\,e^{iAd_{\beta^s_{1J}}(e_{ij})},$$

$$Ad_{\delta^s_{2J}}(e_{ij})\,e^{iAd_{\beta^s_{2J}}(e_{ij})}, Ad_{\delta^s_{3J}}(e_{ij})\,e^{iAd_{\beta^s_{3J}}(e_{ij})})$$

$$= (x_1 - A\,\delta^-_{1J}(e_{ij})\,e^{iA\beta^-_{1J}(e_{ij})}, y_1 - A\,\delta^+_{1J}(e_{ij})\,e^{iA\beta^+_{1J}(e_{ij})},$$

$$x_2 - A\,\delta^-_{1J}(e_{ij})\,e^{iA\beta^-_{2J}(e_{ij})}, y_2 - A\,\delta^+_{2J}(e_{ij})\,e^{iA\beta^+_{2J}(e_{ij})},$$

$$x_3 - A\,\delta^-_{3J}(e_{ij})\,e^{iA\beta^-_{3J}(e_{ij})}, y_3 - A\,\delta^+_{3J}(e_{ij})\,e^{iA\beta^+_{3J}(e_{ij})})$$

$$=(x_1 - c_1, y_1 - c_2, x_2 - c_3, y_2 - c_4, x_3 - c_5, y_3 - c_6) \text{ by (1)}$$

Hence, $A(\zeta)$ is an δ_J -edge regular IVCNGS.

Thus, (2)⇒(2).

Conversely, assume that (1) and (2) are equivalent.

That is, $A(\zeta)$ is an δ_J -edge regular IVCNGS if and only if $A(\zeta)$ is a totally δ_J -edge regular IVCNGS.

We have to prove that δ_J -edge is a constant function.

Suppose that δ_J -edge is not a constant function (3)

$$Ad_{\delta^s_{1J}}(e_{ij})\,e^{iAd_{\beta^s_{1J}}(e_{ij})} = Ad_{\delta^s_{1J}}(e_{rs})\,e^{iAd_{\beta^s_{1J}}(e_{rs})},$$

$$Ad_{\delta^s_{2J}}(e_{ij})\,e^{iAd_{\beta^s_{2J}}(e_{ij})} = Ad_{\delta^s_{2J}}(e_{rs})\,e^{iAd_{\beta^s_{2J}}(e_{rs})},$$

$$Ad_{\delta^s_{3J}}(e_{ij})\,e^{iAd_{\beta^s_{3J}}(e_{ij})} = Ad_{\delta^s_{3J}}(e_{rs})\,e^{iAd_{\beta^s_{3J}}(e_{rs})}$$

for at least one pair of $e_{ij}, e_{rs} \in R_J$.

Let $A(\zeta)$ is an δ_J -edge regular IVCNGS. Then

$$Ad_{\delta_J}(e_{ij})\,e^{iAd_{\beta_J}(e_{ij})} = (p_1, q_1, p_2, q_2, p_3, q_3) \qquad (4)$$

$$Ad_{\delta_J}(e_{ij})\,e^{iAd_{\beta_J}(e_{ij})} = (Ad_{\delta^S_{1J}}(e_{ij}) + A\delta^S_{1J}(e_{ij})\,e^{iAd_{\beta^S_{1J}}(e_{ij}) + A\beta^S_{1J}(e_{ij})},$$

$$Ad_{\delta^S_{2J}}(e_{ij}) + A\delta^S_{2J}(e_{ij})\,e^{iAd_{\beta^S_{2J}}(e_{ij}) + A\beta^S_{2J}(e_{ij})},$$

$$Ad_{\delta^S_{3J}}(e_{ij}) + A\delta^S_{3J}(e_{ij})\,e^{iAd_{\beta^S_{3J}}(e_{ij}) + A\beta^S_{3J}(e_{ij})}) = (\,p_1 + A\delta^-_{1J}(e_{ij})\,e^{iA\beta^-_{1J}(e_{ij})},$$

$$q_1 + A\delta^+_{1J}(e_{ij})\,e^{iA\beta^+_{1J}(e_{ij})},\; p_2 + A\delta^-_{2J}(e_{ij})\,e^{iA\beta^-_{2J}(e_{ij})}, q\_2 + A\delta^+_{2J}(e_{ij})\,e^{iA\beta^+_{2J}(e_{ij})},$$

$$p_3 + A\delta^-_{3J}(e_{ij})\,e^{iA\beta^-_{3J}(e_{ij})},\; q_3 + A\delta^+_{3J}(e_{ij})\,e^{iA\beta^+_{3J}(e_{ij})})$$

and

$$Ad_{\delta_J}(e_{rs})\,e^{iAd_{\beta_J}(e_{rs})} = (Ad_{\delta^S_{1J}}(e_{rs}) + A\delta^S_{1J}(e_{rs})\,e^{iAd_{\beta^S_{1J}}(e_{rs}) + A\beta^S_{1J}(e_{rs})},$$

$$Ad_{\delta^S_{2J}}(e_{rs}) + A\delta^S_{2J}(e_{rs})\,e^{iAd_{\beta^S_{2J}}(e_{rs}) + A\beta^S_{2J}(e_{rs})},$$

$$Ad_{\delta^S_{3J}}(e_{rs}) + A\delta^S_{3J}(e_{rs})\,e^{iAd_{\beta^S_{3J}}(e_{rs}) + A\beta^S_{3J}(e_{rs})}) = (\,p_1 + A\delta^-_{1J}(e_{rs})\,e^{iA\beta^-_{1J}(e_{rs})},$$

$$q_1 + A\delta^+_{1J}(e_{rs})\,e^{iA\beta^+_{1J}(e_{rs})},\; p_2 + A\delta^-_{2J}(e_{rs})\,e^{iA\beta^-_{2J}(e_{rs})}, q\_2 + A\delta^+_{2J}(e_{rs})\,e^{iA\beta^+_{2J}(e_{rs})},$$

$$p_3 + A\delta^-_{3J}(e_{rs})\,e^{iA\beta^-_{3J}(e_{rs})},\; q_3 + A\delta^+_{3J}(e_{rs})\,e^{iA\beta^+_{3J}(e_{rs})})$$

Since,

$$Ad_{\delta^S_{1J}}(e_{ij})\,e^{iAd_{\beta^S_{1J}}(e_{ij})} \neq Ad_{\delta^S_{1J}}(e_{rs})\,e^{iAd_{\beta^S_{1J}}(e_{rs})},$$

$$Ad_{\delta^S_{2J}}(e_{ij})\,e^{iAd_{\beta^S_{2J}}(e_{ij})} \neq Ad_{\delta^S_{2J}}(e_{rs})\,e^{iAd_{\beta^S_{2J}}(e_{rs})},$$

$$A\,d_{\delta_{3J}^{S}}(e_{ij})\,e^{iAd_{\beta_{3J}^{S}}(e_{ij})} \neq A\,d_{\delta_{3J}^{S}}(e_{rs})\,e^{iAd_{\beta_{3J}^{S}}(e_{rs})}$$

$\Rightarrow A(\zeta)$ is not a totally δ_J -edge regular IVCNGS.

$\Rightarrow$ it is a contradiction to our assumption.

Hence, δ_J -edge is a constant function.

Theorem 20 Let $A\zeta = \{A\delta_1, A\delta_2, \ldots, A\delta_k\}$ be an adjacency matrix of a IVCNGS $\zeta = \{\eta, \delta_1, \delta_2, \ldots, \delta_k\}$ is both δ_J -edge regular and totally δ_J -edge regular. Then δ_J -edge constant function.

Proof By Theorem-19, the result is trivial.

Note: The converse of the above Theorem-19 is not true.

Theorem 21 Let $A\zeta = \{A\delta_1, A\delta_2, \ldots, A\delta_k\}$ be an adjacency matrix of a IVCNGS $\zeta = \{\eta, \delta_1, \delta_2, \ldots, \delta_k\}$ and $A(\zeta)$ is an δ_J regular IVCNGS. Then $A(\zeta)$ is a totally δ_J -edge regular IVCNGS.

Proof Let $A\zeta = \{\, A\delta_1,\ A\delta_2, \ldots, A\delta_k\}$ be an adjacency matrix of a IVCNGS $\zeta = \{\, \eta,\ \delta_1,\ \delta_2, \ldots, \delta_k\}$.

Then $A\,d_{\delta_J}(u\_i)\,e^{iAd_{\beta_J}}$ $(a_1, b_1,\ a_2, b_2, a_3, b_3)$ for all $u_i \in Q$ Given that δ_J are constants.

That is, $A\,d_{\delta_J}(e_{ij})\,e^{iAd_{\beta_J}(e_{ij})} = (c_1, c_2, c_3, c_4, c_5, c_6)$ for all $e_{ij} \in R_J$ where $c_1, c_2, c_3, c_4, c_5, c_6$ are constant.

We have to prove that $A(\zeta)$ is a totally δ_J -edge regular IVCNGS.

By Definition-14 of totally δ_J -edge degree, we have

$$tA\,d_{\delta_J}(e_{ij})\,e^{itA\beta_J(e_{ij})}$$

$$=(\,tA\,d_{\delta_{1J}^{S}}(e_{ij})\,e^{itAd_{\beta_{1J}^{S}}(e_{ij})},\ tA\,d_{\delta_{2J}^{S}}(e_{ij})\,e^{itAd_{\beta_{2J}^{S}}(e_{ij})}, tA\,d_{\delta_{3J}^{S}}(e_{ij})\,e^{itAd_{\beta_{3J}^{S}}(e_{ij})})$$

$$tA\,d_{\delta_{1J}^{S}}(e_{ij})\,e^{iAd_{\beta_{1J}^{S}}(e_{ij})} = A\,d_{\delta_{1J}^{S}}(u_i) + A\,d_{\delta_{1J}^{S}}(u_j)$$

$$-\ 2A\,d_{\delta_{1J}^{S}}(e_{ij})\,e^{i\,Ad_{\beta_{1J}^{S}}(u_i) + Ad_{\beta_{1J}^{S}}(u_j) - 2Ad_{\beta_{1J}^{S}}(e_{ij})} = 2a_1 - c_1, \forall\ e_{ij} \in R_J$$

Similarly, we solve the equation

$$tA\,d_{\delta_J}(e_{ij})\,e^{itA\beta_J(e_{ij})} = (2a_1 - c_1, 2b_1 - c_2, 2a_2 - c_3, 2b_2 - c_4, 2a_3 - c_5, 2b_3 - c_6)$$

Hence, $A(\zeta)$ is a totally δ_J -edge regular IVCNGS.

Theorem 21 Let $A\zeta = \{A\delta_1, A\delta_2, \ldots, A\delta_k\}$ be an adjacency matrix of a IVCNGS $\zeta = \{\eta, \delta_1, \delta_2, \ldots, \delta_k\}$ on a δ_J regular crisp graph $\tilde{\zeta}$ of GS. Then δ_J is a constant if and only if $A(\zeta)$ is both δ_J regular and δ_J -edge regular IVCNGS.

Proof Let $A\zeta = \{A\delta_1, A\delta_2, \ldots, A\delta_k\}$ be an adjacency matrix of a IVCNGS $\zeta = \{\eta, \delta_1, \delta_2, \ldots, \delta_k\}$ on a δ_J regular crisp graph $\tilde{\zeta}$ of GS.

Assume that δ_J is a constant functions, that is $Ad_{(\delta_J)}(e_{ij}) = (c_1, c_2, c_3, c_4, c_5, c_6)$ for all e_{ij}\in R_J where $c_1, c_2, c_3, c_4, c_5, c_6$ are constant.

To prove: $A(\zeta)$ is both δ_J regular and δ_J -edge regular IVCNGS.

$$Ad_{\delta_J}(e_{ij})\, e^{iA\beta_J(e_{ij})} = (Ad_{\delta_{1J}^S}(e_{ij})\, e^{iAd_{\beta_{1J}^S}(e_{ij})}, Ad_{\delta_{2J}^S}(e_{ij})\, e^{iAd_{\beta_{2J}^S}(e_{ij})}, Ad_{\delta_{3J}^S}(e_{ij})\, e^{iAd_{\beta_{3J}^S}(e_{ij})})$$

$$=(\sum_{e_{ij}\in R_J} A\delta_{1J}^S(e_{ij})\, e^{i\sum_{e_{ij}\in R_J} A\beta_{1J}^S(e_{ij})}, \sum_{e_{ij}\in R_J} A\delta_{2J}^S(e_{ij})\, e^{i\sum_{e_{ij}\in R_J} A\beta_{2J}^S(e_{ij})},$$

$$\sum_{e_{ij}\in R_J} A\delta_{3J}^S(e_{ij})\, e^{i\sum_{e_{ij}\in R_J} A\beta_{3J}^S(e_{ij})})$$

$$=\sum_{e_{ij}\in R_J} c_1, \sum_{e_{ij}\in R_J} c_2, \sum_{e_{ij}\in R_J} c_3, \sum_{e_{ij}\in R_J} c_4, \sum_{e_{ij}\in R_J} c_5, \sum_{e_{ij}\in R_J} c_6)$$

$$= (x_1 c_1, y_1 c_2, x_2 c_3, y_2 c_4, x_3 c_5, y_3 c_6)$$

Hence, $A(\zeta)$ is δ_J regular IVCNGS.

$$tAd_{\delta_J}(e_{ij})\, e^{itA\beta_J(e_{ij})}$$

$$=(tAd_{\delta_{1J}^S}(e_{ij})\, e^{itAd_{\beta_{1J}^S}(e_{ij})}, tAd_{\delta_{2J}^S}(e_{ij})\, e^{itAd_{\beta_{2J}^S}(e_{ij})}, tAd_{\delta_{3J}^S}(e_{ij})\, e^{itAd_{\beta_{3J}^S}(e_{ij})})$$

$$tAd_{\delta_{1J}^S}(e_{ij})\, e^{iA\beta_{1J}^S(e_{ij})} = \sum_{u_i,u_k\in R_J, k\neq j} A\delta_{1J}^S(e_{ik}) + \sum_{u_k u_j\in R_J, k\neq i} A\delta_{1J}^S(e_{kj}) + A\delta_{1J}^S(e_{ij})$$

$$e^{i\sum_{u_i,u_k\in R_J, k\neq j} A\beta_{1J}^S(e_{ik}) + \sum_{u_k u_j\in R_J, k\neq i} A\beta_{1J}^S(e_{kj}) + A\beta_{1J}^S(e_{ij})}$$

$$=\sum_{u_i,u_k\in R_J, k\neq j} c_1 + \sum_{u_k u_j\in R_J, k\neq i} c_1 + c_1$$

$= c_1(x_1 - 1) + c_1(x_1 - 1) + c_1, \forall\ e_{ij} \in\ R_J = c_1(2x_1 - 1), \forall\ e_{ij} \in R_J$

Similarly, we solve the equation

$$tA\,d_{\delta^S_{1J}}(e_{ij})\, e^{iA\beta^S_{1J}(e_{ij})} =$$
$$(c_1(2x_1 - 1),\ c_2(2y_1 - 1),\ c_3(2x_2 - 1),\ c_4(2y_2 - 1), c_5(2x_3 - 1),\ c_6(2y_3 - 1))$$

Hence, $A(\zeta)$ is also totally δ_J -edge regular IVCNGS.
Conversely, assume that $A(\zeta)$ is both δ_J regular and δ_J -edge regular IVCNGS.
To prove: δ_J is a constant functions
Since, $A(\zeta)$ is δ_J regular IVCNGS.
Also, $A(\zeta)$ is totally δ_J -edge regular IVCNGS.
Then $tA\,d_{\delta^S_{1J}}(e_{ij})\, e^{iA\beta^S_{1J}(e_{ij})} = (x_1, y_1, x_2, y_2, x_3, y_3)$, for all $e_{ij} \in R_J$. By Definition-12

$$tA\,d_{\delta_J}(e_{ij})\, e^{itA\beta_J(e_{ij})}$$

$$=(\ tA\,d_{\delta^S_{1J}}(e_{ij})\, e^{itAd_{\beta^S_{1J}}(e_{ij})},\ tA\,d_{\delta^S_{2J}}(e_{ij})\, e^{itAd_{\beta^S_{2J}}(e_{ij})}, tA\,d_{\delta^S_{3J}}(e_{ij})\, e^{itAd_{\beta^S_{3J}}(e_{ij})}),$$

where

$$tA\,d_{\delta^S_{1J}}(e_{ij})\, e^{itAd_{\beta^S_{1J}}(e_{ij})} = A\,d_{\delta^S_{1J}}(u_i) + A\,d_{\delta^S_{1J}}(u_j)$$

$$-\ 2A\,\delta^S_{1J}(e_{ij})\, e^{i\ Ad_{\beta^S_{1J}}(u_i) +\ Ad_{\beta^S_{1J}}(u_j) - 2A\beta^S_{1J}(e_{ij})}$$

x_1=a_1+a_1- $2A\,\delta^S_{1J}(e_{ij})\, e^{A\beta^S_{1J}(e_{ij})}, \forall\ e_{ij} \in R_J$

$$A\,\delta^S_{1J}(e_{ij})\, e^{A\beta^S_{1J}(e_{ij})} = 2a_1 - x_1, \forall\ e_{ij} \in R_J$$

Similarly, we solve the equation

$$tA\,d_{\delta_J}(e_{ij})\, e^{itA\beta_J(e_{ij})} = (2a_1 - x_1,\ 2b_1 - y_1, 2a_2 - x_2,\ 2b_2 - y_2, 2a_3 - x_3,\ 2b_3 - y_3)$$

Hence, δ_J is a constant functions.

4. APPLICATION

In this section, we examined the impact of the growing popularity of social media platforms such as Facebook, Instagram, Twitter, WhatsApp, Telegram and Wechat, using our proposed IVCNGS the methodology. Due to its founding in 1996, social media has succeeded in to reach over sixty percent of the world's 8.06 billion population. Social media has become an essential component of our daily lives. It has been integrated into many aspects of human life in various human societies, allowing it to be used for a wide range of purposes, including business, games and entertainment, and all other work activities in figure-4.

Figure 4. Activity on social media

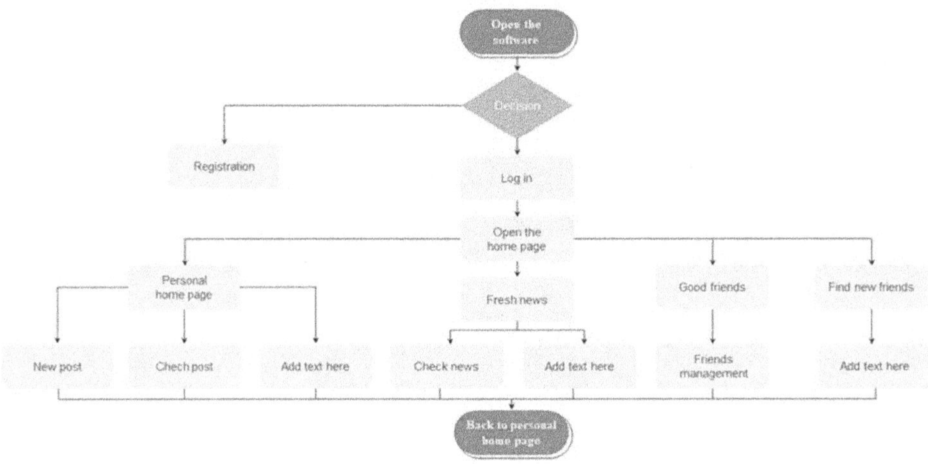

It is used in human activity, and depending on gender and age, these preferences differ significantly. We proceed to use our method to find the most popular social media platform. Figures 4 and 5, 6 illustrate the research's findings, which indicate that younger generations are more likely to list Instagram as their "favourite" social media platform, while older generations are more likely to list Facebook and WhatsApp. Here, the membership function of nodes and edges is considered in the following manner.

- The two distinct strengths and operating styles in each of the social media platforms depicted in figures 5 and 6 are represented by the phase terms and amplitude terms of the node's Inter-valued truth-membership degree, which are taken into consideration for female and male activity on social media platforms between the ages of 18 and 27, respectively.

- The two distinct strengths and operating styles in each of the social media platforms depicted in figures 5 and 6 are represented by the phase terms and amplitude terms of the node's Inter-valued indeterminate-membership degree, which are taken into consideration for female and male activity on social media platforms between the ages of 28 and 37, respectively.
- The two distinct strengths and operating styles in each of the social media platforms depicted in figures 5 and 6 are represented by the phase terms and amplitude terms of the node's Inter-valued false-membership degree, which are taken into consideration for female and male activity on social media platforms between the ages of 38 and 47, respectively.

Figure 5. Female internet users' favorite social media platforms

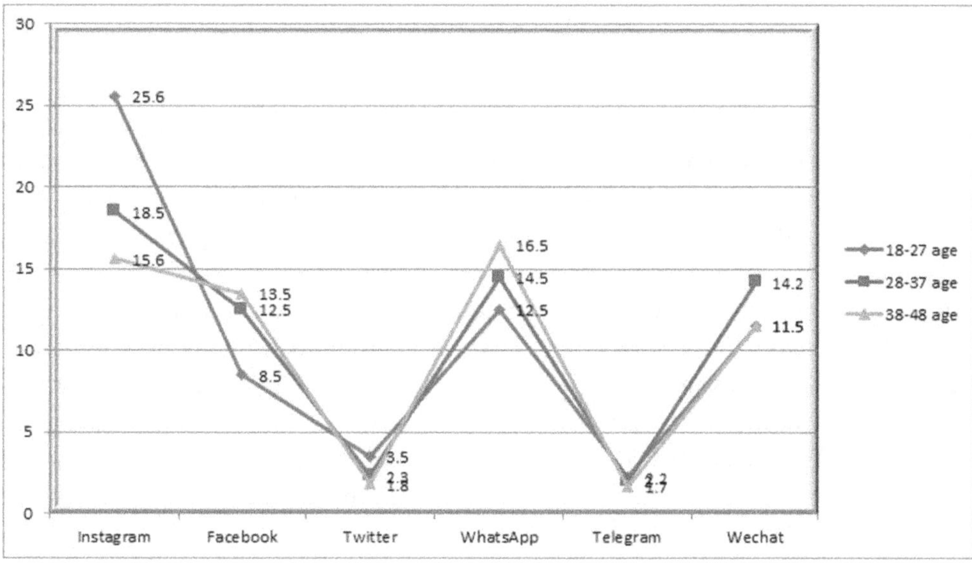

Figure 6. Male internet users' favorite social media platforms

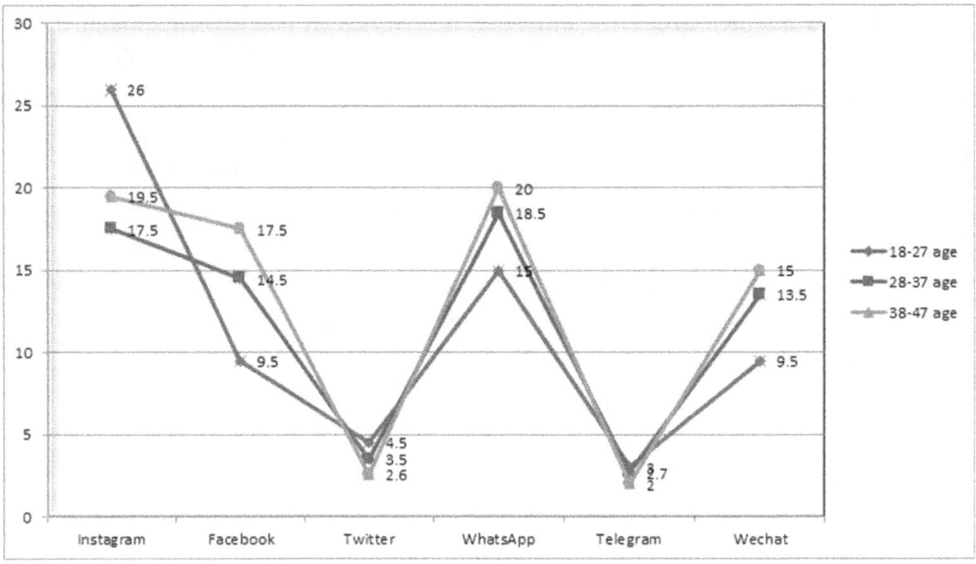

It aids us in communicating with customers, effective social and political campaigns, future events, and online marketing. Social networks are also employed as crucial tools for raising public awareness by rapidly disseminating information sabout any natural disaster and criminal act to a large audience. complex relationships in online organisational networking, most of which are made up of weak ties and temporal change. We use our IVCNGS to compare the data to other information to identify which one is the best. The analysis of these ideas includes a numerous system relationship example. In this example, we examine the network structures of the most widely used social media platforms, such as Facebook (F), Instagram (I), Twitter (T), WhatsApp (W), Telegram (TE), and Wechat (WE), are examined in this example along with their vertices and membership values, as shown in table 1.

Table 1.

social media platform	$\mu^-_{A_1}(a)$	$\mu^+_{A_1}(a)$	$\mu^-_{A_1}(a)$	$\mu^+_{A_2}(a)$	$\mu^-_{A_3}(a)$	$\mu^+_{A_3}(a)$
Instagram (I)	$.23e^{i.24\pi}$	$.25e^{i.36\pi}$	$.15e^{i.16\pi}$	$.18e^{i.17\pi}$	$.13e^{i.18\pi}$	$.15e^{i.19\pi}$
Facebook (F)	$.07e^{i.08\pi}$	$.08e^{i.09\pi}$	$.11e^{i.13\pi}$	$.12e^{i.14\pi}$	$.12e^{i.16\pi}$	$.13e^{i.17\pi}$
Twitter (T)	$.02e^{i.35\pi}$	$.03e^{i.4\pi}$	$.01e^{i.25\pi}$	$.02e^{i.3\pi}$	$.01e^{i.15\pi}$	$.015e^{i.2\pi}$
WhatsApp (W)	$.11e^{i.13\pi}$	$.12e^{i.15\pi}$	$.13e^{i.17\pi}$	$.14e^{i.18\pi}$	$.14e^{i.18\pi}$	$.16e^{i.2\pi}$
Telegram (TE)	$.018e^{i.18\pi}$	$.02e^{i.3\pi}$	$.016e^{i.2\pi}$	$.018e^{i.25\pi}$	$.015e^{i.17\pi}$	$.17e^{i.2\pi}$

social media platform	$\mu^{-}_{A_1}(a)$	$\mu^{+}_{A_1}(a)$	$\mu^{-}_{A_1}(a)$	$\mu^{+}_{A_2}(a)$	$\mu^{-}_{A_3}(a)$	$\mu^{+}_{A_3}(a)$
Wechat (WE)	$.10e^{i.08\pi}$	$.11e^{i.09\pi}$	$.13e^{i.12\pi}$	$.14e^{i.13\pi}$	$.11e^{i.13\pi}$	$.12e^{i.15\pi}$

In this case, we consider a vertex set Q and a set of relations R_j. Consider Q={I, F, T, W, TE, WE} and To study the preference relations R_j for each of these platforms, i=1,2,3, we invited three relations in the field of social media platform issues.

Table 2.

R_i	(I, F)	(I, W)	(I, TE)
R_1	$(.07e^{i.08\pi}, .08e^{i.09\pi}, .14e^{i.15\pi}, .16e^{i.16\pi}, .12e^{i.16\pi}, .13e^{i.17\pi})$,	$(.10e^{i.12\pi}, .12e^{i.4\pi}, .15e^{i.17\pi}, .18e^{i.18\pi}, .14e^{i.18\pi}, .16e^{i.2\pi})$,	$(.018e^{i.18\pi}, .02e^{i.3\pi}, .11e^{i.17\pi}, .12e^{i.2\pi}, .1e^{i.15\pi}, .11e^{i.16\pi})$,
R_2	$(.06e^{i.07\pi}, .07e^{i.08\pi}, .15e^{i.16\pi}, .18e^{i.17\pi}, .13e^{i.18\pi}, .15e^{i.19\pi})$,	$(.11e^{i.13\pi}, .13e^{i.5\pi}, .14e^{i.16\pi}, .17e^{i.17\pi}, .13e^{i.17\pi}, .15e^{i.18\pi})$,	$(.018e^{i.18\pi}, .02e^{i.3\pi}, .10e^{i.16\pi}, .11e^{i.18\pi}, .1e^{i.14\pi}, .12e^{i.18\pi})$,
R_3	$(.07e^{i.08\pi}, .08e^{i.09\pi}, .14e^{i.11\pi}, .16e^{i.12\pi}, .11e^{i.16\pi}, .13e^{i.17\pi})$,	$(.11e^{i.13\pi}, .13e^{i.5\pi}, .14e^{i.16\pi}, .16e^{i.16\pi}, .13e^{i.16\pi}, .14e^{i.18\pi})$,	$(.01e^{i.16\pi}, .016e^{i.2\pi}, .15e^{i.2\pi}, .18e^{i.25\pi}, .13e^{i.18\pi}, .15e^{i.2\pi})$

R_i	(F, T)	(F, W)	(F, WE)
R_1	$(.01e^{i.07\pi}, .02e^{i.08\pi}, .11e^{i.25\pi}, .12e^{i.3\pi}, .12e^{i.16\pi}, .13e^{i.17\pi})$,	$(.07e^{i.08\pi}, .08e^{i.09\pi}, .11e^{i.15\pi}, .12e^{i.16\pi}, .12e^{i.15\pi}, .14e^{i.16\pi})$,	$(.07e^{i.08\pi}, .08e^{i.09\pi}, .14e^{i.12\pi}, .12e^{i.13\pi}, .11e^{i.15\pi}, .12e^{i.17\pi})$,
R_2	$(.02e^{i.08\pi}, .03e^{i.09\pi}, .10e^{i.2\pi}, .11e^{i.28\pi}, .11e^{i.15\pi}, .12e^{i.16\pi})$,	$(.07e^{i.08\pi}, .08e^{i.09\pi}, .12e^{i.16\pi}, .13e^{i.17\pi}, .13e^{i.17\pi}, .15e^{i.18\pi})$,	$(.06e^{i.06\pi}, .07e^{i.08\pi}, .13e^{i.13\pi}, .14e^{i.14\pi}, .11e^{i.16\pi}, .12e^{i.17\pi})$,
R_3	$(.02e^{i.08\pi}, .03e^{i.09\pi}, .09e^{i.18\pi}, .10e^{i.2\pi}, .10e^{i.14\pi}, .12e^{i.15\pi})$,	$(.06e^{i.06\pi}, .07e^{i.08\pi}, .13e^{i.17\pi}, .14e^{i.18\pi}, .14e^{i.18\pi}, .16e^{i.2\pi})$,	$(.07e^{i.08\pi}, .08e^{i.09\pi}, .13e^{i.13\pi}, .14e^{i.14\pi}, .10e^{i.16\pi}, .12e^{i.17\pi})$,

R_i	(W, T)	(W, TE)	(W, WE)
R_1	$(.02e^{i.13\pi}, .03e^{i.15\pi}, .11e^{i.15\pi}, .12e^{i.17\pi}, .13e^{i.11\pi}, .14e^{i.2\pi})$,	$(.018e^{i.13\pi}, .02e^{i.2\pi}, .12e^{i.2\pi}, .13e^{i.25\pi}, .13e^{i.17\pi}, .16e^{i.18\pi})$,	$(.08e^{i.07\pi}, .10e^{i.08\pi}, .13e^{i.17\pi}, .14e^{i.23\pi}, .11e^{i.18\pi}, .16e^{i.2\pi})$,
R_2	$(.02e^{i.13\pi}, .03e^{i.15\pi}, .12e^{i.16\pi}, .13e^{i.17\pi}, .13e^{i.14\pi}, .15e^{i.2\pi})$,	$(.016e^{i.12\pi}, .018e^{i.18\pi}, .13e^{i.3\pi}, .14e^{i.25\pi}, .14e^{i.18\pi}, .17e^{i.2\pi})$,	$(.10e^{i.08\pi}, .11e^{i.08\pi}, .12e^{i.16\pi}, .13e^{i.2\pi}, .1e^{i.16\pi}, .14e^{i.18\pi})$,
R_3	$(.01e^{i.11\pi}, .02e^{i.14\pi}, .13e^{i.17\pi}, .14e^{i.18\pi}, .14e^{i.15\pi}, .16e^{i.2\pi})$,	$(.018e^{i.13\pi}, .02e^{i.2\pi}, .11e^{i.18\pi}, .12e^{i.2\pi}, .13e^{i.16\pi}, .14e^{i.18\pi})$,	$(.10e^{i.08\pi}, .11e^{i.08\pi}, .11e^{i.15\pi}, .12e^{i.2\pi}, .1e^{i.15\pi}, .13e^{i.17\pi})$

- Failure growth increase the phase terms and amplitude terms of the edge's Inter-valued truth-membership degree for the 18–27 age range represent the two different social media platform issues.

- Failure growth increase the phase terms and amplitude terms of the edge's Inter-valued indeterminate-membership degree for the 28–37 age range represent the two different social media platform issues.
- Failure growth increase the phase terms and amplitude terms of the edge's Inter-valued false-membership degree for the 38–47 age range represent the two different social media platform issues.

The membership value of each pair of social media platforms is ascertained through using the definition-5. We can now define the three relations that can be defined on R_1, R_2, and R_3, as we have the set Q={I, F, T, W, TE, WE} defined. As a result, the element of the relationship R_1, R_2, and R_3 whose membership value is most compatible with the other relationships under comparison would be selected.

R_1={(I, W), (F, T), (W, WE)}, R_2={(I,F), (F, WE), (W, TE)}, R_3

={(I,TE), (F, W), (W, T)}

And the corresponding IVCNS are:

δ_1= {(I, W) ($.10e^{i.12\pi}$, $.12e^{i.4\pi}$,$.15e^{i.17\pi}$,$.18e^{i.18\pi}$,$.14e^{i.18\pi}$, $.16e^{i.2\pi}$), (F, T) ($.01e^{i.07\pi}$, $.02e^{i.08\pi}$,$.11e^{i.25\pi}$,$.12e^{i.3\pi}$,$.12e^{i.16\pi}$, $.13e^{i.17\pi}$), (W, WE)} ($.08e^{i.07\pi}$, $.10e^{i.08\pi}$,$.13e^{i.17\pi}$, $.14e^{i.23\pi}$,$.11e^{i.18\pi}$, $.16e^{i.2\pi}$)},

δ_2={(I,F) ($.06e^{i.07\pi}$, $.07e^{i.08\pi}$,$.15e^{i.16\pi}$, $.18e^{i.17\pi}$,$.13e^{i.18\pi}$, $.15e^{i.19\pi}$), (F, WE) ($.06e^{i.06\pi}$, $.07e^{i.08\pi}$,$.13e^{i.13\pi}$, $.14e^{i.14\pi}$,$.11e^{i.16\pi}$, $.12e^{i.17\pi}$), (W, TE) ($.016e^{i.12\pi}$, $.018e^{i.18\pi}$,$.13e^{i.3\pi}$, $.14e^{i.25\pi}$,$.14e^{i.18\pi}$, $.17e^{i.2\pi}$)},

δ_3= {(I,TE) ($.01e^{i.16\pi}$, $.016e^{i.2\pi}$,$.15e^{i.2\pi}$, $.18e^{i.25\pi}$,$.13e^{i.18\pi}$, $.15e^{i.2\pi}$), (F, W) ($.06e^{i.06\pi}$, $.07e^{i.08\pi}$,$.13e^{i.17\pi}$, $.14e^{i.18\pi}$,$.14e^{i.18\pi}$, $.16e^{i.2\pi}$), (W, T) ($.01e^{i.11\pi}$, $.02e^{i.14\pi}$,$.13e^{i.17\pi}$, $.14e^{i.18\pi}$,$.14e^{i.15\pi}$, $.16e^{i.2\pi}$)}

Figure 7. $\zeta = \{\eta, \delta_1, \delta_2, \delta_3\}$

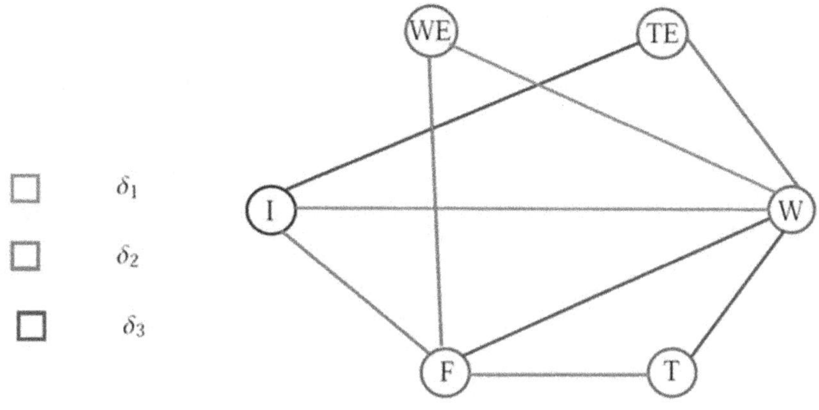

Therefore, the IVCNGS represented in **Figure-7** is $\zeta = \{\eta, \delta_1, \delta_2, \delta_3\}$ is IVCNGS of a GS $\zeta^* = (Q, R_1, R_2, R_3)$. To assess each of these We gave two relation $e_k (k = 1, 2, 3)$, Interval-Valued Complex Neutrosophic Preference relations (IVCNRs) instructions to increase the degree of strength and weakness.

Amplitude Term

The weight of each expert can then be calculate as follows:

$$w_J = \left(\frac{\sum_{e_{ij}\in R_J} Ad_{\delta^S_{1J}}(e_{ij})}{n}, \frac{\sum_{e_{ij}\in R_J} Ad_{\delta^S_{2J}}(e_{ij})}{n}, \frac{\sum_{e_{ij}\in R_J} Ad_{\delta^S_{3J}}(e_{ij})}{n}\right),$$

$\forall n$=number of R_J – edges, S= -,+ and J=1,2,…,k.

The adjacency matrix of amplitude term of a IVCNGS given in given in Figure-7 is

Table 3.

$A\delta_1$	*I*	*F*	*T*	*W*	*TE*	*WE*
I	$\begin{pmatrix}0&0\\0&0\\0&0\end{pmatrix}$	$\begin{pmatrix}0&0\\0&0\\0&0\end{pmatrix}$	$\begin{pmatrix}0&0\\0&0\\0&0\end{pmatrix}$	$\begin{pmatrix}.10&.12\\.15&.18\\.14&.16\end{pmatrix}$	$\begin{pmatrix}0&0\\0&0\\0&0\end{pmatrix}$	$\begin{pmatrix}0&0\\0&0\\0&0\end{pmatrix}$
F	$\begin{pmatrix}0&0\\0&0\\0&0\end{pmatrix}$	$\begin{pmatrix}0&0\\0&0\\0&0\end{pmatrix}$	$\begin{pmatrix}.01&.02\\.11&.12\\.12&.13\end{pmatrix}$	$\begin{pmatrix}0&0\\0&0\\0&0\end{pmatrix}$	$\begin{pmatrix}0&0\\0&0\\0&0\end{pmatrix}$	$\begin{pmatrix}0&0\\0&0\\0&0\end{pmatrix}$
T	$\begin{pmatrix}0&0\\0&0\\0&0\end{pmatrix}$	$\begin{pmatrix}.01&.02\\.11&.12\\.12&.13\end{pmatrix}$	$\begin{pmatrix}0&0\\0&0\\0&0\end{pmatrix}$	$\begin{pmatrix}0&0\\0&0\\0&0\end{pmatrix}$	$\begin{pmatrix}0&0\\0&0\\0&0\end{pmatrix}$	$\begin{pmatrix}0&0\\0&0\\0&0\end{pmatrix}$
W	$\begin{pmatrix}.10&.12\\.15&.18\\.14&.16\end{pmatrix}$	$\begin{pmatrix}0&0\\0&0\\0&0\end{pmatrix}$	$\begin{pmatrix}0&0\\0&0\\0&0\end{pmatrix}$	$\begin{pmatrix}0&0\\0&0\\0&0\end{pmatrix}$	$\begin{pmatrix}0&0\\0&0\\0&0\end{pmatrix}$	$\begin{pmatrix}.08&.10\\.13&.14\\.11&.16\end{pmatrix}$
TE	$\begin{pmatrix}0&0\\0&0\\0&0\end{pmatrix}$	$\begin{pmatrix}0&0\\0&0\\0&0\end{pmatrix}$	$\begin{pmatrix}0&0\\0&0\\0&0\end{pmatrix}$	$\begin{pmatrix}0&0\\0&0\\0&0\end{pmatrix}$	$\begin{pmatrix}0&0\\0&0\\0&0\end{pmatrix}$	$\begin{pmatrix}0&0\\0&0\\0&0\end{pmatrix}$
WE	$\begin{pmatrix}0&0\\0&0\\0&0\end{pmatrix}$	$\begin{pmatrix}0&0\\0&0\\0&0\end{pmatrix}$	$\begin{pmatrix}0&0\\0&0\\0&0\end{pmatrix}$	$\begin{pmatrix}.08&.10\\.13&.14\\.11&.16\end{pmatrix}$	$\begin{pmatrix}0&0\\0&0\\0&0\end{pmatrix}$	$\begin{pmatrix}0&0\\0&0\\0&0\end{pmatrix}$

$A\delta_2$	*I*	*F*	*T*	*W*	*TE*	*WE*
I	$\begin{pmatrix}0&0\\0&0\\0&0\end{pmatrix}$	$\begin{pmatrix}.06&.07\\.15&.18\\.13&.15\end{pmatrix}$	$\begin{pmatrix}0&0\\0&0\\0&0\end{pmatrix}$	$\begin{pmatrix}0&0\\0&0\\0&0\end{pmatrix}$	$\begin{pmatrix}0&0\\0&0\\0&0\end{pmatrix}$	$\begin{pmatrix}0&0\\0&0\\0&0\end{pmatrix}$
F	$\begin{pmatrix}.06&.07\\.15&.18\\.13&.15\end{pmatrix}$	$\begin{pmatrix}0&0\\0&0\\0&0\end{pmatrix}$	$\begin{pmatrix}0&0\\0&0\\0&0\end{pmatrix}$	$\begin{pmatrix}0&0\\0&0\\0&0\end{pmatrix}$	$\begin{pmatrix}0&0\\0&0\\0&0\end{pmatrix}$	$\begin{pmatrix}.06&.07\\.13&.14\\.11&.12\end{pmatrix}$
T	$\begin{pmatrix}0&0\\0&0\\0&0\end{pmatrix}$	$\begin{pmatrix}0&0\\0&0\\0&0\end{pmatrix}$	$\begin{pmatrix}0&0\\0&0\\0&0\end{pmatrix}$	$\begin{pmatrix}0&0\\0&0\\0&0\end{pmatrix}$	$\begin{pmatrix}0&0\\0&0\\0&0\end{pmatrix}$	$\begin{pmatrix}0&0\\0&0\\0&0\end{pmatrix}$
W	$\begin{pmatrix}0&0\\0&0\\0&0\end{pmatrix}$	$\begin{pmatrix}0&0\\0&0\\0&0\end{pmatrix}$	$\begin{pmatrix}0&0\\0&0\\0&0\end{pmatrix}$	$\begin{pmatrix}0&0\\0&0\\0&0\end{pmatrix}$	$\begin{pmatrix}.016&.018\\.13&.14\\.14&.17\end{pmatrix}$	$\begin{pmatrix}0&0\\0&0\\0&0\end{pmatrix}$
TE	$\begin{pmatrix}0&0\\0&0\\0&0\end{pmatrix}$	$\begin{pmatrix}0&0\\0&0\\0&0\end{pmatrix}$	$\begin{pmatrix}0&0\\0&0\\0&0\end{pmatrix}$	$\begin{pmatrix}.016&.018\\.13&.14\\.14&.17\end{pmatrix}$	$\begin{pmatrix}0&0\\0&0\\0&0\end{pmatrix}$	$\begin{pmatrix}0&0\\0&0\\0&0\end{pmatrix}$
WE	$\begin{pmatrix}0&0\\0&0\\0&0\end{pmatrix}$	$\begin{pmatrix}.06&.07\\.13&.14\\.11&.12\end{pmatrix}$	$\begin{pmatrix}0&0\\0&0\\0&0\end{pmatrix}$	$\begin{pmatrix}0&0\\0&0\\0&0\end{pmatrix}$	$\begin{pmatrix}0&0\\0&0\\0&0\end{pmatrix}$	$\begin{pmatrix}0&0\\0&0\\0&0\end{pmatrix}$

$A\delta_3$	*I*	*F*	*T*	*W*	*TE*	*WE*
I	$\begin{pmatrix}0&0\\0&0\\0&0\end{pmatrix}$	$\begin{pmatrix}0&0\\0&0\\0&0\end{pmatrix}$	$\begin{pmatrix}0&0\\0&0\\0&0\end{pmatrix}$	$\begin{pmatrix}0&0\\0&0\\0&0\end{pmatrix}$	$\begin{pmatrix}.01&.016\\.15&.18\\.13&.15\end{pmatrix}$	$\begin{pmatrix}0&0\\0&0\\0&0\end{pmatrix}$
F	$\begin{pmatrix}0&0\\0&0\\0&0\end{pmatrix}$	$\begin{pmatrix}0&0\\0&0\\0&0\end{pmatrix}$	$\begin{pmatrix}0&0\\0&0\\0&0\end{pmatrix}$	$\begin{pmatrix}.06&.07\\.13&.14\\.14&.16\end{pmatrix}$	$\begin{pmatrix}0&0\\0&0\\0&0\end{pmatrix}$	$\begin{pmatrix}0&0\\0&0\\0&0\end{pmatrix}$
T	$\begin{pmatrix}0&0\\0&0\\0&0\end{pmatrix}$	$\begin{pmatrix}0&0\\0&0\\0&0\end{pmatrix}$	$\begin{pmatrix}0&0\\0&0\\0&0\end{pmatrix}$	$\begin{pmatrix}.01&.02\\.13&.14\\.14&.16\end{pmatrix}$	$\begin{pmatrix}0&0\\0&0\\0&0\end{pmatrix}$	$\begin{pmatrix}0&0\\0&0\\0&0\end{pmatrix}$
W	$\begin{pmatrix}0&0\\0&0\\0&0\end{pmatrix}$	$\begin{pmatrix}.06&.07\\.13&.14\\.14&.16\end{pmatrix}$	$\begin{pmatrix}.01&.02\\.13&.14\\.14&.16\end{pmatrix}$	$\begin{pmatrix}0&0\\0&0\\0&0\end{pmatrix}$	$\begin{pmatrix}0&0\\0&0\\0&0\end{pmatrix}$	$\begin{pmatrix}0&0\\0&0\\0&0\end{pmatrix}$
TE	$\begin{pmatrix}.01&.016\\.15&.18\\.13&.15\end{pmatrix}$	$\begin{pmatrix}0&0\\0&0\\0&0\end{pmatrix}$	$\begin{pmatrix}0&0\\0&0\\0&0\end{pmatrix}$	$\begin{pmatrix}0&0\\0&0\\0&0\end{pmatrix}$	$\begin{pmatrix}0&0\\0&0\\0&0\end{pmatrix}$	$\begin{pmatrix}0&0\\0&0\\0&0\end{pmatrix}$
WE	$\begin{pmatrix}0&0\\0&0\\0&0\end{pmatrix}$	$\begin{pmatrix}0&0\\0&0\\0&0\end{pmatrix}$	$\begin{pmatrix}0&0\\0&0\\0&0\end{pmatrix}$	$\begin{pmatrix}0&0\\0&0\\0&0\end{pmatrix}$	$\begin{pmatrix}0&0\\0&0\\0&0\end{pmatrix}$	$\begin{pmatrix}0&0\\0&0\\0&0\end{pmatrix}$

$$Ad_{\delta_1}(e_{I,W}) = (.08,.10,.13,.14,.11,.16),$$

$$Ad_{\delta_1}(e_{F,T}) = (0,0,0,0,0,0),$$

$$Ad_{\delta_1}(e_{W,WE}) = (.10,.12,.15,.18,.14,.16),$$

$$Ad_{\delta_1}(e_{T,W}) = (.18,.24,.39,.44,.37,.45),$$

$$Ad_{\delta_1}(e_{F,W}) = (.19,.24,.39,.44,.37,.45),$$

$$Ad_{\delta_1}(e_{I,TE}) = (.10,.12,.15,.18,.14,.16),$$

$$Ad_{\delta_1}(e_{I,F}) = (.11,.14,.26,.3,.26,.29),$$

$$Ad_{\delta_1}(e_{F,WE}) = (.09,.12,.24,.26,.23,.29),$$

$$Ad_{\delta_1}(e_{W,TE}) = (.18,.22,.28,.32,.25,.32),$$

$$Ad_{\delta_2}(e_{I,W}) = (.076,.088,.28,.32,.27,.32),$$

$$Ad_2(e_{F,T}) = (.12,.14,28,.32,.24,.27),$$

$$Ad_2(e_{W,WE}) = (.076,.088,.26,.28,.25,.29),$$

$$Ad_2(e_{T,W}) = (.016,.018,.13,.14,.14,.17),$$

$$Ad_{\delta_2}(e_{F,W}) = (.136,.158,.41,.46,.38,.44),$$

$$Ad_{\delta_2}(e_{I,TE}) = (.076,.088,.27,.32,.27,.32),$$

$$Ad_2(e_{I,F}) = (.06,.07,.13,.14,.11,.12),$$

$$Ad_{\delta_2}(e_{F,WE}) = (.06,.07,.15,.18,.13,.15),$$

$$Ad_{\delta_1}(e_{W,TE}) = (0,0,0,0,0,0),$$

$$Ad_{\delta_3}(e_{I,W}) = (.08,.106,.41,.46,.41,.47),$$

$$Ad_{\delta_3}(e_{F,T}) = (.07,.09,.26,.28,.28,.32) = Ad_{\delta_3}(e_{W,WE}) ,$$

$$Ad_{\delta_3}(e_{T,W}) = (.06,.07,.13,.14,.14,.16),$$

$$Ad_{\delta_3}(e_{F,W}) = (.01,.02,.13,.14,.14,.16),$$

$$Ad_{\delta_3}(e_{I,TE}) = (0,0,0,0,0,0),$$

$$Ad_{\delta_3}(e_{I,F}) = (.07,.076,.28,.32,.27,.31),$$

$$Ad_{\delta_3}(e_{F,WE}) = (.06,.07,.13,.14,.14,.16),$$

$$Ad_{\delta_3}(e_{W,TE}) = (.08,.106,.41,.46,.41,.47).$$

$$W_1 = (0.3433,0.4333,0.6633,0.7533,0.6233,0.77),$$

$$W_2 = (0.2067,0.24,0.6367,0.72,0.5967,0.6933)$$

$$W_3 = (0.1667,0.2093,0.67,0.74,0.69,0.79)$$

We use the aggregation operator to combine all individual IVCNWA $M = \left(u_{ij}^J\right)_{9\times 9}$, (J=1,2,3) into the collective $M = (u_{ij})_{9\times 9}$. We use the Interval-Valued Complex Neutrosophic Weighted Averaging (IVCNWA) Operator [38] to combine all individual IVCNRs in amplitude term.

$$u_i^k = IVCNWA\left(u_{ij}^1, u_{ij}^2, \ldots, u_{ij}^s\right) = \left(1 - \left(\prod_{J=1}^{3} (1 - \left(A\delta_{1J}^{-}(e_k)\right)_{ij}{}^2\right)^{W_J}\right),$$

$$1-\left(\prod_{J=1}^{3}((1-(A\delta_{2J}^{+}(e_k))_{ij}{}^{2})^{W_J}\right)),\left(1-\left(\prod_{J=1}^{3}((1-(A\delta_{3J}^{-}(e_k))_{ij}{}^{2})^{W_J}\right)\right),$$

$$1-\left(\prod_{J=1}^{3}((1-(A\delta_{3J}^{+}(e_k))_{ij}{}^{2})^{W_J}\right))$$

The aggregated value for u_{12} is shown as follows:

Therefore, u_{12}= (0.0881, 0.1492, 0.0143, 0.0234, 0.0156, 0.0156).

Similarly, we can use IVCNWA to calculate other aggregated values. M shows overall aggregated values.

Table 4.

M	*I*	*F*	*T*	*W*	*TE*	*WE*
I	$\begin{pmatrix}0&0\\0&0\\0&0\end{pmatrix}$	$\begin{pmatrix}.0881&.1492\\.0143&.0234\\.0101&.0156\end{pmatrix}$	$\begin{pmatrix}0&0\\0&0\\0&0\end{pmatrix}$	$\begin{pmatrix}.0034&.0062\\.0014&.0245\\.0122&.0197\end{pmatrix}$	$\begin{pmatrix}.0000&.0001\\.0149&.0245\\.0105&.0173\end{pmatrix}$	$\begin{pmatrix}0&0\\0&0\\0&0\end{pmatrix}$
F	$\begin{pmatrix}.0881&.1492\\.0143&.0234\\.0101&.0156\end{pmatrix}$	$\begin{pmatrix}0&0\\0&0\\0&0\end{pmatrix}$	$\begin{pmatrix}.0000&.0001\\.0080&.0108\\.0075&.0130\end{pmatrix}$	$\begin{pmatrix}.0006&.0010\\.0113&.0145\\.0135&.0207\end{pmatrix}$	$\begin{pmatrix}0&0\\0&0\\0&0\end{pmatrix}$	$\begin{pmatrix}.0007&.0011\\.0107&.0141\\.0072&.0100\end{pmatrix}$
T	$\begin{pmatrix}0&0\\0&0\\0&0\end{pmatrix}$	$\begin{pmatrix}.0000&.0001\\.0080&.0108\\.0075&.0130\end{pmatrix}$	$\begin{pmatrix}0&0\\0&0\\0&0\end{pmatrix}$	$\begin{pmatrix}.0000&.0000\\.0113&.0145\\.0135&.0207\end{pmatrix}$	$\begin{pmatrix}0&0\\0&0\\0&0\end{pmatrix}$	$\begin{pmatrix}0&0\\0&0\\0&0\end{pmatrix}$
W	$\begin{pmatrix}.0034&.0062\\.0014&.0245\\.0122&.0197\end{pmatrix}$	$\begin{pmatrix}.0006&.0010\\.0113&.0145\\.0135&.0207\end{pmatrix}$	$\begin{pmatrix}.0000&.0000\\.0113&.0145\\.0135&.0207\end{pmatrix}$	$\begin{pmatrix}0&0\\0&0\\0&0\end{pmatrix}$	$\begin{pmatrix}.0000&.0000\\.0107&.0141\\.0117&.02012\end{pmatrix}$	$\begin{pmatrix}.0022&.0043\\.0112&.0148\\.0075&.0197\end{pmatrix}$
TE	$\begin{pmatrix}.0000&.0001\\.0149&.0245\\.0105&.0173\end{pmatrix}$	$\begin{pmatrix}0&0\\0&0\\0&0\end{pmatrix}$	$\begin{pmatrix}0&0\\0&0\\0&0\end{pmatrix}$	$\begin{pmatrix}.0000&.0000\\.0107&.0141\\.0117&.02012\end{pmatrix}$	$\begin{pmatrix}0&0\\0&0\\0&0\end{pmatrix}$	$\begin{pmatrix}0&0\\0&0\\0&0\end{pmatrix}$
WE	$\begin{pmatrix}0&0\\0&0\\0&0\end{pmatrix}$	$\begin{pmatrix}.0007&.0011\\.0107&.0141\\.0072&.0100\end{pmatrix}$	$\begin{pmatrix}0&0\\0&0\\0&0\end{pmatrix}$	$\begin{pmatrix}.0022&.0043\\.0112&.0148\\.0075&.0197\end{pmatrix}$	$\begin{pmatrix}0&0\\0&0\\0&0\end{pmatrix}$	$\begin{pmatrix}0&0\\0&0\\0&0\end{pmatrix}$

Displays the results as an aggregate M. Using the δ_J- degree of IVCNGSWA Operator, compute a collective IVCNGSE u_i (i=1,2,...,6) of the I (u_1), F (u_2), T (u_3), W (u_4), TE (u_5), WE (u_6).

$$Md_{\delta_J}(u) = (\mathrm{Md}_{\delta_{1J}^{-}}(\mathrm{u}), \mathrm{Md}_{\delta_{1J}^{+}}(\mathrm{u}),$$

$$\mathrm{Md}_{\delta_{2J}^{-}}(\mathrm{u}), \mathrm{Md}_{\delta_{2J}^{+}}(\mathrm{u}), \mathrm{Md}_{\delta_{3J}^{-}}(\mathrm{u}), \mathrm{Md}_{\delta_{3J}^{+}}(\mathrm{u})),$$

where

$$\mathrm{Md}_{\delta_{1J}^{-}}(\mathrm{u}) = \sum \delta_{1J}^{-}(\mathrm{u}_{\mathrm{jz}})_{\mathrm{z}=1}^{\mathrm{k}},$$

$$\mathrm{Md}_{\delta_{1J}^{+}}(\mathrm{u}) = \sum \delta_{1J}^{+}(\mathrm{u}_{\mathrm{jz}})_{\mathrm{z}=1}^{\mathrm{k}},$$

$$\mathrm{Md}_{\delta_{2J}^{-}}(\mathrm{u}) = \sum \delta_{2J}^{-}(\mathrm{u}_{\mathrm{jz}})_{\mathrm{z=1}}^{\mathrm{k}},$$

$$\mathrm{Md}_{\delta_{2J}^{+}}(\mathrm{u}) = \sum \delta_{2J}^{+}(\mathrm{u}_{\mathrm{jz}})_{\mathrm{z=1}}^{\mathrm{k}},$$

$$\mathrm{Md}_{\delta_{3J}^{-}}(\mathrm{u}) = \sum \delta_{3J}^{-}(\mathrm{u}_{\mathrm{jz}})_{\mathrm{z=1}}^{\mathrm{k}},$$

$$Md_{\delta_J}(u_2) = (.0894, .1514, .0443, .0628, .0383, .0593),$$

$$Md_{\delta_J}(u_3) = (.0000, .0001, .0193, .0253, .0243, .0337),$$

$$Md_{\delta_J}(u_4) = (.0062, .0115, .0459, .0824, .0584, .1009),$$

Evaluate the score function

$$S(u_k)$$

$$= \left((Md_{\delta_{1J}^{-}})^2 - (Md_{\delta_{1J}^{+}})^2 + (Md_{\delta_{2J}^{-}})^2 - (Md_{\delta_{2J}^{+}})^2 + (Md_{\delta_{3J}^{-}})^2 - (Md_{\delta_{3J}^{+}})^2 \right)$$

of u_k (k=1,2,3,4,5,6) and rated all the management organization modules I (u_1), F (u_2), T (u_3), W (u_4), TE (u_5), WE (u_6).

$S(u_5) = 0.0010$, $S(u_6) = 0.0007$,

Then $S(u_4) > S(u_3) > S(u_5) > S(u_6) > S(u_2) > S(u_1)$. Therefore, when compared to other facilities, the best ones for managing all sorts of technology are user and organization is correct valued data more efficiently and extremely secure (u_4).

Similarly, we can verify the phase terms.

4.1 Algorithm

We now explain the detailed mathematical procedure of our method, which is used in the algorithm that follows.

1. Put the membership values $\eta = ([\eta_1^- e^{i\alpha_1^-}, \eta_1^+ e^{i\alpha_1^+}], [\eta_2^- e^{i\alpha_2^-}, \eta_2^+ e^{i\alpha_2^+}], [\eta_3^- e^{i\alpha_3^-}, \eta_3^+ e^{i\alpha_3^+}])$ in the set $Q = \{a_1, a_2, \ldots, a_n\}$ of the social media platforms (vertices).
2. Input the membership values

$$\delta_J = (\delta_{1J}, \delta_{2J}, \delta_{3J})$$
$$= \left([\delta_{1J}^- e^{i\beta_{1J}^-},\ \delta_{1J}^+ e^{i\beta_{1J}^+}],\ [\delta_{2J}^- e^{i\beta_{2J}^-},\ \delta_{2J}^+ e^{i\beta_{2J}^+}],\ [\delta_{3J}^- e^{i\beta_{3J}^-},\ \delta_{3J}^+ e^{i\beta_{3J}^+}] \right)$$

of the edges $a_i a_j \in R_J$ such that

$$\delta_{1J}^-(a,b)\, e^{i\beta_{1J}^-(ab)} \le min\{\eta_1^-(a), \eta_1^-(b)\}\, e^{i min\{\alpha_1^-(a),\ \alpha_1^-(b)\}},$$

$$\delta_{1J}^+(a,b)\, e^{i\beta_{1J}^+(ab)} \le min\{\eta_1^+(a), \eta_1^+(b)\}\, e^{i min\{\alpha_1^+(a),\ \alpha_1^+(b)\}},$$

$$\delta_{2J}^-(a,b)\, e^{i\beta_{2J}^-(ab)} \le max\{\eta_2^-(a), \eta_2^-(b)\}\, e^{i max\{\alpha_2^-(a),\ \alpha_2^-(b)\}},$$

$$\delta_{2J}^+(a,b)\, e^{i\beta_{2J}^+(ab)} \le max\{\eta_2^+(a), \eta_2^+(b)\}\, e^{i max\{\alpha_2^+(a),\ \alpha_2^+(b)\}},$$

$$\delta_{3J}^-(a,b)\, e^{i\beta_{3J}^-(ab)} \le max\{\eta_3^-(a), \eta_3^-(b)\}\, e^{i max\{\alpha_3^-(a),\ \alpha_3^-(b)\}},$$

$$\delta_{3J}^+(a,b)\, e^{i\beta_{3J}^+(ab)} \le max\{\eta_3^+(a), \eta_3^+(b)\}\, e^{i max\{\alpha_3^+(a),\ \alpha_3^+(b)\}}$$

$$\delta_{1J}^+(a,b) + \delta_{2J}^+(a,b) + \delta_{3J}^+(a,b) \le 3,\ \forall\ (a,b) \in R_J \text{ and } J = 1, 2, \ldots, k.$$

3. Create relations $R_1, R_2, \ldots, R_k$ between the set of social media platforms Q that are mutually disjoint, reflexive, and symmetric, and find each relationship as illustrative of a certain stage of development between those two social media platforms.
4. Construct a graph structure using a set of social media platforms that are related, then determine the degree of a R_J edge for each $AR_1, AR_2, \ldots, AR_k$.
5. Enter a calculation, such as "weight of each exper"
6. Calculate IVCNA \ref{0.2} and IVCNWA.

7. By assessing the score function

$$= \left(\left(Md_{\delta_{1J}^{-}} \right)^2 - \left(Md_{\delta_{1J}^{+}} \right)^2 + \left(Md_{\delta_{2J}^{-}} \right)^2 - \left(Md_{\delta_{2J}^{+}} \right)^2 + \left(Md_{\delta_{3J}^{-}} \right)^2 - \left(Md_{\delta_{3J}^{+}} \right)^2 \right)$$

of u_k (k=1,2,3,4,5,6), it is possible to identify the facilities that, in comparison to other facilities, are the best at managing all social media platforms at a high level.

Discussion

E. Sampathkumar (2006) introduced the idea of Generalized GSs, and T. Dinesh et al. (2010) introduced the idea of Generalized FGSs. The SVNGS concept was developed recently by Akram (2017). Edge Regular Intuitionistic FGS was first proposed by M.G. Karunambigai et al. (2010). But understanding the IVCNGS with adjacency matrix edge regular concept is crucial when an IVCNGS develops in a real-world scenario. The research's findings could have a variety of uses, especially for the identification of optimal functions. The Application section contains its manifestations. Moreover, we found some advantages and isomorphic characteristics of the edges adjacency matrix of δ_J for a particular relationship in this study.

5. CONCLUSION AND FUTURE WORKS

In comparison to traditional fuzzy sets, the Set IVCNS, an extension of the IVNS, provides a more realistic description of uncertainty. Through fuzzy control, it can be used in a variety of ways. In this study work, we also introduce the IVCNGS adjacency matrix concept and the notion of an isomorphic adjacency matrix. Additionally introduced are IVCNGS. Using an example, we examine certain IVCNGS adjacency matrix properties. Additionally, we introduce the concepts of an IVCNGS adjacency matrix that is edge regular and totally edge regular. It is described under what circumstances the edge regular adjacency matrix IVCNGS and totally edge regular adjacency matrix IVCNGS are equal. To help explain our suggested IVCNGS principles, we outline the advantages of the IVCNGS and show how it can be applied in social environments to investigate the impacts of the growing use of social media platforms. We also create an algorithm that improves the readability of the application's main functions. Future work in this area could take many different paths if the adjacency matrix IVCNGS is applied. Determine the Wiener index, connectivity index, and edge regular properties using IVCNGS.

REFERENCES

Akram, M., & Akmal, R. (2016). operations on Intuitionistic Fuzzy Graph Structures. *Fuzzy Inf.Eng*, 8(4), 389–410. DOI:10.1016/j.fiae.2017.01.001

Akram, M., Bashir, A., & Samanta, S. (2020). Article. *International Journal of Applied and Computational Mathematics*, 6–58.

Akram, M., Koam, A. N. A., & Liu, P. (2020). Decision-Making Analysis Based on Fuzzy Graph Structures. *Hindawi Mathematical Problems in Engineering*.

Akram, M., & Naz, S. (2019). A Novel Decision-Making Approach under Complex Pythagorean Fuzzy Environment. *Mathematical & Computational Applications*, 24(3), 73. DOI:10.3390/mca24030073

Akram, , & Sarwar, . (2017a). Novel multiple criteria decision making methods based on bipolar neutrosophic sets and bipolar neutrosophic graphs. *International Journal of Pure and Applied Mathematics*, 38, 368–389.

Akram, , & Sarwar, . (2017b). Bipolar neutrosophic graph structures. *J. Indones. Math. Soc*, 23(1), 55–76.

Akram, M., Sattar, A., Karaaslan, F., & Samanta, S. (2021). Extension of competition graphs under complex fuzzy environment. *Complex & Intelligent Systems*, 7(1), 539–558. DOI:10.1007/s40747-020-00217-5

Ali, Dat, Son, Smarandache. (2018). Interval Complex Neutrosophic Set: Formulationand Applications in Decision-Making. *Int. J. Fuzzy Syst, 20*(3).

Alkouri, A., & Salleh, A. (2012). Complex intuitionistic fuzzy sets. *AIP Conference Proceedings*, 14, 464–470. DOI:10.1063/1.4757515

Arumugam, S., & Velammal, S. (1998). Edge domination in graphs. *Taiwanese Journal of Mathematics*, 2(2), 177–196. DOI:10.11650/twjm/1500406930

Atanassov, K. T. (1986). Intuitionistic fuzzy sets. *Fuzzy Sets and Systems*, 20(1), 87–96. DOI:10.1016/S0165-0114(86)80034-3

Atanassove, K. T., & Gargov, G. (1989). Interval valued intuitionistic fuzzy sets. *Fuzzy Sets and Systems*, 31(3), 343–349. DOI:10.1016/0165-0114(89)90205-4

Dinesh, T., & Ramakrishnan, T. V. (2011). Generalised Fuzzy Graph Structures. *Applied Mathematical Sciences*, 5(4), 173–180.

Ezhilmaran, D., & Sankar, K. (2015). Morphism of bipolar intuitionistic fuzzy graphs. *Journal of Discrete Mathematical Sciences and Cryptography*, 18(5), 605–621. DO I:10.1080/09720529.2015.1013673

Garg, H., & Rani, D. (2019). Complex Interval-Valued Intuitionistic Fuzzy Sets and their Aggregation Operator. *Fundamenta Informaticae*, 164(1), 61–101. DOI:10.3233/FI-2019-1755

Greenfield, S., Chiclana, F., & Dick, S. (2016). Interval-valued complex fuzzy logic. *Proceedings of the IEEE International Conference on Fuzzy Systems.*

Hussain, Broumi, & Jun. (2019). Intuitionistic Bipolar neutrosophic set and its Application to Intuitionistic Bipolar neutrosophic Graph. *Annals of Communications in Mathematics, 2*(2), 121-140.

Karunambigai, Palanivel, & Sivasankar. (2015). Edge Regular Intuitionistic Fuzzy Graph. *Advances in Fuzzy sets and Systems, 20*(1), 25-46.

Lee, K.-M. (2000). Bipolar-valued fuzzy sets and their basic operations. *Proc. Int. Conf.*

Milo, D., Fiedman, R., & Kandel, M. (2002). Complex fuzzy sets. *IEEE Transactions on Fuzzy Systems*, 10(2), 171–186. DOI:10.1109/91.995119

Mordeson, J. N., & Peng, C. S. (1994). Operations on fuzzy graphs. *Information Sciences*, 79(3-4), 159–170. DOI:10.1016/0020-0255(94)90116-3

Muhammad Akram, S. (2019). Simplified interval-valued Pythagorean fuzzy graphs with application. *Complex & Intelligent Systems*, 5(2), 229–253. DOI:10.1007/s40747-019-0106-3

Nagoor Gani, A., & Radha, K. (2008). On Regular Fuzzy Graphs. *The Journal of Physiological Sciences; JPS*, 12, 33–40.

Ramot, D., Friedman, M., Langholz, G. A., & Kandel, A. (2003). Kandel, Complex fuzzy logic. *IEEE Transactions on Fuzzy Systems*, 11(4), 450–461. DOI:10.1109/TFUZZ.2003.814832

Rani, D., & Garg, H. (2017). Distance measures between the complex intuitionistic fuzzy sets and its applications to the decision-making process. *International Journal for Uncertainty Quantification*, 7(5), 423–439. DOI:10.1615/Int.J.UncertaintyQuantification.2017020356

Rani, D., & Garg, H. (2018). Complex intuitionistic fuzzy power aggregation operators and their applications in multi-criteria decision making. *Expert Systems: International Journal of Knowledge Engineering and Neural Networks*, 35(6), e12325. DOI:10.1111/exsy.12325

Rosenfeld, A. (1975). Fuzzy graphs. In *Fuzzy Sets and their Applications*. Academic Press.

Sampathkumar, E. (2006). Generalized graph structures. *Bulletin of Kerala Mathematics Association*, 3(2), 65–123.

Satham Hussain, S. (2021). Interval intuitionistic neutrosophic sets with its applications to interval intuitionistic neutrosophic graphs and climatic analysis. *Computational & Applied Mathematics*, 40(4), 121. DOI:10.1007/s40314-021-01504-8

Shamim Kaiser, M. (2018). Article. *IEEE Transactions on Intelligent Transportation Systems*, 1524–9050.

Shannon & Atanassov. (1994). A first stap to a theory of the Intuitionistic fuzzy graph. *Proceeding of FUBEST*, 59-61.

Smarandache, F. (1998). *Neutrosophy, Neutrosophic Probability, Set, and Logic, Amer*. Res. Press.

Smarandache, F. (2010). Neutrosophic set, a generalisation of the intuitionistic fuzzy sets. *International Journal of Pure and Applied Mathematics*, 24, 289–297.

Turksen, I. B. (1986). Turksen, Interval valued fuzzy sets based on normal forms. *Fuzzy Sets and Systems*, 20(2), 191–10. DOI:10.1016/0165-0114(86)90077-1

Ullah, Mahmood, Ali, & Jan. (2019). On some distance measures of complex Pythagorean fuzzy sets and their applications in pattern recognition. *Complex Intell. Syst.*

Yager, R. R. (2013). Pythagorean fuzzy subsets. *Proceedings of the Joint IFSA World Congress and NAFIPS Annual Meeting*.

Yager, R. R. (2014). Pythagorean membership grades in multi-criteria decision making. *IEEE Transactions on Fuzzy Systems*, 22(4), 958–965. DOI:10.1109/TFUZZ.2013.2278989

Yager, R. R., & Abbasov, A. M. (2013). Pythagorean membership grades, complex numbers, and decision making. *International Journal of Intelligent Systems*, 28(5), 436–452. DOI:10.1002/int.21584

Yazdanbakhsh, O., & Dick, S. (2018). A systematic review of complex fuzzy sets and logic. *Fuzzy Sets and Systems*, 338, 1–2. DOI:10.1016/j.fss.2017.01.010

Zadeh, L. A. (1965). Fuzzy sets. *Information and Control*, 8(3), 338–353. DOI:10.1016/S0019-9958(65)90241-X

Zadeh, L. A. (1971). Similarity Relations and fuzzy Ordering. *Information and Control*, 3, 177–200.

Zadeh, L. A. (1975). The concept of a linguistic and application to approximate reasoning I. *Information Sciences*, 8(3), 199–249. DOI:10.1016/0020-0255(75)90036-5

Zhang, W. R. (1994). Bipolar fuzzy sets and relations: a computational framework for cognitive modeling and multi agent decision analysis. *Proceedings of IEEE Conf.*, 305-309.

Zhang, W. R. (1998). Bipolar fuzzy sets. *Proc. of FUZZ-IEEE*, 835-840.

Zhang & Xu. (2014). Extension of TOPSIS to multiple-criteria decision making with Pythagorean fuzzy sets. *Int. J. Intell. System, 29*.

Chapter 6
An Approach of Selecting Best School Using Neutrosophic Hyper Soft Set

S. Santhi
VISTAS, India

S. Sandhiya
VISTAS, India

K. Srinivasan
VISTAS, India

ABSTRACT

Decision-making analysis is one of the best ways to choose the perfect alternative for any specified purpose. Fuzzy theory overcomes the vague and uncertain conditions. Neutrosophic set was an extension of fuzzy set theory. Application of neutrosophic hyper soft set is a major tool in solving the multi-criteria decision-making problem. In this chapter, a numerical example has been framed to select the best school in the certain locality using the proposed algorithm. The parameters have been given in the form of neutrosophic hyper soft set. Comparison was done with the existing method.

DOI: 10.4018/979-8-3693-2085-3.ch006

1. INTRODUCTION

In many real life situations some of the collective data and information are vague and uncertain. Zadeh (Zadeh, 1965) introduced the idea of Fuzzy Set theory. It paves an important way to solve the difficulty in dealing with uncertainty. Fuzzy set contains the degree of membership conferring the elements belongs to the set entirely. The membership belong to the unit interval (Abbas, Murtaza, Smarandache, 2020). In fuzzy set theory the membership values are converted into crisp values by using different ranking functions. In many situations the decision maker may overcome the information about the belongings and non – belongings of the objects. In such cases fuzzy system needs an extension to overcome the situations. Atanassov (Atanassov, 1986) developed the idea of Intuitionistic Fuzzy set to deal with inaccurate information in membership and non- membership function. Since there is a possibility to exceed the value of unit interval, the notion of Pythagorean Fuzzy Set was developed. Later many authors introduced various operational laws and several aggregation operators.

Molodtsov defined the concept of Soft Set theory to deal with the parameterised family of the set of universe .Soft sets has been used to construct the connection between alternatives and attributes in Multi criteria Decision Making problems . Maji et al further prolonged the idea with basic operations and their properties. Many decision making ideas had been done with the combination of Fuzzy Set and Soft Set. Similarly Intuitionistic Fuzzy Soft Set were also developed to overcome decision making theory and many aggregation operators has been applied to solve the problems.

To deal with indertermine information apart from belonging and non-belonging of the information Florentin Smarandache defined the concept of Neutrosophic Fuzzy Set. Maji et al (Maji, Biwas, Roy, 2003) proposed many basic operations and properties to solve Neutrosophic Fuzzy Soft Sets. When the decision making problems contains the subattributes of the attributes Smarandache (Smarandache, 2018) proposed the idea of Hyper Soft Set from the idea of soft set. Generally Fuzzy Soft set has been framed in the matrix form. A decision matrix is a list of values in rows and columns that allows an analyst to systematically identify, analyse, and rate the performance of relationships between sets of values and information. There are many criteria involved in the decision making process such as Maxmin, Maximax, Laplace, Hurwich criteria etc.,

Generally fuzzy numbers measures the range of uncertainty, intuitionistic fuzzy numbers measures truth and falsity, while Neutrosophic fuzzy set measures the indeterminacy value of the observations. Here Neutrosophic Hyper Soft Sets has been applied to select the best school in a locality under various criteria.

2. PRELIMINARIES

2.1 Fuzzy Set

If X is a collection of objects denoted generically by x, then fuzzy set $\widetilde{A}$ in X is a set of ordered pairs: $\widetilde{A} = \{(x, \mu_{\widetilde{A}}(x)|x \in X)\}$

$\mu_{\widetilde{A}}(x)$ is called the membership function which maps X to the membership space M and $\mu_{\widetilde{A}}(x)$ is the grade of membership (also degree of compatibility or degree of truth) of x in A.

$$\mu_{\widetilde{A}}(x) = \begin{Bmatrix} 1 \; if x \in X \\ 0 \; if x \notin X \end{Bmatrix}$$

In the theory of fuzzy sets, the degree of membership is determined by generalising the characteristic function and is called the membership function. Instead of the set {0,1}, the interval [0,1] is used and the membership function is expressed as $\mu_{\widetilde{A}}(x):x \rightarrow [0,1]$ (or) $0 \leq \mu_{\widetilde{A}}(x) \geq 1$. $\mu_{\widetilde{A}}(x) = 0$ indicates that x is not a member of A and $\mu_{\widetilde{A}}(x) = 1$ indicates that x is a member of A.

2.2 Neutrosophic Sets

Let X be an universal set and $x \in X$. A Neutrosophic set A in X is characterized by a truth, indeterminacy and falsity membership function which are respectively denoted as T_A, I_A *and* F_A are real standard elements of [0,1] and denoted by A = $\{ \langle x, T_A(x), I_A(x), F_A(x) \rangle | x \in X, T_A, I_A, F_A \in]0^-, 1^+[\}$. There is no restriction on the sum of $T_A(x), I_A(X)$ and $F_A(X)$, so

$$0^- \leq T_A(X) + I_A(X) + F_A(X) \leq 3^+$$

2.3 Soft Sets

Let X be a universal set, $P(X)$ be the power set of X and E be the set of all parameters. A soft set (φ, E) on X is defined by

$$(\varphi, E) = \{(e, \varphi(e)) : e \in E, \varphi(e) \in P(X)\} \; where \varphi : E \rightarrow P(X).$$

2.4 Fuzzy Soft Sets

Let X be a universal set, $IP(X)$ be the set of all fuzzy sets of X and E be the set of all parameters. Then a pair (φ, E) is called a fuzzy soft set on X, where $\varphi : E \rightarrow I(X)$.

2.5 Neutrosophic Soft Sets

Let X be the universal set and E be the set of attributes with respect to X. Let $P(X)$ be the set of neutrosophic values of X and $A \subseteq E$. A pair (φ, A) is called a neutrosophic soft set over X and its mapping is given by $\varphi : A \rightarrow P(X)$

2.6 Hypersoft Sets

Let X be the universal set and $P(X)$ be the power set of X. Consider $e_1, e_2, e_3, \ldots,$ e_n, for $n \geq 1$ be n well defined attributes, whose corresponding sub-attributes of e_i are respectively the sets $E_1, E_2, E_3, \ldots, E_n$ with $E_i \cap E_j = \emptyset$ for $i \neq j$ and $i,j \in \{1,2,3\ldots,n\}$ then the pair $(\varphi, E_1 \times E_2 \times \ldots \times E_n)$ is said to be hypersoft set over X where $\varphi : E_1 \times E_2 \times \ldots \times E_n \rightarrow P(X)$.

2.7 Fuzzy Hypersoft Sets

Let X be the universal set and $FP(X)$ be a family of all fuzzy set over X and $E_1, E_2, E_3, \ldots E_n$ the pairwise disjoint sets of parameters. Let A_i be the nonempty subset of E_i for each $i = 1,2,3\ldots n$. A fuzzy hypersoft set defined as the pair $(\varphi, A_1 \times A_2 \times \ldots \times A_n)$ where $\varphi : A_1 \times A_2 \times \ldots \times A_n \rightarrow FP(X)$.

Examples: Consider the universe of discourse $X = \{x_1 x_2, x_3\}$ be the set of all students enrolled in the university and and $\{e_1 = \textit{University A},\ e_2 = \textit{University B},\ e_3 = \textit{University C}\}$ be a collection of attributes with following corresponding attributes value;

$$\textit{University A} = E_1 = \{a_{11} = CSE, a_{12} = IT\},$$

$$\textit{University B} = E_2 = \{a_{21} = CIVIL, a_{22} = ECE, a_{23} = EEE\}$$

and $\textit{University C} = E_3 = \{a_{31} = \textit{Data Science},\ a_{32} = AIML\}$.

Let $\widehat{A} = E_1 \times E_2 \times E_3$ be a set of attributes

$$\widehat{A} = E_1 \times E_2 \times E_3 = \{a_{11}, a_{12}\} \times \{a_{21}, a_{22}, a_{23}\} \times \{a_{31}, a_{32}\}$$

$$\left\{ \begin{array}{l} (a_{11}, a_{21}, a_{31}), (a_{11}, a_{21}, a_{32}), (a_{11}, a_{22}, a_{31}), (a_{11}, a_{22}, a_{32}), (a_{11}, a_{23}, a_{31}), (a_{11}, a_{23}, a_{32}) \\ (a_{12}, a_{21}, a_{31}), (a_{12}, a_{21}, a_{32}), (a_{12}, a_{22}, a_{31}), (a_{12}, a_{22}, a_{32}), (a_{12}, a_{23}, a_{31}), (a_{12}, a_{23}, a_{32}) \end{array} \right\}$$

where

$$\left\{\begin{array}{c}\widehat{a_1} = (a_{11},a_{21},a_{31})\ ;\widehat{a_2} = (a_{11},a_{21},a_{32});\widehat{a_3} = (a_{11},a_{22},a_{31});\widehat{a_4} = (a_{11},a_{22},a_{32})\ ;\\ \widehat{a_5} = (a_{11},a_{23},a_{31});\widehat{a_6} = (a_{11},a_{23},a_{32});\widehat{a_7} = (a_{12},a_{21},a_{31});\widehat{a_8} = (a_{12},a_{21},a_{32})\ ;\\ \widehat{a_9} = (a_{12},a_{22},a_{31})\ ;\widehat{a_{10}} = (a_{12},a_{22},a_{32})\ ;\widehat{a_{11}} = (a_{12},a_{23},a_{31})\ ;\widehat{a_{12}} = (a_{12},a_{23},a_{32})\end{array}\right\}$$

$\widehat{A} = \{\widehat{a_1},\widehat{a_2},\widehat{a_3},\widehat{a_4},\widehat{a_5},\widehat{a_6},\widehat{a_7},\widehat{a_8},\widehat{a_9},\widehat{a_{10}},\widehat{a_{11}},\widehat{a_{12}}\}$ then the hypersoft sets is given by:

$$(\varphi,\widehat{A}) = \left\{\begin{array}{c}(\widehat{a_1},(x_1,0.3),(x_2,0.6)),\\ (\widehat{a_2},(x_3,0.5),(x_1,0.2)),\\ (\widehat{a_3},(x_1,0.7),(x_3,0.2))),(\widehat{a_4},(x_1,0.6),(x_2,0.3))),\\ (\widehat{a_5},(x_2,0.5),(x_3,0.2))),\\ (\widehat{a_6},(x_2,0.4),(x_3,0.3))),(\widehat{a_7},(x_1,0.7)),(\widehat{a_8},(x_2,0.8)),(\widehat{a_9},(x_3,0.5)),(\widehat{a_{10}},(x_1,0.6)),\\ (\widehat{a_{11}},(x_1,0.3),(x_2,0.2),(x_3,0.3))),(\widehat{a_{12}},(x_1,0.6),(x_2,0.2),(x_3,0.1))\end{array}\right\}$$

then the fuzzy hypersoft sets over X is given as follows

$$(\varphi,\widehat{A}) = \left\{\begin{array}{c}(\widehat{a_1},(x_1,0.5),(x_2,0.3),(x_3,0.6)),(\widehat{a_2},(x_1,0.3),(x_2,0.5),(x_3,0.4))\\ (\widehat{a_3},(x_1,0.6),(x_2.0.2),(x_3,0.7)),(\widehat{a_4},(x_1,0.7),(x_2,0.4),(x_3,0.6))\\ (\widehat{a_5},(x_1,0.2),(x_2,0.7),(x_3,0.6)),(\widehat{a_6},(x_1,0.3),(x_2,0.5),(x_3,0.8))\\ (\widehat{a_7},(x_1,0.3),(x_2,0.5),(x_3,0.8)),(\widehat{a_8},(x_1,0.2),(x_2,0.7),(x_3,0.6))\\ (\widehat{a_9},(x_1,0.3),(x_2,0.6),(x_3,0.4)),(\widehat{a_{10}},(x_1,0.5),(x_2,0.1),(x_3,0.7))\\ (\widehat{a_{11}},(x_1,0.5),(x_2,0.6),(x_3,0.4)),(\widehat{a_{12}},(x_1,0.6),(x_2,0.3),(x_3,0.8)\end{array}\right\}$$

2.8 Linguistic Variable

A linguistic variable is a variable whose values are words or sentences in a natural or artificial language. These linguistic variables can be expressed in positive triangular fuzzy numbers.

2.9 Decision Theory

Decision Making Under Certainty

This is a Deterministic Model, here for each situation the alternatives and the consequences of each alternatives is known in advance with complete certainty. Eg: Linear Programming, Sequencing etc.

Decision Making Under Risk

This is a stochastic model, here each alternative are known but their consequences are in doubt. Therefore the consequences are not certain but having a probability. Eg: Replacment Model, Stochastic Model in Inventory.

Decision Making Under Uncertainty

Here for each alternative their corresponding are unknown. The probabilities of the consequences are also unknown. Eg: Market research for a new product with no competitors.

Decision Making Under Conflict

This follows the competitive strategies. Here for each situation the consequences of each act of the decision maker are influenced by the act of the opponent. Eg: Game theory.

Decision Matrix

A decision matrix is a list of values in rows and columns that allows an analyst to systematically identif, analyse and rate the performance of relationships.

2.10 Maxi Max Criterion

In this criteria the decision maker achieves the greatest possible payoff or lowest possible cost by choosing the maximum among the maximum element of each row.

2.11 Maximin Criterion

"Maximin" means "Maximize the Minimum Payoff". This criterion is appropriate for Pessimist persons. Using this criterion, the decision-maker looks at the worst that can happen under each action and then choose the action that has the largest payoff for the worst-case scenario.

2.12 Laplace Criterion

This criteria choose the maximum value obtained by taking the average of each row.

2.13 Regret Criterion

This criteria choose the maximum value obtained by subtracting each element of the matrix from the maximum value of each row.

3. PROPOSED ALGORITHM

Here the idea of Neutrosophic Hyper Soft Set has been used to evaluate the Multi Criteria Decision Making problem. The problem involves the selection of best school in certain locality with some attributes. For this, construct a Neutrosophic hyper soft sets (φ, S)over X is a mapping $\varphi: S \rightarrow P(X)$. This Neutrosophic hyper soft sets gives a relation matrix X in which the element denotes the schools with different attributes. Then construct another Neutrosophic Hyper soft sets (ψ, Z) over Y is a mapping $\psi: Z \rightarrow P(Y)$. This gives a relation matrix Y same as X where these entries are also Neutrosophic numbers.

Algorithm

Step 1: Construct the Neutrosophic hyper soft sets (φ, S) to obtain the matrix X (Decision – maker 1).

Step 2: Construct the Neutrosophic hyper soft set (ψ, Z) to obtain the matrix Y (Decision – maker 2).

Step3: Calculate the value matrix of X and Y, by using $(1 - T)(1 - I)(1 - F)$

Step 4: Prepare the matrix D by taking the average of each corresponding cells from matrix X and Y.

Step 5: Apply the proposed formula $\frac{Max.Value - Min.Value}{Max.Value + Min.Value}$ for each row and identify the maximum value of the calculated values.

Step 6: Comparison with existing criteria such as Maxi max and Laplace criteria.

4. FORMULATION OF THE PROBLEM

Generally, the decision making analysis exist in our day – to – day life. Here to admit the child in a school parents usually suggest many ideas to select the best school around their area, like infrastructure of the school, fees, quality teachers and distance etc.

Let **U** be the universe of discourse consisting of selected schools in the surrounding area, where

$$\boldsymbol{U} = \{\boldsymbol{S}_1, \boldsymbol{S}_2, \boldsymbol{S}_3, \boldsymbol{S}_4, \boldsymbol{S}_5\}$$

The attributes of the schools, chosen for the decision are $\boldsymbol{e}_1, \boldsymbol{e}_2, \boldsymbol{e}_3, \boldsymbol{e}_4$

$$\boldsymbol{e}_1 = infrastructure, e_2 = fees,\ e_3 = faculties\ experience\ e_4 = distance$$

The attribute values of $\boldsymbol{e}_1, \boldsymbol{e}_2, \boldsymbol{e}_3, \boldsymbol{e}_4$ belong to the sets $\boldsymbol{E}_1, \boldsymbol{E}_2, \boldsymbol{E}_3, \boldsymbol{E}_4$ respectively.

$$E_1 = \{AC(i_1), NonAC(i_2), NonAC\ with\ furnished(i_3), AC\ with\ furnished(i_4)\}$$

$$E_2 = \{\ low(f_1), medium(f_2), high(f_3)\}$$

$$E_3 = \{3(q_1), 4(q_2), 8(q_3), 10 + (q_4)\}$$

$$E_4 = \{near(d_1), very\ near(d_2), far(d_3), toofar(d_4)\}$$

Let the function be $\boldsymbol{\varphi} : \boldsymbol{E}_1 \times \boldsymbol{E}_2 \times \boldsymbol{E}_3 \times \boldsymbol{E}_4 \rightarrow \boldsymbol{P}(\boldsymbol{U})$

Let us assume the relation

$$\varphi(E_1 \times E_2 \times E_3 \times E_4) = \{\varphi(\text{NonAC with furnished}(i_3), \text{medium}(f_2)), 10 + (q_4), \text{near}(d_1)\}$$

which is the actual requirement for selecting a school. Five schools $\{\boldsymbol{S}_1, \boldsymbol{S}_2, \boldsymbol{S}_3, \boldsymbol{S}_4, \boldsymbol{S}_5\}$ are selected on the basis of the above relation.

The Decision Maker 1(X) and Decision Maker 2(Y) select on the above basis. These people give their opinion in the form of Neutrosophic hyper soft sets separately as

$$\text{X} = \{\varphi(\text{NonAC with furnished}(i_3), \text{medium}(f_2)), 10 + (q_4), \text{near}(d_1))\}$$

$$\begin{Bmatrix} \varphi(S_1) &=& \{i_3(0.7,0.1,0.2), f_2(0.5,0.2,0.3), q_4(0.8,0.2,0.1), d_1(0.2,0.1,0.1)\} \\ \varphi(S_2) &=& \{i_3(0.6,0.2,0.1), f_2(0.4,0.1,0.2), q_4(0.7,0.2,0.3), d_1(0.4,0.2,0.3)\} \\ \varphi(S_3) &=& \{i_3(0.8,0.2,0.3), f_2(0.6,0.1,0.2), q_4(0.6,0.2,0.1), d_1(0.3,0.2,0.4)\} \\ \varphi(S_4) &=& \{i_3(0.9,0.1,0.1), f_2(0.5,0.2,0.3), q_4(0.2,0.3,0.4), d_1(0.4,0.2,0.2)\} \\ \varphi(S_5) &=& \{i_3(0.7,0.2,0.3), f_2(0.6,0.4,0.3), q_4(0.7,0.1,0.3), d_1(0.5,0.2,0.3)\} \end{Bmatrix}$$

$$\mathrm{Y} = \{\varphi(\text{NonAC with furnished}(i_3), \text{medium}(f_2)), 10+(q_4), \text{near}(d_1))\}$$

$$\begin{Bmatrix} \varphi(S_1) &=& \{i_3(0.6,0.2,0.3), f_2(0.7,0.1,0.4), q_4(0.9,0.2,0.5), d_1(0.3,0.2,0.5)\} \\ \varphi(S_2) &=& \{i_3(0.8,0.1,0.4), f_2(0.8,0.2,0.5), q_4(0.5,0.4,0.3), d_1(0.6,0.2,0.3)\} \\ \varphi(S_3) &=& \{i_3(0.7,0.1,0.2), f_2(0.8,0.2,0.3), q_4(0.5,0.1,0.2), d_1(0.7,0.1,0.2)\} \\ \varphi(S_4) &=& \{i_3(0.8,0.1,0.4), f_2(0.7,0.1,0.4), q_4(0.7,0.2,0.3), d_1(0.5,0.4,0.3)\} \\ \varphi(S_5) &=& \{i_3(0.7,0.2,0.3), f_2(0.8,0.2,0.5), q_4(0.8,0.1,0.4), d_1(0.2,0.3,0.4)\} \end{Bmatrix}$$

Step 1: Let us construct the Neutrosophic hyper soft (φ, S) to obtain the matrix $X(\varphi)$

$$X\left(\varphi\right) = \begin{bmatrix} i_3(0.7,0.1,0.2), f_2(0.5,0.2,0.3), q_4(0.8,0.2,0.1), d_1(0.2,0.1,0.1) \\ i_3(0.6,0.2,0.1), f_2(0.4,0.1,0.2), q_4(0.7,0.2,0.3), d_1(0.4,0.2,0.3) \\ i_3(0.8,0.2,0.3), f_2(0.6,0.1,0.2), q_4(0.6,0.2,0.1), d_1(0.3,0.2,0.4) \\ i_3(0.9,0.1,0.1), f_2(0.5,0.2,0.3), q_4(0.2,0.3,0.4), d_1(0.4,0.2,0.2) \\ i_3(0.7,0.2,0.3), f_2(0.6,0.4,0.3), q_4(0.7,0.1,0.3), d_1(0.5,0.2,0.3) \end{bmatrix}$$

Step 2: Now let us construct the Neutrosophic hyper soft set (ψ, Z) to obtain the matrix $Y(\psi)$

$$Y\left(\psi\right) = \begin{bmatrix} i_3(0.6,0.2,0.3), f_2(0.7,0.1,0.4), q_4(0.9,0.2,0.5), d_1(0.3,0.2,0.5) \\ i_3(0.8,0.1,0.4), f_2(0.8,0.2,0.5), q_4(0.5,0.4,0.3), d_1(0.6,0.2,0.3) \\ i_3(0.7,0.1,0.2), f_2(0.8,0.2,0.3), q_4(0.5,0.1,0.2), d_1(0.7,0.1,0.2) \\ i_3(0.8,0.1,0.4), f_2(0.7,0.1,0.4), q_4(0.7,0.2,0.3), d_1(0.5,0.4,0.3) \\ i_3(0.7,0.2,0.3), f_2(0.8,0.2,0.5), q_4(0.8,0.1,0.4), d_1(0.2,0.3,0.4) \end{bmatrix}$$

Step 3: Now calculate the value matrix

$\boldsymbol{X} = (1-T)(1-I)(1-F)$ and $\boldsymbol{Y} = (1-T)(1-I)(1-F)$

$$X = \begin{bmatrix} 0.216 & 0.2800.144 & 0.648 \\ 0.288 & 0.4320.168 & 0.336 \\ 0.112 & 0.2880.288 & 0.336 \\ 0.081 & 0.2800.336 & 0.384 \\ 0.168 & 0.1680.189 & 0.280 \end{bmatrix} Y = \begin{bmatrix} 0.224 & 0.1620.040 & 0.280 \\ 0.108 & 0.0800.210 & 0.224 \\ 0.216 & 0.1120.360 & 0.216 \\ 0.108 & 0.1620.168 & 0.210 \\ 0.168 & 0.0800.108 & 0.336 \end{bmatrix}$$

Step 4: Prepare the matrix D by taking the average of each corresponding cells from matrix X and Y.

$$D = \begin{bmatrix} 0.220 & 0.2210.092 & 0.464 \\ 0.198 & 0.2560.189 & 0.280 \\ 0.164 & 0.2000.324 & 0.276 \\ 0.094 & 0.2210.252 & 0.297 \\ 0.168 & 0.1240.148 & 0.308 \end{bmatrix}$$

Step 5: Apply the formula $\frac{Max.Value - Min.Value}{Max.Value + Min.Value}$ for each row and identify the maximum value of the calculated values

$$D = \begin{bmatrix} 0.220 & 0.2210.092 & 0.464 \\ 0.198 & 0.2560.189 & 0.280 \\ 0.164 & 0.2000.324 & 0.276 \\ 0.094 & 0.2210.252 & 0.297 \\ 0.168 & 0.1240.148 & 0.308 \end{bmatrix} \begin{matrix} 0.669 \\ 0.194 \\ 0.327(0.425) \\ 0.519 \\ 0.425 \end{matrix}$$

From the above table the maximum value of each row lies in second row corresponds tp S_1.

Therefore the decision makers are willing to choose the S_1.

Step 6: Comparison with existing criterion.

Maxi Max Criterion

Selecting the maximum value among the maximum element of each row.

$$D = \begin{bmatrix} 0.220 & 0.2210.092 & 0.464 \\ 0.198 & 0.2560.189 & 0.280 \\ 0.164 & 0.2000.324 & 0.276 \\ 0.094 & 0.2210.252 & 0.297 \\ 0.168 & 0.1240.148 & 0.308 \end{bmatrix} \begin{matrix} 0.464 \\ 0.280 \\ 0.324(0.308) \\ 0.297 \\ 0.308 \end{matrix}$$

Here the maximum value occurs corresponding to S_1

Laplace Criterion

Selecting the maximum value among the average of all the elements of each row.

$$D = \begin{bmatrix} 0.220 & 0.2210.092 & 0.464 \\ 0.198 & 0.2560.189 & 0.280 \\ 0.164 & 0.2000.324 & 0.276 \\ 0.094 & 0.2210.252 & 0.297 \\ 0.168 & 0.1240.148 & 0.308 \end{bmatrix} \begin{matrix} 0.249 \\ 0.230 \\ 0.241(0.187) \\ 0.216 \\ 0.187 \end{matrix}$$

Here the maximum value occurs corresponding to S_1

Maxi Min Criterion

Selecting the maximum value among the minimum element of each row.

$$D = \begin{bmatrix} 0.220 & 0.2210.092 & 0.464 \\ 0.198 & 0.2560.189 & 0.280 \\ 0.164 & 0.2000.324 & 0.276 \\ 0.094 & 0.2210.252 & 0.297 \\ 0.168 & 0.1240.148 & 0.308 \end{bmatrix} \begin{matrix} 0.092 \\ 0.189 \\ 0.164(0.124) \\ 0.094 \\ 0.124 \end{matrix}$$

Here the maximum value occurs corresponding to S_2

Regret Criterion

Selecting the minimum value among the values obtained by subtracting each element of the column by the maximum element of the corresponding column.

$$D = \begin{bmatrix} 0.220 & 0.2210.092 & 0.464 \\ 0.198 & 0.2560.189 & 0.280 \\ 0.164 & 0.2000.324 & 0.276 \\ 0.094 & 0.2210.252 & 0.297 \\ 0.168 & 0.1240.148 & 0.308 \end{bmatrix}$$

$$=D = \begin{bmatrix} 0. & 0.0350.232 & 0.000 \\ 0.022 & 0.0000.135 & 0.184 \\ 0.056 & 0.0560.000 & 0.188 \\ 0.126 & 0.0350.072 & 0.167 \\ 0.052 & 0.1320.176 & 0.156 \end{bmatrix} \begin{matrix} 0.232 \\ 0.184 \\ 0.188(0.176) \\ 0.167 \\ 0.176 \end{matrix}$$

Here the minimum entry lies in S_4

Therefore the result of the proposed criterion coincides with maxi max and Laplace criterion.

5. CONCLUSION

Decision making analysis is the best way of choosing one act from a set of possible act. The basic objective of the theory is to give a systematic way of approaching decision to get the desired outcome where the possibility of occurrence of different outcomes are evaluated in advance. Here selecting a suitable school under different criterion has been done with Neutrosophic Hyper Soft Set. The result obtained from the proposed method coincide with the majority of the existing criterion. Therefore selecting S_1 is the best decision of the multi criteria decision making problem.

REFERENCES

Abbas, M., Murtaza, G., & Smarandache, F. (2020). *Basic operations on hypersoft sets and hypersoft point.Neutrosophic Sets and Systems, 35*(1), 407-421.

Abd, K., Abhary, K., & Marian, R. (2013). Application of Fuzzy Logic to Multi-Objective Scheduling Problems in Robotic Flexible Assembly Cells. *Automation Control and Intelligent Systems.*, 1(3), 34–4. DOI:10.11648/j.acis.20130103.11

Atanassov, K. (1986). Intuitionistic fuzzy sets. *Fuzzy Sets and Systems*, 20(1), 87–96. DOI:10.1016/S0165-0114(86)80034-3

Cagman, N., Enginoglu, S., & Citak, F. (2011). Fuzzy soft set theory and its applications. *Iranian Journal of Fuzzy Systems, 8*(3), 137-147. DOI:10.22111/IJFS.2011.292

Celik & Yamak. (2013). *Fuzzy soft set theory applied to medical diagnosis using fuzzy arithmetic operations.*DOI:10.1186/1029-242X-2013-82

Jafar & Saeed. (2022). Matrix theory for neutrosophic hypersoft set and applications in multiattributive multicriteria decision-making problems. *Journal of Mathematics*. .DOI:10.1155/2022/6666408

Kong, Z., Wang, L., & Wu, Z. (2011). Application of fuzzy soft set in decision making problems based on grey theory. *Journal of Computational and Applied Mathematics*, 236(6), 1521–1530. DOI:10.1016/j.cam.2011.09.016

Maji, P. K., Biswas, R., & Roy, A. R. (2001). *Fuzzy soft sets. Journal of Fuzzy Mathematics, 9*, 589-602.

Maji, P. K., Biswas, R., & Roy, A. R. (2003). Soft set theory. *Computers & Mathematics with Applications (Oxford, England)*, 45(4-5), 555–562. DOI:10.1016/S0898-1221(03)00016-6

Majumdar, P., & Samanta, S. K. (2010). Generalised fuzzy soft sets. *Computers & Mathematics with Applications (Oxford, England)*, 59(4), 1425–1432. DOI:10.1016/j.camwa.2009.12.006

Majumdar, P., & Samanta, S. K. (2014). On similarity and entropy of neutrosophic sets. *Journal of Intelligent & Fuzzy Systems*, 26(3), 1245–1252. DOI:10.3233/IFS-130810

Saeed, M., Ahsan, M., Siddique, M. K., & Ahmad, M. R. (2020). A study of the fundamentals of hypersoft set theory. *Int. Sci. Eng. Res.*, 11, 320–329. DOI:10.5281/zenodo.6779592

Sanchez, E. (1979). Inverse of fuzzy relations, application to possibility distributions and medical diagnosis. *Fuzzy Sets and Systems*, 2(1), 75–78. DOI:10.1016/0165-0114(79)90017-4

Smarandache, F. (2004). Neutrosophic set, a generalization of the intutionistic fuzzy sets. *International Journal of Pure and Applied Mathematics*, 24(3), 287–297.

Smarandache, F. (2018). Extension of soft sets to hypersoft set, and then to plithogenic hypersoft set. *Neutrosophic Sets and system, 22*, 168-170. DOI:10.5281/zenodo.1408740

Zadeh, L. A. (1965). Fuzzy sets. *Information and Control*, 8(3), 338–353. DOI:10.1016/S0019-9958(65)90241-X

Chapter 7
A Python Toolbox for Single-Valued and Interval-Valued Fermatean Neutrosophic Matrices

Said Broumi
https://orcid.org/0000-0002-1334-5759
University Hassan II, Morocco

González-Caballero Erick
Technological University of Havana, Cuba

ABSTRACT

Neutrosophic sets are a type of mathematical object that can be used to model indeterminacy and inconsistent information. They are defined using three degrees of membership: truthfulness, indeterminacy, and falsity. Single-valued Fermatean neutrosophic sets (SVFNSs) and interval-valued Fermatean neutrosophic sets (IVFNSs) are two specific cases of neutrosophic sets that have been shown to be useful in a variety of applications. In this chapter, a new Python toolbox is proposed under the neutrosophic environment, which consists in some Python code for single-valued Fermatean neutrosophic matrices and interval-valued Fermatean neutrosophic matrices. Some definitions of interval-valued Fermatean neutrosophy are vague sets such as union, complement, and intersection, which are presented. Furthermore, the related examples are included.

DOI: 10.4018/979-8-3693-2085-3.ch007

1. INTRODUCTION.

The idea of fuzzy sets was introduced by Zadeh, (Zadeh, 1965). He proposed that each element in a fuzzy set has a degree of membership. Based on this idea Prof. Atanassov (Atanassov,1986) introduced the concept of intuitionistic fuzzy set on a universe X as a generalization of fuzzy set. His concept is based on two degrees of belonging for each element: the degree of membership and degree of non-membership.

Later on, Prof. Smarandache (Smarandache,1998) originally gave the definition of a neutrosophic set and neutrosophic logic. The concept of neutrosophic set is based on three degrees for each element totally independent: the degree of membership, the degree of indetermination and the degree of non-membership. In (Wang et al, 2014) they proposed the concept of single-valued neutrosophic sets, which is an extensin of Neutrosophic set. In addition, the authors in (Zhang et al.,2014) developped a new extension termed as interval-valued neutrosophic set.

Several scholars have done remarkable achievements in this area (http://fs.gallup .unm.edu/NSS/). Recently, Jansi et al. introduced a new class of single-valued neutrosophic set called Pythagorean neutrosophic set (PyNS) (Jansi et al., 2019). PyNSs are characterized by the fact that the square sum of the membership value, indeterminacy value and non-membership value is equal to or less than two. This makes PyNSs more flexible than Pythagorean fuzzy sets, which can be used to represent a wider range of uncertain information. The concept of Pythagorean neutrosophic sets (PyNSs) comprises independent and dependent membership.

In addition, Antony, Crispin, Sweety, and Jansi defined a new type of neutrosophic set called Fermatean neutrosophic sets (FNSs) (Antony, Crispin, Sweety, and Jansi, 2021). The Fermatean neutrosophic sets generalises the concept of Pythagorean neutrosophic sets. Broumi et al. proposed the concept of interval-valued pythagorean neutrosophic sets as a generalisation of Pythagorean neutrosophic sets and explored the concept of interval-valued Pythagorean neutrosophic graphs (Broumi et al., 2023).

Ajay and Chellamani introduced a new type of graph called a Pythagorean neutrosophic fuzzy graph (Ajay and Chellamani, 2020). This graph is a special case of a neutrosophic graph, but it restricts the independent memberships of the vertices. In other words, it makes sure that the square sum of the membership, non-membership, and indeterminacy values of each vertex is less than or equal to 2. The same author in (Ajay et al.,2021) presented the labelling of Pythagorean neutrosophic fuzzy graphs and investigate their properties. In (Chellamani, et al.,2021) they have initiated the Pythagorean neutrosophic Dombi fuzzy graphs with an application to Multicriteria Decision Making (MCDM). In (Ajay et al.,2022) they studied regular

Pythagorean neutrosophic graphs and introduced a new MCDM method based on the Pythagorean neutrosophic graphs.

Later, Broumi et al. defined the Interval-Valued Pythagorean Neutrosophic Graph (IVPNG) (Broumi et al., 2023). The IVPNG comprises independent and dependent membership elements of interval entries. Murugappan et al. studied neighbourly edge irregularity on interval-valued Pythagorean neutrosophic graphs (Murugappan et al., 2023). They investigated two types of irregularities in interval-valued Pythagorean neutrosophic graphs: neighborly edge irregularity and neighborly edge totally irregularity. They also explored the relationships between these two types of irregularities and other irregular property-bearing graphs.

Ramya et al. introduced the concept of Fermatean quadripartitioned neutrosophic set, this concept is a combination of quadripartitioned neutrosophic set and Fermatean sets, these authors presented some definitions of Fermatean quadripartitioned neutrosophic sets such as union, complement and intersection, including the basic operations, and studied some of their properties with numerical examples (Ramya et al., 2022).

In (Kaya et al.,2022), they combined the two approaches, both rough sets and pentapartitioned neutrophic sets, and constructed new sets to deal with Fermatean structures. In (Broumi et al., 2023) it was solved the shortest path problems using an ant colony algorithm with triangular neutrosophic arc weights.

In (Sasikala et al., 2023) it was initiated the Fermatean Neutrosophic Dombi Fuzzy Graphs. In (Raut et al., 2023) they solved the shortest path problem on Fermatean Neutrosophic Networks. Additionaly, in (Asim Basha et al., 2023) it was solved the neutrosophic Pythagorean fuzzy shortest path in a network. Gonul Bilgin et al. redefined the concept of Fermatean neutrosophic sets and introduced a topological structure for Fermatean neutrosophic sets, they addressed a decision-making problem using the neutrosophic Kano method (Gonul Bilgin et al., 2022). In (Manirathinam et al., 2023) Manirathinam et al. applied Fermatean neutrosophic fuzzy and AHP-MARCOS approach for solving the sustainable renewable energy system selection for self-sufficient households. Joice et al. generalized pre-closed sets in Fermatean neutrosophic hypersoft topological spaces (Joice et al., 2023).

In (Stephy and Helen, 2023) they presented a new set called the interval-valued Fermatean neutrosophic set of second type, and developped some basic properties of them like union, intersection, direct sum, direct product, complement, scalar multiplication and power. In (Broumi et al, 2017a, 2017b) it was developped a Matlab Toolbox for computing operational matrices in Neutrosophic Environments.

In (El-Ghareeb, 2019) it was developped python programs for solving operations on neutrosophic numbers including single-valued neutrosophic numbers and interval-valued neutrosophic numbers. Gayathri et al defined neutrosophic vague measure using python (Gayathri et al, 2020). Bui et al. developed a python package for sequence of neutrosophic soft sets (Bui et al., 2022). Next, Sleem et al. developed a python-based tool for interval-valued neutrosophic operations and normalization (Sleem et al., 2020). The weakness of these python programs is that they cannot deal with neutrosophic matrices. For this reason, Topal et al. created a python tool for implementations on bipolar neutrosophic matrices (Topal et al., 2019). In (Broumi et al., 2020) developed a novel python toolbox for single and interval-valued neutrosophic matrices.

Kandasamy and Smarandache defined the concept of the neutrosophic matrices and square neutrosophic fuzzy matrices, whose elements belong to a neutrosophic field $K(I)$ (Kandasamy and Smarandache, 2014). They also investigated some properties of these matrices. In the literature there are two types of neutrosophic matrices, the first one is based on literal neutrosophic numbers of the form $(a + Ib)$ and the second one is based on numerical neutrosophic numbers of the form (T, I, F). Both types of neutrosophic matrices can be used to represent incomplete or indeterminate information. In the second type of neutrosophic matrices, the three components T, I, and F are totally independents. Recently, Broumi and Prabha in (Broumi and Prabha, 2023) defined a special case of neutrosophic matrix called Fermatean neutrosophic matrix where the entries satisfy the condition $0 \leq T^3 + I^3 + F^3 \leq 2$, and $0 \leq T^3 + F^3 \leq 1$, where T and F are dependent each other, and I is independent of the entry, respectively. This condition is known as the Fermatean constraint. In addition, a variety of other hybrid neutrosophic matrices theories can be found in (Karaaslan and Khizar, 2018, Dhar, 2020, Khan et al., 2021, Murugadas and Kavitha, 2021, Abobala etal., 2021; 2021a; 2021b, Mahima Poonia and Bajaj, 2021, Salama et al., 2022, Debnath, 2022, Donbosco and Ganesan, 2022, Esther and Shanmugapriya, 2022, Jeni Seles Martina and Deepa, 2023; 2023a, Al-Odhari, 2023, Martina et al., 2023, Lalitha et al., 2023, Anandhkumar et al., 2023, Muthukumaran et al., 2023, Silambarasan, 2023).

So far, to the best of our knowledge, this may be the first time that a python code is developed for computing Fermatean neutrosophic operations. This chapter aims to fill this gap by developing Python codes for computing on single-valued Fermatean numbers, interval-valued Fermatean numbers, single-valued Fermatean matrices, and interval-valued Fermatean matrices.

We have the purpose to support the calculus of Fermatean neutrosophic theory using the Python language. Python is one of the most popular languages used for the computation of mathematical methods. This is a high-level multi-paradigm and multi-platform language. Specifically, we used the object oriented programming paradigm.

The chapter is structured in the following manner. Section 2 presents some basic mathematical concepts to enhance the understanding of single-valued Fermatean neutrosophic sets and interval-valued Fermatean neutrosophic sets. Section 3 describes the python programs for operations on single-valued Fermatean neutrosophic numbers and single-valued Fermatean neutrosophic matrices together with numerical examples. Section 4 describes the python programs for operations on interval-valued Fermatean neutrosophic matrices together with numerical examples. Finally, conclusion is stated in section 5.

2. BACKGROUND AND INTERVAL VALUED FERMATEAN NEUTROSOPHIC SETS

In this section, we discuss some definitions regarding neutrosophic sets, single-valued neutrosophic sets, interval-valued neutrosophic sets, the set-theoretic operators on the interval-valued neutrosophic sets and interval-valued neutrosophic matrices, which will be used in the rest of the chaptre. However, for details on the interval-valued neutrosophic sets, one can see (Smarandache, 1998, Wang et al, 2014, Zhang et al, 2014).

Definition 2.1. (Smarandache,1998): Let us suppose ξ is a universal set. The neutrosophic set A on ξ is categorized into three membership functions that are called true T_A (x), indeterminate I_A (x), and false F_A (x), which are contained in real standard or non-standard subset of $]^{-}0, 1^{+}[$, respectively.

$$0 \leq \sup T_A(x) + \sup I_A(x) + \sup F_A(x) \leq 3^{+} \quad (1)$$

Definition 2.2. (Wang et al., 2014): Let us suppose ξ is a universal set. The single-valued neutrosophic set (SVNS) A on the universal ξ is termed as following:

$$A = \{\langle x : T_A(x), I_A(x), F_A(x) \rangle x \in \hat{\imath}\} \quad (2)$$

The functions $T_A(x) \in [0,1]$, $I_A(x) \in [0, 1]$, and $F_A(x) \in [0, 1]$ denote the "degree of membership", the "degree of indeterminacy", and the "degree of non-membership" of x in A, respectively, with the following condition:

$$0 \leq T_A(x) + I_A(x) + F_A(x) \leq 3 \quad (3)$$

Definition 2.3. (Zhang et al.,2014): suppose ξ be a space of points (objects) with a generic element in ξ denoted by x. An interval-valued neutrosophic set (IVNS) A in ξ is characterized by truth-membership function T_A, indeterminacy-membership function I_A, and falsity-membership function F_A. For each point $x \in \xi$, $T_A(x)$, $I_A(x)$, $F_A(x) \subseteq [0, 1]$.

$$A_{\text{IVNS}} = \{[T_A^L(x), T_A^U(x)], [I_A^L(x), I_A^U(x)], [F_A^L(x), F_A^U(x)] : x \in \xi\}$$

with

$$0 \le T_A^U(x) + I_A^U(x) + F_A^U(x) \le 3 \tag{4}$$

Definition 2.4. (Zhang et al., 2014): Suppose there are two interval-valued neutrosophic sets:

$$A_{\text{IVNS}} = \{[T_A^L(x), T_A^U(x)], [I_A^L(x), I_A^U(x)], [F_A^L(x), F_A^U(x)] : x \in \xi\}$$

and

$$B_{\text{IVNS}} = \{[T_B^L(x), T_B^U(x)], [I_B^L(x), I_B^U(x)], [F_B^L(x), F_B^U(x)] : x \in \xi\}$$

the set-theoretic operators on them are defined as follows:

1. An interval-valued neutrosophic set *A* is contained in another interval-valued neutrosophic set *B*, $A_{\text{IVNS}} \subseteq B_{\text{IVNS}}$, if and only if:

$$T_A^L(x) \le T_B^L(x), T_A^U(x) \le T_B^U(x),$$

$$I_A^L(x) \ge I_B^L(x),\ I_A^U(x) \ge I_B^U(x),$$

$$F_A^L(x) \ge F_B^L(x),\ F_A^U(x) \ge F_B^U(x), \text{ for all } x \in \xi.$$

2. Two interval-valued neutrosophic sets *A* and *B* are equal, it is denoted by $A_{\text{IVNS}} = B_{\text{IVNS}}$, if and only if A $\subseteq$ B and B $\subseteq$ A, i.e.,

$$T_A^L(x) = T_B^L(x), T_A^U(x) = T_B^U(x),$$

$$I_A^L(x) = I_B^L(x),\ I_A^U(x) = I_B^U(x),$$

$F_A^L(x) = F_B^L(x),\ F_A^U(x) = F_B^U(x),$

for all x $\in \xi$.

3. An interval-valued neutrosophic set *A* is empty if and only if:

$$T_A^L(x) = T_A^U(x) = 0,$$

$$I_A^L(x) = I_A^U(x) = 1, \text{ and}$$

$$F_A^L(x) = F_A^U(x) = 0,$$

for all x $\in \xi$.

4. The complement of an interval neutrosophic set *A* is denoted by A^c and is defined by

$$A_{\mathrm{IVNS}^c} = \left\{ \begin{matrix} x, \left[F_A^L(x), F_A^U(x)\right], \\ \left[1 - I_A^U(x), 1 - I_A^L(x)\right], :\mathrm{x} \in \mathrm{X} \\ \left[T_A^L(x), F_A^U(x)\right] \end{matrix} \right\},$$

for all *x* in ξ.

5. The intersection of two interval-valued neutrosophic sets *A* and *B* is an interval-valued neutrosophic set $A \cap B$ defined as follows:

$$A_{IVNS} \cap B_{IVNS} = \left\{ \begin{matrix} x, \left[T_A^L(x) \wedge T_B^U(x), T_A^U(x) \wedge T_B^U(x)\right], \\ \left[I_A^L(x) \vee I_B^U(x), I_A^U(x) \vee I_B^U(x)\right], \quad :x \in \xi \\ \left[F_A^L(x) \vee F_B^U(x), F_A^U(x) \vee F_B^U(x)\right. \end{matrix} \right\},$$

for all *x* in ξ.

6. The union of two interval-valued neutrosophic sets *A* and *B* is an interval-valued neutrosophic set $A_{\mathrm{IVNS}} \cup B_{\mathrm{IVNS}}$ defined as follow:

$$A_{IVNS} \cup B_{IVNS} = \left\{ \begin{array}{l} x, \left[T_A^L(x) \vee T_B^L(x), T_A^U(x) \vee T_B^U(x)\right], \\ \left[I_A^L(x) \wedge I_B^L(x), I_A^U(x) \wedge I_B^U(x)\right], \quad :x \in \xi \\ \left[F_A^L(x) \wedge F_B^L(x), F_A^U(x) \wedge F_B^U(x)\right] \end{array} \right\}, \text{ for all } x \text{ in } \xi.$$

7. The difference of two interval-valued neutrosophic sets A and B is an interval-valued neutrosophic set $A_{\mathrm{IVNS}} \ominus B_{\mathrm{IVNS}}$ defined as follows:

$$A \ominus B = \left\langle \left[T^L_{\mathrm{A\ominus B}}, T^U_{\mathrm{A\ominus B}}\right], \left[I^L_{\mathrm{A\ominus B}}, I^U_{\mathrm{A\ominus B}}\right], \left[F^L_{\mathrm{A\ominus B}}, F^U_{\mathrm{A\ominus B}}\right] \right\rangle \tag{5}$$

Where:

$$T^L_{\mathrm{A\ominus_2 B}} = \min\left(T_A^L(x), F_B^L(x)\right), \; T^U_{\mathrm{A\ominus_2 B}} = \min\left(T_A^U(x), F_B^U(x)\right),$$

$$I^L_{\mathrm{A\ominus_2 B}} = \max\left(I_A^L(x), 1 - I_B^U(x)\right), \; I^U_{\mathrm{A\ominus_2 B}} = \max\left(I_A^U(x), 1 - I_B^L(x)\right),$$

$$F^L_{\mathrm{A\ominus_2 B}} = \max\left(F_A^L(x), T_B^L(x)\right), \; F^U_{\mathrm{A\ominus_2 B}} = \max\left(F_A^U(x), T_B^U(x)\right).$$

Karaşan and Cengiz introduced a new difference operation for the interval-valued neutrosophic sets as follows (Karaşan and Cengiz, 2018):

$$A \ominus_2 B = \left\langle \left[T^L_{A\ominus_2 B}, T^U_{A\ominus_2 B}\right], \left[I^L_{A\ominus_2 B}, I^U_{A\ominus_2 B}\right], \left[F^L_{A\ominus_2 B}, F^U_{A\ominus_2 B}\right] \right\rangle \tag{6}$$

Where:

$$T^L_{\mathrm{A\ominus_2 B}} = T_A^L(x) - F_B^U(x), \; T^U_{\mathrm{A\ominus_2 B}} = T_A^U(x) - F_B^L(\mathrm{x}),$$

$$I^L_{\mathrm{A\ominus_2 B}} = \max\left(I_A^L(x), I_B^L(x)\right), \; I^U_{\mathrm{A\ominus_2 B}} = \max\left(I_A^U(x), I_B^U(x)\right),$$

$$F^L_{\mathrm{A\ominus_2 B}} = F_A^L(x) - T_B^U(x) = F^U_{\mathrm{A\ominus_2 B}} = F_A^U(x) - T_B^L(\mathrm{x}).$$

For all x in ξ.

8. The multiplication by a scalar of an interval-valued neutrosophic set A is λA_{IVNS}, defined as follows:

$$\lambda A_{\text{IVNS}} = \left\{ \begin{array}{l} x, \left[\min(\lambda T_A^L(x), 1), \min(\lambda T_A^U(x), 1)\right], \\ \left[\min(\lambda I_A^L(x), 1), \min(\lambda I_A^U(x), 1)\right], \quad : x \in \xi \\ \left[\min(\lambda F_A^L(x), 1), \min(\lambda F_A^U(x), 1)\right] \end{array} \right\} \text{ for all } x \in \xi, \lambda \in \mathbb{R}^+.$$

9. The division by a scalar of interval-valued neutrosophic set A is A_{IVNS}/λ defined as follows

$$A_{\text{IVNS}}/\lambda = \left(\frac{1}{\lambda}\right) A_{\text{IVNS}}$$

for all $x \in \xi, \lambda \in \mathbb{R}^+$.

The convenient method for comparing single-valued neutrosophic and interval-valued neutrosophic numbers can be applied by using the score function.

Definition 2.5. (Nancy & Garg, 2016, Garg and Nancy,2017, Şahin, 2015): Suppose A be an interval-valued neutrosophic number A_{IVNN}, the score functions are defined as follows:

$$\tilde{S}_{IVNN}(x) = \frac{T_A^L(x) + T_A^U(x) + 4 - I_A^L(x) - I_A^U(x) - F_A^L(x) - F_A^U(x)}{6} \tag{7}$$

$$\tilde{S}_{SVNN}(x) = \frac{2 + T_A(x) - I_A(x) - F_A(x)}{3}.$$

Definition 2.6 (Broumi and Prabha, 2023): An interval-valued Fermatean neutrosophic matrix (IVFNM) of order $m \times n$ is defined as:

$$A_{\text{IVFNM}} = \left[< a_{ij}, [a_{ij_T}^L, a_{ij_T}^U], [a_{ij_I}^L, a_{ij_I}^U], [a_{ij_F}^L, a_{ij_F}^U] >\right]_{m \times n}$$

Where:
$a^L_{ij_T}$ is the lower membership value of the element a_{ij} in A.
$a^L_{ij_T}$ is the upper membership value of the element a_{ij} in A.
$a^L_{ij_T}$ is the lower indeterminate-membership value of the element a_{ij} in A.
$a^L_{ij_T}$ is the upper indeterminate-membership value of the element a_{ij} in A.
$a^L_{ij_T}$ is the lower non-membership value of the element a_{ij} in A.
$a^L_{ij_T}$ is the upper non-membership value of the element a_{ij} in A.
For simplicity, we write A as:

$$A_{\text{IVFNM}} = \left[< [a^L_{ij_T}, a^U_{ij_T}], [a^L_{ij_I}, a^U_{ij_I}], [a^L_{ij_F}, a^U_{ij_F}] >\right]_{m\times n} \quad (8)$$

3. COMPUTING THE FERMATEAN NEUTROSOPHIC MATRIX OPERATIONS USING PYTHON LANGUAGE

This section describes how we generated the python program to input and calculate with Fermatean neutrosophic matrices. The steps are as follows:

3.1 Checking the Matrix Is a Fermatean Neutrosophic Matrix (FNM)

We based our code mainly on Object Oriented Programing (OOP) paradigm in python. Thus, we defined two classes on single-valued Fermatean neutrosophic matrices, which are the following:

1. *SVFNN*: is the name of the class for single-valued Fermatean neutrosophic numbers,
2. *SVFNM:* is the name of the class for single-valued Fermatean neutrosophic matrices,

The method *__init__* of *SVFNN* has constrains for defining single-valued Fermatean neutrosophic numbers. Therefore, when the user inputs a wrong *SVFNN* the program launches an error.

Additionally, the method *__init__* of *SVFNM* creates matrices with the dimensions entered by the user, and it has the constraint such that every element is a SVFNN, otherwise the program launches an error.

See the codes below in Figures 1 and 2:

Figure 1. Code of the class SVFNN with the methods __init__ and __str__.

```
class SVFNN:

    def __init__(self,label,T,I,F):
        '''Definition of Single-valued Fermatean Neutrosophic Number
           label: It's optional
           T: Truthfulness
           I: Indeterminacy
           F: Falseness
        '''
        try:
            assert 0 <= T <= 1
            assert 0 <= I <= 1
            assert 0 <= F <= 1
            assert 0<= (T**3)+(F**3)<=1
            assert 0<= (I**3)<=1
            self.label = label
            self.T = T
            self.I = I
            self.F = F
        except AssertionError:
            print("This isn't a SVFNN")

    def __str__(self):
        '''Return a string representation of a Single-Valued Fermatean Neutrosophic Number'''
        if self.label=="":
            return '(%s,%s,%s)'%(self.T, self.I, self.F)
        else:
            return '(%s,%s,%s,%s)'%(self.label,self.T, self.I, self.F)
```

Figure 2. Code of the class SVFNM with the methods __init__ and __str__.

```
class SVFNM:
    '''Class of Single-Valued Fermatean Neutrosophic Matrix'''
    def __init__(self,M):
        '''Enter a matrix M in form of list of lists and the output is a matrix of Single-Valued Fermatean Neutrosophic Numbers'''
        s=[len(m) for m in M] #Check that all the rows have the same length
        L = [l for l in s if(l==s[0])]

        try:
            assert len(s)==len(L)
            self.row = len(M)
            self.column = s[0]
            self.matrix = M

            R = create_matrix(self.row,self.column)

            for i in range(self.row):
                for j in range(self.column):
                    R[i][j]=SVFNN(M[i][j][0],M[i][j][1],M[i][j][2],M[i][j][3])

        except (AssertionError,TypeError):
            print("This isn't a SVFNM")


    def __str__(self):
        '''Output the SVFNM in form of matrix'''
        r=self.row
        c=self.column
        M = self.matrix

        for i in range(r):
            for j in range(c):
                if j == 0:
                    print('[',SVFNN(M[i][j][0],M[i][j][1],M[i][j][2],M[i][j][3]),end=' ')
                elif j==c-1:
                    print(SVFNN(M[i][j][0],M[i][j][1],M[i][j][2],M[i][j][3]),']',end=' ')
                else:
                    print(SVFNN(M[i][j][0],M[i][j][1],M[i][j][2],M[i][j][3]),end=' ')
            print("")
        return ""
```

Let us note that the method *__str__* allows us to output the SVFNN or the SVFNM in a comprehensible way for the user when he/she uses the function *print*.

Also, we defined two functions for creating and printing matrices, they are *create_matrix* and *print_matrix*, respectively, see the code below:

Figure 3. Code of the functions create_matrix and print_matrix.

```
def create_matrix(r,c):
    '''Create a new rxc null matrix'''
    M = []
    for i in range(r):
        M.append([])
        for j in range(c):
            M[i].append(0)
    return M

def print_matrix(M):
    '''Print matrix'''
    r = len(M)
    c = len(M[0])
    for i in range(r):
        for j in range(c):
            if j == 0:
                print('[',M[i][j],end=' ')
            elif j==c-1:
                print(M[i][j],']',end=' ')
            else:
                print(M[i][j],end=' ')
        print("")
    return ""
```

3.2. Finding the Complement of a Single-Valued Fermatean Neutrosophic Matrix

Given a single-valued Fermatean neutrosophic matrix A= $\left[\langle T_{ij}, I_{ij}, F_{ij}\rangle\right]_{m\times n}$, of dimension $m \times n$, its complement is defined as follows:

$$A^c = \left[< \{1\} - T_{ij}, \{1\} - I_{ij}, \{1\} - F_{ij}\right]_{m\times n} \tag{9}$$

$$A^c = \left[< F_{ij}, \{1\} - I_{ij}, T_{ij},\right]_{m\times n} \tag{10}$$

We used Equation 10 for calculating complement,

The Python program for calculating the complement of a SVFNM is shown below:

First we have to calculate the negation of a SVFNN,

Figure 4. Code of the method NOT of SVFNN and SVFNM for calculating complement.

```
def NOT(self):
    '''Negation of one SVFNN with the operator NOT'''
    true = self.F
    indet = 1-self.I
    false = self.T
    if self.label!="":
        l = "not "+self.label
    else:
        l=""
    return SVFNN(l,true,indet,false)
```

```
def NOT(self):
    '''Negation of a SVFNM'''
    R = create_matrix(self.row,self.column)

    P = self.matrix

    for i in range(self.row):
        for j in range(self.column):
            p = SVFNN(P[i][j][0],P[i][j][1],P[i][j][2],P[i][j][3])
            notp = p.NOT()
            R[i][j]=[notp.label,notp.T,notp.I,notp.F]
    return SVFNM(R)
```

3.3. Determining the Score, Accuracy, and Certainty Matrices of Single-Valued Fermatean Neutrosophic Matrix

The Python program for calculating the score, accuracy, and certainty of a SVFNM is shown below, first for SVFNN, and later for SVFNM:

Figure 5. Code of the methods score, accuracy, and certainty of SVFNN (left) and SVFNM (right).

```
def sc(self):
    '''Score of the SVFNN'''
    return (2+self.T-self.I-self.F)/3

def ac(self):
    '''Accuracy of the SVFNN'''
    return self.T-self.I-self.F

def cert(self):
    '''Certainty of the SVFNN'''
    return self.T
```

```
def sc(self):
    '''Score of a SVFNM'''
    R = create_matrix(self.row,self.column)

    P = self.matrix

    for i in range(self.row):
        for j in range(self.column):
            p = SVFNN(P[i][j][0],P[i][j][1],P[i][j][2],P[i][j][3])
            scorep = p.sc()
            R[i][j]=scorep
    print_matrix(R)

def ac(self):
    '''Accuracy of a SVFNM'''
    R = create_matrix(self.row,self.column)

    P = self.matrix

    for i in range(self.row):
        for j in range(self.column):
            p = SVFNN(P[i][j][0],P[i][j][1],P[i][j][2],P[i][j][3])
            accuracyp = p.ac()
            R[i][j]= accuracyp
    print_matrix(R)

def cert(self):
    '''Certainty of a SVFNM'''
    R = create_matrix(self.row,self.column)

    P = self.matrix

    for i in range(self.row):
        for j in range(self.column):
            p = SVFNN(P[i][j][0],P[i][j][1],P[i][j][2],P[i][j][3])
            certaintyp = p.cert()
            R[i][j]= certaintyp
    print_matrix(R)
```

3.4. Computing the Union of Two Single-Valued Fermatean Neutrosophic Matrices

The union of two single-valued neutrosophic matrices A and B is defined as follows:

$$A \cup B = C = \left[\langle c_{ij_T}, c_{ij_I}, c_{ij_F}\rangle\right]_{m\times n} \tag{11}$$

Where:

$$c_{ij_T} = a_{ij_T} \vee b_{ij_T},$$

$$c_{ij_I} = a_{ij_I} \wedge b_{ij_I},$$

$$c_{ij_F} = a_{ij_F} \wedge b_{ij_F}.$$

The Python programs for calculating the union of SVFNNs and SVFNMs are shown in Figure 6:

Figure 6. Code of the method __or__ of SVFNNs and SVFNMs.

```
def __or__(self,y):
    '''Disjunction of two SVFNNs with the operator |'''
    true = max(self.T,y.T)
    indet = min(self.I,y.I)
    false = min(self.F,y.F)
    if self.label!="" and y.label!="":
        l = self.label+" or "+y.label
    else:
        l = ""
    return SVFNN(l,true,indet,false)
```

```
def __or__(self,other):
    '''Disjunction of two SVFNMs'''
    r1 = self.row
    c1 = self.column

    r2 = other.row
    c2 = other.column

    try:
        assert r1 == r2
        assert c1 == c2

        R = create_matrix(self.row,self.column)

        P = self.matrix
        Q = other.matrix

        for i in range(r1):
            for j in range(c1):
                p = SVFNN(P[i][j][0],P[i][j][1],P[i][j][2],P[i][j][3])
                q = SVFNN(Q[i][j][0],Q[i][j][1],Q[i][j][2],Q[i][j][3])
                disj = p|q
                R[i][j]=[disj.label,disj.T,disj.I,disj.F]
        return SVFNM(R)

    except (AssertionError,TypeError):
        print("This operation is invalid")
```

3.5. Computing the Intersection of Two Single-Valued Fermatean Neutrosophic Matrices

The union of two single-valued Fermatean neutrosophic matrices *A* and *B* is defined as follows:

$$A \cap B = D = \left[\left\langle d_{ij_T}, d_{ij_I}, d_{ij_F} \right\rangle\right]_{m\times n} \tag{12}$$

Where:

$$d_{ij_T} = a_{ij_T} \wedge b_{ij_T},$$

$$d_{ij_I} = a_{ij_I} \vee b_{ij_I},$$

$$d_{ij_F} = a_{ij_F} \vee b_{ij_F},$$

The Python program for calculating the intersection of SVFNNs and SVFNMs is shown in Figure 7.

Figure 7. Code of the method__and____ of SVFNNs and SVFNMs.

```
def __and__(self,y):
    '''Conjunction of two SVFNNs with the operator &'''
    true = min(self.T,y.T)
    indet = max(self.I,y.I)
    false = max(self.F,y.F)
    if self.label!="" and y.label!="":
        l = self.label+" and "+y.label
    else:
        l = ""
    return SVFNN(l,true,indet,false)
```

```
def __and__(self,other):
    '''Conjunction of two SVFNMs'''
    r1 = self.row
    c1 = self.column

    r2 = other.row
    c2 = other.column

    try:
        assert r1 == r2
        assert c1 == c2

        R = create_matrix(self.row,self.column)

        P = self.matrix
        Q = other.matrix

        for i in range(r1):
            for j in range(c1):
                p = SVFNN(P[i][j][0],P[i][j][1],P[i][j][2],P[i][j][3])
                q = SVFNN(Q[i][j][0],Q[i][j][1],Q[i][j][2],Q[i][j][3])
                conj = p&q
                R[i][j]=[conj.label,conj.T,conj.I,conj.F]
        return SVFNM(R)

    except (AssertionError,TypeError):
        print("This operation is invalid")
```

3.6. Computing Addition Operation of Two Single-Valued Fermatean Neutrosophic Matrices

The addition of two single-valued Fermatean neutrosophic matrices A and B is defined as follow:

$$A \oplus B = S = \left[\langle s_{ij_T}, s_{ij_I}, s_{ij_F}\rangle\right]_{m\times n} \tag{13}$$

Where:

$$s_{ij_T} = a_{ij_T} + b_{ij_T} - a_{ij_T}.b_{ij_T},$$

$$s_{ij_I} = a_{ij_I}.b_{ij_I},$$

$$s_{ij_F} = a_{ij_F}.b_{ij_F},$$

The Python program for calculating the addition between two SVFNNs and SVFNMs is shown in Figure 8.

Figure 8. Code of the method __add__ of SVFNNs and SVFNMs.

```
def __add__(self,y):
    '''Addition of two SVFNNs with the operator +'''
    true = self.T+y.T-self.T*y.T
    indet = self.I*y.I
    false = self.F*y.F
    if self.label!="" and y.label!="":
        l = self.label+" + "+y.label
    else:
        l = ""
    return SVFNN(l,true,indet,false)
```

```
def __matmul__(self,other):
    '''Multiplication of two SVFNMs with the operator @'''
    r1 = self.row
    c1 = self.column

    r2 = other.row
    c2 = other.column

    try:
        assert r1 == r2
        assert c1 == c2

        R = create_matrix(self.row,self.column)

        P = self.matrix
        Q = other.matrix

        for i in range(r1):
            for j in range(c1):
                p = SVFNN(P[i][j][0],P[i][j][1],P[i][j][2],P[i][j][3])
                q = SVFNN(Q[i][j][0],Q[i][j][1],Q[i][j][2],Q[i][j][3])
                prod = p*q
                R[i][j]=[prod.label,prod.T,prod.I,prod.F]
        return SVFNM(R)

    except (AssertionError,TypeError):
        print("This operation is invalid")
```

3.7. Computing the Product of Two Single-Valued Fermatean Neutrosophic Matrices

The product of two single valued Fermatean neutrosophic matrices A and B is defined as follows:

$$AB = R = [\langle r_{ij_T}, r_{ij_I}, r_{ij_F}\rangle]_{m\times n} \quad (14)$$

Where:

$$r_{ij_T} = a_{ij_T} . b_{ij_T},$$

$$r_{ij_I} = a_{ij_I} + b_{ij_I} - a_{ij_I} . b_{ij_I},$$

$$r_{ij_F} = a_{ij_F} + b_{ij_F} - a_{ij_F} . b_{ij_F},$$

The Python program for calculating the product between two SVFNNs and SVFNMs is shown in Figure 9.

Figure 9. Code of the methods __mul__ and __matmul__ for SVFNNs and SVFNMs, respectively

```
def __mul__(self,y):
    '''Product of two SVFNNs with the operator *'''
    true = self.T*y.T
    indet = self.I+y.I-self.I*y.I
    false = self.F+y.F-self.F*y.F
    if self.label!="" and y.label!="":
        l = self.label+" * "+y.label
    else:
        l = ""
    return SVFNN(l,true,indet,false)
```

```
def __matmul__(self,other):
    '''Multiplication of two SVFNMs with the operator @'''
    r1 = self.row
    c1 = self.column

    r2 = other.row
    c2 = other.column

    try:
        assert r1 == r2
        assert c1 == c2

        R = create_matrix(self.row,self.column)

        P = self.matrix
        Q = other.matrix

        for i in range(r1):
            for j in range(c1):
                p = SVFNN(P[i][j][0],P[i][j][1],P[i][j][2],P[i][j][3])
                q = SVFNN(Q[i][j][0],Q[i][j][1],Q[i][j][2],Q[i][j][3])
                prod = p*q
                R[i][j]=[prod.label,prod.T,prod.I,prod.F]
        return SVFNM(R)

    except (AssertionError,TypeError):
        print("This operation is invalid")
```

3.8. Computing the Transpose of a Single-Valued Fermatean Neutrosophic Matrix

The Python program for calculating the transpose of a SVFNM is shown in Figure 10.

Figure 10. Code of the method __transp__ of the transpose of a SVFNM.

```
def transp(self):
    '''Transpose of a SVFNM'''
    R = create_matrix(self.column,self.row)

    P = self.matrix

    for i in range(self.column):
        for j in range(self.row):
            p = SVFNN(P[j][i][0],P[j][i][1],P[j][i][2],P[j][i][3])
            R[i][j]=[p.label,p.T,p.I,p.F]
    return SVFNM(R)
```

3.9. Comparing Two Single-Valued Fermatean Neutrosophic Matrices

To compare two single-valued Fermatean neutrosophic numbers $A = \langle T_A, I_A, F_A \rangle$ and $B = \langle T_B, I_B, F_B \rangle$ we use the criteria $A \leq B$ if and only if $T_A \leq T_B$, $I_B \leq I_A$, and $F_B \leq F_A$.

The Python program for comparing two SVFNMs, which is a matrix of Boolean values as the result of pair-wise comparing between SVFNN elements, this is shown in Figure 11.

Figure 11. Code of the method __le__ of both, the SVFNNs and SVFNMs.

```
def __le__(self,y):
    '''Compare two SVFNNs with the operator <='''
    if self.T<=y.T and self.I>=y.I and self.F>=y.F:
        return True
    else:
        return False
```

```
def __le__(self,other):
    '''Comparing two SVFNMs'''
    r1 = self.row
    c1 = self.column

    r2 = other.row
    c2 = other.column

    try:
        assert r1 == r2
        assert c1 == c2

        R = create_matrix(self.row,self.column)

        P = self.matrix
        Q = other.matrix

        for i in range(r1):
            for j in range(c1):
                p = SVFNN(P[i][j][0],P[i][j][1],P[i][j][2],P[i][j][3])
                q = SVFNN(Q[i][j][0],Q[i][j][1],Q[i][j][2],Q[i][j][3])
                comp = p<=q
                R[i][j]=comp
        print_matrix(R)
        return ""

    except (AssertionError,TypeError):
        print("This operation is invalid")
```

3.10. An Illustrative Example

Example 1. Let us define two single-valued Fermatean matrices *M* and *N* typed as python lists of lists, and calculate neutrosophic operations on them.

M = [[[“”,.8,.2,.1], [“”,.2,.1,.6], [“”,.1,0,.9]], [[“”,.3,.1,.6], [“A”,.4,.01,.8], [“”,.5,.5,.5]]]

N = [[[“”,.7,.3,.2],[“”,.8,.3,.1], [“”,.4,.6,.6]], [[“”,.7,.01,.3], [“B”,.2,.9,.3], [“”,.4,.4,.6]]]

For dealing with SVFNMs we have to define objects $M = SVFNM(M)$ and $N = SVFNM(N)$

For printing them using *print(M)* and *print(N)*, we have:

[(0.8,0.2,0.1) (0.2,0.1,0.6) (0.1,0,0.9)] [(0.3,0.1,0.6) (A,0.4,0.01,0.8) (0.5,0.5,0.5)]

[(0.7,0.3,0.2) (0.8,0.3,0.1) (0.4,0.6,0.6)] [(0.7,0.01,0.3) (B,0.2,0.9,0.3) (0.4,0.4,0.6)]

For the complement of M we have *print(M.NOT())*, obtaining the following matrix:

[(0.1,0.8,0.8) (0.6,0.9,0.2) (0.9,1,0.1)]

[(0.6,0.9,0.3) (not A,0.8,0.99,0.4) (0.5,0.5,0.5)]

The score, accuracy, and certainty matrices of *M*, using $M.sc()$, $M.ac()$, and $M.cert()$
are the following, respectively:

[0.8333333333333331 0.5 0.4000000000000001] [0.5333333333333332 0.53 0.5]

[0.5000000000000001 -0.5 -0.8] [-0.4 -0.41000000000000003 -0.5]

[0.8 0.2 0.1] [0.3 0.4 0.5]

The result of *print(M|N)* for the union and *print(M&N)* for the intersection are the following:

[(0.7,0.3,0.2) (0.2,0.3,0.6) (0.1,0.6,0.9)] [(0.3,0.1,0.6) (A and B,0.2,0.9,0.8) (0.4,0.5,0.6)]

[(0.8,0.2,0.1) (0.8,0.1,0.1) (0.4,0,0.6)] [(0.7,0.01,0.3) (A or B,0.4,0.01,0.3) (0.5,0.4,0.5)]

For calculating the sum (*print(M+N)*) and the product (*print(M@N)*) we obtained, respectively:

[(0.94,0.06,0.02) (0.84,0.03,0.06) (0.46,0.0,0.54)] [(0.79,0.001,0.18) (A + B,0.52,0.009,0.24) (0.7,0.2,0.3)]

[(0.56,0.44,0.28)(0.16,0.37,0.64) (0.04,0.6,0.96)] [(0.21,0.109,0.72) (A* B,0.08,0.901,0.86) (0.2,0.7,0.8)]

The Transpose of *M*, using *M.transp()*, is the following:

[(0.8,0.2,0.1) (0.3,0.1,0.6)]

[(0.2,0.1,0.6) (A,0.4,0.01,0.8)]

[(0.1,0,0.9) (0.5,0.5,0.5)]

Using *print(M<=N)* we obtained the matrix:

[False False False]
[True False False]

4. COMPUTING THE INTERVAL VALUED FERMATEAN NEUTROSOPHIC MATRIX OPERATIONS USING PYTHON LANGUAGE

4.1 Checking the Matrix Is IVFNM

Similarly to the SVFNM, we defined a class called *IVFNN* for calculating with Interval-Valued Fermatean Neutrosophic Numbers, and *IVFNM* for Interval-Valued Fermatean Neutrosophic Matrices. See Figures 12 and 13.

Figure 12. Code of the class IVFNN with the methods __init__ and __str__.

```
class IVFNN:
    def __init__(self,label,T,I,F):
        '''Definition of  Interval-valued Fermatean Neutrosophic Number
           label: It's optional
           T: Interval of Truthfulness
           I: Interval of Indeterminacy
           F: Interval of Falseness
        '''
        try:
            TL = T[0]
            IL = I[0]
            FL = F[0]
            TU = T[1]
            IU = I[1]
            FU = F[1]
            assert 0 <= TL <= 1
            assert 0 <= IL <= 1
            assert 0 <= FL <= 1
            assert 0<= (TL**3)+(FL**3)<=1
            assert 0<= (IL**3)<=1
            assert 0 <= TU <= 1
            assert 0 <= IU <= 1
            assert 0 <= FU <= 1
            assert 0<= (TU**3)+(FU**3)<=1
            assert 0<= (IU**3)<=1
            assert TL <= TU
            assert IL <= IU
            assert FL <= FU
            self.label = label
            self.T = T
            self.I = I
            self.F = F
        except AssertionError:
            print("This isn't an IVFNN")

    def __str__(self):
        '''Return a string representation of a Interval-Valued Fermatean Neutrosophic Number'''
        if self.label=="":
            return '(%s,%s,%s)'%(self.T,self.I,self.F)
        else:
            return '(%s,%s,%s,%s)'%(self.label,self.T,self.I,self.F)
```

Figure 13. Code of the class IVFNM with the methods __init__ and __str__.

```
class IVFNM:
    '''Class of Interval-Valued Fermatean Neutrosophic Matrix'''
    def __init__(self,M):
        '''Enter a matrix M in form of list of lists and the output is a matrix of Interval-Valued Fermatean Neutrosophic Numbers'''
        s=[len(m) for m in M] #Check that all the rows have the same length
        L = [l for l in s if(l==s[0])]

        try:
            assert len(s)==len(L)
            self.row = len(M)
            self.column = s[0]
            self.matrix = M

            R = create_matrix(self.row,self.column)

            for i in range(self.row):
                for j in range(self.column):
                    R[i][j]=IVFNN(M[i][j][0],M[i][j][1],M[i][j][2],M[i][j][3])

        except (AssertionError,TypeError):
            print("This isn't an IVFNM")


    def __str__(self):
        '''Output the IVFNM in form of matrix'''
        r=self.row
        c=self.column
        M = self.matrix

        for i in range(r):
            for j in range(c):
                if j == 0:
                    print('[',IVFNN(M[i][j][0],M[i][j][1],M[i][j][2],M[i][j][3]),end=' ')
                elif j==c-1:
                    print(IVFNN(M[i][j][0],M[i][j][1],M[i][j][2],M[i][j][3]),']',end=' ')
                else:
                    print(IVFNN(M[i][j][0],M[i][j][1],M[i][j][2],M[i][j][3]),end=' ')
            print("")
        return ""
```

4.2. Determining Complement of an Interval-Valued Fermatean Neutrosophic Matrix

The complement of an interval- valued Fermatean neutrosophic is defined as follow:

$$A^c = \left[< [a^L_{ij_F}, a^U_{ij_F}], [1 - a^U_{ij_I}, 1 - a^L_{ij_I}], [a^L_{ij_T}, a^U_{ij_T}] >\right]_{m\times n} \tag{15}$$

The python code is in Figure 14.

Figure 14. Code of the method NOT of both, IVFNN and IVFNM.

```
def NOT(self):
    '''Negation of one IVFNN with the operator NOT'''
    true = self.F
    indetL = 1-self.I[1]
    indetU = 1-self.I[0]
    indet = [indetL,indetU]
    false = self.T
    if self.label!="":
        l = "not "+self.label
    else:
        l=""
    return IVFNN(l,true,indet,false)
```

```
def NOT(self):
    '''Negation of an IVFNMs'''

    R = create_matrix(self.row,self.column)

    P = self.matrix

    for i in range(self.row):
        for j in range(self.column):
            p = IVFNN(P[i][j][0],P[i][j][1],P[i][j][2],P[i][j][3])
            notp = p.NOT()
            R[i][j]=[notp.label,notp.T,notp.I,notp.F]
    return IVFNM(R)
```

4.3. Determining the Score, Accuracy, and Certainty Matrix of an Interval-Valued Fermatean Neutrosophic Matrix

Figure 15 contains the code for calculating these values.

Figure 15. Code of the scalar values, namely, score, accuracy, and certainty, of both IVFNN and IVFNM.

```
def sc(self):
    '''Score of the IVFNN'''
    true = self.T
    indet = self.I
    false = self.F
    return (4+(true[0]+true[1])-(indet[0]+indet[1])-(false[0]+false[1]))/6

def ac(self):
    '''Accuracy of the IVFNN'''
    true = self.T
    indet = self.I
    false = self.F
    return (true[0]+true[1])-(indet[0]+indet[1])-(false[0]+false[1])

def cert(self):
    '''Certainty of the IVFNN'''
    true = self.T
    return (true[0]+true[1])/2
```

```
def sc(self):
    '''Score of an IVFNM'''
    R = create_matrix(self.row,self.column)

    P = self.matrix

    for i in range(self.row):
        for j in range(self.column):
            p = IVFNN(P[i][j][0],P[i][j][1],P[i][j][2],P[i][j][3])
            scorep = p.sc()
            R[i][j]=scorep
    print_matrix(R)

def ac(self):
    '''Accuracy of an IVFNM'''
    R = create_matrix(self.row,self.column)

    P = self.matrix

    for i in range(self.row):
        for j in range(self.column):
            p = IVFNN(P[i][j][0],P[i][j][1],P[i][j][2],P[i][j][3])
            accuracyp = p.ac()
            R[i][j]= accuracyp
    print_matrix(R)

def cert(self):
    '''Certainty of an IVFNM'''
    R = create_matrix(self.row,self.column)

    P = self.matrix

    for i in range(self.row):
        for j in range(self.column):
            p = IVFNN(P[i][j][0],P[i][j][1],P[i][j][2],P[i][j][3])
            certaintyp = p.cert()
            R[i][j]= certaintyp
    print_matrix(R)
```

4.4. Computing Union of Two Interval-Valued Neutrosophic Matrices

The union of two interval valued Fermatean neutrosophic matrices A and is defined as follow:

$$A \cup B = C = \left[< [c^L_{ij_T}, c^U_{ij_T}], [c^L_{ij_I}, c^U_{ij_I}], [c^L_{ij_F}, c^U_{ij_F}] >\right]_{m\times n} \tag{16}$$

Where,

$$c^L_{ij_T} = a^L_{ij_T} \vee b^L_{ij_T}, \; c^U_{ij_T} = a^U_{ij_T} \vee b^U_{ij_T}$$

$$c^L_{ij_I} = a^L_{ij_I} \wedge b^L_{ij_I}, \; c^U_{ij_I} = a^U_{ij_I} \wedge b^U_{ij_I}$$

$c_{ij_F}^L = a_{ij_F}^L \wedge b_{ij_F}^L,\ c_{ij_F}^U = a_{ij_F}^U \wedge b_{ij_F}^U$

See the python program in Figure 16.

Figure 16. Code of the union between two IVFNNs and IVFNMs.

```
def __or__(self,y):
    '''Disjunction of two IVFNNs with the operator |'''
    trueL = max(self.T[0],y.T[0])
    indetL = min(self.I[0],y.I[0])
    falseL = min(self.F[0],y.F[0])
    trueU = max(self.T[1],y.T[1])
    indetU = min(self.I[1],y.I[1])
    falseU =  min(self.F[1],y.F[1])
    true = [trueL,trueU]
    indet = [indetL,indetU]
    false = [falseL,falseU]

    if self.label!="" or y.label!="":
        l = self.label+" or "+y.label
    else:
        l = ""
    return IVFNN(l,true,indet,false)
```

```
def __or__(self,other):
    '''Disjunction of two IVFNMs'''
    r1 = self.row
    c1 = self.column

    r2 = other.row
    c2 = other.column

    try:
        assert r1 == r2
        assert c1 == c2

        R = create_matrix(self.row,self.column)

        P = self.matrix
        Q = other.matrix

        for i in range(r1):
            for j in range(c1):
                p = IVFNN(P[i][j][0],P[i][j][1],P[i][j][2],P[i][j][3])
                q = IVFNN(Q[i][j][0],Q[i][j][1],Q[i][j][2],Q[i][j][3])
                disj = p|q
                R[i][j]=[disj.label,disj.T,disj.I,disj.F]
        return IVFNM(R)

    except (AssertionError,TypeError):
        print("This operation is invalid")
```

4.5. Computing Intersection of Two Interval-Valued Fermatean Neutrosophic Matrices

The union of two interval valued Fermatean neutrosophic matrices A and B is defined as follow:

$$A \cap B = D = \left[< [d_{ij_T}^L, d_{ij_T}^U], [d_{ij_I}^L, d_{ij_I}^U], [d_{ij_F}^L, d_{ij_F}^U] > \right]_{m \times n} \tag{17}$$

Where,

$d_{ij_T}^L = a_{ij_T}^L \vee b_{ij_T}^L,\ d_{ij_T}^U = a_{ij_T}^U \vee b_{ij_T}^U,$

$d_{ij_I}^L = a_{ij_I}^L \wedge b_{ij_I}^L,\ d_{ij_I}^U = a_{ij_I}^U \wedge b_{ij_I}^U,$

$d_{ij_F}^L = a_{ij_F}^L \wedge b_{ij_F}^L,\ d_{ij_F}^U = a_{ij_F}^U \wedge b_{ij_F}^U.$

The Python program for calculating the intersection of IVFNNs and IVFNMs is shown in Figure 17.

Figure 17. Code of the intersection between two IVFNNs and IVFNMs

```
def __and__(self,y):
    '''Conjunction of two IVFNNs with the operator &'''
    trueL = min(self.T[0],y.T[0])
    indetL = max(self.I[0],y.I[0])
    falseL = max(self.F[0],y.F[0])
    trueU = min(self.T[1],y.T[1])
    indetU = max(self.I[1],y.I[1])
    falseU = max(self.F[1],y.F[1])
    true = [trueL,trueU]
    indet = [indetL,indetU]
    false = [falseL,falseU]

    if self.label!="" and y.label!="":
        l = self.label+" and "+y.label
    else:
        l = ""
    return IVFNN(l,true,indet,false)
```

```
def __and__(self,other):
    '''Conjunction of two IVFNMs'''
    r1 = self.row
    c1 = self.column

    r2 = other.row
    c2 = other.column

    try:
        assert r1 == r2
        assert c1 == c2

        R = create_matrix(self.row,self.column)

        P = self.matrix
        Q = other.matrix

        for i in range(r1):
            for j in range(c1):
                p = IVFNN(P[i][j][0],P[i][j][1],P[i][j][2],P[i][j][3])
                q = IVFNN(Q[i][j][0],Q[i][j][1],Q[i][j][2],Q[i][j][3])
                conj = p&q
                R[i][j]=[conj.label,conj.T,conj.I,conj.F]
        return IVFNM(R)
    except (AssertionError,TypeError):
        print("This operation is invalid")
```

4.6 Computing Power of an Interval-Valued Fermatean Neutrosophic Matrix

The Python program for calculating the power of an IVFNM is shown in Figure 18.

Figure 18. Code of the power of IVFNM

```
def __pow__(self,l):
    '''Power of an IVFNM to a scalar l'''

    R = create_matrix(self.row,self.column)

    P = self.matrix
    try:
        assert 0<=l
        for i in range(self.row):
            for j in range(self.column):
                p = IVFNN(P[i][j][0],P[i][j][1],P[i][j][2],P[i][j][3])
                true = [min([(p.T[0])**l,1]),min([(p.T[1])**l,1])]
                indet = [min([1-(1-p.I[0])**l,1]),min([1-(1-p.I[1])**l,1])]
                false = [min([1-(1-p.F[0])**l,1]),min([1-(1-p.F[1])**l,1])]
                if p.label == "":
                    R[i][j]=[true,indet,false]
                else:
                    R[i][j]=[p.label,true,indet,false]
        print_matrix(R)
    except (AssertionError,TypeError):
        print("This operation is invalid")
    return ""
```

4.7. Computing Addition Operation of Two Interval-Valued Fermatean Neutrosophic Matrices

The addition of two interval valued fermatean neutrosophic matrices *A* and *B* is defined as follows:

$$A \oplus B = S = \left[< [s^L_{ij_T}, s^U_{ij_T}], [s^L_{ij_I}, s^U_{ij_I}], [s^L_{ij_F}, s^U_{ij_F}] >\right]_{m\times n} \tag{18}$$

Where,

$$s^L_{ij_T} = a^L_{ij_T} + b^L_{ij_T} - a^L_{ij_T}.b^L_{ij_T},\ s^U_{ij_T} = a^U_{ij_T} + b^U_{ij_T} - a^U_{ij_T}.b^U_{ij_T},$$

$$s^L_{ij_I} = a^L_{ij_I}.b^L_{ij_I},\ s^U_{ij_I} = a^U_{ij_I}.b^U_{ij_I},$$

$$s^L_{ij_F} = a^L_{ij_F}.b^L_{ij_F},\ s^U_{ij_F} = a^U_{ij_F}.b^U_{ij_F}.$$

The Python program for calculating the addition between two IVFNMs is shown below:

Figure 19. Code of the addition between two IVFNNs and IVFNMs

```python
def __add__(self,y):
    '''Addition of two IVFNNs with the operator +'''
    trueL = self.T[0]+y.T[0]-self.T[0]*y.T[0]
    indetL = self.I[0]*y.I[0]
    falseL = self.F[0]*y.F[0]
    trueU = self.T[1]+y.T[1]-self.T[1]*y.T[1]
    indetU = self.I[1]*y.I[1]
    falseU =  self.F[1]*y.F[1]
    true = [trueL,trueU]
    indet = [indetL,indetU]
    false = [falseL,falseU]

    if self.label!="" and y.label!="":
        l = self.label+" + "+y.label
    else:
        l = ""
    return IVFNN(l,true,indet,false)
```

```python
def __add__(self,other):
    '''Addition of two IVFNMs with the operator +'''
    r1 = self.row
    c1 = self.column

    r2 = other.row
    c2 = other.column

    try:
        assert r1 == r2
        assert c1 == c2

        R = create_matrix(self.row,self.column)

        P = self.matrix
        Q = other.matrix

        for i in range(r1):
            for j in range(c1):
                p = IVFNN(P[i][j][0],P[i][j][1],P[i][j][2],P[i][j][3])
                q = IVFNN(Q[i][j][0],Q[i][j][1],Q[i][j][2],Q[i][j][3])
                ad = p+q
                R[i][j]=[ad.label,ad.T,ad.I,ad.F]
        return IVFNM(R)

    except (AssertionError,TypeError):
        print("This operation is invalid")
```

4.8. Computing Product of Two Interval-Valued Fermatean Neutrosophic Matrices

The product of two interval valued Fermatean neutrosophic matrices *A* and *B* is defined as follows:

$$A\,B \;=\; R \;=\; \left[<\;[r^L_{ij_T}, r^U_{ij_T}], [r^L_{ij_I}, r^U_{ij_I}], [r^L_{ij_F}, r^U_{ij_F}]>\right]_{m\times n} \tag{19}$$

Where,

$$r^L_{ij_T} = a^L_{ij_T}\,.\,b^L_{ij_T},\; r^U_{ij_T} = a^U_{ij_T}\,.\,b^U_{ij_T}$$

$$r^L_{ij_I} = a^L_{ij_I} + b^L_{ij_I} - a^L_{ij_I}\,.\,b^L_{ij_I},\; r^U_{ij_I} = a^U_{ij_I} + b^U_{ij_I} - a^U_{ij_I}\,.\,b^U_{ij_I}$$

$$r^L_{ij_F} = a^L_{ij_F} + b^L_{ij_F} - a^L_{ij_F}\,.\,b^L_{ij_F},\; r^U_{ij_F} = a^U_{ij_F} + b^U_{ij_F} - a^U_{ij_F}\,.\,b^U_{ij_F}$$

The Python program for calculating the product between two IVFNMs is shown below:

Figure 20. Code of the product between two IVFNNs and IVFNMs

```
def __mul__(self,y):
    '''Product of two IVFNNs with the operator *'''
    trueL = self.T[0]*y.T[0]
    indetL = self.I[0]+y.I[0]-self.I[0]*y.I[0]
    falseL = self.F[0]+y.F[0]-self.F[0]*y.F[0]
    trueU = self.T[1]*y.T[1]
    indetU = self.I[1]+y.I[1]-self.I[1]*y.I[1]
    falseU =  self.F[1]+y.F[1]-self.F[1]*y.F[1]
    true = [trueL,trueU]
    indet = [indetL,indetU]
    false = [falseL,falseU]

    if self.label!="" and y.label!="":
        l = self.label+" ⊗ "+y.label
    else:
        l = ""
    return IVFNN(l,true,indet,false)
```

```
def __matmul__(self,other):
    '''Product of two IVFNMs with the operator @'''
    r1 = self.row
    c1 = self.column

    r2 = other.row
    c2 = other.column

    try:
        assert r1 == r2
        assert c1 == c2

        R = create_matrix(self.row,self.column)

        P = self.matrix
        Q = other.matrix

        for i in range(r1):
            for j in range(c1):
                p = IVFNN(P[i][j][0],P[i][j][1],P[i][j][2],P[i][j][3])
                q = IVFNN(Q[i][j][0],Q[i][j][1],Q[i][j][2],Q[i][j][3])
                pr = p*q
                R[i][j]=[pr.label,pr.T,pr.I,pr.F]
        return IVFNM(R)
    except (AssertionError,TypeError):
        print("This operation is invalid")
```

4.9. Computing Transpose of an Interval-Valued Fermatean Neutrosophic Matrix

The Python program for calculating the transpose of an IVFNM is shown below in Figure 21.

Figure 21. Code for calculating the transpose of an IVFNM

```
def transp(self):
    '''Transpose of an IVFNM'''
    R = create_matrix(self.column,self.row)

    P = self.matrix

    for i in range(self.column):
        for j in range(self.row):
            p = IVFNN(P[j][i][0],P[j][i][1],P[j][i][2],P[j][i][3])
            R[i][j]=[p.label,p.T,p.I,p.F]
    return IVFNM(R)
```

4.10. Computing Difference of Two Interval-Valued Fermatean Neutrosophic Matrices

The difference of two interval valued Fermatean neutrosophic matrices A and B is defined as follow:

$$A \ominus_2 B = K = \left[< [r_{ij_T}^L, r_{ij_T}^U], [r_{ij_I}^L, r_{ij_I}^U], [r_{ij_F}^L, r_{ij_F}^U] >\right]_{m \times n} \tag{20}$$

Where,

$$r_{ij_T}^L = a_{ij_T}^L - b_{ij_F}^U,\ r_{ij_T}^U = a_{ij_T}^U - b_{ij_F}^L,$$

$$r_{ij_I}^L = \max\left(a_{ij_I}^L, b_{ij_I}^L\right),\ r_{ij_I}^U = \max\left(a_{ij_I}^U, b_{ij_I}^U\right),$$

$$r_{ij_F}^L = a_{ij_F}^L - b_{ij_T}^U,\ r_{ij_F}^U = a_{ij_F}^U - b_{ij_T}^L.$$

The Python program for calculating the difference between two IVFNMs is shown in Figure 22.

Figure 22. Code for calculating the difference between two IVFNMs

```
def __sub__(self,other):
    '''Difference of two IVFNMs with the operator -'''
    r1 = self.row
    c1 = self.column

    r2 = other.row
    c2 = other.column

    try:
        assert r1 == r2
        assert c1 == c2

        R = create_matrix(self.row,self.column)

        P = self.matrix
        Q = other.matrix

        for i in range(r1):
            for j in range(c1):
                p = IVFNN(P[i][j][0],P[i][j][1],P[i][j][2],P[i][j][3])
                q = IVFNN(Q[i][j][0],Q[i][j][1],Q[i][j][2],Q[i][j][3])
                if p.label!="" and q.label!="":
                    l = p.label+" - "+q.label
                    R[i][j]=[l,[p.T[0]-q.F[1],p.T[1]-q.F[0]],[max([p.I[0],q.I[0]]),max([p.I[1],q.I[1]])],[p.F[0]-q.T[1],p.F[1]-q.T[0]]]
                else:
                    R[i][j]=[[p.T[0]-q.F[1],p.T[1]-q.F[0]],[max([p.I[0],q.I[0]]),max([p.I[1],q.I[1]])],[p.F[0]-q.T[1],p.F[1]-q.T[0]]]
        print_matrix(R)
    except (AssertionError,TypeError):
        print("This operation is invalid")
    return ""
```

4.11. Computing Scalar Multiplication and Division of an Interval-Valued Fermatean Neutrosophic Matrix

The scalar multiplication of an interval-valued neutrosophic matrix A is $A_{\text{IVNM}} . z$ is defined as follows:

$$A_{\text{IVNM}} . z = Q = \left[< [q^L_{ij_T}, q^U_{ij_T}], [q^L_{ij_I}, q^U_{ij_I}], [q^L_{ij_F}, q^U_{ij_F}] >\right]_{m \times n} \tag{21}$$

Where,

$$q^L_{ij_T} = \min(a^L_{ij_T} . z, 1),\ q^U_{ij_T} = \min(a^U_{ij_T} . z, 1)$$

$$q^L_{ij_I} = \min\left(a^L_{ij_I} . z, 1\right),\ q^U_{ij_I} = \min\left(a^U_{ij_I} . z, 1\right)$$

$$q^L_{ij_F} = \min(a^L_{ij_F} . \text{z}, 1),\ q^U_{ij_F} = \min(a^U_{ij_F} . z, 1)$$

The scalar division of an interval-valued Fermatean neutrosophic matrix A is A_{IVNM}/z that is defined as follows:

$$A_{\text{IVNM}} . z = P = \left[< [p^L_{ij_T}, p^U_{ij_T}], [p^L_{ij_I}, p^U_{ij_I}], [p^L_{ij_F}, p^U_{ij_F}] >\right]_{m \times n} \tag{22}$$

where

$$p^L_{ij_T} = \min(a^L_{ij_T} / z, 1),\ p^U_{ij_T} = \min(a^U_{ij_T} / z, 1)$$

$$p^L_{ij_I} = \min\left(a^L_{ij_I} / z, 1\right),\ p^U_{ij_I} = \min\left(a^U_{ij_I} / z, 1\right)$$

$$p^L_{ij_F} = \min(a^L_{ij_F} / \text{z}, 1),\ p^U_{ij_F} = \min(a^U_{ij_F} / z, 1)$$

The Python program for calculating the scalar product and the scalar division of an IVFNM is shown below:

Figure 23. Code for calculating the scalar product and division of an IVFNM with a numerical value

```
def scprod(self,l):
    '''Product of an IVFNM by a scalar l'''

    R = create_matrix(self.row,self.column)

    P = self.matrix
    try:
        assert 0<=l
        for i in range(self.row):
            for j in range(self.column):
                p = IVFNN(P[i][j][0],P[i][j][1],P[i][j][2],P[i][j][3])
                true = [min([l*p.T[0],1]),min([l*p.T[1],1])]
                indet = [min([l*p.I[0],1]),min([l*p.I[1],1])]
                false = [min([l*p.F[0],1]),min([l*p.F[1],1])]
                if p.label == "":
                    R[i][j]=[true,indet,false]
                else:
                    R[i][j]=[p.label,true,indet,false]
        print_matrix(R)
    except (AssertionError,TypeError):
        print("This operation is invalid")
    return ""
```

```
def __truediv__(self,l):
    '''Product of an IVFNM by a scalar l'''

    P = self.matrix
    R = IVFNM(P)
    try:
        assert 0<=l
        R.scprod(1/l)
    except (AssertionError,TypeError):
        print("This operation is invalid")
    return ""
```

4.12. Comparing Two Interval-Valued Neutrosophic Matrices

To compare two Interval-valued Fermatean Neutrosophic Numbers

$A = \langle [T_A^L, T_A^U], [I_A^L, I_A^U], [F_A^L, F_A^U] \rangle$ and $B = \langle [T_B^L, T_B^U], [I_B^L, I_B^U], [F_B^L, F_B^U] \rangle$

we use the criteria $A \leq B$ if and only if

$$T_A^L \leq T_B^L, I_B^L \leq I_A^L, F_B^L \leq F_A^L, T_A^U \leq T_B^U, I_B^U \leq I_A^U, F_B^U \leq F_A^U.$$

The Python program for comparing two IVFNMs, which is a matrix of Boolean values as the result of pair-wise comparing between IVFNN elements, this is shown in Figure 24.

Figure 24. Code for comparing two IVFNNs and IVFNMs

```
def __le__(self,y):
    '''Compare two IVFNNs with the operator <='''
    if self.T[0]<=y.T[0] and self.I[0]>=y.I[0] and self.F[0]>=y.F[0] and self.T[1]<=y.T[1] and self.I[1]>=y.I[1] and self.F[1]>=y.F[1]:
        return True
    else:
        return False

def __le__(self,other):
    '''Comparing two IVFNMs'''
    r1 = self.row
    c1 = self.column

    r2 = other.row
    c2 = other.column

    try:
        assert r1 == r2
        assert c1 == c2

        R = create_matrix(self.row,self.column)

        P = self.matrix
        Q = other.matrix

        for i in range(r1):
            for j in range(c1):
                p = IVFNN(P[i][j][0],P[i][j][1],P[i][j][2],P[i][j][3])
                q = IVFNN(Q[i][j][0],Q[i][j][1],Q[i][j][2],Q[i][j][3])
                comp = p<=q
                R[i][j]=comp
        print_matrix(R)
        return ""
    except (AssertionError,TypeError):
        print("This operation is invalid")
```

4.13. An Example of Calculus With IVFNMs

Example 2. Let us define two interval-valued Fermatean matrices *P* and *Q* as two lists of lists. We used *P* = *IVFNM*(*P*) and *Q* = *SVFNM*(*Q*) for converting them to interval-valued Fermatean neutrosophic matrices:

P = [([0.8, 0.9],[0.2, 0.25],[0, 0.2]) ([0.01, 0.2],[0.1, 0.3],[0.6, 0.61]) ([0.1, 0.3],[0, 1],[0.9, 0.91])]

[([0.3, 0.4],[0.1, 0.5],[0, 0.6]) (A,[0.4, 0.6],[0.01, 0.02],[0.8, 0.9]) ([0.5, 0.5],[0.5, 0.5],[0.5, 0.5])]

Q = [([0.7, 0.71],[0.3, 0.34],[0.2, 0.23]) ([0.5, 0.8],[0.2, 0.3],[0.1, 0.31]) ([0.4, 0.42],[0.6, 0.6],[0.6, 0.6])]

[([0, 0.7],[0.01, 0.7],[0.3, 0.6]) (B,[0.2, 0.5],[0.9, 1],[0.3, 0.4]) ([0.4, 0.7],[0.4, 0.4],[0.6, 0.61])]

For the complement of *P* we used *print(P.NOT())*, the matrix is the following:

[([0, 0.2],[0.75, 0.8],[0.8, 0.9]) ([0.6, 0.61],[0.7, 0.9],[0.01, 0.2]) ([0.9, 0.91],[0, 1],[0.1, 0.3])]

[([0, 0.6],[0.5, 0.9],[0.3, 0.4]) (not A,[0.8, 0.9],[0.98, 0.99],[0.4, 0.6]) ([0.5, 0.5],[0.5, 0.5],[0.5, 0.5])]

The score, accuracy, and certainty matrices of *P*, using *P*.*sc*(), *P*.*ac*(), and *P*.*cert*() are the following, respectively:

[0.8416666666666667 0.43333333333333335 0.26500000000000007]

[0.5833333333333334 0.5449999999999999 0.5],

[1.0500000000000003 -1.4 -2.41]

[-0.5 -0.7300000000000002 -1.0], and,

[0.8500000000000001 0.10500000000000001 0.2]

[0.35 0.5 0.5]

The union of *P* and *Q*, using *print*(*P*|*Q*), is the following:

[([0.8, 0.9],[0.2, 0.25],[0, 0.2]) ([0.5, 0.8],[0.1, 0.3],[0.1, 0.31]) ([0.4, 0.42],[0, 0.6],[0.6, 0.6])]

[([0.3, 0.7],[0.01, 0.5],[0, 0.6]) (A or B,[0.4, 0.6],[0.01, 0.02],[0.3, 0.4]) ([0.5, 0.7],[0.4, 0.4],[0.5, 0.5])]

The intersection of *P* and *Q*, using *print*(*P* & *Q*), is the following:

[([0.7, 0.71],[0.3, 0.34],[0.2, 0.23]) ([0.01, 0.2],[0.2, 0.3],[0.6, 0.61]) ([0.1, 0.3],[0.6, 1],[0.9, 0.91])]

[([0, 0.4],[0.1, 0.7],[0.3, 0.6]) (A and B,[0.2, 0.5],[0.9, 1],[0.8, 0.9]) ([0.4, 0.5],[0.5, 0.5],[0.6, 0.61])]

The sum of *P* and *Q*, with *print*(*P* + *Q*) is:

[([0.94,0.971],[0.06,0.085],[0.0,0.046]) ([0.505, 0.84],[0.02, 0.09],[0.06, 0.1891]) ([0.46, 0.594],[0.0, 0.6],[0.54, 0.546])]

[([0.3, 0.82],[0.001, 0.35],[0.0, 0.36]) (A+B,[0.52, 0.8],[0.009, 0.02],[0.24, 0.36]) ([0.7, 0.85],[0.2, 0.2],[0.3, 0.305])]

The product of P and Q, with $print(P@Q)$ is:

[([0.56, 0.639],[0.44, 0.505],[0.2, 0.384]) ([0.005, 0.16],[0.28, 0.51],[0.64, 0.7309]) ([0.04, 0.126],[0.6, 1.0],[0.96, 0.964])]

[([0.0, 0.28],[0.109, 0.85],[0.3, 0.84]) (A*B,[0.08, 0.3],[0.901, 1.0],[0.86, 0.94]) ([0.2, 0.35],[0.7, 0.7],[0.8, 0.805])]

The transpose of P that is calculated with $print(P.transp())$ is:

[([0.8, 0.9],[0.2, 0.25],[0, 0.2]) ([0.3, 0.4],[0.1, 0.5],[0, 0.6])]

[([0.01, 0.2],[0.1, 0.3],[0.6, 0.61]) (A,[0.4, 0.6],[0.01, 0.02],[0.8, 0.9])]

[([0.1, 0.3],[0, 1],[0.9, 0.91]) ([0.5, 0.5],[0.5, 0.5],[0.5, 0.5])]

The difference using $print(P - Q)$ is:

[[[0.57, 0.7], [0.3, 0.34], [-0.71, -0.5]] [[-0.3, 0.1], [0.2, 0.3], [-0.2, 0.11]] [[-0.5, -0.3], [0.6, 1], [0.48, 0.51]]]

[[[-0.3, 0.1], [0.1, 0.7], [-0.7, 0.6]] ['A - B', [0.0, 0.3], [0.9, 1], [0.3, 0.7]] [[-0.11, -0.1], [0.5, 0.5], [-0.2, 0.1]]]

After, we calculated the scalar product using $P.scprod(2.0)$, the scalar division using $P/2.0$, and the power $P**2.0$, where the scalar is 2.0. The results are shown in the following:

[[[1, 1], [0.4, 0.5], [0.0, 0.4]] [[0.02, 0.4], [0.2, 0.6], [1, 1]] [[0.2, 0.6], [0.0, 1], [1, 1]]]

[[[0.6, 0.8], [0.2, 1.0], [0.0, 1]] ['A', [0.8, 1], [0.02, 0.04], [1, 1]] [[1.0, 1.0], [1.0, 1.0], [1.0, 1.0]]],

[[[0.4, 0.45], [0.1, 0.125], [0.0, 0.1]] [[0.005, 0.1], [0.05, 0.15], [0.3, 0.305]] [[0.05, 0.15], [0.0, 0.5], [0.45, 0.455]]]

[[[0.15, 0.2], [0.05, 0.25], [0.0, 0.3]] ['A', [0.2, 0.3], [0.005, 0.01], [0.4, 0.45]] [[0.25, 0.25], [0.25, 0.25], [0.25, 0.25]]], and,

[[[0.64, 0.81], [0.36, 0.4375], [0.0, 0.36]] [[0.0001, 0.04], [0.19, 0.51], [0.84, 0.8479]] [[0.01, 0.09], [0.0, 1.0], [0.99, 0.9919]]]

[[[0.09, 0.16], [0.19, 0.75], [0.0, 0.84]] ['A', [0.16, 0.36], [0.0199, 0.0396], [0.96, 0.99]] [[0.25, 0.25], [0.75, 0.75], [0.75, 0.75]]]

Finally, for comparing P and Q, using $P < = Q$ it is obtained:

[False False False]

[False False False]

5. CONCLUSION

This chapter proposes some new Python programs for set-theoretic operations on Fermatean and interval valued Fermatean neutrosophic matrices. The package provides some programs such as complement, transpose, scalar multiplication of matrix, scalar division of matrix, computing the union, intersection addition, product, difference and division operations of the proposed special case of neutrosophic matrices. In future work, the complex Fermatean matrices can be studied using the Python language.

ACKNOWLEDGMENT

The authors are very grateful to the chief editor and reviewers for their comments and suggestions, which is helpful in improving the chapter.

REFERENCES

Abobala, M. (2021a). On the representation of neutrosophic matrices by neutrosophic linear transformations. *Journal of Mathematics*, 2021, 1–5. DOI:10.1155/2021/5591576

Abobala, M. (2021b). On refined neutrosophic matrices and their application in refined neutrosophic algebraic equations. *Journal of Mathematics*, 2021, 1–5. DOI:10.1155/2021/5531093

Abobala, M., Bal, M., & Hatip, A. (2021). A Review On Recent Advantages In Algebraic Theory Of Neutrosophic Matrices. *International Journal of Neutrosophic Science*, 68-86.

Ajay, D., & Chellamani, P. (2020). Pythagorean neutrosophic fuzzy graphs. *International Journal of Neutrosophic Science*, 11(2), 108–114.

Ajay, D., Karthiga, S., & Chellamani, P. (2021). A study on labelling of pythagorean neutrosophic fuzzy graphs. *Journal of Computational Mathematics*, 5(1), 105–116. DOI:10.26524/cm97

Al-Odhari, A. (2023). Some Algebraic Structure of Neutrosophic Matrices. *Prospects for Applied Mathematics and data Analysis (PAMDA), 1*(2), 37-44.

Anandhkumar, M., Kamalakannan, V., Chithra, S. M., & Said, B. (2023). Pseudo Similarity of Neutrosophic Fuzzy matrices. In *International Journal of Neutrosophic Science* (Vol. 20, Issue 4, pp. 191–196). DOI:10.54216/IJNS.200415

Antony Crispin Sweety, C., & Jansi, R. (2021). Fermatean Neutrosophic Sets. *International Journal of Advanced Research in Computer and Communication Engineering*, 10(6), 24–27.

Asim Basha, M., Mohammed Jabarulla, M., & Broumi, S. (2023). Neutrosophic Pythagorean Fuzzy Shortest Path in a Network. *Journal of Neutrosophic and Fuzzy Systems*, 6(1), 21–28. DOI:10.54216/JNFS.060103

Broumi, S., & Prabha, S. K. (2023). Fermatean Neutrosophic Matrices and Their Basic Operations. *Neutrosophic Sets and Systems*, 58, 572–595. DOI:10.5281/zenodo.8404536

Broumi, S., Raut, P. K., & Behera, S. P. (2023). Solving shortest path problems using an ant colony algorithm with triangular neutrosophic arc weights. *International Journal of Neutrosophic Science*, 20(4), 128–137. DOI:10.54216/IJNS.200410

Broumi, S., Sundareswaran, R., Shanmugapriya, M., Chellamani, P., Bakali, A., & Talea, M. (2023). Determination of various factors to evaluate a successful curriculum design using interval-valued Pythagorean neutrosophic graphs. *Soft Computing*, 1–20. DOI:10.1007/s00500-023-08996-y

Broumi, S., Topal, S., Bakali, A., Talea, M., & Smarandache, F. (2020). A Novel Python Toolbox for single and interval-valued neutrosophic matrices. In *Neutrosophic Sets in Decision Analysis and Operations Research* (pp. 281–330). IGI Global. DOI:10.4018/978-1-7998-2555-5.ch013

Bui, Q.-T., Ngo, M.-P., Snasel, V., Pedrycz, W., & Vo, B. (2022). The Sequence of Neutrosophic Soft Sets and a Decision-Making Problem in Medical Diagnosis. In *International Journal of Fuzzy Systems* (Vol. 24, Issue 4, pp. 2036–2053). Springer Science and Business Media LLC. https://doi.org/DOI:10.1007/s40815-022-01257-4

Chellamani, P., & Ajay, D. (2021). Pythagorean neutrosophic Dombi fuzzy graphs with an application to MCDM. *Neutrosophic Sets and Systems*, 47, 411–431.

Debnath, S. (2022). Fuzzy quadripartitioned neutrosophic soft matrix theory and its decision-making approach. *Journal of Computational and Cognitive Engineering*, 1(2), 88–93. DOI:10.47852/bonviewJCCE19522514205514

Dhar, M. (2020). Neutrosophic soft block matrices and some of its properties. *Int J Neutrosophic Sci*, 12(1), 39–49.

Donbosco, J. S. M., & Ganesan, D. (2022). The Energy of rough neutrosophic matrix and its application to MCDM problem for selecting the best building construction site. In *Decision Making: Applications in Management and Engineering* (Vol. 5, Issue 2, pp. 30–45). Regional Association for Security and Crisis Management. DOI:10.31181/dmame0305102022d

El-Ghareeb, H. A. (2019). Novel Open Source Python Neutrosophic Package. *Neutrosophic Sets and Systems*, 25, 136–160. DOI:10.5281/zenodo.2631514

Esther, S. P. C., & Shanmugapriya, M. M. (2022). M-Ordering on Generalized Regular Neutrosophic Fuzzy Matrices. *Mathematical Statistician and Engineering Applications*, 71(3), 1150–1158.

Gayathri, N. (n.d.). Coefficient of Correlation of Fermatean Neutrosophic sets. *Multidisciplinary Approach in Arts, Science & Commerce, 2*, 109.

Gayathri, N., Helen, M., & Mounika, P. (2020). On neutrosophic vague measure using python. In *Proceedings of International Conference on Advances in Materials Research (ICAMR - 2019)*. AIP Publishing. DOI:10.1063/5.0017191

Gonul Bilgin, N., Pamučar, D., & Riaz, M. (2022). Fermatean neutrosophic topological spaces and an application of neutrosophic kano method. *Symmetry*, 14(11), 2442. DOI:10.3390/sym14112442

Jansi, R., Mohana, R. K., & Smarandache, F. (2019). Correlation Measure for Pythagorean Neutrosophic Fuzzy Sets with T and F as Dependent Neutrosophic Components. *Neutrosophic Sets and Systems*, 30(1), 202–212.

Jeni Seles Martina, D., & Deepa, G. (2023). Operations on Multi-Valued Neutrosophic Matrices and Its Application to Neutrosophic Simplified-TOPSIS Method. *International Journal of Information Technology & Decision Making*, 22(01), 37–56. DOI:10.1142/S0219622022500572

Jeni Seles Martina, D., & Deepa, G. (2023a). *Some algebraic properties on rough neutrosophic matrix and its application to multi-criteria decision-making*. DOI:10.3934/math.20231230

Joice, P. R., Pricilla, M. T., & Broumi, S. (2023). Generalized Pre-closed Sets in Fermatean Neutrosophic Hypersoft Topological Spaces. *International Journal of Neutrosophic Science*, 20(3), 82–2. DOI:10.54216/IJNS.200308

Kandasamy, W.B.V., & Smarandache, F. (2004). *Fuzzy relational maps and neutrosophic relational maps*. HEXIS.

Khan, M., Anis, S., Bibi, K., Iqbal, S., & Smarandache, F. (2021). Complex Neutrosophic Soft Matrices Framework: An Application in Signal Processing. *Journal of Mathematics* (Vol. 2021, pp. 1–10). DOI:10.1155/2021/8887824

Lalitha, K., Sarguna, S., & Muthuraji, T. (2023, January). Application of Neutrosophic matrix in document retrieval systems. In *2023 Third International Conference on Advances in Electrical, Computing, Communication and Sustainable Technologies (ICAECT)* (pp. 1-5). IEEE. DOI:10.1109/ICAECT57570.2023.10118146

Mahima Poonia, & Bajaj, R. K. (2021). Complex Neutrosophic Matrix with Some Algebraic Operations and Matrix Norm Convergence. *Neutrosophic Sets Syst.*, 47, 165–178. DOI:10.5281/ZENODO.5775110

Manirathinam, T., Narayanamoorthy, S., Geetha, S., Othman, M. F. I., Alotaibi, B. S., Ahmadian, A., & Kang, D. (2023). Sustainable renewable energy system selection for self-sufficient households using integrated fermatean neutrosophic fuzzy stratified AHP-MARCOS approach. *Renewable Energy*, 218, 119292. DOI:10.1016/j.renene.2023.119292

Martina, D. J. S., & Deepa, G. (2023). Some algebraic properties on rough neutrosophic matrix and its application to multi-criteria decision-making. *AIMS Mathematics*, 8(10), 24132–24152. DOI:10.3934/math.20231230

Murugadas, P., & Kavitha, M. (2021, May). Convergence of fuzzy neutrosophic soft circulant matrices. *Journal of Physics: Conference Series*, 1850(1), 012076. DOI:10.1088/1742-6596/1850/1/012076

Murugappan, M., Govindan, V., & Grienggarai, R. (2023). Neighbourly Edge Irregularity on Interval-valued Pythagorean Neutrosophic Graph. International Journal on Robotics. *Automation and Sciences*, 5(2), 54–58.

Muthukumaran, V., Kumar, M. S., Silambarasan, I., Udhayakumar, R., & Broumi, S. (2023). A study on n-HyperSpherical Neutrosophic matrices. *Neutrosophic Sets and Systems*, 55(1), 21.

Ramya, M., Murali, S., Radha, R.(2022). Fermatean Quadripartitioned Neutrosophic Set. *International Journal of Creative Research Thoughts*.

Raut, P. K., Behera, S. P., Broumi, S., & Mishra, D. (2023). Calculation of shortest path on Fermatean Neutrosophic Networks. *Neutrosophic Sets and Systems*, 57(1), 22.

Salama, A., Dalla, R., Al Aswad, M., & Ali, R. (2022). On Some Novel Results About Neutrosophic Square Complex Matrices. *Journal of Neutrosophic and Fuzzy Systems*, 4(01), 21–29. DOI:10.54216/JNFS.040103

Sasikala, D., & Divya, B. (2023). A Newfangled Interpretation on Fermatean Neutrosophic Dombi Fuzzy Graphs. *Neutrosophic Systems with Applications*, 7, 36–53. DOI:10.61356/j.nswa.2023.21

Silambarasan, I. (2023). Some Algebric Structure of Spherical Neutrosophic Matrices. *TWMS J. App. and Eng. Math.*, 13(3), 1177–1189.

Sleem, A., Abdel-Baset, M., & El-henawy, I. (2020). PyIVNS: A python based tool for Interval-valued neutrosophic operations and normalization. *SoftwareX*, 12, 100632. DOI:10.1016/j.softx.2020.100632

Topal, S., Broumi, S., Bakali, A., Talea, M., & Smarandache, F. (2019). A python tool for implementations on bipolar neutrosophic matrices. *Infinite Study*.

Yusuf, Bilgin, & Bozma. (2022). Pentapartitioned Fermatean Neutrosophic Alpha Phi Normal Topological Spaces. *International Sciences and Innovation Congress*, 116-132.

KEY TERMS AND DEFINITIONS

Array: A type of ordered series of things.

Fermatean Neutrosophic Set: Set of neutrosophic elements dependent to a variable.

Implementation: A realization of a technical specification or algorithm as a program.

Interval Valued Fermatean Neutrosophic: Set: Fermatean Neutrosophic set of element components are intervals.

Matrix Operations: Operations that are defined on matrices.

Python: A programming language which is useful for scientific computations and implementations.

Toolbox: Programs or functions accessible from a single menu.

Chapter 8
A Proposed Neutrosophic Probability Model for Normalized DifferenceVegetation Index Using Remote Sensing:
Model Building on Climate

Shan-E-Fatima
Government College University, Lahore, Pakistan

Hina Khan
Government College University, Lahore, Pakistan

Kanwal Javid
https://orcid.org/0000-0003-3143-8868
Government College University, Lahore, Pakistan

ABSTRACT

In this research work, a new neutrosophic probability model named a neutrosophic Topp-Leone exponentiated generalized exponential distribution is proposed to model the normalized difference vegetation index (NDVI) of Pakistan in the year 2022. The MODIS was used in this research, which gave spatial and spectral information on NDVI in the Earth. NDVI maps were produced from the acquired data, and NDVI sensors computed the normalized difference vegetation index. Mathematical char-

DOI: 10.4018/979-8-3693-2085-3.ch008

acteristics of the proposed model of NDVI are derived, including central tendency measures, dispersion estimators, inferential statistics, moment generating function, order statistics, reliability measures, quantile-based statistical measures, and renyi entropy and graphical representations of the density function are also presented. The maximum likelihood technique is used to estimate the parameters for the proposed probability model.

1. INTRODUCTION

A mathematical method known as fuzzy logic enables the representation and processing of hazy or inaccurate data. It is based on the idea of fuzzy sets, which generalize crisp sets in the sense that they permit items to have degrees of membership ranging from 0 to 1. The degree to which an element belongs to a fuzzy set is represented by membership functions, which are given to variables and propositions in fuzzy logic. Depending on the nature of the problem, the membership functions can be defined using a variety of shapes, including triangular, trapezoidal, or Gaussian curves. Fuzzy logic is enhanced by the concept of neutrality or indeterminacy in the neutrosophic sense. Neutrosophic logic includes indeterminate truth values in addition to true and false values to deal with circumstances in which the truth or falsity of a statement cannot be decided or is only partially known. A new division of philosophy is introduced as neutrosophic statistics, which is executed as a generalization of fuzzy logic(Smarandache, 2000) (Rivieccio, 2008). This type of statistics is used for uncertain environments(Kashihara, 1996). It gained significance in utilizing the ambivalent phenomenon and estimating values in intervals instead of single values(Wang, Smarandache, Sunderraman, & Zhang, 2005) (Smarandache & Pramanik, 2016). The set of neutrosophic variables is defined in three components indeterminate (I), valid (T), and false (F) (Smarandache, 2003), (Salama, 2018) uses these three components to improve grayscale images(Salama, Smarandache, & Eisa, 2014) also (Salama, Smarandache, & Kromov, 2022)has developed "Neutrosophic Closed Set and Neutrosophic Continuous Functions" in application to GIS and topology(Vasantha Kandasamy, 2006),(Salama, Smarandache, & Kroumov, 2014), (Salama & Alblowi, 2012),(Smarandache, 2014).A new set theory based on the neutrosophic random variable is derived and named it neutrosophic set theory(Salama & Alblowi, 2012). "Neutrosophic crisp neighbourhoods system for the neutrosophic crisp points" has been established for local neutrosophic functions (Salama, Smarandache, & Alblowi), (Smarandache, 1999). Programming in the most potent, easily assessable software, EXCEL, has been developed to analyze neutrosophic data sets (Salama, El-Ghareeb, Manie, & Smarandache). The effect of neutrosophic random variables in decision trees is a significant area in classical decision-making(Abdel-Basset, Smarandache, & Ye, 2019), (M. Khan et al., 2018)to reach the best decision with more general and accurate information(Olgun & Hatip), (Pramanik & Mondal, 2015). This technique is used for comparison purposes with other different classical methods to reach the most precise decision(Basha, Tharwat, Ahmed, & Hassanien, 2018), (Zeema & Christopher, 2019), (Khalifa, Loey, Chakrabortty, & Taha, 2022), (Jain, Pal Nandi, Gupta, & Tayal, 2020). Development of Neutrosophic Data envelopment (DAE) methods to analyze the performance of organizations, whether private or public (Mao, Guoxi, Fallah, & Edalatpanah). The Neutrosophic Erlang queuing service model is derived to modify its parameters for better data handling (Zeina, 2020).

The development of neutrosophic distributions, along with neutrosophic statistical techniques, played an essential role in analyzing the data efficiently. Neutrosophic lognormal distribution has been developed, and environmental data on nitrogen oxide has been utilized to provide better estimates(Z. Khan, Amin, Khan, & Gulistan, 2021). Neutrosophic Kumaraswamy, Pareto, and Rayleigh distributions have been derived (Ahsan-ul-Haq, 2022), (M. Aslam, Khan, & Al-Marshadi, 2019),(M. A. Aslam, 2020). Neutrosophic one-way and two-wayANOVA is produced to deal with uncertainty in data sets available in the market(Miari, Anan, & Zeina, 2022). NANOVA is used to check the hostility level among university students(M. Aslam, 2019). F test is modified with the assumption that the two counts of the climatology of the U.S. follow distribution, and the data set is based on uncertain events of climate(M. Aslam, 2021b). Neutrosophic analysis of the mean test was developed and compared its efficiency with classical analysis of the mean using the data of wind power data (M. Aslam, 2021a). Neutrosophic beta distribution, along with some mathematical characteristics and application on flood peak data sets of Wheaton River Canada, is analyzed(Rehan A Khan Sherwani et al.). Binomial, Normal, and Weibull distributions are also modified in the neutrosophic version as available data are vague and imprecise (Rehan Ahmad Khan Sherwani et al., 2021), (Alhasan & Smarandache), (Patro & Smarandache). Poisson, Exponential, and Uniform distribution are also generalized under the umbrella of Neutrosophic logic (Alhabib, Ranna, Farah, & Salama, 2018).

Climate change is a big challenge for scientists and researchers. To deal with such changes, which occur every second and affect our environment, new inventions need to be studied and their effects on human life(Z. Khan et al., 2021), (M. Aslam, 2021a, 2021b). Wind speed data from Pakistan is analyzed using newly proposed neutrosophic measures of skewness and kurtosis(M. Aslam, 2021c).

There is a need to track the vegetation index, which is why this research is being done to construct an NDVI structural model. It addresses the creation of the recently suggested NTLEG-E distribution model for NDVI. This study is important because it will aid in the creation of environmental policies and streamline the decision-making procedures. Additionally, the NDVI model provides important details on Pakistan's vegetation. Dependable NDVI models support decision-makers in assessing the effectiveness of interventions and implementing targeted policies to protect the environment and public welfare, which helps in the development of evidence-based guidelines. The rest of this study is organized as the development of the newly proposed NTLEG-E distribution for NDVI of Pakistan, major essential characteristics of the newly proposed model, analysis of NDVI through mapping, and the last section containing the conclusion of the article.

2. MATERIAL AND METHODS

The techniques used to extract data and apply an NDVI model are described in this section.

2.1. Study Area

The terrain in Pakistan includes a complex mixture of plains, deserts, forests, and plateaus, stretching from the southern Indian Ocean coast to the northern mountains of the Karakoram, Hindukush, and Himalayan regions. Pakistan's Sindh and Punjab provinces are located on the northwest corner of the Indian plate. In contrast, Baluchistan and most of Khyber Pakhtunkhwa are situated within the Eurasian plate, primarily made up of the Iranian Plateau.

India borders Pakistan in the east, Afghanistan borders Pakistan in the northwest, Iran borders Pakistan in the west, and China borders Pakistan in the northeast, as seen in Figures 1(a) and (b). The location's latitude and longitude are 30.3753° N and 69.3451° W. Pakistan has an overall area of 803,936 km^2, as seen in Figure 1 (c). Pakistan is located in the temperate zone, directly above the tropic of cancer. There are both tropical and temperate climates. While the Punjab province experiences plentiful rainfall, arid conditions exist in the coastal south, characterized by a monsoon season with sufficient rain and a dry season with less rainfall and significant changes between temperature extremes at specific sites. In various country regions, annual precipitation ranges from less than 10 inches to over 150 inches. Yet, these generalizations should not mask the noticeable variations in specific places.

Figure 1. Maps showing the location and outline of the study area. a) shows the world, b) shows the study area location in South Asia, and c) shows the study area, Pakistan

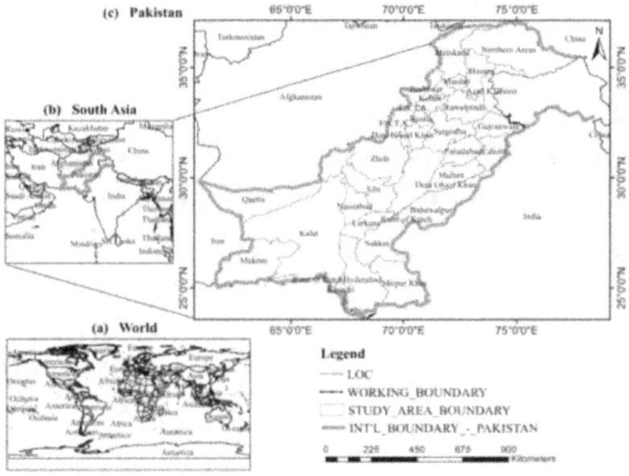

2.2. Acquisition of Data

The National Aeronautics and Space Administration (NASA)-World View provides the data. Data are gathered between January 2022 to December 2022. MOD08_M3 v6.1 using online platform Giovanni (http://disc.sci.gsfc.nasa.gov/giovanni/), which gave spatial and spectral information on NDVI in the Earth of cell size 250m. NDVI sensors compute normalized difference vegetation index. The normalized difference between leaf area and canopy chlorophyll content, or NDVI, is estimated and is commonly used to track leaf senescence in the autumn and spring green-up.

2.3. Neutrosophic Topp-Leone Exponentiated Generalized-Exponential Distribution

In this section, the Probability Density and Distribution Function of NTLEG-E distributions are derived to model NDVI of Pakistan. The four-parameterNTLEG-E distribution's CDF is given by:

$$F_{NTLEG-G}(x) = \left[1 - \left\{1 - \left\{1 - e^{-\lambda_{\Phi N} a_{\Phi N} x}\right\}^{b_{\Phi N}}\right\}^{2}\right]^{\alpha_{\Phi N}} \quad (1)$$

The PDF of NTLEG-E is as follows:

$$f_{NTLEG-G}(x) = 2\alpha_{\Phi N} a_{\Phi N} b_{\Phi N} \lambda_{\Phi N} e^{-\lambda_{\Phi N} a_{\Phi N} x} (1 - e^{-\lambda_{\Phi N} a_{\Phi N} x})^{b_{\Phi N}-1}$$

$$[1 - \{1 - e^{-\lambda_{\Phi N} a_{\Phi N} x}\}^{b_{\Phi N}}] \, [1 - [1 - \{1 - e^{-\lambda_{\Phi N} a_{\Phi N} x}\}^{b_{\Phi N}}]^2]^{(\alpha_{\Phi N}-1)}, \; a_{\Phi N}, b_{\Phi N}, \alpha_{\Phi N}, \lambda_{\Phi N}, x > 0 \tag{2}$$

Where $'a'_{\Phi N}$ is the location parameter, $'b'_{\Phi N}$ *and* $'\lambda'_{\Phi N}$ are scale parameters and' $\alpha'_{\Phi N}$ is the shape parameter. The following figure shows the shapes of PDF on different parametric values of NTLEG-E distribution. The parametric effect on PDF of NTLEG-E distribution is is executed in figure 2.

Figure 2. Effect of parameters on PDF of NTLEG-E distribution

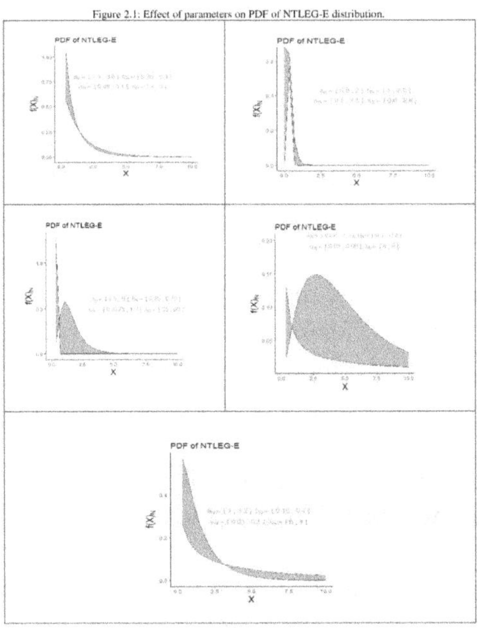

The following table 1 shows the sub-models of NTLEG-E distribution. All the special cases of NTLEG-E probability models are new neutrosophic versions of the developed distributions as follows:

continued on following page

Table 1. Continued

Table 1. New probability models (Special cases) of NTLEG-E distribution

Parametric Values	Sub-Models	New Models
a = 1	$F(x) = [\{(1 - e^{-\lambda_{\Phi N}x})^{b_{\Phi N}}\}^2]^{\alpha_{\Phi N}}$	**NTLEEx**
b = 1	$F(x) = (1 - e^{-2\lambda_{\Phi N}a_{\Phi N}x})^{\alpha_{\Phi N}}$	**NTLEx(a)**
a = **b** = 1	$F(x) = (1 - e^{-2\lambda_{\Phi N}x})^{\alpha_{\Phi N}}$	**NTLEx**
b = **α** = **a** = 1	$F(x) = 1 - e^{-2\lambda_{\Phi N}x}$	**N.Weibull** ($\beta = 2$)
a = **b** = 1	$F(x) = (1 - e^{-2\lambda_{\Phi N}x})^{\alpha_{\Phi N}}$	**NEW** ($\beta = 2$)

2.3.1. Reliability Measures of NTLEG-E Distribution

In this section, essential properties in the reliability theory of NTLEG-E distribution are obtained along with graphs of some characteristics.

• **Survival Rate Function**

If $X \sim NTLEGE(a_{\Phi N}, b_{\Phi N}, \alpha_{\Phi N}, \lambda_{\Phi N})$, the survival function of NTLEG-E can be obtained by using the following formulae (Nzei, Eghwerido, & Ekhosuehi, 2020):

$$S(x,\varnothing) = \overline{F}(x,\varnothing) = 1 - F(x,\varnothing) \tag{3}$$

By using CDF of NTLEG-E distribution in (3), the survival function of TLEG-E distribution is expressed as:

$$S(x) = 1 - \left[1 - \{1 - \{1 - e^{-\lambda_{\Phi N}a_{\Phi N}x}\}^{b_{\Phi N}}\}^2\right]^{\alpha_{\Phi N}} \tag{4}$$

• **Hazard Rate Function**

The instantaneous hazard rate function of a random variable $'X'$ is defined as the ratio of the PDF and survival rate function. The hazard rate is also known as the instantaneous failure rate (Nzei et al., 2020).

$$h(x,\varnothing) = \frac{f(x,\varnothing)}{s(x,\varnothing)}\, s(x,\varnothing) > 0$$

Where

$$S(x,\varnothing) = 1 - F(x,\varnothing)$$

So,

$$h(x) = \frac{f(x,\varnothing)}{1 - F(x,\varnothing)} \tag{5}$$

Substituting equations PDF and CDF in the above equation, the failure rate for the NTLEG-E distribution can be given as:

$$h(x) = \frac{2\alpha_{\Phi N} a_{\Phi N} b_{\Phi N} \lambda_{\Phi N} e^{-\lambda_{\Phi N} a_{\Phi N} x} (1 - e^{-\lambda_{\Phi N} a_{\Phi N} x})^{b_{\Phi N}-1} [1 - \{1 - e^{-\lambda_{\Phi N} a_{\Phi N} x}\}^{b_{\Phi N}}] [1 - [1 - \{1 - e^{-\lambda_{\Phi N} a_{\Phi N} x}\}^{b_{\Phi N}}]^2]^{(\alpha_{\Phi N}-1)}}{1 - [1 - \{1 - \{1 - e^{-\lambda_{\Phi N} a_{\Phi N} x}\}^{b_{\Phi N}}\}^2]^{\alpha_{\Phi N}}} \tag{6}$$

- **Reverse Hazard Rate Function**

The reverse hazard function is derived by using the following formula:(Nzei et al., 2020):

$$\hat{R}\left(x\right) = \frac{f(x)}{1 - S(x)} \tag{7}$$

By substituting PDF and survival function of NTLEG-E distribution in the above formula, the reverse hazard rate function of NTLEG-Eis as follows:

$$\hat{R}\left(x\right) = \frac{2\alpha_{\Phi N} a_{\Phi N} b_{\Phi N} \lambda_{\Phi N} e^{-\lambda_{\Phi N} a_{\Phi N} x} (1 - e^{-\lambda_{\Phi N} a_{\Phi N} x})^{b_{\Phi N}-1} [1 - \{1 - e^{-\lambda_{\Phi N} a_{\Phi N} x}\}^{b_{\Phi N}}] [1 - [1 - \{1 - e^{-\lambda_{\Phi N} a_{\Phi N} x}\}^{b_{\Phi N}}]^2]^{(\alpha_{\Phi N}-1)}}{[1 - \{1 - \{1 - e^{-\lambda_{\Phi N} a_{\Phi N} x}\}^{b_{\Phi N}}\}^2]^{\alpha_{\Phi N}}} \tag{8}$$

- **Cumulative Hazard Rate Function**

The cumulative hazard rate function is obtained by utilizing the following formula(Nzei et al., 2020):

$$\omega(x) = -ln(s(x)) \tag{9}$$

By substituting the survival function in eq.(9), the cumulative hazard function of NTLEG-E is as follows:

$$\omega(x) = -ln\left(1 - [1 - \{1 - \{1 - e^{-\lambda_{\Phi N} a_{\Phi N} x}\}^{b_{\Phi N}}\}^2]^{\alpha_{\Phi N}}\right)$$

2.3.2. Odds Function

The odds function is the ratio of the distribution Function and survival rate function of the distribution. The general formula for the odds function is given as(Nzei et al., 2020):

$$O_{TLEG-E} = \frac{F(x)}{S(x)} \tag{10}$$

By substituting CDF and survival function in the expression mentioned above of the odds function, the odds function of TLEG-E is as follows:

$$O_{TLEGE} = \frac{[1 - \{1 - \{1 - e^{-\lambda_{\Phi N} a_{\Phi N} x}\}^{b_{\Phi N}}\}^2]^{a_{\Phi N}}}{1 - [1 - \{1 - \{1 - e^{-\lambda_{\Phi N} a_{\Phi N} x}\}^{b_{\Phi N}}\}^2]^{a_{\Phi N}}}$$

2.3.4. Quantile Based Characteristics

Quantile-based functions are commonly used in reliability theory. Quantile function is helpful in such situations as they may not need the life-testing tryouts to last until the consumption of all subjects(Parzen, 1979). NTLEG-E distribution is used to derive quantile-based measures.

• Quantiles of NTLEG-E Distribution

The quantile function is a very significant feature of any probability model as it is used to generate data. The quantile function of NTLEG-E when $F(x) = u$ is as follows(Gilchrist, 2000):

$$x = -\frac{ln\left[1 - \{1 - \sqrt{1 - u^{\frac{1}{a_{\Phi N}}}}\}^{\frac{1}{b_{\Phi N}}}\right]}{a_{\Phi N}\lambda_{\Phi N}} \tag{11}$$

The quantile function is used to find the different quantiles. For example, for different values of u first quartile, third quartile, median, and 90th percentiles are obtained in table 2.

Table 2. Quantiles of NTLEG-E Distribution

$Q_1 = -\frac{ln\left[1 - \{1 - \sqrt{1 - (0.25)^{\frac{1}{a_{\Phi N}}}}\}^{\frac{1}{b_{\Phi N}}}\right]}{a_{\Phi N}\lambda_{\Phi N}}$
$\text{Median} = -\frac{ln\left[1 - \{1 - \sqrt{1 - (0.5)^{\frac{1}{a_{\Phi N}}}}\}^{\frac{1}{b_{\Phi N}}}\right]}{a_{\Phi N}\lambda_{\Phi N}}$
$Q_3 = -\frac{ln\left[1 - \{1 - \sqrt{1 - (0.75)^{\frac{1}{a_{\Phi N}}}}\}^{\frac{1}{b_{\Phi N}}}\right]}{a_{\Phi N}\lambda_{\Phi N}}$
$P_{90} = -\frac{ln\left[1 - \{1 - \sqrt{1 - (0.9)^{\frac{1}{a_{\Phi N}}}}\}^{\frac{1}{b_{\Phi N}}}\right]}{a_{\Phi N}\lambda_{\Phi N}}$

• Semi-Inter Quartile Range

The semi-inter-quartile range is half of the inter-quartile which is as follows(Gilchrist, 2000):

$$Q.D = \frac{Q_3 - Q_1}{2}$$

Using formulae of the third and first quartile, the expression of quartile deviation for the NTLEG-E probability model is as follows:

$$Q.D = ln\frac{\left[1-\left\{1-\sqrt{1-(0.25)^{\frac{1}{a_{\Phi N}}}}\right\}^{\frac{1}{b_{\Phi N}}}\right]}{a_{\Phi N}\lambda_{\Phi N}\left[1-\left\{1-\sqrt{1-(0.75)^{\frac{1}{a_{\Phi N}}}}\right\}^{\frac{1}{b_{\Phi N}}}\right]} \quad (12)$$

- **Quantile Hazard Function**

Conferring to Gilchrist (2000), the QF's as the hazard quantile function is as follows:

$$H(u) = \left[(1-u)q(u)\right]^{-1} \quad (13)$$

Where $q(u)$is a quantile density function, and 'u' is a random number. The quantile hazard function of NTLEG-E distribution using equation (13) is:

$H(u) =$

$$\frac{-b_{\Phi N}\sqrt{1-u^{1/a_{\Phi N}}\alpha_{\Phi N}x(1-\sqrt{1-u^{1/a_{\Phi N}}})\left(1-(1-\sqrt{1-u^{1/a_{\Phi N}}})^{1/b_{\Phi N}}\right)a_{\Phi N}\lambda_{\Phi N}}}{(1-u)(1-\sqrt{1-u^{1/a_{\Phi N}}})^{1/b_{\Phi N}}u^{1/a_{\Phi N}}}$$

- **Reverse Hazard Quantile Function**

The general Reverse hazard quantile function is introduced by Nair and Sankaran (2009) which is expressed as:

$$A(u) = (uq(u))^{-1} \quad (14)$$

By substituting the quantile density function in equation (14), the reverse hazard quantile function is given below:

$$A(u) = \frac{-b_{\Phi N}\sqrt{1-u^{1/a_{\Phi N}}\alpha_{\Phi N}x(1-\sqrt{1-u^{1/a_{\Phi N}}})\left(1-(1-\sqrt{1-u^{1/a_{\Phi N}}})^{1/b_{\Phi N}}\right)a_{\Phi N}\lambda_{\Phi N}}}{u(1-\sqrt{1-u^{1/a_{\Phi N}}})^{1/b_{\Phi N}}u^{1/a_{\Phi N}}} \quad (15)$$

2.3.5. Qausi Range (Inter-p Range)

The lower-p deviation ld(p) and upper-p deviation ud(p) can be used for the inter-P range, which is also called quasi-range. It is a spread function.Quasi-range is defined as(Gilchrist, 2000):

$$ipr(p) = \widetilde{Q}(q) - \widetilde{Q}(p) = ld(p) + ud\left(p\right)\frac{r-1}{n} < p \le \frac{r}{n}\, and\, p = \left(1-q\right) \quad (16)$$

where $\widetilde{Q}\left(p\right)$ is empirical quartile function. By substituting ld(p) and ud(p), the ipr(p) for TLEG-E distribution is as follows:

$$ipr(p) = -\frac{1}{a_{\Phi N}\lambda_{\Phi N}}\left[ln\left\{\left[1-\left\{1-\sqrt{1-(0.75)^{\frac{1}{\alpha_{\Phi N}}}}\right\}^{\frac{1}{b_{\Phi N}}}\right]\left[1-\left\{1-\sqrt{1-(0.25)^{\frac{1}{\alpha_{\Phi N}}}}\right\}^{\frac{1}{b_{\Phi N}}}\right]\right\}\right] \quad (17)$$

2.3.6. Mode of NTLEG-E Distribution

The probability density function of NTLEG-E distribution is used to obtain the formulae of mode(A TALAAT, 2018).

$$f_{TLEG-G}(x) = 2\alpha_{\Phi N}a_{\Phi N}b_{\Phi N}\lambda_{\Phi N}e^{-\lambda_{\Phi N}a_{\Phi N}x}(1-e^{-\lambda_{\Phi N}a_{\Phi N}x})^{b_{\Phi N}-1}$$

$$[1-\{1-e^{-\lambda_{\Phi N}a_{\Phi N}x}\}^{b_{\Phi N}}]\,[1-[1-\{1-e^{-\lambda_{\Phi N}a_{\Phi N}x}\}^{b_{\Phi N}}]^2]^{(\alpha_{\Phi N}-1)},\, x > 0$$

Taking natural log on both sides of the equation, then differentiate both sides with respect to x, put $f'(x) = 0$. Since $f(x) > 0$, then the mode can be found numerically by solving the following equation

$$= -\lambda_{\Phi N}a_{\Phi N} + \frac{(b_{\Phi N}-1)\lambda_{\Phi N}a_{\Phi N}e^{-\lambda_{\Phi N}a_{\Phi N}x}}{(1-e^{-\lambda_{\Phi N}a_{\Phi N}x})} - \frac{b_{\Phi N}\{1-e^{-\lambda_{\Phi N}a_{\Phi N}x}\}^{b_{\Phi N}-1}\lambda_{\Phi N}a_{\Phi N}e^{-\lambda_{\Phi N}a_{\Phi N}x}}{[1-\{1-e^{-\lambda_{\Phi N}a_{\Phi N}x}\}^{b_{\Phi N}}]}$$

$$+\frac{2(\alpha_{\Phi N}-1)\lambda_{\Phi N}a_{\Phi N}b_{\Phi N}e^{-\lambda_{\Phi N}a_{\Phi N}x}(1-\{1-e^{-\lambda_{\Phi N}a_{\Phi N}x}\}^{b_{\Phi N}})\{1-e^{-\lambda_{\Phi N}a_{\Phi N}x}\}^{b_{\Phi N}-1}}{[1-[1-\{1-e^{-\lambda_{\Phi N}a_{\Phi N}x}\}^{b_{\Phi N}}]^2]} = 0$$

2.3.7. Moments of TLEG-E Distribution

Moments play an essential role in the measurement of the mean, variance, kurtosis, and skewness. The general expression to define the raw moments of a random variable$X$ is as follows(Nzei et al., 2020)

$$E(x^r) = \int_0^\infty x^r f(x; a_{\Phi N}, b_{\Phi N}, \alpha_{\Phi N}, \lambda_{\Phi N})dx$$

By the definition of complete gamma function, we obtained

$$E(x^r) = \frac{2\alpha_{\Phi N} a_{\Phi N} b_{\Phi N} \lambda_{\Phi N} \sum_{p,q,r=0}^{\infty} (-1)^{p+q+r} \binom{\alpha - 1}{p} \binom{2p+1}{q} \binom{b(q+1)-1}{r}}{\left(-\lambda_{\Phi N} a_{\Phi N} (r+1)\right)^{r+1}} \Gamma r + 1$$

2.3.8. Skewness and Kurtosis

Kurtosis and skewness are fundamental properties of any distribution. These measures accurately define the shape and peak of available data. The two estimates of TLEG-E distribution can be derived through the following formulae of Bowley (B) skewness(Nzei et al., 2020), Galton (G) skewness coefficient by Gilchrist (2000), and Moors (M) kurtosis(Nzei et al., 2020):

$$G = \frac{QR}{IQR}$$

$$B = \frac{Q\left(\frac{3}{4}\right) + Q\left(\frac{1}{4}\right) - 2Q\left(\frac{1}{2}\right)}{Q\left(\frac{3}{4}\right) - Q\left(\frac{1}{4}\right)}$$

and

$$B = \frac{Q\left(\frac{7}{8}\right) - Q\left(\frac{3}{8}\right) - Q\left(\frac{5}{8}\right) + Q\left(\frac{1}{8}\right)}{Q\left(\frac{3}{4}\right) - Q\left(\frac{1}{4}\right)}$$

2.3.9. Moment Generating Function (MGF)

The moment generating a function of the NTLEG-E distribution can be derived by using the following general formula of MGF:(Nzei et al., 2020)

$$M_X(t) = E(e^{tx}) = \int_0^{\infty} e^{tx}.f\left(x; a_{\Phi N}, b_{\Phi N}, \alpha_{\Phi N}, \lambda_{\Phi N}\right) dx$$

By considering the expression of $E(x^r)$ we obtain,

$M_x(t)$

$$= \sum_{s=0}^{\infty} \frac{(t)^s}{s!} \frac{2\alpha_{\Phi N} a_{\Phi N} b_{\Phi N} \lambda_{\Phi N} \sum_{p,q,r=0}^{\infty} (-1)^{p+q+r} \binom{\alpha - 1}{p} \binom{2p+1}{q} \binom{b(q+1)-1}{r}}{\left(-\lambda_{\Phi N} a_{\Phi N} (r+1)\right)^{r+1}} \Gamma r + 1$$

2.3.10. Renyi Entropy

It is a measure of the uncertainty measure of a probability model and the randomness of the data. Renyi entropy if $X \sim f(x)$ is defined as(Nzei et al., 2020):

$$I_R(v) = \frac{1}{1-v} log\left[\int_0^\infty [f(x)]^v dx\right]$$

If $X \sim NTLEG - E\left(x; a_{\Phi N}, b_{\Phi N}, \alpha_{\Phi N}, \lambda_{\Phi N}\right)$ then $I_R(v)$ is:

$$\frac{1}{1-v} log\left[\int_0^\infty [f(x)]^v dx\right]$$

$$= \frac{1}{1-v} log\left[\frac{\left(2\alpha_{\Phi N} a_{\Phi N} b_{\Phi N} \lambda_{\Phi N}\right)^v}{\lambda_{\Phi N} a_{\Phi N} (r+v)}\right] \sum_{p,q,r=0}^{\infty} (-1)^{p+q+r} \binom{v(\alpha - 1)}{p} \binom{2p + v}{q} \binom{bq + (b-1)}{r}$$

2.3.11. Maximum Likelihood Estimates

Suppose $x_1, x_2, x_3, \ldots, x_n$ be a random sample from NTLEG-E distribution, then the log-likelihood function becomes(Mahdavi & Kundu, 2017):

$$L = \prod_{i=1}^{n} f(x)$$

$$L = \prod_{i=1}^{n} 2\alpha_{\Phi N} a_{\Phi N} b_{\Phi N} \lambda_{\Phi N} e^{-\lambda_{\Phi N} a_{\Phi N} x} \left(1 - e^{-\lambda_{\Phi N} a_{\Phi N} x}\right)^{b_{\Phi N} - 1}$$

$$\left[1 - \left\{1 - e^{-\lambda_{\Phi N} a_{\Phi N} x}\right\}^{b_{\Phi N}}\right] \left[1 - \left[1 - \left\{1 - e^{-\lambda_{\Phi N} a_{\Phi N} x}\right\}^{b_{\Phi N}}\right]^2\right]^{(\alpha_{\Phi N} - 1)}$$

The four normal equations for $\hat{a}, \hat{b}, \hat{\lambda}$ *and* $\hat{\alpha}$ are as follows to estimate the parametric values of the TLEG-E distribution.

$$\frac{\partial lnL}{\partial\left(\hat{\alpha}_{\Phi N}\right)} = \frac{n}{\alpha_{\Phi N}} + \sum ln\left[1 - \left\{1 - \left(1 - e^{-\lambda_{\Phi N} a_{\Phi N} x}\right)^{b_{\Phi N}}\right\}^2\right] = 0$$

$$\frac{\partial lnL}{\partial\left(\hat{b}_{\Phi N}\right)} = \frac{n}{b_{\Phi N}} + \sum ln\left(1 - e^{-\lambda_{\Phi N} a_{\Phi N} x}\right) + \sum ln\left[\frac{\left(1 - e^{-\lambda_{\Phi N} a_{\Phi N} x}\right)}{1 - \left(1 - e^{-\lambda_{\Phi N} a_{\Phi N} x}\right)^{b_{\Phi N}}}\right]$$

$$+(\alpha_{\Phi N}-1)\frac{\sum ln[2\{-(1-e^{-\lambda_{\Phi N}a_{\Phi N}x})^{b_{\Phi N}}\}]}{[1-1-\{(1-e^{-\lambda_{\Phi N}a_{\Phi N}x})^{b_{\Phi N}}\}^2]}=0$$

$$\frac{\partial lnL}{\partial(\hat{a}_{\Phi N})}=\frac{n}{a_{\Phi N}}-\sum(\lambda_{\Phi N}x)+(b_{\Phi N}-1)\frac{\sum ln[-e^{-\lambda_{\Phi N}a_{\Phi N}x}(-\lambda_{\Phi N}x)]}{(1-e^{-\lambda_{\Phi N}a_{\Phi N}x})}$$

$$+\frac{\sum ln[-(1-e^{-\lambda_{\Phi N}a_{\Phi N}x})^{b_{\Phi N}}\lambda_{\Phi N}xe^{-\lambda_{\Phi N}a_{\Phi N}x}]}{\{(1-e^{-\lambda_{\Phi N}a_{\Phi N}x})^{b_{\Phi N}}\}}$$

$$+(\alpha_{\Phi N}-1)\frac{\sum ln[-\{1-(1-e^{-\lambda_{\Phi N}a_{\Phi N}x})\}^2\{\lambda_{\Phi N}x(1-e^{-\lambda_{\Phi N}a_{\Phi N}x})(-e^{-\lambda_{\Phi N}a_{\Phi N}x})\}]}{[1-\{1-(1-e^{-\lambda_{\Phi N}a_{\Phi N}x})^{b_{\Phi N}}\}^2]}$$

$$\frac{\partial lnL}{\partial(\hat{\lambda}_{\Phi N})}=\frac{n}{\lambda_{\Phi N}}+\sum(a_{\Phi N}x)+(b_{\Phi N}-1)\frac{\sum ln(a_{\Phi N}xe^{-\lambda_{\Phi N}a_{\Phi N}x})}{(1-e^{-\lambda_{\Phi N}a_{\Phi N}x})}$$

$$+\frac{\sum ln[-(1-e^{-\lambda_{\Phi N}a_{\Phi N}x})a_{\Phi N}xe^{-\lambda_{\Phi N}a_{\Phi N}x}]}{\{1-(1-e^{-\lambda_{\Phi N}a_{\Phi N}x})^{b_{\Phi N}}\}}$$

$$+(\alpha_{\Phi N}-1)\frac{\sum[\{1-(1-e^{-\lambda_{\Phi N}a_{\Phi N}x})^{b_{\Phi N}}\}^2(1-e^{-\lambda_{\Phi N}a_{\Phi N}x})^{b_{\Phi N}}a_{\Phi N}xe^{-\lambda_{\Phi N}a_{\Phi N}x}]}{[1-\{1-(1-e^{-\lambda_{\Phi N}a_{\Phi N}x})^{b_{\Phi N}}\}^2]}=0$$

The equation, as mentioned above, can be solved simultaneously. The Newton-Raphson method may be employed for the Standard algorithm to derive the final expression of these non-linear equations for parametric values. Since it is a simple two-dimensional optimization delinquent, getting some preliminary guesses is also not challenging.

2.4. Results

This section contains the results extracted from the proposed model and the overall situation of NDVI in Pakistan.

2.4.1. Spatial and Temporal Patterns of NDVI

Spatial presentation of NDVI through maps is presented in this section to observe the difference in vegetation index over the year 2022 in Pakistan. The Merra-2 NDVI reanalysis datasets were also acquired from online data visualization tools GIOVANNI (http://disc.sci.gsfc.nasa.gov/giovanni/) for the study area for comparison purposes. Spatial and temporal patterns of NDVI from Merra-2 which is a reanalysis data has been shown as visualization for better understanding of NDVI behavior in the region. The information gives a broad picture of the state and dynamics of the vegetation throughout Pakistan and quantifies the amount of living greenery.

Figure 3a. Monthly Comparison of NDVI of Pakistan

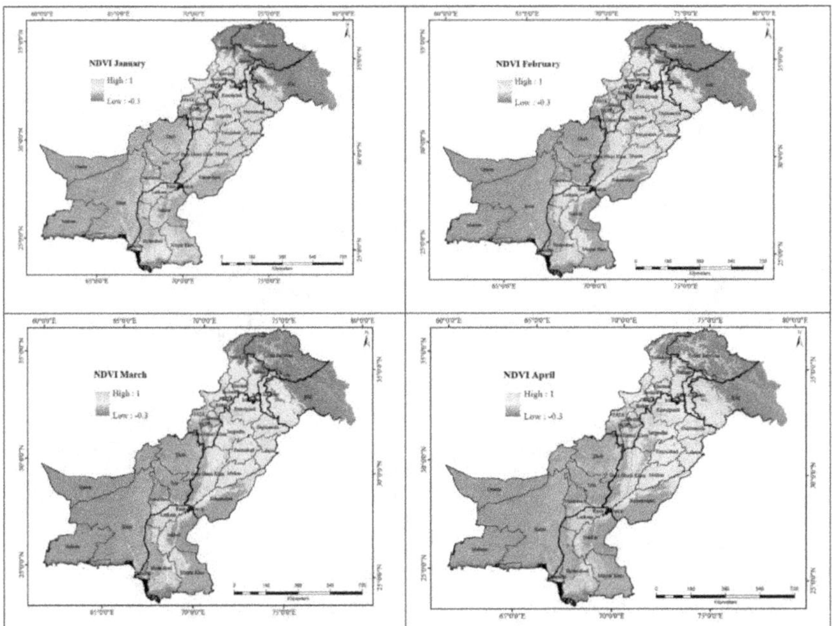

Figure 3b. Monthly Comparison of NDVI of Pakistan

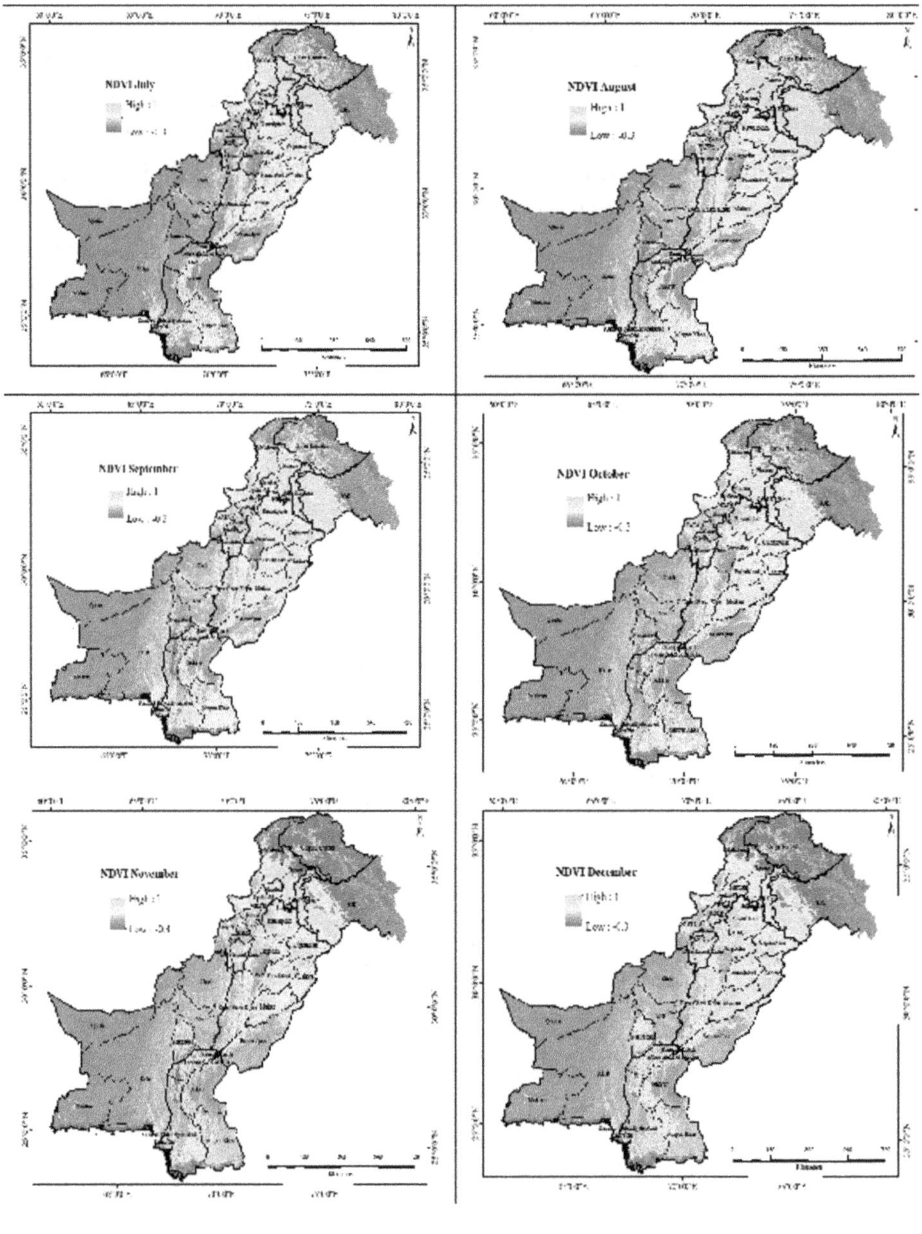

The Merra-2 was used in this research, which gave spatial and spectral information on NDVI in the Earth. NDVI maps were produced from the acquired data, and DVI sensors computed the normalized difference vegetation index. The normalized difference between leaf area and canopy chlorophyll content, or NDVI, is estimated and is commonly used to track leaf senescence in the autumn and spring green-up.NDVI values generally fall between -1.0 and 1.0, with negative values denoting clouds and water, positive values close to zero denoting bare soil, and higher positive values of NDVI ranging from 0.1 to 0.5 representing sparse vegetation to 0.6 and above representing thick green vegetation. In Pakistan, the assessment of seasonal variability in NDVI was evaluated with the help of MISR analysis, which was performed on the collected data by NASA for the year 2022. NDVI is frequently used in forestry, ecology, and agriculture to track the health and growth of vegetation as well as to pinpoint damaged or stressed areas. Moreover, vegetation types can be mapped and classified, and variations in vegetation cover over time can be identified using NDVI readings. In this research, the changes in NDVI were tracked down to observe the density of plants in Pakistan over 2022.

It is observed from figure 3 that from Hyderabad to Malakand, the NDVI value seems to be 1, which shows high greenery from January to March. The trend changes from April onward till June, and maps show low greenery in the south of Pakistan. The green areas in Dera Ghazi Khan to Malakand shrinks in April, whereas from Kashmir to Malakand, it shrinks in May. In May, low greenery levels can also be seen from Hyderabad to Islamabad. However July onward, it is observed that the region of Balochistan and nearby areas become lighter red, and the southeast area of Pakistan becomes green again. So, over the year 2022, it is observed that the northeast regions of Pakistan were greener as compared to the end of the year.

CONCLUSION

A new proposed novel continuous probability model with four parameters called Topp-Leone Exponentiated Generalized--Exponential (TLEG-E) is developed to address the need for modeling NDVI effectively. Special cases of the proposed model, explicit expressions of some important mathematical characteristics,i.e., ordinary moments, moment generating function, reliability measure, quantile function-based measures for fatigue of components, Rényi entropy, and order statistics of new proposed distribution are derived. ML method is employed for estimating the new model parameters for efficient modeling. Mapping of NDVI data of Pakistan is also considered to observe its pattern in 2022. It is observed that the green area in Pakistan shrinks from January to May; however, from July onwards, green areas can be seen, which might be due to the plantation of new trees or seasonal vegetation in those areas.

REFERENCES

Abdel-Basset, M., Smarandache, F., & Ye, J. (2019). Special issue on "Applications of neutrosophic theory in decision making-recent advances and future trends". *Complex & Intelligent Systems*, 5(4), 363–364. DOI:10.1007/s40747-019-00127-1

Ahsan-ul-Haq, M. (2022). Neutrosophic Kumaraswamy Distribution with Engineering Application. *Neutrosophic Sets and Systems*, 49(1), 17.

Alhabib, R., Ranna, M. M., Farah, H., & Salama, A. (2018). Some neutrosophic probability distributions. *Neutrosophic Sets and Systems*, 22, 30–38.

Alhasan, K. F. H., & Smarandache, F. (n.d.). *Neutrosophic Weibull distribution and neutrosophic family Weibull distribution*. Infinite Study.

Aslam, M. (2019). Neutrosophic analysis of variance: Application to university students. *Complex & Intelligent Systems*, 5(4), 403–407. DOI:10.1007/s40747-019-0107-2

Aslam, M. (2021a). Analyzing wind power data using analysis of means under neutrosophic statistics. *Soft Computing*, 25(10), 7087–7093. DOI:10.1007/s00500-021-05661-0

Aslam, M. (2021b). Neutrosophic statistical test for counts in climatology. *Scientific Reports*, 11(1), 1–5. DOI:10.1038/s41598-021-97344-x PMID:34497328

Aslam, M. (2021c). A study on skewness and kurtosis estimators of wind speed distribution under indeterminacy. *Theoretical and Applied Climatology*, 143(3), 1227–1234. DOI:10.1007/s00704-020-03509-5

Aslam, M., Khan, N., & Al-Marshadi, A. H. (2019). Design of variable sampling plan for pareto distribution using neutrosophic statistical interval method. *Symmetry*, 11(1), 80. DOI:10.3390/sym11010080

Aslam, M. A. (2020). *Neutrosophic Rayleigh distribution with some basic properties and application. In Neutrosophic Sets in Decision Analysis and Operations Research*. IGI Global.

Basha, S. H., Tharwat, A., Ahmed, K., & Hassanien, A. E. (2018). *A predictive model for seminal quality using neutrosophic rule-based classification system*. Paper presented at the International conference on advanced intelligent systems and informatics.

Gilchrist, W. (2000). *Statistical modelling with quantile functions*. CRC Press. DOI:10.1201/9781420035919

Jain, A., Pal Nandi, B., Gupta, C., & Tayal, D. K. (2020). Senti-NSetPSO: Large-sized document-level sentiment analysis using Neutrosophic Set and particle swarm optimization. *Soft Computing*, 24(1), 3–15. DOI:10.1007/s00500-019-04209-7

Kashihara, K. (1996). *Comments and topics on Smarandache notions and problems*. Infinite Study.

Khalifa, N. E., Loey, M., Chakrabortty, R. K., & Taha, M. H. N. (2022). Within the Protection of COVID-19 Spreading: A Face Mask Detection Model Based on the Neutrosophic RGB with Deep Transfer Learning. *Neutrosophic Sets and Systems*, 50, 320–335.

Khan, M., Son, L. H., Ali, M., Chau, H. T. M., Na, N. T. N., & Smarandache, F. (2018). Systematic review of decision making algorithms in extended neutrosophic sets. *Symmetry*, 10(8), 314. DOI:10.3390/sym10080314

Khan, Z., Amin, A., Khan, S. A., & Gulistan, M. (2021). Statistical Development of the Neutrosophic Lognormal Model with Application to Environmental Data. *Neutrosophic Sets and Systems*, 47(1), 1.

Mahdavi, A., & Kundu, D. (2017). A new method for generating distributions with an application to exponential distribution. *Communications in Statistics. Theory and Methods*, 46(13), 6543–6557. DOI:10.1080/03610926.2015.1130839

Mao, X., Guoxi, Z., Fallah, M., & Edalatpanah, S. (2020). A neutrosophic-based approach in data envelopment analysis with undesirable outputs. *Mathematical Problems in Engineering*, 2020, 1–8. DOI:10.1155/2020/7626102

Miari, M., Anan, M. T., & Zeina, M. B. (2022). Neutrosophic two way ANOVA. *International Journal of Neutrosophic Science*, 18(3), 73–83. DOI:10.54216/IJNS.180306

Nair, N. U., & Sankaran, P. (2009). Quantile-based reliability analysis. *Communications in Statistics. Theory and Methods*, 38(2), 222–232. DOI:10.1080/03610920802187430

Nzei, L. C., Eghwerido, J. T., & Ekhosuehi, N. (2020). Topp-Leone Gompertz Distribution: Properties and Applications. *Journal of Data Science : JDS*, 18(4), 782–794. DOI:10.6339/JDS.202010_18(4).0012

Olgun, N., & Hatip, A. (n.d.). *The effect of the neutrosophic logic on the decision tree* (Vol. 7). Academic Press.

Parzen, E. (1979). *Density quantile estimation approach to statistical data modelling. In Smoothing Techniques for Curve Estimation*. Springer. DOI:10.21236/ADA068148

Patro, S., & Smarandache, F. (n.d.). *The neutrosophic statistical distribution, more problems, more solutions*. Infinite Study.

Pramanik, S., & Mondal, K. (2015). Interval neutrosophic multi-attribute decision-making based on grey relational analysis. *Neutrosophic Sets and Systems*, 9(1), 13–22.

Rivieccio, U. (2008). Neutrosophic logics: Prospects and problems. *Fuzzy Sets and Systems*, 159(14), 1860–1868. DOI:10.1016/j.fss.2007.11.011

Salama, A. (2018). *Neutrosophic approach to grayscale images domain*. Academic Press.

Salama, A., & Alblowi, S. (2012). Neutrosophic set and neutrosophic topological spaces. *IOSR Journal of Mathematics (IOSR-JM), 3*(4).

Salama, A., Smarandache, F., & Alblowi, S. (n.d.). *New neutrosophic crisp topological concepts*. Infinite Study.

Salama, A., Smarandache, F., & Eisa, M. (2014). *Introduction to image processing via neutrosophic techniques*. Infinite Study.

Salama, A., Smarandache, F., & Kromov, V. (2022). Neutrosophic closed set and neutrosophic continuous functions. *Collected Papers. Volume IX: On Neutrosophic Theory and Its Applications in Algebra*, 25.

Salama, A., Smarandache, F., & Kroumov, V. (2014). *Neutrosophic crisp sets & neutrosophic crisp topological spaces*. Infinite Study.

Sherwani, R. A. K., Aslam, M., Raza, M. A., Farooq, M., Abid, M., & Tahir, M. (2021). Neutrosophic Normal Probability Distribution—A Spine of Parametric Neutrosophic Statistical Tests: Properties and Applications. *NeutrosophicOperations Research*, 153–169.

Sherwani, R. A. K., Naeem, M., Aslam, M., Raza, M., Abid, M., & Abbas, S. (n.d.). *Neutrosophic beta distribution with properties and applications*. Infinite Study.

Smarandache, F. (1999). A unifying field in Logics: Neutrosophic Logic. *Philosophy (London, England)*, 1–141.

Smarandache, F. (2000). Neutrosophy. *arXiv preprint math/0010099.*

Smarandache, F. (2003). *Definiton of neutrosophic logic-a generalization of the intuitionistic fuzzy logic*. Paper presented at the EUSFLAT Conf.

Smarandache, F. (2014). *Neutrosophic Theory and Its Applications, Vol. I: Collected Papers*. Infinite Study.

Smarandache, F., & Pramanik, S. (2016). *New trends in neutrosophic theory and applications* (Vol. 1). Infinite Study.

Talaat, A. (2018). *Marsall Olkin extended Topp–Leone distribution*. Academic Press.

Vasantha Kandasamy, W. (2006). Smarandache Neutrosophic algebraic structures. *arXiv Mathematics e-prints*, math/0603708.

Wang, H., Smarandache, F., Sunderraman, R., & Zhang, Y.-Q. (2005). *Interval neutrosophic sets and logic: theory and applications in computing: Theory and applications in computing* (Vol. 5). Infinite Study.

Zeema, J. L., & Christopher, D. F. X. (2019). Evolving optimized neutrosophic C means clustering using behavioral inspiration of artificial bacterial foraging (ONCMC-ABF) in the prediction of Dyslexia. *Journal of King Saud University. Computer and Information Sciences*.

Zeina, M. B. (2020). Erlang Service Queueing Model with Neutrosophic Parameters. *International Journal of Neutrosophic Science*, 6(2), 106–112. DOI:10.54216/IJNS.060202

Chapter 9
A Viewpoint for Making Decisions via Compact Spaces in Neutrosophic Generalized Topology

A. Yuvarani
https://orcid.org/0000-0002-5755-3429
The American College, India

S. Vijaya
https://orcid.org/0000-0002-4173-0451
Thiagarajar College, Madurai Kamaraj University, India

P. Santhi
The Standard Fireworks Rajaratnam College for Women, India

ABSTRACT

The ramifications of making decisions are more noteworthy due to the abundance and intricacy of data in everyday challenges. Hence, it is imperative to make sound and effective decision by developing innovative mathematical approaches to resolve these tasks. In this chapter, a problem is identified in the current scenario and a novel technique is proposed to make efficacious decision through the utilization of compactness in neutrosophic generalized topology. For that, initially, μN-compact space is introduced, and its characteristics are analyzed. Subsequently, μN-feebly compact space is presented along with its properties and examined its relationships with some existing notions.

DOI: 10.4018/979-8-3693-2085-3.ch009

INTRODUCTION

To pact with indeterminate and inconsistent data, Neutrosophic concept delivers a more realistic mathematical framework. Smarandache (Al-Omeri & Smarandache, 2016; Smarandache, 1999; Smarandache, 2002; Smarandache, 2010) devoted his exertions to delve into the scope of indeterminacy, leading to the development of Neutrosophic Sets (NS). Further, Salama and Albowi (Salama, 2012) paved the way to Neutrosophic Topological Spaces.

Császár (1997, 2002, 2005) originated and studied the characteristics of Generalized Topological Spaces. Drawing inspiration from these works, in 2020, Raksha Ben & Hari Siva Annam (2021) instigated Neutrosophic Generalized Topological Spaces and analyzed its properties.

The conception of compactness in Generalized Topological Spaces is formerly presented and investigated by Jyothis Thomas and Sunil Jacob John in 2012 (Thomas & John, 2012). Later on, K. Bageerathi and P. Jeya Puvaneswari, hosted the idea of compactness in neutrosophic topological spaces in 2019 (Bageerathi & Jeya Puvaneswari, 2019).

Compact sets perform a decisive role in numerous decision-making scenarios, abetting in the depiction of uncertainty, feasible regions, and constraints athwart a wide gamut of applications. Decision-makers can employ them mathematically and logically, to formulate and make decisions thoroughly.

An innovative strategy is proposed in our chapter, by making use of the statistical tools such as logistic regression analysis and Python programming code (Bewick et al., 2003; Embarak, 2018; Nongthombam & Sharma, 2021; Peng et al., 2002), to make effectual decision for a current scenario issue via compactness in Neutrosophic Generalized Topology. For that, μ^N-compact space and μ^N-feebly compact space are introduced along with its properties and its characteristics are analyzed.

PREREQUISITES

2.1 Definition (Al-Omeri & Smarandache, 2016)

Consider **B** as a set $\neq 0_N$. A μ^N-set D in **B**, labelled as $D = \{< \beta, (\mathbf{Y}_D(\beta), \mathbf{U}_D(\beta), \mathbf{N}_D(\beta)) >: \beta \in \mathbf{B}, \mathbf{Y}_D, \mathbf{U}_D, \mathbf{N}_D \in]^-0, 1^+[\}$ where $\mathbf{Y}_D$, $\mathbf{U}_D$ and $\mathbf{N}_D$ are real standard rudiments of [0, 1], represented as degree of membership, neutrality and non-membership respectively. Also, $0 \leq \mathbf{Y}_D(\beta) + \mathbf{U}_D(\beta) + \mathbf{N}_D(\beta) \leq 3$.

2.2 Definition (Al-Omeri & Smarandache, 2016)

Let $\mathbf{B} \neq 0_N$ and let $D = \{< \beta, (\mathbf{Y}_D(\beta), \mathbf{U}_D(\beta), \mathbf{N}_D(\beta)) >\}$ and $E = \{< \beta, (\mathbf{Y}_E(\beta), \mathbf{U}_E(\beta), \mathbf{N}_E(\beta)) >\}$, $\forall\, \beta \in \mathbf{B}$. Then

- Complement of E is $E^c = \{<\beta, \mathbf{N}_E(\beta), 1 - \mathbf{U}_E(\beta), \mathbf{Y}_E(\beta) >: \beta \in \mathbf{B}\}$
- $D \subseteq E \Rightarrow \mathbf{Y}_D(\beta) \leq \mathbf{Y}_E(\beta), \mathbf{U}_D(\beta) \leq \mathbf{U}_E(\beta), \mathbf{N}_D(\beta) \geq \mathbf{N}_E(\beta)$
- $D \subseteq E \Rightarrow \mathbf{Y}_D(\beta) \leq \mathbf{Y}_E(\beta), \mathbf{U}_D(\beta) \geq \mathbf{U}_E(\beta), \mathbf{N}_D(\beta) \geq \mathbf{N}_E(\beta)$
- $D \wedge E = <\beta, \mathbf{Y}_D(\beta) \wedge \mathbf{Y}_E(\beta), \mathbf{U}_D(\beta) \vee \mathbf{U}_E(\beta), \mathbf{N}_D(\beta) \vee \mathbf{N}_E(\beta) >$
- $D \wedge E = <\beta, \mathbf{Y}_D(\beta) \wedge \mathbf{Y}_E(\beta), \mathbf{U}_D(\beta) \wedge \mathbf{U}_E(\beta), \mathbf{N}_D(\beta) \vee \mathbf{N}_E(\beta) >$
- $D \vee E = <\beta, \mathbf{Y}_D(\beta) \vee \mathbf{Y}_E(\beta), \mathbf{U}_D(\beta) \wedge \mathbf{U}_E(\beta), \mathbf{N}_D(\beta) \wedge \mathbf{N}_E(\beta) >$
- $D \vee E = <\beta, \mathbf{Y}_D(\beta) \vee \mathbf{Y}_E(\beta), \mathbf{U}_D(\beta) \vee \mathbf{U}_E(\beta), \mathbf{N}_D(\beta) \wedge \mathbf{N}_E(\beta) >$

2.3 Remark (Al-Omeri & Smarandache, 2016)

- $0_N = \{<\beta, 0, 0, 1 >\}$ or $\{<\beta, 0, 1, 1 >\}$ or $\{<\beta, 0, 1, 0 >\}$ or $\{<\beta, 0, 0, 0 >\}$, $\forall\, \beta \in \mathbf{B}$
- $1_N = \{<\beta, 1, 0, 0 >\}$ or $\{<\beta, 1, 0, 1 >\}$ or $\{<\beta, 1, 1, 0 >\}$ or $\{<\beta, 1,1,1 >\}$, $\forall\, \beta \in \mathbf{B}$

2.4 Definition (Bewick et al., 2003)

Let $(\mathbf{B}, \beta)$ be a μ^N-TS and $\mathbf{B} \neq \phi$. A collection of μ^N-subsets of $\mathbf{B}$ is μ^N-TS if it satisfies

- $0_N \in \beta$
- $D_1 \vee D_2 \in \beta$ for all $D_1, D_2 \in \beta$.

Each μ^N-set in β is termed as a μ^N-open set (μ^N-os) and its complement is termed as a μ^N-closed set (μ^N-cs). A μ^N-set, in $(\mathbf{B}, \beta)$, which is both μ^N-os and μ^N-cs is μ^N-clopen set.

2.5 Definition (Bewick et al., 2003)

Consider a μ^N-subset $D = \{< \beta, (\mathbf{Y}_D(\beta), \mathbf{U}_D(\beta), \mathrm{N}_D(\beta)) >: \beta \in \mathbf{B}\}$ in a μ^N-TS $(\mathbf{B}, \beta)$. Then

- μ^N-Closure of D ($\mu^N c(D)$) $= \wedge \{E: D \subseteq E, E \text{ is } \mu^N\text{-cs}\}$
- μ^N-Interior of D ($\mu^N i(D)$) $= \vee \{F: F \subseteq D, F \text{ is } \mu^N\text{-os}\}$

2.6 Definition (Salama, 2012)

A μ^N-subset, D in a μ^N-TS (**B**, β) is said to be

- $\mu^N\sigma$-open set ($\mu^N\sigma$-os) if $D \le \mu^N c(\mu^N i(D))$,
- $\mu^N\pi$-open set ($\mu^N\pi$-os) if $D \le \mu^N i(\mu^N c(D))$,
- $\mu^N\alpha$-open set ($\mu^N\alpha$-os) if $D \le \mu^N i(\mu^N c(\mu^N i(D)))$,
- μ^Nregular-open set (μ^Nr-os) if $D = \mu^N i(\mu^N c(D))$.

2.7 Definition (Salama, 2012)

The function ϕ: $(\mathbf{B}_1, \beta_1) \rightarrow (\mathbf{B}_2, \beta_2)$ is μ^N-Cts (μ^N-SCts, μ^N-PCts, μ^N-αCts) if ϕ^{-1} of μ^N-cs in $(\mathbf{B}_2, \beta_2)$ is a μ^N-cs (μ^N-σcs, μ^N-πcs, μ^N-αcs) in $(\mathbf{B}_1, \beta_1)$.

μ^N-COMPACT SPACES

Throughout this chapter, μ^N-TS are considered as strong.

3.1 Definition

A collection F of μ^N-subsets of a μ^N-TS (**B**, β) is a μ^N-cover of **B** if $1_N = \vee\{E / E \le F\}$.

3.2 Definition

Let (**B**, β) be a μ^N-TS. A μ^N-sub cover of a μ^N-cover F is a sub collection E of F which itself is a μ^N-cover.

3.3 Definition

A μ^N-cover S of a μ^N-TS (**B**, β) is called a μ^N-open cover if the elements of S are μ^N-os of **B**.

3.4 Definition

A μ^N-TS (**B**, β) is said to be μ^N-compact space ⇔ each μ^N-open cover of **B** has a finite μ^N-open sub cover.

3.5 Theorem

If (**B**, β) is a μ^N-TS which is finite, then **B** is μ^N-compact.

Proof:

Consider S as a μ^N-open covering of $\mathbf{B} = \{b_1, b_2, \ldots, b_n\}$, where (**B**, β) is a finite μ^N-TS. Then every member in **B** belongs to one of the elements of S, say, $b_1 \in E_1$, $b_2 \in E_2, \ldots, b_n \in E_n$ where $E_i \in F$, $i = 1, 2, \ldots, p$, $\Rightarrow$ the collection $\{E_1, E_2, \ldots, E_p\}$ is a finite μ^N-open sub cover of **B** i.e., **B** is μ^N-compact.

3.6 Theorem

A μ^N-TS (**B**, β) is μ^N-compact when $\beta = \{V \leq \mathbf{B}: \mathbf{B} \setminus V$ is finite or all of $\mathbf{B}\}$.

Proof:

Consider S, a μ^N-open cover of a μ^N-TS (**B**, β) and E be an arbitrary member of S. Since $E \in \mu^N$-TS $\Rightarrow \mathbf{B} \setminus E$ is finite. Consider $\mathbf{B} \setminus E = \{e_1, e_2, \ldots, e_k\}$. As S is a μ^N-open cover of **B**, each e_i such that, $e_1 \in E_1$, $e_2 \in E_2, \ldots, e_k \in E_k$ where $E_i \in S$, $i = 1, 2, \ldots, k$, $\Rightarrow$ the collection $\{E, E_1, E_2, \ldots, E_k\}$ is a finite μ^N-open sub cover of **B** i.e., **B** is μ^N-compact.

3.7 Theorem

The μ^N-compactness of a finite union of sets is preserved i.e., if $E_1, E_2, \ldots, E_k$ are μ^N-compact subsets of a μ^N-TS (**B**, β), then $E_1 \vee E_2 \vee \ldots \vee E_k$ is also ì^N-compact.

Proof:

Take any two ì^N-compact subsets S & T of a ì^N-TS (**B**, â). Consider M as a ì^N-open cover of $S \vee T \Rightarrow$ M is a ì^N-open cover of S & T. So, ∃ a finite sub collection of M of ì^N-os, say, $\{S_1, S_2, \ldots, S_k\}$ and $\{T_1, T_2, \ldots, T_p\}$ covering S & T, respectively. Evidently, this collection $\{S_1, S_2, \ldots, S_k, T_1, T_2, \ldots, T_p\}$ is a collection of ì^N-os which is finite, that covers $S \vee T$. Hence, by the hypothesis of induction, the ì^N-compactness of a finite union of sets is preserved.

3.8 Theorem

Every ì^N-cs of a ì^N-compact space (**B**, â) is ì^N-compact.

Proof:

In the ì^N-compact space (**B**, â), consider any ì^N-open cover S of a ì^N-cs T. then the collection $H = (\mathbf{B} \setminus T) \vee S$ is a ì^N-open cover of **B**. As **B** is ì^N-compact, the assortment H has a finite ì^N-open sub cover. If this finite ì^N-open sub cover $\leq \mathbf{B} \setminus T$, abandon it, or else leave the finite ì^N-open sub cover alone, the ensuing collection is a finite ì^N-open sub cover of S.

3.9 Theorem

In a ì^N-compact space (**B**, â), each infinite ì^N-subset has at least one ì^N-cluster point in **B**.

Proof:

Presume E be an infinite ì^N-subset of a ì^N-compact space **B**. Take up that E has no ì^N-cluster points in **B**. Then for every y ∈ **B**, ∃ a ì^N-open set $S_y \ni S_y \wedge E = \{y\}$ or 0_N. Now, the collection $\{S_y: y \in \mathbf{B}\}$ is a ì^N-open covering of **B**. Since **B** is ì^N-compact, ∃ points $y_1, y_2, \ldots, y_n$ in **B** $\ni \vee_{j=1}^{n} S_{y_j}$ =**B.** But ... $= \{y_1\}\{y_2\}\cdot\cdot\cdot\{y_n\}$ or $0_N \Rightarrow (\cdot\cdot\cdot) E = \{y_1, y_2, \ldots, y_n\}$ or $0_N \Rightarrow E = \{y_1, y_2, \ldots, y_n\}$or 0_N, ⇒⇐ that E is infinite.

3.10 Theorem

The ì^N-continuous image of a ì^N-compact space is ì^N-compact.

Proof:

Suppose ($\mathbf{B}_1$, $â_1$) and ($\mathbf{B}_2$, $â_2$) be two ì^N-TS. Let ô: ($\mathbf{B}_1$, $â_1$) → ($\mathbf{B}_2$, $â_2$) be ì^N-continuous from $\mathbf{B}_1$ onto $\mathbf{B}_2$ and $\mathbf{B}_1$ be -compact. If T is a -open cover of $\mathbf{B}_2$, then the family {$ô^{-1}$(S): S ∈ T} is a -open cover of $\mathbf{B}_1$. As $\mathbf{B}_1$ is -compact, ∃ a finite -open subcover of $\mathbf{B}_1$, say, {$ô^{-1}(S_1)$, $ô^{-1}(S_2)$, . . ., $ô^{-1}(S_p)$}, $S_1, S_2, \ldots, S_p$ ∈ T. As ô is onto, the collection $\{S_1, S_2, \ldots, S_p\}$ is a -open subcover of $\mathbf{B}_2$. Hence $\mathbf{B}_2$ be -compact.

3.11 Definition

A collection î of exp(**B**) is said to gratify the finite intersection condition if for each finite sub collection $\{S_1, S_2, \ldots, S_p\}$ of î, the intersection $S_1\ S_2\ \ldots\ S_p$ is $\neq 0_N$.

3.12 Theorem

Let (**B**, â) be a ì^N-TS. Then **B** is ì^N-compact ⇔ for every collection of ì^N-cs in **B**, satisfying the finite intersection condition, the intersection of all the ì^N-cs in the collection is $\neq 0_N$.

Proof:

Presume æ is a collection of ì^N-subsets of **B**. Let î = {**B** \ E: E ∈ æ } be the collection of their complements. Then the equivalent conditions given below holds validity:

(1) æ is a collection of ì^N-os ⇔ î is a collection of ì^N-cs in **B**.
(2) The collection æ is a ì^N-open cover of **B** ⇔ the intersection of all the ì^N-closed elements in î is $= 0_N$ (tracks from DeMorgan's Law).

(3) The finite sub collection $\{S_1, S_2, \ldots, S_p\}$ of æ is a ì^N-open cover of **B** ⇔ the intersection of the corresponding ì^N-closed elements of î is $\neq 0_N$ (tracks from DeMorgan's Law).

Now **B** is ì^N-compact ⇔ given any collection æ of ì^N-os, if æ is a ì^N-open cover of **B**, then ∃ a finite ì^N-open sub collection of æ covers **B** ⇔ given any collection æ of ì^N-os, if ∃ no finite ì^N-open sub collection of æ covers **B**, ⇒ æ is not a ì^N-open cover of **B** ⇔ given any collection î of ì^N-cs, if every finite intersection of ì^N-cs in î is is $\neq 0_N$, then the intersection of all the ì^N-cs in î is is $\neq 0_N$.

3.13 Theorem

A ì^N-TS **B** is ì^N-compact iff ∃ a base B for it ∋ every ì^N-open cover of **B** by elements of B has a ì^N-open sub cover, which is finite.

4. ì^N-FEEBLY COMPACT SPACES

4.1 Definition

A subset A of ì^N-TS (**B**, â) is called as
(i) ì^N-Feebly open set (ì^{N}F-os) if ∃ a ì^N-os S in **B** ∋ $S \leq A \leq$ ì^{N}ó-c(S).
(ii) ì^N-Feebly closed set (ì^{N}F-cs) if ∃ a ì^N-cs S in **B** ∋ ì^{N}ó-i(S) $\leq A \leq S$.

4.2 Definition

A collection ç of ì^{N}F-os in **B** is termed as a ì^N-feebly open cover of a ì^N-subset S of **B** if $S \leq \bigvee\{T_á : T_á \in$ ç $\}$.

4.3 Definition

A ì^N-TS **B** is termed as ì^N-feebly compact if every ì^N-feebly open cover of **B** has a finite ì^N-subcover.

4.4 Definition

A ì^N-subset S of a ì^N-TS **B** is termed as ì^N-feebly compact relative to **B** if each ì^N-feebly open cover of **B** has a finite ì^N-subcover.

4.5 Theorem

Every ì^N-feebly compact space is ì^N-compact.

Proof:

Consider the ì^N-TS (**B**, â) as ì^N-feebly compact. Assume **B** is not ì^N-compact. Then ∃ a ì^N-open cover S of **B** has no finite ì^N-subcover. Since every ì^N-open set is ì^N-feebly open, then ∃ ì^N-feebly open cover S of **B**, that has no finite ì^N-subcover, which ⇒⇐ that **B** is ì^N-feebly compact ⇒ **B** is ì^N-compact.

4.6 Theorem

A ì^N-feebly closed subset of a ì^N-feebly compact space **B** is ì^N-feebly compact relative to **B**.

Proof:

Let S be a ì^{N}F-cs of a ì^N-feebly compact space **B**. Then S^c is ì^{N}F-os in **B**. Take up ç = {S_i: i ∈ I} be a ì^N-feebly open cover of S, ⇒ ç ⋁{S^c} is a ì^N-feebly open cover of **B**. As **B** is ì^N-feebly compact, it has a finite ì^N-subcover say {T_1, T_2, ..., T_p, S^c}. Then {T_1, T_2, ..., T_p} is a finite ì^N-feebly open cover ⇒ S is ì^N-feebly compact relative to **B**.

4.7 Theorem

Let ô: ($\mathbf{B}_1$, $â_1$) → ($\mathbf{B}_2$, $â_2$) be ì^N-feebly continuous surjection and $\mathbf{B}_1$ be ì^N-feebly compact. Then $\mathbf{B}_2$ is ì^N-compact.

Proof:

Let ô: ($\mathbf{B}_1$, $â_1$) → ($\mathbf{B}_2$, $â_2$) be a ì^N-feebly continuous surjection and $\mathbf{B}_1$ be ì^N-feebly compact. Let {$S_á$} be a ì^N-open cover for $\mathbf{B}_2$. Since ô is ì^N-feebly continuous, {$ô^{-1}(S_á)$} is a ì^N-feebly open cover of $\mathbf{B}_1$. Since $\mathbf{B}_1$ is ì^N-feebly compact, {$ô^{-1}(S_á)$} contains a finite ì^N-subcover, namely {$ô^{-1}()$, $ô^{-1}()$, …, $ô^{-1}()$}. Since ô is surjection, {, , …, } is a finite ì^N-subcover for $\mathbf{B}_2$ ⇒ $\mathbf{B}_2$ is ì^N-compact.

4.8 Theorem

Let ô: ($\mathbf{B}_1$, $â_1$) → ($\mathbf{B}_2$, $â_2$) be a ì^N-feebly open function and $\mathbf{B}_2$ be ì^N-feebly compact. Then $\mathbf{B}_1$ is ì^N-compact.

Proof:

Let ô: ($\mathbf{B}_1$, $â_1$) → ($\mathbf{B}_2$, $â_2$) be a ì^N-feebly open function and $\mathbf{B}_2$ be ì^N-feebly compact. Let {$S_á$} be a ì^N-open cover for $\mathbf{B}_1$. As ô is ì^N-feebly open, {ô($S_á$)} is a ì^N-feebly open cover of $\mathbf{B}_2$. Since $\mathbf{B}_2$ is ì^N-feebly compact, {ô($S_á$)} contains a finite sub ì^N-feebly cover, namely {ô(), ô(), …, ô()}. Then {, , …, } is a finite ì^N-subcover for $\mathbf{B}_1$ ⇒ $\mathbf{B}_1$ is ì^N-compact.

4.9 Theorem

The image of a ì^N-compact space is ì^N-feebly compact in a ì^N-continuous map.

Proof:

Let ô: ($\mathbf{B}_1$, $â_1$) → ($\mathbf{B}_2$, $â_2$) be a ì^{N}F-cts map from a ì^N-feebly compact space ($\mathbf{B}_1$, $â_1$) onto a ì^{N}F-TS ($\mathbf{B}_2$, $â_2$). Let {S_i: $i \in$ I} be a ì^N-open cover of ($\mathbf{B}_2$, $â_2$). Since ô is ì^N-cts, {$ô^{-1}(S_i)$: $i \in$ I} is a ì^N-feebly open cover of ($\mathbf{B}_1$, $â_1$). As ($\mathbf{B}_1$, $â_1$) is ì^N-feebly compact, the ì^N-open cover {$ô^{-1}(S_i)$: $i \in$ I} of ($\mathbf{B}_1$, $â_1$) has a finite ì^N-subcover {$ô^{-1}(S_i)$: i=1,2,3,…,p}. Consequently T = (S_i). Then ô(T) = , i.e., V = ⇒ {S_1, S_2, …., S_p} is a finite ì^N-subcover of {S_i: $i \in$ I} for ($\mathbf{B}_2$, $â_2$). Hence ($\mathbf{B}_2$, $â_2$) is ì^N-feebly compact.

APPLICATION: DECISION MAKING VIA ì^N-COMPACT SPACES

Despite the well-established and acknowledged significance of mathematics as a fundamental requirement for numerous subjects, there remains a persistent issue of subpar achievement and a lack of interest in mathematics among students across educational institutions worldwide. Mathematics is consistently perceived as one of the most formidable subjects in schools, contributing to a prevalent dislike to the subject. Moreover, students in the 21st century frequently enter mathematics classrooms with deficiencies in numerical and algebraic manipulation skills, problem-solving abilities, and an overall negative disposition.

Individuals possessing proficient mathematical skills showcase enhanced analytical thinking and superior reasoning abilities. Mathematics stands as a crucial prerequisite for admission to higher education programs, especially in the scientific field, engineering and technology. The decline in participation in advanced mathematics courses has become a cause for concern, resulting in a rise in the number of students entering higher education without adequate mathematical preparation.

The experiences students undergo during their academic journey exert a significant influence on their perceptions and attitudes toward mathematics. Motivation stands out as a pivotal factor in shaping students' perspectives, as those who are motivated tend to display heightened dedication to enhancing their abilities. Also, it makes them to realize, learning Mathematics will improve their logical and analytical skills.

Recognizing the significant influence of motivation, educators can foster an understanding of the real-world applications of Mathematics starting from lower grades. This involves incorporating motivational strategies into their teaching approaches to nurture the development of mathematical skills.

This study investigates the factors contributing to students' abhorrence attitudes toward mathematics, irrespective of their academic performance. A considerable number of students indicated that their dislike for mathematics originated during their school years. The article presents a survey conducted via google form to explore students' reluctance to pursue advanced studies in mathematics. The data collected through questionnaires sheds light on the reasons behind students' hesitancy to choose mathematics for higher education, along with suggestions aimed at fostering interest in learning the subject.

We garnered 669 responses from a diverse group of stakeholders, including students, teachers, and parents. The statistical analysis delved into multiple factors, such as a lack of interest, unwilling to work hard, unaware of scope, wrong guidance, lack of motivation, etc.

Python program coding was utilized for statistical analysis to investigate the relationships among variables. Inferential statistical techniques, including Logistic Regression Analysis, were employed to scrutinize the connections between variables. The research revealed noteworthy correlations between students' self-realization, understanding of the practical applications of mathematics, innovative teaching methodologies, the introduction of job-oriented courses in mathematics, and the utilization of mathematical concepts in other disciplines. Additionally, both teacher and parental encouragement emerged as significant factors influencing students' attitudes toward mathematics.

OBJECTIVES

To enhance the ability of attaining better decision for a real time issue by making use of compactness notion in Neutrosophic Generalized Topology. Our focus centers on addressing a prevalent concern: the declining interest of students in pursuing higher education in Mathematics. We delve into the reasons behind this current trend and offer corresponding suggestions.

The data are collected through the survey on "Why students are not choosing Mathematics for higher education recently? "- Reasons and Suggestions.

To address this issue, we gathered data from various stakeholders and employed statistical tools for analysis. The scrutiny of the collected data is conducted through the application of Compactness in Neutrosophic Generalized Topology. Subsequently, Python programming code is utilized to organize and sort the data. The final step involves decision-making through Regression analysis.

METHODOLOGY

Identification

To begin with, a current societal issue on making appropriate decision in selecting higher education is identified. Our primary concern revolves around tackling a widespread issue: the decreasing enthusiasm among students for pursuing higher education in Mathematics.

Data Collection

Data are collected from various academically related stakeholders regarding this issue through questionnaires.

I. Name:
II. Email:
III. Category: Faculty/Teacher, Parent, Student
IV. Name of the City
V. Reasons for Not choosing Mathematic for Higher Education
   1. Lack of interest in Mathematics
   2. Unwilling to work hard & to do more practice
   3. Unaware about the future scope of Mathematics and its real-life applications
   4. Not ready to learn Mathematics with more concentration
   5. Feels other subjects are easy when compared to Mathematics
   6. Lack of motivation from Parents, Teachers and Friends.
   7. Wrong guidance from seniors to choose non-Mathematics courses for easy learning.
   8. Not knowing that "Learning Mathematics will improve their logical and analytical thinking to get through competitive exams"
   9. Online education in schools (During COVID) reduced their confidence in understanding and learning Mathematics.
   10. Less knowledge about the availability of various high-salaried job opportunities for Mathematics students
VI. Suggestions: (Qn. No. 11-15) How to make students to select Mathematics for higher education?
   11. Introducing innovative Teaching Methodology to create interest in Mathematics.
   12. Providing job-oriented courses in Mathematics to get placed in highly reputed well-paid jobs.

13. Creating awareness about the practical applications of Mathematics from lower classes onwards.
14. Clarifying the usage of mathematical concepts in all other subjects.
15. Making them to realize that learning Mathematics will improve their logical and analytical skills to get through competitive exams.
16. Are you as a (Student / Faculty / Parent) interested or suggest others to choose Mathematics for higher education?

Figure 1.

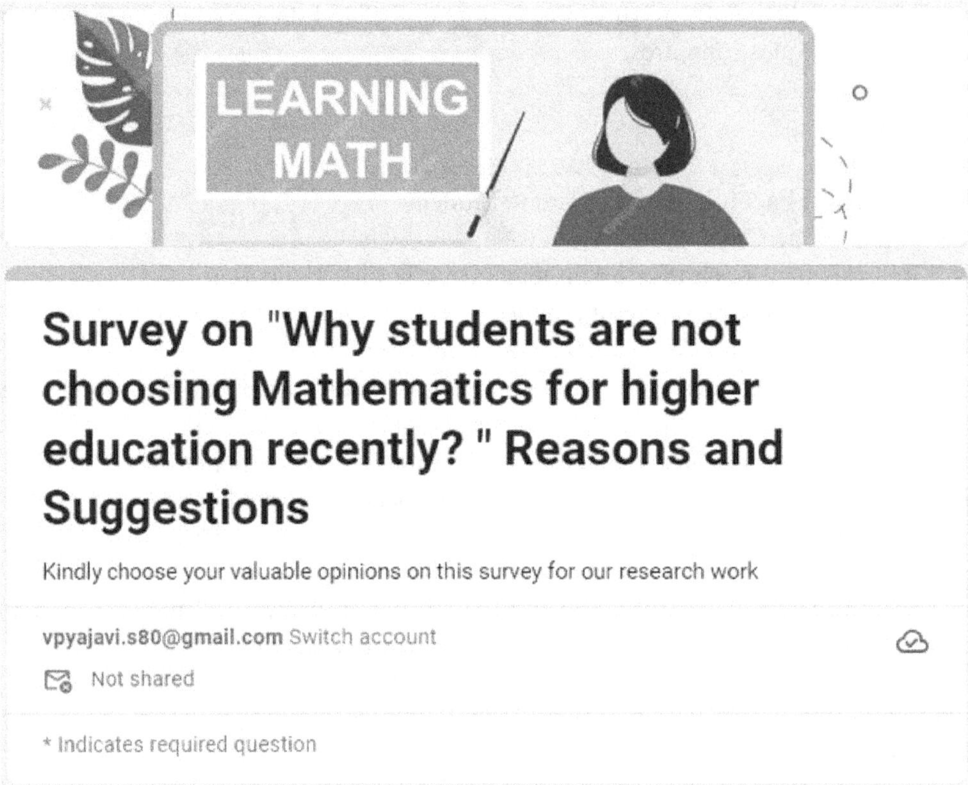

Figure 2.

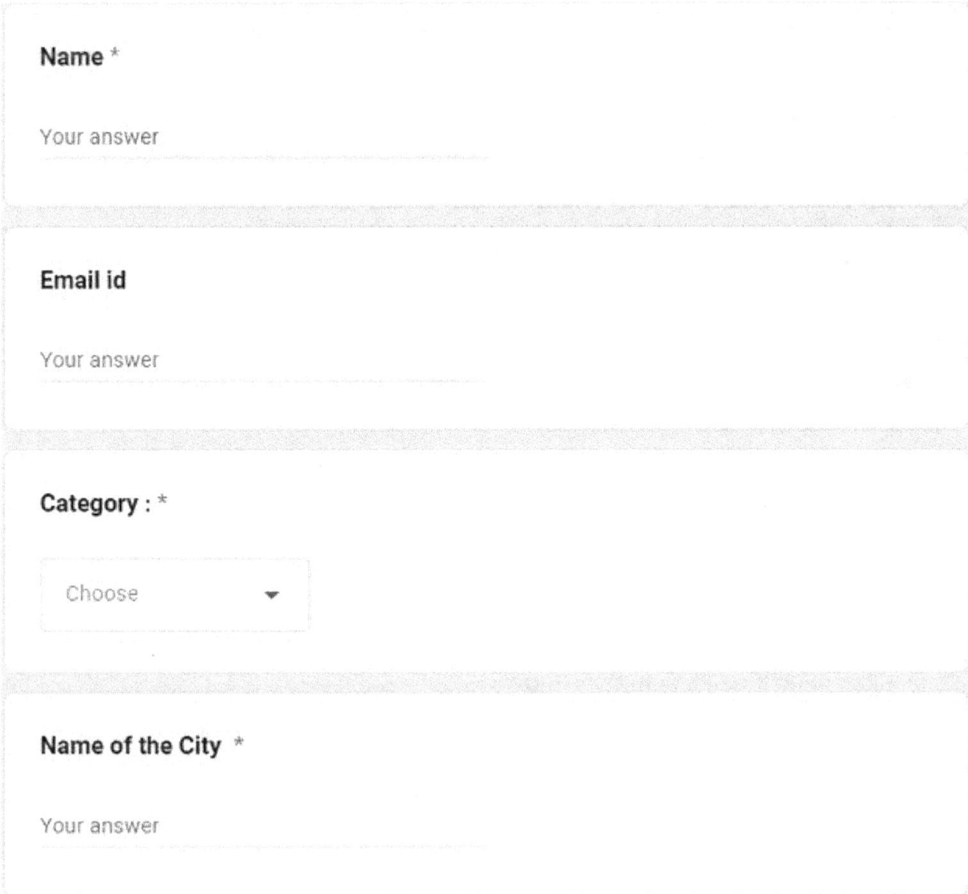

Name *

Your answer

Email id

Your answer

Category : *

Choose

Name of the City *

Your answer

Figure 3.

Reasons: (Qn. No. 1-10) Why the students are not choosing Mathematics for higher education? *

1. Lack of interest in Mathematics

- ○ Exactly True
- ○ May be True
- ○ Definitely No
- ○ No idea

Figure 4.

2. Unwilling to work hard & to do more Practice. *

- ○ Exactly True
- ○ May be True
- ○ Definitely No
- ○ No idea

Figure 5.

3. Unaware about the future scope of Mathematics and its real-life applications. *

- ◯ Exactly True
- ◯ May be True
- ◯ Definitely No
- ◯ No idea

Figure 6.

4. Not ready to learn Mathematics with more concentration. *

- Exactly True
- May be True
- Definitely No
- No idea

5. Feels other subjects are easy when compared to Mathematics. *

- Exactly True
- May be True
- Definitely No
- No idea

Figure 7.

6. Lack of motivation from Parents, Teachers and Friends. *

- ◯ Exactly True
- ◯ May be True
- ◯ Definitely No
- ◯ No idea

7. Wrong guidance from seniors to choose non-Mathematics courses for easy learning. *

- ◯ Exactly True
- ◯ May be True
- ◯ Definitely No
- ◯ No idea

Figure 8.

8. Not knowing that "Learning Mathematics will improve their logical and analytical thinking to get through competitive exams"

- Exactly True
- May be True
- Definitely No
- No idea

9. Online education in schools (During COVID) reduced their confidence in understanding and learning Mathematics.

- Exactly True
- May be True
- Definitely No
- No idea

Figure 9.

10. Less knowledge about the availability of various high-salaried job opportunities for Mathematics students.

- Exactly True
- May be True
- Definitely No
- No idea

Figure 10.

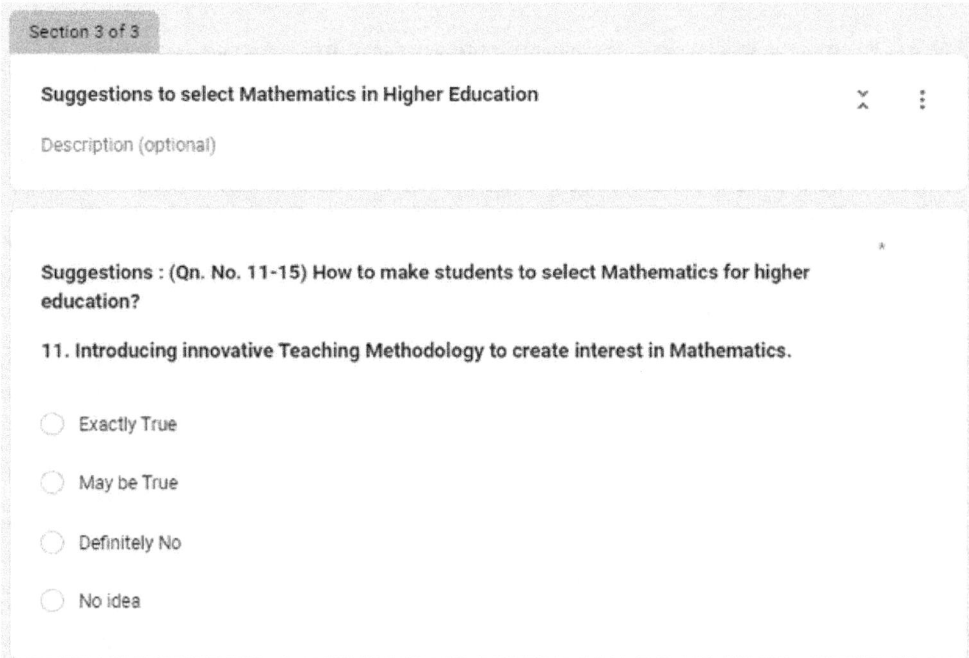

Section 3 of 3

Suggestions to select Mathematics in Higher Education

Description (optional)

Suggestions : (Qn. No. 11-15) How to make students to select Mathematics for higher education?

11. Introducing innovative Teaching Methodology to create interest in Mathematics.

- Exactly True
- May be True
- Definitely No
- No idea

Figure 11.

*

12. Providing job-oriented courses in Mathematics to get placed in highly reputed well-paid jobs.

◯ Exactly True

◯ May be True

◯ Definitely No

◯ No idea

*

13. Creating awareness about the practical applications of Mathematics from lower classes onwards.

◯ Exactly True

◯ May be True

◯ Definitely No

◯ No idea

Figure 12.

14. Clarifying the usage of mathematical concepts in all other subjects. *

- Exactly True
- May be True
- Definitely No
- No idea

15. Making them to realize that learning Mathematics will improve their logical and analytical skills to get through competitive exams. *

- Exactly True
- May be True
- Definitely No
- No idea

Figure 13.

16. Are you as a(Student / Faculty / Parent) interested or suggest others to choose Mathematics for higher education? *

- Yes
- No

The link to the questionnaire utilized to gather data has been included below for reference https://forms.gle/RPCgcwQ3z2XKVgdB9

Algorithm

A step-by-step process is framed to analyze the acquired data and reach apt decisions by means of compactness in Neutrosophic Generalized Topology.

Step:1 Data Preprocessing with appropriate Python code

- Plotting Cook's Distance
- Defining Predictors and Calculating Variance Inflation Factor (VIF) for each predictor

Step:2 Data accuracy evaluation using various models

- OLS Model
- Logistic Regression Model
- Naive Bayes model
- Random Forest Classifier

Step:3 Filtering major predictors

Algorithms Applied on Data With Python Code and Output Screenshots

```
data.info()
```

Output 1.

```
<class 'pandas.core.frame.DataFrame'>
RangeIndex: 669 entries, 0 to 668
Data columns (total 21 columns):
 #   Column                Non-Null Count  Dtype
---  ------                --------------  -----
 0   Timestamp             669 non-null    object
 1   name                  669 non-null    object
 2   email                 669 non-null    object
 3   category              669 non-null    object
 4   city                  669 non-null    object
 5   lack of interest      669 non-null    object
 6   hardworking           669 non-null    object
 7   Unaware_future scope  669 non-null    object
 8   more _concentrate     669 non-null    object
 9   other_sub_easy        669 non-null    object
 10  No_motivation(P/S/T)  669 non-null    object
 11  Wrong_guidance        669 non-null    object
 12  Not_know              669 non-null    object
 13  Online_edu            669 non-null    object
 14  job                   669 non-null    object
 15  S_innovative          669 non-null    object
 16  S_job-oriented        669 non-null    object
 17  S_awareness           669 non-null    object
 18  S_use                 669 non-null    object
 19  S_logical             669 non-null    object
 20  outcome               669 non-null    object
dtypes: object(21)
```

```
import pandas as pd

# List of columns to process

columns_to_process = ['lack of interest', 'hardworking',
'Unaware_future scope', 'more _concentrate',

                        'other_sub_easy', 'No_motiva-
tion(P/S/T)', 'Wrong_guidance', 'Not_know',
```

```
                          'Online_edu', 'job', 'S_innovative',
'S_job-oriented', 'S_awareness',

                          'S_use', 'S_logical']

  # Mapping for each value

  value_mapping = {"Exactly True": 1, "May be True": 2, "No
idea": -1, "Definitely No": 0}

  # Apply mapping to each column

  for column in columns_to_process:

      data[column] = data[column].replace(value_mapping)

  # Display the updated DataFrame

  print(data)
```

Output 2.

```
           Timestamp               name                          email  \
0    11/15/2023 17:14           Santhi P           saayphd.11@gmail.com
1    11/15/2023 17:56           Vijaya.S          vpyajavi.s80@gmail.com
2    11/15/2023 19:06           Varsha L     varshalnarayanan@gmail.com
3    11/15/2023 19:07     Anu Gayathri S       anugayathri04@@gmail.com
4    11/15/2023 21:46   Vijaya Vishwanath          viviphd.11@gmail.com
..                ...                ...                            ...
664  11/16/2023 14:12  Esther Jebarani A      estherjeba.star@gmail.com
665  11/16/2023 14:31         A m.akhash  22cos205@americancollege.edu.in
666  11/16/2023 14:37           Sharmila        lekha19smart@gmail.com
667  11/16/2023 14:39           Vijaya S          viviphd.11@gmail.com
668  11/16/2023 14:54           Difrina S       sdifrina2003@gmail.com
```

```
data['outcome'] = data['outcome'].replace({"Yes": 1, "No": 0})
```

```
print(data['outcome'])
```

Output 3.

```
0      1
1      1
2      0
3      1
4      1
      ..
664    0
665    0
666    0
667    0
668    0
Name: outcome, Length: 669, dtype: int64
```

```
data.drop(columns=['name'], inplace=True)
```

```
data.drop(columns=['city'], inplace=True)
```

```
data.drop(columns=['email'], inplace=True)
```

```
data.drop(columns=['Timestamp'], inplace=True)
```

```
data.info()
```

Output 4.

```
<class 'pandas.core.frame.DataFrame'>
RangeIndex: 669 entries, 0 to 668
Data columns (total 17 columns):
 #   Column                Non-Null Count  Dtype
---  ------                --------------  -----
 0   category              669 non-null    int64
 1   lack of interest      669 non-null    int64
 2   hardworking           669 non-null    int64
 3   Unaware_future scope  669 non-null    int64
 4   more _concentrate     669 non-null    int64
 5   other_sub_easy        669 non-null    int64
 6   No_motivation(P/S/T)  669 non-null    int64
 7   Wrong_guidance        669 non-null    int64
 8   Not_know              669 non-null    int64
 9   Online_edu            669 non-null    int64
 10  job                   669 non-null    int64
 11  S_innovative          669 non-null    int64
 12  S_job-oriented        669 non-null    int64
 13  S_awareness           669 non-null    int64
 14  S_use                 669 non-null    int64
 15  S_logical             669 non-null    int64
 16  outcome               669 non-null    int64
dtypes: int64(17)
```

```
import seaborn as sns

import statsmodels.api as sm

from statsmodels.formula.api import ols

import matplotlib.pyplot as plt

data['outcome'] = data['outcome'].replace({'no': 0})

print(data['outcome'].unique())
```

```
[1 0]

import numpy as np

# Assuming 'data' is your DataFrame

y = data['outcome'].astype(int)

X = data.drop(['outcome'], axis=1)

# Fit the OLS model

model = sm.OLS(y, sm.add_constant(X)).fit()

# Calculate Cook's distance

influence = model.get_influence()

(c, _) = influence.cooks_distance

# Plot Cook's distance

fig = plt.figure(figsize=(12, 8))

plt.stem(np.arange(len(data)), c, markerfmt=",")

plt.title("Cook's Distance Plot")
```

```
plt.xlabel("Observation Index")

plt.ylabel("Cook's Distance")

plt.show()

from statsmodels.stats.outliers_influence import variance_
inflation_factor

# Define your predictors (exclude 'outcome')

predictors = ['category', 'lack of interest', 'hardworking',
'Unaware_future scope',

                'more _concentrate', 'other_sub_easy', 'No_mo-
tivation(P/S/T)',

                'Wrong_guidance', 'Not_know', 'Online_edu',
'job', 'S_innovative',

                'S_job-oriented', 'S_awareness', 'S_use', 'S_
logical']

# Calculate VIF for each predictor

vif = pd.DataFrame()

vif["VIF Factor"] = [variance_inflation_factor(data[predic-
tors].values, i) for i in range(len(predictors))]
```

```
vif["Predictor"] = predictors

print(vif)
```

Output 5.

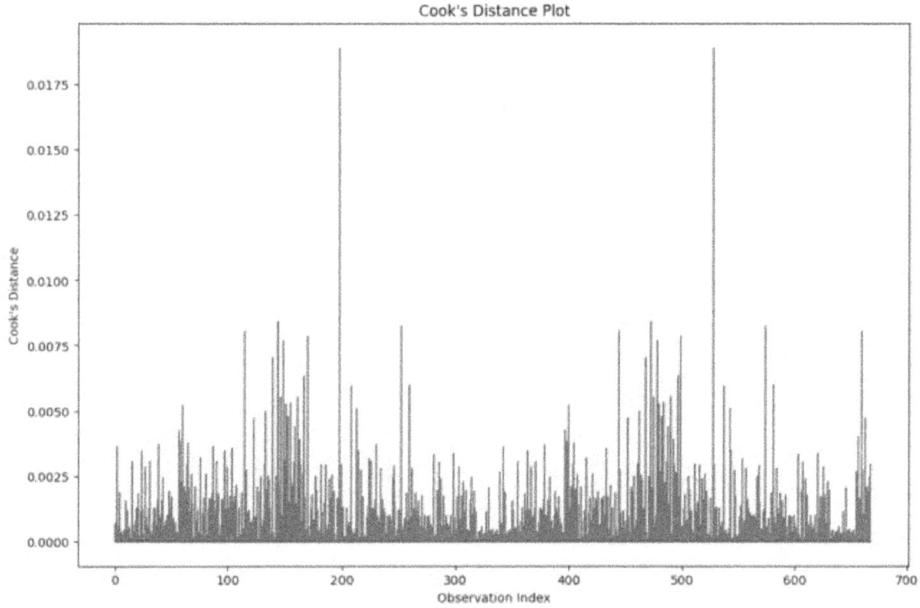


```
x = data[['category', 'lack of interest', 'hardworking',
'Unaware_future scope','more _concentrate', 'other_sub_easy',
'No_motivation(P/S/T)','Wrong_guidance', 'Not_know', 'Online_
edu', 'job', 'S_innovative', 'S_job-oriented', 'S_awareness',
'S_use', 'S_logical']]  # Exclude 'outcome' from predictors

y = data['outcome']

x = sm.add_constant(x)

model = sm.OLS(y,x).fit()

print(model.summary())
```

Output 6.

```
                            OLS Regression Results
==============================================================================
Dep. Variable:                outcome   R-squared:                       0.056
Model:                            OLS   Adj. R-squared:                  0.033
Method:                 Least Squares   F-statistic:                     2.430
Date:                Tue, 05 Dec 2023   Prob (F-statistic):            0.00143
Time:                        06:58:52   Log-Likelihood:                -443.03
No. Observations:                 669   AIC:                             920.1
Df Residuals:                     652   BIC:                             996.7
Df Model:                          16
Covariance Type:            nonrobust
==============================================================================
                          coef    std err          t      P>|t|      [0.025      0.975]
------------------------------------------------------------------------------
const                   0.5235      0.088      5.947      0.000       0.351       0.696
category               -0.1060      0.031     -3.443      0.001      -0.166      -0.046
lack of interest        0.0379      0.023      1.640      0.101      -0.007       0.083
hardworking             0.0437      0.025      1.770      0.077      -0.005       0.092
Unaware_future scope    0.0309      0.027      1.133      0.258      -0.023       0.084
more _concentrate       0.0019      0.023      0.083      0.934      -0.044       0.047
other_sub_easy         -0.0088      0.028     -0.317      0.751      -0.063       0.046
No_motivation(P/S/T)    0.0307      0.021      1.480      0.139      -0.010       0.071
Wrong_guidance          0.0265      0.022      1.204      0.229      -0.017       0.070
Not_know                0.0172      0.028      0.619      0.536      -0.037       0.072
Online_edu             -0.0343      0.027     -1.279      0.201      -0.087       0.018
job                     0.0195      0.026      0.752      0.452      -0.031       0.071
S_innovative           -0.0350      0.031     -1.137      0.256      -0.095       0.025
S_job-oriented          0.0036      0.031      0.119      0.905      -0.056       0.064
S_awareness            -0.0493      0.035     -1.429      0.154      -0.117       0.018
S_use                  -0.0396      0.030     -1.325      0.186      -0.098       0.019
S_logical               0.0980      0.039      2.498      0.013       0.021       0.175
==============================================================================
Omnibus:                     4916.414   Durbin-Watson:                   1.427
Prob(Omnibus):                  0.000   Jarque-Bera (JB):               94.544
Skew:                          -0.518   Prob(JB):                     2.95e-21
Kurtosis:                       1.478   Cond. No.                         23.5
==============================================================================
```

```
data=data.drop(['S_logical'],axis=1)
```

```
from statsmodels.stats.outliers_influence import variance_
inflation_factor
```

```
# Define your predictors (exclude 'outcome')
```

```
predictors = ['category', 'lack of interest', 'hardworking', 'Unaware_future scope',
              'more _concentrate', 'other_sub_easy', 'No_motivation(P/S/T)',
              'Wrong_guidance', 'Not_know', 'Online_edu', 'job', 'S_innovative',
              'S_job-oriented', 'S_awareness', 'S_use']

# Calculate VIF for each predictor
vif = pd.DataFrame()
vif["VIF Factor"] = [variance_inflation_factor(data[predictors].values, i) for i in range(len(predictors))]
vif["Predictor"] = predictors
print(vif)
```

Output 7.

	VIF Factor	Predictor
0	1.742208	category
1	3.532717	lack of interest
2	3.270933	hardworking
3	4.203612	Unaware_future scope
4	3.098865	more _concentrate
5	3.650666	other_sub_easy
6	2.530422	No_motivation(P/S/T)
7	2.678235	Wrong_guidance
8	3.971771	Not_know
9	3.580724	Online_edu
10	4.430191	job
11	4.933114	S_innovative
12	4.989556	S_job-oriented
13	5.471085	S_awareness
14	4.927866	S_use
15	6.513385	S_logical

```
data=data.drop(['S_awareness'],axis=1)

from statsmodels.stats.outliers_influence import variance_
inflation_factor

# Define your predictors (exclude 'outcome')

predictors = ['category', 'lack of interest', 'hardworking',
'Unaware_future scope',

                'more _concentrate', 'other_sub_easy', 'No_mo-
tivation(P/S/T)',

                'Wrong_guidance', 'Not_know', 'Online_edu',
'job', 'S_innovative',
```

```
                'S_job-oriented', 'S_use']

# Calculate VIF for each predictor

vif = pd.DataFrame()

vif["VIF Factor"] = [variance_inflation_factor(data[predic-
tors].values, i) for i in range(len(predictors))]

vif["Predictor"] = predictors

print(vif)
```

Output 8.

```
    VIF Factor             Predictor
0     1.735981              category
1     3.433511      lack of interest
2     3.268557           hardworking
3     4.202548  Unaware_future scope
4     3.098810     more _concentrate
5     3.584710        other_sub_easy
6     2.496041  No_motivation(P/S/T)
7     2.675477        Wrong_guidance
8     3.892556              Not_know
9     3.567042            Online_edu
10    4.429892                   job
11    4.598517          S_innovative
12    4.983682        S_job-oriented
13    5.308029           S_awareness
14    4.795879                 S_use
```

```
data=data.drop(['S_awareness'],axis=1)
```

Output 9.

```
<class 'pandas.core.frame.DataFrame'>
RangeIndex: 669 entries, 0 to 668
Data columns (total 15 columns):
 #   Column                Non-Null Count  Dtype
---  ------                --------------  -----
 0   category              669 non-null    int64
 1   lack of interest      669 non-null    int64
 2   hardworking           669 non-null    int64
 3   Unaware_future scope  669 non-null    int64
 4   more _concentrate     669 non-null    int64
 5   other_sub_easy        669 non-null    int64
 6   No_motivation(P/S/T)  669 non-null    int64
 7   Wrong_guidance        669 non-null    int64
 8   Not_know              669 non-null    int64
 9   Online_edu            669 non-null    int64
 10  job                   669 non-null    int64
 11  S_innovative          669 non-null    int64
 12  S_job-oriented        669 non-null    int64
 13  S_use                 669 non-null    int64
 14  outcome               669 non-null    int64
dtypes: int64(15)
```

```
from statsmodels.stats.outliers_influence import variance_
inflation_factor

# Define your predictors (exclude 'outcome')

predictors = ['category', 'lack of interest', 'hardworking',
'Unaware_future scope',

              'more _concentrate', 'other_sub_easy', 'No_mo-
tivation(P/S/T)',

              'Wrong_guidance', 'Not_know', 'Online_edu',
'job', 'S_innovative',
```

```
                'S_job-oriented', 'S_use']

# Calculate VIF for each predictor

vif = pd.DataFrame()

vif["VIF Factor"] = [variance_inflation_factor(data[predic-
tors].values, i) for i in range(len(predictors))]

vif["Predictor"] = predictors

print(vif)
```

Output 10.

```
    VIF Factor             Predictor
0     1.723326              category
1     3.433510      lack of interest
2     3.166575           hardworking
3     3.958158  Unaware_future scope
4     3.032619     more _concentrate
5     3.498877        other_sub_easy
6     2.484794  No_motivation(P/S/T)
7     2.653641        Wrong_guidance
8     3.856471              Not_know
9     3.558159            Online_edu
10    4.429879                   job
11    4.450345          S_innovative
12    4.883370        S_job-oriented
13    4.743078                 S_use
```

```
columns_to_drop = ['more _concentrate', 'other_sub_easy',
'S_innovative']

data = data.drop(columns=columns_to_drop, axis=1)
```

```
data.info()

<class 'pandas.core.frame.DataFrame'>

RangeIndex: 669 entries, 0 to 668

Data columns (total 12 columns):
```

Output 11.

```
<class 'pandas.core.frame.DataFrame'>
RangeIndex: 669 entries, 0 to 668
Data columns (total 12 columns):
 #   Column                Non-Null Count  Dtype
---  ------                --------------  -----
 0   category              669 non-null    int64
 1   lack of interest      669 non-null    int64
 2   hardworking           669 non-null    int64
 3   Unaware_future scope  669 non-null    int64
 4   No_motivation(P/S/T)  669 non-null    int64
 5   Wrong_guidance        669 non-null    int64
 6   Not_know              669 non-null    int64
 7   Online_edu            669 non-null    int64
 8   job                   669 non-null    int64
 9   S_job-oriented        669 non-null    int64
 10  S_use                 669 non-null    int64
 11  outcome               669 non-null    int64
dtypes: int64(12)
```

Data Analysis

Data accuracy evaluation using various models:

```
model = sm.OLS(y,x).fit()

print(model.summary())
```

Output 12.

```
                                 OLS Regression Results
=========================================================================================
Dep. Variable:                outcome   R-squared (uncentered):                   0.619
Model:                            OLS   Adj. R-squared (uncentered):              0.611
Method:                 Least Squares   F-statistic:                              76.13
Date:                Tue, 05 Dec 2023   Prob (F-statistic):                   4.31e-127
Time:                        07:05:17   Log-Likelihood:                         -471.25
No. Observations:                 669   AIC:                                      970.5
Df Residuals:                     655   BIC:                                      1034.
Df Model:                          14
Covariance Type:            nonrobust
==========================================================================================
                          coef    std err          t      P>|t|      [0.025      0.975]
------------------------------------------------------------------------------------------
category               -0.0761      0.031     -2.449      0.015      -0.137      -0.015
lack of interest        0.0828      0.023      3.567      0.000       0.037       0.128
hardworking             0.0846      0.025      3.436      0.001       0.036       0.133
Unaware_future scope    0.0571      0.027      2.088      0.037       0.003       0.111
more _concentrate       0.0194      0.024      0.816      0.415      -0.027       0.066
other_sub_easy          0.0349      0.028      1.246      0.213      -0.020       0.090
No_motivation(P/S/T)    0.0578      0.021      2.717      0.007       0.016       0.100
Wrong_guidance          0.0199      0.023      0.877      0.381      -0.025       0.065
Not_know                0.0385      0.029      1.349      0.178      -0.018       0.095
Online_edu              0.0258      0.026      0.981      0.327      -0.026       0.077
job                     0.0307      0.027      1.138      0.255      -0.022       0.084
S_innovative            0.0467      0.030      1.574      0.116      -0.012       0.105
S_job-oriented          0.0363      0.031      1.161      0.246      -0.025       0.098
S_use                   0.0161      0.030      0.535      0.593      -0.043       0.075
==============================================================================
Omnibus:                      593.737   Durbin-Watson:                   1.336
Prob(Omnibus):                  0.000   Jarque-Bera (JB):               69.965
Skew:                          -0.500   Prob(JB):                     6.42e-16
Kurtosis:                       1.772   Cond. No.                         8.20
==============================================================================
```

The implementation of a logistic regression model using Python code process the following steps and the corresponding output is displayed.

Imports: Indispensable libraries like pandas for data handling, modules like train_test_split, Logistic Regression from Scikit-learn for model building and metrics such as accuracy_score, confusion_matrix, classification_report for model evaluation are imported.

Data Splitting: The dataset is split into training and testing subsets by means of the train_test_split function.

Model Creation: A logistic regression model is primed using Logistic Regression().

Model Training: The formed model is trained using the fit() function with the training data.

Prediction: Predictions are made on the test data using the predict() function.

Model Evaluation: The model's performance is evaluated using metrics like accuracy_score, confusion_matrix, and classification_report to recognize how well the model predicts outcomes compared to the actual values.

This code sequence illustrates a typical workflow for building, training, and evaluating a logistic regression model in Python using Scikit-learn.

```
Accuracy: 0.6417910447761194

Confusion Matrix:

[[10 37]

 [11 76]]

Classification Report:

              precision    recall  f1-score   support

           0       0.48      0.21      0.29        47

           1       0.67      0.87      0.76        87

    accuracy                           0.64       134

   macro avg       0.57      0.54      0.53       134

weighted avg       0.60      0.64      0.60       134
```

Handling Imbalanced Data in Outcome variable

```
import pandas as pd
```

```
from sklearn.model_selection import train_test_split

from sklearn.preprocessing import LabelEncoder

from sklearn.linear_model import LogisticRegression

from sklearn.metrics import accuracy_score, classification_
report, confusion_matrix

from imblearn.over_sampling import SMOTE
```

Handle Imbalanced Data (SMOTE)

```
# No need to encode target variable 'y' as it is already bi-
nary

y = data['outcome']

# Split the data into training and testing sets

X_train, X_test, y_train, y_test = train_test_split(X, y,
test_size=0.2, random_state=42)

# Apply SMOTE to oversample the minority class

smote = SMOTE(random_state=42)

X_resampled, y_resampled = smote.fit_resample(X_train, y_
train)
```

Train Logistic Regression Model

```
# Initialization

model = LogisticRegression(random_state=42)

# Train on Resampled data

model.fit(X_resampled, y_resampled)

# Predictions making

y_pred = model.predict(X_test)

# Evaluate accuracy

accuracy = accuracy_score(y_test, y_pred)

print(f"Accuracy: {accuracy:.4f}")

# Display confusion matrix and classification report

conf_matrix = confusion_matrix(y_test, y_pred)

print("Confusion Matrix:")

print(conf_matrix)
```

```
class_report = classification_report(y_test, y_pred)

print("Classification Report:")

print(class_report)

Accuracy: 0.5522

Confusion Matrix:

[[19 28]

 [32 55]]

Classification Report:

              precision    recall  f1-score   support

           0       0.37      0.40      0.39        47

           1       0.66      0.63      0.65        87

    accuracy                           0.55       134

   macro avg       0.52      0.52      0.52       134

weighted avg       0.56      0.55      0.56       134
```

Hyperparameter Tuning to improve accuracy

```
from sklearn.model_selection import GridSearchCV

from sklearn.linear_model import LogisticRegression

# Specify the hyperparameter grid

param_grid = {'C': [0.001, 0.01, 0.1, 1, 10],

              'penalty': ['l2']}

# Create logistic regression model

logreg = LogisticRegression(solver='lbfgs')

# Create GridSearchCV

grid_search = GridSearchCV(logreg, param_grid, cv=5)

# Fit the grid search to the data

grid_search.fit(X_train, y_train)

# Print the best hyperparameters and accuracy

print("Best Parameters: ", grid_search.best_params_)
```

```
print("Best Accuracy: ", grid_search.best_score_)

# Evaluate on the test set

test_accuracy = grid_search.score(X_test, y_test)

print("Test Accuracy: ", test_accuracy)
```

Output 13.

	Feature	Coefficient	Absolute Coefficient
0	category	-0.528073	0.528073
15	S_logical	0.350179	0.350179
2	hardworking	0.319669	0.319669
13	S_awareness	-0.241567	0.241567
6	No_motivation(P/S/T)	0.222836	0.222836
11	S_innovative	-0.199897	0.199897
8	Not_know	0.165731	0.165731
1	lack of interest	0.161942	0.161942
12	S_job-oriented	0.130049	0.130049
4	more _concentrate	0.123181	0.123181
7	Wrong_guidance	0.116098	0.116098
14	S_use	-0.056465	0.056465
9	Online_edu	0.040319	0.040319
5	other_sub_easy	-0.023871	0.023871
3	Unaware_future scope	0.022600	0.022600
10	job	0.016353	0.016353

```
import pandas as pd

from statsmodels.stats.outliers_influence import variance_
inflation_factor

import seaborn as sns

import matplotlib.pyplot as plt
```

```
# Assuming 'data' is your DataFrame with predictors (X) and outcome (y)

# Replace 'X' with your set of predictors

# VIF Analysis

def calculate_vif(data_frame):

    vif_data = pd.DataFrame()

    vif_data["Variable"] = data_frame.columns

    vif_data["VIF"] = [variance_inflation_factor(data_frame.values, i) for i in range(data_frame.shape[1])]

    return vif_data

# Call the function with your DataFrame

vif_result = calculate_vif(data)

# Print the VIF values

print(vif_result)
```

Output 14.

```
               Variable       VIF
0              category  1.718003
1      lack of interest  3.301506
2           hardworking  3.009511
3  Unaware_future scope  3.977145
4  No_motivation(P/S/T)  2.479577
5        Wrong_guidance  2.628323
6              Not_know  3.779352
7            Online_edu  3.164389
8                   job  4.290497
9        S_job-oriented  4.610638
10                S_use  4.454295
11              outcome  2.604722
```

```
# Drop 'job' and 'S_job-oriented' columns

data = data.drop(['job', 'S_job-oriented'], axis=1)

import pandas as pd

from statsmodels.stats.outliers_influence import variance_
inflation_factor

import seaborn as sns

import matplotlib.pyplot as plt

# Assuming 'data' is your DataFrame with predictors (X) and
outcome (y)

# Replace 'X' with your set of predictors
```

```
# VIF Analysis

def calculate_vif(data_frame):

    vif_data = pd.DataFrame()

    vif_data["Variable"] = data_frame.columns

    vif_data["VIF"] = [variance_inflation_factor(data_frame.
values, i) for i in range(data_frame.shape[1])]

    return vif_data

# Call the function with your DataFrame

vif_result = calculate_vif(data)

# Print the VIF values

print(vif_result)
```

Output 15.

```
                Variable       VIF
0               category  1.705190
1       lack of interest  3.160788
2            hardworking  2.934098
3  Unaware_future scope  3.727412
4  No_motivation(P/S/T)  2.444332
5         Wrong_guidance  2.520615
6               Not_know  3.630007
7             Online_edu  3.132474
8                  S_use  3.978448
9                outcome  2.581787
```

```
data.info()

<class 'pandas.core.frame.DataFrame'>

RangeIndex: 669 entries, 0 to 668

Data columns (total 10 columns):
```

Output 16.

```
<class 'pandas.core.frame.DataFrame'>
RangeIndex: 669 entries, 0 to 668
Data columns (total 10 columns):
 #   Column                 Non-Null Count  Dtype
---  ------                 --------------  -----
 0   category               669 non-null    int64
 1   lack of interest       669 non-null    int64
 2   hardworking            669 non-null    int64
 3   Unaware_future scope   669 non-null    int64
 4   No_motivation(P/S/T)   669 non-null    int64
 5   Wrong_guidance         669 non-null    int64
 6   Not_know               669 non-null    int64
 7   Online_edu             669 non-null    int64
 8   S_use                  669 non-null    int64
 9   outcome                669 non-null    int64
dtypes: int64(10)
```

```
from sklearn.model_selection import train_test_split

from sklearn.linear_model import LogisticRegression

from sklearn.metrics import accuracy_score, classification_
report, confusion_matrix

# Assuming 'data' is your DataFrame
```

```
X = data.drop('outcome', axis=1)  # Features

y = data['outcome']  # Target variable

# Split the data into training and testing sets

X_train, X_test, y_train, y_test = train_test_split(X, y,
test_size=0.2, random_state=42)

# Initialize the logistic regression model

model = LogisticRegression(random_state=42)

# Fit the model on the training data

model.fit(X_train, y_train)

# Make predictions on the test data

y_pred = model.predict(X_test)

# Evaluate the model

accuracy = accuracy_score(y_test, y_pred)

conf_matrix = confusion_matrix(y_test, y_pred)
```

```
classification_rep = classification_report(y_test, y_pred)

# Display the results

print(f'Accuracy: {accuracy:.4f}\n')

print('Confusion Matrix:')

print(conf_matrix)

print('\nClassification Report:')

print(classification_rep)

# Assuming X and y are your feature matrix and target vari-
able

# Split the data into training and testing sets

X_train, X_test, y_train, y_test = train_test_split(X, y,
test_size=0.2, random_state=42)

# Create a Support Vector Machine classifier

svm_classifier = SVC()

# Train the model on the training data
```

```
svm_classifier.fit(X_train, y_train)

# Make predictions on the test set

y_pred = svm_classifier.predict(X_test)

# Evaluate the model

accuracy = accuracy_score(y_test, y_pred)

conf_matrix = confusion_matrix(y_test, y_pred)

class_report = classification_report(y_test, y_pred)

print(f"Accuracy: {accuracy:.4f}\n")

print(f"Confusion Matrix:\n{conf_matrix}\n")

print(f"Classification Report:\n{class_report}")

Accuracy: 0.6418

Confusion Matrix:

[[ 6 41]

 [ 7 80]]
```

```
Classification Report:

              precision    recall  f1-score   support

           0       0.46      0.13      0.20        47

           1       0.66      0.92      0.77        87

    accuracy                           0.64       134

   macro avg       0.56      0.52      0.48       134

weighted avg       0.59      0.64      0.57       134
```

```
data=data.drop(['S_use'],axis=1)

from sklearn.model_selection import train_test_split

from sklearn.svm import SVC

from sklearn.metrics import accuracy_score, confusion_matrix, classification_report

# Split the data into training and testing sets

X_train, X_test, y_train, y_test = train_test_split(data.drop('outcome', axis=1), data['outcome'], test_size=0.2, random_state=42)
```

```
# Initialize the Naive Bayes model

nb_model = GaussianNB()

# Train the model on the training set

nb_model.fit(X_train, y_train)

# Make predictions on the test set

y_pred = nb_model.predict(X_test)

# Calculate accuracy

accuracy = accuracy_score(y_test, y_pred)

print("Accuracy:", accuracy)

# Display confusion matrix and classification report

conf_matrix = confusion_matrix(y_test, y_pred)

print("\nConfusion Matrix:")

print(conf_matrix)

class_report = classification_report(y_test, y_pred)
```

```
print("\nClassification Report:")

print(class_report)
```

Then, the dataset is processed to perform classification using the Naive Bayes algorithm. A breakdown of what the Python code does is explained below.

Data Preprocessing: Removes the column 'S_use' from the dataset.

Data Splitting: Splits the data into training and testing sets using `train_test_split` from Scikit-learn. The `test_size` parameter defines the proportion of the dataset used for testing.

Model Initialization: Initializes a Naive Bayes (GaussianNB) model.

Model Training: Trains the Naive Bayes model using the training data (X_train and y_train).

Prediction: Uses the trained model to predict outcomes on the test set (X_test).

Performance Evaluation: Calculates the accuracy of the model by comparing predicted labels (y_pred) against actual labels (y_test) using `accuracy_score`.

- Displays the accuracy score.
- Generates and displays a confusion matrix using `confusion_matrix`. The confusion matrix provides insights into the model's performance in terms of true positives, true negatives, false positives, and false negatives.
- Prints a classification report using `classification_report`, which includes metrics like precision, recall, F1-score, and support for each class. It offers a detailed evaluation of the model's performance on different classes within the dataset.

The ensuing output is obtained.

```
Accuracy: 0.7313

Confusion Matrix:

[[19 28]

 [ 8 79]]
```

```
Classification Report:

              precision    recall  f1-score   support

           0       0.70      0.40      0.51        47

           1       0.74      0.91      0.81        87

    accuracy                           0.73       134

   macro avg       0.72      0.66      0.66       134

weighted avg       0.73      0.73      0.71       134
```

```
# Assuming you have already imported necessary libraries and split your data into features (X) and target variable (y)

from sklearn.model_selection import train_test_split

from sklearn.naive_bayes import GaussianNB

from sklearn.metrics import accuracy_score, confusion_matrix, classification_report

import pandas as pd

from statsmodels.stats.outliers_influence import variance_inflation_factor
```

```
import seaborn as sns

import matplotlib.pyplot as plt

# Assuming 'data' is your DataFrame with predictors (X) and outcome (y)

# Replace 'X' with your set of predictors

# VIF Analysis

def calculate_vif(data_frame):

    vif_data = pd.DataFrame()

    vif_data["Variable"] = data_frame.columns

    vif_data["VIF"] = [variance_inflation_factor(data_frame.values, i) for i in range(data_frame.shape[1])]

    return vif_data

# Call the function with your DataFrame

vif_result = calculate_vif(data)

# Print the VIF values
```

```
print(vif_result)

Accuracy: 0.6417910447761194

Confusion Matrix:

[[17 30]

 [18 69]]

Classification Report:

              precision    recall  f1-score   support

           0       0.49      0.36      0.41        47

           1       0.70      0.79      0.74        87

    accuracy                           0.64       134

   macro avg       0.59      0.58      0.58       134

weighted avg       0.62      0.64      0.63       134
```

Output 17.

```
                 Variable       VIF
0                category  1.705178
1        lack of interest  3.065117
2             hardworking  2.815298
3   Unaware_future scope  3.670020
4   No_motivation(P/S/T)  2.405051
5          Wrong_guidance  2.491339
6                Not_know  3.536404
7              Online_edu  3.013012
8                 outcome  2.568386
```

```
from sklearn.compose import ColumnTransformer

from sklearn.pipeline import Pipeline

from sklearn.impute import SimpleImputer

from sklearn.preprocessing import StandardScaler, OneHotEn-
coder

# Identify numerical and categorical columns

numerical_cols = data.select_dtypes(include=['int64']).col-
umns

categorical_cols = []

# Assuming 'category' is a categorical column, modify as
needed

categorical_cols.append('category')
```

```
# Create transformers

numerical_transformer = Pipeline(steps=[

    ('imputer', SimpleImputer(strategy='median')),  # You
can choose 'mean' or 'most_frequent' as well

    ('scaler', StandardScaler())

])

categorical_transformer = Pipeline(steps=[

    ('imputer', SimpleImputer(strategy='most_frequent')),

    ('onehot', OneHotEncoder(handle_unknown='ignore'))

])

# Combine transformers into a preprocessor

preprocessor = ColumnTransformer(

    transformers=[

        ('num', numerical_transformer, numerical_cols),
```

```
        ('cat', categorical_transformer, categorical_cols)

    ])

# Now you can use this preprocessor in your model pipeline

from sklearn.model_selection import train_test_split

from sklearn.naive_bayes import GaussianNB

from sklearn.metrics import accuracy_score, confusion_matrix, classification_report

# Split the data into training and testing sets

X_train, X_test, y_train, y_test = train_test_split(data.drop('outcome', axis=1), data['outcome'], test_size=0.2, random_state=42)

# Initialize the Naive Bayes model

nb_model = GaussianNB()

# Train_model

nb_model.fit(X_train, y_train)

# Predictions
```

```
y_pred = nb_model.predict(X_test)

# Accuracy calculation

accuracy = accuracy_score(y_test, y_pred)

print("Accuracy:", accuracy)

# Demonstrate confusion matrix with classification report

conf_matrix = confusion_matrix(y_test, y_pred)

print("\nConfusion Matrix:")

print(conf_matrix)

class_report = classification_report(y_test, y_pred)

print("\nClassification Report:")

print(class_report)

Accuracy: 0.6417910447761194

Confusion Matrix:

[[17 30]
```

```
 [18 69]]

Classification Report:

              precision    recall  f1-score   support

           0       0.49      0.36      0.41        47

           1       0.70      0.79      0.74        87

    accuracy                           0.64       134

   macro avg       0.59      0.58      0.58       134

weighted avg       0.62      0.64      0.63       134

import pandas as pd

from sklearn.ensemble import RandomForestClassifier

import matplotlib.pyplot as plt

import seaborn as sns

from sklearn.model_selection import GridSearchCV
```

```
# Define hyperparameters to search

param_grid = {

    'n_estimators': [50, 100, 200],

    'max_depth': [None, 10, 20, 30],

    'min_samples_split': [2, 5, 10],

    'min_samples_leaf': [1, 2, 4]

}

# Initialize RandomForestClassifier

rf_model_tuned = RandomForestClassifier(random_state=42)

# Initialize GridSearchCV

grid_search = GridSearchCV(estimator=rf_model_tuned, param_
grid=param_grid, cv=3, scoring='accuracy')

# Fit the model to the training data

grid_search.fit(X_train, y_train)
```

```
# Get the best parameters and the corresponding model

best_params = grid_search.best_params_

best_model = grid_search.best_estimator_

# Make predictions on the test set using the best model

y_pred_tuned = best_model.predict(X_test)

# Calculate accuracy

accuracy_tuned = accuracy_score(y_test, y_pred_tuned)

print("Best Parameters: ", best_params)

print("Tuned Accuracy: ", accuracy_tuned)

Best Parameters:  {'max_depth': None, 'min_samples_leaf': 1,
'min_samples_split': 2, 'n_estimators': 100}

Tuned Accuracy:  0.9104477611940298

import pandas as pd

from sklearn.model_selection import train_test_split
```

```
from sklearn.ensemble import RandomForestClassifier

from sklearn.metrics import accuracy_score, confusion_matrix, classification_report

import matplotlib.pyplot as plt

import seaborn as sns

# Assuming your DataFrame is named 'data'

X = data.drop('outcome', axis=1)

y = data['outcome']

# Split the data into training and testing sets

X_train, X_test, y_train, y_test = train_test_split(X, y, test_size=0.2, random_state=42)

# Initialize the RandomForestClassifier

rf_model = RandomForestClassifier(random_state=42)

# Fit the model to the training data

rf_model.fit(X_train, y_train)
```

```
# Make predictions on the test set

y_pred = rf_model.predict(X_test)

# Calculate accuracy

accuracy = accuracy_score(y_test, y_pred)

print("Accuracy:", accuracy)

# Display Confusion Matrix

conf_matrix = confusion_matrix(y_test, y_pred)

print("\nConfusion Matrix:")

print(conf_matrix)

conf_matrix = confusion_matrix(y_test, y_pred)

plt.figure(figsize=(8, 6))

sns.heatmap(conf_matrix, annot=True, fmt='d', cmap='Blues',
cbar=False,

            xticklabels=['0', '1'], yticklabels=['0', '1'])
```

```
plt.xlabel('Predicted')

plt.ylabel('Actual')

plt.title('Confusion Matrix')

plt.show()

# Display Classification Report

class_report = classification_report(y_test, y_pred)

print("Classification Report:\n", class_report)
```

```
Accuracy: 0.9104477611940298

Confusion Matrix:

[[43  4]

 [ 8 79]]
```

Output 18.

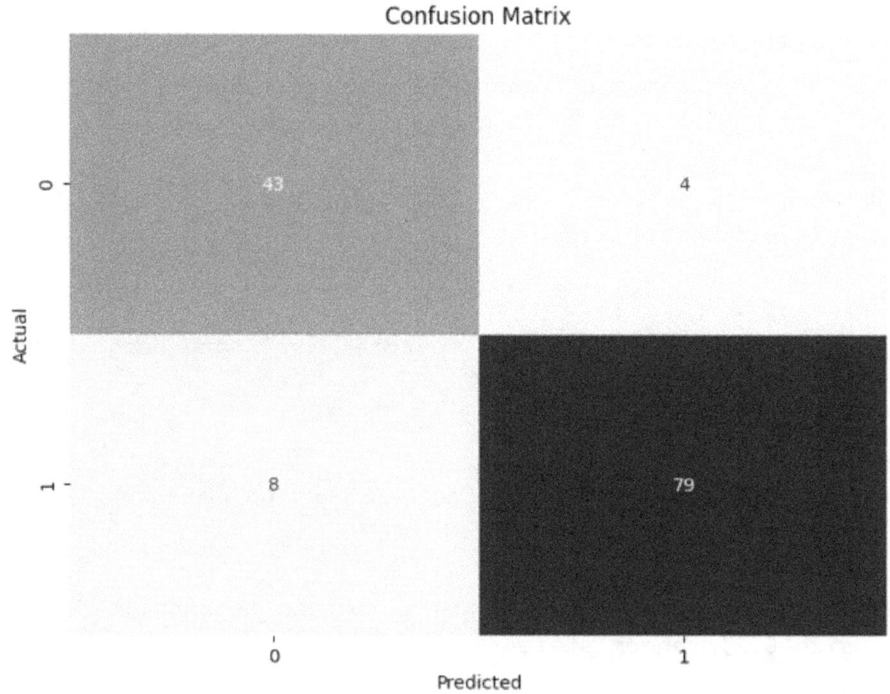

Classification Report:

	precision	recall	f1-score	support
0	0.84	0.91	0.88	47
1	0.95	0.91	0.93	87
accuracy			0.91	134
macro avg	0.90	0.91	0.90	134
weighted avg	0.91	0.91	0.91	134

```
from sklearn.model_selection import train_test_split

from sklearn.ensemble import RandomForestClassifier

from sklearn.metrics import accuracy_score, confusion_ma-
trix, classification_report

# Assuming X and y are your feature matrix and target vari-
able

# Split the data into training and testing sets

X_train, X_test, y_train, y_test = train_test_split(X, y,
test_size=0.2, random_state=42)

# Create a Random Forest classifier

rf_classifier = RandomForestClassifier(random_state=42)

# Train the model on the training data

rf_classifier.fit(X_train, y_train)

# Make predictions on the test set

y_pred = rf_classifier.predict(X_test)

# Evaluate the model
```

```
accuracy = accuracy_score(y_test, y_pred)

conf_matrix = confusion_matrix(y_test, y_pred)

class_report = classification_report(y_test, y_pred)

print(f"Accuracy: {accuracy:.4f}\n")

print(f"Confusion Matrix:\n{conf_matrix}\n")

print(f"Classification Report:\n{class_report}")
```

Final Accuracy Report:

```
Accuracy: 0.9104

Confusion Matrix:

[[43  4]

 [ 8 79]]

Classification Report:

              precision    recall  f1-score   support

           0       0.84      0.91      0.88        47
```

```
           1       0.95      0.91      0.93        87

    accuracy                           0.91       134

   macro avg       0.90      0.91      0.90       134

weighted avg       0.91      0.91      0.91       134
```

```
import pandas as pd

from statsmodels.stats.outliers_influence import variance_
inflation_factor

import seaborn as sns

import matplotlib.pyplot as plt

# Assuming 'data' is your DataFrame with predictors (X) and
outcome (y)

# Replace 'X' with your set of predictors

# VIF Analysis

def calculate_vif(data_frame):

    vif_data = pd.DataFrame()
```

```
    vif_data["Variable"] = data_frame.columns

    vif_data["VIF"] = [variance_inflation_factor(data_frame.
values, i) for i in range(data_frame.shape[1])]

    return vif_data

# Call the function with your DataFrame

vif_result = calculate_vif(data)

# Print the VIF values

print(vif_result)
```

Output 19.

```
                Variable       VIF
0               category  1.705178
1       lack of interest  3.065117
2            hardworking  2.815298
3   Unaware_future scope  3.670020
4   No_motivation(P/S/T)  2.405051
5         Wrong_guidance  2.491339
6               Not_know  3.536404
7             Online_edu  3.013012
8                outcome  2.568386
```

```
from sklearn.ensemble import RandomForestClassifier

import matplotlib.pyplot as plt

import seaborn as sns
```

```
# Assuming 'X' is your feature set and 'y' is your target variable

# Replace 'X' and 'y' with your actual feature set and target variable

# Initialize RandomForestClassifier

rf_model = RandomForestClassifier(random_state=42)

# Fit the model

rf_model.fit(X, y)

# Get feature importances

feature_importances = pd.DataFrame(rf_model.feature_importances_, index=X.columns, columns=['Importance'])

# Sort feature importances in descending order

feature_importances = feature_importances.sort_values(by='Importance', ascending=False)

# Plot feature importances

plt.figure(figsize=(10, 6))
```

```
sns.barplot(x='Importance', y=feature_importances.index, data=feature_importances, palette='viridis')

plt.title('Feature Importances')

plt.xlabel('Importance')

plt.ylabel('Features')

plt.show()
```

Figure 14.

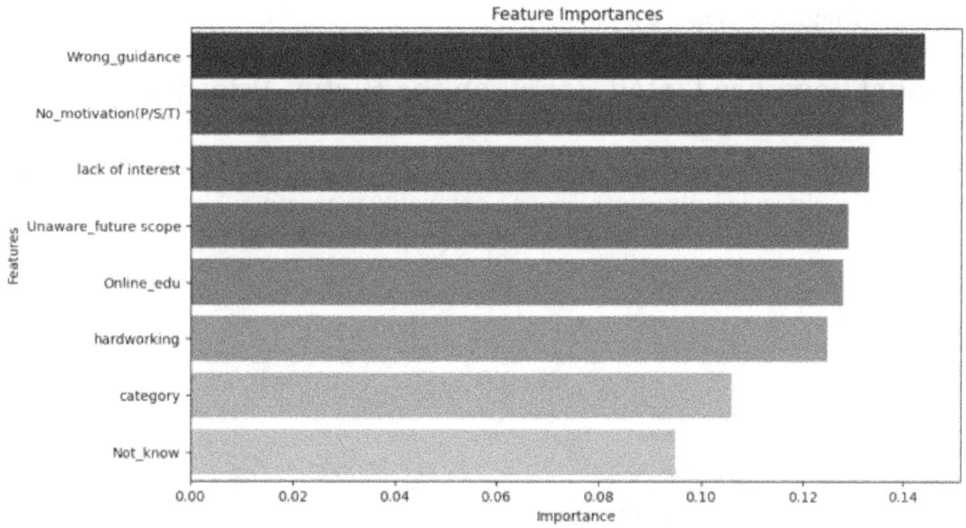

Interpretation

To summarize, the data is graphically represented and suitable decision is interpreted for the documented issue.

From the above analysis report we come to a conclusion that the following features plays a vital role in making decision to choose mathematics for higher education.

- Wrong guidance from seniors to choose non-Mathematics courses for easy learning.
- Lack of motivation from Parents, Teachers and Friends.
- Unaware about the future scope of Mathematics and its real-life applications.
- Online education in schools (During COVID) reduced their confidence in understanding and learning Mathematics.
- Unwilling to work hard & to do more Practice.
- Not knowing that "Learning Mathematics will improve their logical and analytical thinking to get through competitive exams.

The following suggestions are recommended to make students to select Mathematics for higher education:

Suggestions Are Listed Based on the Higher Priority

- Making them to realize that learning Mathematics will improve their logical and analytical skills to get through competitive exams.

Figure 15.

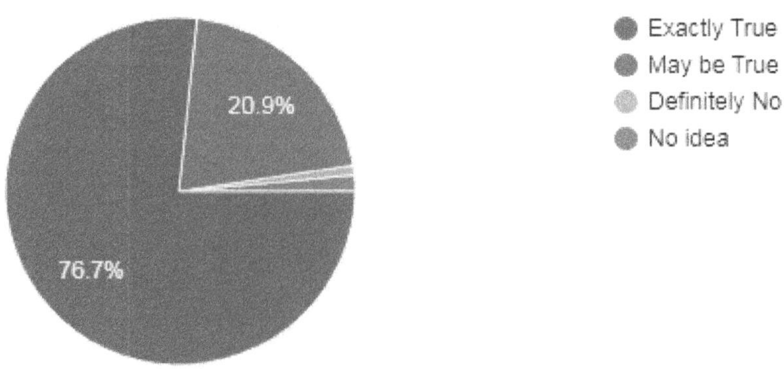

Based on response from stakeholders, **76.7%** of them accorded higher priority to the suggestion given above. In shaping young's mind, Mathematics plays a crucial role. It builds the groundwork that hones their analytical, logical reasoning and problem-solving skills. As a result, helping them recognize that logical and analytical knowledge in Mathematics will aid to achieve in competitive exams.

- Creating awareness about the practical applications of Mathematics from lower classes onwards.

Figure 16.

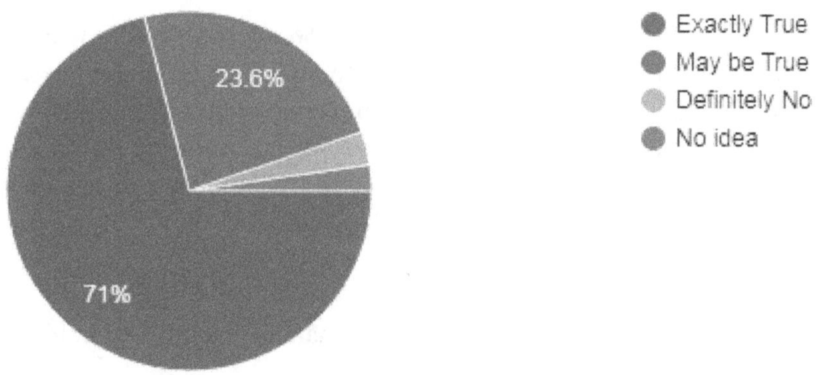

According to participants comment, **71%** assigned significance to the aforementioned proposal. In this highly technological advanced world, practical applications of mathematics are as assorted as they are indispensable, influencing every facet of our up-to-date lives. Hence fostering an understanding of the real time usage of Mathematics from the initial stage of curriculum is vital in formulating entities to grasp its importance in current world scenarios.

- Introducing innovative Teaching Methodology to create interest in Mathematics.

Figure 17.

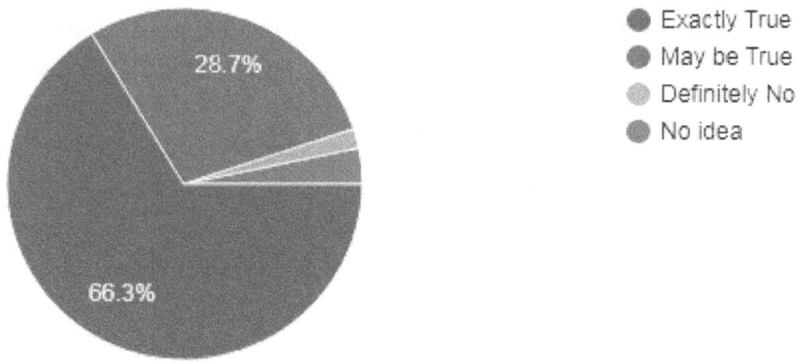

As per the feedback provided by partakers, **66.3%** measured this idea to have reasonable significance. Implementing innovative teaching methodologies, captivate students' critical thinking and creativity to think outside the box, apply knowledge in unconventional ways, increasing their involvement in the educational progression. Thus, embracing ground-breaking teaching techniques equips students with malleable skills essential for the budding demands of the forthcoming workforce, concocting them for victory in a fluctuating world.

- Providing job-oriented courses in Mathematics to get placed in highly reputed well-paid jobs.

Figure 18.

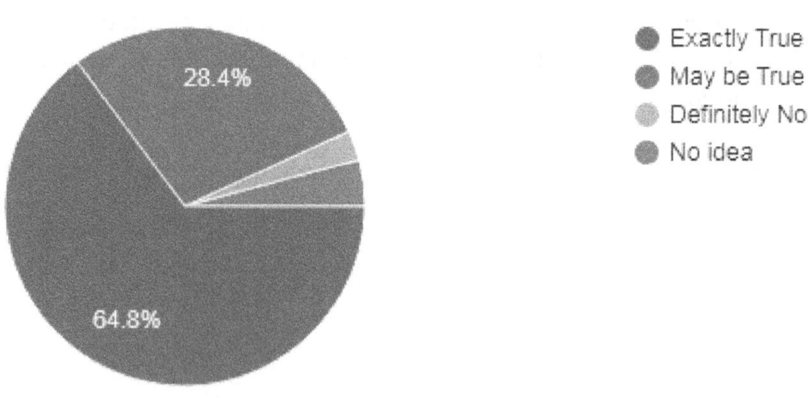

Out of the selections made by the contributors, **64.8%** attributed middling implication to this inkling. Providing career-focused programs in Mathematics tailored to shelter employment in prestigious, high-paying spots. This permits individuals to acclimate to the varying profession markets and chase careers that align with their desires and passions. Thus, offering job-oriented Mathematics courses pointed at forming students for lucrative careers in esteemed, well-paying professions.

- Clarifying the usage of mathematical concepts in all other subjects.

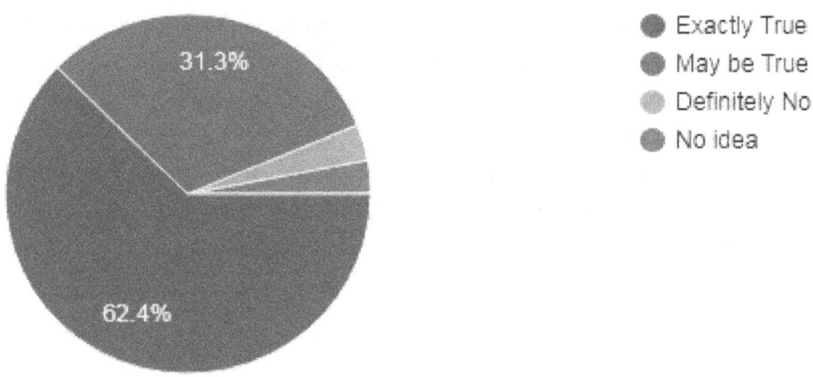

Among the choices made by the backers, **62.4%** assigned moderate significance to this notion. Mathematics is not a remote island but a bridge that links and boosts learning in numerous subjects. Highlighting how mathematics integrates across other subjects, broadens students' outlooks that equips them with essential interdisciplinary skills with a deep mathematical foundation, required for academic success and forthcoming careers.

CONCLUSION

The notions of compact space and feebly compact space in Generalized Topological Spaces through Neutrosophic Sets (ì^{N}-TSs) is introduced in this chapter. After that, specific properties associated with ì^{N}-compact space in ì^{N}-TSs is deliberated.

Additionally, we converse about ì^{N}-feebly compact space. Also, we addressed the characteristics of ì^{N}-feebly compact space within ì^{N}-TSs.

Compact sets perform a pivotal role in numerous decision-making scenarios, aiding in representing uncertainty, feasible regions and constraints across a broad spectrum of applications. Decision-makers can utilize the above concept to implement comprehensive decisions.

Further, we studied on the specific application of present context related to choosing mathematics for higher education, the reasons for not choosing mathematics is considered as open cover for Neutrosophic Generalized Topological space. We examine the factors influencing the decision not to choose mathematics for advanced education.

The collected data is then processed using statistical tools such as logistic regression analysis and Python programming code. The data accuracy is subsequently assessed through various models, including the OLS Model, Logistic Regression Model, Naive Bayes model, and Random Forest Classifier. Following this, the open sub cover for this space is highlighted, leveraging the compactness property to aid in real-life decision-making.

Hence, our chapter employs an innovative strategy to make effective decisions for the identified real-time issue via the application of compactness in Neutrosophic Generalized Topology.

REFERENCES

Al-Omeri, W. F., & Smarandache, F. (2016). New Neutrosophic Sets via Neutrosophic Topological Spaces. *New Trends in Neutrosophic Theory and Applications*, (2), 1–10.

Bageerathi, K., & Jeya Puvaneswari, P. (2019). Neutrosophic Feebly Connectedness and Compactness. *IOSR Journal of Polymer and Textile Engineering, 6*(3), 7-13.

Ben, R. (2021a). Some new open sets in μ^N topological space. *Malaya Journal of Matematik*, 9(1), 89–94. DOI:10.26637/MJM0901/0014

Ben, R. (2021b). Generalized Topological Spaces via Neutrosophic Sets. *J. Math. Comput. Sci.*, 11, 716–734.

Bewick, V., Cheek, L., & Ball, J. (2003). Statistics review 7: Correlation and regression. *Critical Care*, 7(6), 451. DOI:10.1186/cc2401 PMID:14624685

Császár, Á. (1997). Generalized open sets. *Acta Mathematica Hungarica*, 75(1-2), 65–87. DOI:10.1023/A:1006582718102

Császár, Á. (2002). Generalized topology, Generalized continuity. *Acta Mathematica Hungarica*, 96(4), 351–357. DOI:10.1023/A:1019713018007

Császár, Á. (2005). Generalized open sets in Generalized topologies. *Acta Mathematica Hungarica*, 106(1-2), 53–66. DOI:10.1007/s10474-005-0005-5

Embarak. (2018). *Data analysis and visualization using Python*. Springer.

Nongthombam & Sharma. (2021). Data Analysis using Python. *International Journal of Engineering Research & Technology, 10*(7), 463-468.

Peng, Lee, & Gary. (2002). An Introduction to Logistic Regression Analysis and Reporting. *The Journal of Educational Research, 96*(1), 3-14.

Salama, A. (2012). Neutrosophic set and Neutrosophic topological space. *ISOR J. Mathematics*, 3(4), 31–35. DOI:10.9790/5728-0343135

Smarandache, F. (1999). *A Unifying Field in Logic: Neutrosophic Logic. Neutrosophy, Neutrosophic set, Neutrosophic Probability*. American Research Press.

Smarandache, F. (2002). Neutrosophy and Neutrosophic Logic. *First International Conference on Neutrosophy,* Neutrosophic Logic, Set, Probability, and Statistics. University of New Mexico.

Smarandache, F. (2010). Neutrosophic Set: A Generalization of Intuitionistic Fuzzy set. *Journal of Defense Resources Management*, 1, 107–116.

Thomas & John. (2012). ì-Compactness in Generalized Topological Spaces. *Journal of Advanced Studies in Topology, 3*(3), 18-22.

Chapter 10
Single-Valued Neutrosophic ARAS Based on Multi-Criteria Group Decision-Making for a School Selection

Irvanizam Irvanizam
https://orcid.org/0000-0001-8823-6250
Universitas Syiah Kuala, Indonesia

Novi Zahara
Madrasah Aliyah Swasta Ulumul Qur'an, Indonesia

Marzuki Marzuki
https://orcid.org/0000-0002-2178-9253
Universitas Syiah Kuala, Indonesia

ABSTRACT

Education is a crucial aspect in determining the progress of a nation. However, selecting a good school is a challenge. Therefore, the chapter offers a solution by applying the theories of single-valued neutrosophic numbers (S-VNNs) and the additive ratio assessment (ARAS) method for a school evaluation. This performance evaluation is viewed as a process involving a committee of school performance judgments and a list of senior high schools. The committee gives professional assessments of the school's performance by using S-VNNs. To conquer this, the chapter first presents the basic theory of S-VNNs with some of their mathematical operations and their two Einstein aggregation operators. The chapter then proposes an improved

DOI: 10.4018/979-8-3693-2085-3.ch010

ARAS method based on S-VNNs to handle a multi-criteria group decision-making problem. Next, the chapter demonstrates an illustrative example using the improved ARAS method to select the favorite school. Finally, comparison analysis with other decision-making methods is presented to prove the feasibility and capability of the proposed ARAS method.

1. INTRODUCTION

According to Slot *et al.* (2020), schools are made up of groups of people that are coordinated and managed to work toward shared goals. Academic directors oversee, supervise, and set the direction for the schools. Academic directors make decisions regularly while organizing, carrying out, and reviewing routine tasks. To promote student learning, academic directors should have a clear vision, align the curriculum, learning, and assessment, and pay attention to staff and working environment needs (Alm *et al.*, 2019).

The most crucial component and core duty in managing any school is to make judgments by considering other significant aspects into account. For instance, a high concentration of "small" schools may provide several difficulties. Fewer students in each school suggest higher per-student spending. In addition, when focusing on financial constraints, a profusion of "small" schools may indicate that each one lacks fundamental facilities and instructional materials (Dongre and Tewary, 2020).

A school's performance can be investigated based on a variety of aspects. These include teaching atmosphere, academic staff performance, student bullying, and infrastructure quality. However, it is difficult for evaluators to deliver accurate information because of the complexities of the external influences, uncertainty, and limitations of human intervention. It is necessary to have an instrument for proper, realistic, and efficient school assessment in the factual decision-making system (Irvanizam and Zahara, 2023). People commonly rank a particular index or item using natural language terms like "great," "good," "weak," and "bad" when making decisions. A decision-making process that transforms both qualitative and quantitative data is necessary to address the assessment difficulty.

Zadeh (1965) first exhibited the concept of fuzzy set (FS) to express uncertain information by presenting a membership function. The values of its membership value should be in a range between zero and one. Further, Atanassov (1986) revolutionized this theory by introducing an Intuitionistic fuzzy set (IFS) in which he added a non-membership function for each element of the universe of discourse and included a condition the sum of membership and non-membership values should be less than or equal to one. As a result, this extension of FS can handle not only incomplete but also uncertain conditions of data representation (Son *et al.*, 2020). Nevertheless, this concept cannot tackle other issues, such as indeterminate and inconsistent data representation, in which policymakers often face these conditions in many real cases. Therefore, Smarandache (1998) first initiated Neutronosophic set (NS) as an improvement on the notions of FS and IFS. When it comes to solving issues and circumstances involving ambiguous, imprecise, inconsistent, and unclear information, this idea is highly effective. Truth-membership, indeterminacy-membership, and falsity-membership functions can be used to describe it. This inspires a lot of researchers, who then use this idea to solve practical problems in areas like medical image processing, investment, supply chain management, transportation management, banking system evaluation (Biswas *et al.*, 2016; Bui *et al.*, 2023; Garg and Nancy, 2017; Irvanizam *et al.*, 2020; Jana *et al.*, 2020; Kamacı *et al.*, 2021; Paulraj and Tamilarasi, 2022; Tian *et al.*, 2017).

In fact, NS theory was updated to better meet the demands of research and engineering. Designing the single-valued neutrosophic set (S-VNS) concept created by Wang *et al.* (2010) is one of its advancements. Additionally, this sub-NS has evolved into several additional NS forms, including the single-valued trapezoidal neutrosophic set (S-VTraNS), which was first presented by Deli (2018). He also created their fundamental mathematical procedures, a single-valued trapezoidal fuzzy neutrosophic number (S-VTraFNN), and a few S-VTraFNN-related theorems.

A novel tool for the decision-making process that ranks several options based on the weight of the respective criterion is multi-criteria group decision-making (MCGDM). It entails numerous specialists assigning weights to criteria for various options based on their individual assessments. Experts even frequently choose language values while determining the alternatives' criteria. Indecisive and contradictory information can be efficiently addressed with the concept of linguistic values. Nevertheless, some research has demonstrated that combining MCGDM with a decision-making method might lead to more workable, dependable, and appropriate outcomes.

In the last few decades, some famous scholars have initiated innovative traditional decision-making methods such as the Technique for Order Preference by Similarity to Ideal Solution (TOPSIS) (Hwang and Yoon, 1981), VIKOR (Opricovic and Tzeng, 2004), CODAS (Ghorabaee *et al.*, 2016), COPRAS (Zavadskas *et al.*, 1994), and ARAS (Zavadskas and Turskis, 2010). The TOPSIS technique determines which option is preferable by determining the farthest distance from the negative-ideal solution and the shortest distance from the positive-ideal solution. However, according to (Shih *et al.*, 2007), it does not consider how great these distances are in comparison. Without considering the choice hazards, the VIKOR searches for the largest profit and estimates the ideal answer by identifying a certain proximity to the positive-ideal solution (Ouenniche *et al.*, 2021). In a system of weights and values for the elements, the COPRAS approach allows evaluation of the direct and proportional requirements of the significance and utility degree of substitutes. Meanwhile, ARAS is predicated on the notion that straightforward relative comparisons can be used to resolve complex domain phenomena involving competing criteria. The principal benefits of the ARAS approach are as follows: (i) it has a direct and proportionate relationship with criterion weights (Heidary Dahooie *et al.*, 2018); (ii) it can handle problems that are extremely complex (Büyüközkan and Göçer, 2018); and (iii) it consists of simple and straightforward processes that produce results that are reasonable, realistic, and satisfactory when evaluating and prioritizing different alternatives (Ghenai *et al.*, 2020).

In the last five years ago, several popular studies discussed MCGDM under S-VNN circumstances have been constructed (Biswas *et al.*, 2016; Garg and Rani, 2020; Irvanizam *et al.*, 2018). For instance, Riaz *et al.* (2023) developed fair aggregation operators for S-VNN to solve an MCGDM problem and utilized partial weight data to obtain accurate decision results. İ. Deli (2019) investigated MCGDM problems containing S-VNN information and S-VNN criteria weight by proposing a new defuzzification method of S-VNN. Wu *et al.* (2018) developed new S-VNN power aggregation operators based on the possibility degree to finding a solution for green supplier selection problems. L. Wang and Bao (2021) developed normalized aggregation operators for S-VNN as an effective instrument to resolve an MCGDM problem.

On the other hand, many researchers have actively developed the original ARAS method using the approaches of FS and its extension in handling MCGDM problems. For instance, Karagöz *et al.* (2021) utilized Interval type-2 Fuzzy to extend the traditional ARAS to solve the location selection problem of vehicle recycling facilities. Goswami and Behera (2021) integrated ARAS with the Entropy method to implement an adaptive tool for solving an MCGDM problem under fuzzy information. Nithyanandham and Augustin (2023) utilized A bipolar fuzzy p-competition graph to improve the ARAS for selecting an appropriate COVID-19 vaccine. Mishra *et al.* (2022) developed a new similarity measurement for Pythagorean fuzzy sets and integrated this FS extension with ARAS to handle stainable biomass crop selection. Bahrami *et al.* (2019) designed a hybrid model, a combination technique between ARAS and the Best Worst Method (BWM), as a practical tool to map Cu prospectively areas in Iran under uncertain information. As described in previous literature, those techniques have delivered a bit of weakness in expressing indeterminate and inconsistent information, which are recent issues in decision science. In addition, there is still very little research regarding the extension of decision-making methods by integrating the S-VNN idea with the ARAS approach. Considering the benefits of the ARAS and the capability of S-VNNs, an extended ARAS methodology will be a prospective strategy to yield a reliable instrument for tackling problematic MCGDM problems under indeterminate and inconsistent information.

Therefore, we propose an extended ARAS method based on S-VNNs based on an MCGDM framework to reach a trustworthy strategy under indeterminate and incompatible information. The contributions of the chapter are the following:

(a). To develop a new MCGDM framework combining ARAS and S-VNN under indeterminate and incompatible information.
(b). To utilize the integrated S-VNN ARAS method to evaluate five potential schools based on four factors for selecting the favorite school.
(c). To combine the S-VNN and traditional ARAS in tackling the issues of ambiguous, imprecise, and inconsistent for choosing the favorite school.

The remaining portion of this chapter will provide information using S-VNN, an instrument for representing the format of natural language values, and combine it with the conventional ARAS to get the best possible solution. The first section of the chapter highlights the benefits of using the NS and ARAS techniques to solve MCGDM problems. The ideas of NS and S-VNNs are then briefly presented, along with a discussion of their computational processes and mathematical operator laws. In the next section, using an example of an application, the procedures describe how the extended model can list the best possible answer. The last section examines and contrasts them with those from alternative methods to validate the viability and capability of the expanded ARAS and summarizes some conclusions and prospective future studies.

2. PRELIMINARIES

Section 2 re-discusses a short description of some fundamental concepts of NS, S-VNNs, and two S-VNNs aggregation operators, including dynamic S-VNN Einstein weighted arithmetic and dynamic S-VNN Einstein weighted geometric. In addition, this section also characterizes the ideas of how to measure the score functions based on the centroid of S-VNNs.

2.1. Neutrosophic Sets

Definition 1. (Smarandache, 1998) A neutrosophic set (NS) $\mathcal{N}$ on a universal set $\mathcal{U}$ is characterized by

$$N = \left\{n, \left\langle \Im_N(n), \wp_N(n), \aleph_N(n) \right\rangle : n \in N \right\}$$

In which $\mathfrak{I}_N(n)$ is a truth-membership degree (TMSD), $\wp_N(n)$ is an indeterminacy-membership degree (IMSD), and $\aleph_N(n)$ is a falsity-membership degree (FMSD),

$\mathfrak{I}_N(n), \wp_N(n), \aleph_N(n) \in \;]0^-, 1^+[$

and

$0^- \leq \mathfrak{I}_N(n) + \wp_N(n) + \aleph_N(n) \leq 3^+.$

Obviously, the above definition is a bit difficult to utilize for real-world decision-making issues in both the area of science and engineering. Therefore, (H. Wang et al., 2010) simplified the NS by presenting a single-valued neutrosophic set as a new sub-class of the NS.

2.2. Single-Valued Neutrosophic Sets

Definition 3. (H. Wang et al., 2010) Let $\mathfrak{R}$ is a universal disclosure, then a Single-Valued Neutrosophic Set (S-VNS) is depicted as

$$\zeta = \{\nu, \mathfrak{I}_\zeta(\nu), \wp_\zeta(\nu), \aleph_\zeta(\nu) | \nu \in \mathfrak{R}\} \tag{1}$$

Where $\mathfrak{I}_\zeta(\nu)$ is a TMSD, $\wp_\zeta(\nu)$ is an IMSD, and $\aleph_\zeta(\nu)$ is a FMSD, such that

$\mathfrak{I}_\zeta(\nu), \wp_\zeta(\nu), \aleph_\zeta(\nu) \in [0,1]$ and $0 \leq \mathfrak{I}_\zeta(\nu) + \wp_\zeta(\nu) + \aleph_\zeta(\nu) \leq 3.$

Furthermore, we re-call several mathematical rules to aggregate S-VNNs.

Definition 4. (Peng et al., 2016) (Wang et al., 2010) Let $\nu_1 = \langle \mathfrak{I}_1, \wp_1, \aleph_1 \rangle$ and $\nu_2 = \langle \mathfrak{I}_2, \wp_2, \aleph_2 \rangle$ be two S-VNNs and $\eta > 0$, then:

$$\nu_1 \oplus \nu_2 = \langle \mathfrak{I}_1 + \mathfrak{I}_2 - \mathfrak{I}_1 \mathfrak{I}_2, \wp_1 \wp_2, \aleph_1 \aleph_2 \rangle \tag{2}$$

$$\nu_1 \otimes \nu_2 = \langle \mathfrak{I}_1 \mathfrak{I}_2, \wp_1 + \wp_2 - \wp_1 \wp_2, \aleph_1 + \aleph_2 - \aleph_1 \aleph_2 \rangle \tag{3}$$

$$\eta \nu_1 = \langle 1 - (1 - \mathfrak{I}_1)^\eta, \wp_1^\eta, \aleph_1^\eta \rangle \tag{4}$$

$$\nu_1^{\eta} = \langle \mathfrak{I}_1^{\eta}, 1-(1-\wp_1)^{\eta}, 1-(1-\aleph_1)^{\eta} \rangle \tag{5}$$

$$\nu_1 \vee \nu_2 = \langle \max(\mathfrak{I}_1,\mathfrak{I}_2), \min(\wp_1,\wp_2), \min(\aleph_1,\aleph_2) \rangle \tag{6}$$

$$\nu_1 \wedge \nu_2 = \langle \min(\mathfrak{I}_1,\mathfrak{I}_2), \max(\wp_1,\wp_2), \max(\aleph_1,\aleph_2) \rangle \tag{7}$$

$$\nu_1^{c} = \langle \aleph_1, \wp_1, \mathfrak{I}_1 \rangle \tag{8}$$

Definition 5. (Wu et al., 2016) Let $\nu_{\alpha} = \langle \mathfrak{I}_{\alpha}, \wp_{\alpha}, \aleph_{\alpha} \rangle$ and $\nu_{\beta} = \langle \mathfrak{I}_{\beta}, \wp_{\beta}, \aleph_{\beta} \rangle$ be two S-VNNs, then the score-function of ν_{α} denoted by $\mho(\nu_{\alpha})$ is formulated by:

$$\mho(\nu_{\alpha}) = \frac{1}{3} \times (\mathfrak{I}_{\alpha} + 1 - \wp_{\alpha} + 1 - \aleph_{\alpha}) \tag{9}$$

For an order relation between two S-VNNs, ν_{α} and ν_{β}, if $\mho(\nu_{\alpha}) > \mho(\nu_{\beta})$, then $\nu_{\alpha} > \nu_{\beta}$.

Definition 6. (Wang et al., 2010) Let $\nu_{\alpha} = \langle \mathfrak{I}_{\alpha}, \wp_{\alpha}, \aleph_{\alpha} \rangle$ and $\nu_{\beta} = \langle \mathfrak{I}_{\beta}, \wp_{\beta}, \aleph_{\beta} \rangle$ be two S-VNNs and $\eta, \eta_1, \eta_2 > 0$ be any positive numbers, then the following rules are valid.

i. $\nu_{\alpha} \oplus \nu_{\beta} = \nu_{\beta} \oplus \nu_{\alpha}$;
ii. $\nu_{\alpha} \otimes \nu_{\beta} = \nu_{\beta} \otimes \nu_{\alpha}$;
iii. $\eta(\nu_{\alpha} \oplus \nu_{\beta}) = (\eta\nu_{\alpha}) \oplus (\eta\nu_{\beta})$;
iv. $(\nu_{\alpha} \otimes \nu_{\beta})^{\eta} = \nu_{\alpha}^{\eta} \otimes \nu_{\beta}^{\eta}$;
v. $(\eta_1 + \eta_2)\nu_{\beta} = (\eta_1\nu_{\beta}) \oplus (\eta_2\nu_{\beta})$;
vi. $\nu_{\beta}^{\eta_1+\eta_2} = \nu_{\beta}^{\eta_1} \otimes \nu_{\beta}^{\eta_2}$

Definition 6. (Li et al., 2018) Let $\nu_1 = \langle \mathfrak{I}_1, \wp_1, \aleph_1 \rangle$ and $\nu_2 = \langle \mathfrak{I}_2, \wp_2, \aleph_2 \rangle$ be two S-VNNs and $\eta > 0$ be any positive numbers. Then,

i. $\nu_1 \oplus \nu_2 = \left\langle \frac{\mathfrak{I}_1 + \mathfrak{I}_2}{1 + \mathfrak{I}_1 \cdot \mathfrak{I}_2}, \frac{\wp_1 \cdot \wp_2}{1 + (1-\wp_1)\cdot(1-\wp_2)}, \frac{\aleph_1 \cdot \aleph_2}{1 + (1-\aleph_1)\cdot(1-\aleph_2)} \right\rangle$;

ii. $\nu_1 \otimes \nu_2 = \left\langle \frac{\mathfrak{I}_1 \cdot \mathfrak{I}_2}{1 + (1-\mathfrak{I}_1)\cdot(1-\mathfrak{I}_2)}, \frac{\wp_1 + \wp_2}{1 + \wp_1 \cdot \wp_2}, \frac{\aleph_1 + \aleph_2}{1 + \aleph_1 \cdot \aleph_2} \right\rangle$;

iii. $\eta \cdot \nu_1 = \left\langle \frac{(1+\mathfrak{I}_1)^{\eta} - (1-\mathfrak{I}_1)^{\eta}}{(1+\mathfrak{I}_1)^{\eta} + (1-\mathfrak{I}_1)^{\eta}}, \frac{2(\wp_1)^{\eta}}{(2-\wp_1)^{\eta} + (\wp_1)^{\eta}}, \frac{2(\aleph_1)^{\eta}}{(2-\aleph_1)^{\eta} + (\aleph_1)^{\eta}} \right\rangle$;

iv. $\nu_1^{\eta} = \left\langle \frac{2(\mathfrak{I}_1)^{\eta}}{(2-\mathfrak{I}_1)^{\eta} + (\mathfrak{I}_1)^{\eta}}, \frac{(1+\wp_1)^{\eta} - (1-\wp_1)^{\eta}}{(1+\wp_1)^{\eta} + (1-\wp_1)^{\eta}}, \frac{(1+\aleph_1)^{\eta} - (1-\aleph_1)^{\eta}}{(1+\aleph_1)^{\eta} + (1-\aleph_1)^{\eta}} \right\rangle$;

2.3. S-VNNs Aggregation Methodologies

Generally, scientists in decision fields are familiar with two common instruments for gathering neutrosophic or fuzzy information. The two instruments are arithmetic and geometric averaging methodologies. However, this study utilizes those two methodologies based on Einstein approaches to accumulate SVNS information for overcoming a school selection problem as a final goal of the study. The definitions of a dynamic single-valued neutrosophic Einstein weighted arithmetic (DySVNE-WA) and a dynamic single-valued neutrosophic Einstein weighted geometric (DySVNEWG) method are as follows.

Definition 7. (Farid & Riaz, 2023) Let $\tilde{\nu} = \{\nu_1, \nu_2, \nu_3, \ldots, \nu_k\}$ be a positive conglomeration of k S-VNNs in which each $\nu_m = \langle \Im_m, \wp_m, \aleph_m \rangle$ for m=1,2,….,k and $\psi = [\psi_1, \psi_2, \ldots, \psi_k]^T$ be a conglomeration of weights vector of k S-VNNs where $0 \leq \psi_m \leq 1$ and $\sum_{m=1}^{k} \psi_m = 1$, then a DySVNEWA operator is formulated by:

$$DySVNEWA(\tilde{\nu}, \psi) = \left\langle \frac{\prod_{m=1}^{k}(1+\Im_m)^{\psi_m} - \prod_{m=1}^{k}(1-\Im_m)^{\psi_m}}{\prod_{m=1}^{k}(1+\Im_m)^{\psi_m} + \prod_{m=1}^{k}(1-\Im_m)^{\psi_m}}, \right.$$
$$\left. \frac{2\prod_{m=1}^{k}(\wp_m)^{\psi_m}}{\prod_{m=1}^{k}(2-\wp_m)^{\psi_m} + \prod_{m=1}^{k}(\wp_m)^{\psi_m}}, \frac{2\prod_{m=1}^{k}(\aleph_m)^{\psi_m}}{\prod_{m=1}^{k}(2-\aleph_m)^{\psi_m} + \prod_{m=1}^{k}(\aleph_m)^{\psi_m}} \right\rangle \tag{10}$$

Definition 8. (Farid & Riaz, 2023) Let $\tilde{\nu} = \{\nu_1, \nu_2, \nu_3, \ldots, \nu_k\}$ be a positive conglomeration of k S-VNNs in which each $\nu_m = \langle \Im_m, \wp_m, \aleph_m \rangle$ for m=1,2,…,k and $\psi = [\psi_1, \psi_2, \ldots, \psi_k]^T$ be a conglomeration of weights vector of k S-VNNs where $0 \leq \psi_m \leq 1$ and $\sum_{m=1}^{k} \psi_m = 1$, then a DySVNEWG operator is formulated by:

$$DySVNEWG(\tilde{\nu}, \psi) = \left\langle \frac{2\prod_{m=1}^{k}(\Im_m)^{\psi_m}}{\prod_{m=1}^{k}(2-\Im_m)^{\psi_m} + \prod_{m=1}^{k}(\Im_m)^{\psi_m}}, \right.$$
$$\left. \frac{\prod_{m=1}^{k}(1+\wp_m)^{\psi_m} - \prod_{m=1}^{k}(1-\wp_m)^{\psi_m}}{\prod_{m=1}^{k}(1+\wp_m)^{\psi_m} + \prod_{m=1}^{k}(1-\wp_m)^{\psi_m}}, \frac{\prod_{m=1}^{k}(1+\aleph_m)^{\psi_m} - \prod_{m=1}^{k}(1-\aleph_m)^{\psi_m}}{\prod_{m=1}^{k}(1+\aleph_m)^{\psi_m} + \prod_{m=1}^{k}(1-\aleph_m)^{\psi_m}} \right\rangle \tag{11}$$

3. THE EXTENSION OF ARAS METHOD WITH S-VNNS FOR AN MCGDM PROBLEM

This section presents a MCGDM methodology by combining the traditional ARAS with S-VNNs. Let $\{E_1, E_2, \ldots, E_p\}$ be a set of p experts, $\xi = [\xi_1, \xi_2, \ldots, \xi_p]^T$ be an experts' weight vector, $\psi = \{\psi_1, \psi_2, \ldots, \psi_s\}$ be a criteria weight vector, $\{S_1, S_2, \ldots, S_r\}$

be a set of r alternatives, and $\{F_1, F_2, \ldots, F_s\}$ be a set of s criteria, where $\xi_t \in [0,1]$ such that $\sum_{k=1}^{p} \xi_k = 1$, and $\psi_r \in [0,1]$ such that $\sum_{j=1}^{s} \psi_j$. The algorithm of the extended ARAS based on S-VNNs is designed as below and Figure 1 provides the flow chart of the proposed MCGDM strategy.

Algorithm

Step 1. Create S-VNN decision-making matrices $N_w = [n_{ij}^{w}]_{rxs}$ given by p experts, where $n_{ij}^{w} = \langle(\mathfrak{I}_{ij}^{w}, \wp_{ij}^{w}, \aleph_{ij}^{w}\rangle$ is a S-VNN, $\mathfrak{I}_{ij}^{w}, \wp_{ij}^{w}, \aleph_{ij}^{w} \in [0,1], 0 \leq \mathfrak{I}_{ij}^{w} + \wp_{ij}^{w} + \aleph_{ij}^{w} \leq 3$, i=1,2,…,r, j=1,2,…,s, and w=1,2,…,p.

Step 2. Normalize individual S-VNN matrices $\tilde{N}_w = [\tilde{n}_{ij}^{w}]_{rxs}$ by considering two criteria types, benefit (Ω_{Benefit}) and cost (Ω_{Cost}), then entries of the matrix can be yielded by utilizing Expression (12).

$$\tilde{n}_{ij}^{w} = \left\langle \tilde{\mathfrak{I}}_{ij}^{w}, \tilde{\wp}_{ij}^{w}, \tilde{\aleph}_{ij}^{w} \right\rangle = \begin{cases} \left\langle \mathfrak{I}_{ij}^{w}, \wp_{ij}^{w}, \aleph_{ij}^{w} \right\rangle, for\ \Omega_{\text{Benefit}} \\ \left\langle \aleph_{ij}^{w}, \wp_{ij}^{w}, \mathfrak{I}_{ij}^{w} \right\rangle . for\ \Omega_{\text{Cost}} \end{cases} \tag{12}$$

Step 3. Determine an aggregated S-VNN decision matrix $E = [e_{ij}]_{rxs}$ where $e_{ij} = \left\langle \hat{\mathfrak{I}}_{ij}, \hat{\wp}_{ij}, \hat{\aleph}_{ij} \right\rangle$ can be yielded by utilizing Expression (13) for DySVNEWA operator and Expression (14) for DySVNEWG operator.

$$e_{ij} = \left\langle \frac{\prod_{w=1}^{p}\left(1+\mathfrak{I}_{ij}^{w}\right)^{\xi_w} - \prod_{w=1}^{p}\left(1-\mathfrak{I}_{ij}^{w}\right)^{\xi_w}}{\prod_{m=1}^{p}\left(1+\mathfrak{I}_{ij}^{w}\right)^{\xi_m} + \prod_{m=1}^{p}\left(1-\mathfrak{I}_{ij}^{w}\right)^{\xi_m}}, \frac{2\prod_{w=1}^{p}\left(\wp_{ij}^{w}\right)^{\xi_w}}{\prod_{w=1}^{p}\left(2-\wp_{ij}^{w}\right)^{\xi_w} + \prod_{w=1}^{p}\left(\wp_{ij}^{w}\right)^{\xi_w}}, \frac{2\prod_{w=1}^{p}\left(\aleph_{ij}^{w}\right)^{\xi_w}}{\prod_{w=1}^{p}\left(2-\aleph_{ij}^{w}\right)^{\xi_w} + \prod_{w=1}^{p}\left(\aleph_{ij}^{w}\right)^{\xi_w}} \right\rangle \tag{13}$$

$$e_{ij} = \left\langle \frac{2\prod_{w=1}^{p}\left(\mathfrak{I}_{ij}^{w}\right)^{\xi_w}}{\prod_{w=1}^{p}\left(2-\mathfrak{I}_{ij}^{w}\right)^{\xi_w} + \prod_{w=1}^{p}\left(\mathfrak{I}_{ij}^{w}\right)^{\xi_w}}, \frac{\prod_{w=1}^{p}\left(1+\wp_{ij}^{w}\right)^{\xi_w} - \prod_{w=1}^{p}\left(1-\wp_{ij}^{w}\right)^{\xi_w}}{\prod_{w=1}^{p}\left(1+\wp_{ij}^{w}\right)^{\xi_w} + \prod_{w=1}^{p}\left(1-\wp_{ij}^{w}\right)^{\xi_w}}, \frac{\prod_{w=1}^{p}\left(1+\aleph_{ij}^{w}\right)^{\xi_w} - \prod_{w=1}^{p}\left(1-\aleph_{ij}^{w}\right)^{\xi_w}}{\prod_{w=1}^{p}\left(1+\aleph_{ij}^{w}\right)^{\xi_w} + \prod_{w=1}^{p}\left(1-\aleph_{ij}^{w}\right)^{\xi_w}} \right\rangle \tag{14}$$

Step 4. Provide the criteria weight vector $\psi = [\psi_1, \psi_2, .., \psi_s]^T$.

Step 5. Construct an improved S-VNN aggregation matrix as Expression (15) based on the ARAS procedure.

$$E' = \begin{bmatrix} e'_{01} & \cdots & e'_{0j} & \cdots & e'_{0s} \\ \vdots & \ddots & \vdots & \ddots & \vdots \\ e'_{i1} & \cdots & e'_{ij} & \cdots & e'_{is} \\ \vdots & \ddots & \vdots & \ddots & \vdots \\ e'_{r1} & \cdots & e'_{rj} & \cdots & e'_{rs} \end{bmatrix}, (i = 0, 2, ..., r | j = 1, 2, ..., s) \tag{15}$$

Where r is the number of alternatives, s is the number of criteria, $e'_{ij} = \langle \mathfrak{I}'_{ij}, \wp'_{ij}, \aleph'_{ij} \rangle$ is a performance aggregation value of alternative i responding to criterion j with $e'_{ij} = \langle \widehat{\mathfrak{I}}_{ij}, \widehat{\wp}_{ij}, \widehat{\aleph}_{ij} \rangle$, and e'_{0j} is an optimal aggregation value of criterion j. If experts cannot find references, the performance value can be obtained by utilizing Expression (16).

$$e'_{0j} = \left\langle \max_i \left\{ \widehat{\mathfrak{I}}_{ij} \right\}, \min_i \left\{ \widehat{\wp}_{ij} \right\}, \min_i \left\{ \widehat{\aleph}_{ij} \right\} \right\rangle \tag{16}$$

Step 6. Normalized the improved S-VNN aggregation matrix into $\widetilde{E'} = \left[\widetilde{e'}_{ij} \right]_{(r+1) \times s}$ where $\widetilde{e'}_{ij}$ can be computed by using Expression (17).

$$\widetilde{e'}_{ij} = \left\langle \widetilde{\mathfrak{I}'}_{ij}, \widetilde{\wp'}_{ij}, \widetilde{\aleph'}_{ij} \right\rangle = \left\langle \frac{\mathfrak{I}'_{ij}}{\sum_{i=0}^{r} \mathfrak{I}'_{ij}}, \frac{\wp'_{ij}}{\sum_{i=0}^{r} \wp'_{ij}}, \frac{\aleph'_{ij}}{\sum_{i=0}^{r} \aleph'_{ij}} \right\rangle \tag{17}$$

Step 7. Create a weighted normalized S-VNN aggregation matrix $H = \left[h_{ij} \right]_{r \times s}$. We utilize the matrix $\widetilde{E'}$ and the criteria weight vector $\psi = [\psi_1, \psi_2, .., \psi_s]^T$ from Step 5 to yield entries of the matrix H by using $h_{ij} = \psi_j \cdot \left\langle \widetilde{\mathfrak{I}'}_{ij}, \widetilde{\wp'}_{ij}, \widetilde{\aleph'}_{ij} \right\rangle$. So, an entry $h_{ij} = \left\langle \overline{\mathfrak{I}}_{ij}, \overline{\wp}_{ij}, \overline{\aleph}_{ij} \right\rangle$ can be calculated by utilizing Expression (18).

$$h_{ij} = \left\langle \frac{\left(1 + \widetilde{\mathfrak{I}'}_{ij}\right)^{\psi_j} - \left(1 - \widetilde{\mathfrak{I}'}_{ij}\right)^{\psi_j}}{\left(1 + \widetilde{\mathfrak{I}'}_{ij}\right)^{\psi_j} + \left(1 - \widetilde{\mathfrak{I}'}_{ij}\right)^{\psi_j}}, \frac{2\left(\widetilde{\wp'}_{ij}\right)^{\psi_j}}{\left(2 - \widetilde{\wp'}_{ij}\right)^{\psi_j} + \left(\widetilde{\wp'}_{ij}\right)^{\psi_j}}, \frac{2\left(\widetilde{\aleph'}_{ij}\right)^{\psi_j}}{\left(2 - \widetilde{\aleph'}_{ij}\right)^{\psi_j} + \left(\widetilde{\aleph'}_{ij}\right)^{\psi_j}} \right\rangle \tag{18}$$

Step 8. Determine optimality function values.

Optimality function value $\widetilde{O}_i = \langle \mathfrak{I}_i, \wp_i, \aleph_i \rangle = \bigoplus_{j=1}^{s} h_{ij}$ of each alternative can be determined by Expression (19), which is the sum of the S-VNNs (Expression (2)) of the matrix H.

$$\widetilde{O}_i = \left\langle \sum_{j=1}^{s} \overline{\mathfrak{I}}_{ij} - \sum_{j=1}^{s} \sum_{k=i+1}^{s} \overline{\mathfrak{I}}_{ij} \overline{\mathfrak{I}}_{ik} + \prod_{j=1}^{s} \overline{\mathfrak{I}}_{ij}, \prod_{j=1}^{s} \overline{\wp}_{ij}, \prod_{j=1}^{s} \overline{\aleph}_{ij} \right\rangle \tag{19}$$

We then utilize Expression (20) to calculate the score function or defuzzification of $\widetilde{O}_i$ for obtaining the value of O_i.

$$O_i = \mho(\widetilde{O}_i) = \frac{1}{3} \times (\Im_i + 1 - \wp_i + 1 - \aleph_i) \tag{20}$$

Step 9. Compute utility degree for each alternative by comparing the optimal function value with the ideal one O_0. Expression (21) will present the utility degree of alternative i.

$$S_i = \frac{O_i}{O_0}, \forall i = 1,2,..,r \tag{21}$$

Step 10. Rank the alternatives according to the values of utility degree in descending order. We consider the highest value of S_i as the best selected alternative.

4. AN ILLUSTRATIVE EXAMPLE

This section demonstrates a numerical example case for an MCGDM study under an S-VNN environment to exhibit the capability and feasibility of the extended ARAS methodology. In an example of a decision-making issue in an education office for a local government, the head of an education and culture office mandates three education experts (EEs) $E= \{E_1,E_2,E_3\}$ to evaluate five state schools $S= \{S_1,S_2,S_3,S_4,S_5\}$ with various schools' performances and determine the best school in the region. The EEs have required four factors or criteria: teaching atmosphere (F_1), academic staff performance (F_2), student bullying level (F_3), and infrastructure quality (F_4) to be major evaluation assessment factors. The five candidate schools regarded as alternatives will be evaluated utilizing the extended ARAS algorithm based on S-VNNs by three EEs on the four factors with the criteria weight vector of $\psi = [0.189189, 0.11, 0.560811, 0.14]^T$ and the EEs weight vector of $\xi = [0.3781, 0.2951, 0.3268]^T$. Additionally, the EEs have analyzed and decided that only criterion F_3 is categorized as a cost criterion.

4.1. Implementation of the Extended ARAS Method

This section explains the computation steps to select the favorite school using the extended ARAS model according to the MCGDM strategy with S-VNNs. The following describes the detailed computational steps of the proposed ARAS model to solve this MCGDM problem.

Step 1. The EEs evaluate five schools and they give their personal judgements in individual S-VNN decision-making matrices as presented in Tables 1, 2, and 3, respectively.

Table 1. Evaluation assessment of EE_1

Alter-natives	F1	F2	F3	F4
S1	<0.798, 0.355, 0.606>	<0.353, 0.557, 0.207>	<0.46, 0.516, 0.579>	<0.579, 0.444, 0.135>
S2	<0.658, 0.055, 0.457>	<0.556, 0.266, 0.276>	<0.191, 0.246, 0.246>	<0.135, 0.656, 0.358>
S3	<0.404, 0.479, 0.149>	<0.055, 0.488, 0.147>	<0.458, 0.236, 0.454>	<0.076, 0.286, 0.546>
S4	<0.246, 0.021, 0.659>	<0.384, 0.169, 0.492>	<0.373, 0.482, 0.612>	<0.236, 0.166, 0.136>
S5	<0.066, 0.771, 0.136>	<0.381, 0.761, 0.196>	<0.181, 0.616, 0.321>	<0.716, 0.076, 0.236>

Table 2. Evaluation assessment of EE_2

Alter-natives	F1	F2	F3	F4
S1	<0.241, 0.236, 0.621>	<0.461, 0.366, 0.231>	<0.146, 0.441, 0.326>	<0.456, 0.251, 0.346>
S2	<0.416, 0.136, 0.466>	<0.066, 0.256, 0.421>	<0.271, 0.326, 0.321>	<0.546, 0.146, 0.126>
S3	<0.541, 0.456, 0.216>	<0.576, 0.371, 0.166>	<0.456, 0.276, 0.141>	<0.154, 0.436, 0.046>
S4	<0.736, 0.641, 0.166>	<0.381, 0.231, 0.346>	<0.576, 0.356, 0.541>	<0.354, 0.536, 0.366>
S5	<0.566, 0.602, 0.236>	<0.182, 0.541, 0.856>	<0.281, 0.036, 0.131>	<0.455, 0.654, 0.436>

Table 3. Evaluation assessment of EE_3

Alter-natives	F1	F2	F3	F4
S1	<0.376, 0.246, 0.411>	<0.046, 0.153, 0.104>	<0.456, 0.204, 0.326>	<0.426, 0.546, 0.336>
S2	<0.236, 0.446, 0.346>	<0.646, 0.626, 0.636>	<0.631, 0.554, 0.421>	<0.136, 0.336, 0.646>
S3	<0.271, 0.266, 0.176>	<0.836, 0.411, 0.746>	<0.136, 0.153, 0.121>	<0.166, 0.126, 0.334>
S4	<0.121, 0.566, 0.636>	<0.151, 0.316, 0.146>	<0.316, 0.053, 0.641>	<0.466, 0.546, 0.136>
S5	<0.444, 0.655, 0.566>	<0.771, 0.359, 0.666>	<0.721, 0.316, 0.161>	<0.616, 0.116, 0.036>

Step 2. We normalize the individual S-VNN matrices by considering two criteria types, benefit and cost. Tables 4, 5, and 6 shows the normalized individual S-VNN matrices for EE_1, EE_2, and EE_3, respectively.

Table 4. Normalized individual S-VNN matrix of EE_1

Alter-natives	F1	F2	F3	F4
S1	<0.798, 0.355, 0.606>	<0.353, 0.557, 0.207>	<0.579, 0.516, 0.46>	<0.579, 0.444, 0.135>
S2	<0.658, 0.055, 0.457>	<0.556, 0.266, 0.276>	<0.246, 0.246, 0.191>	<0.135, 0.656, 0.358>
S3	<0.404, 0.479, 0.149>	<0.055, 0.488, 0.147>	<0.454, 0.236, 0.458>	<0.076, 0.286, 0.546>
S4	<0.246, 0.021, 0.659>	<0.384, 0.169, 0.492>	<0.612, 0.482, 0.373>	<0.236, 0.166, 0.136>
S5	<0.066, 0.771, 0.136>	<0.381, 0.761, 0.196>	<0.321, 0.616, 0.181>	<0.716, 0.076, 0.236>

Table 5. Normalized individual S-VNN matrix of EE_2

Alter-natives	F1	F2	F3	F4
S1	<0.241, 0.236, 0.621>	<0.461, 0.366, 0.231>	<0.326, 0.441, 0.146>	<0.456, 0.251, 0.346>
S2	<0.416, 0.136, 0.466>	<0.066, 0.256, 0.421>	<0.321, 0.326, 0.271>	<0.546, 0.146, 0.126>
S3	<0.541, 0.456, 0.216>	<0.576, 0.371, 0.166>	<0.141, 0.276, 0.456>	<0.154, 0.436, 0.046>

continued on following page

Table 5. Continued

Alter-natives	F1	F2	F3	F4
S4	<0.736, 0.641, 0.166>	<0.381, 0.231, 0.346>	<0.541, 0.356, 0.576>	<0.354, 0.536, 0.366>
S5	<0.566, 0.602, 0.236>	<0.182, 0.541, 0.856>	<0.131, 0.036, 0.281>	<0.455, 0.654, 0.436>

Table 6. Normalized individual S-VNN matrix of EE_3

Alter-natives	F1	F2	F3	F4
S1	<0.376, 0.246, 0.411>	<0.046, 0.153, 0.104>	<0.326, 0.204, 0.456>	<0.426, 0.546, 0.336>
S2	<0.236, 0.446, 0.346>	<0.646, 0.626, 0.636>	<0.421, 0.554, 0.631>	<0.136, 0.336, 0.646>
S3	<0.271, 0.266, 0.176>	<0.836, 0.411, 0.746>	<0.121, 0.153, 0.136>	<0.166, 0.126, 0.334>
S4	<0.121, 0.566, 0.636>	<0.151, 0.316, 0.146>	<0.641, 0.053, 0.316>	<0.466, 0.546, 0.136>
S5	<0.444, 0.655, 0.566>	<0.771, 0.359, 0.666>	<0.161, 0.316, 0.721>	<0.616, 0.116, 0.036>

Step 3. We create two aggregated S-VNN decision matrices separately both using DySVNEWA and DySVNEWG operators, proposed by (Farid & Riaz, 2023), with the EEs weight of $\xi = [0.3781, 0.2951, 0.3268]^T$. As a result, the DySVNEWA and DySVNEWG matrices can be presented in Tables 7 and 8, respectively.

Table 7. Aggregation matrix using DySVNEWA operator

Alter-natives	F1	F2	F3	F4
S1	<0.548, 0.28, 0.541>	<0.293, 0.332, 0.172>	<0.43, 0.37, 0.334>	<0.496, 0.406, 0.243>
S2	<0.468, 0.055, 0.421>	<0.468, 0.355, 0.418>	<0.327, 0.353, 0.322>	<0.27, 0.352, 0.332>
S3	<0.407, 0.479, 0.176>	<0.544, 0.426, 0.275>	<0.261, 0.215, 0.316>	<0.129, 0.252, 0.238>
S4	<0.391, 0.021, 0.453>	<0.311, 0.228, 0.305>	<0.602, 0.225, 0.405>	<0.35, 0.357, 0.184>
S5	<0.354, 0.771, 0.263>	<0.493, 0.548, 0.48>	<0.214, 0.232, 0.338>	<0.617, 0.175, 0.16>

Table 8. Aggregation matrix using DySVNEWG operator

Alter-natives	F1	F2	F3	F4
S1	<0.456, 0.285, 0.553>	<0.206, 0.381, 0.181>	<0.409, 0.4, 0.373>	<0.49, 0.427, 0.266>
S2	<0.421, 0.215, 0.425>	<0.336, 0.397, 0.45>	<0.319, 0.379, 0.378>	<0.211, 0.426, 0.405>
S3	<0.39, 0.407, 0.178>	<0.303, 0.43, 0.397>	<0.214, 0.221, 0.36>	<0.121, 0.283, 0.344>
S4	<0.284, 0.415, 0.533>	<0.286, 0.236, 0.344>	<0.6, 0.315, 0.421>	<0.335, 0.414, 0.207>
S5	<0.247, 0.69, 0.321>	<0.402, 0.591, 0.614>	<0.198, 0.371, 0.423>	<0.6, 0.289, 0.236>

To obtain the alternatives' ranking order result based on methods proposed by (Farid & Riaz, 2023), we utilize the criteria weight vector of $\psi = [0.189189, 0.11, 0.560811, 0.14]^T$ and Tables 7 and 8 to create a weighted DySVNEWA aggregation matrix and a weighted DySVNEWG aggregation matrix, presented in Tables 9 and 10, respectively. Next, we perform a matrix multiplication operation between the weighted DySVNEWA aggregation matrix and the criteria weight vector to obtain comprehensive performance evaluation results for all alternatives. After calculating score functions for each S-VNN performance evaluation result by using Expression (9), we rank all the alternatives according to the score functions in descending order and select the first ranking of the ordered score functions as the chosen school suggested by the DySVNEWA method. Similarly, we attempt to do the same way for the DySVNEWG aggregation operator. As a result, we can see that Table 11 is a ranking order result generated by DySVNEWA and DySVNEWG methods with their different score functions.

Table 9. Weighted aggregation matrix using DySVNEWA operator

Alter-natives	F1	F2	F3	F4
S1	<0.116, 0.83, 0.906>	<0.033, 0.911, 0.871>	<0.253, 0.607, 0.578>	<0.076, 0.905, 0.862>
S2	<0.096, 0.675, 0.876>	<0.056, 0.916, 0.927>	<0.188, 0.593, 0.568>	<0.039, 0.892, 0.887>
S3	<0.081, 0.891, 0.782>	<0.067, 0.928, 0.899>	<0.149, 0.468, 0.562>	<0.018, 0.865, 0.861>
S4	<0.078, 0.595, 0.884>	<0.035, 0.888, 0.906>	<0.372, 0.478, 0.633>	<0.051, 0.894, 0.841>
S5	<0.07, 0.956, 0.823>	<0.059, 0.946, 0.937>	<0.122, 0.485, 0.581>	<0.1, 0.837, 0.831>

Table 10. Weighted aggregation matrix using DySVNEWG operator

Alter-natives	F1	F2	F3	F4
S1	<0.093, 0.832, 0.909>	<0.023, 0.921, 0.874>	<0.239, 0.629, 0.609>	<0.075, 0.909, 0.869>
S2	<0.085, 0.802, 0.877>	<0.038, 0.923, 0.932>	<0.183, 0.614, 0.613>	<0.03, 0.909, 0.904>
S3	<0.078, 0.872, 0.783>	<0.034, 0.929, 0.923>	<0.121, 0.474, 0.599>	<0.017, 0.874, 0.89>
S4	<0.055, 0.874, 0.904>	<0.032, 0.89, 0.914>	<0.37, 0.561, 0.645>	<0.049, 0.906, 0.85>
S5	<0.048, 0.939, 0.845>	<0.047, 0.952, 0.955>	<0.112, 0.607, 0.647>	<0.097, 0.876, 0.86>

Table 11. Ranking results and various score functions based on DySVNEWA and DySVNEWG methods

Methods	Ranking Results	Score Functions
DySVNEWA	S4 > S3 > S1 > S2 > S5	0.6046 > 0.5356 > 0.5324 > 0.5318 > 0.5224
DySVNEWG	S4 > S1 > S3 > S2 > S5	0.5336 > 0.5048 > 0.5030 > 0.4784 > 0.4486

Step 4. The criteria weight vector $\psi = [0.189189, 0.11, 0.560811, 0.14]^T$ is the criteria weight that has been agreed by the EEs is.

Step 5. Based on the procedure of traditional ARAS method and the result of Table 7, we modified the construction of improved S-VNN aggregation matrix by utilizing Expression (15) . Table 12 shows the result of the improved S-VNN aggregation matrix.

Table 12. The improved S-VNN aggregation matrix

Alter-natives	F1	F2	F3	F4
S0*)	<0.548, 0.021, 0.176>	<0.544, 0.228, 0.172>	<0.602, 0.215, 0.316>	<0.617, 0.175, 0.16>
S1	<0.548, 0.28, 0.541>	<0.293, 0.332, 0.172>	<0.43, 0.37, 0.334>	<0.496, 0.406, 0.243>
S2	<0.468, 0.055, 0.421>	<0.468, 0.355, 0.418>	<0.327, 0.353, 0.322>	<0.27, 0.352, 0.332>
S3	<0.407, 0.479, 0.176>	<0.544, 0.426, 0.275>	<0.261, 0.215, 0.316>	<0.129, 0.252, 0.238>
S4	<0.391, 0.021, 0.453>	<0.311, 0.228, 0.305>	<0.602, 0.225, 0.405>	<0.35, 0.357, 0.184>

continued on following page

Table 12. Continued

Alter-natives	F1	F2	F3	F4
S5	<0.354, 0.771, 0.263>	<0.493, 0.548, 0.48>	<0.214, 0.232, 0.338>	<0.617, 0.175, 0.16>

Note that: S0*) is an optimal aggregation value of criterion for each criterion

Step 6. The extended ARAS algorithm then normalizes the improved S-VNN aggregation matrix using Expression (17) shows the result as in Table 13.

Table 13. The normalization result of the improved S-VNN aggregation matrix

Alter-natives	F1	F2	F3	F4
S0*)	<0.202, 0.013, 0.087>	<0.205, 0.108, 0.094>	<0.247, 0.134, 0.155>	<0.249, 0.102, 0.121>
S1	<0.202, 0.172, 0.267>	<0.11, 0.157, 0.094>	<0.177, 0.23, 0.165>	<0.2, 0.237, 0.185>
S2	<0.172, 0.034, 0.207>	<0.177, 0.168, 0.229>	<0.134, 0.219, 0.159>	<0.109, 0.205, 0.252>
S3	<0.15, 0.294, 0.087>	<0.205, 0.201, 0.151>	<0.107, 0.134, 0.155>	<0.052, 0.147, 0.181>
S4	<0.144, 0.013, 0.223>	<0.117, 0.108, 0.167>	<0.247, 0.14, 0.199>	<0.141, 0.208, 0.14>
S5	<0.13, 0.474, 0.13>	<0.186, 0.259, 0.264>	<0.088, 0.144, 0.166>	<0.249, 0.102, 0.121>

Note that: S0*) is an normalized optimal aggregation value of criterion for each criterion

Step 7. We then perform a matrix multiplication operation between the matrix provided by Table 13 and the criteria weight vector from Step 4 to obtain a weighted matrix from Table 13. The result is presented in Table 14.

Table 14. The weighted normalized S-VNN aggregation matrix

Alter-natives	F1	F2	F3	F4
S0*)	<0.039, 0.557, 0.715>	<0.023, 0.844, 0.836>	<0.141, 0.371, 0.4>	<0.036, 0.798, 0.81>
S1	<0.039, 0.78, 0.825>	<0.012, 0.865, 0.836>	<0.1, 0.483, 0.411>	<0.028, 0.86, 0.841>
S2	<0.033, 0.634, 0.799>	<0.02, 0.869, 0.888>	<0.076, 0.472, 0.404>	<0.015, 0.849, 0.865>

continued on following page

Table 14. Continued

Alter-natives	F1	F2	F3	F4
S3	<0.029, 0.835, 0.715>	<0.023, 0.88, 0.863>	<0.06, 0.371, 0.4>	<0.007, 0.824, 0.84>
S4	<0.027, 0.557, 0.806>	<0.013, 0.844, 0.869>	<0.141, 0.38, 0.451>	<0.02, 0.85, 0.821>
S5	<0.025, 0.89, 0.753>	<0.021, 0.896, 0.897>	<0.049, 0.385, 0.413>	<0.036, 0.798, 0.81>

Note that: S0*) is a weighted normalized optimal aggregation value of criterion for each criterion

Step 8. The extended ARAS algorithm utilizes Expression (19) to determine optimal function values for each alternative and uses Expression (20) to compute their score functions. Table 15 demonstrates an optimal function vector with their score functions.

Table 15. The optimal function vector with their score functions

Alter-natives	Optimal Function Values	Score Function (O_i)
S0*)	<0.221, 0.139, 0.194>	0.629
S1	<0.169, 0.28, 0.239>	0.550
S2	<0.137, 0.221, 0.248>	0.556
S3	<0.114, 0.225, 0.207>	0.561
S4	<0.191, 0.152, 0.259>	0.593
S5	<0.124, 0.245, 0.226>	0.551

Note that: S0*) is an optimal function value of criterion for each criterion

Step 9. We finally calculate utility degree for each alternative by comparing the optimal function value with the ideal one O_0 which is 0.629. Table 16 presents the utility degree for each alternative.

Table 16. The optimal function vector with their score functions

U	S0*)	S1	S2	S3	S4	S5
Utility Degree	1	0.874	0.884	0.891	0.943	0.876

Note that: S0*) is utility degree of the optimal function

Step 10. Based on the values of utility degree of S1, S2, S3, S4, and S5, we rank the alternatives and select the first alternative as the favorite school suggested by our proposed ARAS method. The final ranking result is S4 > S3 > S2 > S5 > S1.

4.2. Comparative Analysis

This subsection presents a comparative analysis between our proposed ARAS method with others S-VNN aggregation operators to reflect the feasibility and benefits of the proposed ARAS methodology based on S-VNNs for school assessment and school selection. The methods used for comparison include the DySVNEWA and DySVNEWG operator-based-on S-VNNs proposed by (Farid & Riaz, 2023), and S-VNN fairly aggregation (S-VNNFA) operator introduced by (Riaz et al., 2023). The proposed technique is utilized to examine the school performance factors' ranking, utility degree, and priority based on the combined performance examination data and the significance of the criterion evaluation. Meanwhile, the other abovementioned techniques are used to examine the school performance factors and their priorities without considering the utility degrees of the alternatives. Table 13 shows the comparative results. In addition, Figures 1 and 2 show representation graphics to exhibit various score function values and the ranking results, respectively.

Table 17. The optimal function vector with their score functions

Methods	Score Function Values					Ranking
	S1	S2	S3	S4	S5	
DySVNEWA	0.5324	0.5318	0.5356	0.6046	0.5224	S4 > S3 > S1 > S2 > S5
DySVNEWG	0.5048	0.4784	0.5030	0.5336	0.4486	S4 > S1 > S3 > S2 > S5
S-VNNFA	0.405	0.416	0.428	0.432	0.397	S4 > S3 > S2 > S1 > S5
Our proposed ARAS	0.874	0.884	0.891	0.943	0.876	S4 > S3 > S2 > S5 > S1

Figure 1. Comparison Analysis Based-on Score Function Values

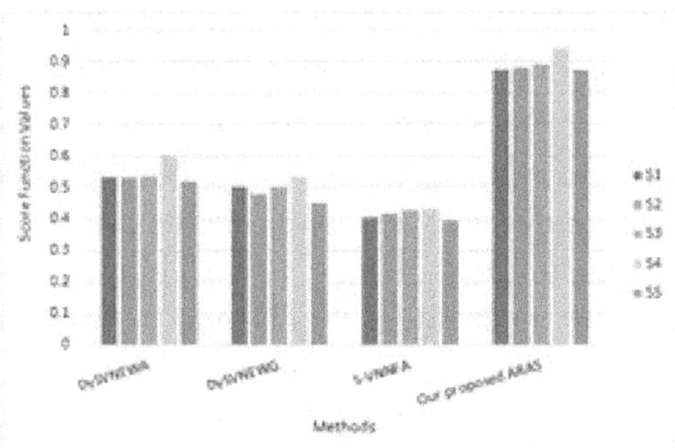

Figure 2. Alternatives' Ranking Results

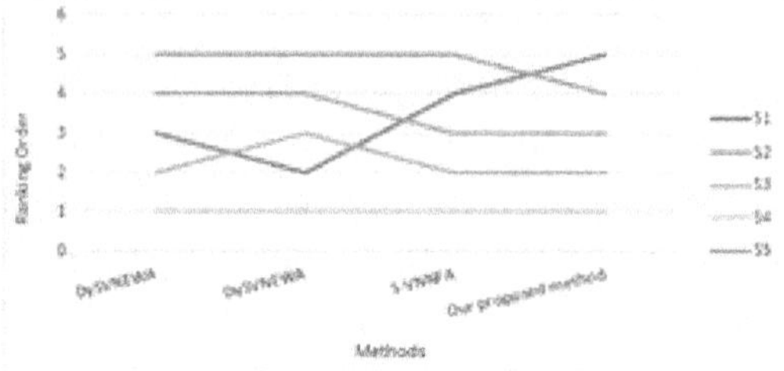

Based on the result from Table 15, all the above-mentioned techniques suggest the same alternative, which is alternative S5 as the favorite school. However, the values of the score function generated by those techniques have various and fluctuating values. Our proposed technique tends to calculate score function values higher than the others. It might be a utility degree measurement effect, but it did not impact the alternative selection result. So, based on the comparison results, it indicates that the proposed ARAS model has the capability and feasibility to overcome school assessment and school selection problems.

5. CONCLUSION

A synthetic and effective instrument for assessing and ranking viable alternatives, the ARAS methodology has been used in many different contexts. Nevertheless, because the original ARAS still relies on numerical data to evaluate the decision-making process, it has many shortcomings when it performs risk assessment and ranking under uncertain and imprecise information. Therefore, this study presented the novel ARAS model based on S-VNNs by integrating the DySVNEWA operator, the S-VNN operator, and ARAS procedures under the S-VNNs environment to overcome the above drawbacks and improve the effectiveness of the traditional ARAS methodology. The EE committee used S-VNNs in the suggested ARAS model to express the uncertain preference and assessments for the school's performance indicators over each evaluated school.

Then, we used a consensus technique to decide the weights of the risk criteria and the members of the EE committee. Additionally, an enhanced ARAS technique integrated by the DySVNEWA and S-VNN operators was introduced to evaluate and rank schools' performance utilizing S-VNN information. It can simultaneously account for the flexibility of the integration process and the relation between examination variables. Next, an application to evaluate the schools in the performance selection system verified the actual ability and feasibility of the proposed ARAS framework. Eventually, the comparative analyses were conducted to elaborate on the stability and dominance of the proposed S-VNN-ARAS model.

Further studies will be arranged according to the following directions. To overcome the gaps in the ARAS model, it is first necessary to address the shortcomings of the original ARAS technique. Then, using S-VNN information, the previously presented ARAS model can be used to address additional confusing and unclear performance assessment and prioritization issues. Furthermore, some novelty-improved ARAS models should be investigated under various imprecise and vague circumstances, such as spherical fuzzy numbers (Kutlu Gündoğdu & Kahraman, 2019b, 2019a, 2020), Spherical Trapezoidal Fuzzy Numbers (I. Deli & Çağman, 2021), probabilistic double hierarchy linguistic term sets (X. Wang et al., 2022), Trapezoidal Fuzzy Neutrosophic Numbers (Irvanizam & Zi, 2022), and so on. Additionally, it would also be an interesting study direction to develop a novel ARAS model by incorporating the consensus-reaching process and social-network large-scale group decision methodology with complex-linguistic information (Ji et al., 2023; Sun et al., 2023).

REFERENCES

Alm, S., Låftman, S. B., Sandahl, J., & Modin, B. (2019). School effectiveness and students' future orientation: A multilevel analysis of upper secondary schools in Stockholm, Sweden. *Journal of Adolescence*, 70(1), 62–73. DOI:10.1016/j.adolescence.2018.11.007 PMID:30544017

Atanassov, K. T. (1986). Intuitionistic fuzzy sets. *Fuzzy Sets and Systems*, 20(1), 87–96. DOI:10.1016/S0165-0114(86)80034-3

Bahrami, Y., Hassani, H., & Maghsoudi, A. (2019). BWM-ARAS: A new hybrid MCDM method for Cu prospectivity mapping in the Abhar area, NW Iran. *Spatial Statistics*, 33, 100382. DOI:10.1016/j.spasta.2019.100382

Biswas, P., Pramanik, S., & Giri, C. B. (2016). Value and ambiguity index based ranking method of single-valued trapezoidal neutrosophic numbers and its application to multi-attribute decision making. *Neutrosophic Sets and Systems, 12*, 127–138. http://fs.unm.edu/NSS2/index.php/111/article/view/687

Bui, Q.-T., Ngo, M.-P., Snasel, V., Pedrycz, W., & Vo, B. (2023). Information measures based on similarity under neutrosophic fuzzy environment and multi-criteria decision problems. *Engineering Applications of Artificial Intelligence*, 122, 106026. DOI:10.1016/j.engappai.2023.106026

Büyüközkan, G., & Göçer, F. (2018). An extension of ARAS methodology under Interval Valued Intuitionistic Fuzzy environment for Digital Supply Chain. *Applied Soft Computing*, 69, 634–654. DOI:10.1016/j.asoc.2018.04.040

Deli, I. (2018). Operators on Single Valued Trapezoidal Neutrosophic Numbers and SVTN-Group Decision Making. *Neutrosophic Sets and Systems, 22*, 131–150. http://fs.unm.edu/NSS2/index.php/111/article/view/277

Deli, İ. (2019). A novel defuzzification method of SV-trapezoidal neutrosophic numbers and multi-attribute decision making: A comparative analysis. *Soft Computing*, 23(23), 12529–12545. DOI:10.1007/s00500-019-03803-z

Deli, I., & Çağman, N. (2021). Spherical fuzzy numbers and multi-criteria decision-making. In *Decision Making with Spherical Fuzzy Sets* (pp. 53–84). Springer International Publishing. DOI:10.1007/978-3-030-45461-6_3

Dongre, A., & Tewary, V. (2020). Pain without gain? Impact of school rationalisation in India. *International Journal of Educational Development*, 72, 102142. DOI:10.1016/j.ijedudev.2019.102142

Farid, H. M. A., & Riaz, M. (2023). Single-valued neutrosophic dynamic aggregation information with time sequence preference for IoT technology in supply chain management. *Engineering Applications of Artificial Intelligence*, 126, 106940. DOI:10.1016/j.engappai.2023.106940

Garg, H., & Nancy, . (2017). Some New Biparametric Distance Measures on Single-Valued Neutrosophic Sets with Applications to Pattern Recognition and Medical Diagnosis. *Information (Basel)*, 8(4), 162. Advance online publication. DOI:10.3390/info8040162

Garg, H., & Rani, D. (2020). Robust Averaging–Geometric Aggregation Operators for Complex Intuitionistic Fuzzy Sets and Their Applications to MCDM Process. *Arabian Journal for Science and Engineering*, 45(3), 2017–2033. DOI:10.1007/s13369-019-03925-4

Ghenai, C., Albawab, M., & Bettayeb, M. (2020). Sustainability indicators for renewable energy systems using multi-criteria decision-making model and extended SWARA/ARAS hybrid method. *Renewable Energy*, 146, 580–597. DOI:10.1016/j.renene.2019.06.157

Ghorabaee, M. K., Zavadskas, E. K., Turskis, Z., & Antucheviciene, J. (2016). A new combinative distance-based assessment (CODAS) method for multi-criteria decision-making. *Economic Computation and Economic Cybernetics Studies and Research*, 50(3), 25–44. https://econpapers.repec.org/RePEc:cys:ecocyb:v:50:y:2016:i:3:p:25-44

Goswami, S. S., & Behera, D. K. (2021). Implementation of ENTROPY-ARAS decision making methodology in the selection of best engineering materials. *Materials Today: Proceedings*, 38, 2256–2262. DOI:10.1016/j.matpr.2020.06.320

Heidary Dahooie, J., Beheshti Jazan Abadi, E., Vanaki, A. S., & Firoozfar, H. R. (2018). Competency-based IT personnel selection using a hybrid SWARA and ARAS-G methodology. *Human Factors and Ergonomics in Manufacturing*, 28(1), 5–16. DOI:10.1002/hfm.20713

Hwang, C.-L., & Yoon, K. (1981). Methods for Multiple Attribute Decision Making. In *Multiple Attribute Decision Making: Methods and Applications A State-of-the-Art Survey* (pp. 58–191). Springer Berlin Heidelberg. DOI:10.1007/978-3-642-48318-9_3

Irvanizam, I., Marzuki, M., Patria, I., & Abubakar, R. (2018). An Application for Smartphone Preference Using TODIM Decision Making Method. *Proceedings - 2nd 2018 International Conference on Electrical Engineering and Informatics, ICELTICs 2018*. DOI:10.1109/ICELTICS.2018.8548820

Irvanizam, I., Usman, T., Iqbal, M., Iskandar, T., & Marzuki, M. (2020). An Extended Fuzzy TODIM Approach for Multiple-Attribute Decision-Making with Dual-Connection Numbers. *Advances in Fuzzy Systems*, 2020, 1–10. Advance online publication. DOI:10.1155/2020/6190149

Irvanizam, I., & Zahara, N. (2023). *An Extended EDAS Based on Multi-Attribute Group Decision Making to Evaluate Mathematics Teachers With Single-Valued Trapezoidal Neutrosophic Numbers*. DOI:10.4018/978-1-6684-7836-3.ch003

Irvanizam, I., & Zi, N. N. (2022). *Improved MABAC Method for Multicriteria Group Decision Making With Trapezoidal Fuzzy Neutrosophic Numbers*. DOI:10.4018/978-1-7998-7979-4.ch030

Jana, C., Pal, M., Karaaslan, F., & Wang, J. Q. (2020). Trapezoidal neutrosophic aggregation operators and their application to the multi-attribute decision-making process. *Scientia Iranica*, 27(3), 1655–1673. DOI:10.24200/sci.2018.51136.2024

Ji, F., Wu, J., Chiclana, F., Wang, S., Fujita, H., & Herrera-Viedma, E. (2023). The Overlapping Community-Driven Feedback Mechanism to Support Consensus in Social Network Group Decision Making. *IEEE Transactions on Fuzzy Systems*, 31(9), 3025–3039. DOI:10.1109/TFUZZ.2023.3241062

Kamacı, H., Garg, H., & Petchimuthu, S. (2021). Bipolar trapezoidal neutrosophic sets and their Dombi operators with applications in multicriteria decision making. *Soft Computing*, 25(13), 8417–8440. DOI:10.1007/s00500-021-05768-4

Karagöz, S., Deveci, M., Simic, V., & Aydin, N. (2021). Interval type-2 Fuzzy ARAS method for recycling facility location problems. *Applied Soft Computing*, 102, 107107. DOI:10.1016/j.asoc.2021.107107

Kutlu Gündoğdu, F., & Kahraman, C. (2019a). A novel fuzzy TOPSIS method using emerging interval-valued spherical fuzzy sets. *Engineering Applications of Artificial Intelligence*, 85, 307–323. DOI:10.1016/j.engappai.2019.06.003

Kutlu Gündoğdu, F., & Kahraman, C. (2019b). Spherical fuzzy sets and spherical fuzzy TOPSIS method. *Journal of Intelligent & Fuzzy Systems*, 36(1), 337–352. DOI:10.3233/JIFS-181401

Kutlu Gündoğdu, F., & Kahraman, C. (2020). A novel spherical fuzzy analytic hierarchy process and its renewable energy application. *Soft Computing*, 24(6), 4607–4621. DOI:10.1007/s00500-019-04222-w

Li, B., Wang, J., Yang, L., & Li, X. (2018). A Novel Generalized Simplified Neutrosophic Number Einstein Aggregation Operator. *ViXra*. https://api.semanticscholar.org/CorpusID:49381119

Mishra, A. R., Rani, P., Cavallaro, F., & Mardani, A. (2022). A similarity measure-based Pythagorean fuzzy additive ratio assessment approach and its application to multi-criteria sustainable biomass crop selection. *Applied Soft Computing*, 125, 109201. DOI:10.1016/j.asoc.2022.109201

Nithyanandham, D., & Augustin, F. (2023). A bipolar fuzzy p-competition graph based ARAS technique for prioritizing COVID-19 vaccines. *Applied Soft Computing*, 146, 110632. DOI:10.1016/j.asoc.2023.110632

Opricovic, S., & Tzeng, G.-H. (2004). Compromise solution by MCDM methods: A comparative analysis of VIKOR and TOPSIS. *European Journal of Operational Research*, 156(2), 445–455. DOI:10.1016/S0377-2217(03)00020-1

Ouenniche, J., Bouslah, K., Perez-Gladish, B., & Xu, B. (2021). A new VIKOR-based in-sample-out-of-sample classifier with application in bankruptcy prediction. *Annals of Operations Research*, 296(1), 495–512. DOI:10.1007/s10479-019-03223-0 PMID:34812215

Paulraj, S., & Tamilarasi, G. (2022). Generalized ordered weighted harmonic averaging operator withtrapezoidal neutrosophic numbers for solving MADM problems. *Journal of Ambient Intelligence and Humanized Computing*, 13(8), 4089–4102. DOI:10.1007/s12652-021-03509-x PMID:34659583

Peng, J., Wang, J., Jing, W., Zhang, H., & Chen, X. (2016). Simplified neutrosophic sets and their applications in multi-criteria group decision-making problems. *International Journal of Systems Science*, 47(10), 2342–2358. DOI:10.1080/00207721.2014.994050

Riaz, M., Farid, H. M. A., Ashraf, S., & Kamacı, H. (2023). Single-valued neutrosophic fairly aggregation operators with multi-criteria decision-making. *Computational & Applied Mathematics*, 42(3), 104. DOI:10.1007/s40314-023-02233-w

Shih, H.-S., Shyur, H.-J., & Lee, E. S. (2007). An extension of TOPSIS for group decision making. *Mathematical and Computer Modelling*, 45(7), 801–813. DOI:10.1016/j.mcm.2006.03.023

Slot, E. M., Bronkhorst, L. H., Wubbels, T., & Akkerman, S. F. (2020). The role of school in adolescents' interest in daily life. *International Journal of Educational Research*, 104, 101643. DOI:10.1016/j.ijer.2020.101643

Smarandache, F. (1998). *Neutrosophy: Neutrosophic Probability, Set, and Logic: Analytic Synthesis & Synthetic Analysis*. American Research Press.

Son, L. H., Ngan, R. T., Ali, M., Fujita, H., Abdel-Basset, M., Giang, N. L., Manogaran, G., & Priyan, M. K. (2020). A New Representation of Intuitionistic Fuzzy Systems and Their Applications in Critical Decision Making. *IEEE Intelligent Systems*, 35(1), 6–17. DOI:10.1109/MIS.2019.2938441

Sun, J., Gong, Z., Zhang, D., Xu, Y., & Wei, G. (2023). A robust ordinal regression feedback consensus model with dynamic trust propagation in social network group decision-making. *Information Fusion*, 100, 101952. DOI:10.1016/j.inffus.2023.101952

Tian, Z., Wang, J., Wang, J., & Zhang, H. (2017). An improved MULTIMOORA approach for multi-criteria decision-making based on interdependent inputs of simplified neutrosophic linguistic information. *Neural Computing & Applications*, 28(1), 585–597. DOI:10.1007/s00521-016-2378-5

Wang, H., Smarandache, F., Zhang, Y. Q., & Sunderraman, R. (2010). Single valued neutrosophic set. *Multisp Multistructure*, 4, 410–413.

Wang, L., & Bao, Y.-L. (2021). Multiple-Attribute Decision-Making Method Based on Normalized Geometric Aggregation Operators of Single-Valued Neutrosophic Hesitant Fuzzy Information. *Complexity*, 5580761, 1–15. Advance online publication. DOI:10.1155/2021/5580761

Wang, X., Xu, Z., & Gou, X. (2022). The Interval probabilistic double hierarchy linguistic EDAS method based on natural language processing basic techniques and its application to hotel online reviews. *International Journal of Machine Learning and Cybernetics*, 13(6), 1517–1534. DOI:10.1007/s13042-021-01463-w

Wu, X., Qian, J., Peng, J., & Xue, C. (2018). A Multi-Criteria Group Decision-Making Method with Possibility Degree and Power Aggregation Operators of Single Trapezoidal Neutrosophic Numbers. *Symmetry*, 10(11), 590. Advance online publication. DOI:10.3390/sym10110590

Wu, X., Wang, J., Peng, J., & Chen, X. (2016). Cross-Entropy and Prioritized Aggregation Operator with Simplified Neutrosophic Sets and Their Application in Multi-Criteria Decision-Making Problems. *International Journal of Fuzzy Systems*, 18(6), 1104–1116. DOI:10.1007/s40815-016-0180-2

Zadeh, L. A. (1965). Fuzzy sets. *Informes de la Construcción*, 8(3), 338–353.

Zavadskas, E., Kaklauskas, A., & Šarka, V. (1994). The new method of multicriteria complex proportional assessment of projects. *Technological and Economic Development of Economy*, 1, 131–139.

Chapter 11
Correlating Resonance: Configurational Analysis, Neutrosophy, and Wickedness

Geoff Brian Ebbs
https://orcid.org/0000-0003-0002-5841
Griffith University, Australia

Louis Sanzogni
Griffith University, Australia

Luke Houghton
https://orcid.org/0000-0002-7461-6591
Griffith University, Australia

ABSTRACT

The complex problems facing the world today resist solutions. The reasons are the complex, multidisciplinary, interdependent variables, and the non-optimal behaviour of stakeholders that lead to unsolvable "wicked" problems. Analysis of these complex situations requires methodologies that can deal with this complex, incomplete, and inconsistent data. Neutrosophy has evolved specifically to deal with the indeterminate nature of such data. Some researchers have considered both configurational analysis and neutrosophy. Neutrosophy examines the neutralities and the interplays between opposites whereas configurational analysis isolates the neutralities and focuses on the interplay between opposites. This chapter examines a configurational approach that is simple and arithmetic in nature and does not preclude a focus on the neutralities, so is compatible with neutrosophic logic, statistics, and probability analysis.

DOI: 10.4018/979-8-3693-2085-3.ch011

INTRODUCING RESONANT CORRELATIONS

Resonant Correlations is a method developed to bring quantitative rigour and automation to quantitative analysis of complex problems. In addition to these quantitative advantages, it was developed to address the inter-dependent, multi-valued variables present in complex problems that resist analysis. This method assumes that the available data may be irrelevant, incomplete, contradictory, or indeterminate. Rather than attempting to determine the accuracy of an individual datapoint to facilitate statistical analysis, it determines the significance of each datapoint by considering its relationship with other datapoints. Thus, it takes all data at face value rather than their accuracy and reliability and examines the resonance and dissonance between data points based on the aggregation of their correlation to each element of the data set. Regardless of the accuracy and or reliability of an individual datapoint, the resonance between clusters of data highlights concepts (values) that regularly appear together and so likely to be related. Further, dissonant clusters reveal mutually exclusive values. By focusing on the resonant, dissonant, and neutral clusters of correlations we find configurations of patterns in the data that offers a starting point for further exploration. This statistical analysis of the qualitative data reveals groupings that suggest potential significance.

This approach evolved as a quantitative method that confirms and clarifies the thematic analysis of qualitative research and is an extension of the Systematic Qualitative Literature Review (SQLR) (Pickering & Byrne, 2014). Because of that history, the data discussed in this paper are concepts or themes, identified in bodies of text. It is proposed that the method could be useful for other data types, such as quantitative data in physical experiments. The use of a similar approach to identify relevant content in web searches (Ebbs, 2018) supports this proposal. In addition to documenting and mapping the process by which themes emerge during qualitative analysis, this method provides the opportunity to rigorously explore possible relationship that have been missed by the qualitative researcher. It also provides scope for the comparative analysis of the emergent clusters between populations of texts, allowing a rigorous comparison of the concepts that contribute to the meaning and beliefs inherent in different bodies of data.

Examining the resonance and dissonance between concepts within and across datasets, highlights those concepts that contribute to a commonly held paradigm and those which undermine such understanding and contribute to the wickedness of the problem. This is useful for facilitation of policy intended to address wicked problems, such as the sustainable development goals (SDGs). While the example provided here analyses two sets of research papers examining sustainable development in small business, the method has been subsequently tested against a body of 186 submissions to the Australian Parliamentary Inquiry into Food Security with meaningful results. This article focuses on the identification of clusters within a single dataset (in this case, a body of texts).

The structure of this article is to introduce the methodology, its development and then its validation. That sets the scene for a discussion of its limitations, its value and future refinement.

RESONANT CORRELATIONS AND CLUSTER ANALYSIS

Cluster analysis is a technique useful for organising different conceptual approaches (Preiser, Biggs, De Vos, & Folke, 2018). Most forms of cluster analysis examine an entire set of data to isolate those elements of a dataset that have the most in common, i.e., are "closest". The method of Resonant Correlations differs from standard cluster analysis in two ways. Firstly, it examines the relationships between concepts (as opposed to the relationships between texts based on one or more concepts). Secondly, it takes a configurational approach, seeking only to identify those concepts (or more specifically, correlations between concepts) that resonate because of common relationships with a distinct subset of other concepts. This resonance distinguishes one set of beliefs from another and paradigms may be mutually exclusive (dissonant) or overlap. In that regard, it has strong similarities with Kelly's Personal Construct Theory (Kelly, 1977).

In a standard thematic analysis, tens to hundreds of papers are analysed to determine threads of meaning that run through the papers, developing a taxonomy as a framework to understand how the papers are grouped based on various concepts that are related. This is often accompanied by a qualitative analysis of the frequency of various concepts to validate the structure of the taxonomy. Sovacool's 2017 *Ordering of theories* is typical of this approach, teasing out the relationships between various theories of sustainable transitions (Sovacool & Hess, 2017). The taxonomy and its qualitative information about frequency may be replaced by the researcher's expert knowledge. Göpel's refinement of the multilevel protocol used to explain sustainability transitions follows this tradition, referring to a body of literature and applying the author's knowledge to comment on it (Göpel, 2016).

This research complements those processes by recording the frequency of correlation between qualitative concepts across the body of papers. It then explores the clusters of those correlations, and the resonance and dissonance between those clusters. The research on which this example is based, focused on the relationships between concepts relating to transitions by business toward sustainable development. The approach was developed specifically to examine the wicked nature of the problem rather than the reasons that specific practitioners struggled with those transitions. We wanted to note if there were common patterns in those struggles and if those patterns resonated with the findings of previous research into the area. Because of the interdependent, multi-valued and sub-optimal nature of the data it was important that this focus on patterns across the data set, rather than the conclusions of any particular case study or piece of research, provided an aggregate view that circumvented the need to individually determine the relevance or accuracy of each element of the data set. That does not preclude the possibility of using a neutrosophical approach to enrich the data before it is aggregated, but it provides a way of dealing with a "spread" of data that occurs because of imprecision or unreliability.

In addition to providing distance, this abstraction allowed us to focus on the resonant reoccurrence of correlations between key concepts. By examining the details of this resonance and dissonance, we can distinguish the significant factors that lead to particular outcomes. In this case, we can identify the points of view that are consistent with certain intentions and lead to a preference for certain responses.

What is unusual about that capacity is that it addresses one of the challenges of wicked problems, the complex, namely the interdependent nature of the variables (Peter & Swilling, 2014), exacerbated by the sub-optimal behaviour of individual stakeholders (Grubb et al., 2017). In the research used to provide the example given here we confirmed the obvious finding; that business owners and radical change advocates have different definitions of sustainable development, desire different outcomes and so respond differently to the same stimuli. While this is not unexpected, it has confounded policy makers who previously had no way to address these divergent views. Importantly, it also allows, for independent, overlapping correlations that identify alternative clusters. In this way, Resonant Correlations also identifies independent variables that are important to one group but neutral to another. It provides a map for navigating possible solutions to find common, or uncontroversial ground. Again, there is nothing in the method that would preclude its application to quantitative data involving complex problems in hard science, or challenges in interface design, for example, which involve a mixture of hard coding and subjective responses.

In summary, Resonant Correlations is an algorithm built from a series of relatively simple arithmetic operations that approximates, documents, and extends the qualitative process of performing a thematic analysis. We skip the initial processes involved in coding a systematic qualitative literature review, as that is already well defined elsewhere (Pickering & Byrne, 2014).

nVivo Cross Tabs

This step is a straightforward example of thematic analysis and is only included here to establish the nomenclature used subsequently. A simple cross tab operation listing the number of words to which a specific term is coded in each document produces a grid of papers ($P_{1..i..x}$) by terms ($T_{1..n..z}$) with a whole number in each cell (P_i, T_n) of the grid that represents the number of times the term (T_n) appears in the paper (P_i). The maximum, total and average numbers of terms in each paper e.g. Sum(P_i, $T_{1..n..z}$) and occurrences of a term across all papers e.g. Avg($P_{1..i..z}$, T_n) are calculated for potential use in future calculations. The *coverage* of each term is estimated by dividing the frequency of a particular code by the maximum number of words coded in each document. A threshold (in this case, the overall average Avg($P_{1..z}$, $T_{1..z}$)) identifies those concepts that are considered "important" reducing the grid of papers ($P_{1..i..x}$, $T_{1..n..z}$) to the Boolean table shown in Figure 1 in which important concepts are shown by a dark (red/black) pixel.

While this representation of the data is hardly unusual, it is not generally considered important. Researchers collapse, separate, delete and add codes to their initial "open coding" set of data, without documenting or analysing the relationships between codes. Even in bibliometric analysis, which relies totally on the quantitative analysis of the relationships between concepts and papers, the process of refining the original codes is not generally part of the research documentation and reporting, despite the exhortations of (Onwuegbuzie, Leech, & Collins, 2012). In Resonant Correlations, this is the starting point for the arithmetic steps that will reveal the resonance and dissonance between concepts. The visual representation of this process is a precursor to the development of algorithms that would allow its automation as well as an explanatory tool to describe the process.

Sum of Products

We now seek to identify the relevance of each code to the others using a sum of products. As a Boolean function a sum of products resolves a truth table by taking the OR of the minterms in a row to find all the input combinations that produce a 1 output.

Figure 1. Concepts (columns) considered important by papers (rows) typical output of an SQLR (© authors)

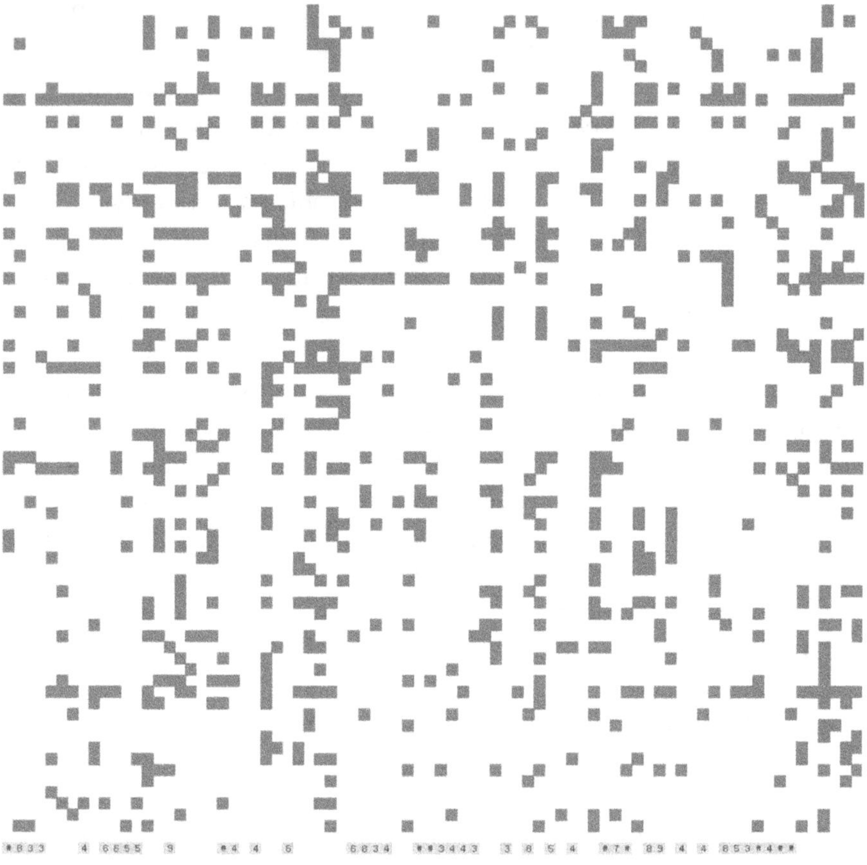

The Excel Sum of Products calculation multiplies (ANDs) the contents of each cell in a pair of columns or rows and adds (ORs) the products together. In this way, it counts the number of times that a 1 occurs in both columns, providing a measure of the correlation between the two concepts.

In this methodology, the sum of products is applied to the grid of papers by tables to correlate the importance of each pair of concepts. The sum of products applied to a pair of columns provides a count of the number of times the two concepts both appear as important in the same paper. Literally =(SUMPRODUCT('Threshhold binary'!P_nT_1:P_nT_z,'Threshhold binary'! P_mT_1:P_mT_z)). This is a perfectly square and symmetrical table of values showing how each correlation is related to itself. Naturally, the diagonal, the relationship between a concept and itself, is the maximum, occurring as many times as the concept. A discussion about the determination of thresholds appears in the section Development and validation, below.

TF-IDF and Directionality

By definition, a sum-of-products produces a symmetrical relationship between any two pair of variables that incorporates a count of the frequency of their occurrence. There are two separate limitations on the usefulness of those data.

One is that the most frequently mentioned concepts may be the most important ones overall but may not be the most significant in determining the differences between conceptual frameworks involved. What we need is a method that isolates those concepts that are mentioned frequently in a subset of documents but not in all documents. This paper refers to that process as "weighting". The relevance of this is that we seek the terms that "differentiate" clusters rather than the terms that are most important. This has similarities to the concept of Total Frequency by Inverse Document Frequency (TF-IDF) which identifies those terms that are notably frequent in a subset of documents as opposed to simply more frequent across the dataset. Note also that TF-IDF identifies the significance of the concept in the population of texts, which is different from its significance among the population of concepts. Note also that we do not employ the term "vectorisation", which has a different meaning in proximity analysis that does not imply directionality.

Because we seek to find clusters of papers with similar concerns, we want to identify whether papers that consider one term important, also consider a set of other terms as important. For example, all research that considers "management tools" and "internal capacity" as important might also be concerned with "business profitability" but the reverse may not be true. "Business profitability" would then operate in the role of "club", grouping "member" categories that are important to that general field of enquiry. We use "club" rather than "parent" because individual members (concepts) may belong to multiple clubs, whereas parental relationships are usually exclusive. That is, the term "parents" assumes a hierarchy of concepts, "clubs" allows for heterarchical relationships. To be truly heterarchical, all concepts are potentially both clubs and members.

Figure 2. A Boolean representation of the weighted inverse hamming distance (WIHD) correlates concepts indicating relative importance. (© authors) Note that it is roughly, but not perfectly symmetrical around the TL/BR diagonal.

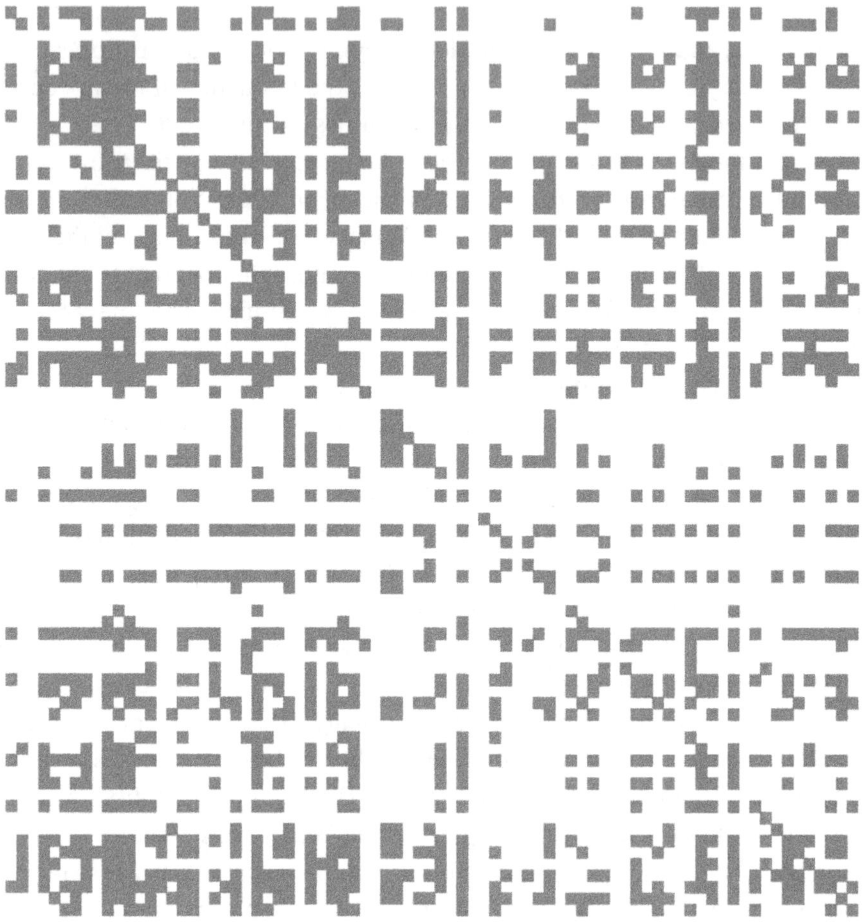

This potential for a bidirectional relationship calls for specific analysis, i.e., for each datapoint that considers term A important, we note whether term B is important and sum the results to determine the importance of term B to term A. We can then compare this outcome to the inverse, are A and B important to each other, or does the importance flow in one direction only. The relevance of this is that we want to prioritise those concepts that are *significant* in establishing differentiation from those concepts that are participatory in differentiation. The common characteristics that define the rules of membership for any given "club" are the findings from this method. It is these relationships that allow us to tease apart the messy relationships that confound traditional methods of analysis.

The method selected to calculate the significance of any given correlation, $Significance(T_n, T_m)$, is $(Correlation(T_n, T_m))^2/(Max(Coverage(T_n, P_{1-x})) * Avg(Coverage(T_{1-z}, P_{1-x})))$ The resulting grid appears in Figure 2 and is referred to below as WIHD for the Weighted Inverse Hamming Distance.

Initial Clustering

All clustering is iterative, and the iterations proceed until some measure of the "strength" of the clustering is considered sufficient, usually because it has plateaued. The holes and clumps in the data displayed in Figure 2, clearly reveal some clusters of concepts. Some will be synonyms that could potentially be grouped together. At this stage we are visually (or arithmetically) identifying these clusters without knowing what concepts are involved, documenting the process of grouping values, and identifying correlations numerically, rather than conceptually, thereby explicitly documenting the assumptions made by the researcher. Figure 4, shows the result of that iterative process.

A detailed discussion of the iterative process used to consolidate the clusters appears in Development and validation, suffice to say that the process is essentially on of refining the sorted data to eliminate as many "holes" as possible.

Interpretation

While the findings of this study are beyond the scope of this article, an overview may assist the reader in grasping the application of this approach. Despite the blurred boundaries, the distinctions between categories with mutually exclusive patterns of "importance" is quite clear. As this chapter appears in colour online and in monochrome in print, the term *Dark* has been used to represent red (online) or black (print), and the term *Shaded* has been used to present blue and green (online) and grey (print). The patterns that define the major clusters in Figure 4 are Cluster1 = Dark, Dark, Dark, Cluster 2 = Dark, Dark, Shaded, and Cluster 3 = Dark, Shaded, Dark. The unshaded areas in Figure 4, show scattered importance (Dark pixels), and the concepts that are considered completely unimportant (White pixels only) have been excluded from the diagram. We will focus on the three areas defined above, identifying the groups of concepts and any differences between the grouping that forms the "club" and its "members".

With the major clusters identified, we can consider the concepts that make up the significant clusters. Club 1 includes the following concepts (Sustainable urban development, governance, power, Networking, Societal transformation, systemic transitions, Business – corporate, Consumption, Green growth. The members of that club include most of those concepts plus culture. The core of Club 2 (that is focusing on the concepts which are not snuggled up next to Group 1) includes: "Resource availability", "Public sector", "sustainable entrepreneurship", "Ecopreneurs & social-enterprise", "External support" and "Localisation". Its rogue members (which are closer to Group 1) are "SMEs", "barriers financial", "intermediaries", and "organisational characteristics". Group 3 predominantly focus on concepts related to food and health with the addition of "business model innovation", "visioning", and "diverse economies". Its membership involves similar concerns, with the exception of "external support" and "drivers and opportunities". Noting the presence of these concepts implies correlation rather than causality, we must turn to a narrative analysis of the text to understand the nature of their relationship.

Figure 3. A primary sort reveals some obvious clusters that can be iteratively refined

That analysis identifies a cluster of concepts that represent systemic concerns about the need for policy on sustainable development and the concerns around delivery of that policy, including implementation by corporations. The next cluster focuses on the concerns of businesses and social enterprises attempting to implement those policies and the final cluster addresses urban food advocates, focused on the role of urban agriculture in contributing to those sustainable transitions. These clusters then can be considered as related to types of organisations: corporations focused on high level policy; government, SMEs, entrepreneurs, and social enterprise are more concerned about the organisational response to problems of implementation. By contrast, the urban food providers and health advocates are primarily focused on the technical and social complexity of producing food in that space, the health and well-being of their customers and the vision and passion for this focus.

Figure 4. After initial sorting, the results are iteratively consolidated and the clusters identified. Only then are the names of the concepts revealed so the analysis can begin.

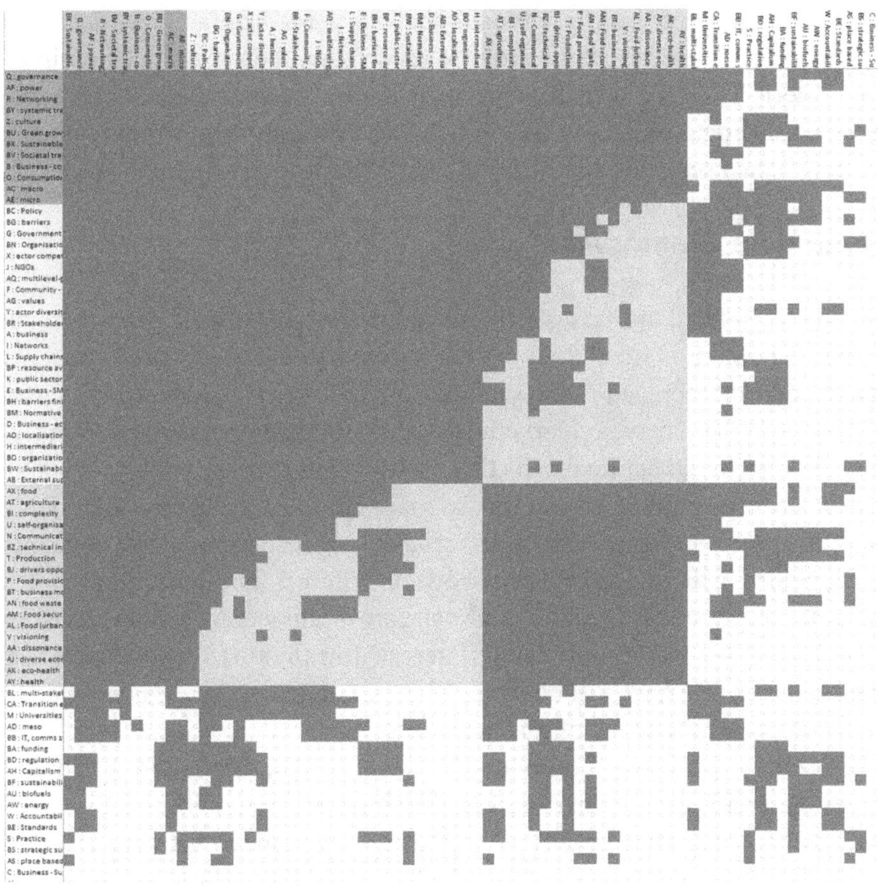

Given that this analysis would likely match the primary observations that would be made by any reader of the set of papers that produced this table it raises the question of what the Resonant Correlations method has added to the process. Not only does it quantitatively and objectively confirm the qualitative findings, but it also reveals configurations that were initially missed by the researcher, as detailed in *Initial Clustering*, below. The initial interpretation identified the major difference between practitioners in for-profit and not-for-profit organisations but did not notice the difference between environmentally-driven small business and social entrepreneurs on one hand, and health advocates and systemic-change advocates on the other. Similarly, the free agents and guerilla groups trying to change the system from the grassroots, were invisible until the clustering was reorganised as discussed under *Comparative cluster analysis* below.

Importantly, we have not yet considered the obvious patterns appearing outside the large, shaded area of Figure 4 that has been our focus up until now. Rather than trying to group those additional, smaller clusters while maintaining our initial focus, it is better to simply focus on them, excluding the clusters we have identified so far. This is an advantage of configurational analysis using heterarchical data. We can simply pick a new starting point and rule for sorting, then seek meaning in the resulting pattern. Thus, we have the capacity to compare two sets of clusters emerging within the same data set. A separate process can be employed to compare clusters between two data sets, but that is the subject of a future paper.

Comparative Cluster Analysis

Having considered the most significant concepts based on the general frequency as a starting point, it is worth looking for patterns within the "spare" concepts, the odds and ends not included in the shaded zone of Figure 4, analysed in the section immediately above. There is clearly the potential for further clustering of these concepts, but its scattered nature means that it is difficult to identify significant blocks of resonance, especially if we attempt to maintain the correlations just identified. To start this process, we can simply re-sort the data, focused on those concepts that are not included in the shaded zone as shown in Figure 5. The conceptual challenges raised by this representation of the same data, are discussed in detail in *Development and validation*, but we are ultimately interested in the differences between these clusters and those we have just observed. Again, a quick overview is provided here, simply to illustrate the value of this approach.

The primary difference in this organisation of concepts is the distribution or the types of organisations considered and the intended outcome. The first cluster is primarily concerned with governance, education, and green growth, and involves government. The second group is concerned with building culture and involves community, SMEs, and NGOs. The third group focuses on values, systemic change, and societal transformation and involves the public sector and universities. Corporates and social enterprise are in the final cluster and consider issues around health, food production, and diverse economies.

What we don't see in this initial, raw sort is the dissonance within the groups. Visually there are lots of stripes indicating mutually exclusive values within each cluster. Sorting within each cluster will produce more meaningful findings. These stripes are a remnant of the previous sort appearing within identical values in the new sort. We provide the initial re-sorting here, to indicate the how a simple arithmetic organisation of the data can reveal the resonance and dissonance in the data.

When we begin to compare the clusters between Figure 4 and Figure 5 it is also apparent that the role of "power", of critical importance to systemic change makers, is also somewhat significant in every other sector. Without this alternative sorting, it would simply be dismissed as a generally important concept that is not useful in distinguishing "clubs" of concepts.

Figure 5. Simply sorting by the number of dark squares in white areas provides a different group of clusters (© authors)

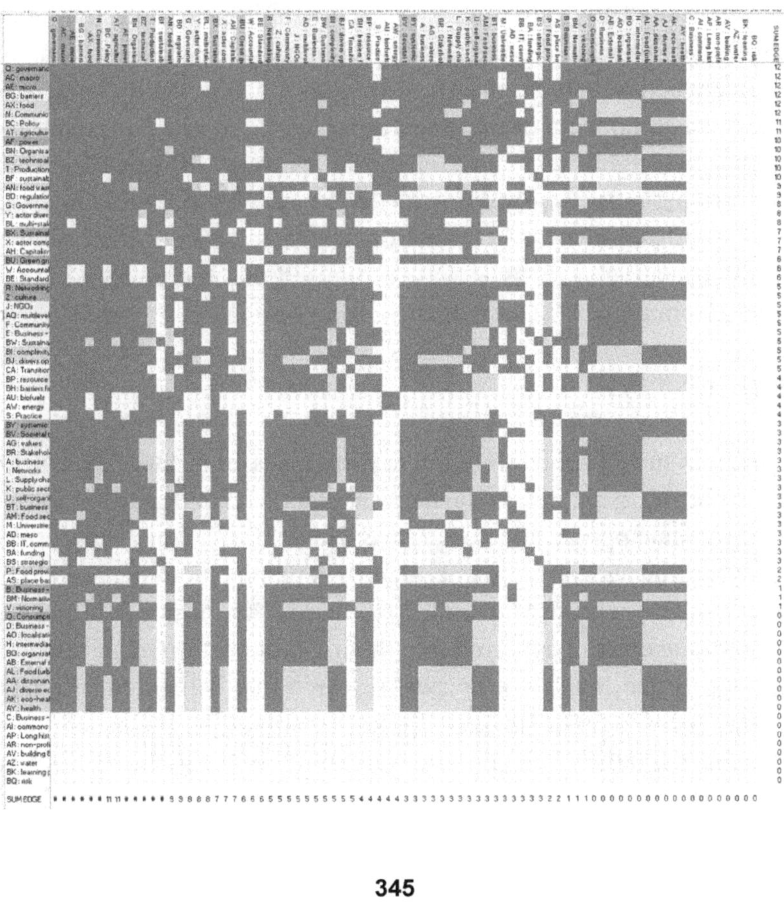

An extended example of the application of this technique is available online (Ebbs, 2023), in which the authors advised the Australian Government on navigating the complex field of competing interests in considering issues approaches to food security in the face of climate change and an increasingly unstable geopolitical environment. While this text and the online example are both qualitative, similar reasoning can be applied, for example, to software management of documents that need to go to multiple people across different groups in a web-based document management system, which rely on a hard-coded rules, as opposed to this somewhat subjective interpretation.

DEVELOPMENT AND VALIDATION

This section of the chapter steps through the process of developing and validating the Resonant Correlations method. It works through the process in the same order that it is performed rather than as it was chronologically developed, and so some examples make use of different data sets.

As previously stated, this research set out to rigorously record the process of thematic analysis, to ensure that the research can be duplicated. This was inspired by Gioia, who noted the importance of documenting the decisions made when collapsing, expanding and deleting codes (Gioia, Corley, & Hamilton, 2013) and Onwuegbuzie who pointed out that the decisions made in the literature review are, in fact, a critical component of the researcher's world view that frames and shapes the research (Onwuegbuzie et al., 2012). That approach led to the development of the algorithms that most simply duplicated the manual process being documented. Because the algorithm revealed correlations between concepts that had been overlooked in the narrative analysis, it was recognised that there was additional value to be derived from the application of these methods.

Background

Research into sustainable development recognises large gaps between the theory and practice (Grubb et al., 2017; Prashar & Sunder M, 2020) partly due to the wide range of theoretical approaches (Sovacool & Hess, 2017), which has resulted in the mapping of research agenda (Köhler et al., 2019) that includes the need for practice-led research (Bijl-Brouwer & Malcolm, 2020; Popa, Guillermin, & Dedeurwaerdere, 2015). A lot of the existing research into the implementation of sustainability transitions is not practice-led, it is empirical research that is theoretically based. As a result, it often focused on the integrity of the theory, or the impact of the transition on the organisation rather than on the sustainability of the global environment. The need for practice-led research, including action research and case studies is that it sets out to build theory from the ground up, identifying "what we don't know we don't know" (Bourner & Simpson, 2005). Despite this, the role of the researcher in action case studies is rarely uninformed by theory (Halecker, 2015) and, in fact, the practitioner may expect and actively seek knowledge from the researcher (Gibson-Graham & ProQuest, 2006). It is therefore important that there be a methodology that can cope with the complex, interdependent, multivariate nature of sustainability and effectively capture the themes emerging from the theoretical research, the theoretically-based research into practice, and the practice-led research.

Sparsely populated, heterarchical matrices are one tool for analysing complexity without enforcing a positivist order upon the data (Peter & Swilling, 2014). There is some overlap with Serin's mapping of the urban development literature (Serin, 2018, p. 1) whose approach provides a worked example of the way in which the typology emerging from the SQLR of sustainability transitions frameworks can be used to frame the disparate literature studying SME responses to sustainability.

Indeed, the SQLR methodology (Pickering & Byrne, 2014) uses a set of columns with binary values identifying whether each paper in the review has or has not a specific characteristic. As these concepts are initially not related or grouped, it is inherently heterarchical, multi-value and scalable. It can also be sparsely populated, so does not require a response to every variable for every item (in this case, research paper) under consideration. Importantly, it conceptually matches the approach taken by text-coding applications such as nVivo.

This research, then, began with a systematic literature review and then sought ways to build a typology of concepts contained in that literature that could be used as the basis of comparative cluster analysis with a similar typology of concepts formed from surveys and interviews with practitioners.

Quantifying Systemic Literature Reviews

The methodology was developed using data from the coding of papers using a systematic literature review, to the synthesis of a taxonomy following Gioia (Gioia et al., 2013) and then the failure of "off the shelf" cluster analysis to reveal any particular grouping of papers.

A series of trial-and-error experiments was undertaken until meaningful clusters appeared, and then the assumptions made during those trials were individually tested through further experiments to isolate and remove subjective manipulation of the process to subjectively create outcomes useful for the broader research.

The methods employed in the approach were then analysed and substitutes trialled to further refine test and strengthen the process. While each variation of the method produces small variations in the contents of the cluster, it was considered relatively unimportant to examine those differences in detail while developing the method. Those differences are explored in *Testing the methodology*, below.

Once a robust, repeatable, and verifiable method was laid out, the results were then examined for resonance and dissonance with the qualitative analysis. The details of that comparison are beyond the scope of this paper, but the findings are relevant to identify potential benefits and shortcomings of this methodology. This section discusses in detail the evolution of each method described above, with an overview of the precursors to developing the method.

Precursors

The approach of this research was informed by a review of the literature researching theoretical frameworks that describe the process of transforming industry and society to achieve sustainable development. Some researchers in the "Sustainable Transitions" field had already researched the frequency of various concepts and identified relationships between them as a way of grouping the papers, theories, and outcomes (Ljungkvist & Andersén, 2021; Sovacool & Hess, 2017). Sovacool uses a frequency analysis to group and organise theories, Ljungkvist uses comparative cluster analysis to identify cultural approaches to sustainability in business and strategies that are relevant to each approach. Kuokkannen identified similar cultural responses using a qualitative analysis of a variety of research examining disruptive innovation in the food sustainability space (Kuokkanen, Uusitalo, & Koistinen, 2019).

These various approaches and their convergent findings indicated both the relevance of the enquiry and the potential of comparative cluster analysis. While Kuokkanen used qualitative analysis alone to provide insights into the field, the potential of quantitative methods to reveal relationships that are not obvious in a qualitative analysis was sufficient temptation to develop the hypothesis that clusters of concepts across different populations of text might reveal meaning that would otherwise be difficult to pinpoint or justify. The other tempting prize available from a quantitative process is the potential automation of the extraction of meaning through studying conceptual relationships. A key component in this is establishing some measure of "importance".

Crosstabs

A cross tab of the number of references for nVivo was used as a proxy for importance during the development of the methodology with the following considerations.

nVivo offers an output of the percentage of text coded by each concept, rather than a count of the number of paragraphs coded to each concept. That percentage was not used to calculate "coverage" as there is a large discrepancy between texts with large portions of uncoded end matter and those with none. That discrepancy is removed by comparing each code with the maximum number of paragraphs coded. The assumption is that there will generally be one code which applies to the vast bulk of the article. That could be standardised in a formal application of the methodology by introducing a variable coding all paragraphs determined as relevant. This would not be available when the analysis is applied to existing datasets coded by other researchers and so was not adopted as a standard.

Initially, the coverage of the concept in each paper was reduced to a binary important/unimportant using an arbitrary threshold adjusted to get between one third and two thirds of the correlations considered as important. After some trial and error this was refined by using the average of all concepts across all papers as the threshold, which provided reasonable results in all the datasets used in the trials. Importantly, the adjustment of the threshold fine tunes rather than alters the outcome. It has a focusing impact on the results, bringing more or less detail into view, rather than changing the correlations that emerge.

Sum of Products

To identify the number of times any two concepts were both considered in the same paper across all papers in the population, a sum of products calculation was used. This results in a totally symmetric count correlating the concepts to each other that emphasises the most frequently occurring concepts because they occur most often and so, naturally, are more likely to correlate. This led to a significant investigation into the weighting of correlations and a separate investigation into the directionality of importance, which are discussed below.

Again, the arbitrary nature of thresholds emerged as significant. To avoid an arbitrary threshold, we trialled calculating the sum of products using the raw count of each term in each paper. This created similar patterns in the correlations but also produced anomalies as shown in Figure 6 and so could not be skipped. The key highlighted cells show that using raw integers to calculate the sum of products indicates that, when weighted, some concepts appear to be more important to a given concept than itself, which is clearly illogical.

Directionality and Weighting

The weighting of correlations to determine the relative importance is subtle but important. A worked example outlines the concept. In this example, four papers discuss four concepts; two of them relating to fruit and two relating to the vendor. The numbers in each of the three steps shown in Table 1, indicate respectively the number of times each paper mentions the concept, the number of times the two terms are both considered as important (> average), then the percentage of times a paper considering one concept important (the column) considers the other important (the row). This is referred to in the remainder of this document as "simple weighting".

Table 1. Sample of correlating co-located concepts

	Apple	Orange	Supermarket	Farmers markets
Mentions per paper				
Fruits of the world	9	7	2	1
Sales of fruits	7	6	9	7
The power of the supermarket	1	0	9	4
The rise of the farmer's market	5	1	5	9
The number of references to four terms in four papers				
Raw count (papers)				
Apple	3	2	2	2
Orange	2	2	1	0
Supermarket	2	1	3	2
Farmers market	2	1	2	2
The co-location of important (>4) terms across the papers				
% weighted				
Apple	100	100	66	100
Orange	66	100	33	0
Supermarket	66	50	100	100
Farmers market	66	50	66	100

Simple weighting by the number of times the column considers the row important

Figure 6. Using raw numbers rather than counting values above a threshold leads to perverse outcomes

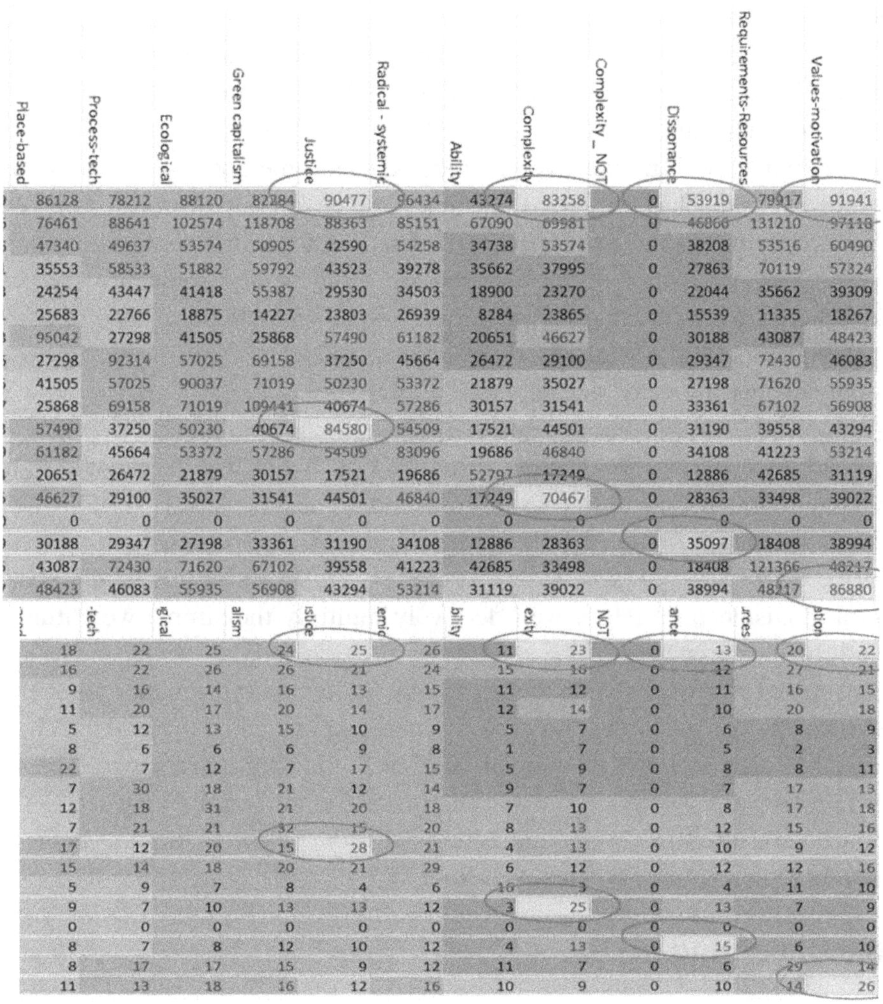

Place-based	Process-tech	Ecological	Green capitalism	Justice	Radical - systemic	Ability	Complexity	Complexity _ NOT	Dissonance	Requirements-Resources	Values-motivation
86128	78212	88120	82284	90477	96434	43274	83258	0	53919	79917	91941
76461	88641	102574	118708	88363	85151	67090	69981	0	46866	131210	97118
47340	49637	53574	50905	42590	54258	34738	53574	0	38208	53516	60490
35553	58533	51882	59792	43523	39278	35662	37995	0	27863	70119	57324
24254	43447	41418	55387	29530	34503	18900	23270	0	22044	35662	39309
25683	22766	18875	14227	23803	26939	8284	23865	0	15539	11335	18267
95042	27298	41505	25868	57490	61182	20651	46627	0	30188	43087	48423
27298	92314	57025	69158	37250	45664	26472	29100	0	29347	72430	46083
41505	57025	90037	71019	50230	53372	21879	35027	0	27198	71620	55935
25868	69158	71019	109441	40674	57286	30157	31541	0	33361	67102	56908
57490	37250	50230	40674	84580	54509	17521	44501	0	31190	39558	43294
61182	45664	53372	57286	54509	83096	19686	46840	0	34108	41223	53214
20651	26472	21879	30157	17521	19686	52797	17249	0	12886	42685	31119
46627	29100	35027	31541	44501	46840	17249	70467	0	28363	33498	39022
0	0	0	0	0	0	0	0	0	0	0	0
30188	29347	27198	33361	31190	34108	12886	28363	0	35097	18408	38994
43087	72430	71620	67102	39558	41223	42685	33498	0	18408	121366	48217
48423	46083	55935	56908	43294	53214	31119	39022	0	38994	48217	86880

...ased	-tech	...gical	...alism	...stice	...emic	...bility	...exity	NOT	...ance	...rces	...ation
18	22	25	24	25	26	11	23	0	13	20	22
16	22	26	26	21	24	15	16	0	12	27	21
9	16	14	16	13	15	11	12	0	11	16	15
11	20	17	20	14	17	12	14	0	10	20	18
5	12	13	15	10	9	5	7	0	6	8	9
8	6	6	6	9	8	1	7	0	5	2	3
22	7	12	7	17	15	5	9	0	8	8	11
7	30	18	21	12	14	9	7	0	7	17	13
12	18	31	21	20	18	7	10	0	8	17	18
7	21	21	32	15	20	8	13	0	12	15	16
17	12	20	15	28	21	4	13	0	10	9	12
15	14	18	20	21	29	6	12	0	12	12	16
5	9	7	8	4	6	16	3	0	4	11	10
9	7	10	13	13	12	3	25	0	13	7	9
0	0	0	0	0	0	0	0	0	0	0	0
8	7	8	12	10	12	4	13	0	15	6	10
8	17	17	15	9	12	11	7	0	6	29	14
11	13	18	16	12	16	10	9	0	10	14	26

Thus, we see that all papers that treat oranges as important also consider apples important, but the reverse is not true. Only 66% of the papers that consider apples significant have the same view of oranges. Similarly, the papers that focus on supermarkets appear to consider apples and farmers markets as somewhat significant but rarely mention oranges, whereas supermarkets are considered important in most papers that discuss either fruit. Supermarkets are also considered significant in all papers that discuss farmers markets. In this paper we refer to the columns as the "clubs", which focus on certain "members". As prolific members belonging to many clubs, the concepts of apples and supermarkets are not particularly useful as pointers to specific areas of interest.

This is a trivial example designed to show the approach for calculating weighted importance. As such it does not reveal any correlations between the configuration of the importance. At best, you might cluster the vendors and the types of produce more successfully than you would through simply examining the papers.

Having established the concept of weighting correlations to determine directionality of importance, it remained to establish a useful method of consistently doing so. Multiple approaches were tried, starting with the raw correlation as a percentage of the maximum (as shown in Table 1.). One reason for adding a weighting factor at all, regardless of directionality, is that concepts that occur infrequently (remember that frequency is a percentage of mentions, not an absolute number) will correlate with themselves (and potentially other concepts) 100 percent of the time even if they only appear in one or two papers.

An indication of this bias appears in Table 1, which rates Apples as important as supermarkets in all concepts excepts supermarkets themselves. Because of this, it is worth maintaining some emphasis on frequency. Thus, the squaring of the denominator in the final formula. WIHD = Significance$(T_n, T_m) = (Correlation(T_n, T_m))^2 / (Max(Coverage(T_{n,} P_{1\text{-}x})) * Avg(Coverage(T_{1\text{-}z}, P_{1\text{-}x})))$. To obtain the Weighted Inverse Hamming Distance (WIHD), we effectively multiply the simple weighting from Table 1, by the percentage of the specific correlation and then divide it by the table wide average (effectively using that as a constant to maintain smaller numbers). To determine that this is optimal, multiple formulae were applied to raw data, clustered using kMeans clustering and compared to each other for consistency. The results of this process are shown in Figure 7 and discussed in the following section. Most approaches resulted in similar outcomes, with the selected formula being more consistent than any of the others.

Initial Clustering

Initially, kMeans clustering was employed to determine clusters of correlations. That did not reflect the qualitative findings found in the initial thematic analysis. Going back to first principles, we recognised that we sought some method of identifying the patterns of correlations that stood out as being mutually exclusive. The first version of this process involved manually selecting columns that contained rows with similar “stripes”. Having identified those columns that “resonated”, we could then identify other columns with the opposite “stripes” and were therefore “dissonant”. We emphasised this by ignoring those rows that did not visually support the clustering. The repetition and refinement of this process eventually led to the process described above.

Along the way, kMeans clustering provided a quick method of comparing formulae, and comparing the application of the final clusters back to the texts. Three different methods of applying the clusters of concepts to the tests were employed as part of this testing. One method simply used kMeans clustering of the texts. Another sorted the texts using the average of the frequencies of concepts in each cluster and then graded them against calculated the average of the values of the same cluster in the WHID. A third used the Hamming Distance between the text and the average of the cluster. The results portrayed a similar pattern with internal variations.

A tabulation of these different methods and their results is shown in Figure 7, below. The texts appear in the left-hand block with the percentage coverage for each concept identifying most frequent and somewhat frequent in pink/dark grey and yellow/light grey. The three columns in the centre of the diagram show the "clubs" of concepts used to distinguish clusters according to colour. The dark (red/black) cells in this diagram are of low importance, the shaded (green/grey) cells are of high importance. White cells are neutral. The patters are cluster one shaded/shaded/shaded, cluster two shaded/dark/dark. Cluster 3 mixed/dark/mixed, Cluster 4 mixed/dark/dark and Cluster 5 dark/dark/dark. A sixth cluster mixed/mixed/dark emerged during this analysis, which was quite exciting as it was a finding missed in the qualitative analysis, that emerged from a manual selection of three clusters involving only ten concepts.

To the right of the three clubs is a faint, single column that represents the kMeans clusters identified in the WIHD and used to colour code the titles of the texts in the left-hand column. Note that kMeans clustering did not identify the sixth cluster! Note also that the boundaries between the middle three clusters are somewhat soft; similar to what we have seen in the application of the final method.

The three groups of four columns to the right of Figure 7, identify the correlation between the frequency of references to concepts in the text, with the method of weighting the WIHD and the method of calculating "closeness" of the text to the cluster in which it has been placed. Green indicates a strong correlation, white some correlation and red very poor correlation. We see that there is almost no red in the left-hand edges of the two right hand columns. This confirms the validity of the chosen formula for weighting, and a greater accuracy for manually calculating the correlation. As the Hamming Distance produces a result, almost as good, and is fully automated, we nominate it as the preferred method for grouping texts based on the results of the final clusters. This is based on the long-term view that this method will be useful for automated analysis of large data sets.

Having discussed the process of validating and selecting the weighting method and approaches to clustering, it is important to pay attention to some details of the semi-manual process of iteratively refining the clusters. The process used to go from Figure 2 to Figure 3 is relatively straightforward and can be simply automated. There remain some arbitrary aspects of the process, however.

The iterative process employed in this example was semi manual as we work toward defining the optimal algorithm. One method of doing this is to identify the most "significant" holes by counting the number of white squares within the upper left triangle and then sorting on the variable. This quickly consolidates the upper left triangle (and conversely can be used to consolidate the lower right, white triangle), the other method focuses on those groups of holes that occur most commonly. After one or two applications of these rules to an overall sorting, we continued to apply human judgement to "tidy up the edges".

Note that there is an arbitrary selection for the starting point, which becomes the intersection between the first and second triangle. Similarly, there is a blurring of the boundaries between clusters because of the untidy nature of the "edges". There is also a limit to the capacity to tidy up the edges. This is apparent when we reach the point when each change we make introduces as many "holes" as it closes. For example, the dark (red/black) square that appears in two shaded (blue/grey) rectangles could be moved up and left to place them into the triangular block of dark pixels but that simply creates a new cluster of orphans that sit in the shaded rectangle. Thus, there is no significance to where the exceptions sit within a cluster, simply that these concepts blur the line between the distinct clusters.

Figure 7. A tabulation of four different methods of clustering concepts verified against texts (© authors)

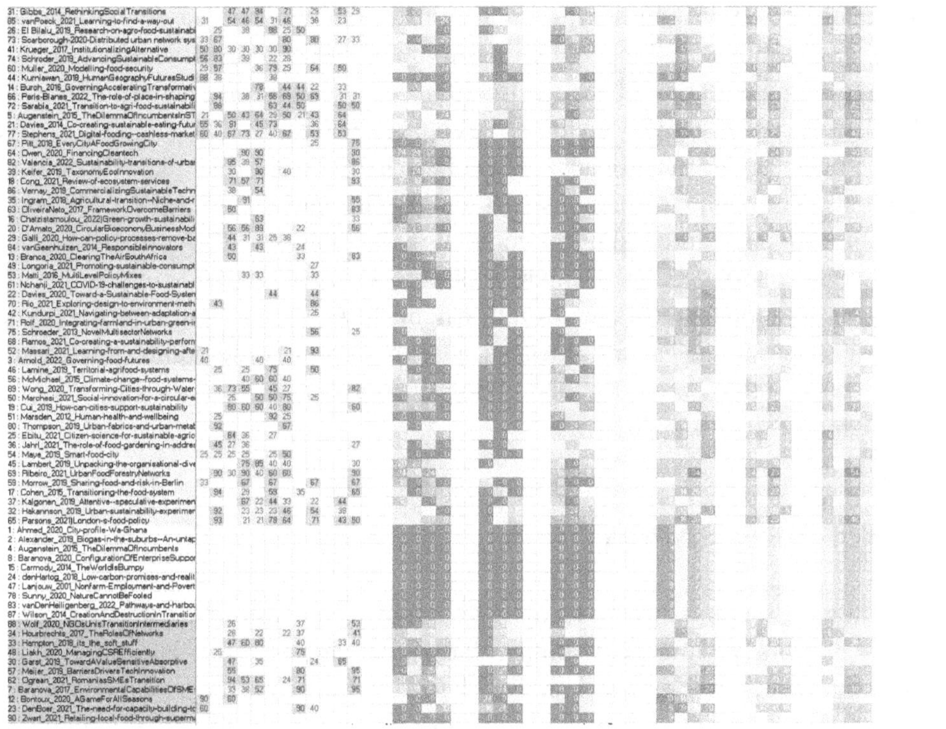

While there is the requirement to draw a line between clusters, and acknowledgement that such a line will be arbitrary, it is important to remember that in configurational analysis we can focus on those "clubs" and "members" that are distinct, i.e., that are completely resonant internally and dissonant externally and use them to drive the clustering of research subjects (whether that is arithmetic by Hamming Distance, or visually by colour coding). Such an approach would provide clarity and the expense of inclusion. It would identify those examples (in this case, papers) that closely resonated with the cluster and ignore those on the edges.

The fact that variables exist that do not exhibit this clear distinction does not reduce the value of the analysis, it simply identifies those concepts that might help bridge the gap between two groups that have some mutually exclusive principles, by identifying areas where their concerns overlap. The appropriate application of the method will depend on the nature of the research.

Comparative Cluster Analysis

Figure 5 presents conceptual challenges that reveal important characteristics of this approach. If we begin to group the clusters shown here based on their colour, for example moving all the white lines to be near each other, then we simply drift back toward a variation of Figure 4, with resulting similarity between the clusters. Thus, we focus exclusively on the white columns and rows, to avoid this convergence on the major points of resonance. This tendency indicates that, like other clustering methods, Resonant Correlations will tend to find the major clusters aligned with overall frequency and assign the remaining datapoints to a cluster based on their relative unimportance. It is a feature of this process that the small clusters that feature in Figure 5 contribute to our overall insight. In fact, this method explicitly seeks the exceptions to the general rules, because they identify the points of tension – the dissonance – that reveal the underlying friction between various points of view (Houghton & Tuffley, 2015).

FUTURE RESEARCH

The scope of this paper and the analysis it outlines is restricted to the identification of the clusters of concepts within an individual dataset. The opportunity exists to perform a comparative cluster analysis between the resonant correlations that occur in different data sets. Thus we might contribute to meta studies of large data sets that measure different values and so cannot be directly compared by comparing the clustering of those values where appropriate. This capacity is a function of the use of a sparse matrix to store heterarchical data, allowing for configurational analysis of the common elements. That expands the possibility of dealing with more complex inputs in which different variables have been interrogated in different ways, but there are sufficient values in common to identify resonance and dissonance between the data sets.

This approach can be also extended to "on-the-fly" search algorithms, where a data set can be potentially filtered through iterative adjustments to the relative significance of various concepts as the user rates individual pieces of content. The high-level algorithm for such an approach would involve iterative filtering and recalculation of the significant concepts, using a simple "Tinder-like" swipe-right or swipe-left approach, to determine relevance, along with the injection of small numbers of random papers to avoid "in-breeding", and the iterative analysis of rejected papers to provide a useful adjunct to the major process.

DECLARATIONS

Compliance With Ethical Standards

Ethics Approval

The data was collected in compliance with the University Ethics Policy and approved under the University Ethics Committee ref 2021/284.

Consent to Participate

The subjects were provided with information about the process and use of their information and agreed in writing prior to participating.

Consent to Publish

The subjects gave permission for their responses to the survey and interviews in which they participated to be published anonymously as part of the research findings.

Funding

No external funding was provided to carry out the research.

The authors declare that they have no financial or non-financial interests in this research.

The corresponding author has subsequently joined the Board of a company related to one of the participants in the survey in an honorary capacity which is complementary to the research and represents no conflict of interest.

Availability of Data and Materials

Anonymised and normalised research data is available to other researchers via email request from the corresponding author.

REFERENCES

Bijl-Brouwer, M., & Malcolm, B. (2020). Systemic Design Principles in Social Innovation: A Study of Expert Practices and Design Rationales. *She Ji: The Journal of Design, Economics, and Innovation*, 6(3), 386–407. DOI:10.1016/j.sheji.2020.06.001

Bourner, T., & Simpson, P. (2005). Practitioner-centred research and the Ph.D. *Action Learning*, 2(2), 133–151. DOI:10.1080/14767330500206789

Ebbs, G. (2018). *Visualising database content using Metadata* (Masters Interactive Media Exegesis). Griffith University, Brisbane, Australia. Retrieved from https://github.com/giobono/metadex/blob/master/GEbbs_s2980212_Exegesis.pdf

Ebbs, G. (2023). *Analysis of submissions to Food Security Inquiry*. Retrieved from Canberra Australia: https://www.aph.gov.au/DocumentStore.ashx?id=34221367-8589-40fe-a628-07b47ccb435f&subId=744530

Gibson-Graham, J. K. (2006). *A postcapitalist politics*. Minneapolis: University of Minnesota Press.

Gioia, D. A., Corley, K. G., & Hamilton, A. L. (2013). Seeking Qualitative Rigor in Inductive Research: Notes on the Gioia Methodology. *Organizational Research Methods*, 16(1), 15–31. DOI:10.1177/1094428112452151

Göpel, M. (2016). *The Great Mindshift*. Retrieved from https://resolver.ebscohost.com/Redirect/PRL?EPPackageLocationID=4476.11747448.43334445&epcustomerid=s2947694

Grubb, M., McDowall, W., & Drummond, P. (2017). On order and complexity in innovations systems: Conceptual frameworks for policy mixes in sustainability transitions. *Energy Research & Social Science*, 33, 21–34. DOI:10.1016/j.erss.2017.09.016

Halecker, B. (2015). Action case study - A research strategy based on abduction for relevant and rigorous management research. *International Journal of Business Research, 15*(4), 23-32. DOI:10.18374/IJBR-15-4.3

Houghton, L., & Tuffley, D. (2015). Towards a Methodology of Wicked Problem Exploration through Concept Shifting and Tension Point Analysis. *Systems Research and Behavioral Science*, 32(3), 283–297. DOI:10.1002/sres.2223

Kelly, G. A. (1977). Personal construct theory and the psychotherapeutic interview. *Cognitive Therapy and Research*, 1(4), 355–362. DOI:10.1007/BF01663999

Köhler, J., Geels, F. W., Kern, F., Markard, J., Onsongo, E., Wieczorek, A., Alkemade, F., Avelino, F., Bergek, A., Boons, F., Fünfschilling, L., Hess, D., Holtz, G., Hyysalo, S., Jenkins, K., Kivimaa, P., Martiskainen, M., McMeekin, A., Mühlemeier, M. S., & Wells, P. (2019). An agenda for sustainability transitions research: State of the art and future directions. *Environmental Innovation and Societal Transitions*, 31, 1–32. DOI:10.1016/j.eist.2019.01.004

Korucuk, S., Demir, E., Karamasa, C., & Stević, Ž. (2020). *Determining the dimensions of the innovation ability in logistics sector by using plithogenic-critic method: An application in Sakarya Province*. Academic Press.

Kuokkanen, A., Uusitalo, V., & Koistinen, K. (2019). A framework of disruptive sustainable innovation: An example of the Finnish food system. *Technology Analysis and Strategic Management*, 31(7), 749–764. DOI:10.1080/09537325.2018.1550254

Ljungkvist, T., & Andersén, J. (2021). A taxonomy of ecopreneurship in small manufacturing firms: A multidimensional cluster analysis. *Business Strategy and the Environment*, 30(2), 1374–1388. DOI:10.1002/bse.2691

Onwuegbuzie, A. J., Leech, N. L., & Collins, K. M. T. (2012). Qualitative analysis techniques for the review of the literature. *Qualitative Report, 17*(28), 1. Retrieved from https://go.exlibris.link/HY73SsLl

Peter, C., & Swilling, M. (2014). Linking complexity and sustainability theories: Implications for modeling sustainability transitions. *Sustainability (Basel)*, 6(3), 1594–1622. DOI:10.3390/su6031594

Pickering, C., & Byrne, J. (2014). The benefits of publishing systematic quantitative literature reviews for PhD candidates and other early-career researchers. *Higher Education Research & Development*, 33(3), 534–548. DOI:10.1080/07294360.2013.841651

Popa, F., Guillermin, M., & Dedeurwaerdere, T. (2015). A pragmatist approach to transdisciplinarity in sustainability research: From complex systems theory to reflexive science. *Futures*, 65, 45–56. DOI:10.1016/j.futures.2014.02.002

Prashar, A., & Sunder M, V. (2020). A bibliometric and content analysis of sustainable development in small and medium-sized enterprises. *Journal of Cleaner Production, 245*. DOI:10.1016/j.jclepro.2019.118665

Smarandache, F. (2005). *A unifying field in logics: neutrosophic logic. Neutrosophy, neutrosophic set, neutrosophic probability: neutrsophic logic. Neutrosophy, neutrosophic set, neutrosophic probability*. Infinite Study.

Sovacool, B. K., & Hess, D. J. (2017). Ordering theories: Typologies and conceptual frameworks for sociotechnical change. *Social Studies of Science*, 47(5), 703–750. DOI:10.1177/0306312717709363 PMID:28641502

UNESA. (2023). *Global Sustainable Development Report 2023: Times of crisis, times of change: Science for accelerating transformations to sustainable development*. DOI:10.5281/zenodo.3951672

Compilation of References

Abbas, M., Murtaza, G., & Smarandache, F. (2020). *Basic operations on hypersoft sets and hypersoft point.Neutrosophic Sets and Systems, 35*(1), 407-421.

Abdel-Basset, M., Smarandache, F., & Ye, J. (2019). Special issue on "Applications of neutrosophic theory in decision making-recent advances and future trends". *Complex & Intelligent Systems*, 5(4), 363–364. DOI:10.1007/s40747-019-00127-1

Abd, K., Abhary, K., & Marian, R. (2013). Application of Fuzzy Logic to Multi-Objective Scheduling Problems in Robotic Flexible Assembly Cells. *Automation Control and Intelligent Systems.*, 1(3), 34–4. DOI:10.11648/j.acis.20130103.11

Abobala, M., Bal, M., & Hatip, A. (2021). A Review On Recent Advantages In Algebraic Theory Of Neutrosophic Matrices. *International Journal of Neutrosophic Science*, 68-86.

Abobala, M. (2021a). On the representation of neutrosophic matrices by neutrosophic linear transformations. *Journal of Mathematics*, 2021, 1–5. DOI:10.1155/2021/5591576

Abobala, M. (2021b). On refined neutrosophic matrices and their application in refined neutrosophic algebraic equations. *Journal of Mathematics*, 2021, 1–5. DOI:10.1155/2021/5531093

Afzal. (2023). New Statistical Methodology for Capacitor Data Analysis via LCR Meter. *Neutrosphic System With Applications, 8*, 26-34. Doi.org/10.61356/j.nsw .2023.19

Agrawal, A., Stehlé, S., & Yadav, A. (2022). Round-optimal lattice-based threshold signatures, revisited. *49th EATCS International Conference on Automata, Languages, and Programming*.

Ahmad, M. R., Saeed, M., Afzal, U., & Yang, M. S. (2020). A novel MCDM method based on plithogenic hypersoft sets under fuzzy neutrosophic environment. *Symmetry*, 12(11), 1855. DOI:10.3390/sym12111855

Ahsan-ul-Haq, M. (2022). Neutrosophic Kumaraswamy Distribution with Engineering Application. *Neutrosophic Sets and Systems*, 49(1), 17.

Ajay, D., & Chellamani, P. (2020). Pythagorean neutrosophic fuzzy graphs. *International Journal of Neutrosophic Science*, 11(2), 108–114.

Ajay, D., Karthiga, S., & Chellamani, P. (2021). A study on labelling of pythagorean neutrosophic fuzzy graphs. *Journal of Computational Mathematics*, 5(1), 105–116. DOI:10.26524/cm97

Akram, M., Koam, A. N. A., & Liu, P. (2020). Decision-Making Analysis Based on Fuzzy Graph Structures. *Hindawi Mathematical Problems in Engineering*.

Akram, M., & Akmal, R. (2016). operations on Intuitionistic Fuzzy Graph Structures. *Fuzzy Inf.Eng*, 8(4), 389–410. DOI:10.1016/j.fiae.2017.01.001

Akram, M., Amjad, U., Alcantud, J. C. R., & Santos-García, G. (2023). Complex fermatean fuzzy N-soft sets: A new hybrid model with applications. *Journal of Ambient Intelligence and Humanized Computing*, 14(7), 8765–8798. DOI:10.1007/s12652-021-03629-4 PMID:35136452

Akram, M., Bashir, A., & Samanta, S. (2020). Article. *International Journal of Applied and Computational Mathematics*, 6–58.

Akram, M., Bibi, R., & Deveci, M. (2023). An outranking approach with 2-tuple linguistic Fermatean fuzzy sets for multi-attribute group decision-making. *Engineering Applications of Artificial Intelligence*, 121, 105992. DOI:10.1016/j.engappai.2023.105992

Akram, M., & Naz, S. (2019). A Novel Decision-Making Approach under Complex Pythagorean Fuzzy Environment. *Mathematical & Computational Applications*, 24(3), 73. DOI:10.3390/mca24030073

Akram, M., Sattar, A., Karaaslan, F., & Samanta, S. (2021). Extension of competition graphs under complex fuzzy environment. *Complex & Intelligent Systems*, 7(1), 539–558. DOI:10.1007/s40747-020-00217-5

Akram, , & Sarwar, . (2017a). Novel multiple criteria decision making methods based on bipolar neutrosophic sets and bipolar neutrosophic graphs. *International Journal of Pure and Applied Mathematics*, 38, 368–389.

Akram, , & Sarwar, . (2017b). Bipolar neutrosophic graph structures. *J. Indones. Math. Soc*, 23(1), 55–76.

Alenezi, M., Wardat, S., & Akour, M. (2023). The Need of Integrating Digital Education in Higher Education: Challenges and Opportunities. *Sustainability (Basel)*, 15(6), 4782. DOI:10.3390/su15064782

Alhabib, R., Ranna, M. M., Farah, H., & Salama, A. (2018). Some neutrosophic probability distributions. *Neutrosophic Sets and Systems*, 22, 30–38.

Alhasan, K. F. H., & Smarandache, F. (n.d.). *Neutrosophic Weibull distribution and neutrosophic family Weibull distribution*. Infinite Study.

Ali, Dat, Son, Smarandache. (2018). Interval Complex Neutrosophic Set: Formulationand Applications in Decision-Making. *Int. J. Fuzzy Syst, 20*(3).

Ali, M. I., Feng, F., Liu, X., Min, W. K., & Shabir, M. (2009). On some new operations in soft set theory. *Computers & Mathematics with Applications (Oxford, England)*, 57(9), 1547–1553. DOI:10.1016/j.camwa.2008.11.009

Alkouri, A., & Salleh, A. (2012). Complex intuitionistic fuzzy sets. *AIP Conference Proceedings*, 14, 464–470. DOI:10.1063/1.4757515

Alm, S., Låftman, S. B., Sandahl, J., & Modin, B. (2019). School effectiveness and students' future orientation: A multilevel analysis of upper secondary schools in Stockholm, Sweden. *Journal of Adolescence*, 70(1), 62–73. DOI:10.1016/j.adolescence.2018.11.007 PMID:30544017

Al-Odhari, A. (2023). Some Algebraic Structure of Neutrosophic Matrices. *Prospects for Applied Mathematics and data Analysis (PAMDA), 1*(2), 37-44.

Al-Omeri, W. F., & Smarandache, F. (2016). New Neutrosophic Sets via Neutrosophic Topological Spaces. *New Trends in Neutrosophic Theory and Applications*, (2), 1–10.

Al-Quran, A., & Hassan, N. (2018). The complex neutrosophic soft expert relation and its multiple attribute decision-making method. *Entropy (Basel, Switzerland)*, 20(2), 101. DOI:10.3390/e20020101 PMID:33265192

Anandhkumar, M., Kamalakannan, V., Chithra, S. M., & Said, B. (2023). Pseudo Similarity of Neutrosophic Fuzzy matrices. In *International Journal of Neutrosophic Science* (Vol. 20, Issue 4, pp. 191–196). DOI:10.54216/IJNS.200415

Angel, N., Pandiammal, P., Gandhi, N. R., Martin, N., & Smarandache, F. (2023). PCM with Linguistic Contradiction Degree Representations in Decision making on Academic Stress causing Factors. *International Journal of Neutrosophic Science*, 21(3), 126–26. DOI:10.54216/IJNS.210312

Antony Crispin Sweety, C., & Jansi, R., R. (2021). Fermatean Neutrosophic Sets. *International Journal of Advanced Research in Computer and Communication Engineering*, 10(6), 24–27.

Arumugam, S., & Velammal, S. (1998). Edge domination in graphs. *Taiwanese Journal of Mathematics*, 2(2), 177–196. DOI:10.11650/twjm/1500406930

Asim Basha, M., Mohammed Jabarulla, M., & Broumi, S. (2023). Neutrosophic Pythagorean Fuzzy Shortest Path in a Network. *Journal of Neutrosophic and Fuzzy Systems*, 6(1), 21–28. DOI:10.54216/JNFS.060103

Aslam, M. (2019). Neutrosophic analysis of variance: Application to university students. *Complex & Intelligent Systems*, 5(4), 403–407. DOI:10.1007/s40747-019-0107-2

Aslam, M. (2021a). Analyzing wind power data using analysis of means under neutrosophic statistics. *Soft Computing*, 25(10), 7087–7093. DOI:10.1007/s00500-021-05661-0

Aslam, M. (2021b). Neutrosophic statistical test for counts in climatology. *Scientific Reports*, 11(1), 1–5. DOI:10.1038/s41598-021-97344-x PMID:34497328

Aslam, M. (2021c). A study on skewness and kurtosis estimators of wind speed distribution under indeterminacy. *Theoretical and Applied Climatology*, 143(3), 1227–1234. DOI:10.1007/s00704-020-03509-5

Aslam, M. A. (2020). *Neutrosophic Rayleigh distribution with some basic properties and application. In Neutrosophic Sets in Decision Analysis and Operations Research.* IGI Global.

Aslam, M., Khan, N., & Al-Marshadi, A. H. (2019). Design of variable sampling plan for pareto distribution using neutrosophic statistical interval method. *Symmetry*, 11(1), 80. DOI:10.3390/sym11010080

Atanassove, K. T., & Gargov, G. (1989). Interval valued intuitionistic fuzzy sets. *Fuzzy Sets and Systems*, 31(3), 343–349. DOI:10.1016/0165-0114(89)90205-4

Atanassov, K. T. (1986). Intutionistic fuzzy sets. *Fuzzy Sets and Systems*, 20(1), 87–96. DOI:10.1016/S0165-0114(86)80034-3

Atanassov, K. T. (2012). *On intuitionistic fuzzy sets theory* (Vol. 283). Springer. DOI:10.1007/978-3-642-29127-2

Avanzi. (2021). CRYSTALS-Kyber (version 3.02) – Submission to round 3 of the NIST post-quantum project. Specification document (update from August 2021).

Bageerathi, K., & Jeya Puvaneswari, P. (2019). Neutrosophic Feebly Connectedness and Compactness. *IOSR Journal of Polymer and Textile Engineering, 6*(3), 7-13.

Bahrami, Y., Hassani, H., & Maghsoudi, A. (2019). BWM-ARAS: A new hybrid MCDM method for Cu prospectivity mapping in the Abhar area, NW Iran. *Spatial Statistics*, 33, 100382. DOI:10.1016/j.spasta.2019.100382

Basha, S. H., Tharwat, A., Ahmed, K., & Hassanien, A. E. (2018). *A predictive model for seminal quality using neutrosophic rule-based classification system.* Paper presented at the International conference on advanced intelligent systems and informatics.

Bellman, R. E., & Zadeh, L. A. (1970). Decision-making in a fuzzy environment. *Management Science*, 17(4), B-141–B-164. DOI:10.1287/mnsc.17.4.B141

Ben, R. (2021a). Some new open sets in μ^N topological space. *Malaya Journal of Matematik*, 9(1), 89–94. DOI:10.26637/MJM0901/0014

Ben, R. (2021b). Generalized Topological Spaces via Neutrosophic Sets. *J. Math. Comput. Sci.*, 11, 716–734.

Bewick, V., Cheek, L., & Ball, J. (2003). Statistics review 7: Correlation and regression. *Critical Care*, 7(6), 451. DOI:10.1186/cc2401 PMID:14624685

Bijl-Brouwer, M., & Malcolm, B. (2020). Systemic Design Principles in Social Innovation: A Study of Expert Practices and Design Rationales. *She Ji: The Journal of Design, Economics, and Innovation*, 6(3), 386–407. DOI:10.1016/j.sheji.2020.06.001

Biswas, P., Pramanik, S., & Giri, C. B. (2016). Value and ambiguity index based ranking method of single-valued trapezoidal neutrosophic numbers and its application to multi-attribute decision making. *Neutrosophic Sets and Systems, 12*, 127–138. http://fs.unm.edu/NSS2/index.php/111/article/view/687

Boole, G. (1957). *An investigation of the laws of thought, on which are founded the mathematical theories of logic and probabilities*. Dover Publications, Inc.

Borah, M. J., Neog, T. J., & Sut, D. K. (2012). Relations on fuzzy soft sets. *J. Math. Comput. Sci.*, 2(3), 515–534.

Bos. (2022). Dilithium for memory constrained devices. *Lecture Notes in Comput. Sci., 13503.*

Bourner, T., & Simpson, P. (2005). Practitioner-centred research and the Ph.D. *Action Learning*, 2(2), 133–151. DOI:10.1080/14767330500206789

Broumi, S. (2013). *Generalized neutrosophic soft set*. Infinite Study. https://doi.org//arXiv.1305.2724DOI:10.48550

Broumi, S., & Smarandache, F. (2013). Intuitionistic neutrosophic soft set. *Infinite Study*, 130-140.

Broumi, S. (2013). Generalized neutrosophic soft set. *International Journal of Computer Science Engineering and Information Techonology*, 3(2), 17–30.

Broumi, S. (2023). Fermatean Neutrosophic Matrices and Their Basic Operations. *Neutrosophic Sets and Systems*, 58(1), 35.

Broumi, S., Mohanaselvi, S., Witczak, T., Talea, M., Bakali, A., & Smarandache, F. (2023). Complex fermatean neutrosophic graph and application to decision making. *Decision Making: Applications in Management and Engineering*, 6(1), 474–501. DOI:10.31181/dmame24022023b

Broumi, S., & Prabha, S. K. (2023). Fermatean Neutrosophic Matrices and Their Basic Operations. *Neutrosophic Sets and Systems*, 58, 572–595. DOI:10.5281/zenodo.8404536

Broumi, S., Prabha, S., & Uluçay, V. (2023). Interval-Valued Fermatean Neutrosophic Shortest Path Problem via Score Function. *Neutrosophic Systems with Applications*, 11, 1–10. DOI:10.61356/j.nswa.2023.83

Broumi, S., Raut, P. K., & Behera, S. P. (2023). Solving shortest path problems using an ant colony algorithm with triangular neutrosophic arc weights. *International Journal of Neutrosophic Science*, 20(4), 128–137. DOI:10.54216/IJNS.200410

Broumi, S., Sundareswaran, R., Shanmugapriya, M., Chellamani, P., Bakali, A., & Talea, M. (2023). Determination of various factors to evaluate a successful curriculum design using interval-valued Pythagorean neutrosophic graphs. *Soft Computing*, 1–20. DOI:10.1007/s00500-023-08996-y

Broumi, S., Topal, S., Bakali, A., Talea, M., & Smarandache, F. (2020). A Novel Python Toolbox for single and interval-valued neutrosophic matrices. In *Neutrosophic Sets in Decision Analysis and Operations Research* (pp. 281–330). IGI Global. DOI:10.4018/978-1-7998-2555-5.ch013

Budaghyan. (2018). Arithmetic of finite fields. *7th International Workshop, WAIFI 2018.*

Bui, Q. T., Ngo, M. P., Snasel, V., Pedrycz, W., & Vo, B. (2022). The sequence of neutrosophic soft sets and a decision-making problem in medical diagnosis. *International Journal of Fuzzy Systems*, 24(4), 2036–2053. DOI:10.1007/s40815-022-01257-4

Bui, Q.-T., Ngo, M.-P., Snasel, V., Pedrycz, W., & Vo, B. (2023). Information measures based on similarity under neutrosophic fuzzy environment and multi-criteria decision problems. *Engineering Applications of Artificial Intelligence*, 122, 106026. DOI:10.1016/j.engappai.2023.106026

Bustince, H., & Burillo, P. (1996). Structures on intuitionistic fuzzy relations. *Fuzzy Sets and Systems*, 78(3), 293–303. DOI:10.1016/0165-0114(96)84610-0

Butin, A. V., Tselykovskiy, A. A., Kuzenkov, S. E., & Pogodina, E. K. (2023, June). Transformation of the Education System in the Context of Digitalization. In *2023 3rd International Conference on Technology Enhanced Learning in Higher Education (TELE)* (pp. 294-296). IEEE. DOI:10.1109/TELE58910.2023.10184366

Büyüközkan, G., & Göçer, F. (2018). An extension of ARAS methodology under Interval Valued Intuitionistic Fuzzy environment for Digital Supply Chain. *Applied Soft Computing*, 69, 634–654. DOI:10.1016/j.asoc.2018.04.040

Cagman, N., Enginoglu, S., & Citak, F. (2011). Fuzzy soft set theory and its applications. *Iranian Journal of Fuzzy Systems, 8*(3), 137-147. DOI:10.22111/IJFS.2011.292

Carlet, C. (2020). *Boolean functions for cryptography and coding theory*. Cambridge University Press.

Carlet, C., Dalai, D. K., Gupta, K. C., & Maitra, S. (2006). Algebraic immunity for cryptographically significant Boolean functions: analysis and construction. *IEEE Trans. Inform. Theory, 52*(7), 3105–3121.

Carlet, C. (2006). Vectorial Boolean functions for cryptography. In *Boolean Methods and Models*. Cambridge Univ. Press. Available http://www-roc.inria.fr/secret/Claude.Carlet/pubs.html

Celik & Yamak. (2013). *Fuzzy soft set theory applied to medical diagnosis using fuzzy arithmetic operations.*DOI:10.1186/1029-242X-2013-82

Chellamani, P., & Ajay, D. (2021). Pythagorean neutrosophic Dombi fuzzy graphs with an application to MCDM. *Neutrosophic Sets and Systems*, 47, 411–431.

Chidinmma, A. E., & Matthew, O. O. (2023). Revitalizing Education through Digitalization: Its Pros and Cons. *Journal of Advances in Education and Philosophy*, 7(2), 52–55. DOI:10.36348/jaep.2023.v07i02.004

Christianto, V., Boyd, R. N., & Smarandache, F. (2020). *Three possible applications of neutrosophic logic in fundamental and applied sciences.* Infinite Study. https://doi.org/DOI:10.5281/zenodo.3692037

Courtois & Meier. (2003). Algebraic attacks on stream ciphers with linear feedback. Advances in cryptology—EUROCRYPT 2003, 345–359.

Császár, Á. (1997). Generalized open sets. *Acta Mathematica Hungarica*, 75(1-2), 65–87. DOI:10.1023/A:1006582718102

Császár, Á. (2002). Generalized topology, Generalized continuity. *Acta Mathematica Hungarica*, 96(4), 351–357. DOI:10.1023/A:1019713018007

Császár, Á. (2005). Generalized open sets in Generalized topologies. *Acta Mathematica Hungarica*, 106(1-2), 53–66. DOI:10.1007/s10474-005-0005-5

Cusick & Stănică. (2009). *Cryptographic Boolean functions and applications*. Elsevier/Academic Press.

Dalkılıç, O. (2021). Relations on neutrosophic soft set and their application in decision making. *Journal of Applied Mathematics & Computing*, 67(1-2), 257–273. DOI:10.1007/s12190-020-01495-5

Davronovich, A. D., & Mansurjonovich, J. M. (2023). Important Advantages Of Organizing The Educational Process In A Digital Technology Environment. *Galaxy International Interdisciplinary Research Journal*, 11(2), 149–154.

Debnath, S. (2022). Fuzzy quadripartitioned neutrosophic soft matrix theory and its decision-making approach. *Journal of Computational and Cognitive Engineering*, 1(2), 88–93. DOI:10.47852/bonviewJCCE19522514205514

Decru, T. Panny, L., & Vercauteren, F. (2019). Faster SeaSign signatures through improved rejection sampling. *Post-quantum cryptography*, 271–285.

Deli, I. (2018). Operators on Single Valued Trapezoidal Neutrosophic Numbers and SVTN-Group Decision Making. *Neutrosophic Sets and Systems, 22*, 131–150. http://fs.unm.edu/NSS2/index.php/111/article/view/277

Deli, I., & Broumi, S. (2015). Neutrosophic soft relations and some properties. *Annals of Fuzzy Mathematics and Informatics, 9*(1), 169-182.

Deli, İ. (2019). A novel defuzzification method of SV-trapezoidal neutrosophic numbers and multi-attribute decision making: A comparative analysis. *Soft Computing*, 23(23), 12529–12545. DOI:10.1007/s00500-019-03803-z

Deli, I., & Çağman, N. (2021). Spherical fuzzy numbers and multi-criteria decision-making. In *Decision Making with Spherical Fuzzy Sets* (pp. 53–84). Springer International Publishing. DOI:10.1007/978-3-030-45461-6_3

Devi, R. N., & Muthumari, G. (2022, November). Dominating energy in neutrosophic over topologized graphs. In AIP Conference Proceedings: Vol. 2516. *No. 1* (p. 210010). AIP Publishing LLC. DOI:10.1063/5.0108812

Devi, R., & Muthumari, G. (2021). View On Neutrosophic Over Topologized Domination Graphs. *Neutrosophic Sets and Systems, 47*(1), 33. https://dio.org/10.5281/zenodo.5775174

Dhar, M. (2020). Neutrosophic soft block matrices and some of its properties. *Int J Neutrosophic Sci*, 12(1), 39–49.

Di Nola, A., Pedrycz, W., & Sessa, S. (1988). Fuzzy relation equations with equality and difference composition operators. *Fuzzy Sets and Systems*, 25(2), 205–215. DOI:10.1016/0165-0114(88)90188-1

Dillon, J. F. (1974). *Elementary Hadamard difference-sets* [PhD Thesis]. University of Maryland.

Dinda, B., & Samanta, T. K. (2012). Relations on intuitionistic fuzzy soft sets. *arXiv preprint arXiv:1202.4649.*

Dinesh, T., & Ramakrishnan, T. V. (2011). Generalised Fuzzy Graph Structures. *Applied Mathematical Sciences*, 5(4), 173–180.

Donbosco, J. S. M., & Ganesan, D. (2022). The Energy of rough neutrosophic matrix and its application to MCDM problem for selecting the best building construction site. In *Decision Making: Applications in Management and Engineering* (Vol. 5, Issue 2, pp. 30–45). Regional Association for Security and Crisis Management. DOI:10.31181/dmame0305102022d

Dongre, A., & Tewary, V. (2020). Pain without gain? Impact of school rationalisation in India. *International Journal of Educational Development*, 72, 102142. DOI:10.1016/j.ijedudev.2019.102142

Ducas. (2021). CRYSTALS-Dilithium – Algorithm Specifications and Supporting Documentation (Version 3.1). Specification document (update from February 2021).

Dutta, S., & Chakraborty, M. K. (2015). Fuzzy relation and fuzzy function over fuzzy sets: A retrospective. *Soft Computing*, 19(1), 99–112. DOI:10.1007/s00500-014-1356-z

Ebbs, G. (2018). *Visualising database content using Metadata* (Masters Interactive Media Exegesis). Griffith University, Brisbane, Australia. Retrieved from https://github.com/giobono/metadex/blob/master/GEbbs_s2980212_Exegesis.pdf

Ebbs, G. (2023). *Analysis of submissions to Food Security Inquiry*. Retrieved from Canberra Australia: https://www.aph.gov.au/DocumentStore.ashx?id=34221367-8589-40fe-a628-07b47ccb435f&subId=744530

El-Ghareeb, H. A. (2019). Novel Open Source Python Neutrosophic Package. *Neutrosophic Sets and Systems*, 25, 136–160. DOI:10.5281/zenodo.2631514

Embarak. (2018). *Data analysis and visualization using Python*. Springer.

Esther, S. P. C., & Shanmugapriya, M. M. (2022). M-Ordering on Generalized Regular Neutrosophic Fuzzy Matrices. *Mathematical Statistician and Engineering Applications*, 71(3), 1150–1158.

Ezhilmaran, D., & Sankar, K. (2015). Morphism of bipolar intuitionistic fuzzy graphs. *Journal of Discrete Mathematical Sciences and Cryptography*, 18(5), 605–621. DOI:10.1080/09720529.2015.1013673

Farid, H. M. A., & Riaz, M. (2023). Single-valued neutrosophic dynamic aggregation information with time sequence preference for IoT technology in supply chain management. *Engineering Applications of Artificial Intelligence*, 126, 106940. DOI:10.1016/j.engappai.2023.106940

Feng, F., Li, C., Davvaz, B., & Ali, M. I. (2010). Soft sets combined with fuzzy sets and rough sets: A tentative approach. *Soft Computing*, 14(9), 899–911. DOI:10.1007/s00500-009-0465-6

Garg, H., & Nancy, . (2017). Some New Biparametric Distance Measures on Single-Valued Neutrosophic Sets with Applications to Pattern Recognition and Medical Diagnosis. *Information (Basel)*, 8(4), 162. Advance online publication. DOI:10.3390/info8040162

Garg, H., & Rani, D. (2019). Complex Interval-Valued Intuitionistic Fuzzy Sets and their Aggregation Operator. *Fundamenta Informaticae*, 164(1), 61–101. DOI:10.3233/FI-2019-1755

Garg, H., & Rani, D. (2020). Robust Averaging–Geometric Aggregation Operators for Complex Intuitionistic Fuzzy Sets and Their Applications to MCDM Process. *Arabian Journal for Science and Engineering*, 45(3), 2017–2033. DOI:10.1007/s13369-019-03925-4

Gayathri, N. (n.d.). Coefficient of Correlation of Fermatean Neutrosophic sets. *Multidisciplinary Approach in Arts, Science & Commerce, 2*, 109.

Gayathri, N., Helen, M., & Mounika, P. (2020). On neutrosophic vague measure using python. In *Proceedings of International Conference on Advances in Materials Research (ICAMR - 2019)*. AIP Publishing. DOI:10.1063/5.0017191

Ghenai, C., Albawab, M., & Bettayeb, M. (2020). Sustainability indicators for renewable energy systems using multi-criteria decision-making model and extended SWARA/ARAS hybrid method. *Renewable Energy*, 146, 580–597. DOI:10.1016/j.renene.2019.06.157

Ghorabaee, M. K., Zavadskas, E. K., Turskis, Z., & Antucheviciene, J. (2016). A new combinative distance-based assessment (CODAS) method for multi-criteria decision-making. *Economic Computation and Economic Cybernetics Studies and Research*, 50(3), 25–44. https://econpapers.repec.org/RePEc:cys:ecocyb:v:50:y:2016:i:3:p:25-44

Gibson-Graham, J. K. (2006). *A postcapitalist politics*. Minneapolis: University of Minnesota Press.

Gilchrist, W. (2000). *Statistical modelling with quantile functions*. CRC Press. DOI:10.1201/9781420035919

Gioia, D. A., Corley, K. G., & Hamilton, A. L. (2013). Seeking Qualitative Rigor in Inductive Research: Notes on the Gioia Methodology. *Organizational Research Methods*, 16(1), 15–31. DOI:10.1177/1094428112452151

Gomathy, S., Rajkumar, A., Nagarajan, D., & Said, B. (2023). Plıthogenıc Combıned Dısjoınt Block Fuzzy Cognıtıve Maps (Pcdbfcm). *International Journal of Neutrosophic Science*, 20(1).

Gonul Bilgin, N., Pamučar, D., & Riaz, M. (2022). Fermatean neutrosophic topological spaces and an application of neutrosophic kano method. *Symmetry*, 14(11), 2442. DOI:10.3390/sym14112442

Göpel, M. (2016). *The Great Mindshift*. Retrieved from https://resolver.ebscohost.com/Redirect/PRL?EPPackageLocationID=4476.11747448.43334445&epcustomerid=s2947694

Goswami, S. S., & Behera, D. K. (2021). Implementation of ENTROPY-ARAS decision making methodology in the selection of best engineering materials. *Materials Today: Proceedings*, 38, 2256–2262. DOI:10.1016/j.matpr.2020.06.320

Greenfield, S., Chiclana, F., & Dick, S. (2016). Interval-valued complex fuzzy logic. *Proceedings of the IEEE International Conference on Fuzzy Systems.*

Grubb, M., McDowall, W., & Drummond, P. (2017). On order and complexity in innovations systems: Conceptual frameworks for policy mixes in sustainability transitions. *Energy Research & Social Science*, 33, 21–34. DOI:10.1016/j.erss.2017.09.016

Gunduz, Ç., Ozturk, T. Y., & Bayramov, S. (2019). Separation axioms on neutrosophic soft topological spaces. *Turkish Journal of Mathematics*, 43(1), 498–510. DOI:10.3906/mat-1805-110

Halecker, B. (2015). Action case study - A research strategy based on abduction for relevant and rigorous management research. *International Journal of Business Research, 15*(4), 23-32. DOI:10.18374/IJBR-15-4.3

Heidary Dahooie, J., Beheshti Jazan Abadi, E., Vanaki, A. S., & Firoozfar, H. R. (2018). Competency-based IT personnel selection using a hybrid SWARA and ARAS-G methodology. *Human Factors and Ergonomics in Manufacturing*, 28(1), 5–16. DOI:10.1002/hfm.20713

Houghton, L., & Tuffley, D. (2015). Towards a Methodology of Wicked Problem Exploration through Concept Shifting and Tension Point Analysis. *Systems Research and Behavioral Science*, 32(3), 283–297. DOI:10.1002/sres.2223

Hussain, Broumi, & Jun. (2019). Intuitionistic Bipolar neutrosophic set and its Application to Intuitionistic Bipolar neutrosophic Graph. *Annals of Communications in Mathematics, 2*(2), 121-140.

Hussain, A., & Shabir, M. (2015). Algebraic structures of neutrosophic soft sets. *Neutrosophic Sets and Systems*, 7, 53–61.

Hwang, C.-L., & Yoon, K. (1981). Methods for Multiple Attribute Decision Making. In *Multiple Attribute Decision Making: Methods and Applications A State-of-the-Art Survey* (pp. 58–191). Springer Berlin Heidelberg. DOI:10.1007/978-3-642-48318-9_3

Irvanizam, I., Marzuki, M., Patria, I., & Abubakar, R. (2018). An Application for Smartphone Preference Using TODIM Decision Making Method. *Proceedings - 2nd 2018 International Conference on Electrical Engineering and Informatics, ICELTICs 2018.* DOI:10.1109/ICELTICS.2018.8548820

Irvanizam, I., Usman, T., Iqbal, M., Iskandar, T., & Marzuki, M. (2020). An Extended Fuzzy TODIM Approach for Multiple-Attribute Decision-Making with Dual-Connection Numbers. *Advances in Fuzzy Systems*, 2020, 1–10. Advance online publication. DOI:10.1155/2020/6190149

Irvanizam, I., & Zahara, N. (2023). *An Extended EDAS Based on Multi-Attribute Group Decision Making to Evaluate Mathematics Teachers With Single-Valued Trapezoidal Neutrosophic Numbers*. DOI:10.4018/978-1-6684-7836-3.ch003

Irvanizam, I., & Zi, N. N. (2022). *Improved MABAC Method for Multicriteria Group Decision Making With Trapezoidal Fuzzy Neutrosophic Numbers*. DOI:10.4018/978-1-7998-7979-4.ch030

Jafar & Saeed. (2022). Matrix theory for neutrosophic hypersoft set and applications in multiattributive multicriteria decision-making problems. *Journal of Mathematics*. .DOI:10.1155/2022/6666408

Jain, A., Pal Nandi, B., Gupta, C., & Tayal, D. K. (2020). Senti-NSetPSO: Large-sized document-level sentiment analysis using Neutrosophic Set and particle swarm optimization. *Soft Computing*, 24(1), 3–15. DOI:10.1007/s00500-019-04209-7

Jana, C., Pal, M., Karaaslan, F., & Wang, J. Q. (2020). Trapezoidal neutrosophic aggregation operators and their application to the multi-attribute decision-making process. *Scientia Iranica*, 27(3), 1655–1673. DOI:10.24200/sci.2018.51136.2024

Jansi, R., Mohana, R. K., & Smarandache, F. (2019). Correlation Measure for Pythagorean Neutrosophic Fuzzy Sets with T and F as Dependent Neutrosophic Components. *Neutrosophic Sets and Systems*, 30(1), 202–212.

Jeni Seles Martina, D., & Deepa, G. (2023). Operations on Multi-Valued Neutrosophic Matrices and Its Application to Neutrosophic Simplified-TOPSIS Method. *International Journal of Information Technology & Decision Making*, 22(01), 37–56. DOI:10.1142/S0219622022500572

Jeni Seles Martina, D., & Deepa, G. (2023a). *Some algebraic properties on rough neutrosophic matrix and its application to multi-criteria decision-making*. DOI:10.3934/math.20231230

Ji, F., Wu, J., Chiclana, F., Wang, S., Fujita, H., & Herrera-Viedma, E. (2023). The Overlapping Community-Driven Feedback Mechanism to Support Consensus in Social Network Group Decision Making. *IEEE Transactions on Fuzzy Systems*, 31(9), 3025–3039. DOI:10.1109/TFUZZ.2023.3241062

Joice, P. R., Pricilla, M. T., & Broumi, S. (2023). Generalized Pre-closed Sets in Fermatean Neutrosophic Hypersoft Topological Spaces. *International Journal of Neutrosophic Science*, 20(3), 82–2. DOI:10.54216/IJNS.200308

Kamacı, H., Garg, H., & Petchimuthu, S. (2021). Bipolar trapezoidal neutrosophic sets and their Dombi operators with applications in multicriteria decision making. *Soft Computing*, 25(13), 8417–8440. DOI:10.1007/s00500-021-05768-4

Kandasamy, W.B.V., & Smarandache, F. (2004). *Fuzzy relational maps and neutrosophic relational maps*. HEXIS.

Karagöz, S., Deveci, M., Simic, V., & Aydin, N. (2021). Interval type-2 Fuzzy ARAS method for recycling facility location problems. *Applied Soft Computing*, 102, 107107. DOI:10.1016/j.asoc.2021.107107

Karunambigai, Palanivel, & Sivasankar. (2015). Edge Regular Intuitionistic Fuzzy Graph. *Advances in Fuzzy sets and Systems, 20*(1), 25-46.

Kashihara, K. (1996). *Comments and topics on Smarandache notions and problems*. Infinite Study.

Kaushik. (2023). Post Quantum Public and Private Key Cryptography Optimized for IoT Security. *Wireless Pers Commun, 129*, 893–909. https://doi.org/DOI:10.1007/s11277-022-10162-w

Kavut. (2008). *Boolean functions with excellent cryptographic properties in autocorrelation and walsh spectra* [PhD thesis]. Middle East Technical University.

Kelly, G. A. (1977). Personal construct theory and the psychotherapeutic interview. *Cognitive Therapy and Research*, 1(4), 355–362. DOI:10.1007/BF01663999

Khalifa, N. E., Loey, M., Chakrabortty, R. K., & Taha, M. H. N. (2022). Within the Protection of COVID-19 Spreading: A Face Mask Detection Model Based on the Neutrosophic RGB with Deep Transfer Learning. *Neutrosophic Sets and Systems*, 50, 320–335.

Khan, M., Anis, S., Bibi, K., Iqbal, S., & Smarandache, F. (2021). Complex Neutrosophic Soft Matrices Framework: An Application in Signal Processing. *Journal of Mathematics* (Vol. 2021, pp. 1–10). DOI:10.1155/2021/8887824

Khan, M., Son, L. H., Ali, M., Chau, H. T. M., Na, N. T. N., & Smarandache, F. (2018). Systematic review of decision making algorithms in extended neutrosophic sets. *Symmetry*, 10(8), 314. DOI:10.3390/sym10080314

Khan, Z., Amin, A., Khan, S. A., & Gulistan, M. (2021). Statistical Development of the Neutrosophic Lognormal Model with Application to Environmental Data. *Neutrosophic Sets and Systems*, 47(1), 1.

Kiptum, C. K., Bouraima, M. B., Badi, I., Zonon, B. I. P., Ndiema, K. M., & Qiu, Y. (2023). Assessment of the Challenges to Urban Sustainable Development Using an Interval-Valued Fermatean Fuzzy Approach. *Systemic Analytics*, 1(1), 11–26. DOI:10.31181/sa1120233

Kirişci, M. (2022). Novel Multi-Attribute Group-Decision Making Method with TOPSIS: A Fermatean Fuzzy Hypersoft Sets and Correlation Coefficients Approach. In *Applied Mathematics, Modeling and Computer Simulation* (pp. 952-960). IOS Press. DOI:10.3233/ATDE221119

Köhler, J., Geels, F. W., Kern, F., Markard, J., Onsongo, E., Wieczorek, A., Alkemade, F., Avelino, F., Bergek, A., Boons, F., Fünfschilling, L., Hess, D., Holtz, G., Hyysalo, S., Jenkins, K., Kivimaa, P., Martiskainen, M., McMeekin, A., Mühlemeier, M. S., & Wells, P. (2019). An agenda for sustainability transitions research: State of the art and future directions. *Environmental Innovation and Societal Transitions*, 31, 1–32. DOI:10.1016/j.eist.2019.01.004

Kolmogorov & Yushkevich. (1992). *Mathematics of the 19th century, Mathematical logic Algebra Number Theory Probability theory*. Springer Basel AG.

Kong, Z., Wang, L., & Wu, Z. (2011). Application of fuzzy soft set in decision making problems based on grey theory. *Journal of Computational and Applied Mathematics*, 236(6), 1521–1530. DOI:10.1016/j.cam.2011.09.016

Korucuk, S., Demir, E., Karamasa, C., & Stević, Ž. (2020). *Determining the dimensions of the innovation ability in logistics sector by using plithogenic-critic method: An application in Sakarya Province*. Academic Press.

Kuokkanen, A., Uusitalo, V., & Koistinen, K. (2019). A framework of disruptive sustainable innovation: An example of the Finnish food system. *Technology Analysis and Strategic Management*, 31(7), 749–764. DOI:10.1080/09537325.2018.1550254

Kutlu Gündoğdu, F., & Kahraman, C. (2019a). A novel fuzzy TOPSIS method using emerging interval-valued spherical fuzzy sets. *Engineering Applications of Artificial Intelligence*, 85, 307–323. DOI:10.1016/j.engappai.2019.06.003

Kutlu Gündoğdu, F., & Kahraman, C. (2019b). Spherical fuzzy sets and spherical fuzzy TOPSIS method. *Journal of Intelligent & Fuzzy Systems*, 36(1), 337–352. DOI:10.3233/JIFS-181401

Kutlu Gündoğdu, F., & Kahraman, C. (2020). A novel spherical fuzzy analytic hierarchy process and its renewable energy application. *Soft Computing*, 24(6), 4607–4621. DOI:10.1007/s00500-019-04222-w

Lalitha, K., Sarguna, S., & Muthuraji, T. (2023, January). Application of Neutrosophic matrix in document retrieval systems. In *2023 Third International Conference on Advances in Electrical, Computing, Communication and Sustainable Technologies (ICAECT)* (pp. 1-5). IEEE. DOI:10.1109/ICAECT57570.2023.10118146

Lee, K.-M. (2000). Bipolar-valued fuzzy sets and their basic operations. *Proc. Int. Conf.*

Li, B., Wang, J., Yang, L., & Li, X. (2018). A Novel Generalized Simplified Neutrosophic Number Einstein Aggregation Operator. *ViXra*. https://api.semanticscholar.org/CorpusID:49381119

Ljungkvist, T., & Andersén, J. (2021). A taxonomy of ecopreneurship in small manufacturing firms: A multidimensional cluster analysis. *Business Strategy and the Environment*, 30(2), 1374–1388. DOI:10.1002/bse.2691

Mahdavi, A., & Kundu, D. (2017). A new method for generating distributions with an application to exponential distribution. *Communications in Statistics. Theory and Methods*, 46(13), 6543–6557. DOI:10.1080/03610926.2015.1130839

Mahima Poonia, & Bajaj, R. K. (2021). Complex Neutrosophic Matrix with Some Algebraic Operations and Matrix Norm Convergence. *Neutrosophic Sets Syst.*, 47, 165–178. DOI:10.5281/ZENODO.5775110

Maji, P. K. (2015). An application of weighted neutrosophic soft sets in a decision-making problem. In *Facets of Uncertainties and Applications: ICFUA, Kolkata, India, December 2013* (pp. 215-223). Springer India. DOI:10.1007/978-81-322-2301-6_16

Maji, P. K., Biswas, R. K., & Roy, A. (2001a). *Fuzzy soft sets*. Academic Press.

Maji, P. K., Biswas, R., & Roy, A. R. (2001). *Fuzzy soft sets. Journal of Fuzzy Mathematics, 9*, 589-602.

Maji, P. K., Biswas, R., & Roy, A. R. (2001b). Intuitionistic fuzzy soft sets. *Journal of Fuzzy Mathematics, 9*(3), 677-692.

Maji, P. K. (2013). Neutrosophic soft set. *Ann. Fuzzy Math. Inform.*, 5(1), 157–168.

Maji, P. K., Biswas, R., & Roy, A. R. (2003). Soft set theory. *Computers & Mathematics with Applications (Oxford, England)*, 45(4-5), 555–562. DOI:10.1016/S0898-1221(03)00016-6

Majumdar, P., & Samanta, S. K. (2010). Generalised fuzzy soft sets. *Computers & Mathematics with Applications (Oxford, England)*, 59(4), 1425–1432. DOI:10.1016/j.camwa.2009.12.006

Majumdar, P., & Samanta, S. K. (2014). On similarity and entropy of neutrosophic sets. *Journal of Intelligent & Fuzzy Systems*, 26(3), 1245–1252. DOI:10.3233/IFS-130810

Manirathinam, T., Narayanamoorthy, S., Geetha, S., Othman, M. F. I., Alotaibi, B. S., Ahmadian, A., & Kang, D. (2023). Sustainable renewable energy system selection for self-sufficient households using integrated fermatean neutrosophic fuzzy stratified AHP-MARCOS approach. *Renewable Energy*, 218, 119292. DOI:10.1016/j.renene.2023.119292

Mao, X., Guoxi, Z., Fallah, M., & Edalatpanah, S. (2020). A neutrosophic-based approach in data envelopment analysis with undesirable outputs. *Mathematical Problems in Engineering*, 2020, 1–8. DOI:10.1155/2020/7626102

Martin, N., & Smarandache, F. (2020). *Introduction to combined plithogenic hypersoft sets*. Infinite Study. https://digitalrepository.unm.edu/nss_journal/vol35/iss1/28

Martin, N., & Smarandache, F. (2020). *Plithogenic cognitive maps in decision making*. Infinite Study.

Martin, N., Priya, R., & Smarandache, F. (2021). *New Plithogenic sub cognitive maps approach with mediating effects of factors in COVID-19 diagnostic model.* Infinite Study.

Martin, N., Smarandache, F., & Broumi, S. (2021). Covid-19 decision-making model using extended plithogenic hypersoft sets with dual dominant attributes. *International Journal of Neutrosophic Science, 13*(2), 75-86. https://dio.org/10.5281/zenodo.4553562

Mehmood, A., Abdullah, S., & Park, C. (2022). A New Approach to Vague Soft Bi-Topological Spaces. *CMES-Computer Modeling in Engineering & Sciences, 131*(1).

Miari, M., Anan, M. T., & Zeina, M. B. (2022). Neutrosophic two way ANOVA. *International Journal of Neutrosophic Science*, 18(3), 73–83. DOI:10.54216/IJNS.180306

Milo, D., Fiedman, R., & Kandel, M. (2002). Complex fuzzy sets. *IEEE Transactions on Fuzzy Systems*, 10(2), 171–186. DOI:10.1109/91.995119

Mishra, A. R., Rani, P., Cavallaro, F., & Mardani, A. (2022). A similarity measure-based Pythagorean fuzzy additive ratio assessment approach and its application to multi-criteria sustainable biomass crop selection. *Applied Soft Computing*, 125, 109201. DOI:10.1016/j.asoc.2022.109201

Molodtsov, D. (1999). Soft set theory first results. *Computers & Mathematics with Applications (Oxford, England)*, 37(4-5), 19–31. DOI:10.1016/S0898-1221(99)00056-5

Mordeson, J. N., & Peng, C. S. (1994). Operations on fuzzy graphs. *Information Sciences*, 79(3-4), 159–170. DOI:10.1016/0020-0255(94)90116-3

Muhammad Akram, S. (2019). Simplified interval-valued Pythagorean fuzzy graphs with application. *Complex & Intelligent Systems*, 5(2), 229–253. DOI:10.1007/s40747-019-0106-3

Mukhitdinova, N. A. (2023). The Importance of Implementing Digitalization into Educational System and its Impact on the Development of Teaching Process. Best Journal of Innovation in Science. *Research for Development*, 2(7), 27–32.

Murugadas, P., & Kavitha, M. (2021, May). Convergence of fuzzy neutrosophic soft circulant matrices. *Journal of Physics: Conference Series*, 1850(1), 012076. DOI:10.1088/1742-6596/1850/1/012076

Murugappan, M., Govindan, V., & Grienggarai, R. (2023). Neighbourly Edge Irregularity on Interval-valued Pythagorean Neutrosophic Graph. International Journal on Robotics. *Automation and Sciences*, 5(2), 54–58.

Muthukumaran, V., Kumar, M. S., Silambarasan, I., Udhayakumar, R., & Broumi, S. (2023). A study on n-HyperSpherical Neutrosophic matrices. *Neutrosophic Sets and Systems*, 55(1), 21.

Nagoor Gani, A., & Radha, K. (2008). On Regular Fuzzy Graphs. *The Journal of Physiological Sciences; JPS*, 12, 33–40.

Nair, N. U., & Sankaran, P. (2009). Quantile-based reliability analysis. *Communications in Statistics. Theory and Methods*, 38(2), 222–232. DOI:10.1080/03610920802187430

Nithyanandham, D., & Augustin, F. (2023). A bipolar fuzzy p-competition graph based ARAS technique for prioritizing COVID-19 vaccines. *Applied Soft Computing*, 146, 110632. DOI:10.1016/j.asoc.2023.110632

Nongthombam & Sharma. (2021). Data Analysis using Python. *International Journal of Engineering Research & Technology, 10*(7), 463-468.

Nzei, L. C., Eghwerido, J. T., & Ekhosuehi, N. (2020). Topp-Leone Gompertz Distribution: Properties and Applications. *Journal of Data Science : JDS*, 18(4), 782–794. DOI:10.6339/JDS.202010_18(4).0012

Olgun, N., & Hatip, A. (n.d.). *The effect of the neutrosophic logic on the decision tree* (Vol. 7). Academic Press.

Onwuegbuzie, A. J., Leech, N. L., & Collins, K. M. T. (2012). Qualitative analysis techniques for the review of the literature. *Qualitative Report, 17*(28), 1. Retrieved from https://go.exlibris.link/HY73SsLl

Opricovic, S., & Tzeng, G.-H. (2004). Compromise solution by MCDM methods: A comparative analysis of VIKOR and TOPSIS. *European Journal of Operational Research*, 156(2), 445–455. DOI:10.1016/S0377-2217(03)00020-1

Ouenniche, J., Bouslah, K., Perez-Gladish, B., & Xu, B. (2021). A new VIKOR-based in-sample-out-of-sample classifier with application in bankruptcy prediction. *Annals of Operations Research*, 296(1), 495–512. DOI:10.1007/s10479-019-03223-0 PMID:34812215

Ozturk, T. Y. (2018). Soft Mappings on soft generalized topological spaces. *Creat. Math. Inform, 27*(2).

Ozturk, T. Y., Aras, C. G., & Bayramov, S. (2019). *A new approach to operations on neutrosophic soft sets and to neutrosophic soft topological spaces*. Infinite Study.

Ozturk, T. Y. (2016). On defining soft spaces by weak soft neighborhood systems. *New Trends in Mathematical Sciences*, 4(2), 113–124. DOI:10.20852/ntmsci.2016217822

Ozturk, T. Y., & Bayramov, S. (2017). Topology on soft continuous function spaces. *Mathematical & Computational Applications*, 22(2), 32. DOI:10.3390/mca22020032

Ozturk, T. Y., Benek, A., & Ozkan, A. (2021b). Neutrosophic soft compact spaces. *Afrika Matematika*, 32(1-2), 301–316. DOI:10.1007/s13370-020-00827-9

Ozturk, T. Y., Karataş, E., & Yolcu, A. (2021a). On neutrosophic soft continuous mappings. *Turkish Journal of Mathematics*, 45(1), 81–95. DOI:10.3906/mat-1912-113

Pandey. (2017). Count and cryptographic properties of generalized symmetric Boolean functions. *Ital. J. Pure Appl. Math., 37*, 173–182.

Parzen, E. (1979). *Density quantile estimation approach to statistical data modelling. In Smoothing Techniques for Curve Estimation*. Springer. DOI:10.21236/ADA068148

Patro, S., & Smarandache, F. (n.d.). *The neutrosophic statistical distribution, more problems, more solutions*. Infinite Study.

Paulraj, S., & Tamilarasi, G. (2022). Generalized ordered weighted harmonic averaging operator withtrapezoidal neutrosophic numbers for solving MADM problems. *Journal of Ambient Intelligence and Humanized Computing*, 13(8), 4089–4102. DOI:10.1007/s12652-021-03509-x PMID:34659583

Peng, Lee, & Gary. (2002). An Introduction to Logistic Regression Analysis and Reporting. *The Journal of Educational Research, 96*(1), 3-14.

Peng, J., Wang, J., Jing, W., Zhang, H., & Chen, X. (2016). Simplified neutrosophic sets and their applications in multi-criteria group decision-making problems. *International Journal of Systems Science*, 47(10), 2342–2358. DOI:10.1080/00207721.2014.994050

Peter, C., & Swilling, M. (2014). Linking complexity and sustainability theories: Implications for modeling sustainability transitions. *Sustainability (Basel)*, 6(3), 1594–1622. DOI:10.3390/su6031594

Pickering, C., & Byrne, J. (2014). The benefits of publishing systematic quantitative literature reviews for PhD candidates and other early-career researchers. *Higher Education Research & Development*, 33(3), 534–548. DOI:10.1080/07294360.2013.841651

Popa, F., Guillermin, M., & Dedeurwaerdere, T. (2015). A pragmatist approach to transdisciplinarity in sustainability research: From complex systems theory to reflexive science. *Futures*, 65, 45–56. DOI:10.1016/j.futures.2014.02.002

Pramanik, S., & Mondal, K. (2015). Interval neutrosophic multi-attribute decision-making based on grey relational analysis. *Neutrosophic Sets and Systems*, 9(1), 13–22.

Prashar, A., & Sunder M, V. (2020). A bibliometric and content analysis of sustainable development in small and medium-sized enterprises. *Journal of Cleaner Production, 245*. DOI:10.1016/j.jclepro.2019.118665

Priya, R., & Martin, N. (2021). *Induced Plithogenic Cognitive Maps with Combined Connection Matrix to investigate the glitches of online learning system*. Infinite Study.

Priya, R., Martin, N., & Kishore, T. E. (2022, May). Plithogenic cognitive analysis on instigating spiritual intelligence in smart age youth for humanity redemption. In *AIP Conference Proceedings* (Vol. 2393, No. 1). AIP Publishing. DOI:10.1063/5.0074105

Qahtan, S., Alsattar, H. A., Zaidan, A. A., Deveci, M., Pamucar, D., Delen, D., & Pedrycz, W. (2023). Evaluation of agriculture-food 4.0 supply chain approaches using Fermatean probabilistic hesitant-fuzzy sets based decision making model. *Applied Soft Computing*, 138, 110170. DOI:10.1016/j.asoc.2023.110170

Ramot, D., Friedman, M., Langholz, G. A., & Kandel, A. (2003). Kandel, Complex fuzzy logic. *IEEE Transactions on Fuzzy Systems*, 11(4), 450–461. DOI:10.1109/TFUZZ.2003.814832

Ramya, M., Murali, S., Radha, R. (2022). Fermatean Quadripartitioned Neutrosophic Set. *International Journal of Creative Research Thoughts*.

Rani, D., & Garg, H. (2017). Distance measures between the complex intuitionistic fuzzy sets and its applications to the decision-making process. *International Journal for Uncertainty Quantification*, 7(5), 423–439. DOI:10.1615/Int.J.UncertaintyQuantification.2017020356

Rani, D., & Garg, H. (2018). Complex intuitionistic fuzzy power aggregation operators and their applications in multi-criteria decision making. *Expert Systems: International Journal of Knowledge Engineering and Neural Networks*, 35(6), e12325. DOI:10.1111/exsy.12325

Raut, P. K., Behera, S. P., Broumi, S., & Mishra, D. (2023). Calculation of shortest path on Fermatean Neutrosophic Networks. *Neutrosophic Sets and Systems*, 57(1), 22.

Regev. (2009). Oded On lattices, learning with errors, random linear codes, and cryptography. *J. ACM, 56*(6).

Riaz, M., Farid, H. M. A., Ashraf, S., & Kamacı, H. (2023). Single-valued neutrosophic fairly aggregation operators with multi-criteria decision-making. *Computational & Applied Mathematics*, 42(3), 104. DOI:10.1007/s40314-023-02233-w

Rivas, A. (2023). The platformization of education: A framework to map the new directions of hybrid education systems 1. In *The New Digital Education Policy Landscape* (pp. 191–209). Routledge. DOI:10.4324/9781003373018-13

Rivieccio, U. (2008). Neutrosophic logics: Prospects and problems. *Fuzzy Sets and Systems*, 159(14), 1860–1868. DOI:10.1016/j.fss.2007.11.011

Rosenfeld, A. (1975). Fuzzy graphs. In *Fuzzy Sets and their Applications.* Academic Press.

Rothaus, O. S. (1976). On “bent” functions. *J. Combinatorial Theory Ser., A20*(3), 300–305.

Sadjadi, E. N. (2023). Challenges and Opportunities for Education Systems with the Current Movement toward Digitalization at the Time of COVID-19. *Mathematics*, 11(2), 259. DOI:10.3390/math11020259

Saeed, M., Ahsan, M., Siddique, M. K., & Ahmad, M. R. (2020). A study of the fundamentals of hypersoft set theory. *Int. Sci. Eng. Res.*, 11, 320–329. DOI:10.5281/zenodo.6779592

Saeed, M., Nisa, M. U., Saeed, M. H., Alballa, T., & Khalifa, H. A. E. W. (2023). Detecting Patterns of Infection-Induced Fertility Using Fermatean Neutrosophic Set with Similarity Analysis. *IEEE Access : Practical Innovations, Open Solutions*, 11, 112320–112333. DOI:10.1109/ACCESS.2023.3323024

Salama, A. (2018). *Neutrosophic approach to grayscale images domain*. Academic Press.

Salama, A., & Alblowi, S. (2012). Neutrosophic set and neutrosophic topological spaces. *IOSR Journal of Mathematics (IOSR-JM), 3*(4).

Salama, A., Smarandache, F., & Alblowi, S. (n.d.). *New neutrosophic crisp topological concepts*. Infinite Study.

Salama, A., Smarandache, F., & Eisa, M. (2014). *Introduction to image processing via neutrosophic techniques*. Infinite Study.

Salama, A., Smarandache, F., & Kromov, V. (2022). Neutrosophic closed set and neutrosophic continuous functions. *Collected Papers. Volume IX: On Neutrosophic Theory and Its Applications in Algebra*, 25.

Salama, A., Smarandache, F., & Kroumov, V. (2014). *Neutrosophic crisp sets & neutrosophic crisp topological spaces*. Infinite Study.

Salama, A. (2012). Neutrosophic set and Neutrosophic topological space. *ISOR J. Mathematics*, 3(4), 31–35. DOI:10.9790/5728-0343135

Salama, A., Dalla, R., Al Aswad, M., & Ali, R. (2022). On Some Novel Results About Neutrosophic Square Complex Matrices. *Journal of Neutrosophic and Fuzzy Systems*, 4(01), 21–29. DOI:10.54216/JNFS.040103

Sampathkumar, E. (2006). Generalized graph structures. *Bulletin of Kerala Mathematics Association*, 3(2), 65–123.

Sanchez, E. (1979). Inverse of fuzzy relations, application to possibility distributions and medical diagnosis. *Fuzzy Sets and Systems*, 2(1), 75–78. DOI:10.1016/0165-0114(79)90017-4

Sankar, C., Sujatha, R., & Nagarajan, D. (2020). *Topsis by using plithogenic set in COVID-19 decision making*. Infinite Study. htts://DOI:10.5281/zenodo.4011772

Sasikala, D., & Divya, B. (2023). A Newfangled Interpretation on Fermatean Neutrosophic Dombi Fuzzy Graphs. *Neutrosophic Systems with Applications*, 7, 36–53. DOI:10.61356/j.nswa.2023.21

Satham Hussain, S. (2021). Interval intuitionistic neutrosophic sets with its applications to interval intuitionistic neutrosophic graphs and climatic analysis. *Computational & Applied Mathematics*, 40(4), 121. DOI:10.1007/s40314-021-01504-8

Senapati, T., & Yager, R. R. (2020). Fermatean fuzzy sets. *Journal of Ambient Intelligence and Humanized Computing*, 11(2), 663–674. DOI:10.1007/s12652-019-01377-0

Shamim Kaiser, M. (2018). Article. *IEEE Transactions on Intelligent Transportation Systems*, 1524–9050.

Shannon & Atanassov. (1994). A first stap to a theory of the Intuitionistic fuzzy graph. *Proceeding of FUBEST*, 59-61.

Sherwani, R. A. K., Naeem, M., Aslam, M., Raza, M., Abid, M., & Abbas, S. (n.d.). *Neutrosophic beta distribution with properties and applications*. Infinite Study.

Sherwani, R. A. K., Aslam, M., Raza, M. A., Farooq, M., Abid, M., & Tahir, M. (2021). Neutrosophic Normal Probability Distribution—A Spine of Parametric Neutrosophic Statistical Tests: Properties and Applications. *NeutrosophicOperations Research*, 153–169.

Shih, H.-S., Shyur, H.-J., & Lee, E. S. (2007). An extension of TOPSIS for group decision making. *Mathematical and Computer Modelling*, 45(7), 801–813. DOI:10.1016/j.mcm.2006.03.023

Silambarasan, I. (2023). Some Algebric Structure of Spherical Neutrosophic Matrices. *TWMS J. App. and Eng. Math.*, 13(3), 1177–1189.

Sleem, A., Abdel-Baset, M., & El-henawy, I. (2020). PyIVNS: A python based tool for Interval-valued neutrosophic operations and normalization. *SoftwareX*, 12, 100632. DOI:10.1016/j.softx.2020.100632

Slot, E. M., Bronkhorst, L. H., Wubbels, T., & Akkerman, S. F. (2020). The role of school in adolescents' interest in daily life. *International Journal of Educational Research*, 104, 101643. DOI:10.1016/j.ijer.2020.101643

Smarandache, F. (2000). Neutrosophy. *arXiv preprint math/0010099*.

Smarandache, F. (2003). *A unifying field in logics: neutrosphic logic, neutrosophy, neutrosphic set, neutrosphic probability*. Academic Press.

Smarandache, F. (2003). *Definiton of neutrosophic logic-a generalization of the intuitionistic fuzzy logic*. Paper presented at the EUSFLAT Conf.

Smarandache, F. (2005). *A unifying field in logics: neutrosophic logic. Neutrosophy, neutrosophic set, neutrosophic probability: neutrsophic logic. Neutrosophy, neutrosophic set, neutrosophic probability*. Infinite Study.

Smarandache, F. (2014). *Neutrosophic Theory and Its Applications, Vol. I: Collected Papers*. Infinite Study.

Smarandache, F. (2018). *Plithogenic set, an extension of crisp, fuzzy, intuitionistic fuzzy, and neutrosophic sets-revisited.* Infinite Study.

Smarandache, F., & Pramanik, S. (2016). *New trends in neutrosophic theory and applications* (Vol. 1). Infinite Study.

Smarandache, F. (1998). *Neutrosophy, Neutrosophic Probability, Set, and Logic, Amer*. Res. Press.

Smarandache, F. (1998). *Neutrosophy: Neutrosophic Probability, Set, and Logic: Analytic Synthesis & Synthetic Analysis*. American Research Press.

Smarandache, F. (1999). *A Unifying Field in Logic: Neutrosophic Logic. Neutrosophy, Neutrosophic set, Neutrosophic Probability*. American Research Press.

Smarandache, F. (1999). A unifying field in Logics: Neutrosophic Logic. In *Philosophy* (pp. 1–141). American Research Press.

Smarandache, F. (1999). A unifying field in Logics: Neutrosophic Logic. *Philosophy (London, England)*, 1–141.

Smarandache, F. (2002). Neutrosophy and Neutrosophic Logic. *First International Conference on Neutrosophy,* Neutrosophic Logic, Set, Probability, and Statistics. University of New Mexico.

Smarandache, F. (2004). Neutrosophic set, a generalization of the intutionistic fuzzy sets. *International Journal of Pure and Applied Mathematics*, 24(3), 287–297.

Smarandache, F. (2010). Neutrosophic set, a generalisation of the intuitionistic fuzzy sets. *International Journal of Pure and Applied Mathematics*, 24, 289–297.

Smarandache, F. (2010). Neutrosophic Set: A Generalization of Intuitionistic Fuzzy set. *Journal of Defense Resources Management*, 1, 107–116.

Smarandache, F. (2013). *A unifying field in logics: neutrosphic logic, neutrosophy, neutrosphic set, neutrosphic probability*. American Research Press.

Smarandache, F. (2018). *Plithogenic set, an extension of crisp, fuzzy, intuitionistic fuzzy, and neutrosophic sets-revisited.* Infinite Study. https://doi.org/DOI:10.5281/zenodo.1408740

Smarandache, F. (2019). Introduction to NeutroAlgebraic Structures and AntiAlgebraic Structures. In *Advances of Standard and Nonstandard Neutrosphic Theories*. Academic Press.

Smarandache, F. (2020a). Introduction to NeutroAlgebraic Structures and AntiAlgebraic Structures (revisited). *Neutrosphic Sets and Systems*, 31, 1–16.

Smarandache, F. (2020b). NeutroAlgebra is a Generalization of Partial Algebra. *International Journal of Neutrosphic Science*, 2(1), 8–17.

Son, L. H., Ngan, R. T., Ali, M., Fujita, H., Abdel-Basset, M., Giang, N. L., Manogaran, G., & Priyan, M. K. (2020). A New Representation of Intuitionistic Fuzzy Systems and Their Applications in Critical Decision Making. *IEEE Intelligent Systems*, 35(1), 6–17. DOI:10.1109/MIS.2019.2938441

Sovacool, B. K., & Hess, D. J. (2017). Ordering theories: Typologies and conceptual frameworks for sociotechnical change. *Social Studies of Science*, 47(5), 703–750. DOI:10.1177/0306312717709363 PMID:28641502

Stanica & Martinsen. (2011). Octal Bent Generalized Boolean Functions. arXiv:1102.4812v2

Sujatha, R., Poomagal, S., Kuppuswami, G., & Broumi, S. (2020). *An Analysis on Novel Corona Virus by a Plithogenic Approach to Fuzzy Cognitive Map*. Infinite Study.

Sun, J., Gong, Z., Zhang, D., Xu, Y., & Wei, G. (2023). A robust ordinal regression feedback consensus model with dynamic trust propagation in social network group decision-making. *Information Fusion*, 100, 101952. DOI:10.1016/j.inffus.2023.101952

Tække, J. (2023, July). Digitalization of education-the theory of the three waves. In *7 International ISEKI-Food Conference* (p. 1). Academic Press.

Talaat, A. (2018). *Marsall Olkin extended Topp–Leone distribution*. Academic Press.

Tăndăreanu, N. (1981). On generalized Boolean functions. *I. Discrete Math., 34*(3), 293–299.

Thomas & John. (2012). ì-Compactness in Generalized Topological Spaces. *Journal of Advanced Studies in Topology, 3*(3), 18-22.

Tian, Z., Wang, J., Wang, J., & Zhang, H. (2017). An improved MULTIMOORA approach for multi-criteria decision-making based on interdependent inputs of simplified neutrosophic linguistic information. *Neural Computing & Applications*, 28(1), 585–597. DOI:10.1007/s00521-016-2378-5

Timotheou, S., Miliou, O., Dimitriadis, Y., Sobrino, S. V., Giannoutsou, N., Cachia, R., Monés, A. M., & Ioannou, A. (2023). Impacts of digital technologies on education and factors influencing schools' digital capacity and transformation: A literature review. *Education and Information Technologies*, 28(6), 6695–6726. DOI:10.1007/s10639-022-11431-8 PMID:36465416

Topal, S., Broumi, S., Bakali, A., Talea, M., & Smarandache, F. (2019). A python tool for implementations on bipolar neutrosophic matrices. *Infinite Study*.

Tran, T. B., Ngo, M. P., Bui, Q. T., Snasel, V., & Vo, B. (2022). A new approach for operations on neutrosophic soft sets based on the novel norms for constructing topological structures. *AIMS Mathematics*, 7(6), 9603–9626. DOI:10.3934/math.2022534

Turksen, I. B. (1986). Turksen, Interval valued fuzzy sets based on normal forms. *Fuzzy Sets and Systems*, 20(2), 191–10. DOI:10.1016/0165-0114(86)90077-1

Ullah, Mahmood, Ali, & Jan. (2019). On some distance measures of complex Pythagorean fuzzy sets and their applications in pattern recognition. *Complex Intell. Syst.*

UNESA. (2023). *Global Sustainable Development Report 2023: Times of crisis, times of change: Science for accelerating transformations to sustainable development*. DOI:10.5281/zenodo.3951672

Vadiraja. (2022). Classical Balanced, Anti Balanced and Neutro Balanced functions. *Neutrosphic Sets and Systems, 48*, 386-398. Retrieved from https://fs.unm.edu/NSS2/index.php/111/article/view/2111

Vasantha Kandasamy, W. (2006). Smarandache Neutrosophic algebraic structures. *arXiv Mathematics e-prints*, math/0603708.

Wang, H., Smarandache, F., Sunderraman, R., & Zhang, Y.-Q. (2005). *Interval neutrosophic sets and logic: theory and applications in computing: Theory and applications in computing* (Vol. 5). Infinite Study.

Wang, H., Smarandache, F., Zhang, Y. Q., & Sunderraman, R. (2010). Single valued neutrosophic set. *Multisp Multistructure*, 4, 410–413.

Wang, L., & Bao, Y.-L. (2021). Multiple-Attribute Decision-Making Method Based on Normalized Geometric Aggregation Operators of Single-Valued Neutrosophic Hesitant Fuzzy Information. *Complexity*, 5580761, 1–15. Advance online publication. DOI:10.1155/2021/5580761

Wang, X., Xu, Z., & Gou, X. (2022). The Interval probabilistic double hierarchy linguistic EDAS method based on natural language processing basic techniques and its application to hotel online reviews. *International Journal of Machine Learning and Cybernetics*, 13(6), 1517–1534. DOI:10.1007/s13042-021-01463-w

Wu, X., Qian, J., Peng, J., & Xue, C. (2018). A Multi-Criteria Group Decision-Making Method with Possibility Degree and Power Aggregation Operators of Single Trapezoidal Neutrosophic Numbers. *Symmetry*, 10(11), 590. Advance online publication. DOI:10.3390/sym10110590

Wu, X., Wang, J., Peng, J., & Chen, X. (2016). Cross-Entropy and Prioritized Aggregation Operator with Simplified Neutrosophic Sets and Their Application in Multi-Criteria Decision-Making Problems. *International Journal of Fuzzy Systems*, 18(6), 1104–1116. DOI:10.1007/s40815-016-0180-2

Yager, R. R. (2013). Pythagorean fuzzy subsets. *Proceedings of the Joint IFSA World Congress and NAFIPS Annual Meeting.*

Yager, R. R. (2014). Pythagorean membership grades in multi-criteria decision making. *IEEE Transactions on Fuzzy Systems*, 22(4), 958–965. DOI:10.1109/TFUZZ.2013.2278989

Yager, R. R., & Abbasov, A. M. (2013). Pythagorean membership grades, complex numbers, and decision making. *International Journal of Intelligent Systems*, 28(5), 436–452. DOI:10.1002/int.21584

Yazdanbakhsh, O., & Dick, S. (2018). A systematic review of complex fuzzy sets and logic. *Fuzzy Sets and Systems*, 338, 1–2. DOI:10.1016/j.fss.2017.01.010

Yolcu, A., & Ozturk, T. Y. (2021). Fuzzy hypersoft sets and its application to decision-making. *Theory and application of hypersoft set, 50.*

Yolcu, A., Karatas, E., & Ozturk, T. Y. (2021b). A new approach to neutrosophic soft mappings and application in decision making. *Neutrosophic Operational Research: Methods and Applications*, 291-313.

Yolcu, A., Smarandache, F., & Ozturk, T. Y. (2021a). Intuitionistic fuzzy hypersoft sets. *Communications Faculty of Sciences University of Ankara Series A1 Mathematics and Statistics, 70*(1), 443-455..

Yolcu, A., Benek, A., & Ozturk, T. Y. (2023a). A new approach to neutrosophic soft rough sets. *Knowledge and Information Systems*, 65(5), 2043–2060. DOI:10.1007/s10115-022-01824-z

Yolcu, A., & Büşra, A. K. A. (2023b). On Neutrosophic Soft Multisets and Neutrosophic Soft Multi Topological Spaces. *Erzincan University Journal of Science and Technology*, 16(1), 89–109. DOI:10.18185/erzifbed.1114721

Yolcu, A., & Ozturk, T. Y. (2022). Separation axioms and connectedness on fuzzy parameterized fuzzy soft topological spaces. In *Handbook of research on advances and applications of fuzzy sets and logic* (pp. 412–427). IGI Global. DOI:10.4018/978-1-7998-7979-4.ch019

Yusuf, Bilgin, & Bozma. (2022). Pentapartitioned Fermatean Neutrosophic Alpha Phi Normal Topological Spaces. *International Sciences and Innovation Congress*, 116-132.

Zadeh, L. A. (1965). Fuzzy sets. *Information and Control*, 8(3), 338–353. DOI:10.1016/S0019-9958(65)90241-X

Zadeh, L. A. (1965). Fuzzy sets. *Informes de la Construcción*, 8(3), 338–353.

Zadeh, L. A. (1971). Similarity Relations and fuzzy Ordering. *Information and Control*, 3, 177–200.

Zadeh, L. A. (1975). The concept of a linguistic and application to approximate reasoning I. *Information Sciences*, 8(3), 199–249. DOI:10.1016/0020-0255(75)90036-5

Zadeh, L. A. (1978). Fuzzy sets as a basis for a theory of possibility. *Fuzzy Sets and Systems*, 1(1), 3–28. DOI:10.1016/0165-0114(78)90029-5

Zaman, M., Ghani, F., Khan, A., Abdullah, S., & Khan, F. (2023). Complex Fermatean fuzzy extended TOPSIS method and its applications in decision making. *Heliyon*, 9(9), e19170. DOI:10.1016/j.heliyon.2023.e19170 PMID:37809522

Zavadskas, E., Kaklauskas, A., & Šarka, V. (1994). The new method of multicriteria complex proportional assessment of projects. *Technological and Economic Development of Economy*, 1, 131–139.

Zeema, J. L., & Christopher, D. F. X. (2019). Evolving optimized neutrosophic C means clustering using behavioral inspiration of artificial bacterial foraging (ONCMC-ABF) in the prediction of Dyslexia. *Journal of King Saud University. Computer and Information Sciences*.

Zeina, M. B. (2020). Erlang Service Queueing Model with Neutrosophic Parameters. *International Journal of Neutrosophic Science*, 6(2), 106–112. DOI:10.54216/IJNS.060202

Zhang & Xu. (2014). Extension of TOPSIS to multiple-criteria decision making with Pythagorean fuzzy sets. *Int. J. Intell. System, 29*.

Zhang, W. R. (1994). Bipolar fuzzy sets and relations: a computational framework for cognitive modeling and multi agent decision analysis. *Proceedings of IEEE Conf.*, 305-309.

Zhang, W. R. (1998). Bipolar fuzzy sets. *Proc. of FUZZ-IEEE*, 835-840.

Zheng, Z., Wang, A., & Qin, L. (2021). Rejection sampling revisit: how to choose parameters in lattice-based signature. *Math. Probl. Eng.*

About the Contributors

Mohamed Abdel-Basset received his B.Sc. and M.Sc from Faculty of Computers and Informatics, Zagazig University, Egypt. Received his Ph.D from Faculty of Computers and Informatics, Menoufia University, Egypt. Currently, Mohamed is Associate Professor at Faculty of Computers and Informatics, Zagazig University, Egypt. His current research interests are Optimization, Operations Research, Data Mining, Computational Intelligence, Applied Statistics, Decision support systems, Robust Optimization, Engineering Optimization, Multi-objective Optimization, Swarm Intelligence, Evolutionary Algorithms, and Artificial Neural Networks. He is working on the application of multi-objective and robust meta-heuristic optimization techniques. He is also an/a Editor/reviewer in different international journals and conferences. He holds the program chair in many conferences in the fields of decision making analysis, big data, optimization, complexity and internet of things, as well as editorial collaboration in some journals of high impact.

Florentin Smarandache, PhD, PostDocs, is an Emeritus Professor of Mathematics at the University of New Mexico, United States. He got his MSc in Mathematics and Computer Science from the University of Craiova, Romania, PhD in Mathematics from the State University of Kishinev, and Postdoctoral in Applied Mathematics from Okayama University of Sciences, Japan, and The Guangdong University of Technology, Guangzhou, China. He is the founder of neutrosophy (generalization of dialectics), neutrosophic set, logic, probability and statistics since 1995 and has published hundreds of papers and books on neutrosophic physics, superluminal and instantaneous physics, unmatter, quantum paradoxes, absolute theory of relativity, redshift and blueshift due to the medium gradient and refraction index besides the Doppler effect, paradoxism, outerart, neutrosophy as a new branch of philosophy, Law of Included Multiple-Middle, multispace and multistructure, HyperSoft set, TreeSoft Set, IndetermSoft Set and IndetermHyperSoft Set, SuperHyperGraph, SuperHyperTopology, SuperHyperAlgebra, SuperHyperFunction, Neutrosophic SuperHyperAlgebra, degree of dependence and independence between neutrosophic components, refined neutrosophic set, neutrosophic over-under-off-set, plithogenic set / logic / probability / statistics, symbolic plithogenic algebraic structures, neutrosophic triplet and duplet structures, quadruple neutrosophic structures, extension of algebraic structures to NeutroAlgebra and AntiAlgebra, NeutroGeometry and AntiGeometry, NeutroTopology and AntiTopology, Refined Neutrosophic Topology, Refined Neutrosophic Crisp Topology, Dezert-Smarandache Theory and so on to many peer-reviewed international journals and many books and he presented papers and plenary lectures to many international conferences around the world. In addition, he published many books of poetry, dramas, children stories, translations, essays, a novel, folklore collections, traveling memories, and art albums.

* * *

N. Angel is a research scholar in the Department of Mathematics, Madurai Kamaraj University, Madurai, India.

Aysun Benek graduated from the Department of Mathematics, Faculty of Science and Letter, Kafkas University, Kars, Turkey, in 2018. She received her MSc from Kafkas University in 2021. Currently, she is doing her PhD at Kafkas University. Her research interest focuses mainly on soft set, fuzzy set, rough set, neutrosophic soft set, neutrosophic sets and topological structures of this notions.

Said Broumi was born in Casablanca, Morocco in 1978, is a PHD of university Hassan II - Casablanca. He received his M.Sc. in Industrial Automatic from Hassan II University Ain chok-Casablanca. His search major field is on neutrosophic graph theory, soft set theory, fuzzy theory, intuitionistic fuzzy theory, neutrosophic theory, neutrosophic soft set theory and neutrosophic decision making problem, networking. He published over 200 articles. Memberships: -Neutrosophic science International Association, USA - Associate Editor of Neutrosophic Sets and Systems Journal - Editor in Chief of International Journal of Neutrosophic Science.

Geoff Ebbs is an author, publisher, data architect and environmental consultant working with the regenerative food sector to implement strategic change at a policy level. He has been teaching at Griffith University as an industry consultant since 2016 and is in the process of completing his PhD research into the impact that the experience of food practitioners can have on sustainability transitions theory.

N. Ramila Gandhi is currently working as an Associate Professor in the Department of Mathematics, PSNA College of Engineering & Technology, Dindigul, India. Her areas of interest are Fuzzy and Neutrosophic Algebra.

Erick González Caballero received his PhD degree (2013) in technical science from the Technological University of Havana in Cuba, and his BS degree (1998) in Mathematics from the University of Havana. After graduating, he works as a scientist or teacher at various universities and research centers in Cuba. In 2011 he continued his teaching and scientific activities at the Technological University of Havana. He was a Postdoctoral Visitor (2016) at the University of Oviedo, Spain. His research interests include, decision-making under uncertainty, rough sets, fuzziness, image processing, expert systems, cooperative game theory, among others. He has published in important journals like "Group Decision and Negotiation", "International Journal of Computational Intelligence Systems", and "Journal of Intelligent & Fuzzy Systems", also in book chapters of Atlantis Press and Springer.

Luke Houghton is an Associate Professor in Management and Information Systems in the Griffith Business School in Griffith University. Luke is actively engaged in research in management problem solving with over 80 publications in this field. His research follows three key streams. The first stream looks at how framing and sensemaking influence problem-solving in messy management environments. The second stream is the feral information systems project which looks at the social, technical, and organisation impacts of workarounds. The third stream involves a study of communities of practice and technology use as well as the practices of blended learning in higher education contexts. His main passion is thinking about how cognitive models (thinking patterns) affect the way we solve problems and make decisions. Luke has completed more than 20 research higher degrees with the great majority (16) of those being PhD candidates. He has also been published in top journals such as: Information Systems Journal, the Journal of Industrial Ecology, The Journal of the Operations Research Society as well as a host of other Q1 Scimago ranked publications.

Irvanizam was born in Teupin Raya, Pidie, Aceh, Indonesia, in 1981. He received the B.Sc. degree in mathematics science majoring in informatics from Universitas Syiah Kuala, Banda Aceh, Indonesia, in 2002, and the M.Sc. degree in computer science from the Free University of Bozen-Bolzano, Bolzano, Italy, in 2010. He is currently a PhD student in Computer Science from Universitas Sumatera Utara, Medan, Indonesia. From 2014 to 2022, he was the Deputy Chairman of the Department of Informatics, Universitas Syiah Kuala, where he was the Head of the Laboratory for Database and Data Mining, Department of Informatics, from 2010 to 2014. He is currently an Associate Professor in applied informatics or computer science with the Department of Informatics, Universitas Syiah Kuala. He is also the author of publications in international journals and conference proceedings, many of which are indexed by Scopus and Web of Science, such as Expert Systems with Applications, IEEE Access, Applied Computational Intelligence and Soft Computing, Axioms, Advances in Fuzzy Systems, and some marvelous IEEE proceedings. He published a book chapter titled "Improved MABAC Method for Multicriteria Group Decision Making with Trapezoidal Fuzzy Neutrosophic Numbers" in the "Handbook of Research on Advances and Applications of Fuzzy Sets and Logic" (IGI Global, 2022) edited by Dr. Said Broumi. His current research interests include neutrosophic sets, decision support systems, fuzzy sets and its application, soft computing, multiple-attribute decision making, and multiple-criteria group decision making. Mr. Irvanizam is currently a member of some professional associations, such as the International Association of Engineers (IAENG) society of computer science, the Institute of Electrical and Electronics Engineers (IEEE), the Association of Higher Education of Informatics and Computer (APTIKOM), and the Institute of Engineers Indonesia (PII). He regularly serves as a Reviewer for some prestigious technical and international journals, such as Expert Systems with Applications, Artificial Intelligence Review, Soft Computing, Case Studies in Thermal Engineering, Systems and Soft Computing, Machine Learning with Applications, Operations Research and Decisions, International Journal of Information Technology and Web Engineering (IJITWE), Journal of Computational and Applied Mathematics, and Mathematical Biosciences and Engineering (MBE).

Marzuki completed his bachelor degree from the Department of Mathematics, Universitas Syiah Kuala in 2000 and earned a master degree in Statistics from Bogor Agricultural University (IPB) in 2005. He has published some scientific articles in statistics at four national journals since 2005 as well as national and international proceedings since 2007.

Taha Yasin Öztürk has a BSc (2008) and MSc (2010) from Kafkas University Turkey. PhD (2013) from Ataturk University Turkey. Currently, associate professor in Department of Mathematics, Faculty of Sciences and Letter, Kafkas University, Turkey. Now he is working as Professor at Kafkas University. His research interest focuses soft set, fuzzy set, bipolar soft set, neutrosophic set and topological structures of this notions.

Shashi Kant Pandey is working at SETS as a Scientist and has received his Ph.D. from the Department of Mathematics, University of Delhi. He has completed a Master of Science (Mathematics) From Banaras Hindu University. His research focuses on Boolean functions and, more specifically, on the cryptographic and combinatorial characterization of Boolean functions. Some other verticals of his research are Post Quantum Cryptography and Privacy-Preserving technology. Mathematics, poetry, and music are his other fascinations. His project 'Poetic Presentation of Mathematics and its Pedagogy' received a National Award from NCERT, Delhi.

P. Pandiammal is currently working as an Assistant Professor in the Department of Mathematics, G.T.N Arts College, Dindigul, India. Her areas of interest are Fuzzy and Neutrosophic Algebra.

Louis Sanzogni is a member of Faculty at Griffith University in Brisbane Australia where he currently lectures in Management and Management Information System. His research interests are in the areas of Diffusion of Innovation and Technology Adoption. In his more recent publications Dr Sanzogni explored the effects of user perceptions on the adoption of innovations proposing a number of successful variations in pre-established as well as newly developed adoption models.

Adem Yolcu graduated from the Department of Mathematics, Faculty of Science and Letter, Kafkas University, Kars, Turkey in 2014. He received MSc from Kafkas University in 2016. Then, he received PhD from Kafkas University in 2020. Now he is working as Associate Professor at Kafkas University. His research interest focuses mainly soft set, fuzzy set, intuitionistic fuzzy set, neutrosophic sets and topological structures of this notions.

Novi Zahara was born in Teupin Raya, Pidie, Aceh, Indonesia, in 1984. She is a mathematics teacher at an Islamic senior high school or Madrasah Aliyah Swasta Ulumul Qur'an, Pagar Air, Banda Aceh. She obtained her B.Ed degree in Mathematics Education from Institute Agama Islam Negeri (IAIN) Ar-raniry, Banda Aceh, Indonesia, in 2008. She is currently a deputy principal for academic and teaching affairs at the madrasah. Her current research interests include algebra, mathematical analysis, statistics, and geometry.

Index

Symbols

A

B

C

D

F

I

L

N

P

www.ingramcontent.com/pod-product-compliance
Lightning Source LLC
LaVergne TN
LVHW080629011026
849160LV00014B/1165